Listening to MUSIC

EDITION 8

Craig Wright

Yale University

CENGAGE
Learning·

Australia • Brazil • Canada • Mexico • Singapore • United Kingdom • United States

Listening to Music, Eighth Edition
Craig Wright

Product Director: Monica Eckman

Product Manager: Sharon Adams Poore

Senior Content Developer: Sue Gleason Wade

Associate Content Developer: Erika Hayden

Product Assistant: Rachael Bailey

Media Developer: Chad Kirchner

Marketing Manager: Jillian Borden

Content Project Manager: Lianne Ames

Art Director: Diana H. Graham

Manufacturing Planner: Julio Esperas

IP Analyst: Christina Ciaramella

IP Project Manager: Farah J. Fard

Production Service: Thistle Hill Publishing Services

Compositor: Cenveo® Publisher Services

Text and Cover Designer: Lisa Kuhn, Curio Press, LLC, www.curiopress.com

Cover Image: Scala/Ministero per i Beni e le Attività culturali / Art Resource, NY.

For product information and technology assistance, contact us at **Cengage Learning Customer & Sales Support, 1-800-354-9706**

For permission to use material from this text or product, submit all requests online at **www.cengage.com/permissions**. Further permissions questions can be emailed to **permissionrequest@cengage.com**.

Library of Congress Control Number: 2015949011

Student Edition ISBN: 978-1-305-58707-6

Book-only ISBN: 978-1-305-58700-7

Loose-leaf Edition ISBN: 978-1-305-86760-4

Loose-leaf Book-only Edition ISBN: 978-1-305-86761-1

Cengage Learning
20 Channel Center Street
Boston MA 02210
USA

Cengage Learning is a leading provider of customized learning solutions with employees residing in nearly 40 different countries and sales in more than 125 countries around the world. Find your local representative at **www.cengage.com**.

To learn more about Cengage Learning Solutions, visit **www.cengage.com**.

Purchase any of our products at your local college store or at our preferred online store **www.cengagebrain.com**.

Printed in the United States of America
Print Number: 05   Print Year: 2021

For Clark Baxter—innovator, publisher, and valued friend

BRIEF CONTENTS

The following part of the text is available online only, in MindTap.

CONTENTS

The following part of the text is available online only, in MindTap.

PART VIII GLOBAL MUSIC

Elements of the Music
Bossa Nova
Antonio Carlos Jobim (1927–1994)

LISTENING GUIDE
Jobim (lyrics by Vinicius de Moraes; English lyrics by
Norman Gimbel), "The Girl from Ipanema" (1963)

A MEXICAN MARIACHI PERFORMANCE
Mariachi

LISTENING GUIDE
"El burro" (nineteenth-century traditional)

CONCLUSION

ABOUT THE AUTHOR

Craig M. Wright received his Bachelor of Music degree at the Eastman School of Music in 1966 and his Ph.D. in musicology from Harvard University in 1972. He began his teaching career at the University of Kentucky and for the past forty-three years has been teaching at Yale University, where he is currently the Henry L. and Lucy G. Moses Professor of Music. At Yale, Wright's courses include his perennially popular introductory course, Listening to Music (also part of the offerings of Open Yale Courses, which can be viewed on YouTube); his large lecture course, Exploring the Nature of Genius; and most recently, his Coursera course, Introduction to Classical Music, which has been viewed by nearly 70,000 learners worldwide. He is the author of numerous scholarly books and articles on composers ranging from Leoninus to Bach. Wright also has been the recipient of many awards, including a Guggenheim Fellowship, the Einstein and Kinkeldey Awards of the American Musicological Society, and the Dent Medal of the International Musicological Society. In 2004, he was awarded the honorary degree Doctor of Humane Letter from the University of Chicago. In 2010, he was elected a member of the American Academy of Arts and Sciences, joining fellow inductee banjo player Steve Martin.

In addition to *Listening to Music* and *Listening to Western Music*, Wright has also published *The Essential Listening to Music*, Second Edition (Cengage Learning, 2016); *Listening to Music*, Chinese Edition (Schirmer Cengage Learning/Three Union Press, 2012), translated and simplified by Professors Li Xiujung (China Conservatory, Beijing) and Yu Zhigang (Central Conservatory, Beijing), both of whom worked with Wright at Yale; and *Music in Western Civilization, Media Update* (Schirmer Cengage Learning, 2010), with coauthor Bryan Simms. He is currently at work on a volume titled *Mozart's Brain: Exploring the Nature of Genius*.

PREFACE

Listening to music isn't just the title of this book. It is a sincere wish that all persons on this planet come to experience the joy and expressive power of classical music, and make it part of their lives. Now it is possible to do so through this book.

Most music appreciation textbooks treat music, not as an opportunity for personal engagement through listening, but as a history of music. Students are required to learn something of the technical workings of music (what a tonic chord is, for example) and specific facts (how many symphonies Beethoven wrote), but they are not asked to become personally engaged in the act of listening to music. What listening there is, is passive, not active. *Listening to Music*, Eighth Edition, however, is different. Here, students are encouraged—indeed, required—to become active participants in a musical dialogue through a variety of means both between the covers of this book and beyond them. Online technology now makes this possible.

Indeed, whether your musical education occurs in a traditional classroom or online, technology drives the need for newer editions, including this one. Today, instructors are not as "textbook dependent" as they were five to ten years ago. The Internet has made possible instant access to a wealth of media that can enhance students' interest by making the musical experience immediate and relevant to their world. Textbooks themselves are increasingly becoming hybrids—a combination book and media center. The book also can be experienced entirely online, with links to a wealth of electronic resources embedded therein. The job of the textbook today is to assure not only that students have access to these resources but also that the almost limitless number of audio and video tracks and clips available globally have been reduced to a manageable number of the very best. Finally, the textbook of today must not only inform and link students to the outside world but also be educationally creative.

Video games, animations, and exercises of all sorts are the newest modes of educational engagement in the twenty-first century. Instead of viewing these electronic experiences as unwanted distractions, *Listening to Music*, Eighth Edition, has embraced them. Many new drills, games, and animations are built into the MindTap platform that accompanies the book. In every way, this new edition of *Listening to Music* is written for the digital age. Its aim is to take what is essentially a past culture (Western classical music) and present it in the mode of delivery of today and tomorrow. Only in this way will students come to see that this past culture is relevant to their current existence; only in this way will students be engaged—indeed, inspired—to learn.

MindTap: An Online Companion

When *Listening to Music* was first under development some thirty years ago, the publisher considered issuing the recordings on vinyl but, instead, dared move to a revolutionary new development: magnetic tape. Thereafter came CDs, now streaming music and downloads. Similarly, some dozen years ago, the publisher and I created an online platform as a necessary companion to the book. Now entitled MindTap, it has grown into an engaging, personalized online environment, accessible on laptops, tablets, and hand-held devices. With relevant assignments that guide students to analyze, apply, and improve their thinking, MindTap also allows instructors to measure skills and outcomes, and record the results, with ease.

A Core Repertoire

What pieces of music are essential for students studying Western music? While we may all debate what should comprise the "canon" of Western music, *Listening to Music*, Eighth Edition, presents a cohort of pieces that many instructors would eagerly adopt. In fact, it is built on the opinions of many music appreciation instructors and on what is now my own nearly fifty years of teaching music appreciation at the college level. Thus, the compositions presented and discussed here are not only the staples of the concert hall today but also pieces that work in the classroom. Through them, the instructor can present all of the genres, processes, and historical changes that have appeared in Western art music during the last millennium.

For instructors who do not wish to cover popular or world music, an alternative volume, *Listening to Western Music*, Eighth Edition—and the audio that accompanies it—is available.

New to This Edition

Although its goals have not changed, this edition of *Listening to Music* incorporates several improvements:

- The full integration of the text pedagogy with MindTap, to provide high-value, gradable activities (Listening Exercises, now for most pieces discussed in the textbook; Chapter Quizzes by Timothy J. Roden of Ohio Wesleyan University; and Critical Thinking Quizzes by James D. Siddons of Liberty University), as well as opportunities to engage with the content and practice what has been learned.

- The points on the MindTap learning path are, wherever appropriate, cued in the text to remind users to take advantage of its rich resources.

  - **NEW** learning objectives preview each chapter's core concepts for students.

  - **NEW** YouTube videos, as well as animations by Stephen Malinowski, of Music Animation Machine, serve as chapter-opening engagement activities, which are compatible with class discussion boards.

  - **NEW** Critical Thinking Quizzes in each chapter challenge and sometimes call on students to apply information from previous chapters to the chapter at hand.

  - Additional practice is available, including videos and an Active Listening Guide for each musical selection.

- **NEW** instant audio is only a click away for most notated examples in the book.
- **More than 20 NEW** Listening Exercises provide in-depth quizzes on even more individual selections.

- Twenty musical works are **NEW** to this Eighth Edition, spanning eras from Classical to Postmodernist, and including three examples of well-known film music from *Gone with the Wind* to *Star Wars*.

- Chapter 4 now includes a discussion of the *Dies irae*, which will return again and again in later chapters.

- In Chapter 5, the *Kyrie* from Palestrina's *Missa Papae Marcelli* replaces its *Gloria* and *Agnus Dei*.

- Chapter 6 now includes the Prologue to Monteverdi's *Orfeo* as an example of early opera recitative.

- Chapter 8 now covers the second movement of Bach's *Wachet auf, ruft uns die Stimme:* "Er kommt."

- Chapter 9 adds "Behold, a Virgin shall conceive" and "O thou that tellest good tidings to Zion" to the sections of Handel's *Messiah*.

- Chapter 11 discusses Mozart's Piano Concerto in C major, accompanied by a Murray Perahia recording.

- Robert Schumann's "Träumerei" from *Kinderszenen* and Franz Liszt's "Un sospiro" now grace Chapter 19 with more accessible selections.

- Chapter 23 includes a more accessible Mahler selection: Symphony No. 1's third movement, "Funeral March."

- Chapter 26 now includes the "saddest piece ever written"—Barber's Adagio for Strings—and returns Ellen Taaffe Zwilich's *Concerto Grosso 1985* to the text.

- Chapter 27 includes "Passacaglia" by young Pulitzer Prize winner Caroline Shaw, as well as a unique bonus capstone activity, calling for students to apply what they have learned to prepare their own Listening Guide for the fifth movement (*Amhrán*) of Christopher Rouse's Flute Concerto.

- Quire Cleveland's movingly pure recording of the traditional "Amazing Grace" now launches Chapter 28.

- Chapter 29, which now combines postwar jazz and Broadway, features jazz greats doing covers: Charlie Parker and Dizzy Gillespie applying bebop to "My Melancholy Baby," and John Coltrane applying modal jazz to "My Favorite Things."

- Chapter 30, created especially for this edition by Julie Hubbert of the University of South Carolina, is sure to capture students' interest with film music discussions ranging from early film scores, such as that for *Gone with the Wind*, to experimental work used in *Inception*; TV scores for series such as *The Twilight Zone*; and a fascinating explanation of game music.

- The world music chapters, 32 through 34, are now available online only, in MindTap, as well as in PDF format for custom adoptions.

- There are now five fewer chapters overall, enabling instructors to cover more of the text in class.

Pedagogical Aids

Listening Exercises

Listening to Music was the first music appreciation text on the market to include detailed Listening Exercises. Now online in MindTap, Listening Exercises can be graded electronically and results can be automatically stored in an instructor's gradebook. By means of these, students will embrace hundreds of specific passages of music and make critical decisions about them. The exercises begin by developing basic listening skills: recognizing rhythmic patterns, distinguishing major keys from minor keys, and differentiating various kinds of textures. Students then move on to entire pieces in which they are required to become participants in an artistic exchange, the composer communicating with the listener, and the listener reacting over a span of time. Ultimately, equipped with these newly developed listening skills, students will move comfortably to the concert hall, listening to classical and popular music with greater confidence and enjoyment. To be sure, this book is for the present course, but its aim—like any good educational experience—is to prepare students for a lifetime of learning, in this case, of musical listening and enjoyment. Text cues highlight the availability of online Listening Exercises.

Listening Guides

Listening Guides continue to contain such key information as genre and form, a concise suggestion of "What to Listen For," and MindTap cues to interactive streaming music, Active Listening Guides, Listening Exercises, and sometimes a video.

Chapter 27 includes a unique capstone activity, in which students are challenged to create their own Listening Guide after being given very little information about Christopher Rouse's moving Flute Concerto, fifth movement. Rather than step through the usual timed annotations, its Active Listening Guide works with students to tease out an understanding of the piece.

Ancillaries for Students

Streaming and Downloads

All of the musical content discussed in the book, printed on the inside covers, is available streaming in MindTap and as free downloads, accessible via the Music Download Card that is packaged with each copy of the textbook.

Active Listening Guides

The Active Listening Guides in MindTap contain full-color interactive and streaming listening guides for every selection, along with listening quizzes and background information.

Other MindTap Features

MindTap offers several creative and challenging features, including a timed "drop-the-needle" trivia game that provides more practice identifying music, flash cards, ReadSpeaker, and opportunities for instructors to add their own teaching materials to the learning path.

In addition, MindTap contains numerous YouTube videos; video demonstrations of keyboard instruments; eighteen iAudio podcasts on difficult musical concepts; a checklist of musical styles with integrated musical style comparisons; musical elements, genres, and forms tutorials; an online discussion of writing concert reports; and grade management for instructors.

Students may access MindTap using a passcode either bundled with their text or purchased online at www.cengagebrain.com.

For Instructors: Instructor's Companion Site

Accompanying *Listening to Music*, Eighth Edition, is an Instructor Companion Website where you will find an *Instructor's Resource Manual*, Cengage Learning Testing Powered by Cognero®, and Microsoft® PowerPoint® presentations.

The extensive ***Instructor's Resource Manual***, written by Timothy J. Roden of Ohio Wesleyan University, supplements the textbook.

Cengage Learning Testing Powered by Cognero® is a flexible, cloud-based system that allows you to

- Author, edit, and manage test bank content from multiple Cengage Learning products.

- Create multiple test versions in an instant.

- Deliver tests from your LMS, your classroom, or wherever you prefer.

The **Microsoft® PowerPoint® presentations**, created for this edition by Vicki Curry of James Madison University, are predesigned for use with the book. They include full-color images, music clips, and web links, and they are fully customizable.

Acknowledgments

I am especially indebted to the following reviewers, who provided invaluable in-depth feedback on both the text and MindTap:

Michael Adduci, San Jose State University
Warren Arnold, Spartanburg Community College
Valentin Bogdan, Arizona Western College
Michael Boyle, Oklahoma City Community College
Mary Collins, Eastman School of Music of the University of Rochester
Vicki Curry, James Madison University
Mark DeBellis, Columbia University
Noe Dinnerstein, John Jay College of Criminal Justice, CUNY
Steven Edwards, Delgado Community College
Gregory Gardner, Norfolk State University
Patricia Grutzmacher, Kent State University
Nora Kile, University of Tennessee at Chattanooga
Jason Lester, Wharton County Junior College
Andrew Tomasello, Baruch College, CUNY
Elizabeth Waterbury, Shasta College

I have also benefited from the help and good will of the staff of the Yale Music Library, as well as James Park, also at Yale, who accuracy-checked and developed many of the materials that appear in MindTap. Professor Timothy Roden (Ohio Wesleyan University), the author of much of the web material, the *Instructor's Manual*, and the Test Bank, has corrected errors and saved me from myself on numerous occasions.

Certainly, not to be overlooked are the important contributions of, most recently, Professor Julie Hubbert (University of South Carolina), who prepared the new Chapter 30; Professor Andrew Tomasello (Baruch College, CUNY), who prepared Chapter 31; and Professor Anthony DeQuattro (Quinnipiac University), who drafted large portions of Chapters 32 and 34.

As always, it has been a privilege to work with publisher Clark Baxter and his successor, product manager Sharon Poore, as well as with the experienced team at Cengage Learning—Liz Newell, Erika Hayden, Rachael Bailey, Brian Giordano, Chad Kirchner, Jillian Borden, Lianne Ames, Andrea Archer, and Angela Urquhart—and especially Tom Laskey at SONY, who has provided valuable advice on recordings and has helped usher this book into the era of downloads. Behind the scenes for more than fifteen years has been Sue Gleason Wade, the shining yet silent star around whom all of these *Listening to Music* projects revolve. My heartiest thanks to all of you!

Craig Wright
Yale University

Introduction to LISTENING

part ONE

The Power
of MUSIC

START... experiencing this chapter's topics with an online video activity.

LEARNING OBJECTIVES

After studying the material in this chapter, you should be able to:

1 Describe how we perceive music.
2 Compare popular and classical music.
3 Know the primary genres (types) and venues (places) of classical music.
4 Consider in what ways music is a "language" of its own.
5 Recognize where and how to listen to music.
6 Test the capacity of classical music to move you by exploring two of its most famous examples.

W hy do we listen to music? Does it keep us in touch with the latest musical trends, help get us through our morning exercise, or relax us in the evening? Each day almost everyone in the industrialized world listens to music, whether intentionally or not. The global expenditure for commercial music is about $40 billion annually, if we include ticket sales, concert merchandise, and website advertising. Whereas in earlier centuries a music lover needed to seek out a concert or other live performance, now almost everyone can listen to music from a smartphone. Do you have an "app" for ballet or painting? Likely not. But probably you have one or more for music—iTunes, Spotify, Shazam, and Pandora among them. Turn on the radio, and what do we hear: drama or poetry? No, usually just music; the radio is basically a transmission tool for music. Whether we get it from FM radio waves or shorter electromagnetic waves carrying digital information, we choose to let music penetrate our lives.

But why is music so appealing? What is its attraction? Does it perpetuate the human species? Does it shelter us from the elements? No. Does it keep us warm? Not unless we dance. Is music some sort of drug or aphrodisiac?

Oddly, yes. Neuroscientists at Harvard University have done studies that show that, when we listen to music, we engage processes in the brain that are "active in other euphoria inducing stimuli such as food, sex, and drugs of abuse."[1] These same researchers have explained the neural processes through which listening to particular pieces of music can give us goose bumps. There is a chemical change in the human brain, as blood flow increases in some parts and decreases in others. In this way, music can lower the heart rate and reduce levels of stress. Although listening to music today may or may not be necessary for survival, it does alter our chemical composition and our mental state. It is pleasurable and rewarding, as well as therapeutic.

It is also powerful—yet mysterious. Here's a riddle: "You can't see it; you can't touch it. But it can touch you; it can make you cry or lift you up and out of your seat." What is it? Music, of course! Indeed, music has an inspirational power. Think of a religious service, or a wedding or funeral, or a parade or commencement, without music. Think of the four-note "rally" motive played at professional sports events to get the crowd energized. Think of the refined sounds of Mozart in a commercial that is intended to convince us to buy an expensive watch. Plato (*The Republic*) once said what advertisers practice today: "To control the people, control the music."

Sound perception is, in fact, the most powerful sense we possess, likely because it *was* once essential to our survival—who is coming and from where? Friend or foe? Flight or fight? We get frightened at horror films, not when the images on the screen become vivid, but when the music starts to turn ominous. In short, sounds rationally organized in a pleasing or frightening way—music—profoundly affect how we feel and behave.

Music, the Ear, and the Brain

Briefly defined, **music** is the rational organization of sounds and silences passing through time. Tones must be arranged in some consistent, logical, and (usually) pleasing way before we can call these sounds "music" instead of "noise."

---

[1]Anne Blood and Robert Zatorre, "Intensely Pleasurable Responses to Music Correlate with Activity in Brain Regions Implicated in Reward and Emotion," *Proceedings of the National Academy of Sciences,* Vol. 98, No. 20 (Sept. 25, 2001), pp. 11818–11823.

FIGURE 1.1

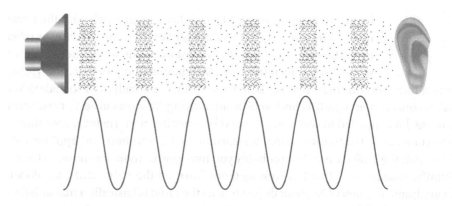

A representation of air molecules showing six vibrations of a single cycle of a sound wave. The more dots, the more compact the molecules. For the musical pitch middle C on the piano, such a cycle repeats 256 times per second—the strings on the piano are vibrating that quickly.

Like all sound, music is a disturbance of the atmosphere, one that creates **sound waves**, vibrations that reflect differences in air pressure. But music is special: Its sound waves come in regular patterns. Air molecules are compressed and expanded in consistently recurring cycles (Figure 1.1). And they repeat with shocking speed. When we play the pitch called middle C on the piano, a string vibrates (compressing and decompressing air molecules) 256 times per second; for the pitch A above it, this happens 440 times per second. The speed of the vibration determines what we perceive as high and low pitches. The faster the vibration the higher the pitch.

When we hear music, sound waves make their way from our outer to our inner ear, where they are transformed into electrochemical impulses (Figure 1.2). Here the "central processor" is a small organ called the **basilar membrane**, which recognizes sound patterns by frequency and sends the information, via the auditory nerve, to the brainstem and from there to the brain itself.

Given all of the love songs in the world, we might think that music is an affair of the heart. But both love and music are domains of a far more complex vital organ: the brain (Figure 1.3). When sound-stimulated impulses reach the brain, neurons go to work analyzing them for pitch, color, loudness, duration, and direction of source, among other things. Most processing of sound (music as well as language)

FIGURE 1.2

Sounds travel from (1) the outer ear to the inner ear, where sound waves are converted into electrochemical impulses in (2) the basilar membrane. The (3) primary auditory nerve transmits the signal to the (4) brainstem and, finally, to (5) the auditory cortex.

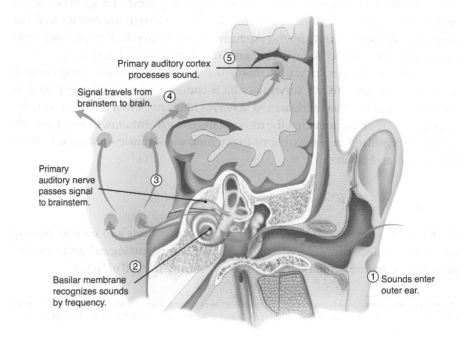

Primary auditory cortex ⑤ processes sound.

Signal travels from ④ brainstem to brain.

Primary auditory nerve passes signal to brainstem. ③

Basilar membrane ② recognizes sounds by frequency.

① Sounds enter outer ear.

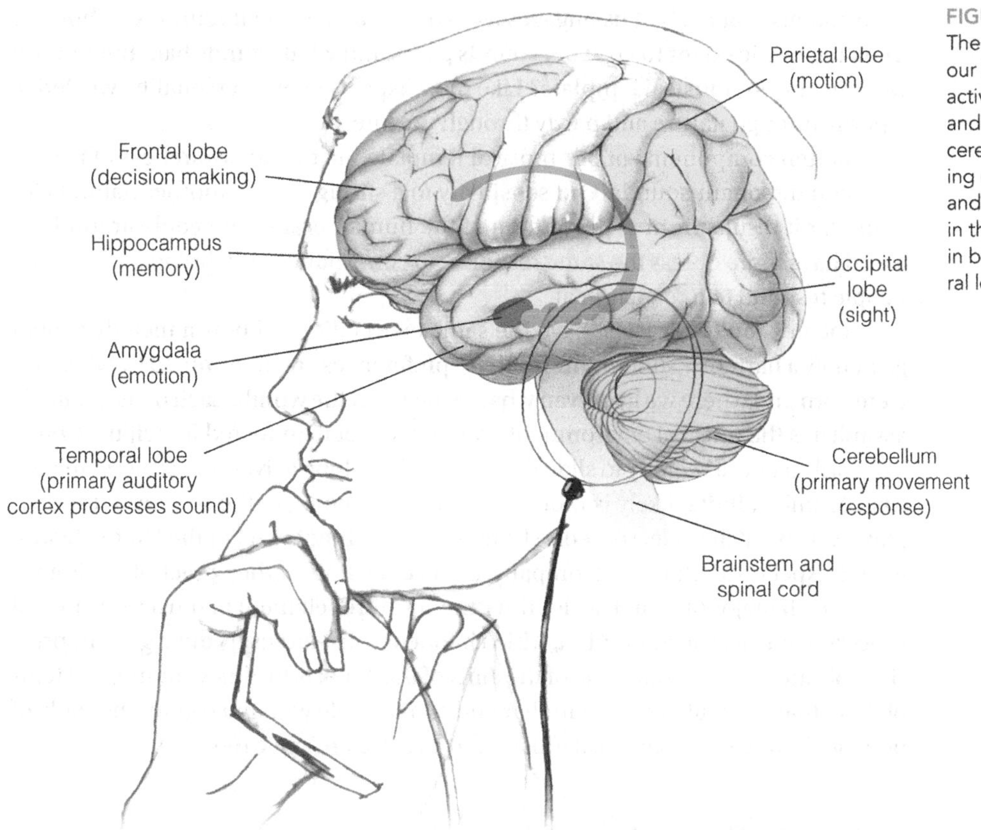

FIGURE 1.3
The processing of music in our brain is a hugely complex activity involving many areas and associated links. The first cerebral recognition and sorting of sounds, both musical and linguistic, occurs largely in the primary auditory cortex in both left and right temporal lobes.

Frontal lobe
(decision making)

Hippocampus
(memory)

Amygdala
(emotion)

Temporal lobe
(primary auditory
cortex processes sound)

Parietal lobe
(motion)

Occipital
lobe
(sight)

Cerebellum
(primary movement
response)

Brainstem and
spinal cord

takes place in the **primary auditory cortex** of the temporal lobe. If we are imagining how the next line of a song will go, that decision is usually reached in the frontal lobe. If we are playing an instrument, we engage the motor cortex (parietal lobe) to move our fingers and tap our foot, and the visual center (occipital lobe) to read the notes. That takes care of musical cognition, but what about emotion?

How do we *feel* about the music we hear? What creates those inner, private emotions we all experience? Emotions are generated mostly by a subregion of the brain called the **limbic system**, especially in a small area named the **amygdala**. As the music proceeds, the limbic system stores feelings as memories and constantly updates the information it receives, hundreds of times per second. At a speed of more than 250 miles per hour, associative neurons integrate all the data into a single perception of the sound. The chemical composition of our brain is altered, causing us to feel sad, to relax, or, if the impulses come strongly at regular intervals, to get up and dance.

In sum, the process of listening to music involves a continuum moving from instrument, or voice, to sound wave, to ear, to brain, and, finally, to our body and limbs as we start to clap, sing along, or dance with joy.

WATCH... a YouTube video on music and the brain, online.

Our Musical Template: Why We Like What We Like

What's your favorite piece of music—your favorite song or symphony? What types of music do you like? That depends on who you are and on the kind of musical template you have in your head. A **musical template** is simply a set of musical expectations that each of us engages as we listen to a piece; it reminds us how we think the music ought to go, what sounds good, and what sounds bad. But how do we come by our musical template? Like most aspects of our personality, we derive it partly through nature and partly through nurture.

Natural components of our musical template include an awareness of consonant and dissonant sounds. Our sensitivity to a strong beat is another natural element, for it results from the evolution of the human brain. All people around the world have more or less the same response to consonance and dissonance, and all people respond to a regular beat.

Not all people, however, have the same expectations of how a melody should go or how a harmony should sound. These preferences are determined by where we were born and where we live, even what we heard in the womb. Each of us gradually assimilates the musical environment around us. A person reared in Beijing, China, likely will expect a melody to slide through pitches along a five-note scale; someone from Mumbai, India, likely is more comfortable listening to the sounds of the sitar playing a six-pitch scale; someone from Nashville, Tennessee, in the United States, would expect a guitar to accompany a voice singing, rather precisely, within a seven-pitch major or minor scale. Thus, the "nurture" element in music is a gradual process of musical acculturation, which happens most intensely during the impressionable adolescent years. One of the aims of this book is to alter your musical template so that you will become familiar and comfortable with the sounds, not only of pop music, but also of classical music, and eager to embrace more.

Listening to Whose Music?

Today, most of the music that we hear isn't "live" music, but recorded sound. Sound recording began in the 1870s with Thomas Edison's phonograph machine, which first played metal cylinders and then vinyl disks, or "records." During the 1930s, magnetic tape recorders appeared and grew in popularity until the early 1990s, when they were superseded by a new technology, digital recording. In digital recording, all the components of musical sound—pitch, tone, duration, volume, and more—are analyzed thousands of times per second, and that information is stored on compact discs (CDs) or in computers as sequences of binary numbers. When it is time to play the music, these digital data are reconverted to electrical impulses that are amplified and pushed through speakers, headphones, or earbuds, as sound waves, to our ears. The process of listening has begun.

Today, most music is no longer sold as a commodity you can see or hold—as sheet music, a vinyl recording, or a CD. Rather, it sits out there in electronic space, stored somewhere on a "cloud." When we want to listen, we download or, more often, stream the music as MP3 or M4A files. While the audio quality is not as good as "live" acoustic sound, surely the trade off has been worth it. What had been an expensive experience for a lucky few (listening to live music at a concert) can now be enjoyed by almost anyone, anywhere, any time. This holds true for popular and classical music alike.

Popular or Classical?

Popular music is rightly named—it's an easily assimilated music that most people want to hear. Downloads and streams of pop outsell those of classical by more than twenty to one. But why are so many people, and young people in particular, attracted to popular music? Two immediate answers: the power of the beat (see below and Chapter 2) and the message of the lyrics.

Classical music, too, can be a powerful force. Hearing the huge, majestic sound of a mass of acoustic instruments—a symphony orchestra—can be an overwhelming experience. Classical music is often regarded as "old" music, written by "dead white men." But this isn't entirely true: No small amount of it has been written by women, and many composers of both sexes are very much alive and well today. In truth, however, much of the classical music that we hear—the music of Bach, Beethoven, and Brahms, for example—*is* old. That is why, in part, it is called "classical." In the same vein, we refer to clothes, furniture, and cars as "classics" because they have timeless qualities of expression, proportion, and balance. Broadly defined, **classical music** is the traditional music of any culture, usually requiring long years of training; it is "high art" or "learned," timeless music that is enjoyed generation after generation.

Popular and Classical Music Compared

Today, Western classical music is taught in conservatories around the world, from Paris to Beijing to Singapore. Western pop music enjoys even greater favor; in many places, Western pop music has replaced local pop traditions, so that all that remains are the local lyrics sung in the native tongue. But what are the essential differences between the music we call popular and the music we call classical (Figure 1.4)? Cutting to the quick, here are six ways in which they differ:

- Popular music often uses electric enhancements (via electric guitars, synthesizers, and so on) to amplify and transform vocal and instrumental sounds. Much of classical music uses **acoustic instruments** that produce sounds naturally.

- Popular music is primarily vocal, involving **lyrics** (accompanying text that tells listeners what the music is about and suggests how they should feel). Classical music is more often purely instrumental, performed on a piano or by a symphony orchestra, for example, and it employs its own language of pure sound to express meaning to the listener.

- Popular songs tend to be short and involve exact repetition, which makes them catchy and memorable. Classical compositions can be long, sometimes thirty to forty minutes in duration, and most repetitions are varied in some way.

- Popular music is performed by memory, not from a written score (have you ever seen music stands at a rock concert?), and each performer can interpret the work as he or she sees fit (hence the proliferation of "cover songs"). Classical music, even if played by memory, is initially generated from a written score, and there is typically one commonly accepted mode of interpretation— the piece exists, almost frozen in time, as a work of art.

- Popular music we associate with the performer who made it famous. Classical music we remember by the composer who created it.

- Finally, popular music has a strong beat that makes us want to move in sync with it. Classical music often subordinates the beat in favor of melody and harmony.

FIGURE 1.4
What helps make popular music popular? No previous experience is required! Classical music, on the other hand, necessitates years of training on an instrument and knowledge of often-complicated music theory. Some musicians are equally at home in the worlds of popular and classical music. Juilliard School of Music–trained Wynton Marsalis can record an album of New Orleans–style jazz one week and a Baroque trumpet concerto the next. He has won nine Grammy awards—seven for various jazz categories and two for classical albums.

This last point is important: Music with a regularly recurring beat has a powerful effect on our psyche, causing us to dance or motivating us to exercise. Cognitive neuroscientists have yet to fully explain the power of the beat. They suggest, however, that sounds with forcefully recurring patterns are processed in the "time-measuring" neurons of the cerebellum, one of the earliest parts of the brain to develop during human evolution. These neurons connect with motor neurons, causing us to move, a physical response to the regularly recurring stimulation of the beat. That explains how a great deal of pop music, especially dance music, "works." But what about classical music?

How Does Classical Music Work?

Explaining how classical music works requires an entire book—this one. But some preliminary observations are in order.

Genres and Venues of Classical Music

Genre in musical terminology is simply a word for "type of music." Needless to say, there are almost endless types of popular music: rap, hip-hop, blues, R&B, country, EDM (electronic dance music), and Broadway show tunes among them. **Venue** is merely a fancy word for place. Genre and venue are interrelated (Table 1.1). The place where we go to hear music determines the type of music we hear. If we go to a bar, we will likely hear a blues or rock band, and there will be room for dancing, or at least swaying. If we go to a chamber music hall, we may hear one of several musical genres—perhaps a string quartet or a piano sonata—and no one will move very much.

The venues for classical music are of three main types: opera houses and theaters for opera and ballet; concert halls for symphony orchestras; and chamber halls for smaller, solo ensembles. Opera houses and theaters are large, often public, venues providing a home for entertainment besides opera and ballet. Concert halls are also large, accommodating 2,000 to 3,000 listeners, and tend to be "music only"; excellent examples include the Disney Center in Los Angeles, the Schermerhorn Symphony Center in Nashville (Figure 1.6), and the famous Carnegie Hall in New York. Chamber or recital halls, for solo performing groups, are smaller, accommodating perhaps 200 to 700 lovers of classical music (Figure 1.5).

Finally, genre and venue determine how we dress and behave—social convention has made it so. A fan goes to hear Kanye West at the River Rock Casino in Las Vegas dressed casually, ready to dance and make a lot of noise. Yet that same person would likely attend a concert of the Boston Symphony Orchestra in Symphony Hall attired in suit and tie; any "fan" noise would only distract the orchestra. In sum, venue dictates genre and comportment: Where we go determines what we hear, what we wear, and how we behave.

TABLE 1.1 Venues for Classical Music with Typical Genres

Opera Houses and Theaters	Concert Halls	Chamber Halls
Opera	Symphony	Art song
Ballet	Concerto	String quartet
	Oratorio	Piano sonata

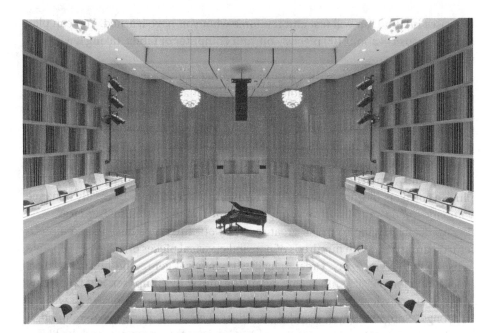

FIGURE 1.5
Some concerts require a large hall that can seat 2,000 to 3,000 listeners (such as the Schermerhorn Symphony Center in Nashville, Tennessee, shown in Figure 1.6). For other performances, a smaller venue with 200 to 700 seats is more appropriate, as we see here in the Hatch Recital Hall at the Eastman School of Music in Rochester, NY, which has exactly 222 seats for listeners.

The Language of Classical Music

Communication involves sending a message that generates a response. If a friend rushed up to you and said, "Your dog was just run over by a truck," you'd probably react with shock and profound sadness. In this case, a verbal language conveys meaning and elicits an emotional reaction.

But music, too, is a means of communication, one older than spoken language. Spoken language, many evolutionary biologists tell us, is simply a specialized subset of music. Over the centuries, composers of classical music have created a language that also can convey shock and sadness. This language of music is a collection of audible gestures that express the world of feelings and sensations in ways that words cannot. The Romantic composer Gustav Mahler said it best when he wrote, "If a composer could say what he had to say in words, he would not bother trying to say it in music."

Music lessons are not required to understand the language of music; we have been passively assimilating it since birth, each of us forming our musical template. We intuit, for example, that music that gets faster and rises in pitch communicates growing excitement, because we have heard these gestures frequently, as in "chase scenes" in films and on TV. Another piece might sound like a funeral march. But why? Because the composer is communicating this to us by using a slow *tempo*, low *tessitura*, regular *beat*, and *minor key*. Understanding musical terms such as these will allow us to simplify complex issues of perception and emotion, and thereby penetrate to the heart of the seemingly mysterious nature of music.

WATCH... YouTube videos comparing pop and classical music, online.

Where and How to Listen

All of the music discussed in this book is available streaming in MindTap and for downloading via a special access card packaged with each new book. For each piece, an Active Listening Guide can be found in MindTap that will lead you second by second, minute by minute, through the work. Finally, frequent Listening

Exercises in MindTap will test and reinforce what you have learned. You can play all of this music—about 100 pieces—on your computer or tablet, taking it with you wherever you go.

That's the good news. The bad news is that with ease of accessibility and mobility comes a decline in audio quality. The quality of sound available from MP3 and M4A formats is not as good as when the digital information was placed on and played from a CD; it has been compressed and many small details eliminated. Similarly, the means of projection is less sharp on a computer than it was back when quality audio (bigger files) was heard on large, stereophonic speakers. Consequently, when listening from a device such as a computer or a tablet, separate plug-in speakers or quality headphones are a necessity. They will greatly enhance your enjoyment—and improve your performance on the Listening Exercises.

Ironically, having so much great music at our fingertips has created a problem: organization. With hundreds of pop and classical pieces on a device, separate categories are a necessity. Create playlists by musical genre and be sure to have at least one for classical music, arranging the music by composer. But be careful. Most of the classical pieces that you will buy, despite what iTunes says, will not be "songs." Songs have lyrics, and a great deal of classical music, as mentioned, is purely instrumental: instrumental symphonies, sonatas, concertos, and the like.

Finally, performances of all the pieces discussed in this book can be found on YouTube. Watching the performers of a symphony orchestra offers an advantage: The listener gains familiarity with the sounds of the various instruments by associating a particular sound with a visual image. Visual listening also humanizes the experience; the viewer can witness the performer struggle with and (usually) overcome seemingly impossible technical challenges. The skill of the performers on YouTube varies enormously, from rank amateur to gifted professional. For the classical repertoire, seek big-name artists (Luciano Pavarotti and Renée Fleming among them) and top-of-the-line orchestras (the New York Philharmonic or the Chicago Symphony Orchestra, for example).

Live in Concert

Pop megastars now make more money from live concerts than they do from recording royalties, and so, too, with classical musicians. Indeed, for classical musicians and listeners alike, there is nothing better than a live performance. First, there is the emotional impact of bonding with the artist(s) on stage. Second and equally important, the sound will be magnificent because it is pure, usually acoustic, music.

Compared to pop or rock concerts, however, performances of classical music (Figures 1.5 and 1.6) can be rather staid affairs. For one thing, people dress "up," not "down." For another, throughout the event, the classical audience sits quietly, saying nothing to friends or to the performers on stage. No one sways, dances, or sings along to the music. Only at the end of each composition does the audience express itself, clapping respectfully.

But classical concerts weren't always so formal. In fact, they were at one time more like professional wrestling matches. In the eighteenth century, for example, the audience talked during performances and yelled words of encouragement to the players. Dogs wandered about, as vendors sold pitchers of wine. The audience clapped at the end of each movement of a symphony and often in the middle of the movement as well. After an exceptionally pleasing performance, listeners

FIGURE 1.6
Schermerhorn Symphony Center, Nashville, Tennessee. Constructed between 2003 and 2006 at a cost of $123 million, the 2,000-seat auditorium is home to the Nashville Symphony as well as concerts of pop, cabaret, choral, jazz, and blues music. If that isn't enough for music lovers visiting Nashville, right across the street is the Country Music Hall of Fame.

would demand that the piece be repeated immediately in an **encore**. If, on the other hand, the audience didn't like what it heard, it might express its displeasure by throwing fruit and other debris at the stage. Our more dignified modern classical concert was a creation of the nineteenth century, when musical compositions came to be considered works of high art worthy of reverential silence.

Thinking and Writing about Music: The Concert Report

Whether you are a student taking a course that requires you to attend a concert or a lifelong learner just going for pleasure, you may benefit from the author's "Insider's Guide to Writing a Concert Report." In this guide, you will learn how to prepare for the concert by listening in advance at YouTube or Spotify and reading at Oxford Music Online, a service to which most colleges and public libraries subscribe. You'll also learn what to think and write about and what is irrelevant. Whatever type of concert you attend—classical, pop, jazz, or world music—focus on the music, not on the life of the composer or the dress and hairdo of the performer. Perhaps most important, show your instructor (and yourself) that you have learned something; incorporate in your thinking the musical vocabulary and concepts to which you have been exposed in this book.

READ... "Insider's Guide to Writing a Concert Report" online.

Getting Started:
No Previous Experience Required

"I'm tone deaf, I can't sing, and I'm no good at dancing." Most likely this isn't true of you. What *is* true is that some people have a remarkable memory for sounds, whether musical or linguistic. Mozart, who had perfect pitch, could hear a piece

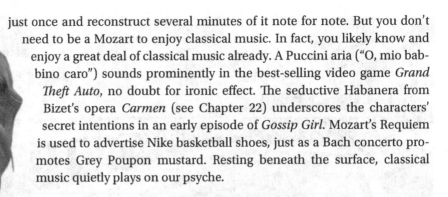

just once and reconstruct several minutes of it note for note. But you don't need to be a Mozart to enjoy classical music. In fact, you likely know and enjoy a great deal of classical music already. A Puccini aria ("O, mio babbino caro") sounds prominently in the best-selling video game *Grand Theft Auto*, no doubt for ironic effect. The seductive Habanera from Bizet's opera *Carmen* (see Chapter 22) underscores the characters' secret intentions in an early episode of *Gossip Girl*. Mozart's Requiem is used to advertise Nike basketball shoes, just as a Bach concerto promotes Grey Poupon mustard. Resting beneath the surface, classical music quietly plays on our psyche.

Take the Classical Music Challenge

To test the capacity of classical music to move you, try a simple comparison: Taylor versus Renée. Watch a YouTube video of Taylor Swift (Figure 1.7) singing "Shake It Off" from her album *1989* (2014), followed by a recent video clip of soprano Renée Fleming (Figure 1.8) singing Puccini's aria "O, mio babbino caro." How much of the effect of these performances is due to beat, electronic enhancements, orchestral sound, visual effects, vocal training, and lyrics? Which would you want to listen to again and again? Which, if either, would you be able to shake off? Or, listen to Coldplay's latest hit next to a rendition of Richard Wagner's "Ride of the Valkyries" (see Chapter 21), to compare the sound of a rock band with that of a symphony orchestra. Which piece gives you chills, and which one just leaves you cold? Were you moved by the classical video clips?

Two Classical Favorites

If you weren't moved by the preceding experiment, try listening to two other famous moments in the history of classical music. The first is the beginning of Ludwig van Beethoven's Symphony No. 5 (see Listening Guide), perhaps the best-known moment in all of classical music, which you've already seen in animated form in this chapter's opening video online. Its "short-short-short-long" (SSSL) gesture (duh-duh-duh-DUHHH) is as much an icon of Western culture as the "To be, or not to be" soliloquy in Shakespeare's *Hamlet*. Beethoven (see Figure 1.9 and Chapter 15 for his biography) wrote this symphony in 1808 when he was thirty-seven and had become almost totally deaf. (Like most great musicians, the nearly deaf Beethoven could hear with an "inner ear"—he could create and rework melodies in his head without relying on external sound.) Beethoven's **symphony**—an instrumental genre for orchestra—is actually a composite of four separate instrumental pieces,

FIGURE 1.7
Taylor Swift at the Academy of Country Music Awards in 2014

WATCH... a YouTube video of Taylor Swift singing "Shake It Off" online. Compare it with Renée Fleming singing "O, mio babbino caro."

LISTEN TO... a podcast about learning how to listen, online.

FIGURE 1.8
Renée Fleming led the singing of "The Star-Spangled Banner" at 2014's Super Bowl XLVIII. Needless to say, the high notes didn't pose a problem.

Ludwig van Beethoven, Symphony No. 5 in C minor (1808)　　　　　　Download 1 (1:29)

First movement, *Allegro con brio* (fast with gusto)

WHAT TO LISTEN FOR: The ever-changing appearance of the four-note motive as the force of the music waxes and wanes

0:00	Opening "short-short-short-long" motive	
0:22	Music gathers momentum and moves forward purposefully.	
0:42	Pause; French horn solo	
0:46	New, lyrical melody sounds forth in strings and is then answered by winds.	
1:08	Rhythm of opening motive returns.	
1:17	Opening motive reshaped into more heroic-sounding melody	

LISTEN TO ... this selection streaming online.

WATCH ... an Active Listening Guide of this selection online.

each called a **movement**. A symphony is played by an **orchestra**, and because an orchestra plays symphonies more than any other musical genre, it is called a **symphony orchestra**. The orchestra for which Beethoven composed his Fifth Symphony was made up of about sixty players, including those playing string, wind, brass, and percussion instruments.

Beethoven begins his symphony with the musical equivalent of a punch in the nose. The four-pitch rhythm (SSSL) comes out of nowhere and hits hard. This SSSL figure is a musical **motive**, a short, distinctive musical unit that can stand by itself. After this "sucker punch," we regain our equilibrium as Beethoven takes us on an emotionally wrenching, thirty-minute, four-movement symphonic journey dominated by his four-note motive.

Turn now to this opening section (in Download 1, as well as in this chapter's streaming music online) and to its Listening Guide above. You will see written music, or **musical notation**, representing the principal musical events. This notation may seem alien to you (the essentials of musical notation will be explained in Chapter 2). But don't panic. Millions of people enjoy

FIGURE 1.9
Ludwig van Beethoven

Richard Strauss, *Also sprach Zarathustra* (1896)   Download 2 (1:32)

Genre: One-movement tone poem

WHAT TO LISTEN FOR: A gradual transition from the nothingness of murky darkness to shafts of light (trumpets) and, finally, to the incandescent power of the full symphony orchestra

0:00	Rumbling of low string instruments, organ, and bass drum
0:14	Four trumpets ascend, moving from bright to dark (major to minor key).

0:26	A drum (timpani) pounds forcefully.
0:30	Four trumpets ascend again, moving from dark to light (minor to major key).

0:44	A drum (timpani) pounds forcefully again.
0:50	Four trumpets ascend a third time.
1:06	Full orchestra joins in to add substance to impressive succession of chords.
1:15	Grand climax by full orchestra at high pitches

LISTEN TO ... this selection streaming online.

WATCH ... an Active Listening Guide of this selection online.

DO ... Listening Exercise 1.1, Musical Beginnings, online.

classical music every day without looking at a shred of written notation. For the moment, simply listen to the music and follow along according to the minute and second counter on your music player. If you prefer a more animated version of this Listening Guide (and all other guides in this book), you will find Active Listening Guides online.

Finally, for the grandest of all sounds, popular or classical, we turn to the beginning of an orchestral work by Richard Strauss, *Also sprach Zarathustra* (*Thus Spoke Zarathustra*). The German title sounds intimidating, but the idea is very simple: the advent of a superhero, backlit by a sunrise (Figure 1.10).

How do you depict the advent of a superhero and a sunrise through music? Strauss tells us by means of a few very simple techniques that express musical

FIGURE 1.10
Strauss attempts to replicate in music the coming of a superhero, the apex of human development, who ascends with the rising of the sun.

meaning. The music ascends in pitch, gets louder, and grows in warmth (more instruments). Moreover, the leading instrument is the trumpet, the sound of which has traditionally been associated with heroic deeds. The climax sounds with the great volume of the full orchestra—in this case, the large Romantic orchestra of the late nineteenth century. So impressive is this passage that it has been borrowed for use in countless radio and TV commercials (to sell digital TV and phone delivery services, insurance, carpets, and storm windows, among other things). The aim is to astound you, the consumer, with the power, durability, and brilliance of the product. In contrast to Beethoven's composition, Strauss's piece isn't a symphony in four movements but, rather, a one-movement work for orchestra called a **tone poem**. If you think classical music is for wimps, think again!

KEY WORDS

music (3)
sound wave (4)
basilar membrane (4)
primary auditory cortex (5)
limbic system (5)
amygdala (5)

musical template (5)
popular music (6)
classical music (7)
acoustic instrument (7)
lyrics (7)
genre (8)

venue (8)
encore (11)
symphony (12)
movement (13)
orchestra (13)
symphony orchestra (13)

motive (13)
musical notation (13)
tone poem (15)

 Join us on Facebook at Listening to Music with Craig Wright

PRACTICE ... your understanding of this chapter's concepts by working once more with the chapter's Active Listening Guides online.

DO ... online multiple-choice and critical thinking quizzes that your instructor may assign for a grade.

Rhythm, Melody, and
HARMONY

START... experiencing this chapter's topics with an online video activity.

LEARNING OBJECTIVES

After studying the material in this chapter, you should be able to:

1 Outline the basics of the first of the fundamental elements of music: rhythm.
2 Distinguish different levels of rhythmic activity in different pieces of music.
3 Recognize the melodic contour of different pieces of music.
4 Differentiate major from minor.
5 Identify consonance and dissonance, and then cadences.
6 Identify chord changes in harmony.

M usic is an unusual art. You can't see it or touch it. But it has matter—compressed air molecules yielding sounding pitches—and these pitches are organized in three main ways: as rhythms, as melodies, and as harmonies. Rhythm, melody, and harmony, then, are the three primary elements—the *what*—of music.

READ... the complete chapter text in a rich, interactive online platform.

LISTEN TO... a podcast about tempo online.

WATCH... Michael Jackson respond to and redefine the beat in a YouTube video online. Compare with screen actor Christopher Walken in action.

Rhythm

Humans are rhythmic beings. Our heartbeat, brain waves, and breathing are all rhythmic. How fundamental is rhythm? Remember that recognition of the beat, as mentioned in Chapter 1, is mainly a function of the cerebellum, that part of the brain to develop first in human evolution. Consider, too, that we heard the beat of our mother's heart before we were aware of any sort of melody or tune. Consequently, our brain reacts powerfully and intuitively to a regularly recurring, strongly articulated "beat" and a catchy, repeating rhythmic pattern. We have a direct, even physical, response to rhythm, especially as expressed in pop music (Figure 2.1). We move, exercise, and dance to its pulse.

The basic pulse of music is the **beat**, a regularly recurring sound that divides the passing of time into equal units. **Tempo** is the speed at which the beat sounds. Some tempos are fast (*allegro*) or very fast (*presto*), and some are slow (*lento*) or very slow (*grave*). Sometimes the tempo speeds up, producing an ***accelerando***, and sometimes it slows down, creating a ***ritard***. But oddly, whether the tempo proceeds rapidly or slowly, undifferentiated streams of anything aren't appealing to us humans. We organize passing time into seconds, minutes, hours, days, years, and centuries. We subconsciously group the chirping of a seatbelt warning chime into units of two or three "dings." So, too, with the undifferentiated stream of musical beats: Our psyche demands that we organize the musical beats into groups, each containing two, three, four, or more pulses. The first beat in each unit is called the **downbeat**, and it gets the greatest **accent**, or stress. Organizing beats into groups produces **meter** in music, just as arranging words in a consistent pattern of emphasis produces meter in poetry. In music, each group of beats is called a **measure** (or **bar**). Although there are several different kinds of meter in music, about 90 percent of the music we hear falls into either a **duple meter** or a **triple meter** pattern. We mentally count "ONE-two" or "ONE-two-three." There's a quadruple pattern as well, but in most instances, our ear perceives this as simply a double duple meter pattern.

Rhythmic Notation

About 800 years ago, in thirteenth-century Paris to be precise, musicians began to devise a system to notate the beats, meters, and rhythms of their music. They created visual symbols that stood for long or longer, and short or shorter, durations. Over the centuries, these visual symbols developed into the notational symbols that we use today, as seen in Example 2.1.

FIGURE 2.1
When we listen to a song with a strong beat, auditory neurons stimulate motor neurons, causing us to dance. In the realm of pop song and dance, perhaps no one was better at this immediate connection between the auditory and the motor than Michael Jackson. Although he died in 2009, the estate of the "King of Pop" still generates about $100 million annually from the sale of music and merchandise.

EXAMPLE 2.1 Notational symbols for rhythmic durations

(whole note) ○ = ♩ ♩ (2 half notes = 4 beats)

(half note) ♩ = ♩ ♩ (2 quarter notes = 2 beats)

(quarter note) ♩ = ♪ ♪ (2 eighth notes = 1 beat)

(eighth note) ♪ = ♪ ♪ (2 sixteenth notes = ½ beat)

To help the performer keep the beat when playing, the smaller note values—specifically, those with flags on the vertical stem—are beamed, or joined together, in groups of two or four (Example 2.2).

EXAMPLE 2.2 Short durations grouped

♩ ♪♪♩ ♪♪♪♪ becomes ♩ ♫♩ ♬

Today, the symbol that usually represents, or "carries," one beat in music is the quarter note (♩). Normally, it moves along roughly at the rate of the average person's heartbeat. As you might suspect from its name, the quarter note is shorter in length than the half note and the whole note, but it is longer than the eighth note and the sixteenth note. There are also signs, called **rests**, to indicate the absence of sound for different lengths of time.

If music proceeded only with beats organized into meter, it would be dull indeed—like the endless sound of a bass drum (ONE-two, ONE-two, or ONE-two-three, ONE-two-three). In fact, what we hear in music by way of duration is **rhythm**, the division of time into compelling patterns of long and short sounds (see Listening Cue, "The Basics of Rhythm"). Rhythm emerges from, and rests upon, the durational grid set by the beat and the meter. In fact, no one actually plays just the beat, except perhaps a drummer; rather, we hear a mass of musical rhythms, and our brain extracts the beat and the meter from them. To see how this works, let's look at a patriotic song from the time of the American Revolution in duple ($\frac{2}{4}$) meter, in Example 2.3.

EXAMPLE 2.3 Beat and rhythm in duple meter

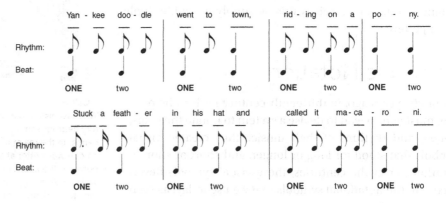

Example 2.4 shows another patriotic song, "America" (first known in England and Canada as "God Save the King"—or "Queen"), arranged the same way. It is in triple ($\frac{3}{4}$) meter.

EXAMPLE 2.4 Beat and rhythm in triple meter

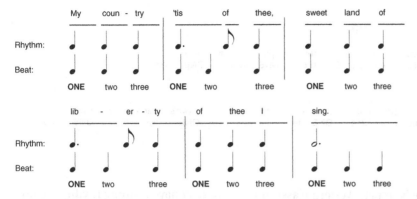

The numbers $\frac{2}{4}$ and $\frac{3}{4}$ aren't fractions but, rather, **meter signatures** (also called **time signatures**). A meter signature tells the performer how the beats of the music are grouped to form a meter. The bottom number of the signature (usually a 4, representing the quarter note) indicates what note value receives the beat, and the top number tells how many beats there are in each measure. The small vertical lines in the preceding examples are called **bar lines**; they help performers keep the music of one measure, or bar, separate from the next and thus tell the performers how to keep the beat. Although all of this terminology of music theory might seem intimidating, the important question is this: Can you hear the downbeat and then recognize a duple meter (as in a ONE-two, ONE-two march) contrasted with a triple meter (as in a ONE-two-three, ONE-two-three waltz)? If so, you're well on your way to grasping the rhythmic element of music.

Hearing Meters

One way you can improve your ability to hear a given meter is to establish some sort of physical response to the music: Keep time with your foot, stomping hard on the downbeat and tapping softly on the weak beats; or conduct with your hand (Figure 2.2), using a conductor's pattern (down-up, or down-over-up), as shown in Example 2.5.

EXAMPLE 2.5 Conducting patterns for duple and triple meter

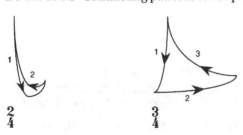

FIGURE 2.2
Marin Alsop, musical director of the Baltimore Symphony Orchestra, conducts during a rehearsal.

One final observation about meters and conducting patterns: Almost all music that we hear, especially dance music, has a clearly identifiable meter and a strong

LISTEN TO... a podcast about the basics of hearing meter online.

downbeat. But not all music *starts* with the downbeat. Often a piece will begin with an upbeat. An upbeat at the very beginning of a piece is called a pickup. The **pickup** is usually only a note or two, but it gives a little momentum or extra push into the first downbeat, as can be seen, in Example 2.6, at the beginning of two other patriotic songs.

EXAMPLE 2.6 Pickup

Oh	beau-	ti-	ful	for	spa-	cious	skies	
two	**ONE**	two	**ONE**	two	**ONE**	two	**ONE**	two

Oh	say	can	you	see		by	the		dawn's	ear -	ly	light	
three	**ONE**	two	three	**ONE**	two	three			**ONE**	two	three	**ONE**	two

Syncopation

Surprisingly, much Western classical music *doesn't* have a strong rhythmic component; rather, the beauty of the music rests in the melody and harmony. Popular music, on the other hand, is often irresistible, not only because of a strong beat, but also because of a catchy rhythm, created by syncopation. In most music, the accent, or musical emphasis, falls directly on the beat, with the downbeat getting the greatest emphasis of all. **Syncopation**, however, places the accent either on a weak beat or between beats—literally, it's "off beat." This unexpected, offbeat moment in the music creates the catchy "hook" of the tune, the part that pops up when you least expect it and sticks in your head.

A short example of syncopation can be heard in bar 2 of the chorus of The Beatles' song "Lucy in the Sky with Diamonds." The arrows in Example 2.7 show the moments of syncopation.

EXAMPLE 2.7 Simple syncopation

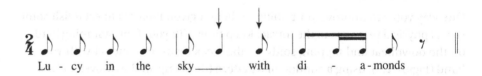

A far more complex example of syncopation can be found in Example 2.8, the popular theme song to *The Simpsons*.

EXAMPLE 2.8 Complex syncopation

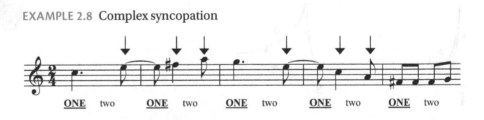

If you're a fan of jazz, Afro-Cuban music, or Latin music, you may be responding to the syncopation that gives these styles their bounce or lift.

Melody

A **melody**, simply put, is the tune. It's the part we sing along with, the part we like, the part we're willing to listen to again and again. Amazon and iTunes offer album downloads of "50 All-Time Favorite Melodies," yet there are no similar collections devoted to rhythms or harmonies. Needless to say, Beyoncé, Adele, Taylor Swift, Sam Smith, and Renée Fleming sing the melody. They, and it, are the stars.

Every melody is composed of a succession of pitches, usually energized by a rhythm. **Pitch** is the relative position, perceived high or low, of a musical sound. We traditionally assign letter names (A, B, C, and so on) to identify specific pitches. When an instrument produces a musical tone, it sets into motion vibrating sound waves that travel through the air to reach the listener's ears. A faster vibration will produce a higher pitch, and a slower one, a lower pitch. Pressing the lowest key on the piano sets a string vibrating back and forth 27 cycles (times) per second, while the highest key does the same at a dizzying 4,186 times per second. Low pitches lumber along and sound "fuzzy," whereas high pitches are clear but fleeting. A low note can convey sadness; a high one, excitement (we don't usually hear a high-pitched piccolo as sad, for example). In Western music, melodies move along from one discrete pitch to another. In other musical cultures—Chinese, for example—melody often "slides," and much of its beauty resides *between* the pitches.

Have you ever noticed, when singing a succession of tones up or down, that the melody reaches a tone that sounds like a duplication of an earlier pitch but is higher or lower? That duplicating pitch is called an **octave**, for reasons that will become clear shortly, and it's usually the largest distance between notes that we encounter in a melody. When a melody leaps up an octave, our spirits soar.

Pitches that are an octave apart sound similar because the frequency of vibration of the higher pitch is precisely twice that of the lower pitch. The ancient Greeks, from whom much of our Western civilization derives, knew of the octave and its 2:1 ratio, and they divided it into seven pitches using other ratios. Their seven pitches plus the eighth (the octave) yield the white keys of the modern keyboard. When early musicians reached the repeating pitch, the octave, they began to repeat the A, B, C letter names for the pitches. Eventually, five additional notes were inserted. Notated with symbols called **flats** (♭) and **sharps** (♯), they correspond to the black keys of the keyboard (Figure 2.3).

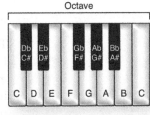

FIGURE 2.3
An octave

When a tune moves from one pitch to another, it moves across a melodic **interval**. Some of these distances are small; others, such as the octave, are large. Melodies with large leaps are usually difficult to sing, whereas those with repeated or neighboring pitches are easier. Example 2.9 shows the beginning of a well-known melody based on a large interval; both phrases of the tune begin with an ascending leap of an octave. To hear the octave, try singing "Take me..." to yourself.

LISTEN TO...

Example 2.9 online.

EXAMPLE 2.9 An octave in "Take Me Out to the Ball Game"

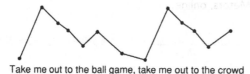

Take me out to the ball game, take me out to the crowd

Now, Example 2.10 shows the opening to Beethoven's famous *Ode to Joy* from his Symphony No. 9 (1823), in which almost all of the pitches are adjacent. It is known and beloved around the world because it is tuneful and singable. Try it—you'll recognize the melody. If you're not comfortable with the words, try singing the syllable "la" to each pitch.

LISTEN TO...

Example 2.10 online.

EXAMPLE 2.10 Adjacent pitches in *Ode to Joy*

Praise to   Joy   the   God   de - scend - ed, Daugh - ter   of   E - ly - si - um.

Ray   of   mirth   and   rap - ture   blend - ed,   God - dess   to   thy   shrine   wel - come.

DO... Listening Exercise 2.2, Hearing Melodies, online.

"Take Me Out to the Ball Game" and Beethoven's *Ode to Joy* are very different in both intervallic structure and mood. Indeed, using all possible combinations of rhythms and pitches, an almost endless number of melodies can be created.

Melodic Notation

The type of notation used above for "Take Me Out to the Ball Game" and *Ode to Joy* is useful if we need only to be reminded of how a melody goes, but it isn't precise enough to allow us to sing it if we don't already know it. When the melody goes up, how *far* up does it go? Around the year 1000, even before the advent of rhythmic notation, church musicians added precision to pitch notation in the West. They started to write black and, later, white circles on horizontal lines and spaces so that the exact distance between these notes could be judged immediately. This grid-work of lines and spaces came to be called a **staff**. The higher on the staff a note is placed, the higher its pitch (Example 2.11).

EXAMPLE 2.11 Pitches on a staff

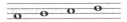

Over the course of centuries, the note heads also came to imply different durations, by means of stems and flags. Example 2.12A shows low, slow pitches that become gradually higher and faster, while Example 2.12B shows the reverse.

EXAMPLE 2.12A Pitches becoming higher and faster

EXAMPLE 2.12B Pitches becoming lower and slower

In notated music, the staff is always provided with a **clef** sign to show the range of pitch in which the melody is to be played or sung (Example 2.13). One clef, called the **treble clef**, designates the upper range and is appropriate for higher-sounding instruments, such as the trumpet and the violin, or a woman's voice. A second clef, called the **bass clef**, covers the lower range and is used for lower-sounding instruments, such as the tuba and the cello, or a man's voice.

EXAMPLE 2.13 Clefs

Treble clef

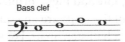

Bass clef

For a single vocal part or a single instrument, a melody could easily be placed on either of these two clefs. But for two-handed keyboard music with a greater range, both clefs are used, one on top of the other (Figure 2.4). The performer looks at this combination of clefs, called the **great staff** (also **grand staff**), and relates the

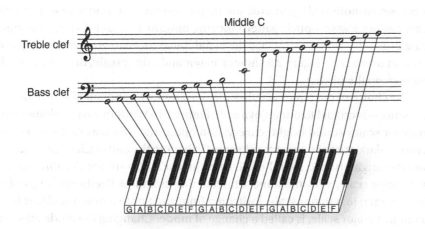

FIGURE 2.4
The great staff

notes to the keys beneath the fingers. The two clefs join at middle C (the middle-most C key on the piano).

Each musical pitch can be represented by a particular line or space on the great staff as well as by a letter name (like C). We use only seven letter names (in ascending order, A, B, C, D, E, F, and G) because, as we've seen, melodies are made up of only seven pitches within each octave. As a melody reaches and extends beyond the range of a single octave, the series of letter names is repeated (see Figure 2.4, bottom). The note above G, then, is an A, which lies exactly one octave above the previous A. In Example 2.14, "Twinkle, Twinkle, Little Star" is notated on the great staff, with the pitches doubled at the octave, as might happen when male and female voices sing together—the women an octave higher than the men.

LISTEN TO...

Example 2.14 online.

EXAMPLE 2.14 "Twinkle, Twinkle, Little Star"

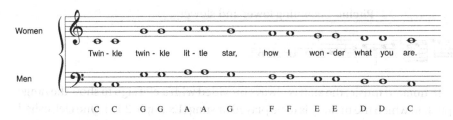

Scales, Modes, Tonality, and Key

When we listen to music, our brain hears a succession of pitches spaced out on a grid. That grid is a **scale**, a fixed pattern of tones within the octave that ascends and descends. Think of the scale as a ladder with eight rungs, or steps, between the two fixed points, low and high, formed by the octave. You can go up or down the ladder, but not all the steps are an equal distance apart. Five are a full step apart, but two are only a half step apart. For example, the distance between A and B is a full step, but the distance between B and C is only a half step—that's just the way the ancient Greeks built their musical ladder, an odd arrangement that Western musical culture retains to the present day.

The position of the two half steps functions something like an aural global positioning system (GPS), providing both a general and an exact location. Specifically, it tells us what kind of scale is in play and where we are within that scale. Since the seventeenth century, almost all Western melodies have been written following one of two seven-note scale patterns: the major one and the minor one. The **major scale** follows a seven-pitch pattern moving upward 1-1-½-1-1-1-½. The **minor scale** goes 1-½-1-1-½-1-1. Once the eighth pitch (octave) is reached, the pattern can start over again. Figure 2.5 shows a major and minor scale, first on the pitch C and then on the pitch A.

The choice of the scale (whether major or minor)—and our ability to hear the difference—is crucial to our enjoyment of music. To Western ears, melodies based on major scales sound bright, cheery, and optimistic, whereas minor ones come across as dark, somber, and even sinister. Go back to the end of Chapter 1 and compare the bright, heroic sound of Richard Strauss's *Also sprach Zarathustra*, built on a major scale, with the almost-threatening sound of Beethoven's Symphony No. 5, written in a minor scale. Switching from a major to a minor scale, or from a minor to a major scale, is called a change of **mode**. Changing the mode affects the mood of the music. To prove the point, listen to the familiar tunes in Example 2.15.

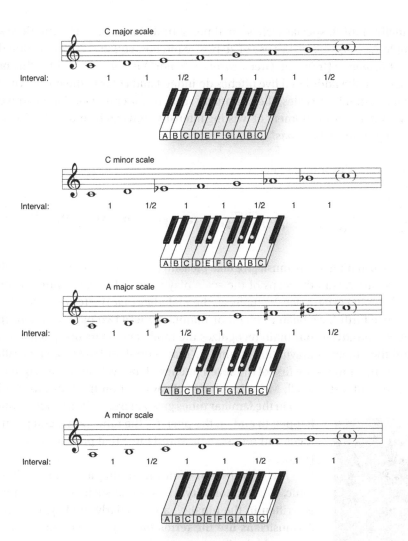

FIGURE 2.5
Major and minor scales

LISTEN TO... audio of
Figure 2.5 online.

The mode has been changed from major to minor by inserting a flat into the scale near the last pitch (C), thereby switching from the beginning of the major scale (1–1–½) to that of the minor (1–½–1). Notice how this alteration sucks all the happiness, joy, and sunshine out of these formerly major melodies.

EXAMPLE 2.15 Major melodies become minor melodies

Joy to the world, the Lord is come

You are my sun-shine, my on-ly sun - shine

Hap- py birth - day to you

LISTEN TO...
Example 2.15 online.

DO... Listening
Exercise 2.3, Hearing
Major and Minor, online.

LISTEN TO... a podcast
about hearing major and
minor online.

Finally, a third, special scale sometimes sounds in music: a **chromatic scale** (Example 2.16), which makes use of all twelve pitches, equally divided, within the octave. *Chromatic* (from the Greek *chroma*, "color") is a good word for this pattern, because the additional five pitches do indeed add color to the music. Unlike the major and minor scales, the chromatic scale is not employed for a complete melody, but only for a moment of twisting intensity. You can hear it in the first line of the song "White Christmas."

LISTEN TO...

Example 2.16 online.

EXAMPLE 2.16 Chromatic scale

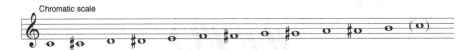

When listening to any music, we take pleasure, consciously or not, in knowing where we are. Again, the steps of the scale play a crucial role, orienting us during the listening experience. Virtually all the melodies that Western listeners have heard since birth have been in major or minor, so these two patterns are deeply ingrained. Intuitively, our brain recognizes the mode and hears one pitch as central and the others as gravitating around it. That central, or home, pitch is called the tonic. The **tonic** is the first of the seven pitches of the scale and, consequently, the eighth and last as well. Melodies almost always end on the tonic, as can be seen in the familiar tunes given in Example 2.15, all of which happen to end on the pitch C. The tonic provides a point of focus and repose, a powerful force that pulls us back home (Figure 2.6).

The organization of music around a central pitch, the tonic, is called **tonality**. We say that such and such a piece is written in the tonality, and similarly the **key**, of C or of A (musicians use the terms *tonality* and *key* almost interchangeably). Composers—classical composers, in particular—like to move temporarily from the home scale and home tonality to another, just for the sake of variety. Such a change is called a **modulation**. In any musical journey, we enjoy traveling away from our tonic "home," but we experience even greater satisfaction arriving back home. Again, almost all music, pop as well as classical, ends on the tonic pitch.

FIGURE 2.6
Planets rotate around and are pulled toward the sun, just as outlying pitches are pulled toward the tonic pitch.

Finally, the greatest musical mystery of all: What makes a good melody? Why are some pieces ("Greensleeves" and Beethoven's *Ode to Joy*) timeless and others immediately forgettable? Although there is no certain recipe for composing a great tune, consider the following: Most have an overall arch (shape), are composed of symmetrical phrases (subsections of 4, 8, or 16 bars), progress to a climax, and end with a final affirmation of the home pitch (the tonic). Beyond this, it's anyone's guess.

Harmony

Perhaps because of the long history of the piano and organ in the West—keyboard instruments that can play several pitches at once—Western music is exceptional among musical cultures in its emphasis on harmony. Simply said, **harmony** is the sound of one or more pitches that support and enhance a melody. Almost always, the pitches of the melody are higher than those of the accompanying harmony. At the piano, for example, the "higher" right hand usually plays the melody and the left hand plays the harmony (see Example 2.17). Although a melody can stand by itself, an accompanying harmony adds a richness to it, just as the dimension of depth adds a rich backdrop to a painting.

EXAMPLE 2.17 Harmony supporting a melody

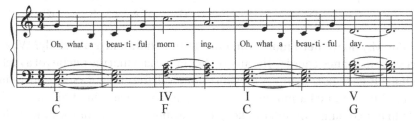

FIGURE 2.7
Claude Monet, *Waterlily Pond: Pink Harmony* (1900). Monet's painting of this famous bridge at Giverny, France, reveals not only the harmonious qualities of nature but also the painter's ability to harmonize various colors into a blend of pastels.

By definition, every harmony must be harmonious (Figure 2.7). From this truism we can see that there are two meanings of *harmony*. First, *harmony* means "a general sense that things work or sound well together"; second, *harmony* specifically denotes an exact musical accompaniment, as when we say "the harmony changes here to another chord."

Building Harmony with Chords

Chords are the building blocks of harmony. A **chord** is simply a group of two or more pitches that sound at the same time. The basic chord in Western music is the **triad**, so called because we construct it using three pitches arranged in a very specific way. Let's start with a C major scale, beginning with the tonic note C. To form a triad (Figure 2.8), we take one pitch, skip one pitch, and take one pitch—in other words, we select the pitches C, E, G (skipping D and F) and sound them together.

Triads can be constructed in a similar fashion on every pitch of the scale. But, given the irregularity of the scale (remember, not all steps on our musical ladder are the same distance apart), some triads will be major and others, minor. A major triad has its middle pitch a half step closer to its top pitch than to its bottom one; conversely, a minor triad has its middle pitch a half step closer to its bottom pitch than to its top one. While this may seem complicated, the difference between a major and a minor triad is immediately audible. Major triads sound bright; minor ones, dark. Example 2.18 shows triads built on every note of the C major scale. Each is assigned a Roman numeral to indicate on which pitch of the scale it is built.

FIGURE 2.8
A triad

These triads provide all the basic chords necessary to harmonize a melody in C major.

EXAMPLE 2.18 Triads of the C major scale

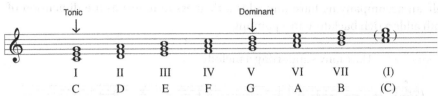

LISTEN TO...

Example 2.18 online.

But why do we need more than one chord to harmonize a melody? Why is it necessary to change chords? The answer lies in the fact that the pitches of a melody continually change, sometimes moving through all the notes of a scale. But a single triadic chord can be harmonious, or consonant, only with the three notes of the scale that it contains. In order to keep the harmony consonant with the melody, then, chords must continually change.

As chords change in a purposeful fashion beneath a melody, they create what is called a **chord progression**. Chords, other than the tonic, are unstable. They want to reach the tonic, "pulling" each other along. One gives way to the next, all gravitating toward the powerful tonic triad. Along the path of the progression, a surprising, unexpected chord might sound, and this can cause a sudden, powerful emotional response. The end of a chord progression is called a **cadence**. Usually, at a cadence, a triad built on degree V of the scale, called the **dominant** triad, will yield to the tonic triad. This is a powerful harmonic move, one conveying a strong feeling of conclusion, as if to say, "THE END."

WATCH... YouTube online to hear how thirty-six pop songs have been constructed on the same chord progression.

To sum up, in Western music, melodies are supported by an enriching, chordal accompaniment—a harmony. The harmony gains force and enriches the melody as the chords move in a purposeful progression. It is necessary to change chords in a harmony so as to avoid unwanted dissonance.

Consonance and Dissonance

What is art? Art can be seen as a parallel life outside of ourselves. As we engage the external work of art, we experience another life of the emotions within us. And just as emotional life is full of consonance and dissonance, so, too, with music.

LISTEN TO... a podcast about consonance and dissonance online.

You've undoubtedly noticed, when you're pressing the keys of the piano at one time or another, that some combinations of keys produce a harsh, jarring sound, whereas others are pleasing and harmonious. The former chords are characterized by **dissonance** (pitches sounding momentarily disagreeable and unstable), and the latter by **consonance** (pitches sounding agreeable and stable). Generally speaking, chords that contain pitches that are very close to one another, just a half or a whole step apart (C joined to D, for example), sound dissonant. On the other hand, chords built with the somewhat larger interval of a third (C joined to E) are consonant, as is the case for each triad in Example 2.18. But culture, and even personal taste, play a role in dissonance perception, too; what might be an unpleasantly spicy, distasteful dissonance to one listener might be a delight to another. While some, for example, find the loud, aggressive distortion of heavy metal bands such as Metallica intolerable, others thrive on it.

But whatever the music, dissonance adds a feeling of tension and anxiety, while consonance produces a sense of calmness and stability (see Listening Cue).

Dissonant chords are unstable, and thus they seek out—they want to move to—consonant resolutions. The continual flux between dissonant and consonant chords gives Western music a sense of drama, as a piece moves between moments of tension to longed-for resolution. We humans try not to end the day with an unresolved argument; nor do we want to end our music with unresolved dissonance.

Hearing the Harmony

If you were asked to listen to a new song by your favorite pop artist and sing it back, you'd undoubtedly sing back the melody. The tuneful melody is invariably the line with the highest-sounding pitches. Thus, we've become trained, consciously or unconsciously, to focus on the top part of any musical texture. To hear and appreciate harmony, however, we've got to "get down" with the bass. Chords are usually built on the bass note, and a change in the bass from one pitch to another may signal a change of chord. The bass is the foundation of the chord and determines where the harmony is going, more so than the higher melody. Some pop artists, such as Paul McCartney and Sting, control both the upper melody and the lower harmony simultaneously. While they sing the tune, they play electric bass, setting the bass pitches for the rhythm guitar to fill out as accompanying triads.

To begin to hear the harmony beneath a melody, let's start with two completely different pieces, one from the world of popular music and the other, a well-known classical favorite. The first one is a bit of soul music called doo-wop. **Doo-wop** emerged in the 1950s as an outgrowth of the gospel hymns sung in African American churches in urban Detroit, Chicago, Philadelphia, and New York. Often doo-wop was improvised **a cappella** (voices only; that is, unaccompanied) on the street because it was direct and repetitive—the accompanying singers could easily hear and form a harmony against the melody. And because the lyrics that the accompanying singers sang were often little more than "doo wop, doo wah," the name "doo-wop" stuck to describe these songs. Finally, doo-wop harmony used a short chord progression, most commonly a sequence of triads moving I-VI-IV-V-(I) that repeated over and over again (for these four repeating chords, see Listening Guide, "Harmony (Chord Changes)".

In music, any element (rhythm, melody, or harmony) that continually repeats is called an **ostinato** (from the Italian word meaning "obstinate thing"). In the doo-wop song "Duke of Earl," we hear the bass voice lead, not with "doo, doo, doo," but with "Duke, Duke, Duke," setting the foundation for the chords that soon enter in the other voices. The tempo is moderately fast, and each of the four chords lasts for four beats. Every time the harmony voices sing "Earl," the chords change. The I-VI-IV-V-(I) chord progression lasts for about nine seconds and then repeats over

LISTEN TO... a podcast about hearing the bass line online.

LISTEN TO... a podcast about chord changes online.

LISTENING GUIDE

Harmony (Chord Changes)   Download 3 (2:33)

Gene Chandler, "Duke of Earl" (1962)

WHAT TO LISTEN FOR: A harmony that repeats as a four-bar ostinato. The bass singer first sets the bass line, and the other singers then add a chordal harmony in support of the melody.

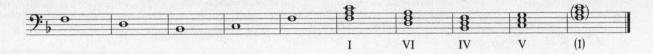

| | | | | | I | VI | IV | V | (I) |

0:00	Bass leads with:
	Duke, Duke, Duke, Duke of Earl, Duke, Duke, Duke of Earl, Duke, Duke, Duke of Earl
	I----------------------------VI----------------------------IV----------------------------V
0:09	Other voices and instruments enter, filling out harmony
0:18	Voice of Gene Chandler enters with lyrics
0:27	Further statement of harmonic pattern
0:37	Each chord now holds for two bars rather than one.
0:54 (and 1:03)	Each chord again holds for one bar.
1:13	Each chord again holds for two bars rather than one.
1:32 (and 1:41)	Each chord again holds for one bar.

For the rest, you're on your own!

LISTEN TO ... this selection streaming online.

WATCH ... an Active Listening Guide of this selection online.

WATCH... Vitamin C's "Graduation (Friends Forever)," in which you can hear the Pachelbel harmony very clearly.

DO... Listening Exercise 2.4, Hearing the Bass Line and Harmony, online.

and over again. As you listen to this doo-wop classic, sing along with the bass, no matter what your vocal range. Anyone can hear this harmony change.

Finally, for a similar, but slightly more complex, piece from the classical repertoire, we turn to the famous Pachelbel Canon. (See also "Pachelbel and His Canon" in Chapter 7.) Johann Pachelbel (1653–1706), who lived in Germany and was a mentor to musicians in the Bach family, composed this piece for four musical lines. The top three, here played by violins, are performed as a **canon** (a "round" in which one voice starts out and the others duplicate it exactly, as in "Three Blind Mice"). Below, the three-part canon is a harmonic ostinato, this one consisting of eight chords. So popular has Pachelbel's harmony become that it has been "borrowed" by countless pop singers, including The Beatles ("Let It Be"), U2 ("With or Without You"), and Vitamin C ("Graduation [Friends Forever]"). For Pachelbel, musical imitation has been an endless form of flattery.

KEY WORDS

beat (17)	meter signature (19)	clef (23)	harmony (26)
tempo (17)	time signature (19)	treble clef (23)	chord (27)
accelerando (17)	bar line (19)	bass clef (23)	triad (27)
ritard (17)	pickup (20)	great staff (grand staff) (23)	chord progression (28)
downbeat (17)	syncopation (20)	scale (24)	cadence (28)
accent (17)	melody (21)	major scale (24)	dominant (28)
meter (17)	pitch (21)	minor scale (24)	dissonance (28)
measure (bar) (17)	octave (21)	mode (24)	consonance (28)
duple meter (17)	flat (♭) (21)	chromatic scale (26)	doo-wop (29)
triple meter (17)	sharp (♯) (21)	tonic (26)	a cappella (29)
rest (18)	interval (22)	tonality (key) (26)	ostinato (29)
rhythm (18)	staff (22)	modulation (26)	canon (30)

 Join us on Facebook at Listening to Music with Craig Wright

PRACTICE ... your understanding of this chapter's concepts by reviewing the elements of music and working once more with the chapter's Active Listening Guides online.

DO ... online multiple-choice and critical thinking quizzes that your instructor may assign for a grade.

Color, Texture, Form, and STYLE

START... experiencing this chapter's topics with an online video activity.

LEARNING OBJECTIVES

After studying the material in this chapter, you should be able to:

1 Recognize the different voice parts and musical instruments within their families.

2 Distinguish the three primary musical textures.

3 Recognize how musical form is created by the use of statement, repetition, contrast, or variation.

4 Experience an overview of musical style from various historical eras.

I f rhythm, melody, and harmony are the *what* of music, then color, texture, form, and style are the *how*. Rhythm, melody, and harmony are the surface details of musical sound that catch our attention and evoke an emotional response. Color, texture, and form refer not so much to the musical idea itself but, instead, to the way the musical idea is presented. Style in music is the distinctive sound created as an expression of all these other elements of music.

Musical **dynamics** (louds and softs) also influence our reaction to music. Heroic themes are usually played loudly, and mournful ones are usually played quietly, for example, so as to create the desired mood. Because Italian musicians once dominated the Western musical world, most of our musical terminology is drawn from that language. Thus, we refer to loud and very loud as *forte* (pronounced FOUR-tay) and *fortissimo*, and to soft and very soft as *piano* and *pianissimo*. But changes in dynamics need not be sudden and abrupt. They can also be gradual and extend over a long period of time. A gradual increase in the volume of sound is called a **crescendo**, whereas a gradual decrease is called either a **decrescendo** or a **diminuendo**. An impressive crescendo sounds at the beginning of Richard Strauss's *Also sprach Zarathustra* (Download 2 or second Active Listening Guide in Chapter 1), as the full orchestra enters and gains momentum. Spectacular moments like these remind us that in music, as in marketing, the medium (here, powerful dynamics and color) can be the message. When heard as background music for a TV commercial, the viewer is led to conclude, "This product *sounds* great!"

Color

Simply stated, **color** in music is the tone quality of any sound produced by a voice or an instrument. **Timbre** (pronounced TAM-ber) is another term for the tone quality of musical sound. We can all hear that a clarinet produces a much different tone quality than does a trombone. Similarly, the voice of pop singer Sam Smith has a different timbre than that of opera star Placido Domingo, even when the two produce the same pitch.

The Voice

How many different voices can you recognize? Perhaps as many as a hundred. Each of us has a uniquely constructed set of vocal cords (two folds of mucous membrane within the throat). When we talk or sing, we send air through them, creating vibrations that reach the ear as sounds of a distinctive timbre. We need to hear only a few notes of a song to recognize that this is the voice of Blake Shelton, for example, and not that of Bono.

Musical voices are classified by range into four principal parts. The two women's vocal parts are the **soprano** and the **alto**, and the two men's vocal parts are the **tenor** and the **bass**. (Men's vocal cords are longer and thicker than women's, so for that reason, the sound of the mature male voice is lower.) Midway between the soprano and the alto voice is the **mezzo-soprano**, and midway between the tenor and the bass is the **baritone**. Most male pop singers—John Mayer, Michael Bublé, and Blake Shelton, for instance—are baritones; a few voices, such as those of Justin Timberlake, Bruno Mars, and the late Michael Jackson, are more in the tenor range.

READ... the complete chapter text in a rich, interactive online platform.

LISTEN TO... a podcast about dynamics online.

Musical Instruments

Have you ever wondered why a flute or a violin sounds the way it does—why it has a distinctive timbre? In brief, instruments are constructed in different shapes, with different materials of different densities. Even when they sound the same pitch, they emit slightly different vibrations, which our brain perceives as distinctive musical colors. Having heard those distinctive vibrations and *seen* a particular instrument as it creates them, we come to associate a particular sound with a particular instrument.

Musical instruments come in groups, or families—instruments of one general type having the same general shape and made of the same materials. The Western symphony orchestra traditionally includes four such groups—the four "food groups" of classical music, so to speak: strings, woodwinds, brasses, and percussion. In addition, there is a fifth group of instruments, the keyboard instruments (piano, organ, and harpsichord), instruments not normally part of the symphony orchestra.

Strings

If you travel to Beijing to hear a traditional Chinese orchestra, most of the instruments (erhu, pipa, and qinqin, for example) will be string instruments. If you attend the Bonnaroo Arts & Music Festival in Manchester, Tennessee, the rock bands there play electric bass and a variety of guitars—all string instruments. Visit the Country Music Hall of Fame in nearby Nashville, Tennessee, and you'll likely hear a fiddle and perhaps a mandolin added to the guitar ensemble. Watch the San Francisco Symphony on stage at Davies Symphony Hall, and you'll notice the majority of its performers playing, again, string instruments. In sum, string instruments, whether plucked or bowed, dominate musical ensembles around the world.

Violin Group

The violin group—violins, violas, cellos, and double basses—constitutes the core of the Western symphony orchestra. A large orchestra can easily include as many as one hundred members, at least sixty of whom play one of these four instruments.

The **violin** (Figure 3.1, center) is chief among the string instruments. It is also the smallest—it has the shortest strings and therefore produces the highest pitch. Because the tune usually sounds in the highest part of the musical texture, the violin generally plays the melody. In an orchestra, violins are usually divided into groups known as firsts and seconds. The seconds play a part slightly lower in pitch and subordinate in function to the firsts.

The **viola** (Figure 3.1, left) is about six inches longer than the violin, and it produces a somewhat lower sound. If the violin is the string counterpart of the soprano voice, then the viola has its parallel in the alto voice. Its tone is darker, richer, and more somber than that of the brilliant violin.

You can easily spot the **cello** (Figure 3.1, right) in the orchestra because the player sits with the instrument placed between his or her legs. The pitch of the cello is well below that of the viola. It can provide a low bass sound as well as a lyrical melody. When played in its middle range by a skilled performer, the cello can produce an indescribably rich, expressive tone.

WATCH... the instruments of the symphony orchestra as they sound in Prokofiev's popular musical narrative, *Peter and the Wolf.*

LISTEN TO... the violin streaming online.

LISTEN TO... the viola streaming online.

FIGURE 3.1
This photo of the American group, the Brentano String Quartet, shows the relative size of the violin (center), viola (left), and cello (right). Founded in 1992, the group is currently in residence as performers and teachers at Yale University.

The **double bass** (Figure 3.2) gives weight and power to the bass line in the orchestra. Because at first it merely doubled the notes of the cello an octave below, it was called the double bass. As you can see, the double bass is the largest, and hence the lowest-sounding, of the string instruments. Its job in the orchestra, and even in jazz bands, is to help set a solid base/bass for the musical harmony.

The members of the violin group all generate pitches in the same way: A bow is drawn across a tight string. This produces the familiar penetrating string sound. In addition, a number of other effects can be created by using different playing techniques.

- **Vibrato**: If you see the left hand of a string player shaking during a performance, the cause isn't too much caffeine. Shaking the left hand as it stops the string produces a controlled "wobble" in the pitch. This adds richness to the tone of the string because, in fact, it creates a blend of two or more pitches.

- **Pizzicato**: Instead of bowing the strings, the performer plucks them. With this technique, the resulting sound has a sharp attack, but it dies away quickly.

- **Tremolo**: The performer creates a musical "tremor" by rapidly repeating the same pitch with quick up-and-down strokes of the bow. Tremolo creates a feeling of heightened tension and excitement when played loudly and a velvety, shimmering backdrop when performed quietly.

- **Trill**: The performer rapidly alternates between two distinctly separate but neighboring pitches. Most instruments, not just the strings, can play trills.

LISTENING CUE

Instruments of the Orchestra: Strings

WHAT TO LISTEN FOR: The distinctive timbres and techniques of the string instruments

WATCH ... an Active Listening Guide of the strings online.

The Harp

Although originally a folk instrument, the **harp** (Figure 3.3) is sometimes added to the modern symphony orchestra. Its role is to lend its distinctive color to the orchestral sound and sometimes to create special effects, the most striking of which is a rapid run up or down the strings, called a **glissando**. When the notes of a triad are played in quick succession, up or down, an **arpeggio** results, a term derived from the Italian word for harp (*arpa*).

Woodwinds

The name "woodwind" was originally given to this family of instruments because they emit sound when air is blown through a wooden tube or pipe. Today, however,

some of these "wooden" instruments are made entirely of metal. Flutes, for example, are constructed of silver and sometimes of gold or even platinum. As with the violin group, there are four principal woodwind instruments in every modern symphony orchestra: flute, oboe, clarinet, and bassoon (Figure 3.4). In addition, each of these has a close relative that is larger or smaller in size and that possesses a somewhat different timbre and range. The larger the instrument or length of pipe is, of course, the lower the sound.

The lovely, silvery tone of the **flute** is probably familiar to you. The instrument can be rich in the lower register and light and airy at the top. It is especially agile, capable of playing tones rapidly and moving quickly from one range to another.

The smaller cousin of the flute is the **piccolo**. (*Piccolo* comes from the Italian *flauto piccolo*, meaning "little flute.") It can produce higher notes than any other orchestral instrument. And though the piccolo is very small, its sound is so piercing that it can always be heard, even when the full orchestra is playing loudly.

The **clarinet** produces sound when the player blows air under a single reed fitted to the mouthpiece. The tone of the clarinet is an open, hollow sound. It can be mellow in its low notes but shrill in its high notes. It also has the capacity to slide or glide smoothly between pitches, which allows for a highly expressive style of playing. A lower, larger version of the clarinet is the bass clarinet.

FIGURE 3.4
(from left to right) A flute, two clarinets, an oboe, and a bassoon. The flute, clarinet, and oboe are about the same length, and they play approximately the same range of pitches. The bassoon is nearly twice their size, and its pitches are much lower.

The **oboe** is equipped with a double reed—two reeds tied together with an air space in between. When the player blows air between them and into the instrument, the resulting vibrations create a nasal, slightly exotic sound. It is invariably the oboe that gives the pitch at the beginning of a symphony concert. Not only was the oboe the first nonstring instrument to be added to the orchestra, it is also a difficult instrument to tune (regulate the pitch). Thus it's better to have the other instruments tune to the oboe than to try to have the oboe adjust to them.

Related to the oboe is the **English horn**. Unfortunately, it is wrongly named, for the English horn is neither English nor a horn. It is simply a larger (hence, lower-sounding) version of the oboe which originated on the continent of Europe.

The **bassoon** functions among the woodwinds much as the cello does among the strings: It adds weight to the lowest sound or acts as a soloist. When played moderately fast or with rapid passages as a solo instrument, it has a dry, almost comical tone. There is also a double bassoon, called the **contrabassoon**, which can play notes lower than any other orchestral instrument.

LISTEN TO... the oboe streaming online.

LISTEN TO... the bassoon streaming online.

Brasses

Like the woodwind and string groups of the orchestra, the brass family consists of four primary instruments: trumpet, trombone, French horn, and tuba (Figure 3.5). Brass players use no reeds but, instead, blow into their instruments through a cup-shaped **mouthpiece** (Figure 3.6). By adjusting valves or moving a slide, the performer can make the length of pipe on the instrument longer or shorter, and hence the pitch lower or higher.

FIGURE 3.5
Members of the Canadian Brass, with the French horn player at the left and the tuba player at the right

FIGURE 3.6
Three mouthpieces for brass instruments

Instruments of the Orchestra: Brasses

WHAT TO LISTEN FOR: The distinctive timbres and techniques of the brasses

WATCH ... an Active Listening Guide of the brasses online.

LISTEN TO... the trumpet and a muted trumpet streaming online.

LISTEN TO... the trombone streaming online.

LISTEN TO... the French horn streaming online.

LISTEN TO... a tuba streaming online.

Everyone has heard the high, bright, cutting sound of the **trumpet**. Whether played in a football stadium or an orchestral hall, the trumpet is an excellent solo instrument because of its agility and penetrating tone. Sometimes the trumpeter is required to play with a **mute** (a plug placed in the bell of the instrument) to lessen its piercing sound.

Although distantly related to the trumpet, the **trombone** (Italian for "large trumpet") plays in the middle range of the brass family. Its sound is large and full. Most important, the trombone is the only brass instrument to generate sounds by moving a slide in and out in order to produce higher or lower pitches. Needless to say, the trombone can easily slide from pitch to pitch, sometimes for comical effect.

The **French horn** (originally called just "horn") was the first brass instrument to join the orchestra, in the late seventeenth century. Because the French horn, like the trombone, sounds in the middle range of the brasses, these two instruments are often almost impossible to distinguish. The French horn, however, has a slightly mellower, more "veiled" sound than does the clearer, "in your face" trombone.

The **tuba** is the largest and lowest-sounding of the brass instruments. It produces a full, though sometimes muffled, tone in its lowest notes. Like the double bass of the violin group, the tuba is most often used to set a base, or foundation, for the melody.

Percussion

Want to make your own percussion instrument? Just find a metal trash can and strike its side with your hand. Percussion instruments are simply resonating objects that sound when hit or scraped with an implement in one fashion or another. Some percussion instruments, like the timpani (kettledrums), produce a specific pitch, while others generate a sound that, while rhythmically precise, has no recognizable

FIGURE 3.7
Tympanist Jonathan Haas of the American Symphony Orchestra

musical pitch. It is the job of the percussion instruments to sharpen the rhythmic contour of the music. They can also add density to the sounds of other instruments and, when played loudly, can heighten the sense of climax in a piece. Percussion instruments work well outdoors, and they never need amplification.

The **timpani** (Figure 3.7) is the percussion instrument most often heard in classical music. Whether struck in single, detached strokes or hit rapidly to produce a thunder-like roll, the function of the timpani is to add depth, tension, and drama to the music. Timpani usually come in pairs, one instrument tuned to the tonic and the other to the dominant. Playing only these pitches, the timpani feature prominently at the beginning of Strauss's *Also sprach Zarathustra* (Download 2 or second Active Listening Guide in Chapter 1).

The "rat-a-tat-tat" sound of the **snare drum**, the dull thud of the **bass drum**, and the crashing ring of the **cymbals** are sounds well known from marching bands and jazz ensembles, as well as the classical orchestra. None of them produces a specific musical tone.

Keyboard Instruments

Keyboard instruments, which are unique to Western music, boast highly intricate mechanisms. They are all "fixed-pitch" instruments—you don't "tune up" before you play them. The **pipe organ** (Figure 3.8), the most complex of all musical instruments, developed during the late Middle Ages in the context of the religious music of the Western church. When the player depresses a key, air rushes into a pipe, thereby generating sound. The pipes are arranged in separate groups, called ranks, each producing a full range of musical pitches with one particular timbre (the sound of the trumpet, for example). When the organist wants to add a

LISTEN TO... the timpani, snare drum, bass drum, and cymbals streaming online.

WATCH... a video of all the orchestral instruments, in Benjamin Britten's *Young Person's Guide to the Orchestra.*

LISTEN TO... a podcast about identifying instruments online.

WATCH... a video demonstration of the pipe organ.

FIGURE 3.8
A three-manual (keyboard) pipe organ with only small pipes visible. Notice the stops (small circular objects on either side of the manual keyboards) and the pedal keyboard below.

A two-manual (-keyboard) harpsichord built by Pascal Taskin (Paris, 1770), preserved in the Yale University Collection of Musical Instruments, New Haven, Connecticut

WATCH... a video demonstration of the harpsichord.

WATCH... a video demonstration of the piano.

FIGURE 3.10
Pianist Lang Lang is known for his flamboyant interpretations of classical favorites.

distinctive musical color to a piece, he or she simply pulls a knob, called a **stop**. The most colorful, forceful sound occurs when all of the stops have been activated (thus the expression "pulling out all the stops"). The several keyboards of the organ make it possible to play several colorful lines at once, each with its own timbre. There is even a keyboard for the feet to play. The largest fully functioning pipe organ in the world is the Wannamaker Organ in the Macy's Center in Philadelphia. It has 463 ranks and 28,604 pipes, activated by six keyboards.

The **harpsichord** (Figure 3.9) appeared in northern Italy as early as 1400 but reached its heyday during the Baroque era (1600–1750). When a key is depressed, it drives a lever upward that, in turn, forces a pick to pluck a string, thereby creating a bright, jangling sound. The harpsichord has one important shortcoming, however: The lever mechanism does not allow the performer to control the force with which the string is plucked. Each string always sounds at the same volume, no matter how hard the player strikes the key.

The **piano** (Figure 3.10) was invented in Italy around 1700, in part to overcome the sound-producing limitations of the harpsichord. The strings of a piano are not plucked; they are hit by soft hammers. A lever mechanism makes it possible for the player to regulate how hard each string is struck: Touch lightly and a soft sound results; bang hard and you hear a loud one. Thus, the original piano was called the *pianoforte*, the "soft-loud." During Mozart's lifetime (1756–1791), the piano replaced the harpsichord as the favorite domestic musical instrument. By the nineteenth century, every aspiring household had to have a piano, whether as an instrument for real musical enjoyment or as a symbol of affluence.

Today, the piano reigns supreme in both home and concert hall. But it has one natural predator that may someday make it extinct: the **electric keyboard**. This computer-driven synthesizer can, with the push of a button, alter the sound we hear from piano to harpsichord, or choir or trombones, or to any acoustic instrument. The compact size and versatility of the electric keyboard make it a favorite of rock and pop bands.

The Symphony Orchestra

The modern Western symphony orchestra is one of the largest and certainly the most colorful of all musical ensembles. When at full strength, the symphony orchestra can include upwards of 100 performers and nearly 30 different instruments, from the high, piping piccolo down to the rumbling contrabassoon. (The New York Philharmonic Orchestra currently has 106 musicians under union contract, with a base salary of about $140,000.) A typical seating plan for an orchestra is given in Figure 3.11. To achieve the best balance of sound, strings are placed toward the front, and the more powerful brasses and percussion are placed at the back.

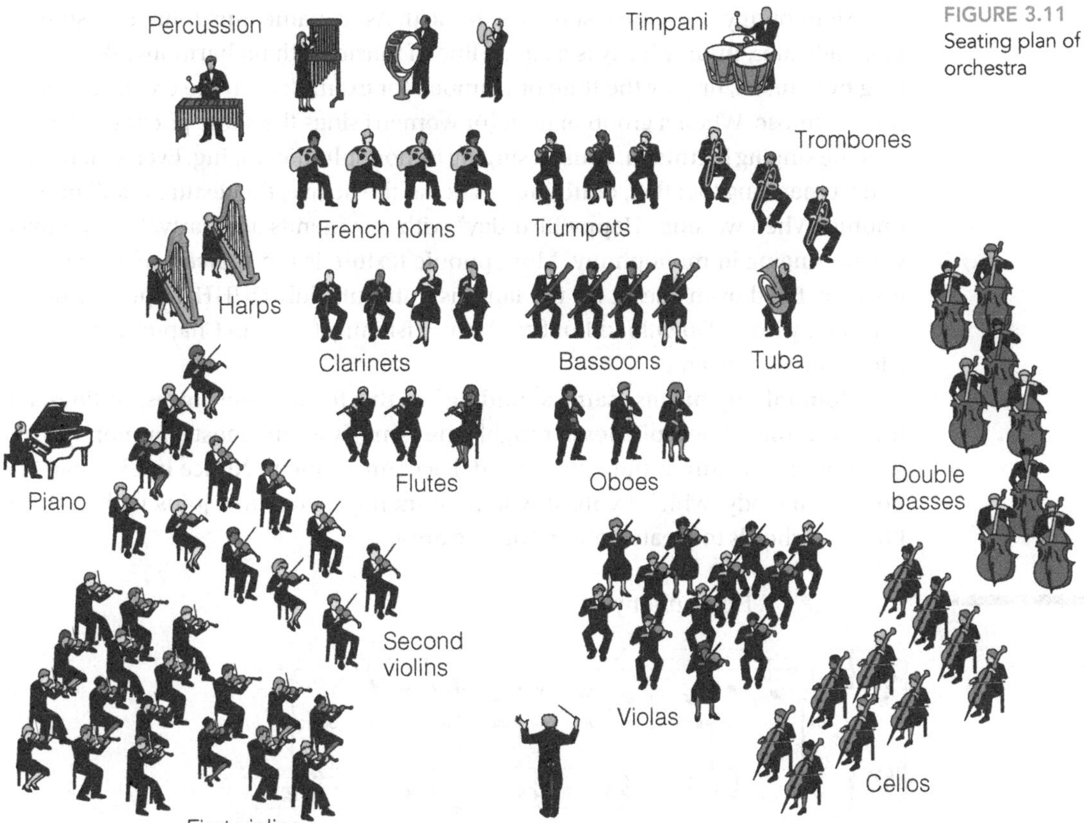

FIGURE 3.11
Seating plan of a symphony
orchestra

When the orchestra first originated in the seventeenth century, it had no separate conductor. The group was small enough for the players to play on their own, usually following the lead of the principal violinist. But around the time of Beethoven (1770–1827), when the orchestra was already 200 years old and had expanded to include some sixty players, it became necessary to have someone stand before the orchestra and direct it. Indeed, the **conductor** functions something like a musical traffic cop: He or she makes sure that the cellos don't overshadow the violins and that the French horns yield to the clarinet at the proper moment, so the melody can be heard. The conductor reads from an **orchestral score** (a composite of all the parts) and must be able to immediately pick out any incorrectly played pitches and rhythms. To do this, the conductor must have an excellent musical ear.

Texture

When a painter or a weaver arranges material on a canvas or a loom, he or she creates a texture: **Texture** is the density and arrangement of artistic elements. Look at Vincent van Gogh's *Branch of an Almond Tree in Blossom* (1890), shown at this chapter's opening. Here the painter has used lines and spaces to create a texture that is heavy at the bottom but light at the top, projecting an image that is well grounded but airy. So, too, a composer creates effects with musical lines—also called parts or voices, even though they might not be sung. There are three primary textures in music, depending on the interaction of vocal parts, or lines, involved: monophonic, homophonic, and polyphonic.

DO... Listening Exercise 3.1, Hearing the Instruments of the Orchestra: Identifying a Single Instrument, online.

DO... Listening Exercise 3.2, Hearing the Instruments of the Orchestra: Identifying Two Instruments, online.

DO... Listening Exercise 3.3, Hearing the Instruments of the Orchestra: Identifying Three Instruments, online.

LISTEN TO... a podcast about texture online.

Monophony is the easiest texture to hear. As its name, meaning "one sounding," indicates, **monophony** is a single line of music, with no harmony. When you sing by yourself, or play the flute or trumpet, for example, you are creating monophonic music. When a group of men (or women) sings the same pitches together, they are singing in **unison**. Unison singing is monophonic singing. Even when men and women sing together, doubling pitches at the octave, the texture is still monophonic. When we sing "Happy Birthday" with our friends at a party, for example, we are singing in monophony. Monophonic texture is the sparsest of all musical textures. Beethoven uses it for the famous duh-duh-duh-DUHHH opening of his Symphony No. 5 (Download 1 or first Active Listening Guide in Chapter 1) to create a lean, sinewy effect.

Homophony means "same sounding." In this texture, the voices, or lines, all move together to new pitches at roughly the same time. The most common type of homophonic texture is tune plus chordal accompaniment. Notice in Example 3.1 how the melody, which by itself would be monophonic, now joins with vertical blocks of chords to create homophonic texture.

LISTEN TO...
Example 3.1 online.

EXAMPLE 3.1 Homophony

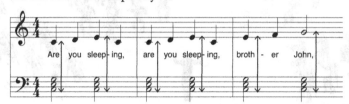

Holiday carols, hymns, folksongs, and almost all pop songs have this sort of tune-plus-chordal-accompaniment texture when sung with harmony. Can you hear in your mind's ear a band playing "The Star-Spangled Banner"? That's homophonic texture.

As we might suppose from its name, which means "many sounding," **polyphony** requires two or more lines in the musical fabric. In addition, the term *polyphonic* implies that each of the lines will be free and independent, and enter at different times. Thus, polyphonic texture has a strong linear (horizontal) thrust, whereas in homophonic texture, the fabric is structured more vertically as blocks of accompanying chords (compare the arrows in Examples 3.1 and 3.2). In polyphonic texture, the voices are of equal importance, moving against one another to create what is called **counterpoint**, the harmonious opposition of two or more independent musical lines. (Musicians often use the terms *polyphony* and *counterpoint* interchangeably.) Finally, there are two types of counterpoint: free and imitative. In free counterpoint, the voices are highly independent and go their separate ways; much jazz improvisation is done in free counterpoint. In imitative counterpoint, on the other hand, a leading voice begins, followed by one or more other voices that duplicate what the first voice has presented. If the followers copy exactly, note for note, what the leader plays or sings, then a canon results. Think of "Three Blind Mice," "Are You Sleeping?" ("Frère Jacques"), and "Row, Row, Row Your Boat," and remember how each voice enters in turn, imitating the first voice from beginning to end (see Example 3.2). These are all short canons, or rounds, a type of strictly imitative counterpoint popular since the Middle Ages. A much longer canon, as we have seen in Listening Exercise 2.4, plays out in the upper three lines of Johann Pachelbel's well-known Canon in D major.

LISTEN TO... an excerpt from Pachelbel's Canon online.

EXAMPLE 3.2 Polyphony

Of course, composers are not limited to just one of these three musical textures in a given piece—they can move from one to another, as George Frideric Handel does brilliantly in the justly famous "Hallelujah" chorus (see Listening Guide) from his oratorio *Messiah*.

LISTEN TO...
Example 3.2 online.

LISTENING GUIDE

George Frideric Handel, *Messiah*, "Hallelujah" chorus (1741)   Download 4 (3:34)

WHAT TO LISTEN FOR: Handel's skillful manipulation of the musical texture to achieve variety and generate excitement. Notice at the very end, before the last "Hallelujah," how the composer introduces a brief example of a fourth texture: silence. Indeed, a thundering silence!

0:06	"Hallelujah! Hallelujah!"	Homophony
0:23	"For the Lord God Omnipotent reigneth"	Monophony
0:30	"Hallelujah! Hallelujah!"	Homophony
0:34	"For the Lord God Omnipotent reigneth"	Monophony
0:40	"Hallelujah! Hallelujah!"	Homophony
0:44	"For the Lord God Omnipotent reigneth," together with "Hallelujah"	Polyphony
1:09	"The Kingdom of this world is become"	Homophony
1:27	"And He shall reign for ever and ever"	Polyphony
1:48	"King of Kings and Lord of Lords," together with "Hallelujah"	Homophony
2:28	"And He shall reign for ever and ever"	Polyphony
2:40	"King of Kings and Lord of Lords," together with "Hallelujah"	Homophony
2:48	"And He shall reign for ever and ever"	Polyphony
2:55	"King of Kings and Lord of Lords," together with "Hallelujah"	Homophony

LISTEN TO ... this selection streaming online.

WATCH ... an Active Listening Guide of this selection online.

DO ... Listening Exercise 3.4, Hearing Musical Textures, online.

Form

LISTEN TO... a podcast about musical form online.

Form in music is the arrangement of musical events. In architecture, sculpture, and painting, objects are situated in physical space to create a pleasing design. Similarly, in music, a composer directs that important sonic events come in an order that creates a compelling pattern. We don't see the form but, rather, hear it as the sounds pass by in time.

To create form in music, a composer employs one of four processes: statement, repetition, contrast, and variation. A **statement**, of course, is the presentation of an important musical idea. **Repetition** validates the statement by reiterating it. Nothing would be more bewildering for a listener than a steady stream of ever-new music. How would we make sense of it? Recurring musical ideas function as formal markers; each return is an important musical event—and a reassuring return to stability.

Contrast, on the other hand, takes us away from the familiar and into the unknown. Contrasting melodies, rhythms, textures, and moods can be used to provide variety and even to create conflict. In music, as in life, we need novelty and excitement; contrast invigorates us, making the eventual return to familiar ideas all the more satisfying.

Variation stands midway between repetition and contrast. The original melody returns but is altered in some way. For example, the tune may now be more complex, or new instruments may be added against it to create counterpoint. The listener has the satisfaction of hearing the familiar melody yet is challenged to recognize how it has been changed, or disguised.

Needless to say, memory plays an important role in hearing musical form. We live forward, but we understand backward. Whether in history or in music, our memory puts the pieces together to help us understand the whole. To simplify this pattern processing, musicians have developed a system to visualize forms by using letters to represent musical units—seeing is usually easier than hearing. The first statement of a musical idea is designated **A**. Subsequent contrasting sections are labeled **B, C, D**, and so on. If the first of any other musical unit returns in varied form, then that variation is indicated by a superscript number or a prime—A^1 and **B'**, for example. Subdivisions of each large musical unit are shown by lowercase letters **a, b**, and so forth. How this works will become clear in the examples used throughout this book.

Strophic Form

This is the most familiar of all musical forms because our hymns, carols, folksongs, and pop tunes invariably make use of it. In **strophic form**, the composer sets the words of the first poetic stanza (strophe) and then uses the same entire melody for all subsequent stanzas. Moreover, in many pop songs, each strophe begins with a verse of text and ends with a **chorus**—a textual **refrain** that repeats. (A chorus is so called because, in the Middle Ages, a group entered at that point to sing the refrain along with the soloist.) In Jay-Z and Alicia Keys's "Empire State of Mind," he raps the verse, and she then sings the refrain. The strophe (verse and chorus) is then repeated two more times, with the music always the same for each strophe. We can't provide the lyrics of "Empire State of Mind" because of its "explicit content," so let's move back to the 1860s to a hymn text that served as a rallying point for the Union (Northern) forces during the American Civil War: "The Battle Hymn of the Republic," with text by Julia Ward Howe (1862).

Johannes Brahms, *Wiegenlied* (*Lullaby*; 1868)   Download 5 (1:43)

WHAT TO LISTEN FOR: An exact repeat of the music of strophe 1 for strophe 2

WHAT NOT TO LISTEN FOR: A chorus—there is none!

0:00	Gut' Abend, gut Nacht,	Good evening, good night,
	Mit Rosen bedacht,	Covered with roses,
	Mit Näglein besteckt,	Adorned with carnations,
	Schlüpf unter die Deck':	Slip under the covers:
	Morgen früh, wenn Gott will,	Tomorrow early, if God so wills,
	Wirst du wieder geweckt.	You will awake again.
0:48	Gut' Abend, gut Nacht,	Good evening, good night,
	Von Englein bewacht,	Watched over by angels,
	Die zeigen im Traum	Who in dreams show
	Dir Christkindleins Baum.	You the Christ child's tree.
	Schlaf nun selig und süss,	Now sleep blissful and sweetly,
	Schau im Traum's Paradies.	Behold Paradise in your dreams.

LISTEN TO ... this selection streaming online.

WATCH ... an Active Listening Guide of this selection online.

WATCH ... an animation of an equally beautiful strophic song by Brahms, online.

Strophe 1

(Verse) Mine eyes have seen the glory of the coming of the Lord:
He is trampling out the vintage where the grapes of wrath are stored;
He hath loosed the fateful lightning of His terrible swift sword:
His truth is marching on.

(Chorus) Glory, glory, hallelujah! Glory, glory, hallelujah!
Glory, glory, hallelujah! His truth is marching on.

A similar use of the word *glory* as the basis for a chorus can be heard in the Academy Award–winning song "Glory" (2014).

Now, listen to the first two strophes of the equally well known *Wiegenlied (Lullaby)* of Johannes Brahms (see Listening Guide). Each strophe, again, is sung to the same music, but here there is no chorus.

Theme and Variations

The working of **theme and variations** form is obvious: one musical idea continually returns but is varied in some fashion, by a change in the melody, harmony, texture, rhythm, or timbre. In classical music, the more variations the composer writes, the more obscure the theme becomes; the listener is increasingly challenged to hear

FIGURE 3.12
The Opera House in the harbor of Sydney, Australia. Here we see a theme (a rising, pointed arch) that displays a new variation each time it appears in a different position.

TABLE 3.1 Theme and Variations Form

Statement of Theme	Variation 1	Variation 2	Variation 3	Variation 4
A	A¹	A²	A³	A⁴

the new as an outgrowth of the old. Theme and variations form can be visualized as in Table 3.1.

When Mozart was a young man, he lived briefly in Paris, where he heard the French folksong, "Ah, vous dirai-je Maman." We know it today as "Twinkle, Twinkle, Little Star" (see Listening Guide). Upon this charming tune (**A**) he later composed a set of variations for piano (discussed in full in Chapter 12).

Binary Form

As the name indicates, **binary form** consists of two contrasting units, **A** and **B** (see Figure 3.13). In length and general shape, **A** and **B** are constructed to balance and complement each other. Variety is usually introduced in **B** by means of a dissimilar mood, key, or melody. Sometimes in binary form, both **A** and **B** are immediately repeated, note for note. Musicians indicate exact repeats by means of the following sign: ‖: :‖ Thus, when binary form appears as ‖:A:‖‖:B:‖ it is performed **AABB**. Joseph Haydn created a perfect example of binary form in music for the second movement of his Symphony No. 94 (see Listening Guide) and then wrote a set of variations upon this theme (discussed in full in Chapter 12).

FIGURE 3.13
The essence of binary form, or **AB** form, can be seen in this Japanese wood carving. Here, the two figures are distinctly different yet mutually harmonious.

Ternary Form

If the most prevalent form in pop songs is strophic form, in classical music it is **ternary form**; the musical journey home-away-home (**ABA**) has satisfied composers and listeners for centuries (see Figure 3.14). In the "Dance of the Reed Pipes" from Peter Tchaikovsky's famous ballet *The Nutcracker* (see Listening Guide), the **A** section is bright and cheery because it makes use of the major mode as well as silvery flutes. However, the **B** section is dark and low, even ominous, owing to the minor

LISTENING GUIDE

Wolfgang Amadeus Mozart, Variations on "Twinkle, Twinkle, Little Star" (c. 1781)   Download 6 (2:58)

WHAT TO LISTEN FOR: How the theme is altered, one way or another, within each new variation

0:00	**A**	Tune played without ornamentation; melody above, harmony below
0:30	**A¹**	Variation 1: Tune above decorated with florid, fast-moving figurations
0:59	**A²**	Variation 2: Tune above undecorated; florid, fast-moving figurations now in bass
1:29	**A³**	Variation 3: Tune above decorated with graceful arpeggios

LISTEN TO ... this selection streaming online.

WATCH ... an Active Listening Guide of this selection online.

DO ... Listening Exercise 3.5, Mozart, Variations on "Twinkle, Twinkle, Little Star," online.

Joseph Haydn, Symphony No. 94, the "Surprise" (1792)   Download 7 (1:06)

Theme from second movement, *Andante* (moving)

WHAT TO LISTEN FOR: A charming **A** theme followed by a complementary **B** theme

0:00	**A** presented by strings
0:17	**A** repeated, with surprise *sforzando* at end
0:33	**B** presented by strings
0:50	**B** repeated, with flutes added to melody

LISTEN TO ... this selection streaming online.

WATCH ... an Active Listening Guide of this selection online.

---

mode and the insistent ostinato (repeated pattern) in the bass. Not wishing to leave us quaking in the dark, Tchaikovsky takes us back home—to the spritely **A** section.

Rondo Form

Rondo form involves a simple principle: A refrain (**A**) alternates with contrasting music. Usually in a rondo, there are at least two contrasting sections (**B** and **C**). Perhaps because of its simple but pleasing design (Figure 3.15), rondo form has been favored by musicians of every age—medieval monks,

FIGURE 3.14
Ternary form, or **ABA** form, can clearly be seen in the architecture of the cathedral of Salzburg, Austria, where Mozart and his father frequently performed.

Peter Tchaikovsky, *The Nutcracker*, "Dance of the Reed Pipes" (1891)   Download 8 (2:34)

WHAT TO LISTEN FOR: The bright, dancing music of **A**; the change to the dark, minor **B**; and the return to an abbreviated **A**

0:00	**A**	Flutes play melody above low string pizzicato.
0:35		English horn and then clarinet add counterpoint.
0:51		Melody repeats, with violins now adding counterpoint.
1:22	**B**	Change to minor mode: trumpets play melody above two-note bass ostinato.
1:36		Violins join melody.
1:57	**A¹**	Return to flute melody (with violin counterpoint) in major mode.

LISTEN TO ... this selection streaming online.

WATCH ... an Active Listening Guide of this selection online.

FIGURE 3.15
The chateau of Chambord, France, has a formal design equivalent to **ABACABA** structure, a pattern often encountered in music in rondo form.

A   B   A   C   A   B   A

classical symphonists such as Mozart and Haydn, and even contemporary pop artists like Sting (see end of Chapter 12). Although the principle of a recurring refrain is a constant, composers have written rondos in several different formal patterns, as seen below. The hallmark of each, however, is a refrain (**A**).

ABACA   ABACABA   ABACADA

You may already be familiar with a rondo composed by Jean-Joseph Mouret (1682–1738), made famous as the theme music for *Masterpiece Theatre* (now *Masterpiece*), America's longest-running prime-time drama series, on PBS (see Listening Guide). It is discussed in full in Chapter 7.

WATCH... Mozart's famous *Rondo alla Turca* in a spritely version for orchestra.

WATCH... a fast, fun romp through musical styles over the centuries.

Styles of Classical Music

Finally, musical style. Cultural historians use **style** as a catchall term for the common attributes that unite similar works of art. When we walk into an art gallery, we look around and try to make an educated guess about what we see, based on style. Similarly, when we turn on the audio mode in our airplane seat or the car radio, or

LISTENING GUIDE

Jean-Joseph Mouret, Rondeau, from *Suite de symphonies* (1729)   Download 9 (1:55)

WHAT TO LISTEN FOR: The regular appearance of theme **A** played by a brilliant trumpet

0:00	**A**	Refrain played by full orchestra, including trumpet and drums, and then repeated (at 0:12)
0:24	**B**	Quieter contrasting section played by strings and woodwinds
0:37	**A**	Refrain returns but without repeat.
0:50	**C**	New contrasting section played by strings and woodwinds
1:22	**A**	Refrain returns and is repeated (at 1:35).

LISTEN TO ... this selection streaming online.

WATCH ... an Active Listening Guide of this selection online.

TABLE 3.2 Musical Style Periods

Middle Ages: 476–1450	Romantic: 1820–1900
Renaissance: 1450–1600	Impressionist: 1880–1920
Baroque: 1600–1750	Modern: 1900–1985
Classical: 1750–1820	Postmodern: 1945–present

walk into Starbucks and listen, we must guess about style. We listen and try to compare what we hear to what we know. Is it Bach or Beethoven, Beyoncé or Bono? Probably what we are hearing in Starbucks comes from Pandora, today a source of listening for nearly 90 million people.

But, oddly enough, Pandora, too, relies on musical style—to give us more of the music we like. We choose a piece of music, and as we listen, a computer mines data about that piece—about the rate of information (tempo and beat), instrumental color, volume, and pitch frequencies of the melody and harmony. These data are then matched with other pieces with similar data (style features), and that's how the site suggests new songs for us. Style, then, is an amalgam of all the surface details of the music.

Singers have styles, bands have styles, and entire historical epochs have styles. Music historians identify eight style periods, extending from the Middle Ages to the Postmodern era (Table 3.2). In so doing, they confirm that all the music within a certain lengthy period possesses common attributes of rhythm, melody, harmony, texture, and color. General designations such as "Baroque style" or "Romantic style" help us quickly make sense of the sonic world.

KEY WORDS

dynamics (33)
forte (33)
piano (33)
crescendo (33)
decrescendo (diminuendo) (33)
color (33)
timbre (33)
soprano (33)
alto (33)
tenor (33)
bass (33)

mezzo-soprano (33)
baritone (33)
vibrato (35)
pizzicato (35)
tremolo (35)
trill (35)
glissando (35)
arpeggio (35)
mouthpiece (37)
mute (38)
stop (40)

conductor (41)
orchestral score (41)
texture (41)
monophony (42)
unison (42)
homophony (42)
polyphony (42)
counterpoint (42)
form (44)
statement (44)
repetition (44)

contrast (44)
variation (44)
strophic form (44)
chorus (refrain) (44)
theme and variations (45)
binary form (46)
‖:‖ (indication to performer to repeat the music) (46)
ternary form (46)
rondo form (47)
style (48)

 Join us on Facebook at Listening to Music with Craig Wright

PRACTICE ... your understanding of this chapter's concepts by reviewing the elements of music, comparing Checklists of Musical Style for all historic eras, and working once more with the chapter's Active Listening Guides online.

DO ... online multiple-choice and critical thinking quizzes that your instructor may assign for a grade.

The Middle Ages and **RENAISSANCE,** part TWO 476–1600

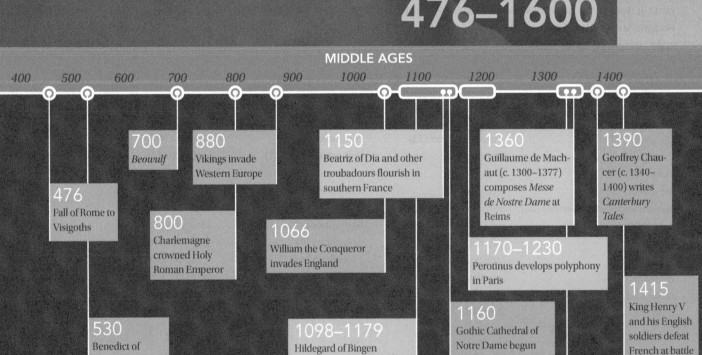

MIDDLE AGES

400   500   600   700   800   900   1000   1100   1200   1300   1400

700
Beowulf

880
Vikings invade
Western Europe

1150
Beatriz of Dia and other
troubadours flourish in
southern France

1360
Guillaume de Mach-
aut (c. 1300–1377)
composes *Messe
de Nostre Dame* at
Reims

1390
Geoffrey Chau-
cer (c. 1340–
1400) writes
*Canterbury
Tales*

476
Fall of Rome to
Visigoths

800
Charlemagne
crowned Holy
Roman Emperor

1066
William the Conqueror
invades England

1170–1230
Perotinus develops polyphony
in Paris

1415
King Henry V
and his English
soldiers defeat
French at battle
of Agincourt

530
Benedict of
Nursia founds
monastic order

1098–1179
Hildegard of Bingen
musician, poet, visionary

1160
Gothic Cathedral of
Notre Dame begun
in Paris

1348–1350
Black Death

Historians use the term *Middle Ages* as a catchall phrase to refer to the thousand years of history between the fall of the Roman Empire (476) and the dawn of the Age of Discovery (mid-1400s, culminating in the voyages of Christopher Columbus). It was a period of monks and nuns, of knightly chivalry and brutal warfare, of sublime spirituality and deadly plagues, and of soaring cathedrals amidst abject poverty. Two institutions vied for political control: the Church and the court. From our modern perspective, the medieval period appears as a vast chronological expanse dotted by outposts of dazzling architecture, stunning stained glass, and equally compelling poetry and music.

Renaissance means literally "rebirth." Historians use the term to designate a period of intellectual and artistic flowering that occurred first in Italy, then in France, and finally in England, during the years 1350–1600. Music historians apply the term more narrowly to musical developments in those same countries during the period 1450–1600. The Renaissance was an age in which writers, artists, and architects looked back to classical Greece and Rome to find models for personal and civic expression. Musicians reengaged ancient Greek drama, and from this emerged a new relationship between music and text—specific sounds came to amplify specific words. Finally, attributing creativity to human accomplishment as well as to God, Renaissance composers began to fashion secular music for the home as well as traditional religious music for the church.

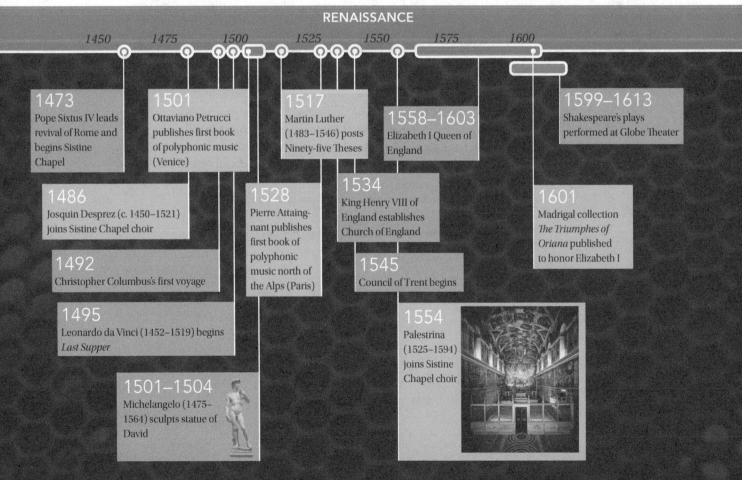

RENAISSANCE

1450   1475   1500   1525   1550   1575   1600

1473
Pope Sixtus IV leads revival of Rome and begins Sistine Chapel

1501
Ottaviano Petrucci publishes first book of polyphonic music (Venice)

1517
Martin Luther (1483–1546) posts Ninety-five Theses

1558–1603
Elizabeth I Queen of England

1599–1613
Shakespeare's plays performed at Globe Theater

1486
Josquin Desprez (c. 1450–1521) joins Sistine Chapel choir

1528
Pierre Attaingnant publishes first book of polyphonic music north of the Alps (Paris)

1534
King Henry VIII of England establishes Church of England

1601
Madrigal collection *The Triumphes of Oriana* published to honor Elizabeth I

1492
Christopher Columbus's first voyage

1545
Council of Trent begins

1495
Leonardo da Vinci (1452–1519) begins *Last Supper*

1554
Palestrina (1525–1594) joins Sistine Chapel choir

1501–1504
Michelangelo (1475–1564) sculpts statue of David

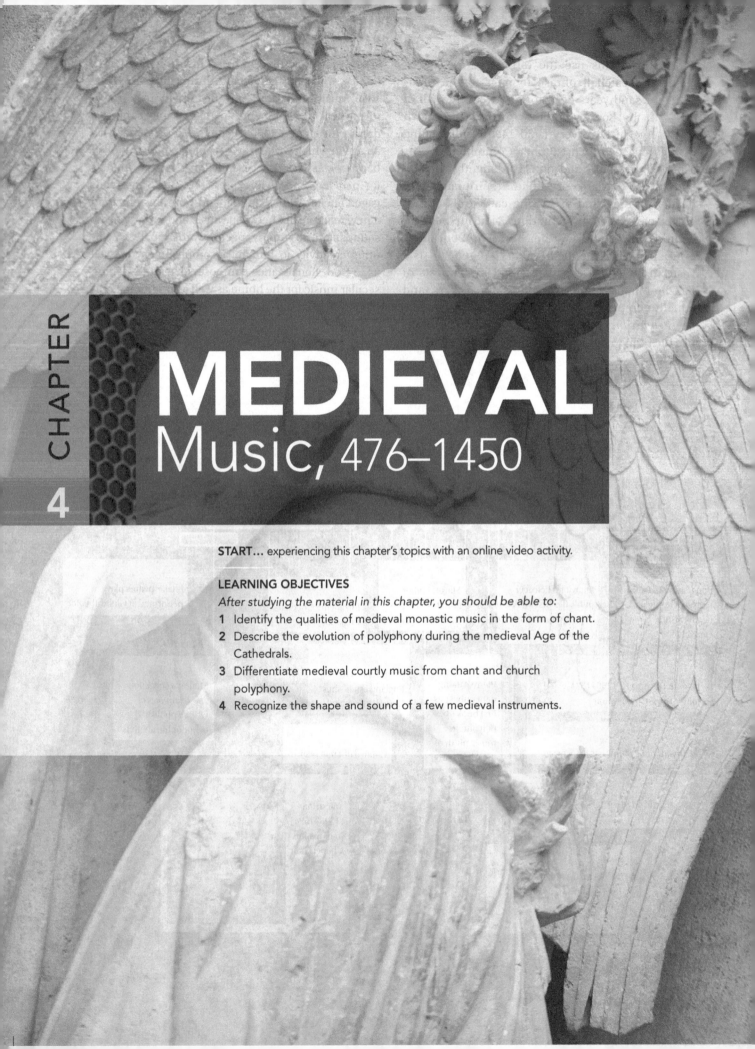

MEDIEVAL
Music, 476–1450

START... experiencing this chapter's topics with an online video activity.

LEARNING OBJECTIVES

After studying the material in this chapter, you should be able to:

1 Identify the qualities of medieval monastic music in the form of chant.
2 Describe the evolution of polyphony during the medieval Age of the Cathedrals.
3 Differentiate medieval courtly music from chant and church polyphony.
4 Recognize the shape and sound of a few medieval instruments.

For the interconnected inhabitant of the twenty-first century, it is difficult to imagine an isolated, solitary life revolving around prayer. But in the Middle Ages a large portion of the population (monks and nuns) defined their lives with two simple tasks: work and prayer. They worked to feed their bodies, and they prayed to save their souls. Indeed, the Middle Ages was a profoundly spiritual period, because life on earth was uncertain and often brief. If you got an infection, you likely died (there were no antibiotics); if insects ate your crops, you likely starved (no insecticides); if your village caught fire, it likely burned to the ground (no fire trucks). With seemingly little control over their own destiny, people turned to an outside agent (God) for help. And they did so mainly through organized religion—the Roman Catholic Church, the dominant spiritual and administrative force in medieval Europe.

READ... the complete chapter text on a rich, interactive online platform.

Music in the Monastery

Most medieval society was overwhelmingly agricultural, and thus religion was centered in isolated, rural monasteries (for monks) and convents (for nuns). The clergy worked in the fields and prayed in the church. Religious services usually began well before dawn and continued at various other times throughout the day in an almost unvarying cycle. The most important service was **Mass**, a symbolic reenactment of the Last Supper, celebrated at about nine o'clock in the morning.

Gregorian Chant

The music for these services was what we today call **Gregorian chant** (or **plainsong**)—a unique collection of thousands of religious songs, sung in Latin, which carry the theological message of the Church. Although this music bears the name of Pope Gregory the Great (c. 540–604), this pontiff actually wrote very little of it. Instead, Gregorian chant was created by many people, male and female, before, during, and after Gregory's reign.

To record chant and pass it from one community to the next, medieval monks and nuns created a wholly new medium of communication: **musical notation**. At first, the system used only a few dashes and dots, called *notae* (Latin for "notes"), which suggested the upward and downward motion of the melody. But exactly how *far* up or down did the pitch go? To represent the melodic distance, church musicians around the year 1000 began to put the notes on a grid of lines and spaces that were identified by letter names: space A, line B, space C, and so forth. Initially created to preserve the repertoire of Gregorian chant, this combination of symbols (notes) on a grid (the staff) formed the basis of the musical pitch notation that we still use today.

Gregorian chant is like no other music. It has a timeless, otherworldly quality that in part arises from its lack of meter and regular rhythms. True, some notes are longer or shorter than others, but pitches do not recur in obvious patterns that would allow us to clap our hands or tap our feet. Because all voices sing in unison, Gregorian chant is monophonic music. There is no instrumental accompaniment; nor, as a rule, are men's and women's voices mixed. For all these reasons, Gregorian chant has a consistently uniform, monochromatic sound, far more conducive to meditation than to dancing. The faithful are not to hear the music per se but, rather, to use the music as a vehicle to enter a spiritual state, to reach communion with God.

FIGURE 4.1

As the dead arise from their tombs, Archangel Michael weighs souls before the Lord in this vivid Last Judgment scene, painted by Hans Memling (c. 1430–1494).

Perhaps the best known of all medieval chants, then and now, is the *Dies irae* (*Day of Wrath;* see Listening Guide). Why is this chant so well known? The **Dies irae** served as the signature melody of the burial service of the Church, which did not lack for corpses during the plague-riddled Middle Ages. Written no later than the thirteenth century, the text speaks of the Day of Judgment, when the Last Trumpet will summon all to rise and stand before the Lord to be judged (Figure 4.1). Both text and music are structurally clear: The text unfolds in a pattern of three four-word phrases, and the accompanying music in pairs of statement and immediate repetition, as seen in Example 4.1.

EXAMPLE 4.1 *Dies irae*

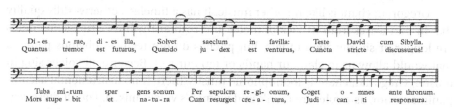

Di - es i - rae, di - es illa, Solvet saeclum in favilla: Teste David cum Sibylla.
Quantus tremor est futurus, Quando ju - dex est venturus, Cuncta stricte discussurus!

Tuba mi - rum spar - gens sonum Per sepulcra re - gi - onum, Coget o - mnes ante thronum.
Mors stupe - bit et na - tu - ra Cum resurget cre - a - tura, Judi - can - ti responsura.

What scares us so in the *Dies irae*: the text or the music? While the words resonate with terrifying images of hellfire and brimstone, the melody sounds serene, even bland. Typical of chant, there is no beat, and the melody moves mostly in simple,

LISTENING GUIDE

Anonymous, Gregorian chant, *Dies irae*

Download 10 (1:17)

Genre: Chant

Texture: Monophonic

WHAT TO LISTEN FOR: An undulating, generally restful melody that carries a frightful text

0:00	**A**	Dies irae, dies illa,	Day of wrath, day of anger,
		Solvet saeclum in favilla	Will dissolve the earth in ashes
		Teste David cum Sibylla.	As foretold by David and the Sibyl Prophets.
0:16	**A repeated**	Quantus tremor est futurus,	What dread there will be,
		Quando judex est venturus,	When the Judge shall come,
		Cuncta stricte discussurus!	All chains will be broken!
0:32	**B**	Tuba mirum spargens sonum	A trumpet spreading a wondrous sound
		Per sepulcra regionum,	Through the graves of all lands,
		Coget omnes ante thronum.	Will drive mankind before the throne.
0:51	**B repeated**	Mors stupebit et natura	Death and Nature shall be astonished
		Cum resurget creatura	When all creation rises again
		Judicanti responsura.	To answer to the Judge.

(The chant continues in a similar vein.)

LISTEN TO ... this selection streaming online.

WATCH ... an Active Listening Guide of this selection online.

---

stepwise intervals. Here, words and music operate on separate levels, as is true of medieval music generally. (Not until the Renaissance [1450–1600] would musicians begin to harness music to text to underscore and intensify verbal meaning—to work *with* the text and not independent of it.) In subsequent centuries, the medieval *Dies irae* would sound in countless Masses and other musical genres (see Chapter 20), and even in thriller films down to the present day. But wherever it appears, it is the text of the *Dies irae*, not the music, that literally scares the hell out of us.

WATCH... a YouTube video of the *Dies irae*, used as the musical theme of the thriller *The Shining*, online.

The Gregorian Chant of Hildegard of Bingen (1098–1179)

One of the most remarkable contributors to the repertoire of Gregorian chant was Hildegard of Bingen (1098–1179; Figure 4.2), from whose fertile pen we received seventy-seven chants. Hildegard was the tenth child of noble parents, who gave her to the Church as a tithe (a donation of a tenth of one's worldly goods). She was educated by Benedictine nuns and then, at the age of fifty-two, founded her own convent near the small town of Bingen, Germany, on the west bank of the Rhine. Over time, Hildegard manifested her extraordinary intellect and imagination as a playwright, poet, musician, naturalist, pharmacologist, and spiritual visionary.

Ironically, then, the first "Renaissance man" was really a medieval woman: Hildegard of Bingen.

Hildegard's *O rubor sanguinis* (*O Redness of Blood;* see Listening Guide) possesses many qualities typical of her chants, and of chant generally (Example 4.2). First, it has a starkly vivid text, which Hildegard herself created. Honoring St. Ursula and a group of 11,000 Christian women believed slain by marauding Huns in the fourth or fifth century, the poem envisages martyred blood streaming in the heavens and virginal flowers unsullied by serpentine evil. Each phrase of text receives its own phrase of music, but the phrases are not of the same length. Occasionally, a passage of **syllabic singing** (only one or two notes for each syllable of text; see "rubor sanguinis") will give way to one of **melismatic singing** (many notes sung to just one syllable; see the twenty-nine notes for "num" of "numquam"). Even today, some pop singers, such as Christina Aguilera, Mariah Carey, and Beyoncé, are referred to as "melismatic singers" owing to their penchant for spinning out just one syllable with many, many pitches.

Hildegard's chant, *O rubor sanguinis*, is sweeping yet solidly grounded tonally, as each phrase ends with the first (tonic) or fifth (dominant) degree of the scale, with D or A (colored red in Example 4.2). Notice, too, that after an initial jump (D to A), the chant proceeds mostly in stepwise motion (neighboring pitches). This was, after all, choral music to be sung by the full community of musically unsophisticated nuns or monks, so it had to be easy. Finally, as with most chants, this piece has no overt rhythm or meter. The unaccompanied, monophonic line and the absence of pulsating rhythm allow a restful, meditative mood to develop. Hildegard did not see herself as an "artist" as we think of one today, but in the spirit of medieval anonymity as a mere vessel through which divine revelation came to earth. Indeed, she styled herself simply as "a feather floating on the breath of God."

FIGURE 4.2
Today, we receive information over the Internet, but during the Middle Ages, people believed in the power of divine revelation. This twelfth-century illumination depicts Hildegard of Bingen receiving divine inspiration, perhaps a spiritual vision or a chant, directly from the heavens. To the right, her secretary, the monk Volmar, peers in at her in amazement.

EXAMPLE 4.2 Hildegard, *O rubor sanguinis*

LISTENING GUIDE

Hildegard of Bingen, *O rubor sanguinis* (c. 1150)   Download 11 (1:21)

Genre: Chant

Texture: Monophonic

WHAT TO LISTEN FOR: A transcendental experience. Does the absence of instruments and a beat relax you, allow you to "defocus"? Does Hildegard's chant carry you away, too, like "a feather floating on the breath of God"?

0:00	O rubor sanguinis,	O redness of blood,
0:14	qui de excelso illo fluxisti,	which flowed down from on high,
0:29	quod divinitas tetigit;	touched by divinity;
0:36	Tu flos es	You are the flower
0:41	quem hyems de flatu serpentis numquam lesit.	that the wintry breath of the serpent never wounded.
0:57	(Note the long melisma on "numquam.")	

LISTEN TO ... this selection streaming online.

WATCH ... an Active Listening Guide of this selection online.

Music in the Cathedral

The future of art music within the Church lay not in isolated monasteries, however, but in city-based cathedrals. Monasteries were rural, inward looking, and run by an abbot; cathedrals were urban, outward looking, and ruled by a bishop. The job of the bishop and his clergy was to administer to the spiritual needs of the citizens of the expanding urban centers. During the twelfth century, cities such as Milan, Paris, and London, among others, grew significantly, as trade and commerce increased. Much of the commercial wealth generated in the cities was used to construct splendid new cathedrals that served as both houses of worship and municipal civic centers. So substantial was this building campaign that the period 1150–1350 is often called the "Age of the Cathedrals." It started in northern France with cathedrals possessing elements of what we now call the **Gothic style**: pointed arches, high ceiling vaults, flying buttresses, and richly colored stained glass.

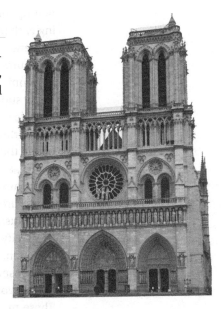

FIGURE 4.3
The cathedral of Notre Dame of Paris, begun c. 1160, was one of the first to be built in the new Gothic style of architecture. Innovative polyphony was composed there as the building was being constructed.

Notre Dame of Paris

The epicenter for the new Gothic style in northern France was Paris. The cathedral of Paris (Figure 4.3), dedicated to Notre Dame (Our Lady), was begun about 1160, yet not completed until more than a hundred years later. Throughout this period, Notre Dame was blessed with a succession of churchmen who were not only theologians and philosophers but also poets and musicians. Foremost among these was Master Perotinus, called the Great (fl. 1198–1236). Perotinus helped

FIGURE 4.4

Perotinus's four-voice *Viderunt omnes* for Christmas Day. Notice how the chant in the tenor voice (staffs 4, 8, and 12) provides a long-note foundation (a tenor) for the three voices above.

create a new style of music called **organum**, the name given generally to early church polyphony. The novelty here rested in the fact that composers added one, two, or three voices on top of the existing chant. In this musical development, we see an early instance of a creative spirit breaking free of the ancient authority (the chant) of the Church.

Perotinus: Organum *Viderunt omnes*

The surviving documents from Paris suggest that Perotinus the Great served as director of the choir at Notre Dame of Paris. To lend special splendor to the celebration of Mass on Christmas morning in the year 1198, Perotinus composed a four-voice organum for Mass, *Viderunt omnes* (*All the Ends of the Earth;* see Listening Guide). He took the centuries-old chant and added three new voices above it (Figure 4.4). Compared to the new upper voices, the old borrowed chant moved very slowly, drawing out or holding each pitch. Because of this, the sustaining line with the chant came to be called the **tenor** voice (from the Latin *teneo*, French *tenir*, "to hold"). As you listen to the organum of Perotinus, you will clearly hear the sustaining chant that provides a harmonic support for the upper voices, just as a massive pillar in a Gothic church might support the delicate movement of the arches above (see Figure 4.5). Equally audible is a novel sound, the sprightly triple-meter rhythms.

Earlier in the Middle Ages, when almost all written music was monophonic chant, there was little need to specify rhythm—all pitches were roughly the same length, and the singers could easily stick together as they moved from one note to the next. When as many as three or four separate parts sang together, however, more direction was needed. Thus, during the thirteenth and fourteenth centuries, musicians devised a system called **mensural notation** (measured notation) to specify precisely musical rhythm as well as pitch. To the note heads indicating pitch, musicians added various sorts of stems and flags to specify duration. Composers could now write for two, three, or four voices together, and each singer would know how long to sustain the pitch so as to make good harmony. These medieval stems and flags are still with us today, in our half, quarter, and eighth notes.

Notre Dame of Reims

Thirteenth-century Paris was the first home of the new Gothic polyphony, but by the fourteenth century, its primacy, both in music and in architecture, was challenged by Reims (pronounced "Rance"). The city of Reims, 100 miles east of Paris in

Master Perotinus the Great, organum built on Gregorian chant, *Viderunt omnes* (1198)   Download 12 (2:15)

Genre: Organum

Texture: Polyphonic

WHAT TO LISTEN FOR: First, polyphony: Three new voices have been added to the chant. Second, the jaunty triple meter: All early polyphony written in rhythmic notation was composed in triple meter to do honor, the music theorists of the time tell us, to the Holy Trinity. Because Perotinus sustains the chant in long notes in his setting of *Viderunt omnes*, a composition of great length—eleven to twelve minutes—results. Thus, only the beginning of his organum is given here. The singers relate that all the ends of the earth have seen ("Viderunt") the Christian Savior.

0:00	Syllable "Vi-" of "Viderunt"; all voices hold on open sound of fifth and octave.
0:06	Upper three voices proceed in rocking triple meter as tenor sustains first note of chant, with all voices singing the "Vi-" syllable.
0:47	Tenor changes to next pitch, and all change to syllable "-de-" of "Viderunt."
1:10	Tenor changes to next pitch, and all change to syllable "-runt" of "Viderunt."
2:06	End of word "Viderunt"

(Continuing organum not included in this text's music compilation)

LISTEN TO ... this selection streaming online.

WATCH ... an Active Listening Guide of this selection online.

the Champagne region of France, boasted a cathedral (Figure 4.5) as impressive as and, indeed, larger than the one that graced Paris. In the fourteenth century, Reims benefited from the service of a poetically and musically talented churchman, Guillaume de Machaut (c. 1300–1377). Judging by his nearly 150 surviving literary works, not only was Machaut (pronounced "ma-SHOW") the most important composer of his day, he was equally esteemed as a poet. Today, historians of literature place him on a pedestal next to his slightly younger English counterpart, Geoffrey Chaucer (c. 1340–1400), author of *The Canterbury Tales*. Indeed, Chaucer knew and borrowed heavily from the poetic works of Machaut.

FIGURE 4.5
Interior of the cathedral of Reims looking from floor to ceiling. The pillars carry the eye up to the ribbed vaults of the roof, creating a feeling of great upward movement, just as the Mass of Machaut, with four superimposed voices, has a new sense of verticality.

Machaut: *Messe de Nostre Dame*

Machaut's *Messe de Nostre Dame* (*Mass of Our Lady*) is deservedly the best-known polyphonic work in the entire repertoire of medieval music. It is impressive for its twenty-five minute length as well as for the novel way it applies music to the text of the Mass. Machaut was the first composer to set what is called the **Ordinary of the Mass**, five sung portions of the Mass, specifically the *Kyrie, Gloria, Credo, Sanctus,* and *Agnus Dei*, with texts that do not change from day to day (other texts change depending on which saint was honored). From Machaut's work onward, composing a Mass meant setting the five texts of the Ordinary and finding some way to tie them together into an integrated whole. Bach, Mozart, Beethoven, and Stravinsky were just a few of the later composers to follow Machaut's lead in this regard.

To construct his Mass, Machaut proceeded as follows. First, he took a chant in honor of the Virgin Mary and placed it in long notes in the tenor voice. Above the foundational tenor Machaut composed two new lines, called the *superius* and the *contratenor altus*, and from these we get our terms *soprano* and *alto*. Below the tenor he composed a *contratenor bassus*, whence our term *bass*. Unlike Perotinus, who bunched his voices around middle C, Machaut spread these voices out over two and a half octaves, becoming the first composer to exploit nearly the full vocal range of a chorus.

As you listen to the foreign sound of this Gothic work, you likely will be struck by two things: (1) the alternation of chant and polyphony—for some portions of his *Kyrie* (see Listening Guide), Machaut allowed the monophonic chant to stand unaltered; and (2) the disparity between rhythm and harmony. The rhythmic patterns unfold within a lilting triple meter, but the harmony is mostly dissonant. At the ends of musical phrases, however, Machaut stretches out the dissonances into open, consonant chords (see the asterisk in Example 4.3). These longed-for consonances are especially satisfying in an echo-filled medieval cathedral, in which the sound can endlessly reverberate around the bare stone walls.

LISTENING GUIDE

Guillaume de Machaut, *Kyrie of Messe de Nostre Dame* (c. 1360)   Download 13 (2:18)

Genre: Mass

Texture: Polyphonic and monophonic

WHAT TO LISTEN FOR: The alternation between polyphony and chant, and the interplay between passages of dissonant chords and consonant ones, the latter coming at the ends of phrases

0:00	Kyrie eleison (sung three times)	Lord have mercy upon us
2:16	Christe eleison (sung three times)	Christ have mercy upon us
3:37	Kyrie eleison (sung three times)	Lord have mercy upon us

LISTEN TO ... this selection streaming online.

WATCH ... an Active Listening Guide of this selection online.

DO ... Listening Exercise 4.1, Machaut, *Kyrie* of *Messe de Nostre Dame*, online.

EXAMPLE 4.3 Machaut's *Kyrie*

Music at the Court

Outside the walls of the cathedral, there was yet another musical world: one of popular song and dance, centered at the court. If the music of the Church was calculated to move the soul toward spiritual reflection, that of the court was meant to move the body to sing and dance. The court emerged as a center for the patronage of the arts during the years 1150–1400, as kings, dukes, counts, and lesser nobles increasingly assumed responsibility for the defense of the land and regulating social behavior. The court embraced forms of public entertainment not permitted by Church authorities. Here, itinerant actors, jugglers, jesters, and animal acts provided welcome diversions at banquets and feasts. Minstrels wandered from castle to castle, playing instruments and bringing with them the latest tunes, along with the news and gossip of the day.

Troubadours and *Trouvères*

France was the center of this new courtly art, though French customs quickly spread to Spain, Italy, and Germany as well. The poet-musicians who flourished in the courts of southern France were called **troubadours,** and those in the north ***trouvère***. These names are distant ancestors of the modern French word *trouver* ("to find"). Indeed, the troubadours and *trouvères* were "finders," or inventors, of a new genre of vocal expression called the **chanson** (French for "song"). In all, the troubadours and *trouvères* created several thousand chansons. Most are monophonic love songs that extol the courtly ideals of faith and devotion, whether to the ideal lady, the just seigneur (lord), or the knight crusading in the Holy Land. Almost all are in strophic form. The origins of the troubadours and *trouvères* were varied. Some were sons of bakers and drapers, others were members of the nobility, many were clerics who had left the rigors of the monastery, and not a few were women.

In the Middle Ages, women were not allowed to sing in church, except in convents, owing to the biblical command of St. Paul: "A woman must be silent in the church." But at court, women often recited poetry, sang, and played musical instruments. A few, such as Beatriz, Countess of Dia (Figure 4.6), were composers in their own right. Beatriz lived in southern France in the mid-twelfth century. She was married to Count William of Poitiers but fell in love with a fellow troubadour, Raimbaut d'Orange (1146–1173). In her chanson, *A chantar m'er* (*I Must Sing;* see Listening Guide), Beatriz complains of unrequited love (presumably hers toward

WATCH... a modern-day troubadour online.

FIGURE 4.6
Beatriz, Countess of Dia, as depicted in a manuscript of troubadour and *trouvère* poetry

LISTENING GUIDE

Countess of Dia, *A chantar m'er* (c. 1175)   Download 14 (1:55)

Genre: Chanson

Texture: Monophonic

WHAT TO LISTEN FOR: An introductory instrumental solo played by a vielle (medieval fiddle) and then the entry of the voice, which sings the first strophe of a monophonic chanson

0:00   Improvised introduction played on vielle (medieval fiddle)

0:26   Solo voice enters and sings first of five strophes

 I must sing of that which I'd rather not,

So bitter do I feel toward him

Whom I love more than anything.

But with him kindness and courtliness get me nowhere,

Neither my beauty, nor my worth, nor my intelligence.

In this way am I cheated and betrayed,

Just as I would be if I were ugly.

LISTEN TO ... this selection streaming online.

WATCH ... an Active Listening Guide of this selection online.

Raimbaut) and does so from a woman's perspective. Like most medieval songsters, Beatriz employs strophic form, a medieval tradition that continues in pop songs today. Here, she constructs the single melody to serve all strophes in a clear **a b a b c d b** form.

A Battle Carol for the English Court

A single song from medieval England, the Agincourt Carol, is a valuable relic on several counts: (1) It tells us something about medieval history; (2) it suggests how we received the most common form for today's pop songs (verse and chorus); and (3) it's exciting music.

Although England was geographically separate from continental Europe, there, too, music was patronized primarily by the Church and the court. The most important English court, of course, was that of the king, and the most illustrious English king in the late Middle Ages was Henry V (1386–1422). Immortalized in three plays by Shakespeare (*Henry IV*, Parts I and II, and *Henry V*), Henry reigned during the **Hundred Years' War (1337–1453)**, the name given to a century-long series of military conflicts between the French and the English. Henry's greatest victory came near the small town of Agincourt on October 25, 1415, where his fast-moving army of 10,000 soldiers overcame a force four times that size (Figure 4.7). With the French defenses weakened, Henry moved southeast to Paris to be crowned king of France (as well as England) in Notre Dame of Paris.

Henry V's stunning victory at the Battle of Agincourt was soon celebrated in a genre of music called the carol. In the Middle Ages, a **carol** was a song in the local language that marked Christmas, Easter, or even, as here, a military victory. Most carols use strophic form (see the section "Strophic Form" in Chapter 3), but in addition, they are characterized by the presence of a chorus—each strophe is composed of a verse (new text), followed by a chorus (repeating text). The verse is sung by one or more soloists, and the chorus is sung by everyone, whence our term *chorus*. As the Agincourt Carol shows, strophic form incorporating verse and chorus became common in English popular music during the Middle Ages and has remained so in pop songs to the present day. As occasionally happens with Western Christmas carols, the verse of the Agincourt Carol is in English (medieval "middle English"), and the chorus in Latin.

Medieval Musical Instruments

In the late Middle Ages, the principal musical instrument of the monastery and cathedral was the large pipe organ. In fact, the organ was the only instrument admitted by church authorities. At court, however, a variety of instrumental sounds could be heard. Some, such as the trumpet and early trombone, were rightly

FIGURE 4.7
A remarkably accurate depiction of the Battle of Agincourt, showing the English archers on the left cutting down the French cavalry on the right. The artist clearly shows the English flag, with lions rampant (left), and the French one, with *fleurs de lis* (right).

Anonymous, Agincourt Carol (c. 1415)   Download 15 (3:56)

Genre: Carol

Form: Strophic

WHAT TO LISTEN FOR: The narrative quality of the verses as they tell the tale of King Henry's victory and the louder, celebratory sounds of the chorus as all singers rejoice as one

0:00	Deo gratias, Anglia, redde pro Victoria!	Chorus
	[England, render thanks to God for this victory!]	

Strophe 1

0:13	Our king went forth to Normandy	Verse
	With grace and might of chivalry;	
	There God for him wrought marv'lously	
	Wherefore England may call and cry. Deo gratias.	
	Deo gratias, Anglia, redde pro Victoria!	Chorus

Strophe 2

0:57	He sette a sege, forsothe to say,	Verse
	To Harflu [Harfleur] towne with ryal array;	
	That toune he wan and made affray	
	That Fraunce shal rewe tyl domesday. Deo gratias.	
	Deo gratias, Anglia, redde pro Victoria!	Chorus

Strophe 3

1:40	Then went hym forth, owre king comely,	Verse
	In Agincourt feld he faught manly;	
	Thorw grace of Gode most marvelously,	
	He had both feld and victory. Deo gratias.	
	Deo gratias, Anglia, redde pro Victoria!	Chorus

Strophe 4

2:23	Ther lordys, erles and barone	Verse
	Were slayne and taken and that full soon,	
	And summe were broght into Lundone [London]	
	With joye and blisse and gret renone. Deo gratias.	
	Deo gratias, Anglia, redde pro Victoria!	Chorus

Strophe 5

3:06	Almighty God he keep owre kynge,	Verse
	His peple, and all his well-syllynge,	
	And give them grace without ending;	
	Then may we call and savely syng: Deo gratias.	
	Deo gratias, Anglia, redde pro Victoria!	Chorus

LISTEN TO ... this selection streaming online.

WATCH ... an Active Listening Guide of this selection online.

DO ... Listening Exercise 4.2, Agincourt Carol, online.

identified as loud (*haut*). Others, such as the harp, lute, flute (recorder), fiddle (vielle), and small portable organ (Figure 4.8), were classified as soft (*bas*).

Figure 4.8 shows a group of angels playing musical instruments of the late Middle Ages. Moving from left to right, we see a straight-pipe trumpet, early trombone, small portative organ, harp, and vielle. The **vielle** (pronounced like the letters "V-L") was a distant ancestor of the modern violin. It usually had five strings that were tuned in a way that made it very easy to play block chords, the same way that guitars today can easily produce basic triads, or "bar chords." In fact, in medieval society, the easily portable vielle served the function of our modern guitar: Not only could it play a melody, it could also provide a basic chordal accompaniment for songs and dances. To hear the sound of the vielle, return to the Listening Guide "Countess of Dia, *A chantar m'er* (c. 1175)" (Download 14), where it provides a solo introduction and then an accompaniment to the voice.

FIGURE 4.8
Hans Memling (c. 1430–1494), musical angels painted for the walls of a hospital in Bruges, Belgium. The depiction of the instruments is remarkably detailed.

KEY WORDS

Mass (53)	syllabic singing (56)	mensural notation (58)	Hundred Years' War
Gregorian chant	melismatic singing (56)	Ordinary of the Mass (60)	(1337–1453) (63)
(plainsong) (53)	Gothic style (57)	troubadour (61)	carol (63)
musical notation (53)	organum (58)	*trouvère* (61)	vielle (65)
Dies irae (54)	tenor (58)	chanson (61)	

 Join us on Facebook at Listening to Music with Craig Wright

PRACTICE ... your understanding of this chapter's concepts by comparing Checklists of Musical Style for all historic eras and working once more with the chapter's Active Listening Guides online.

DO ... online multiple-choice and critical thinking quizzes that your instructor may assign for a grade.

CHECKLIST OF MUSICAL STYLE *Middle Ages: 476–1450*

REPRESENTATIVE COMPOSERS

Anonymous (the most prolific of all)	Hildegard of Bingen	Perotinus	Countess of Dia
	Leoninus	Machaut	

PRINCIPAL GENRES

Gregorian chant	troubadour and *trouvère* songs	popular song	instrumental dance
polyphonic Mass		carol	

Melody	Moves mostly by step within narrow range; rarely uses chromatic notes of the scale.
Harmony	Most surviving medieval music, notably Gregorian chant and troubadour and *trouvère* songs, is monophonic—consisting of a single melodic line without harmonic support. Medieval polyphony (Mass, organum, and carol) has dissonant phrases ending with open, hollow-sounding chords.
Rhythm	Gregorian chant as well as troubadour and *trouvère* songs sung mainly in notes of equal value without clearly marked rhythms. Medieval polyphony is composed mostly in triple meter (in honor of the Holy Trinity, theorists said) and uses repeating rhythmic patterns.
Color	Mainly vocal sounds (choir or soloists) within the church. Popular music might include instruments like the trumpet, trombone, fiddle, or harp.
Texture	Mostly monophonic. Gregorian chant and troubadour and *trouvère* songs are monophonic melodies. Medieval polyphony (two, three, or four independent lines) is mainly contrapuntal.
Form	Gregorian chant has no large-scale form, but each phrase of text generally receives its own phrase of music: strophic form in troubadour and *trouvère* songs; rondo form in the French chanson.

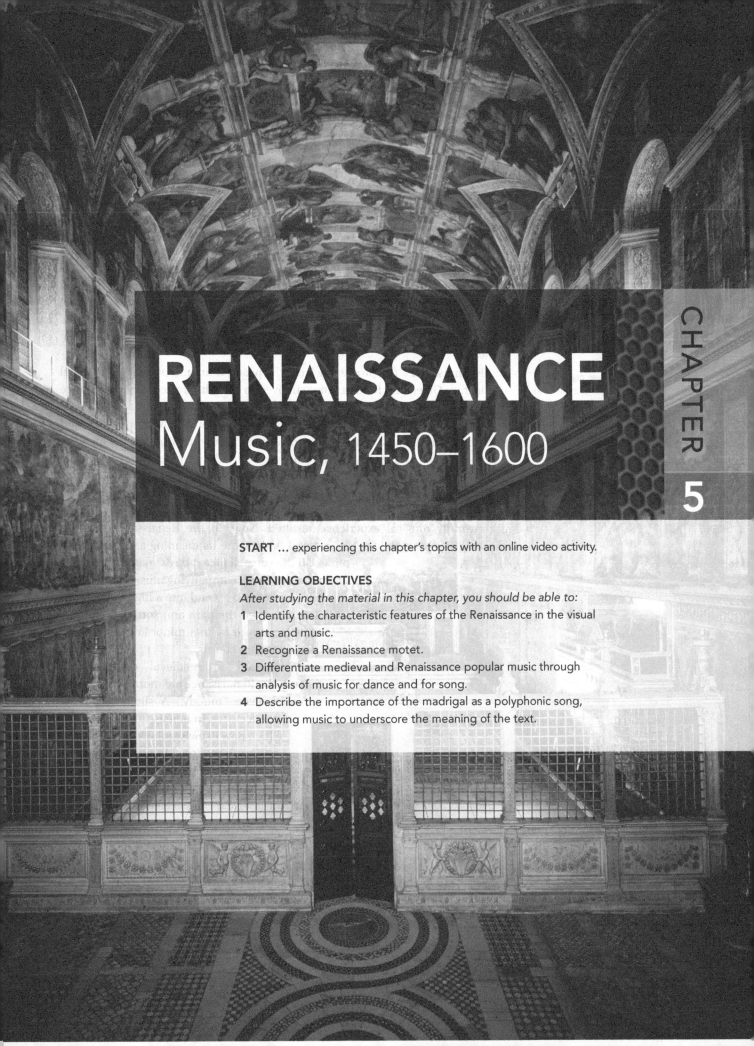

RENAISSANCE
Music, 1450–1600

START ... experiencing this chapter's topics with an online video activity.

LEARNING OBJECTIVES
After studying the material in this chapter, you should be able to:

1 Identify the characteristic features of the Renaissance in the visual arts and music.
2 Recognize a Renaissance motet.
3 Differentiate medieval and Renaissance popular music through analysis of music for dance and for song.
4 Describe the importance of the madrigal as a polyphonic song, allowing music to underscore the meaning of the text.

FIGURE 5.1
Andrea Palladio's Villa Rotunda (c. 1550) near Vicenza, Italy, clearly shows the extent to which classical architecture was reborn during the Renaissance. Elements of the ancient Greek and Roman style include the columns with capitals, triangular pediments, central rotunda, and roof statuary.

READ... the complete chapter text in a rich, interactive online platform.

Renaissance means literally "rebirth." Historians use the term broadly to designate a period of intellectual and artistic flowering that occurred first in Italy, then in France, and finally in England during the years 1350–1600. Music historians, however, apply the term more narrowly to musical developments in those same countries during the period 1450–1600. But what was being reborn?

During the Renaissance, writers, artists, and architects (see Figure 5.1) rediscovered the classical world of Greece and Rome, searching for models for civic and personal expression. How should city government operate? What should a building look like? What about the sculpture erected within it? How should a poet construct a poem? How ought an orator fashion a speech or a musician a song? The remains of classical antiquity, some of which were just then being unearthed, provided the answer.

For musicians, the process of "rebirth" posed a unique problem: No actual music from Greek and Roman times survived to be rediscovered! So, Renaissance intellectuals turned to the writings of Greek philosophers, dramatists, and music theorists, which contained accounts of how ancient music was constructed and performed. In this way, Renaissance musicians came to realize that the ancients had one primary article of faith regarding music: It had enormous expressive power.

To recapture the lost power of music, Renaissance musicians worked to forge a wholly new alliance between text and music. In the Middle Ages, text and music had coexisted on independent emotional levels, and an abstract, almost otherworldly musical experience resulted. Now, in the Renaissance, the job of music was to work with the text and underscore its meaning at every turn of phrase. If the verse depicted birds soaring gracefully in the sky, the accompanying music should be in a major key and ascend into a high range; if the text lamented the pain and sorrow of sin, the music ought to be in a minor key, full of dark and dissonant chords.

Compared to medieval compositions, those of the Renaissance are more overtly emotional, even "moody." A similar development occurred in Renaissance visual arts, which now likewise allowed for a greater range of emotional intensity. Compare, for example, the highly contrasting moods of two paintings created within a few years of each other: the peaceful serenity of Leonardo da Vinci's *The Lady with the Ermine* (Figure 5.2) and the painful intensity of Mathias Grünewald's *Saint John and the Two Marys* (Figure 5.3).

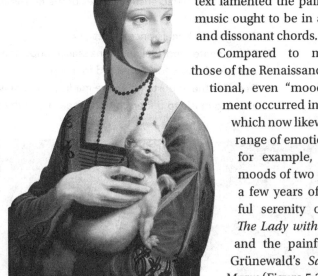

FIGURE 5.2
Leonardo da Vinci's portrait of Cecilia Gallerani, called *The Lady with the Ermine* (1496). Cecilia was the mistress of the duke of Milan, Leonardo's patron, and she clearly enjoyed the finer things of this earthly world, including clothing, jewelry, and exotic animals like the ermine, or mink, that she holds.

Attending the rebirth of the arts and letters of classical antiquity was a renewed interest in humankind itself. We have come to call this enthusiastic self-interest humanism. Simply said, **humanism** is the belief that people are more than mere puppets dangling from divine strings and that they have the capacity to shape their own world and to create things that are both good and beautiful. The culture of the Middle Ages, as we have seen, was fostered by the Church, which emphasized a collective submission to the Almighty, hiding the individual human form beneath layers of clothing. The culture of the Renaissance, by contrast, rejoiced in the human form in all its fullness, expressed in works such as Michelangelo's *David* (Figure 5.4). This culture looked outward and indulged a passion for invention and discovery. Today, when college students take courses in the "humanities," they study such arts, letters, ideas, and institutions that have enriched—and marked the best of—the human experience over the centuries.

While "Master Anonymous" was the most prolific artist of the Middle Ages, creators such as Leonardo, Michelangelo, and Shakespeare—artists with a name—dominate the Renaissance. If inspiration still came from God, it could be shaped in individual ways by an innovative creator. Renaissance artists demanded independence, recognition, and something more: money. Now a gifted artist might vie for the highest-paying commission, just as a sought-after composer might play one patron off against another for the highest salary. Money, it appeared, could prime the pump of creativity and lead to greater productivity. The prolific Michelangelo left an estate worth some $10 million in terms of today's money.

If artists were paid more in the Renaissance, it was because art was now thought to be more valuable. For the first time in the Christian West, there emerged the concept of a "work of art": the belief that an object might not only serve as a religious symbol but also be a creation of purely aesthetic value and enjoyment. Music in the Renaissance was composed by proud artists who aimed to give pleasure. Their music conversed, not with eternity, but with the listener. It was judged good or bad only to the degree that it pleased fellow human beings. Music and the other arts could now be freely evaluated, and composers and painters could be ranked according to their greatness. Artistic judgment, appreciation, and criticism entered Western thought for the first time in the humanistic Renaissance.

FIGURE 5.3
The expressive grief of the Virgin, Saint John, and Mary Magdalene mark this portion of an altarpiece (1510–1515), painted by Mathias Grünewald.

FIGURE 5.4
Michelangelo's giant statue, *David* (1501–1504), stands like a church to man's greatness, where even today pilgrims line up outside to venerate a monument to humankind in near-perfect form. Like Leonardo da Vinci, Michelangelo made a careful study of human anatomy.

Josquin Desprez (c. 1455–1521) and the Renaissance Motet

Josquin Desprez (pronounced "josh-CAN day-PRAY") was one of the greatest composers of the Renaissance (Figure 5.5), the Mozart or Beethoven of his day. Josquin was born somewhere near the present border between France and Belgium about 1455, and died in the same region in 1521. Yet, like so many musicians of northern France, Josquin was drawn to Italy to pursue fame and fortune. Between 1484 and 1504, he worked for dukes in Milan and Ferrara, and in Rome in the **Sistine Chapel**, the pope's private chapel in the Vatican (Figure 5.6). Evidence suggests that Josquin had a temperamental, egotistical personality, typical of many artists of the Renaissance. He would fly into a rage when singers tampered with his music; he composed only when he, not his patron, wished; and he demanded a salary twice that of composers only slightly less gifted. Yet Josquin's contemporaries recognized his genius. Martin Luther said of him: "Josquin is master of the notes, which must express what he desires; other composers can do only what the notes dictate." And Florentine humanist Cosimo Bartoli compared him to the great Michelangelo (1475–1564):

> Josquin may be said to have been a prodigy of nature, as our Michelangelo Buonarroti has been in architecture, painting, and sculpture; for just as there has not yet been anyone who in his compositions approaches Josquin, so Michelangelo, among those active in his arts, is still alone and without a peer. Both Josquin and Michelangelo have opened the eyes of all those who delight in these arts or are to delight in them in the future.

Josquin composed in all of the musical genres of his day—secular as well as sacred—but he excelled in writing motets. The Renaissance **motet** is a composition for a polyphonic choir, setting a Latin text on a sacred subject and intended to be sung either at a religious service in a church or in private devotion at home. While composers of the Renaissance continued to set the prescribed text of the Mass, they

FIGURE 5.5
The only surviving portrait of Josquin Desprez

FIGURE 5.6
Interior of the Sistine Chapel. The high altar and Michelangelo's *Last Judgment* are at the far end; the balcony for the singers, including Josquin Desprez, is inside the screen at the lower right. Josquin carved his name on the door to this balcony, and the graffito remains there to this day.

Josquin Desprez, *Ave Maria* (c. 1485)

Download 16 (4:41)

Genre: Motet

Texture: Polyphonic

WHAT TO LISTEN FOR: Opening using imitation, five sections commemorating the events in the life of the Virgin Mary, and a final plea for salvation

0:00	All four voices present each two-word phrase in turn.	Ave Maria, gratia plena. Dominus tecum, virgo serena.	Hail Mary, full of grace. The Lord be with you, serene Virgin.
0:46	Soprano and alto are imitated by tenor and bass; then all four voices work to a peak on "laetitia" ("joy").	Ave cujus conceptio, Solemni plena gaudio, Coelestia, terrestria, Nova replet laetitia.	Hail to you whose conception, With solemn rejoicing, Fills heaven and earth With new joy.
1:20	Imitation in pairs; soprano and alto answered by tenor and bass	Ave cujus nativitas Nostra fuit solemnitas, Ut lucifer lux oriens Verum solem praeveniens.	Hail to you whose birth Was to be our solemnity, As the rising morning star Anticipates the true sun.
1:58	More imitation by pairs of voices; soprano and alto followed by tenor and bass	Ave pia humilitas, Sine viro foecunditas, Cujus annuntiatio Nostra fuit salvatio.	Hail pious humility, Fruitful without man, Whose annunciation Was to be our salvation.
2:26	Chordal writing; meter changes from duple to triple.	Ave vera virginitas, Immaculata castitas, Cujus purificatio Nostra fuit purgatio.	Hail true virginity, Immaculate chastity, Whose purification Was to be our purgation.
3:03	Return to duple meter; soprano and alto imitated by tenor and bass	Ave praeclara omnibus Angelicis virtutibus, Cujus fuit assumptio Nostra glorificatio.	Hail shining example Of all angelic virtues, Whose assumption Was to be our glorification.
3:58	Strict chordal writing; clear presentation of text	O Mater Dei, Memento mei. Amen.	O Mother of God, Be mindful of me. Amen.

LISTEN TO ... this selection streaming online.

WATCH ... an Active Listening Guide of this selection online.

DO ... Listening Exercise 5.1, Josquin, *Ave Maria*, online.

increasingly turned to the more colorful, dramatic texts in the Old Testament of the Bible—specifically, in the expressive Psalms and the mournful Lamentations. A vivid text cried out for an equally vivid musical setting, allowing the composer to fulfill a mandate of Renaissance humanism: Use music to heighten the meaning of the word.

Josquin's motet, *Ave Maria* (*Hail Mary*, c. 1485; see Listening Guide) honors the Virgin Mary and employs the standard four voice parts: soprano, alto, tenor,

THE RENAISSANCE CHOIR: WHO SANG WHAT?

As mentioned in our discussion of medieval music (Chapter 4), women were allowed to sing in the early Roman Catholic Church in cloistered convents but not in any public church. Similarly, women were not permitted to appear in public in theatrical productions within territories under strict Church control. Thus, most church choirs in the Middle Ages and Renaissance were exclusively male. But who, then, sang the soprano and alto parts when polyphony was performed? The most common practice was to assign these parts to adult males who sang in what is called "head voice," or **falsetto voice**. Alternatively, choirboys might be used, but they were expensive to house and educate. Finally, beginning in 1562, the **castrato** (castrated male) voice was introduced into the papal chapel, mainly as a money-saving measure—a single castrato could produce as much volume as two falsettists or three or four boys. Castrati were renowned for their power and their great lung capacity, which allowed them to execute unusually long phrases in a single breath. Surprisingly, castrati sopranos remained a hallmark of the papal chapel until 1903, when they were officially banned by Pope Pius X. The voice of one castrato, Alessandro Moreschi, known as the "Last Castrato," was captured on a phonograph recording between 1902 and 1904, and is readily available for listening today.

In our recordings of works by Josquin and Palestrina, women take the soprano part, while male falsettists and women share the alto part. To make their sound as close as possible to that of a choirboy, the women sing with almost no vibrato.

Although public church choirs in the Middle Ages and Renaissance were all-male ensembles, women could be heard at home and at court. And women, too, sang in churches, but only in those churches that were within cloistered convents, where they performed all of the chant and, when required, polyphony. This illumination from a fifteenth-century English manuscript shows nuns singing from their choir stalls.

An all-male choir with choirboys for the soprano part, as depicted in a sixteenth-century Italian fresco.

WATCH ... Alessandro Moreschi, the "Last Castrato," online.

and bass (S, A, T, and B in Example 5.1). As the motet unfolds, the listener hears the voices enter in succession with the same musical motive. This process is called **imitation**, a polyphonic procedure whereby one or more voices duplicate in turn the notes of a melody for a short period of time.

EXAMPLE 5.1 Imitation

Josquin also sometimes has one pair of voices imitate another—the tenor and bass, for example, imitating what the alto and soprano have just sung, as highlighted by the arrows (Example 5.2).

EXAMPLE 5.2 Paired imitation

Josquin builds his *Ave Maria* much as a humanistic orator would construct a persuasive speech. The work begins with a salutation to the Virgin Mary, sung in imitation. Thereafter, a key word, *Ave* ("Hail"), sparks a succession of salutes to the Virgin, each making reference to one of her principal feast days during the church year (Conception, Nativity, Annunciation, Purification, and Assumption). Along the way, the music overtly mimics the text; for example, on the words *Coelestia, terrestria, nova replet laetitia* ("Fills heaven and earth with new joy"), Josquin raises the pitch of all voices excitedly. Then he takes this gesture one step further, literally jumping for joy, by leaping upward an octave on the Latin *laetitia* ("joy"). At the end of the motet comes a final exclamation, "O Mater Dei, memento mei. Amen" ("O Mother of God, be mindful of me. Amen"). These last words are set to striking chords, with each syllable of text receiving a new chord. The chordal, homophonic treatment allows this final phrase to stand out with absolute clarity. Here, Josquin declaims the basic principle of musical humanism: Text and music must work together to persuade and move the listener. Most important, they must also persuade the Virgin Mary, for they plead with her to intercede on behalf of the needy soul at the hour of death.

Finally, notice in our recording of Josquin's *Ave Maria* that no instruments accompany the voices. This unaccompanied mode of performance is called **a cappella** singing, a style that has been a hallmark of the Sistine Chapel (see Figure 5.6) since its foundation in the late fifteenth century. Even today, the pope's Sistine Chapel sings all its religious music—chant, Masses, and motets—without organ or any other instruments. If you belong to an a cappella singing group today, you are perpetuating this ancient style of performance.

The Counter-Reformation and Palestrina (1525–1594)

On October 31, 1517, an obscure Augustinian monk named Martin Luther nailed to the door of the castle church at Wittenberg, Germany, ninety-five complaints against the Roman Catholic Church—his famous ninety-five theses. With this defiant act, Luther began what has come to be called the Protestant Reformation. Luther and his fellow reformers sought to bring an end to corruption within the Roman Catholic Church, typified by the practice of selling indulgences (forgiving sin in exchange for money). By the time the Protestant Reformation had run its course, most of Germany, Switzerland, and the Low Countries, and all of England, as well as parts of France, Austria, Bohemia, Poland, and Hungary, had gone over to the Protestant cause. There were now two branches of Christianity in the West: Catholic and Protestant. The established Roman Catholic Church was shaken to its very foundations.

In response to the Protestant Reformation, the leaders of the Church of Rome gathered in northern Italy to discuss their own reform in what proved to be a two-decades-long conference, the **Council of Trent** (1545–1563). Here began the **Counter-Reformation**, a conservative, sometimes austere, movement that changed not only religious practices but also art, architecture, and music. With regard to music, the reformers of the Church of Rome were particularly alarmed by the incessant entry of voices in musical imitation; they feared that excessively dense counterpoint was burying the word of the Lord. As one well-placed bishop said mockingly:

> Nowadays composers have put all their labor and effort into writing imitative passages, so that while one voice sings "Sanctus," another says "Sabaoth," and still another "Gloria tua," with howling, bellowing, and stammering, so that they all together sound more like cats in January than flowers in May.

One important composer who got caught up in this debate about the appropriate style for church music was Giovanni Pierluigi da Palestrina (1525–1594; Figure 5.7). In 1555, Palestrina composed a *Missa Papae Marcelli (Mass for Pope Marcellus)* that conformed to all the requirements for proper church music prescribed by the Council of Trent. His polyphonic Mass was devoid of a strong beat and "catchy" rhythms, and it privileged simple counterpoint over complex, imitative polyphony, qualities that allowed the text to project with great clarity. Although the fathers of the Council of Trent had once considered banning all polyphony from the services of the Church, they now came to see that this somber, serene style of religious music could be a useful vehicle to inspire the faithful to greater devotion. For his role in securing a place for composed polyphony within the established Church, Palestrina came to be called, perhaps with some exaggeration, the "savior of church music."

The *Kyrie* that opens Palestrina's *Missa Papae Marcelli* (see Listening Guide) makes it easy to follow the words because there are only four: *Kyrie eleison, Christe eleison* (Greek for "Lord have mercy upon us, Christ have mercy upon us"). Palestrina begins with imitation in gently overlapping lines, showing that beauty and clarity of expression are not mutually exclusive. Each phrase of text is kept separate from the next so that the words remain clearly audible. All voices are equal in melodic importance, and the dynamic level, too, remains unchanging from beginning to end. No pounding beat tries to seduce the ear. No instruments vie for attention. Finally, whereas medieval religious polyphony was usually marked by frequent, biting dissonance (compare it with the *Kyrie* of Machaut, Download 13, in the Listening Guide "Guillaume de Machaut, *Kyrie* of *Messe de Nostre Dame*"), Palestrina's newer Renaissance style rests on an almost total reliance on consonant triads. In this way, Palestrina creates a consistent, almost celestial sweetness. With its uniform homogenous sound, Palestrina's *Kyrie* does everything possible *not* to call attention to itself but, rather, to God.

FIGURE 5.7
Portrait of Giovanni Pierluigi da Palestrina, the first important composer of the Church to have been a layman rather than a cleric in holy orders.

WATCH... a performance of Palestrina's *Missa Papae Marcelli* online.

LISTENING GUIDE

Giovanni Pierluigi da Palestrina, *Kyrie* of the *Missa Papae Marcelli* (1555)   Download 17 (4:03)

Genre: Mass

Texture: Lightly polyphonic

WHAT TO LISTEN FOR: Almost nothing, for there are few contrasts to attract the listener's attention. Rather, surrender to the peaceful soundscape that emerges as the devout listener is transported to a higher spiritual realm.

0:00	Six-voice a cappella choir unfolds short phrases in imitation.	Kyrie eleison.	Lord, have mercy upon us.
1:21	Choir continues but creates a more homophonic style.	Christe eleison.	Christ, have mercy upon us.
2:50	Imitative polyphony returns.	Kyrie eleison.	Lord, have mercy upon us.

LISTEN TO ... this selection streaming online.

WATCH ... an Active Listening Guide of this selection online.

Palestrina's serene music best captures the somber, restrained spirit of the Counter-Reformation, embodying in its quiet simplicity all that Roman Catholic authority thought proper church music should be. After his death in 1594, the legend of Palestrina, "savior of church music," continued to grow. Later, composers such as Bach (Mass in B minor, 1733) and Mozart (Requiem Mass, 1791) incorporated elements of Palestrina's style into their religious compositions. Even in our universities today, courses in counterpoint for advanced music students usually include some practice in composing in the pure, contrapuntally correct style of Palestrina. Thus, the spirit of the Counter-Reformation, distilled into a set of contrapuntal rules, continued to influence musicians long after the Renaissance came to an end.

Popular Music in the Renaissance

The motets and Masses of Josquin and Palestrina represent the "high" art of the Renaissance—learned music for the Church. But there was popular music as well, and, unlike much of the popular music of the Middle Ages, we have a good general sense of how it sounded. During the Middle Ages, most popular musicians, like pop musicians today, worked without benefit of written musical notation. In fact, most people in the Middle Ages couldn't read—text or music—and manuscripts (by definition, copied by hand) were exceedingly expensive.

All this began to change, however, when Johannes Gutenberg invented printing with movable type around 1460. Printing revolutionized the world of information in the late fifteenth century no less than the computer did in the late twentieth century. Hundreds of copies of a book could be produced quickly and cheaply once the type had been set. The first printed book of music appeared in Venice in 1501, and to this important event can be traced the origins of today's music industry. The standard press run for a printed book of music then was usually 500 copies. Mass production put the music book within reach of the banker, merchant, lawyer, and shopkeeper. "How-to" manuals encouraged ordinary men and women to learn to read musical notation, so as to sing and to play an instrument at home. The learned amateur had arrived.

Dance Music

Our fascination with dance didn't begin with *Dancing with the Stars*. Dancing had existed, of course, since the beginning of time, although almost none of its music survives because it was passed along orally and not in written form. During the Renaissance, however, musicians came to benefit from the growth of literacy. Publishers now issued collections of dance music in notation, rightly assuming that many among the newly emergent middle class could read the notes and were ready to play and dance at home. Not wishing to miss a single sale, they issued volumes for wind instruments, keyboard instruments, "and any other instruments that might seem appropriate." A favorite ensemble—something akin to the Renaissance dance band (Figure 5.8)—included an early trombone and a predecessor of the modern oboe, called the **shawm**. Its piercing tone made the melody easy to hear.

By far the most popular genre of dance in the mid-sixteenth century was the **pavane**, a slow, gliding dance in duple meter performed by couples holding hands. It was often followed by a contrasting **galliard**, a fast, leaping dance in triple meter. (For a painting believed to show Queen Elizabeth I leaping in a galliard, see Figure 5.10.) Around 1550, the French publisher Jacques Moderne issued a collection of twenty-five anonymous dances that included several pavanes and galliards. Moderne titled this collection *Musique de joye* (*Music of Joy*)—listen (see Listening Guide) and you'll understand why.

The Madrigal

About 1530, a new kind of popular, polyphonic song took Europe by storm: the madrigal. A **madrigal** is a piece for several solo voices (usually four or five) that sets a vernacular poem, most often about love, to music. The madrigal arose in Italy but soon spread to northern European countries. So popular did the madrigal become that by 1630 some 40,000 pieces had been printed by publishers eager to satisfy public demand. The madrigal was a truly social art, one that both men and women could enjoy (Figure 5.9).

FIGURE 5.8
The band of municipal musicians employed by the city of Nuremberg, Germany, as painted by Georg Eberlein, c. 1500, after a mural by Albrecht Dürer in the Nuremberg Town Hall. The core instruments are the two early trombones and two shawms; also visible are a cornetto (left), recorder, and drum.

Of all the musical genres of the Renaissance, the madrigal best exemplifies the humanist requirement that music express the meaning of the text. In a typical madrigal, each word or phrase of poetry receives its own musical gesture. Thus, when the madrigal text says "chase after" or "follow quickly," the music becomes fast, and one voice chases after another in musical imitation. For words such as "pain," "anguish," "death," and "cruel fate," the madrigal composer almost invariably employs a twisting chromatic scale or a biting dissonance. This practice of depicting the text by means of a descriptive musical gesture, whether subtly or

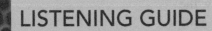

Jacques Moderne, publisher, *Musique de joye* (c. 1550), Pavane and Galliard   Download 18 (2:37)

Genre: Instrumental dance

Texture: Homophonic

WHAT TO LISTEN FOR: Wind instruments (called shawms) play a succession of symmetrical phrases of four measures plus four measures, making it easy for the dancers to match their steps to the music.

Pavane (slow duple meter)		Galliard (fast triple meter)	
0:00	Phrase 1	1:43	Phrase 1
0:21	Phrase 1 repeated but with top line ornamented	1:54	Phrase 1 repeated
0:37	Phrase 2	2:02	Phrase 2
0:53	Phrase 2 repeated but with top line ornamented	2:10	Phrase 2 repeated
1:09	Phrase 3	2:17	Phrase 3
1:26	Phrase 3 repeated but with top line ornamented	2:25	Phrase 3 repeated

LISTEN TO ... this selection streaming online.

WATCH ... an Active Listening Guide of this selection online.

DO ... Listening Exercise 5.2, Pavane and Galliard, online.

FIGURE 5.9
Singers of a four-part madrigal during the mid-sixteenth century. Women were very much a part of this secular, nonreligious music making.

jokingly as a musical pun, is called **word painting**. Word painting became all the rage with madrigal composers in Italy and England. Even today, such musical clichés as a falling melody for "fainting" and a dissonance for "pain" are called **madrigalisms**.

Although the madrigal was born in Italy, popular favor soon carried it over the Alps into Germany, Denmark, the Low Countries, and the England of Shakespeare's day. A single madrigal with English text will allow us to explore the one-to-one relationship between music and word.

In 1601, musician Thomas Morley published a collection of twenty-four madrigals in honor of Virgin Queen Elizabeth (1533–1603), which he entitled *The Triumphes of Oriana*. (Oriana, a legendary British princess and maiden, was a poetic nickname of Queen Elizabeth.) Among these madrigals was *As Vesta Was from Latmos Hill Descending* (see Listening Guide), composed by royal organist Thomas Weelkes (1576–1623). The text of the madrigal, likely fashioned by Weelkes himself, is a rather confused mixture of images from classical mythology: The Roman goddess Vesta, descending the Greek mountain of Latmos, spies Oriana (Elizabeth) ascending the hill; the

LISTENING GUIDE

Thomas Weelkes, *As Vesta Was from Latmos Hill Descending* (1601)　　　Download 19 (3:21)

Genre: Madrigal

Texture: Changes according to the dictates of the text

WHAT TO LISTEN FOR: A one-to-one relationship between text and music in which the music acts out, like a mime, each word or phrase of the text

0:00	Opening homophonic chords give way to falling pitches on "descending."	As Vesta was from Latmos Hill descending,
0:12	Imitation falls, then rises, on word "ascending."	She spied a maiden Queen the same ascending,
0:32	Simple repeating notes suggest simple country swains.	Attended on by all the shepherds' swain;
0:49	All voices come "running down amain."	To whom Diana's darlings came running down amain,
1:13	Two voices exemplify "two by two" then three "three by three."	First two by two, then three by three together,
1:23	Solo voice highlights "all alone."	Leaving their goddess all alone, hasted thither;
1:35	Imitative entries suggest "mingling."	And mingling with the shepherds of her train,
1:42	Light, rapid singing produces "mirthful tunes."	With mirthful tunes her presence did entertain.
1:58	Stark chords announce final acclamation.	Then sang the shepherds and nymphs of Diana:
2:10	Long life to the queen is declaimed endlessly.	Long live fair Oriana.

LISTEN TO ... this selection streaming online.

WATCH ... an Active Listening Guide of this selection online.

DO ... Listening Exercise 5.3, Weelkes, *As Vesta Was from Latmos Hill Descending*, online.

nymphs and shepherds attending the goddess Diana desert her to sing the praises of Oriana. The sole virtue of this doggerel is that it provides frequent opportunity for word painting in music. As the text commands, the music descends, ascends, runs, mingles imitatively, and offers "mirthful tunes" to the maiden queen. Elizabeth herself played lute and harpsichord, and loved to dance (Figure 5.10). Weelkes saw fit to end his madrigal with cries of "Long live fair Oriana." Indeed, the fair queen did enjoy a long and glorious reign of some forty-five years—thus our term "Elizabethan Age."

Madrigals such as Weelkes's *As Vesta Was from Latmos Hill Descending* were popular because they were fun to sing. Vocal lines were written within a comfortable range, melodies were often triadic, rhythms were catchy, and the music was full of puns. When Vesta descends the mountain, so, too, her music moves down the scale; when Oriana (Queen Elizabeth) ascends, her music does likewise; when

FIGURE 5.10
A painting believed to show
Queen Elizabeth dancing
with the Duke of Leicester

Diana, the goddess of virginity, is all alone—you guessed it, we hear a solo voice. With sport like this to be had, no wonder the popularity of the madrigal endured beyond the Renaissance. Today, the madrigal remains a staple of a cappella singing groups and university glee clubs.

The importance of the madrigal—and Renaissance music generally—is that it established a "vocabulary" of expression for music. Listeners came to expect that certain kinds of music would heighten the meaning of certain phrases of text: Fast, rising music would accompany and signal growing excitement, for example. By the succeeding era (the Baroque period), these gestures had become so well established that the musical message could be conveyed without the text, namely, in purely instrumental pieces. This language of expressive gestures, an outgrowth of Renaissance humanism, continued to be spoken by composers into the twenty-first century. It remains today the basis of our TV music and film scores.

KEY WORDS

Renaissance (68)	falsetto voice (72)	Council of Trent (75)	galliard (77)
humanism (69)	castrato (72)	Counter-Reformation (75)	madrigal (77)
Sistine Chapel (70)	imitation (73)	shawm (77)	word painting (78)
motet (70)	a cappella (74)	pavane (77)	madrigalism (78)

 Join us on Facebook at Listening to Music with Craig Wright

PRACTICE ... your understanding of this chapter's concepts by comparing Checklists of Musical Style for all historic eras, completing a Musical Style Quiz for the Middle Ages and Renaissance, and working once more with the chapter's Active Listening Guides online.

DO ... online multiple-choice and critical thinking quizzes that your instructor may assign for a grade.

CHECKLIST OF MUSICAL STYLE *Renaissance: 1450–1600*

REPRESENTATIVE COMPOSERS

Anonymous (now less prolific)	Josquin Desprez	Palestrina	Weelkes

PRINCIPAL GENRES

polyphonic Mass   sacred motet   instrumental dances   secular song and madrigal
                                                (pavane and galliard)

Melody	Mainly stepwise motion within moderately narrow range; still mainly diatonic, but some intense chromaticism found in madrigals from end of period
Harmony	More careful use of dissonance than in Middle Ages as the triad, a consonant chord, becomes the basic building block of harmony
Rhythm	Duple meter is now as common as triple meter; rhythm in sacred vocal music (Mass and motet) is relaxed and without strong downbeats; rhythm in secular music (madrigal and instrumental dance) usually lively and catchy
Color	Although more music for instruments alone has survived, the predominant sound remains that of unaccompanied (a cappella) vocal music, whether for soloists or for choir
Texture	Mainly polyphonic: imitative counterpoint for four or five vocal lines heard throughout Masses, motets, and madrigals; occasional passages of chordal homophonic texture are inserted for variety
Form	Strict musical forms are not often used; most Masses, motets, madrigals, and instrumental dances are through composed—they have no musical repetitions and hence no standard formal plan

The
BAROQUE part THREE Period, 1600–1750

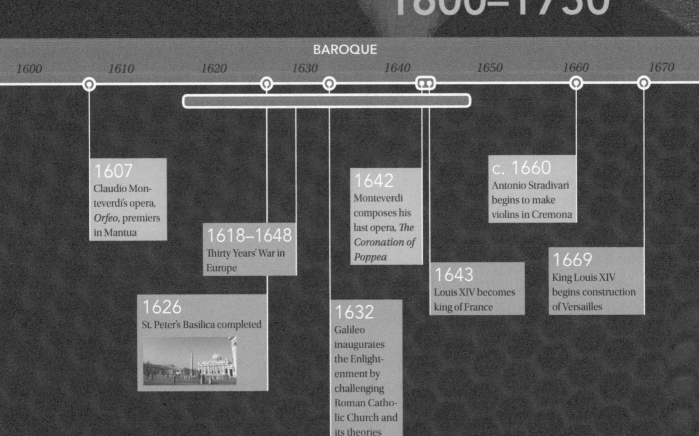

BAROQUE

1600   1610   1620   1630   1640   1650   1660   1670

1607
Claudio Monteverdi's opera, *Orfeo*, premiers in Mantua

1618–1648
Thirty Years' War in Europe

1626
St. Peter's Basilica completed

1642
Monteverdi composes his last opera, *The Coronation of Poppea*

1643
Louis XIV becomes king of France

1632
Galileo inaugurates the Enlightenment by challenging Roman Catholic Church and its theories on celestial bodies

c. 1660
Antonio Stradivari begins to make violins in Cremona

1669
King Louis XIV begins construction of Versailles

The dominant style of architecture, painting, sculpture, music, and dance in the period 1600–1750 is called Baroque. It originated first in Rome, as a way to glorify the Counter-Reformation Catholic Church, and then spread beyond Italy to Spain, France, Germany, Austria, the Low Countries, and England. The artists who created Baroque art worked mainly for the pope and important rulers throughout Europe. Thus, Baroque art is akin to the "official" art of the ruling establishment. Whereas the music of the Renaissance is marked by classical balance and rational restraint, that of the Baroque era is full of grandeur, extravagance, drama, and overt sensuality. This is as true for the music of Claudio Monteverdi at the beginning of the Baroque period as it is for that of Bach and Handel at the end. Finally, during the Baroque period, several new musical genres emerge: Opera, cantata, and oratorio enter the realm of vocal music, and sonata and concerto appear among the instrumental types.

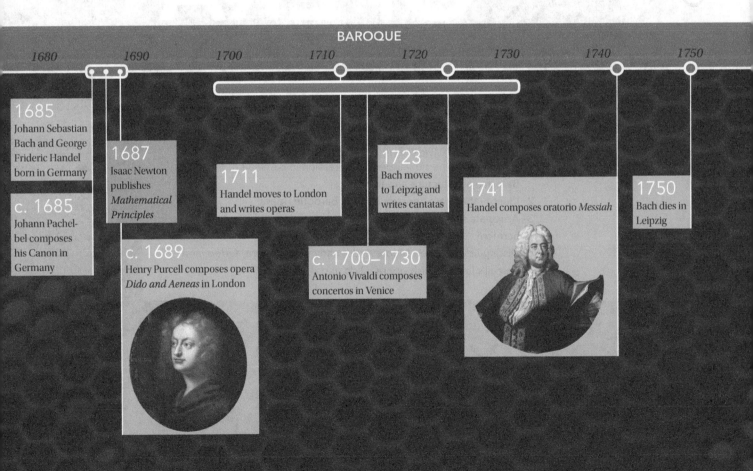

BAROQUE

1680   1690   1700   1710   1720   1730   1740   1750

1685
Johann Sebastian Bach and George Frideric Handel born in Germany

c. 1685
Johann Pachelbel composes his Canon in Germany

1687
Isaac Newton publishes *Mathematical Principles*

c. 1689
Henry Purcell composes opera *Dido and Aeneas* in London

1711
Handel moves to London and writes operas

c. 1700–1730
Antonio Vivaldi composes concertos in Venice

1723
Bach moves to Leipzig and writes cantatas

1741
Handel composes oratorio *Messiah*

1750
Bach dies in Leipzig

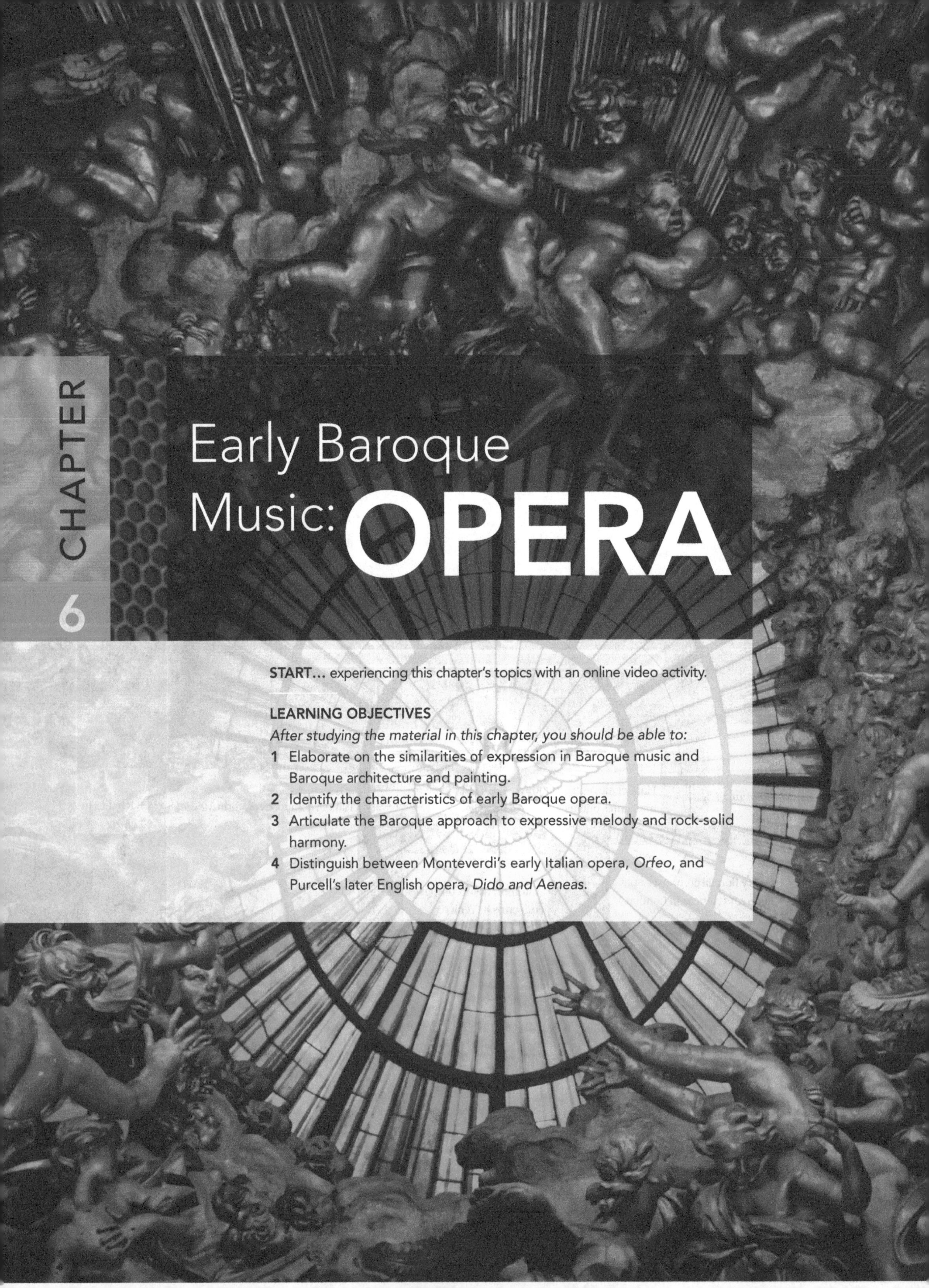

Early Baroque Music: OPERA

START... experiencing this chapter's topics with an online video activity.

LEARNING OBJECTIVES

After studying the material in this chapter, you should be able to:

1 Elaborate on the similarities of expression in Baroque music and Baroque architecture and painting.
2 Identify the characteristics of early Baroque opera.
3 Articulate the Baroque approach to expressive melody and rock-solid harmony.
4 Distinguish between Monteverdi's early Italian opera, *Orfeo*, and Purcell's later English opera, *Dido and Aeneas*.

M usic historians agree, with unusual unanimity, that Baroque music first appeared in Italy in the early seventeenth century. Around 1600, the established equal-voice choral polyphony of the Renaissance receded in importance as a new, more flamboyant style gained popularity. Eventually, the new style was given a new name: Baroque.

Baroque is the term employed to describe the arts generally during the period 1600–1750. It derives from the Portuguese word *barroco*, referring to a pearl of irregular shape then used in jewelry and in fine decorations. Critics applied the term *baroque* to indicate excessive ornamentation in the visual arts and a rough, bold instrumental sound in music. Thus, originally, *baroque* had a negative connotation: It signified distortion, excess, and extravagance. Only during the twentieth century, with a newfound appreciation of the painting of Peter Paul Rubens (1577–1640) and the music of J. S. Bach (1685–1750), among others, has the term *baroque* come to assume a positive meaning in Western cultural history.

Baroque Architecture and Music

What strikes us most when standing before a monument of Baroque design, such as the basilica of St. Peter in Rome or the palace of Versailles outside of Paris, is the grandiose scale. The plazas, buildings, colonnades, gardens, and fountains are all massive. Look at the ninety-foot-high altar canopy inside St. Peter's Basilica in Rome (Figure 6.1), designed by Gian Lorenzo Bernini (1598–1680), and see how it dwarfs the people barely visible below. Outside the basilica, a circle of colonnades forms a courtyard large enough to encompass several football fields (Figure 6.2). Or, consider the French king's palace of Versailles, constructed during the reign of Louis XIV (1643–1715), so monumental in scope that it formed a small independent city, home to several thousand court functionaries (see Figure 7.3).

FIGURE 6.1
The high altar at St. Peter's Basilica, Rome, with baldachin by Gian Lorenzo Bernini. Standing ninety feet high, this canopy is marked by twisted columns and curving shapes, color, and movement, all typical of Baroque art.

FIGURE 6.2
St. Peter's Square, designed by Bernini in the mid-seventeenth century. The expanse is so colossal that it dwarfs people, cars, and buses.

FIGURE 6.3
The Baroque church of Our Lady of Victory in Rome (1603–1675). The powerful pillars and arches set a strong structural framework, while the painted ceiling and elaborately sculpted angels add decoration and energy. Even the organ at the back lends a sense of exuberance to the space.

The music composed for performance in such vast expanses could be equally grandiose. While at first the Baroque orchestra was small, under King Louis XIV it occasionally swelled to more than eighty players. Similarly, choral works for Baroque churches sometimes required twenty-four, forty-eight, or even fifty-three separate lines or parts. These compositions for massive choral forces epitomize the grand or "colossal" Baroque—art on steroids, if you will.

Once the exteriors of the large Baroque palaces and churches were built, the artists of the time rushed to fill these expanses with abundant, perhaps even excessive, decoration. It was as if the architect had created a large vacuum and into it raced the painter, sculptor, and carver to fill the void. Look again at the interior of St. Peter's (Figure 6.1) and notice the ornamentation on the ceiling, as well as the elaborate twists and turns of Bernini's canopy. Or consider the church of Our Lady of Victory in Rome, where Bernini also worked (Figure 6.3). Every square inch is covered with decoration of one sort or another. The riot of sculpture and painting add both warmth and energy to what would otherwise be a vast void.

Similarly, when expressed in the music of the Baroque era, this love of energetic detail within large-scale compositions took the form of a highly ornamental melody set upon a solid chordal foundation. Sometimes the decoration almost seems to overrun the fundamental harmonic structure of the piece. Notice in Example 6.1 the abundance of melodic flourishes in just a few measures of music for violin by Italian composer Arcangelo Corelli (1653–1713). Such ornaments were equally popular with the singers of the early Baroque period, when the cult of the vocal virtuoso first emerged.

EXAMPLE 6.1 Ornamentation of melody above solid foundation

Baroque Painting and Music

Many of the principles at work in Baroque architecture are also found in Baroque painting and music. Baroque canvases are usually large and colorful. Most important, they are overtly dramatic. Drama in painting is created by contrast: Bright light is set against darkness; bold colors are juxtaposed; and lines are placed at right angles, thereby evoking tension and energetic movement. Figure 6.4 depicts a horrific scene: the woman Judith visiting retribution upon the Assyrian general Holofernes, as painted by Artemisia Gentileschi (1593–1656). Here, the play of light and dark creates a dramatic effect, the stark blue and red colors add intensity, while the head of the victim, set at a right angle to his body, suggests an unnatural motion. Baroque art sometimes delights in the pure shock value of presenting gruesome events from history or myth in a dramatic way.

Baroque music is also highly dramatic. We observed in the music of the Renaissance (1450–1600) the humanistic desire to have music reinforce the text so as to sway, or affect, the emotions, as ancient Greek drama had once done. In the early seventeenth century, this desire culminated in a new aesthetic theory, called the Doctrine of Affections. The **Doctrine of Affections** held that different musical moods could and should be used to influence the emotions, or affections, of the listener—be it rage, revenge, sorrow, joy, or love. When composers transferred these vocally delivered emotions to the stage, they created a powerful new medium: opera.

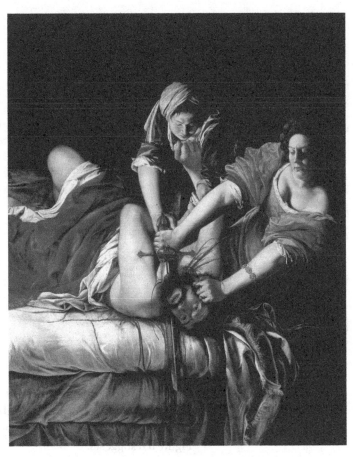

Judith Beheading Holofernes (c. 1615) by Artemisia Gentileschi. The grisly scene of Judith slaying the tyrant general was painted several times by Gentileschi, perhaps as a vivid way of demonstrating her abhorrence of aggressive male domination.

Early Baroque Opera

Given the popularity of opera today—and the fact that opera has existed in China and Japan since the thirteenth century—it is surprising that this genre of music emerged comparatively late in the history of Western European culture. Not until around 1600 did opera appear in Europe, and its native soil was Italy.

An **opera** is basically a stage play (a drama) expressed through music. The term *opera* means literally "a work," and it first appeared in the Italian phrase *opera drammatica in musica,* "a dramatic work set to music." Opera demands singers who can act or, in some cases, actors who can sing. Indeed, in opera, every word of the text (called the **libretto**) is sung. Such a requirement might strike us as unnatural. After all, we don't usually sing to our roommate, "Get out of the shower, I need to get to class this morning." But in opera, what we lose in credibility we more than recoup in expressive power. Set to music, the text of a song, whether a pop hit or an opera aria, gains emotional force. Find a good drama, add music to the words, call the audience to attention with a stirring instrumental piece (an **overture**), throw in a chorus and some instrumental mood music, and, voilà, you've got an opera. Ironically, the inventors of this new genre thought they were resurrecting something old—ancient Greek drama.

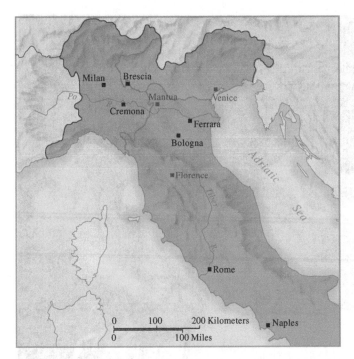

The origins of opera can be traced to late-sixteenth-century Italy, specifically to the cities of Florence, Mantua, and Venice (Figure 6.5). There, progressive musicians continued to pursue the humanist ideals of the Renaissance: They sought to re-create the emotive powers of classical Greek theater. They aimed to do so, however, with modern musical means: employing expressive solo song rather than old-fashioned choral polyphony. Among these pioneering musicians was Vincenzo Galilei (ca. 1525–1591), a noted music theorist and father of the famous astronomer, Galileo Galilei (1564–1642). The elder Galilei and his followers believed that the power of Greek drama owed much to the fact that every line was sung, not spoken. These pioneers of the theater aimed to bring ancient Greek drama to life through expressive, accompanied solo song.

FIGURE 6.5
The major musical centers in northern Italy in the seventeenth century. Opera first developed in Florence, Mantua, and Venice.

Expressive Melody: Monody

The music of the Renaissance, as we saw in Chapter 5, was dominated by polyphonic religious music in which the voices of a choir spun out a web of imitative counterpoint. The nature and importance of each of the lines was about equal, as Figure 6.6 suggests.

FIGURE 6.6
Imitative counterpoint

An equal-voice choir might be a useful medium to convey the abstract religious thoughts of the multitudes. To communicate the raw human emotions of the individual, however, a direct appeal by a soloist seemed more appropriate. In early Baroque music, then, all voices are not created equal. Rather, a polarity develops in which the music projects more strongly from the top and the bottom. In between, the middle voices do little more than fill out the texture (Figure 6.7).

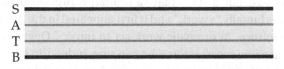

FIGURE 6.7
Soprano-bass polarity

This new structure facilitated a new kind of solo song, called **monody** (from the Greek term meaning "solo song"). A single singer stepped forward, supported only by a bass line and one or more accompanying instruments, to project a highly charged text. With the spotlight squarely on the soloist, a more elaborate, indeed showy, style of singing developed. Notice in Example 6.2 how the vocalist ascends rapidly (densely packed black notes) with a long and difficult melisma. Notice, too, that this heavenly flight underscores the word *paradiso* ("paradise"), the music reinforcing the meaning of the text.

EXAMPLE 6.2 An elaborately expressive Baroque melody

Tan - ta bel - lez-za il pa-ra-di - - - - - - - - - so ha se - co.
(Wherever so much beauty resides contains paradise.)

Rock-Solid Harmony

To prevent the high-flying melodies of Baroque music from spinning out of control, a strong harmonic support was needed. This bass-driven chordal support is called the ***basso continuo*** ("continuous bass"), music created by a small accompanying force. Early in the Baroque era, the accompanying instrument was most often a large lute (Figure 6.8).

By the end of the Baroque period, however, the *basso continuo* was usually provided by a low string instrument and a harpsichord working together. A glance at Figure 6.9 shows a solo singer, two violinists, and a violist supported by a large double bass (to the left), which plays the bass line, and a harpsichord, which improvises chords built above that bass line. The singer projects the melody, while the double bass plays the bass line and the harpsichord fills in the chords above the bass pitch.

What chords did the Baroque lutenist or harpsichordist fill in? These were suggested to the performer by means of **figured bass**—a numerical shorthand placed below the bass line. A player familiar with chord formations would look at the bass line, such as that given in

FIGURE 6.8
A Woman Playing the Theorbo-Lute and a Cavalier (c. 1658) by Gerard ter Borch. The bass strings at the top of the instrument play the bass line, while the upper strings are strummed to fill out chords. In the early Baroque a large lute like this was enough to provide the *basso continuo*.

WATCH... a demonstration of early Baroque violin music

FIGURE 6.9
Antonio Visentini (1688–1782), *Concert at the Villa*. Notice how the double bass player at the left turns his head to read the bass (bottom) line in the score on the harpsichord; together they provide the *basso continuo*.

Example 6.3A, and improvise chords along the lines of those given in Example 6.3B. These improvised chords, generated from the bass according to the numerical code, support a melody above. Here, a modern parallel exists in the alphanumerical code found in "fake sheets" used by jazz musicians and studio guitarists today, which suggests which chords to play beneath the written melody.

LISTEN TO...
Example 6.3A online.

LISTEN TO...
Example 6.3B online.

EXAMPLE 6.3A Figured bass

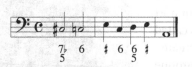

EXAMPLE 6.3B Improvised chords

becomes

Finally, for the general listener, hearing the *basso continuo* is the key to recognizing that music is in Baroque style. The constant plucking of a lute or tinkling of a harpsichord in step with a strong bass line immediately gives it away. As the name suggests, the Baroque *basso continuo* is continual, indeed relentless! With the concepts of monody and *basso continuo* now in mind, let's go on to hear both as we meet the first important composer of opera, Claudio Monteverdi.

Claudio Monteverdi (1567–1643)

The life of Claudio Monteverdi (Figure 6.10) unfolded in northern Italy: first in Cremona, where he was born in 1567, and then in Mantua and Venice (see Figure 6.5), where he was successively employed as a performer and a composer. Monteverdi is known today primarily as a creator of opera, and his first, *Orfeo* (1607), is generally considered the first true example of the genre. Because the aim of early opera was to reproduce elements of ancient Greek drama, not surprisingly Monteverdi's plots draw upon stories from classical Greek mythology. *Orfeo* is essentially a "rescue drama."

The hero, Orfeo (Orpheus), descends into the realm of Hades (the Greek equivalent of Hell) to rescue his new bride, Euridice, who has languished there since her sudden, unexpected death. To accomplish his mission, Orfeo charms and disarms hellish demons with a singularly formidable weapon: his beautiful singing (Figure 6.11). Indeed, the theme of *Orfeo* is the divine power of music.

Like all operas, *Orfeo* begins with a purely instrumental work that serves as a curtain raiser. Although such instrumental introductions are usually called overtures, Monteverdi called his musical preamble a **toccata** (see Listening Guide). The term *toccata* (literally, "a touched thing") refers to an instrumental piece, for keyboard or other instruments, requiring great technical dexterity of the performers. It is, in other words, an instrumental showpiece. Here, the trumpet races up and down the scale, while many of the lower parts rapidly articulate repeating pitches.

FIGURE 6.10
Portrait of Claudio Monteverdi by Bernardo Strozzi (1581–1644)

FIGURE 6.11
Orfeo charms the guardians of Hades with his voice and lyre—a detail from a painting by Nicolas Poussin (1594–1665)

LISTENING GUIDE

Claudio Monteverdi, *Orfeo* (1607), Toccata   Download 20 (1:40)

WHAT TO LISTEN FOR: The brilliant sounds of the early trumpets and trombones—is there any better music with which to grab a listener's attention?

0:00	Trumpet highlights highest part.
0:33	Repeat of toccata with low strings added
1:05	Repeat of toccata with full orchestra

LISTEN TO ... this selection streaming online.

WATCH ... an Active Listening Guide of this selection online.

Monteverdi calls for the toccata to be sounded three times. Brief as it is, this toccata is long enough to suggest the richness and variety of instrumental sounds available to a composer in the early Baroque. Its theatrical function, of course, is to call the audience to attention, to signal that the action is about to begin.

What is this opera *Orfeo* about? The Prologue (see Listening Guide) tells us. La Musica (the allegorical figure of Music) steps onto the stage dressed in clothing befitting an ancient Greek drama. (In fact, the stage for Monteverdi's premiere in Mantua was a platform around which some 200 guests gathered and stood for all five acts of the production.) La Musica, one of the mythological gods of Mount Helicon (south of modern-day Athens), possesses, as she says, the power to "make peaceful every troubled heart." Her task is literally to set the stage, and she does so in a five-strophe monody.

LISTENING GUIDE

Claudio Monteverdi, *Orfeo* (1607)   Download 21 (6:33)

Prologue, "Del mio Permesso amato"

Character: La Musica (the personification of Music, one of the nine muses of Greek mythology)

Situation: Offering a preview of the coming drama, La Musica tells of the powers of the demi-god Orfeo, who, employing the strength of music, will defeat the forces of darkness and reclaim his beloved.

WHAT TO LISTEN FOR: The tug of war between the soothing sounds of the ritornello and the increasingly intense, passionate, and highly emotive expression of the singer as she moves from one strophe to the next

0:00	Ritornello (instrumental refrain) with repeat	
	Strophe 1	
0:41	Dal mio Permesso amato à voi ne vegno,	From my beloved Permessus to you I come,
	Incliti Eroi, sangue gentil de' Regi,	Glorious Heroes, noble bloodline of Kings,
	Di cui narra la Fama eccelsi pregi,	Of whom Fame relates celestial praise,
	Nè giunge al ver, perch'è tropp' alto il segno.	Not quite attaining the truth, as it is too high a mark.
1:31	Ritornello reiterated	

(Continued)

1:47	Io la Musica son, ch'a i dolci accenti,	I am Music, who in sweet accents,
	Sò far tranquillo ogni turbato core,	Can make peaceful every troubled heart,
	Ed hor dì nobil ira, e hor d'amore,	Sometimes with noble anger, and sometimes with love,
	Posso infiammar le più gelate menti.	Can I inflame the coldest minds.
2:32	Ritornello reiterated	

Strophe 3

2:49	Io sù Cetera d'or cantando soglio	Singing with my golden Lyre, I like
	Mortal orecchio lusingar talhora,	To charm mortal ears from time to time,
	E in questa guisa a l'armonia sonora	And in this way with the resounding harmony
	De la lira del Ciel più l'alme invoglio.	Of the Heavenly Lyre I set their souls on fire.
3:38	Ritornello reiterated	

Strophe 4

3:56	Quinci à dirvi d'Orfeo desio mi sprona,	Hence desire spurs me to tell you of Orfeo,
	D'Orfeo che trasse al suo cantar le fere,	Of Orfeo who with his song tamed wild beasts,
	E servo fè l'Inferno a sue preghiere,	And made Hades answer his prayers,
	Gloria immortal di Pindo e d'Elicona.	To the immortal glory of Pindus and Helicon.
4:37	Ritornello reiterated	

Strophe 5

4:55	Hor mentre i canti alterno hor lieti, hor mesti,	While I vary my songs, now happy, now sad,
	Non si mova augellin fra queste piante,	No small bird shall move among these bushes,
	Nè s'oda in queste rive onda sonante,	Nor on these banks a sounding wave be heard,
	Ed ogni auretta in suo cammin s'arresti.	And every breeze shall stay its journey.
5:48	Ritornello reiterated and then repeated with full orchestra	

LISTEN TO ... this selection streaming online.

WATCH ... an Active Listening Guide of this selection online.

WATCH ... a performance of this selection online.

DO ... Listening Exercise 6.1, Monteverdi, *Orfeo*, Prologue, online.

A monody in five strophes might get boring. Monteverdi avoids this trap by keeping the harmony the same for each strophe but varying the melody, thereby producing what is called **strophic variation**, a form in which the music is slightly varied from one strophe to the next. The emotional experience is one of excitement (the ever-new melody) balanced by stability (the repeating harmony). Monteverdi provides additional solidity by surrounding each strophe with one and the same **ritornello**. The psychological purpose of this instrumental insert is to produce a soothing refrain, which is exactly what *ritornello* ("something that returns") means in Italian. Once the musical "trailer" (the Prologue) has finished, the action of the opera can begin.

As the seventeenth century progressed, Monteverdi and his successors increasingly divided operatic monody into two distinctive types: recitative and aria. **Recitative**, from the Italian word *recitativo* ("something recited"), is musically heightened speech. Generally, an opera composer employs recitative to narrate the plot of the opera. Recitative mirrors the natural rhythms of everyday speech and thus has no perceptible meter or beat—you can't tap your foot to it. In Baroque opera, recitative is accompanied only by the *basso continuo*. Such sparsely accompanied recitative is called **simple recitative** (*recitativo semplice* in Italian; also called *recitativo secco*, "dry recitative"). Later, in the nineteenth century, recitative accompanied by the full orchestra, called *recitativo accompagnato*, would become the norm.

If recitative tells us what's going on, an aria serves to tell us what the characters are *feeling*, to showcase the emotional high points of the drama. Whereas the text of the recitative is usually in prose, the aria is always written in poetry, which suggests that the preceding Prologue, with its **abba** rhyme scheme, is less akin to a recitative than to an aria.

An **aria** (Italian for "song" or "air") is more passionate, more expansive, and more tuneful than a recitative. Here, all or part of the orchestra enters to join the *basso continuo* and thereby provide a strong sonic support, saying, in effect, "Listen, everyone, this solo song is an important moment!" In fact, judging from contemporary accounts, the Baroque audience usually talked during most of the recitatives and listened only during the arias. Finally, whereas a recitative often involves a rapid-fire delivery of text, an aria will work through it at a more leisurely pace; words are repeated to heighten their dramatic effect, and important vowels are extended by vocal melismas to increase their emotional power. These moments not only express feeling, they are also moments of musical beauty. Then, as now, the audience leaves the opera house humming, not the speech-like recitative, but the tuneful arias.

Perhaps because it originated there, Italy has always nurtured opera, from the time of Monteverdi, through Verdi and Puccini (see Chapters 20 and 22), to the present day. Indeed, opera has most frequently been written in the Italian language, not only because of the genre's Italian origins, but also because of the pleasing, evenly spaced vowels of this "mother tongue." But early on, opera began to spread from Italy over the Alps to German-speaking countries, to France, and eventually to England. The first English opera worthy of notice is Henry Purcell's *Dido and Aeneas*.

An Opera in English: Henry Purcell's *Dido and Aeneas* (1689)

Henry Purcell (1659–1695; Figure 6.12) has been called the "greatest of all English composers." Indeed, only the late Baroque composer George Frideric Handel (who was actually German-born) and pop songwriter Paul McCartney can plausibly challenge Purcell for this title. Purcell was born in London, the son of one of the king's singers. In 1679, the younger Purcell obtained the position of organist at Westminster Abbey, and then, in 1682, he became organist for the

FIGURE 6.12
Henry Purcell, by an anonymous painter

FIGURE 6.13

A detail from the painting, *The Death of Dido*, by Guercino (1599–1666). The servant Belinda bends over the dying Dido, who has fallen on Aeneas's formidable sword.

WATCH... a walk-through of the score of "Thy hand, Belinda" and "When I am laid in earth," online.

king's Chapel Royal as well. But London has always been a vital theater town, and Purcell increasingly devoted his attention to works for the public stage.

One of Purcell's stage works that still enjoys public favor today is his opera *Dido and Aeneas*, written not for the royal family but, rather, for a private girls' boarding school in the London suburb of Chelsea. The girls presented one major stage production annually, something like the senior class play of today. In *Dido and Aeneas*, they sang the numerous choruses and danced in the equally frequent dance numbers. All nine solo parts save one (the role of Aeneas) were written for female voices. The libretto of the opera, one appropriate for a school curriculum steeped in classical Latin, is drawn from Virgil's *Aeneid*. Surely the girls had studied this epic poem in Latin class, and likely they had memorized parts of it. Surely, too, they knew the story of the soldier-of-fortune Aeneas, who seduces proud Dido, queen of Carthage, but then deserts her to fulfill his destiny—sailing on to found the city of Rome. Betrayed and alone, Dido vents her feelings in an exceptionally beautiful aria, "When I am laid in earth," and then expires. In Virgil's original story, Dido stabs herself with the sword of Aeneas (Figure 6.13). In Purcell's opera, she dies of a broken heart: Her pain is poison enough.

By the time of Purcell's *Dido and Aeneas* (1689), the growing dichotomy between speech-like recitative and song-like aria is clear. Purcell introduces Dido's final aria with a brief example of simple recitative (accompanied by *basso continuo* only): "Thy hand, Belinda." Normally, simple recitative is a business-like process that moves the action along through direct declamation. In this passage, however, recitative transcends its typically routine role. Notice the remarkable way Purcell sets the English language. He understood where the accents fell in the text of his libretto, and he knew how to replicate them effectively in the music. In Example 6.4, the stressed words in the text generally appear in long notes and on the downbeat of each measure. Equally important, notice how the vocal line descends a full octave, passing through chromatic notes along the way. (Chromaticism is another device composers use to signal pain and grief.) As the voice twists chromatically downward, we share the pain of the abandoned Dido. By the end, she has slumped into the arms of her servant Belinda.

EXAMPLE 6.4 Simple recitative "Thy hand, Belinda"

Thy hand, Be-lin-da! Dark - - ness shades me; on thy bo-som let me rest. More I would, but Death in-vades me: Death is now a wel-come guest.

From the recitative, "Thy hand, Belinda," Purcell moves imperceptibly to the climactic aria, "When I am laid in earth," in which Dido sings of her impending death (see Listening Guide). Because this high point of the opera is a lament, Purcell chooses, in the Baroque tradition, to build it upon a *basso ostinato*.

A melody, harmony, or rhythm that repeats continually throughout a musical composition is an **ostinato**. When the repetition occurs in the bass, we have a ***basso ostinato***. The term *ostinato* comes from an Italian word meaning "obstinate," "stubborn," or "pig-headed." English composers called the *basso ostinato* the **ground bass** because the repeating bass provided a solid foundation, or grounding, on which an entire composition could be built. The ground bass that Purcell composed for Dido's lament consists of two sections: (1) a chromatic stepwise descent over the interval of a fourth (G, F♯, F, E, E♭, D) and (2) a two-measure cadence returning to the tonic G (B♭, C, D, G). This fourth-wise descent in a repeating bass became a symbol for grief or lamentation, especially when presented, as here, in a minor key. At the first sounds of this figure, the audience would know, just as if a banner had been held up: "Here comes an aria dealing with despair!"

The text of Dido's lament consists of a short, one-stanza poem (remember, arias always have a poetic text) with an **aba** rhyme scheme. Here, brevity begets eloquence.

> When I am laid in earth, may my wrongs create
> No trouble in thy breast.
> Remember me, but ah! Forget my fate.

Each line of text is repeated, as are many individual words and pairs of words. (Such repetition of text is typical of an aria but not of recitative.) In this case, Dido's repetitions are perfectly appropriate to her emotional state: She can communicate in fragments, but cannot articulate her feelings in complete sentences. Here, the listener cares less about grammatical correctness, however, and more about the emotion of the moment. No fewer than six times does Dido plead with Belinda, and with us, to remember her. And, indeed, we do remember, for this plaintive aria is one of the most moving pieces in all of opera.

LISTENING GUIDE

Henry Purcell, *Dido and Aeneas* (1689)   Download 22 (4:04)

Recitative, "Thy hand, Belinda," and aria, "When I am laid in earth"

Characters: Dido, queen of Carthage; Belinda, her servant

Situation: Having been deserted by her lover, Aeneas, Dido sings farewell to Belinda (and to all) before dying of a broken heart.

WHAT TO LISTEN FOR: Dido's recitative, accompanied by a *basso continuo* (cello and large lute), giving way to her mournful aria, built on a *basso ostinato* and accompanied by full orchestra

Brief recitative

0:00	Continuo played by large lute and cello	Thy hand, Belinda! Darkness shades me;
		on thy bosom let me rest.
		More I would, but Death invades me:
		Death is now a welcome guest.

(Continued)

Aria

0:58 *Basso ostinato* alone in cellos and double basses

1:10 *Basso ostinato* with voice and strings

1:27 *Basso ostinato* repeats beneath voice.

1:44 *Basso ostinato* repeats beneath voice.

2:02 *Basso ostinato* repeats beneath voice.

2:17 *Basso ostinato* repeats beneath voice.

2:37 *Basso ostinato* repeats beneath voice.

2:53 *Basso ostinato* repeats beneath voice.

3:10 *Basso ostinato* repeats beneath voice.

3:29 *Basso ostinato* alone with strings

3:46 *Basso ostinato* alone with strings

LISTEN TO ... this selection streaming online.

WATCH ... an Active Listening Guide of this selection online.

DO ... Listening Exercise 6.2, Purcell, "Thy hand, Belinda" and "When I am laid in earth," online.

ELTON JOHN AND *BASSO OSTINATO*

For an up-to-date example of ostinato bass, we turn to an aria-lament by a more recent English composer, Elton John: "Sorry Seems to Be the Hardest Word" (1976; covered more recently by Ray Charles, Mary J. Blige, and Diana Krall, among others). Although not built exclusively on an ostinato figure, this song has one striking affinity to the aria by Purcell: The chorus makes use of Purcell's *basso ostinato* and sets it to a very, very sad text. The ostinato pattern begins on G, with a chromatically descending fourth, followed by a one-measure cadence:

It's sad (so sad), it's a sad, sad situation
Bass
G   F#   F   E

                  And it's getting more and more absurd
          E♭   D   F♯GAD
                         (cadence)

Compare Elton John's bass line with Purcell's *basso ostinato* and note that both laments are set in the key of G minor. Although one might accuse Elton John of artistic "theft," borrowing and improving has been part of the creative process since time immemorial.

Elton John (Sir Reginald Dwight), the pop artist, who studied for five years at the Royal Academy of Music in London, where the music of Purcell is regularly taught, was inspired by the famous aria of his equally well-coiffed countryman (see Figure 6.12).

WATCH... a YouTube video of "Sorry Seems to Be the Hardest Word" online.

KEY WORDS

Baroque (85)	monody (88)	ritornello (93)	*basso ostinato* (95)
Doctrine of Affections (87)	*basso continuo* (89)	recitative (93)	ground bass (95)
opera (87)	figured bass (89)	simple recitative (93)	
libretto (87)	toccata (90)	aria (93)	
overture (87)	strophic variation (92)	ostinato (95)	

 Join us on Facebook at Listening to Music with Craig Wright

PRACTICE ... your understanding of this chapter's concepts by comparing Checklists of Musical Style for all historic eras and working once more with the chapter's Active Listening Guides online.

DO ... online multiple-choice and critical thinking quizzes that your instructor may assign for a grade.

Toward Late Baroque
INSTRUMENTAL MUSIC

START… experiencing this chapter's topics with an online video activity.

LEARNING OBJECTIVES

After studying the material in this chapter, you should be able to:

1 Trace the transition from vocally to instrumentally dominated classical music during the seventeenth century.

2 Sketch the development of the orchestra for Western classical music as it evolved during the seventeenth century.

3 Differentiate three musical forms found in middle Baroque instrumental music: rondo form in Baroque trumpet music; canon; and ritornello form in the Baroque concerto.

When we think of classical music today, we usually think of instrumental music and instrumental performing groups—a symphony orchestra or a string quartet, for example. The equation classical = instrumental, though certainly not entirely true, nonetheless has some validity—about 80 percent of the Western classical repertoire is instrumental. Statistics prove the point. During the Renaissance, the number of prints of vocal music outsold those of instrumental music by almost ten to one; by the end of the seventeenth century, on the other hand, instrumental publications outnumbered vocal ones by about three to one. The majority of this instrumental music was intended for members of the violin family.

During the seventeenth century, the violin came to be the most important of Western string instruments and the leader in the emerging Western orchestra. Originating in the late Renaissance as a cheaper and easier-to-play cousin of the six-string viol, the violin (*violino*, or "little viol," as it was called in Italian) had only four strings, no frets, and a louder, more penetrating tone. At first used for playing dances in taverns, the lowly violin was soon domesticated as an instrument appropriate for chamber music at home and, ultimately, promoted to leader of the orchestra, mainly because it played the melody. The best violin maker of the Baroque era was Antonio Stradivari (1644–1737), whose instruments (Figure 7.1) today sell for millions of dollars.

Accompanying the growing importance of the violin was an awareness that it—and, indeed, all instruments—had strengths and weaknesses. A violin, for example, was an excellent vehicle for running up and down a scale, whereas a trumpet was particularly good at leaping an octave. Accordingly, composers began to engage in **idiomatic writing** (well-suited writing), composing in a way that exploited the strengths and avoided the weaknesses of particular instruments.

Finally, during the Baroque era, not only did the emphasis shift from vocal to instrumental music, but the means of expression that had developed for Renaissance vocal music also came to be applied to Baroque instrumental music. By adopting devices used in the Renaissance madrigal, for example, composers now made purely instrumental music express rage (with tremolos and rapidly racing scales, for example); despair (with a swooning melody above a lament bass); or a bright spring day (by such means as trills and other "chirps" high in the violins and flutes). Even without the benefit of a text, instrumental music could tell a story or describe a scene, as Antonio Vivaldi does in his "Spring" Concerto. Henceforth, by means of such gestures, composers expressed meaning in music, not only in songs, but also in large, purely instrumental pieces.

The Baroque Orchestra

The symphony orchestra as we know it today had its origins in seventeenth-century Italy and France. Originally, the term *orchestra* referred to the area occupied by the musicians in the ancient Greek theater, between the audience and the stage; eventually, it came to mean the musicians themselves. By the mid-seventeenth century, the core of the orchestra was formed by the violin family—violins, violas, cellos, and the related double bass. To this string nucleus were added woodwinds: oboes and then bassoons and an occasional flute. Sometimes trumpets would be included to provide extra brilliance. When trumpets appeared, so, too, usually did timpani—trumpets and drums having traditionally sounded together on the battlefield.

FIGURE 7.1
Antonio Stradivari made every sort of string instrument, even guitars. About 600 of his violins survive today and are very valuable; one sold at auction in 2011 for $15.9 million.

FIGURE 7.2
Detail of an orchestra playing for a Baroque opera, as seen in Pietro Domenico Olivero's *Interior of the Teatro Regio*, Turin (1740). From left to right are a bassoon, two French horns, a cello, a double bass, a harpsichord, and then violins, violas, and oboes. Again, notice how the cellist and the double bass player are looking at the score from which the harpsichordist is playing. Those three performers constitute the *basso continuo*, the accompanying underpinning that holds the full orchestra together.

WATCH... a YouTube video demonstrating how the harpsichord creates sound, online.

FIGURE 7.3
This view of the front of Versailles gives a sense of the grandeur of the palace that King Louis XIV began there in 1669. Versailles was both a court and a small city, full of courtiers and their servants, as well as court functionaries, including musicians.

Finally, by the end of the seventeenth century, composers sometimes added a pair of hunting horns (we now call them "French" horns) to the orchestra, to give it more sonic resonance. Supporting the entire ensemble was the ever-present *basso continuo*, usually consisting of a harpsichord to provide chords and a low string instrument to play the bass line (Figure 7.2). The orchestra for Western classical music, then, can be said to be an ensemble of musicians, organized around a core of strings, with added woodwinds and brasses, playing under a leader.

Most Baroque orchestras were small, usually with no more than twenty performers, and none of the parts was doubled—that is, no more than one instrumentalist was assigned to a single written line. Yet, while the typical Baroque orchestra had no more than twenty players, there were exceptions, especially toward the end of the seventeenth century. At some of the more splendid courts around Europe, the orchestra might swell to more than eighty instrumentalists for special occasions. Foremost among these was the court of French king Louis XIV.

Of all the courts of Baroque Europe, that of King Louis XIV (reigned 1643–1715) was the most splendid. Louis styled himself the "Sun King," after Apollo, the god of the sun and of music. Outside Paris, near the small town of Versailles, Louis built himself a palace, the largest court complex ever constructed (Figure 7.3). There,

Louis not only shone forth in all his glory but also ruled absolutely: As he famously said, "I *am* the state" ("L'État, c'est moi").

Perhaps the greatest gift that King Louis gave, indirectly, to music was a new genre: the French overture. A **French overture**—so called because it then opened all the musical-dramatic productions at the French court—consists of two sections. The first is set in a slow duple meter, with stately dotted rhythms suggesting a royal procession; the second is set in a fast triple meter and features much imitation among the various musical lines. Although developed at the court of Louis XIV, the French overture quickly spread to Germany and England. Bach began many of his orchestral and keyboard suites with a French overture, as did Handel, who also famously opened his English oratorio *Messiah* in this fashion.

Mouret and Trumpet Music for the French Court

Following an unprecedented reign of seventy-two years, Louis XIV was succeeded by his grandson Louis XV (1715–1774). Among the musicians employed by this younger Louis was Jean-Joseph Mouret (1682–1738). In truth, Mouret was only a minor figure in the history of music. He would be totally forgotten today were it not for one small twist of fate. In 1971, PBS's *Masterpiece Theater* chose the Rondeau from Mouret's *Suite de symphonies* (*Succession of Harmonious Pieces*, 1729; see Listening Guide) to be its theme. *Masterpiece Theater* (now *Masterpiece*) went on to become the longest-running drama series in television history, and over the course of more than forty years, Mouret's music (but not the composer's name) came to be known by millions.

What accounts for the popularity of this music? First, the rhythm. Baroque music, in general—and instrumental music, in particular—is characterized by a

LISTENING GUIDE

Jean-Joseph Mouret, Rondeau from *Suite de symphonies* (1729)   Download 9 (1:55)

Form: Rondo (**ABACA**)

Texture: Homophonic

WHAT TO LISTEN FOR: The continually returning refrain (**A**) of the rondo, performed by a brilliant trumpet

0:00	**A**	Refrain played by full orchestra, including trumpet and drums, and then repeated (at 0:13)
0:25	**B**	Quieter contrasting section played by strings and woodwinds
0:37	**A**	Refrain returns but without repeat.
0:50	**C**	New contrasting section played by strings and woodwinds
1:22	**A**	Refrain returns and is repeated (at 1:35).

LISTEN TO ... this selection streaming online.

WATCH ... an Active Listening Guide of this selection online.

DO ... Listening Exercise 7.1, Mouret, Rondeau from *Suite de symphonies*, online.

strong recurring beat. It pushes the music forward and creates, in contemporary terms, a "groove." This tendency toward rhythmic clarity and drive becomes more pronounced as the Baroque period proceeds, and culminates in the rhythmically propulsive music of Vivaldi and Bach.

Most important, as with so much music and commerce generally, in Mouret's Rondeau, the medium is the message. Mouret aimed to showcase the newly brilliant French orchestra and especially the sound of the trumpet—more idiomatic writing. Would this Rondeau be as memorable if the opening melody were assigned to a low, less-penetrating cello or double bass? Surely not. Music is a combination of durational patterns (rhythm), a configuration of frequencies (pitches), and a medium conveying them (tone color). In this case, what catches our ear and what we remember is the tone color—the brilliant, piercing sound of the trumpet.

Pachelbel and His Canon

Contemporary pop songs invariably are supported by chordal harmonies that move in a predictable way. They follow certain sequences of chords, called chord progressions (see the section "Building Harmony with Chords" in Chapter 2), which by now are so deeply engrained in our aural psyche that we scarcely notice them. These chord progressions first emerged during the Baroque era. Composers such as Purcell and Pachelbel, for example, began to build their music around set patterns of chords, all gravitating toward the tonic. Such stock patterns became well known, and many composers borrowed them or created new but similar chord progressions themselves. A melody might be entirely original, but the harmony would be, consciously or not, drawn from a common pool of accompanying chord patterns. Indeed, so universal have these progressions become since the Baroque period that they have engendered a principle of U.S. copyright law: You can successfully sue someone for stealing your melody but not for expropriating your harmony.

Today, most of us remember the name Johann Pachelbel (rhymes with Taco Bell) only because of a single musical composition, his Canon in D major (see Listening Guide). In his day, however, Pachelbel was known as a composer of a great deal of instrumental music and as a respected teacher (he taught Bach's older brother). Although almost everyone knows the Pachelbel Canon, there is an oddity about it: We don't hear the imitative canon, or at least we don't focus on it. Pachelbel has not used orchestration to help guide the listener's ear. He composed the three canonic voices all in the same range and assigned a violin to play each one. Because the lines don't stand out from one another by range or color, the unfolding of the canon (round) is difficult to hear. Instead, we perceive the bass line churning inexorably in the low strings, working in harmony with the chord-filling harpsichord, both thereby creating the *basso continuo* (Example 7.1). A strong bass is typical of Baroque music generally, but Pachelbel's bass is unforgettable. It has a pleasing intervallic pattern to it (fourths alternate with steps), and it gravitates strongly away from the tonic and back to the tonic in an eight-pitch cycle.

Pachelbel knew that he was onto a good thing, so he gives us this same bass line and harmony twenty-eight times, a classic example of a *basso ostinato*. The allure of the bass is such that later classical composers (Handel, Haydn, and Mozart among them) borrowed it, as have pop musicians in recent times, such

LISTENING GUIDE

Johann Pachelbel, Canon in D major (c. 1690)   Download 23 (4:47)

Texture: Polyphonic

Form: Canon above, ostinato below

WHAT TO LISTEN FOR: We can all hear the *ostinato* bass and harmony, but try to follow the unfolding of the canon (round): A violin will play a phrase, then another will repeat it, and another will repeat it again.

0:00	*Basso continuo* begins.
0:12	Violin 1 enters.
0:24	Violin 2 enters in imitation.
0:35	Violin 3 enters in imitation.

0:57   Violin 1 followed by violins 2 and 3 at two-bar intervals

1:44   Violin 1 followed by violins 2 and 3 at two-bar intervals

2:30   Violin 1 followed by violins 2 and 3 at two-bar intervals

3:18   Violin 1 followed by violins 2 and 3 at two-bar intervals

4:04   Violin 1 followed by violins 2 and 3 at two-bar intervals

LISTEN TO ... this selection streaming online.

WATCH ... an Active Listening Guide of this selection online.

WATCH ... a performance of Pachelbel's Canon online.

as Blues Traveler, Vitamin C, Coolio, and Pet Shop Boys. The full composition has served as background music in numerous TV commercials and films. Why is its appeal so timeless? Most likely it's because of an irresistible interplay of opposites: The regular, almost plodding *basso ostinato* provides a rock-solid foundation that allows the violin lines above to soar.

EXAMPLE 7.1 Pachelbel's Canon

Not only did stock harmonic patterns emerge in the Baroque era, but so, too, did our modern "two-key" (or "two-mode") system. During the Middle Ages and Renaissance, Western music had employed many different scales (called the "church modes"). During the seventeenth century, however, these were gradually reduced to just two patterns: major and minor. The two modes create sharply, indeed dramatically, different sounds, which can be used for expressive purposes. Just as a painter might contrast light and dark (see Figure 6.4) for dramatic effect, so, too, might a composer contrast bright major (for jaunty spring) and dark minor (for a gathering storm), as Vivaldi did in his "Spring" Concerto.

Last but not least, sudden contrast in Baroque music was effected by quick shifts in levels of sound. In the early seventeenth century, composers for the first time began to specify dynamic levels in their pieces, writing into their scores two basic words: *piano* (soft) and *forte* (loud). Sudden shifts were more prized than gradual crescendos and diminuendos, possibly because the harpsichord could play at only one, two, or, at most, three dynamic levels (see the section "Keyboard Instruments" in Chapter 3), and nothing in between. The practice of quickly shifting the volume of sound from one level to another is called **terraced dynamics**. Vivaldi's "Spring" Concerto is a showcase for both alternating major and minor keys and terraced dynamics, all with the aim of generating the one thing prized above all others in Baroque art: drama.

Vivaldi and the Baroque Concerto

The concerto was to the Baroque era what the symphony would later become to the Classical period: the showpiece of orchestral music. A **concerto** (from the Latin *concertare*, "to strive together") is a musical composition marked by a friendly contest or competition between one or more soloists and an orchestra. When only one soloist confronts the orchestra, the work is a **solo concerto**. When a small group of soloists works together, performing as a unit against the full orchestra, the piece is called a **concerto grosso**. In a concerto grosso, the smaller group of two, three, or four soloists forms the **concertino** ("little concert"), which does battle with the larger group, the core orchestra, called the concerto grosso ("big concert"). Playing together, the two groups constitute the full orchestra, called the **tutti** (meaning "all" or "everybody"). The contrast between a full group and soloists was desirable, said a contemporary, "so that the ear might be astonished by the alternation of loud and soft ... as the eye is dazzled by the alternation of light and shade."

As written by Vivaldi and Bach, the solo concerto and the concerto grosso usually have three movements: fast-slow-fast. The fast first movement is invariably composed in ritornello form, a structure popularized by Vivaldi. Indeed, so consistent was Vivaldi in applying this form that composer Igor Stravinsky later said, "Vivaldi didn't write 500 concertos, he wrote one concerto 500 ways!"

In **ritornello form**, all or part of the main theme—the ritornello (refrain)—returns again and again, played by the tutti, or full orchestra. In most ways, then, ritornello form is identical to rondo form, as we just heard in Mouret's Rondeau, but the concerto grosso has the additional element of a contrast between the many (tutti) and the few (concertino). Indeed, much of the excitement of a Baroque concerto comes from the tension between the tutti's reaffirming ritornello (home) and the soloists' flights of fancy (away). Needless to say, we always end back home.

The popularity of the concerto grosso peaked about 1730 and then all but ended around the time of Bach's death (1750), but the solo concerto continued to be cultivated during the Classical and Romantic periods, becoming increasingly a showcase in which a single soloist could display his or her technical mastery of an instrument.

Antonio Vivaldi (1678–1741)

No composer was more influential, and certainly none more prolific, in the creation of the Baroque concerto than Antonio Vivaldi (Figure 7.4). Born in Venice, Vivaldi was the son of a part-time barber and substitute musician at the famous basilica of St. Mark. Although he became a skilled performer on the violin, young Vivaldi also entered Holy Orders, ultimately becoming an ordained priest. Vivaldi's life, however, was by no means saintly. He concertized on the violin throughout Europe; he wrote and produced nearly fifty operas, which brought him a great deal of money; and he lived for fifteen years with an Italian opera star.

Ultimately, the "scandalous" life of *il prete rosso* (the red-haired priest) provoked a response from the authorities of the Roman Catholic Church. In 1737, Vivaldi was forbidden to practice his musical artistry in papally controlled lands, which then constituted a large portion of Italy. This ban affected his income as well as his creativity. He died poor and obscure in 1741 in Vienna, where he had gone in search of a post at the imperial court.

From 1703 until 1740, Vivaldi worked in Venice at the *Ospedale della Pietà* (Hospice of Mercy), an orphanage for the care and education of young women. One of four such charitable institutions in Venice, the Hospice of Mercy accepted abandoned, mostly illegitimate, girls who, as several reports state, "otherwise would have been thrown in the canals." By 1700, music had been made to serve an important role in the religious and social life of the orphanage. Each Sunday afternoon, its orchestra of young women offered public performances for the well-to-do of Venice (see Figure 7.5). Also attending these concerts were foreign visitors—Venice was already a tourist city—among them a French diplomat, who wrote in 1739:

> These girls are educated at the expense of the state, and they are trained solely with the purpose of excelling in music. That is why they sing like angels and play violin, flute, organ, oboe, cello, and bassoon; in short, no instrument is so big as to frighten them. They are kept like nuns in a convent. All they do is perform concerts, always in groups of about

FIGURE 7.4
Portrait of a violinist and composer believed by some to be the musician Antonio Vivaldi

forty girls. I swear to you that there is nothing as pleasant as seeing a young and pretty nun, dressed in white, with a little pomegranate bouquet over her ears, conducting the orchestra with all the gracefulness and incredible precision one can imagine.

FIGURE 7.5
Foreign visitors attend a concert performed by orphan girls assembled from various orphanages around Venice, as depicted by Gabriele Bella about 1750. The Hospice of Mercy was the most musically intense of the Venetian orphanages. Here, girls who showed a special talent for music were placed within a prestigious ensemble of forty musicians. Their musical education included tutelage in singing, ear training, and counterpoint, as well as instruction on at least two musical instruments. Antonio Vivaldi was one of the teachers.

Violin Concerto in E major, the "Spring" (early 1700s)

The "Spring" Concerto is Vivaldi's most popular piece and, indeed, the best-known composition in the entire repertoire of Baroque music. As the name suggests, the "Spring" Concerto is one of a set of four concertos that Vivaldi called *The Four Seasons*. What Vivaldi meant by this was that each of the four concertos, in turn, represents the feelings, sounds, and sights of one of the four seasons of the year, beginning with spring. To avoid ambiguity regarding what sensations and events the music depicts at any given moment, Vivaldi first composed a poem (an "illustrative sonnet," as he called it) about each season. Then he placed each line of the poem at the point in the music where that particular event or feeling was to be expressed, even specifying at one point that the violins were to sound "like barking dogs." In so doing, Vivaldi showed that not only voices but also instruments could create a mood and sway the emotions. Vivaldi also fashioned a landmark in what is called instrumental program music (for more on program music, see Chapter 18)—music that plays out a story or a series of events or moods.

You have no doubt heard the jaunty opening of the "Spring" Concerto. This ritornello consists of two parts (see Listening Guide). Each part is immediately repeated at a softer dynamic level, an example of terraced dynamics. Between appearances of the ritornello, Vivaldi inserts program music depicting spring: Solo violins chirp on high, undulating strings suggest a babbling brook, and string tremolos ominously portend a gathering storm. Although Vivaldi wrote the full text of the program into the musical score, so onomatopoeic (self-expressive) is the music that the attentive listener won't need it.

Finally, Vivaldi's "Spring" Concerto is marked by a stylistic trait that often projects prominently in his music: melodic sequence. A **melodic sequence** is the repetition of a musical motive at successively higher or lower degrees of the scale. Example 7.2 shows a sequence from the middle of the first movement of this work. In this sequence, the motive is played three times, with each repetition a step lower than the last.

EXAMPLE 7.2 Melodic sequence

LISTENING GUIDE

Antonio Vivaldi, Violin Concerto in E major (the "Spring," early 1700s)   Download 24 (3:43)

First movement, *Allegro* (fast)

Meter: Duple

Texture: Mainly homophonic

Form: Ritornello

WHAT TO LISTEN FOR: The ritornello played by the tutti, alternating and contrasting with the descriptive music of the soloists

0:00	Ritornello part 1 played by tutti	
0:11	Ritornello part 1 repeated by tutti *pianissimo*	
0:19	Ritornello part 2 played by tutti	
0:27	Ritornello part 2 repeated by tutti *pianissimo*	
0:36	Solo violin (aided by two violins from tutti) chirps on high.	"Spring with all its festiveness has arrived And the birds salute it with happy song"
1:10	Ritornello part 2 played by tutti	
1:18	Tutti softly plays running sixteenth notes.	"And the brooks, kissed by the breezes, Meanwhile flow with sweet murmurings"
1:42	Ritornello part 2 played by tutti	
1:50	Tutti plays tremolo, and violins shoot up scale.	"Dark clouds cover the sky Announced by bolts of lightning and thunder"
1:58	Solo violin plays agitated, broken triads while tutti continues with tremolos below.	
2:19	Ritornello part 2 played by tutti	
2:28	Solo violin chirps on high, adding ascending chromatic scale and trill.	"But when all has returned to quiet The birds commence to sing once again their enchanted song"
2:47	Ritornello part 1, slightly varied, played by tutti	
3:00	Solo violin plays rising sixteenth notes.	
3:16	Ritornello part 2 played by tutti	

LISTEN TO ... this selection streaming online.

WATCH ... an Active Listening Guide of this selection online.

DO ... Listening Exercise 7.2, Vivaldi, "Spring" Concerto, online.

Although melodic sequence can be found in music from almost all periods, it is especially prevalent in the late Baroque. It helps propel the music forward and creates the energy that we associate with Baroque style. However, because hearing the same melodic phrase time and again can become a tedious listening experience, Baroque composers usually follow the "three strikes and you're out" rule: The melodic unit appears, as in Example 7.2, three times, but no more.

Though widely admired as both a performer and a composer in his day, Vivaldi was largely forgotten within a few years of his death, a victim of rapidly changing musical tastes. Not until the revival of Baroque music in the 1950s were his scores resurrected from obscure libraries and dusty archives. Now Vivaldi's music is loved for its freshness and vigor, its exuberance and daring. A search of YouTube turns up more than 445,000 hits for "Vivaldi The Four Seasons," and iTunes lists more than 300 different recordings of it. So often is the "Spring" Concerto played that it has passed from the realm of art music into that of "classical pop"—a staple at Starbucks.

KEY WORDS

idiomatic writing (99)	concerto (104)	concertino (104)	ritornello form (105)
French overture (101)	solo concerto (104)	tutti (104)	melodic sequence (106)
terraced dynamics (104)	concerto grosso (104)		

 Join us on Facebook at Listening to Music with Craig Wright

PRACTICE ... your understanding of this chapter's concepts by comparing Checklists of Musical Style for all historic eras and working once more with the chapter's Active Listening Guides online.

DO ... online multiple-choice and critical thinking quizzes that your instructor may assign for a grade.

CHECKLIST OF MUSICAL STYLE *Early and Middle Baroque: 1600–1710*

REPRESENTATIVE COMPOSERS

Monteverdi	Purcell	Pachelbel	Corelli
Mouret	Vivaldi		

PRINCIPAL GENRES

opera	chamber cantata	concerto grosso	dance suite
overture	sonata	solo concerto	

Melody	Less stepwise movement, larger leaps, wider range, and more chromaticism reflect influence of virtuosic solo singing; melodic patterns idiomatic to particular musical instruments emerge
Harmony	Stable, diatonic chords played by *basso continuo* support melody; standard chord progressions begin to emerge at end of the seventeenth century; modes are gradually limited to just two: major and minor
Rhythm	Relaxed, flexible rhythms of the Renaissance gradually replaced by repetitive rhythmic patterns and a strongly articulated beat
Color	Musical timbre becomes enormously varied as traditional instruments are perfected (e.g., harpsichord, violin, and oboe) and new combinations of voices and instruments are explored; string-dominated orchestra begins to take shape; sudden shifts in dynamics (terraced dynamics) reflect dramatic quality of Baroque music
Texture	Chordal, homophonic texture predominates; top and bottom lines are strongest as *basso continuo* creates powerful bass to support melody above
Form	Arias and instrumental works often make use of *basso ostinato* procedure; ritornello form emerges in the concerto; binary form regulates most movements of the sonata and dance suite

The Late Baroque:
BACH

START... experiencing this chapter's topics with an online video activity.

LEARNING OBJECTIVES

After studying the material in this chapter, you should be able to:

1 Outline the structure of the fugue, based on an examination of Johann Sebastian Bach's Fugue in G minor.

2 Trace the development of Bach's Brandenburg Concertos and the role that he played in their first performance.

3 Describe the inner workings of a church cantata, based on a study of Bach's *Wachet auf, ruft uns die Stimme.*

4 Account for Bach's musical activities at the end of his life and the fate of his music immediately after his death.

Understanding what is "high" or "late" art involves a consideration of beginnings and ends. When rap music began in the 1970s, it was the product of a handful of innovators in New York who produced sounds that few understood. Today, the airwaves are full of rappers, and people around the world have a general understanding of how rap should sound. Rap is no longer revolutionary; it is commonplace. Thus, we might say that we are in the "high" or "late" phase of "the rap music period." So, too, with Baroque music: From the ideas of a few innovators in Italy in the early 1600s there gradually spread a common understanding of what a new art music should be. As public acceptance grew, so, too, did the number of composers working in that style. But a common understanding did not mean common abilities. During the late Baroque (roughly 1710–1750), two composers were better than all others—namely, Johann Sebastian Bach and George Frideric Handel.

The early Baroque period had witnessed the creation of several new musical genres, such as opera and concerto. The late Baroque, by contrast, is a period, not of musical innovation, but of consolidation and refinement. Neither Bach nor Handel invented any new genres, forms, or styles; instead, they gave greater weight, length, and polish to those established by their musical predecessors, such as Monteverdi and Vivaldi. Bach and Handel approached the craft of composition with unbounded self-confidence. Their music has a sense of rightness, solidity, and maturity about it. Each time we choose to listen to one of their compositions, we offer further witness to their success in bringing 100 years of musical innovation to a glorious culmination.

Attending the high-water mark of late Baroque music (around 1725) came a flood of new counterpoint. Composers reintroduced polyphony to add richness to musical texture; specifically, they sought to "bulk up" the middle range of what had been previously a top-bottom (soprano-bass) dominated sound (see Chapter 6). The gradual reintegration of counterpoint into the fabric of Baroque music reaches its apex in the rigorously contrapuntal music of Johann Sebastian Bach.

READ... the complete chapter text in a rich, interactive online platform.

Johann Sebastian Bach (1685–1750)

For a period of more than 200 years, roughly 1600 to 1800, nearly 100 musicians with the name Bach worked in central Germany—the longest of all musical dynasties. In fact, the name Bach (German for "brook") was nearly a brand name, like our Kleenex or "to Google." "A Bach" meant "a musician." J. S. Bach (Figure 8.1) was simply the most talented and industrious member of the clan. Although arguably the greatest composer who ever lived, Bach was largely self-taught. To learn his craft, he studied, copied, and arranged the compositions of Vivaldi, Pachelbel, and even long-dead Palestrina. He also learned to play the organ, in part by emulating others, once traveling on foot 400 miles round trip to hear a great performer. Soon Bach became the most renowned organ virtuoso in Germany, and his improvisations on that instrument became legendary.

Of all instruments, the organ is the most suitable for playing polyphonic counterpoint. Most organs have at least two separate keyboards for the hands and an additional one for the feet (see Figures 8.2 and 3.8). Thus, the instrument has the capacity to play several lines simultaneously. More important, each of these keyboards can be set to engage a different group (rank) of pipes, and each of these has

FIGURE 8.1
The only authentic portrait of Johann Sebastian Bach, painted by Elias Gottlob Haussmann in 1746. Bach holds in his hand a six-voice canon, or round, which he created to symbolize his skill as a musical craftsman.

its own color, making it easier for the listener to follow the individual lines of a polyphonic piece. For these reasons, the organ is the instrument par excellence for playing fugues.

Fugue

A **fugue** is a musical form that originated in the Baroque era, and in it polyphonic texture reigns supreme. The word *fugue* itself comes from the Latin *fuga*, meaning "flight." Within a fugue, one voice alone presents a theme—here called the **subject**—and then "flies away," as another voice enters with the same subject. Usually a fugue will have from three to five "voices." These may be actual human voices (soprano, alto, tenor, and bass of a choir), or they may simply be lines played by a group of instruments, or even by a solo instrument like the piano, guitar, or organ, which has the capacity to play several "voices" simultaneously. As the voices enter, they do not imitate or pursue each other exactly—this would produce a canon or a round such as "Row, Row, Row Your Boat." Rather, each voice follows the leader only briefly, presenting the subject, and then goes more or less its own way with free counterpoint. The opening section of a fugue, during which each voice presents the subject successively, is called the **exposition**. A typical exposition of a fugue is suggested at the beginning of Figure 8.3.

Once all voices of the fugue have entered with the subject, there follows a section of free counterpoint called the **episode**. In an episode, the subject is not heard in its entirety—only brief allusions to it. And whereas the subject is firmly *in* a key, an episode modulates from one key to another. To sum up: A fugue begins with an exposition, follows with an episode, and then continues by alternating subject statements, in one voice or another, with modulating episodes, right to the very end. Fortunately, fugues are easier to hear than to describe.

Organ Fugue in G minor (c. 1710)

Bach's favorite instrument was the organ, and in his day he was known more as an organ virtuoso than as a composer—his fame as a composer came, ironically, years after his death. Indeed, Bach composed his G minor organ fugue (see Listening Guide), one

FIGURE 8.2
The organ presently in the choir loft at Bach's St. Thomas Church in Leipzig, Germany. It was from this loft that Bach played and conducted.

WATCH... two examples of modern fugues based on Lady Gaga's "Bad Romance," online.

FIGURE 8.3
An example of a typical formal plan of a fugue

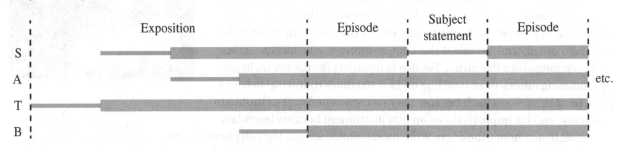

of the nearly 100 that he wrote for that instrument, while working as a court organist for the Duke of Weimar. This fugue has four voices—we'll call them soprano, alto, tenor, and bass—and it begins with a statement of the subject in the soprano (Example 8.1).

LISTEN TO...

Example 8.1 online.

EXAMPLE 8.1 Statement of fugue subject

As fugue subjects go, this is rather a long one, but it is typical of the way Baroque composers liked to "spin out" their melodies. Indeed, melody in late Baroque music is governed by the principle of progressive expansion; an initial idea is set forth and then continually spun out over an ever-lengthening line. Here, the melody sounds very solid in tonality because the subject clearly emphasizes the pitches of the tonic triad in G minor (G, B♭, D), which sound not only in the first measure but also on the strong beats of the following measures. Notice, also, how the subject conveys a sense of gathering momentum, like a train pulling out of the station. It starts moderately with quarter notes and then seems to gain speed as eighth notes and finally sixteenth notes are introduced. This feeling of acceleration is typical of fugue subjects and Baroque rhythmic development generally: Once a rhythmic pattern takes hold, it chugs along energetically, continually driving the music forward.

Our soprano has led the way, setting forth the subject. Now the alto, tenor, and bass take their turn. In a fugue, the voices need not appear in any particular order; here, Bach simply decided to have them enter in succession from top to bottom. Once all voices are in, the exposition is over, and the alternation of episodes and subject statements begins (Figure 8.4). Thereafter, tracking aurally what follows is like playing the musical equivalent of the game, "Where's Waldo?" Is the subject in? Can you hear it? If so, where is it? In which voice is it sounding?

Finally, fugues often make use of a device particularly well suited to the organ—the pedal point. A **pedal point** is a pitch, usually in the bass, that is sustained (or repeated) while harmonies change around it. Such a sustaining tone in the bass derives its name, of course, from the fact that on the organ the note is sounded by a foot holding down a key on the pedal keyboard. In his G minor fugue, Bach prominently inserts a pedal point toward the middle of the piece. Online Listening Exercise 8.1 asks you to identify where this occurs—where a bass note holds for a very long time.

FIGURE 8.4

Fugue (1925) by Josef Albers. Albers's design suggests the "constructivist" or "Lego-like" quality of the fugue, one full of reciprocal relationships and interchangeable parts. The black-and-white units seem to allude to subject and episode, respectively. Notice that if you turn the image upside down, the impact it has on you really doesn't change—as a visual image, it still makes sense.

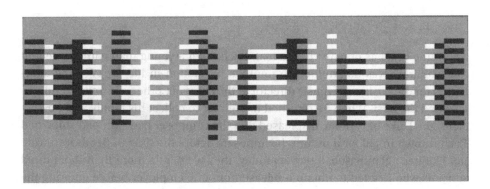

LISTENING GUIDE

Johann Sebastian Bach, Organ Fugue in G minor (c. 1710)   Download 25 (4:08)

Texture: Polyphonic

Form: Fugue

WHAT TO LISTEN FOR: After all voices appear in the exposition with the subject, a succession of episodes and further statements of the subject follows. Can you identify which is which?

Exposition

0:00	Subject alone stated in soprano voice
0:18	Subject in alto; active countersubject in soprano
0:41	Subject in tenor; countersubject above it
0:58	Subject in bass; countersubject in tenor

Alternations of Episodes and Subject Statements

1:15	End of opening exposition and beginning of episode
1:25	Subject begins in tenor, continues in soprano; additional counterpoint in other voices
1:43	Episode
1:52	Subject in alto; countersubject in tenor
2:08	Episode
2:20	Subject in bass; countersubject and long trill above
2:36	Longer episode
2:54	Subject in soprano; countersubject and additional counterpoint below; thick density
3:10	Extended episode
3:40	Subject in bass; countersubject in soprano; additional counterpoint adds thickness.
3:54	Ritard to strong cadence in G major

LISTEN TO ... this selection streaming online.

WATCH ... an Active Listening Guide of this selection online.

WATCH ... a special animation of this selection online.

DO ... Listening Exercise 8.1, Bach, Organ Fugue in G minor, online.

Bach's Orchestral Music

After nine years as organist in Weimar, Bach, then a young man with a wife and four children, was determined to improve his station in life. In 1717, he auditioned for the position of music director at the court of Cöthen, Germany, and was awarded the post. When he returned to Weimar to collect his family and possessions, the Duke of Weimar, displeased that the composer had "jumped ship," had Bach thrown in jail for a month. (Composers before the time of Beethoven were not like free agent baseball players today; they were little more than indentured servants who needed to obtain a release from one employer before entering the service of another.) When freed from jail, Bach fled to Cöthen, where he remained for six years (1717–1723).

At Cöthen, Bach turned his attention from organ music for the church to instrumental music for the court. It was here that he wrote the bulk of his orchestral scores, including more than a dozen solo concertos. The Prince of Cöthen had assembled, with Bach's help, something of an "all-star" orchestra, drawing many top players from the larger city of Berlin. He also ordered a large two-keyboard harpsichord from Berlin and sent Bach to fetch it. About this time, Bach began his *Well-Tempered Clavier* (see end of this chapter) for keyboard, and during these years, he completed six concertos of the concerto grosso type. This set has come to be called the Brandenburg Concertos.

The Brandenburg Concertos (1715–1721)

In 1721, still in Cöthen, Bach began to look for yet another job in the politically more important city of Berlin—specifically, at the court of Margrave Christian Ludwig of Brandenburg. To impress the margrave, Bach gathered together a half dozen of his best concertos and sent them to his prospective employer. Although no job offer was forthcoming, Bach's autograph manuscript survives (Figure 8.5), and in it are six superb examples of the concerto grosso.

The concerto grosso, as we have seen (Chapter 7, "Vivaldi and the Baroque Concerto"), is a three-movement work involving a musical give-and-take between a full orchestra (tutti) and a much smaller group of soloists (concertino). Each of the six Brandenburg Concertos calls for a different group of soloists in the concertino. Together, these concertos constitute an anthology of nearly all instrumental combinations known to the Baroque era.

In Brandenburg Concerto No. 5, the razzle-dazzle projects from a concertino of solo violin, flute, and, most important, harpsichord. Notice here also that Bach's ritornello (see Listening Guide) possesses many characteristics of late Baroque melody: It is idiomatic to the violin (having many repeated notes that the violin can easily play); it is lengthy and somewhat asymmetrical (expanding out over many measures); and it possesses a driving rhythm that propels the music forward.

Although the sound of violins initially dominates the ritornello in this opening movement, the solo harpsichord gradually steals the show. In fact, this work

FIGURE 8.5
The autograph manuscript of the opening of Bach's Brandenburg Concerto No. 5

Johann Sebastian Bach, Brandenburg Concerto No. 5 in D major (c. 1720)   Download 26 (9:34)

First movement

Genre: Concerto grosso

Texture: Polyphonic

Form: Ritornello

WHAT TO LISTEN FOR: The interplay between the tutti and the concertino, as well as the high level of skill required of the performers at every moment. Bach suffered neither fools nor weak players gladly.

0:00	Tutti plays complete ritornello.
0:20	Concertino (violin, Baroque [wooden] flute, and harpsichord) enters.
0:45	Tutti plays ritornello part **A**.
0:50	Concertino varies ritornello part **B**.
1:10	Tutti plays ritornello part **B**.
1:37	Tutti plays ritornello part **B** in minor mode.
1:43	Concertino plays motives derived from ritornello, especially part **B**.
2:24	Tutti plays ritornello part **B**.
2:30	Concertino plays motives derived from ritornello part **B**.
3:20	Cello of tutti joins concertino; plays arpeggios in descending melodic sequence.
3:51	Double bass of tutti repeats single bass pitch (pedal point).
4:09	Tutti plays ritornello part **A**.
4:33	Concertino repeats much of music heard toward beginning (0:20).
4:58	Tutti plays ritornello parts **A** and **B**; sounds very solid.
5:08	Concertino plays motives derived from ritornello part **B**.
5:38	Tutti plays ritornello part **B**.
5:43	Harpsichord plays scales that race up and down keyboard.
6:22	Cadenza: long, brilliant passage for solo harpsichord
8:45	Left hand (bass) of harpsichord repeats one pitch (pedal point).
9:10	Tutti plays complete ritornello.

LISTEN TO ... this selection streaming online.

WATCH ... an Active Listening Guide of this selection online.

DO ... Listening Exercise 8.2, Bach, Brandenburg Concerto No. 5, I, online.

FIGURE 8.6
The Hall of Mirrors at the court of Cöthen, Germany, in which most of Bach's orchestral music was performed while he resided in that town. The bust on the pedestal at the right is of Bach.

might fairly be called the first concerto for keyboard. In earlier concertos, the harpsichord had appeared only as part of the *basso continuo*, not as a solo instrument. But here, toward the end of the movement, all the other instruments fall silent, leaving the harpsichord to sound alone in a lengthy section that is full of brilliant scales and arpeggios. Such a showy passage for soloist alone toward the end of a movement in a concerto is called a **cadenza**. One can easily imagine the great virtuoso Bach performing Brandenburg Concerto No. 5 in the Hall of Mirrors at Cöthen (Figure 8.6), the principal concert hall of the court. There, seated at the large harpsichord he had brought from Berlin, Bach riffed away in this nearly three-minute cadenza, while patron, audience, and fellow performers alike listened in stunned silence to his bravura playing.

Finally, note the length of this movement: more than nine minutes! Typical of Bach's grand musical vision, his movement is three times longer than the usual concerto movement by Vivaldi.

The Church Cantata

In 1723, Bach moved to the central German city of Leipzig, whose population then was about 30,000, to assume the coveted position of cantor of St. Thomas church and choir school (Figure 8.7). Here he stayed until he died at age sixty-five in 1750. Although his new post was prestigious, it was also demanding. As an employee of the town council of Leipzig, the composer was charged with superintending the music of the four principal churches of that city. He also played organ for all funerals, composed any music needed for ceremonies at the University of Leipzig, and sometimes taught Latin grammar to the boys at the choir school of St. Thomas. But by far the most difficult part of his job was composing new music for the church

FIGURE 8.7
Leipzig, St. Thomas Church (center) and choir school (left) from an engraving of 1723, the year in which Bach moved to the city. Bach's large family occupied 900 square feet of the second floor of the choir school. If you look carefully, you can see the choir of the school marching from the schoolhouse and about to turn left to enter the church.

WHAT DID MRS. BACH DO?

Actually, there were two Mrs. Bachs. The first, Maria Barbara, died suddenly in 1720, leaving the composer with four young children (three others had died in infancy). The second, Anna Magdalena, he married in 1722, and she would bear him thirteen more children. Anna Magdalena Bach was a professional singer, earning about as much as her new husband at the court of Cöthen. When the family moved to Leipzig and St. Thomas Church, however, Anna Magdalena curtailed her professional activities. Women did not perform publicly in the Lutheran church at this time; the difficult soprano lines in Bach's religious works were sung by choirboys. Consequently, Anna Magdalena put her musical skills to work as manager of what might be called "Bach Inc."

For almost every Sunday, J. S. Bach was required to produce a cantata, about twenty-five to thirty minutes of new music, week after week, year after year. Writing the music was only part of the high-pressure task. Rehearsals had to be set and music learned by the next Sunday. But composing and rehearsing paled in comparison to the amount of time needed to copy all the parts— these were the days before photocopy machines and software programs were used to notate music. Each of the approximately twelve independent lines of the full score had to be copied, entirely by hand, for each new cantata, along with sufficient copies (parts) for all the singers and players. For this, Bach turned to the members of his household—namely, his wife and children (both sons and daughters), his nephews, and other fee-paying private students who resided in the cantor's quarters at the St. Thomas school (see Figure 8.7). In 1731, the year he composed the cantata *Wachet auf, ruft uns die Stimme*, the roof was taken off the building and two more stories added to accommodate the Bach family and its "music industry."

When Bach died in 1750, some of his most valuable assets (the scores of his cantatas) fell to his wife, with the expectation that she would rent or sell them in the course of time, providing her with an old-age pension. In the end, however, no one wanted these scores! Bach's music was thought to be old-fashioned. Anna Magdalena Bach finished her days in 1760 in poverty, a ward of the city of Leipzig, leaving the cantatas to St. Thomas Church. Not until the mid-nineteenth century did music lovers come to recognize the extraordinary quality of Bach's music.

each Sunday and every religious holiday. How would you like to be responsible for composing, rehearsing, and performing a half hour of new music every week? But Bach did it, and in so doing, he brought an important genre of music, the church cantata, to the highest point of its development.

Like opera, the **cantata** (Italian for "a sung thing") first appeared in Italy during the seventeenth century in the form we call chamber cantata, a form of chamber music in which a soloist sang about some aspect of love or classical mythology. During the early eighteenth century, however, composers in Germany increasingly came to see the cantata as a useful vehicle for religious music in the church.

Bach and his contemporaries created the **church cantata**, a multimovement sacred work, lasting twenty to thirty minutes, which included recitatives, arias, and choruses, all accompanied by a small orchestra. The church cantata became the musical soul of the Lutheran Church, the Protestant religion that then dominated spiritual life in German-speaking lands. Bach wrote nearly 300 cantatas for the citizens of Leipzig. Surrounded by a dozen singers and a small orchestra, all situated in the choir loft above the west door (see Figure 8.2), Bach conducted his cantatas himself, beating time with a roll of paper.

Wachet auf, ruft uns die Stimme (Awake, a Voice Is Calling, 1731)

Bach was a devoted husband, a loving father to twenty children in all, and a respected burgher of Leipzig. Yet, above all, he was a religious man who composed not only for self-expression but also for his fellow Lutherans and the greater glory of God. Bach composed the cantata *Wachet auf, ruft uns die Stimme (Awake, a Voice Is Calling)* in 1731 for a Sunday immediately before the beginning of Advent (four Sundays before Christmas). The text, drawing upon the Gospel of Matthew (25:1–13), speaks opaquely of a bridegroom (Christ) who is arriving to meet the Daughters of Zion (the Christian community). Indeed, immediately before the cantata, a deacon read from the pulpit (Figure 8.8, lower right) the full text of this gospel:

> Then shall the kingdom of heaven be likened unto ten virgins, which took their lamps, and went forth to meet the bridegroom. And five of them were wise, and five were foolish. They that were foolish took their lamps, but took no oil with them. . . . And at midnight there was a cry made, Behold, the bridegroom cometh; go ye out to meet him. Then all those virgins arose, and trimmed their lamps. And the foolish said unto the wise, Give us of your oil; for our lamps are gone out. But the wise answered, saying, Not so; lest there be not enough for us and you: but go ye rather to them that sell, and buy for yourselves. And while they went to buy, the bridegroom came; and they that were ready went in with him to the marriage: and the door was shut. . . . Watch therefore, for ye know neither the day nor the hour wherein the Son of man cometh.

The message to every good Lutheran of Leipzig was clear: Get your spiritual house in order to receive the coming Christ. Thus, Bach's cantatas were intended not as concert entertainment but, rather, as religious instruction for his community—sermons in music.

Like most of Bach's cantatas, *Wachet auf* makes use of a **chorale**, a spiritual melody or religious folksong, of the Lutheran church. (In other denominations, such a melody is called simply a hymn.) Just as many people today know hymn tunes well, so most Lutherans of Bach's day knew their chorales by heart. Chorales,

FIGURE 8.8
Looking across the parishioners' pews and toward the high altar at St. Thomas Church, Leipzig, as it was in the mid-nineteenth century. The pulpit for the sermon is at the right. In Bach's day, nearly 2,500 people would crowd into the church.

like hymns, were meant to be easy to remember; indeed, many of the melodies had begun life as folksongs and popular tunes. And, in keeping with their common origins, the musical forms of these chorales were generally straightforward. *Wachet auf* has **AAB** form (Example 8.2), and the seven musical phrases unfold in the following way: **A** (1, 2, 3) **A** (1, 2, 3) **B** (4–7, 3). To round out the melody, the last phrase of section **A** returns at the very end.

EXAMPLE 8.2 Chorale tune

Bach uses the chorale, *Wachet auf,* to create a clear, large-scale structure, which is typical in his cantatas. Notice the formal symmetry across all seven movements of the work (Table 8.1). The chorale is sung three times to three different stanzas of text, and these presentations appear at the beginning, middle, and end of the work. Between statements of the chorale tune come pairs of recitative and aria, each joyfully announcing the divine love that Christ would bring to the Christian community.

Movement 1

The opening movement of cantata *Wachet auf* is a gigantic choral soundscape that displays a polyphonic mastery that is exceptional even for Bach. Beneath a welter of intricate counterpoint, Bach slowly sounds the chorale melody on high in the sopranos, the voice of tradition, perhaps the voice of God.

Movement 2

The chorale tune is absent for this and all recitatives in church cantatas—recitatives merely set the scene for more musically important movements. In this "scene setter" (see Listening Guide), the Evangelist (the narrator) enjoins the daughters of Zion to

TABLE 8.1 Movements in cantata *Wachet auf*

			Movement			
1	**2**	**3**	**4**	**5**	**6**	**7**
Chorus chorale 1st stanza	Recitative	Aria (duet)	Chorus chorale 2nd stanza	Recitative	Aria (duet)	Chorus chorale 3rd stanza

LISTENING GUIDE

Johann Sebastian Bach, *Wachet auf, ruft uns die Stimme* (1731)

Download 27 (0:51)

Second movement

Genre: Recitative of a cantata

Texture: Homophonic

Form: Through composed (no repetition)

WHAT TO LISTEN FOR: The excited recitation of the Evangelist, supported by a *basso continuo* of low strings and a small organ (which often replaces the harpsichord in the continuo of Baroque religious music)

0:00	Er kommt, er kommt,	He is coming, he is coming,
	der Bräut'gam kommt,	the Bridegroom (Christ) is coming,
	ihr Töchter Zions, kommt heraus.	you daughters of Zion, come forth.
	Sein Ausgang eilet aus der Höhe	His route runs down from the heights
	in euer Mutter Haus.	into your mother's house.
0:20	Der Bräut'gam kommt, der einen Rehe	The Bridegroom comes, who like a roe
	und jungen Hirschen gleich,	and a young stag,
	auf denen Hügeln springt	leaps upon the hills
	und euch das Mahl der Hochzeit bringt.	and invites you to the wedding feast.
	Wacht auf, ermuntert euch,	Arise, be courageous,
	den Bräut'gam zu empfangen;	and receive the Bridegroom;
	dort, sehet, kommt er hergegangen.	look there, He comes this way.

LISTEN TO ... this selection streaming online.

WATCH ... an Active Listening Guide of this selection online.

bond with Christ at the wedding feast, a metaphor for a communal union of spiritual souls. In Bach's religious vocal music, the Evangelist is invariably sung by a tenor.

Movement 3

In this aria (duet) between the Soul (soprano) and Jesus (bass), once again the chorale tune is not used. Rather, the two engage in something akin to a vocal dialogue between master and pupil. It is traditional in German sacred music of the Baroque era to assign the role of Christ—the voice of wisdom and authority—to a solid bass.

Movement 4

For this meeting of Christ and the daughters of Zion (true believers), Bach fashioned one of his loveliest creations. The chorale tune serves as a unifying force, now carrying the second stanza of the chorale text. Once more Bach constructs a musical tapestry for chorus and orchestra, though a less complex one than the first movement. Here, we hear only two central motives. One is the chorale melody sung by the tenors, who represent the watchmen calling on Jerusalem (Leipzig) to awake. The other is the exquisite melody played by all the violins and violas in unison—their togetherness symbolizing the unifying love of Christ for his people. This unison line is a perfect example of a lengthy, ever-expanding Baroque melody and one of the most memorable of the entire era (see Listening Guide). Beneath it we hear the measured tread of the ever-present *basso continuo*, a musical symbol of the inexorable steps of Christ.

A regularly progressing bass such as this goes by a special name: walking bass. A **walking bass** moves at a moderate, steady pace, mostly in equal note values and often stepwise up or down the scale. Falling consistently on the beat, the walking bass provides a solid musical foundation and can, as in Example 8.3, suggest steadily approaching footsteps.

EXAMPLE 8.3 Walking bass

Movement 4 was one of Bach's own favorites and the only cantata movement that he published—all the rest of his Leipzig cantata music was left in handwritten scores at the time of his death.

LISTENING GUIDE

Johann Sebastian Bach, *Wachet auf, ruft uns die Stimme* (1731)   Download 28 (4:16)

Fourth movement

Genre: Cantata movement

Form: **AAB**

WHAT TO LISTEN FOR: Three-part polyphonic texture: melody in violins and violas, chorale tune in tenor voices, and walking bass. Note that the text beginning "Wachet auf" is the *first* strophe of the chorale (like the first stanza of a hymn); here, movement 4 contains the *second* strophe, beginning "Zion hört die Wächter singen" ("Zion hears the watchmen singing").

0:00	Violins and violas play flowing melody above walking bass.		
	Chorale phrases sung by the tenors		
0:43	Chorale phrases 1, 2, and 3	Zion hört die Wächter singen,	Zion hears the watchmen singing,
		Das Herz tut ihr vor Freuden springen.	The heart makes her spring up with joy.
		Sie wachet und steht eilend auf.	She awakes and quickly rises.

1:12	Flowing string melody repeated		
1:53	Chorale phrases 1, 2, and 3 repeated	Ihr Freund kommt vom Himmel prächtig,	Her splendid friend arrives from Heaven,
		Von Gnaden stark, von Wahrheit, mächtig,	Mighty in grace, strong in truth,
2:22	Flowing string melody repeated	Ihr Licht wird hell, ihr Stern geht auf.	Her light grows bright, her star arises.
2:47	Chorale phrases 4, 5, and 6	Nun komm, du werte Kron, Herr Jesu, Gottes Sohn! Hosanna!	Now come, you worthy crown, Lord Jesus, Son of God! Hosanna!
3:09	String melody continues in minor.		
3:28	Chorale phrases 7 and 3	Wir folgen all zum Freudensaal	We will follow all to the banquet hall
		Und halten mit das Abendmahl.	And share in the Lord's supper.
3:56	String melody concludes movement.		

LISTEN TO … this selection streaming online.

WATCH … an Active Listening Guide of this selection online.

DO … Listening Exercise 8.3, Bach, *Wachet auf, ruft uns die Stimme*, online.

Movement 5

In this recitative for Christ (bass), Bach invites the anguished Soul to find comfort in Him.

Movement 6

For this aria for bass and soprano, Bach chose ternary form (**ABA**). An aria in ternary form is often referred to as being in **da capo** form because the performers, when reaching the end of **B**, "take it from the head" and repeat **A**. Here, Christ and the Soul sing a passionate love duet. A religious man who did not compose operas, Bach nonetheless had heard many. In this *da capo* aria, Bach closely approximates the flamboyant vocal style that then ruled the opera house.

Movement 7

Bach's cantatas usually end with a simple, four-voice homophonic setting of the last stanza of the chorale (see Listening Guide). In his closing movements, the composer always places the chorale melody in the soprano part, harmonizing and supporting it with the other three voices below. The instruments of the orchestra have no line of their own and merely double the four vocal parts. But, more important,

Johann Sebastian Bach, *Wachet auf, ruft uns die Stimme*   Download 29 (1:23)

Seventh and last movement

Texture: Homophonic

Form: **AAB**

WHAT TO LISTEN FOR: To truly experience this music as Bach would have, think of musical song as a medium that can unite a community and reinforce a set of common values, be it in a house of worship or in an arena at a rock concert.

0:00	Phrase 1	Gloria sei dir gesungen	May Glory be sung to you
	Phrase 2	Mit Menschen und englischen Zungen	With the tongues of man and angels
	Phrase 3	Mit Harfen und mit Zimbeln schon.	And harps and cymbals too.
0:24	Phrase 1	Von zwölf Perlen sind die Pforten,	The gates are of twelve pearls,
	Phrase 2	An deiner Stadt, wir sind Konsorten	In your city, we are consorts
	Phrase 3	Der Engel hoch um deiner Thron.	Of the angels high above your throne.
0:48	Phrase 4	Kein Aug hat je gespürt,	No eye has ever seen,
	Phrase 5	Kein Ohr hat je gehört	No ear has ever heard
	Phrase 6	Solche Freude.	Such joy.
	Phrase 7	Des sind wir froh,	Let us therefore rejoice,
		Io, io!	Io, io!
	Phrase 3	Ewig in dulci jubilo.	Eternally in sweet jubilation.

LISTEN TO ... this selection streaming online.

WATCH ... an Active Listening Guide of this selection online.

the members of the congregation join in the singing of the chorale melody. Martin Luther had ordained that the community should not merely witness but also participate in the act of worship. At this moment, all congregants bond together to reaffirm through song a simple but basic article of their Christian faith: The coming Christ will reveal to all true believers a vision of better life in the kingdom beyond.

In his last decades, Bach withdrew from the weekly grind of producing a new cantata for every Sunday and retreated into a realm of large-scale contrapuntal projects, including *The Well-Tempered Clavier* and **The Art of Fugue** (1742–1750), an encyclopedic treatment of all known contrapuntal procedures. Bach left the latter work incomplete at the time of his death (Figure 8.9) in 1750—the result of a stroke following a botched surgical operation to remove a cataract. Ironically, the same eye surgeon who operated on Bach also operated on Handel at the end of that composer's life—with the same unsuccessful result.

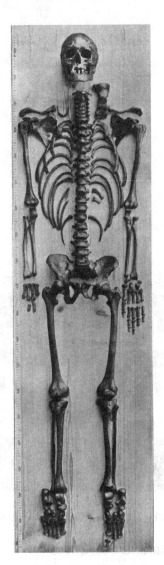

FIGURE 8.9
When Bach died in 1750, he was buried in an outlying parish church, and he and his music were soon forgotten. But, during the nineteenth century, the world came to realize that the citizens of Leipzig had had in their midst a musical genius. By then a theory had developed to the effect that the genius had a misshapen head. So, in 1895, they dug up Bach's grave to measure his skull to see if it was abnormally large or small (it was not), photographed his remains, and repositioned them in a place of honor before the high altar of St. Thomas Church. Bach had gone from forgotten to saint!

KEY WORDS

fugue (112)	episode (112)	cantata (118)	walking bass (122)
subject (112)	pedal point (113)	church cantata (119)	*da capo* form (123)
exposition (112)	cadenza (117)	chorale (119)	*The Art of Fugue* (125)

 Join us on Facebook at Listening to Music with Craig Wright

PRACTICE ... your understanding of this chapter's concepts by comparing Checklists of Musical Style for all historic eras and working once more with the chapter's Active Listening Guides online.

DO ... online multiple-choice and critical thinking quizzes that your instructor may assign for a grade.

The Late Baroque:
HANDEL

START... experiencing this chapter's topics with an online video activity.

LEARNING OBJECTIVES

After studying the material in this chapter, you should be able to:

1   Outline Handel's biography and explain how a very German musician came to be working at the court of an English king.
2   Describe what a dance suite is and how Handel's *Water Music* exemplifies one.
3   Differentiate an opera from an oratorio by George Frideric Handel.
4   Analyze a typical oratorio, as exemplified by Handel's *Messiah*, as well as its "Hallelujah" chorus.

Bach and Handel were born in the same year, 1685, in small towns in central Germany. Other than that commonality and the fact that they shared the same incompetent eye doctor, their careers could not have been more different. While Bach spent his life confined to towns in the region of his birth, the cosmopolitan Handel traveled the world—from Rome, to Venice, to Hamburg, to Amsterdam, to London, to Dublin. Though Bach was most at home playing organ fugues and conducting church cantatas from the choir loft, Handel was a musical entrepreneur working in the theater, by training and temperament a composer of opera. Bach was a musical idealist, writing for God; Handel was a realist, communicating with the people. And, though Bach retreated into a world of esoteric counterpoint and fell into obscurity at the end of his life, Handel's stature only grew larger on the international stage. During his lifetime he became the most famous composer in Europe and a treasured national institution in England.

George Frideric Handel (1685–1759)

George Frideric Handel (Figure 9.1) was born in the town of Halle, Germany, in 1685, and died in London in 1759. Although his father demanded that he become a lawyer, young Handel managed to cultivate his interest in music, sometimes secretly in the attic. At the age of eighteen, he left for the city of Hamburg, where he took a job as second violinist in the orchestra of the city opera. But, because the musical world around 1700 was dominated by things Italian, he soon set off for Italy to learn his trade and broaden his horizons. After living a decade in Italy, Handel returned to North Germany to accept the post of court music director for the Elector of Hanover, but on the condition that he be given an immediate leave of absence to visit London. Arriving in London in 1710, Handel conveniently "forgot" about his obligation to the Hanoverian court. London became the site of his musical activity and the place where he won fame and fortune.

London in the early eighteenth century was the largest and richest city in Europe, boasting a population of 500,000. It was the capital city not only of a country but also of a burgeoning empire of international commerce and trade. London may not have possessed the rich cultural patrimony of Paris or Rome, but it offered opportunity for financial gain, in art as well as commerce. As a friend of Handel then said, "In France and Italy there is something to learn, but in London there is something to earn."

As fate would have it, Handel's continental employer, the Elector of Hanover, became King George I of England in 1714, when this Hanoverian acceded to the throne on the extinction of the Stuart line. (A direct descendant of those same Hanoverians, Queen Elizabeth II, sits on the throne of England today.) Fortunately for Handel, the new German-speaking king bore his truant musician no grudge and called on Handel frequently to compose festival music to entertain the court or provide a "soundtrack" for its events. For these occasions, Handel produced such works as *Water Music* (1717), *Music for the Royal Fireworks* (1749), and the Coronation Service (1727) for King George II and Queen Caroline, parts of which have been used at the coronation of every English monarch since then.

FIGURE 9.1
Thomas Hudson's portrait (1749) of Handel, with the score of *Messiah* visible in the composer's left hand. Handel had a quick temper, could swear in four languages, and liked to eat.

Handel and the Orchestral Dance Suite

The English public has historically had a love-hate affair with its royal family. To curry favor with their subjects, English monarchs often turned to public concerts. Queen Elizabeth II did so in 2012, inviting Elton John and Paul McCartney to her "Diamond Jubilee" celebration at Buckingham Palace and giving away free tickets. Handel's *Water Music* was created for an earlier bit of royal image burnishing. In 1717, the new King George I was an unpopular monarch. He refused to speak a word of English, preferring his native German. His subjects considered George dimwitted—"an honest blockhead," as one contemporary put it.

To improve the king's standing, his ministers organized an evening of music on the Thames River for the lords of Parliament as well as the lesser people of London (Figure 9.2). Thus, on July 17, 1717, George and his court left London, accompanied by a small armada of boats, and progressed up the Thames to the strains of Handel's orchestral music. An eyewitness describes this nautical parade in detail:

> About eight in the evening the King repaired to his barge, into which were admitted the Duchess of Bolton, Countess Godolphin, Madam de Kilmansech [the king's mistress], Mrs. Were and the Earl of Orkney, the Gentleman of the Bedchamber in Waiting. Next to the King's barge was that of the musicians, about 50 in number, who played on all kinds of instruments, to wit trumpets, horns, hautboys [oboes], bassoons, German flutes, French flutes [recorders], violins and basses; but there were no singers. The music had been composed specially by the famous Handel, a native of Halle [Germany], and His Majesty's principal Court Composer. His Majesty so greatly approved of the music that he caused it to be repeated three times in all, although each performance lasted an hour—namely twice before and once after supper. The evening weather was all that could be desired for the festivity, the number of barges and above all of boats filled with people desirous of hearing the music was beyond counting.

FIGURE 9.2
View of London, St. Paul's Cathedral, and the Thames River by Canaletto (1697–1768). Notice the large barges. Crafts such as these could have easily accommodated the fifty musicians reported to have played behind the king as he moved upstream in 1717, listening to Handel's *Water Music*. On June 3, 2012, Queen Elizabeth II made a similar nautical journey up the Thames as part of her "Diamond Jubilee" celebration.

The score that these fifty boat-bound musicians played for King George and hundreds of music lovers on the Thames River was, of course, Handel's *Water Music. Water Music* belongs to a genre called the **dance suite** (from the French word, *suite*, meaning "a succession of things"—in this case, dances). Usually, a suite had two to seven pieces, all in one key, and all were to be played by a full orchestra, trio, or solo. And usually no one actually danced, especially not in boats. These were stylized, abstract dances intended only for the ear. But the trend was significant—as classical music gradually became art music as we know it, dance music began to morph into listening music.

LISTENING GUIDE

George Frideric Handel, *Water Music* (1717)

Download 30 (2:50)

Minuet and Trio

Genre: Dance from dance suite

Form: Binary (**AB**) within larger ternary (**ABCDAB**)

WHAT TO LISTEN FOR: The cheerful sound of the minuet, presented here by various combinations of instruments, contrasted with the somber tones of the trio, played by strings and continuo alone

MINUET (triple meter, major key)

0:00	**A**	French horns introduce part **A**.
0:12	**B**	Trumpets introduce part **B**.
0:29	**A**	Winds and continuo play **A**.
0:42		Full orchestra repeats **A**.
0:55	**B**	Winds and continuo play **B**.
1:08		Full orchestra repeats **B**.

TRIO (triple meter, minor key)

1:28	**C**	Strings and continuo play part **C**.
1:43	**D**	Strings and continuo play part **D**.

MINUET

2:19	**A**	Full orchestra plays **A**.
2:31	**B**	Full orchestra plays **B**.

LISTEN TO ... this selection streaming online.

WATCH ... an Active Listening Guide of this selection online.

DO ... Listening Exercise 9.1, Handel, *Water Music*, Minuet and Trio, online.

Almost all dances of the Baroque period were composed in just one musical form: binary form (**AB**), the two sections of which could be repeated. Some dance movements were followed by a second, complementary dance, called a **trio** (**CD**) because it was originally played by only three instruments. Take, for example, the **minuet**, a stately dance in triple meter. First comes the minuet, followed by a related trio, and then a repeat of the minuet, thereby creating a large-scale ternary arrangement: **AB|CD|AB**. What make the movements of *Water Music* so enjoyable and easy to follow are their tuneful themes and decisive orchestrations. Notice in the Minuet and Trio (see Listening Guide) how Handel asks the French horns and trumpets first to announce both **A** and **B** sections, and then repeats these with the woodwinds, and then again with the full orchestra. Here, instrumentation works to underscore formal clarity.

Handel and Opera

Handel emigrated from Germany to England, not for the chance to entertain the king and certainly not for the cuisine or the climate. Rather, he went to London to make money producing Italian opera. With the rare exception of a work such as Purcell's *Dido and Aeneas* (see Chapter 6), there was no opera in London at this time. The legacy of Shakespeare in England remained strong, and the occasional sonic interlude was about as much music as English audiences tolerated in their spoken plays. Handel aimed to change this. London audiences, he reasoned, were daily growing wealthier and more cosmopolitan, and would welcome the "high art" of imported Italian opera, the way today's New Yorkers welcome Gucci handbags and Armani shoes. Guaranteeing himself a healthy share of the profits, Handel formed an opera company, the Royal Academy of Music, for which he served as composer, director, and producer. He presented his first opera, *Rinaldo*, in 1711 at the Queen's Theater, the same theater where in 1986 Andrew Lloyd Webber premiered his *Phantom of the Opera*.

The type of Italian opera that Handel produced in London is called **opera seria** (literally, "serious—as opposed to comic—opera"), a style that then dominated the operatic stage throughout continental Europe. In three long acts, *opera seria* chronicled the triumphs and tragedies of kings and queens, or gods and goddesses, thus appealing to society's upper crust, namely the nobility. In Handel's day, the leading male roles in *opera seria* were sung by castrati (castrated males with the vocal range of a female; Figure 9.3). Baroque audiences associated high social standing on stage with a high voice, male or female. From 1711 until 1728, Handel had great artistic and some financial success, producing two dozen examples of Italian *opera seria*. Foremost among these was *Giulio Cesare* (*Julius Caesar*, 1724), a recasting of the story of Caesar's conquest of the army of Egypt and Cleopatra's romantic conquest of Caesar (Figure 9.4). As was typical, the male hero (Julius Caesar) was portrayed by a castrato and sang in a high, "womanly" register.

Opera is a notoriously risky business, and in 1728, Handel's Royal Academy of Music went bankrupt, a victim of the exorbitant fees paid to the star singers and the fickle tastes of English theatergoers. Handel continued to write operas into the early 1740s, but he turned his attention increasingly to a musical genre that was less financially volatile than opera: oratorio.

Handel and Oratorio

An **oratorio** is literally "something sung in an oratory," an oratory being a hall or a chapel used specifically for prayer and sometimes prayer with music. Originating in seventeenth-century Italy, oratorio had something in common with today's gospel music: It was sacred music sung in a special hall or chapel and was intended to inspire the faithful to greater devotion. By the time it reached Handel's hands, however, the oratorio had become close to being an unstaged opera with a religious subject.

Both Baroque oratorio and Baroque opera begin with an overture, are divided into acts, and are composed primarily of recitatives and arias. Both genres are

FIGURE 9.3
In 1730, Handel tried (unsuccessfully) to hire the celebrated castrato Farinelli, whose life was chronicled in a film of the same name. For the film, the now-extinct castrato voice was simulated by synthesizing a female soprano with a male falsetto voice.

WATCH... a Handel aria from the film *Farinelli* online.

FIGURE 9.4
Title page of an early English edition of Handel's opera *Julius Caesar*. The musicians form a *basso continuo*.

also long, usually lasting two to three hours. But there are a few important differences between opera and oratorio, aside from the obvious fact that oratorio treats a spiritual subject. Oratorio, being a quasi-religious genre, is performed in a church, a concert hall, or a theater, but it makes no use of acting, staging, or costumes. Because the subject matter is almost always sacred, there is more of an opportunity for moralizing, a dramatic function best performed by a chorus. Thus, the chorus assumes greater importance in an oratorio. It sometimes serves as a narrator but more often functions, like the chorus in ancient Greek drama, as the voice of the people commenting on the action.

By the 1730s, oratorio appeared to Handel to be an attractive alternative to the increasingly unprofitable opera in London. He could do away with the irascible and expensive castrati and prima donnas. He no longer had to pay for elaborate sets and costumes. He could draw on the long-standing English love of choral music, a tradition that extended well back into the Middle Ages. And he could exploit a new, untapped market—the faithful of the Puritan, Methodist, and growing evangelical sects in England, who had viewed the pleasures of foreign opera with distrust and even contempt. And, in contrast to the Italian opera, the oratorio was sung in English, contributing further to the genre's appeal to the general public.

Messiah (1741)

Beginning in 1732 and continuing over a twenty-year period, Handel wrote a total of nearly twenty oratorios. The most famous of these is his *Messiah*, composed in the astonishingly short period of three and a half weeks during the summer of 1741. It was first performed in Dublin, Ireland, the following April as part of a charity benefit, with Handel conducting. Having heard the dress rehearsal, the local press waxed enthusiastic about the new oratorio, saying that it "far surpasses anything of that Nature, which has been performed in this or any other Kingdom." *Messiah* was a hot ticket—so hot, in fact, that ladies were urged not to wear hoop skirts and gentlemen were admonished to leave their swords at home. In this way, Handel squeezed 700 paying customers into a hall with benches usually seating only 600.

Buoyed by his artistic and financial success in Dublin, Handel took *Messiah* back to London, made minor alterations, and performed it in Covent Garden Theater. In 1750, he offered *Messiah* again, this time in the chapel of the Foundling Hospital (Figure 9.5), an orphanage in London, and again there was much popular acclaim for Handel, as well as profit for charity. Thereafter, and down to the present day, Handel's oratorio *Messiah* is equally at home in church, concert hall, and public theater.

In a general way, *Messiah* tells the story of the life of Christ. It is divided into three parts (instead of three acts): (I) the prophecy of His coming and His Incarnation; (II) His Passion and Resurrection, and the triumph of the Gospel; and (III) reflections on the Christian victory over death. Most of Handel's oratorios recount the heroic deeds of characters from the Old Testament; *Messiah* is exceptional because the story comes from the New Testament. There is neither plot action nor "characters" in the dramatic sense, nor are there costumes or staging. The drama is experienced in the mind of the listener.

Put yourself in Handel's shoes for a moment. A librettist has just handed you a script outlining fifty-three numbers (recitatives, arias, and choruses) for an oratorio you must compose. You've reached number 9, an aria text, and see the first line: "O thou that tellest good tidings to Zion, get thee up into the high mountain"

FIGURE 9.5
The chapel of the Foundling Hospital, London, where *Messiah* was performed annually for the benefit of the orphans. Handel himself designed and paid for the organ, which can be seen on the second story at the back of the hall.

(see Listening Guide). What is this about? Someone must go up to a mountaintop and shout the good news of the coming Christ. You read the next line, "O thou that tellest good tidings to Jerusalem, lift up thy voice with strength, lift it up and be not afraid." So far, the text strongly suggests what kind of music you should write to excite and move your listeners. You choose a major key, suitable for "good tidings"; make the melodic line generally ascend, as to a "high mountain"; employ a rising melodic sequence, as if to "lift up thy voice"; and incorporate a consistently high level of volume "with strength." This much we might all intuit. But then what? Just where our aria might have begun to run out of gas, with too much repetition, Handel had a stroke of genius. He handed off the last line of text to a chorus, and, as the voices enter one by one, fugal style, they reinvigorate the music. A team has taken over to carry the soloist to a dramatic—and surprising—end.

When Handel inserted a chorus at the end of the aria "O thou that tellest good tidings to Zion," he revealed where his heart and his strength lay. Indeed, Handel is arguably the finest composer for chorus who ever lived. As a world traveler with an unequaled ear, he absorbed a variety of musical styles from throughout Europe: In Germany, he acquired knowledge of the choral fugue and the Lutheran chorale; in Italy, he immersed himself in the styles of the oratorio and cantata; and, during his years in England, he became familiar with the idioms of the English church **anthem** (a sacred song for chorus sung in English). Most important, having spent a lifetime in the opera theater, Handel had a flair for the dramatic.

"Hallelujah" Chorus

Nowhere is Handel's mastery of the dramatic chorus more evident than in the justly famous "Hallelujah" chorus. In Part II of *Messiah*, we move from the peaceful adoration of the Lamb of God to a triumphant resurrection, climaxing with

LISTENING GUIDE

George Frideric Handel, *Messiah* (1741)　　　　Download 31 (5:39)

Recitative, "Behold, a Virgin shall conceive," and aria, "O thou that tellest good tidings to Zion"

Genre: Recitative and aria (with chorus!)

Form: Strophic variation

WHAT TO LISTEN FOR: A brief recitative that serves as a curtain-raiser for the aria that follows. In the aria, look for moments of "word painting" and the wholly unexpected entry of the chorus.

RECITATIVE (Isaiah 7:14; Matthew 1:23)

0:00　　Behold, a Virgin shall conceive and bear a Son,
　　　　and shall call his name Emmanuel, God with us.

ARIA FOR ALTO VOICE (Isaiah 40:9; Isaiah 60:1)

0:29　　Instrumental ritornello (refrain)

0:52　　O thou that tellest good tidings to Zion,
　　　　get thee up into the high mountain.

1:40　　Instrumental ritornello

1:50　　O thou that tellest good tidings to Jerusalem,
　　　　lift up thy voice with strength;
　　　　lift it up, be not afraid;
　　　　say unto the cities of Judah: Behold your God!
　　　　Arise, shine, for thy light is come,
　　　　and the glory of the Lord is risen upon thee.

2:46　　Instrumental ritornello

2:54　　O thou that tellest good tidings to Zion,
　　　　arise, shine, for thy light is come,
　　　　and the glory of the Lord is risen upon thee.

CHORUS

4:07　　O thou that tellest good tidings to Zion,
　　　　arise, say unto the cities of Judah: Behold your God!
　　　　Behold the glory of the Lord is risen upon thee.

5:12　　Instrumental ritornello concludes.

LISTEN TO ... this selection streaming online.

WATCH ... an Active Listening Guide of this selection online.

WATCH ... Stevie Wonder's take on this aria, online.

DO ... Listening Exercise 9.2, Handel, *Messiah*, "Behold, a Virgin shall conceive" and "O thou that tellest good tidings to Zion," online.

the joyful cry "Hallelujah" (see Listening Guide). Here, Handel displays a variety of choral styles in quick succession: chordal, unison, fugal, and fugal and chordal together (Example 9.1). The opening "Hallelujah" recurs throughout as a powerful refrain, yet each new phrase of text generates its own distinct musical idea. Among them are the following:

EXAMPLE 9.1A Chordal (homophonic) texture

Hal - le - lu - jah,   Hal - le - lu - jah,

EXAMPLE 9.1B Unison (monophonic) texture

For the Lord God om-ni - po-tent reign-eth,

EXAMPLE 9.1C Fugal (polyphonic) texture begins

and he shall   reign for ev - er and   ev - er,

The vivid phrases speak directly to the listener, making the believer an emotional participant in the drama. So moved was King George II when he first heard the great opening chords, the story goes, that he rose to his feet in admiration, thereby establishing the tradition of the audience standing for the "Hallelujah" chorus—for no one sat while the king stood. Indeed, this movement would serve well as a royal coronation march, though in *Messiah*, of course, it is Christ the King who is being crowned.

LISTENING GUIDE

George Frideric Handel, *Messiah*, "Hallelujah" chorus (1741)   Download 4 (3:34)

Genre: Oratorio chorus

WHAT TO LISTEN FOR: The masterful use of contrasting textures (monophonic, homophonic, and polyphonic) to create drama—for at the heart of drama lies vivid contrast

0:00   Brief string introduction

0:06   Chorus enters with two salient motives

Hal - le - lu - jah,   Hal - le - lu - jah,

Hal - le - lu - jah,   Hal - le - lu - jah,

0:14   Five more chordal exclamations of "Hallelujah" motive, but at higher pitch level

0:23	Chorus sings new theme in unison, answered by chordal cries of "Hallelujah"	 For the Lord God omni-po-tent reign-eth,
0:34	Music repeated but at lower pitch	For the Lord God omnipotent reigneth
0:45	Fugal imitation begins with subject	The kingdom of this world is become the
1:09	Quiet and then loud; set in homophonic chords	Kingdom of our Lord…
1:27	New fugal section begins with entry in bass	
		 and he shall reign for ev - er and ev - er,
1:48	Altos and then sopranos begin long ascent in long notes	King of Kings and Lord of Lords
2:28	Basses and sopranos reenter	And he shall reign for ever and ever
2:40	Tenors and basses sing in long notes	King of Kings and Lord of Lords
2:55	Incessant major tonic chord	King of Kings
3:20	Broad final cadence	Hallelujah

LISTEN TO … this selection streaming online.

WATCH … an Active Listening Guide of this selection online.

WATCH … a special animation of this selection online.

DO … Listening Exercise 9.3, Handel, "Hallelujah" chorus, online.

The "Hallelujah" chorus is a strikingly effective work because the large choral force delivers a variety of exciting textures. In fact, however, Handel's chorus for the original Dublin *Messiah* was much smaller than those used today (Figure 9.6).

It included only four singers on each of the alto, tenor, and bass parts, and six choir-boys singing the soprano. The orchestra was equally slight, with only about sixteen players. For the Found-ling Hospital performances of the 1750s, however, the orchestra grew to thirty-five. Then, over the next 100 years, the chorus progres-sively swelled to as many as 4,000, with a balancing orchestra of 500, in what were billed as "Festivals of the People"— a precursor of the modern *Messiah* sing-alongs that we have today.

FIGURE 9.6
Eighteenth-century London was a place of biting satire. Here, in William Hogarth's *The Oratorio Singer* (1732), the chorus of an oratorio is the object of parody. But there is an element of truth here: The chorus for the first performance of *Messiah*, for example, numbered about eighteen males, with choir-boys (front row) taking the soprano part. Women, how-ever, sang soprano and alto for the vocal solos.

FIGURE 9.7
Handel's funeral monument at Westminster Abbey. The composer holds the aria "I know that my Redeemer liveth" from *Messiah*. When Handel was buried, the gravedigger left room to cram in another body immediately adjacent. That space was later filled by the corpse of Charles Dickens.

Just as there was a continual increase in the performing forces for his *Messiah*, so, too, did Handel's fortune and reputation grow. Toward the end of his life, he occupied a squire's house in the center of London; he bought paintings, including a large and "indeed excellent" Rembrandt; and, on his death, he left an estate of nearly £20,000—roughly the equivalent of $5.5 million today. Handel had become the first musical impresario to make a fortune from a paying public—as a music producer. More than 3,000 people attended his funeral in Westminster Abbey on April 20, 1759, and a sculpture of the composer holding an aria from *Messiah* was erected above his grave and is still there (Figure 9.7). As a memento of Handel's music, *Messiah* was an apt choice, for it is still performed each year at Christmas and Easter by countless amateur and professional groups throughout the world.

KEY WORDS

dance suite (128)   minuet (129)   oratorio (130)   anthem (132)

trio (129)   *opera seria* (130)

 Join us on Facebook at Listening to Music with Craig Wright

PRACTICE ... your understanding of this chapter's concepts by comparing Checklists of Musical Style for all historic eras, completing a Musical Style Quiz for the Baroque, and working once more with the chapter's Active Listening Guides online.

DO ... online multiple-choice and critical thinking quizzes that your instructor may assign for a grade.

CHECKLIST OF MUSICAL STYLE *Late Baroque: 1690–1750*

REPRESENTATIVE COMPOSERS

Pachelbel   Vivaldi   Bach   Handel

Corelli   Mouret

PRINCIPAL GENRES

dance suite   solo concerto   opera   prelude

sonata   church cantata   oratorio   fugue

concerto grosso

Melody	Melody is marked by progressive development, growing longer and more expansive; idiomatic instrumental style influences vocal melodies; melodic sequence becomes prevalent
Harmony	Functional chord progressions govern harmonic movement—harmony moves purposefully from one chord to the next; *basso continuo* continues to provide strong bass
Rhythm	Exciting, driving, energized rhythms propel the music forward with vigor; "walking" bass creates feeling of rhythmic regularity
Color	Instruments reign supreme; instrumental sounds, especially of violin, harpsichord, and organ, set musical tone for the era; one tone color used throughout a movement or large section of a movement
Texture	Homophonic texture remains important, but denser, polyphonic texture reemerges in the contrapuntal fugue
Form	Binary form in sonatas and orchestral suites; *da capo* aria (ternary) form in arias; fugal procedure used in fugues; ritornello form in concertos

The
CLASSICAL Period,
1750–1820

part FOUR

CLASSICAL

| 1750 | 1755 | 1760 | 1765 | 1770 | 1775 | 1780 | 1785 |

1763–1766
Mozart family tours
and performs around
Western Europe

1752
Benjamin
Franklin experi-
ments with
electricity

1762
Rousseau publishes out-
line for just government
in *The Social Contract*

1776
American Declaration
of Independence signed
in Philadelphia

1788
U.S. Constitution
ratified

1756–1763
Seven Years' War (French
and Indian War)

1761
Joseph Haydn takes first job at Esterházy
court

1781
Mozart moves to Vienna and
composes operas, symphonies,
concertos, and quartets

1759
Voltaire publishes
Enlightenment
novel *Candide*

During the years 1750–1820, music manifested a style called "Classicism," often termed "Neo-classicism" in the other fine arts. In art and architecture, for example, Neo-classicism aimed to reinstitute the aesthetic values of the ancient Greeks and Romans by incorporating balance and harmonious proportions while avoiding ornate decoration, all leading to a feeling of strength, quiet grace, and noble simplicity. When expressed in music, these same tendencies appeared as balanced phrases, uncluttered textures, and clear, easily audible musical forms. Although composers in cities such as Milan, Paris, and London all wrote symphonies and sonatas with these qualities, the music of this period is often said to be in the "Viennese Classical style." Vienna, Austria, was the capital city of the Holy Roman Empire and the most active center of Classical music in Central Europe. The three principal composers of the Classical era—Joseph Haydn (1732–1809), Wolfgang Amadeus Mozart (1756–1791), and Ludwig van Beethoven (1770–1827)—chose to make Vienna their home because of the city's vibrant musical life. In many ways, Mozart and Haydn created the Classical style, while Beethoven expanded it. Indeed, Beethoven is a transitional figure: Although most of his works fall within the time frame of the Classical era, many also exhibit stylistic characteristics of the succeeding Romantic period.

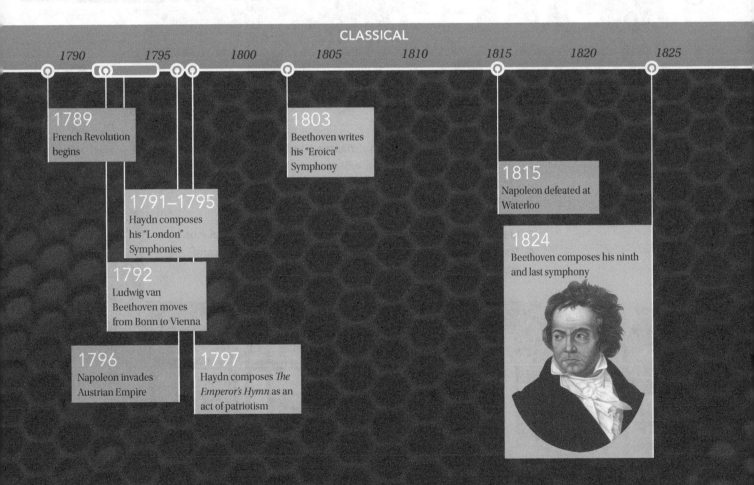

CLASSICAL

1790 1795 1800 1805 1810 1815 1820 1825

1789
French Revolution begins

1803
Beethoven writes his "Eroica" Symphony

1815
Napoleon defeated at Waterloo

1791–1795
Haydn composes his "London" Symphonies

1824
Beethoven composes his ninth and last symphony

1792
Ludwig van Beethoven moves from Bonn to Vienna

1796
Napoleon invades Austrian Empire

1797
Haydn composes *The Emperor's Hymn* as an act of patriotism

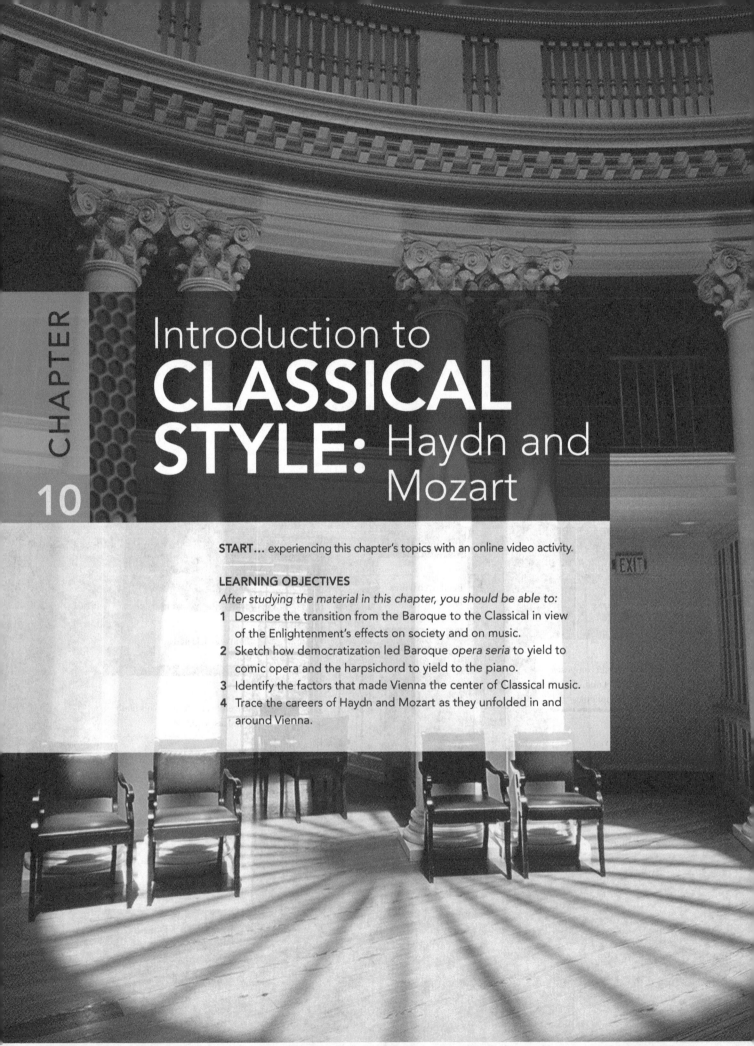

Introduction to
CLASSICAL
STYLE: Haydn and
Mozart

START... experiencing this chapter's topics with an online video activity.

LEARNING OBJECTIVES

After studying the material in this chapter, you should be able to:

1   Describe the transition from the Baroque to the Classical in view of the Enlightenment's effects on society and on music.
2   Sketch how democratization led Baroque *opera seria* to yield to comic opera and the harpsichord to yield to the piano.
3   Identify the factors that made Vienna the center of Classical music.
4   Trace the careers of Haydn and Mozart as they unfolded in and around Vienna.

arketing pitchmen encourage us every day, on TV, on the web, and in print, to buy a particular watch, a suit, or an automobile by saying that it has "classical styling," suggesting that the product possesses a certain timeless beauty. When applied to music, "classical styling" also implies a high-end product. We use the word *classical* to signify the "serious" or "art" music of the West as distinguished from popular and folk music. We call this art music "classical" because there is something about the excellence of its form and style that makes it enduring—it has stood the test of time. Yet, in the same breath, we may refer to "Classical" music (now with a capital C) and by this mean the music of a specific historical period, 1750–1820, the period of the great works of Haydn and Mozart, and the early masterpieces of Beethoven. The creations of these artists have become so identified with musical proportion, balance, and formal correctness—with standards of musical excellence—that this comparatively brief period has given its name to all music of lasting aesthetic worth.

"Classical" derives from the Latin *classicus*, meaning "something of the first rank or highest quality." To the men and women of the eighteenth century, no art was more admirable, virtuous, and worthy of emulation than that of ancient Greece and Rome. Other periods in Western history also have been inspired by classical antiquity—the Renaissance, heavily so (see Chapter 5)—but no era more than the eighteenth century. Classical architecture, with its geometric shapes, balance, symmetrical design, and lack of clutter, became the preferred style for public buildings, not only in Europe, but also in the fledgling United States. Thomas Jefferson (Figure 10.1), while serving as American ambassador to France (1784–1789), traveled to Italy and brought Classical design back home with him. The U.S. Capitol, most state capitols, and countless other governmental and university buildings abound with the well-proportioned columns, porticos, and rotundas of the Classical style (Figures 10.2 and 10.3).

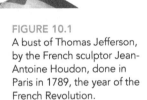

FIGURE 10.1
A bust of Thomas Jefferson, by the French sculptor Jean-Antoine Houdon, done in Paris in 1789, the year of the French Revolution.

FIGURES 10.2 AND 10.3
The Pantheon in Rome and the library of the University of Virginia, designed by Thomas Jefferson. Jefferson had visited Italy and studied ancient ruins while ambassador to France. The library's portico, with columns and triangular pediment, and the central rotunda are all elements of Classical style in architecture.

The Enlightenment

The Classical era in music, art, and architecture overlaps with the period in philosophy and letters known as the **Enlightenment**. During the Enlightenment, also referred to as the Age of Reason, thinkers gave free rein to the pursuit of truth and the discovery of natural laws, formulated largely by Isaac Newton (1642–1727). Science now began to provide as many explanations for the mysteries of life as did religion. In many churches around Europe, the medieval stained glass depicting saintly stories was replaced by clear glass that let in natural light—a literal example of "enlightenment." This is also the age of such scientific advances as the discovery of electricity and the invention of the steam engine. The first *Encyclopedia Britannica* (1771) was inspired by the French *Encyclopédie* (1751–1772), a twenty-four-volume set that aimed to replace medieval faith with modern, scientific reasoning. French encyclopedists Voltaire (1694–1778) and Jean-Jacques Rousseau (1712–1778) espoused the principles of social justice, equality, religious tolerance, and freedom of speech. These Enlightenment ideals subsequently became fundamental to democratic government and were enshrined in the American Constitution (1788).

Needless to say, the notion that all persons are created equal and should enjoy full political freedom put the thinkers of the Enlightenment on a collision course with the defenders of the existing social order, namely the Church and the aristocracy. Spurred on by economic self-interest and enlightened philosophy, an expanding, more confident middle class in France and America rebelled against the monarchy and its supporters. The American colonists—Thomas Jefferson and Benjamin Franklin among them—issued a Declaration of Independence in 1776. In 1789, French citizens stormed the Bastille to seize weapons, thereby precipitating a civil war among the classes. By the end of the eighteenth century, the Age of Reason gave way to the Age of Revolution.

The Democratization of Classical Music and the Rise of "For Profit" Concerts

Music was not exempt from the social changes sweeping eighteenth-century Europe and America. In fact, the century witnessed something of a democratization of classical music. The "audience base" for such music expanded greatly, extending now to the newly affluent middle class. In an earlier day, when art music was performed in only two venues (church and court), the average citizen heard very little of it. By midcentury, however, the bookkeeper, physician, cloth merchant, and stock trader collectively had enough disposable income to organize and patronize their own concerts. In Paris, then a city of 450,000 residents, one could attend, as proclaimed, "the best concerts every day with complete freedom." The most successful Parisian concert series was the *Concert spirituel* (founded in 1725), at which the West's first noncourt orchestra played a regular schedule of performances. The *Concert spirituel* advertised its performances by means of flyers distributed in the streets. To make its offerings accessible to several strata of society, it instituted a two-tiered price scheme for a subscription series (four livres for boxes and two livres for the pit, roughly $200 and $100 in today's money). Children under fifteen were admitted for half price. Thus, we can trace to the middle of the eighteenth century the monetizing of a shared musical experience. The "for profit" concert as we know it today dates from this time.

Public concerts sprang up in London, in the Vauxhall Gardens, the eighteenth-century equivalent of Disney World—which drew as many as 4,500 paying visitors daily. Here, symphonies could be heard inside in the orchestra room or outside when the weather was good. When Leopold Mozart took his young son Wolfgang to concerts there in 1764, he was surprised to see that the audience was not segregated by class. Likewise, in Vienna, the Burgtheater (City Theater) opened in 1759 to any and all paying customers, as long as they were properly dressed and properly behaved (Figure 10.4). Although the allure was music, the hall itself became a place for a leveling of social classes. As their numbers increased, members of the middle class began to compete with the aristocracy for control of high culture—to have a say in the kind of music to be heard.

FIGURE 10.4
A performance at the Burgtheater in Vienna in 1783. The nobility occupied the frontmost seats on the floor, but the area behind them was open to all. So, too, in the galleries, the aristocracy bought boxes low and close to the stage, while commoners occupied higher rungs, as well as the standing room in the fourth gallery. Ticket prices depended, then as now, on proximity to the performers.

Popular Opera Takes Center Stage

Fashions change. At the beginning of the eighteenth century, sophisticated men powdered their faces, painted on "beauty spots," and wore elaborate wigs (see Figure 9.1, portrait of George Frideric Handel). By century's end, a simpler, more natural style was in vogue (see Thomas Jefferson's appearance in Figure 10.1). So, too, did musical style evolve during the eighteenth century. Compared with the relentless, ornate, and often grandiose sound of the Baroque era, Classical music is lighter in tone and more natural. If a single mood dominated a piece in Baroque style, rapid changes between moods (calm to passionate, for example) is more typical of Classical style. This is especially true in the genre of opera.

Social reform in the eighteenth century not only democratized the concert hall but also affected those who went to the opera house and even the characters who populated the stage. A new musical genre, comic opera, appeared and soon drove the established *opera seria* (see Chapter 9) to the wings. Baroque *opera seria* had celebrated the deeds of past kings and heroes, glorifying the aristocracy and solidifying the status quo. By contrast, the new **comic opera**, called *opera buffa* in Italy, championed middle-class values and promoted social change. Comic opera made use of everyday characters and situations; it typically employed spoken dialogue and simple songs in place of recitatives and lengthy arias; and it was liberally spiced with sight gags, bawdy humor, and social satire.

Even a "high-end" composer like Mozart embraced the more natural, down-to-earth spirit of the comic style. Mozart was not always treated fairly by his noble employers, and several of his operas are rife with antiaristocratic sentiment. In *Don Giovanni* (1787), for example, the villain is a leading nobleman of the town (see Chapter 14). In *Le nozze di Figaro* (*The Marriage of Figaro*, 1786), a barber (Figure 10.5) outsmarts a count and exposes him to public ridicule. So seriously did the king of France and the Holy Roman emperor take the threat of such theatrical satire that they banned the play on which *The Marriage of Figaro* was based. Comic theater and comic opera, it seemed, not only reflected social change but could also provoke it.

Popular Opera and a Preview of Classical Style

To witness how a new musical style—and subversive social values—sprang from the operatic stage, we could do no better than to examine Mozart's *The Marriage of Figaro*. Set within the traditional values of a European court, the opera inverts the existing social order; namely, the barber Figaro and his fiancée, the maid Susanna, outwit the morally bankrupt Count Almaviva. The opening scene reveals that the count intends to exercise his *droit du seigneur*—an ancient law allowing the lord of the manor to claim sexual favors from a servant's fiancée. Outraged, Figaro responds with a short aria, "Se vuol ballare" (see Listening Guide). Here, he calls the count by the diminutive "Contino," translated roughly as "Count, you little twerp," and vows to outsmart his master.

Example 10.1 says much about the new, lighter style of Classical music. The melody is simple and tuneful, almost like a folksong. Indeed, during the Classical period, the influence of folk and popular music generally, and dance music in particular, came to influence the melodic structure of art music. Notice the simple arrangement of the musical phrases: four bars and then a matching four bars—a good example of symmetry in classical form. Notice, too, that the texture is entirely homophonic (chordal), another general characteristic of music in the Classical style. Generally speaking, intense polyphony now begins to disappear from the concert hall and stage. If the model of the Baroque period was the polyphonic fugue, that of the Classical era was the symmetrical, tuneful aria sung here by Figaro.

FIGURE 10.5
Bryn Terfel as the combative and cunning barber, Figaro, performs in an English National Opera production of *The Marriage of Figaro*.

EXAMPLE 10.1 Figaro begins

Se vuol bal - la - re, si - gnor Con - ti - no, se vuol bal - la - re, si - gnor Con - ti - no,

staccato

(If you want to dance, Count, you little twerp . . .)

Listening more broadly, we hear Figaro's aria move through four sections: **A**, **B**, **C**, and **D**, with a return to **A** at the end. Although the sections are connected by a measure or two of purely instrumental music, the vocal units of this aria have the proportions 20 + 20 + 20 + 40 + 20—a balanced, "classical" arrangement indeed.

With such serene balance, where is the drama in this opera? Drama is what a great composer like Mozart, in this case literally, brings to the dance. Mozart casts the aria, "Se vuol ballare" ("If you want to dance"), within the context of a stately minuet, the traditional dance of the aristocratic court. Figaro begins in calm, measured steps—all is balance and grace. But the more he thinks about the count's lechery and treachery, the more anxious he becomes. Musically, we hear Figaro's agitation grow through sections **B**, **C**, and **D**, each gaining in intensity. Only at the end does the valet regain his composure, as signaled by the return of the stately minuet (**A**). Here, dance serves as a metaphor for a shuffling of the social order—if the count wants to "dance" (fool around), Figaro, the servant, will call the tune.

LISTENING GUIDE

Wolfgang Amadeus Mozart, "Se vuol ballare," from *Le nozze di Figaro* (1786)   Download 32 (2:24)

Character: Figaro, a clever barber and valet to Count Almaviva

Situation: Figaro has learned that the count intends to seduce his fiancée, Susanna, and Figaro vows to outwit him.

WHAT TO LISTEN FOR: How Mozart depicts through music Figaro's growing agitation and return to composure at the end; classical calm yields to personal passion, and then calm is restored

0:07	Section **A**: Music begins with style of courtly minuet.	Se vuol ballare, Signor Contino, Il chitarrino. Le suonerò.	If you want to dance, Count, you little twerp, I'll sound the guitar. I'll call the tune.
0:28	Section **B**: Music becomes slightly more agitated with fluttering strings.	Se vuol venire Nella mia scuola, La capriole Le insegnerò.	If you want to come To my dancing school, I'll teach you How to caper.
0:55	Section **C**: Music is agitated, with racing strings.	Saprò...ma piano Meglio ogni arcane	I know...but quietly All his secrets
1:13	Music assumes dark, sinister tone, changing to minor.	Dissimulando Scoprir potrò.	Better by trickery I can discover.
1:25	Section **D**: Tempo increases and meter changes to duple.	L'arte schermendo, L'arte adoprando, Di qua pungendo, Di là scherzando, Tutte le maccine	Sometimes concealing, Sometimes revealing, Punching here, Feigning there, All your schemes
1:45	Mozart slows down music.	Rovescierò.	I'll turn against you.
1:52	Music of section **A** returns.	Se vuol ballare, Signor Contino, Il chitarrino. Le suonerò.	If you want to dance, Count, you little twerp, I'll sound the guitar. I'll call the tune.
2:18	Orchestral conclusion		

LISTEN TO ... this selection streaming online.

WATCH ... an Active Listening Guide of this selection online.

WATCH ... a performance of this selection online.

WATCH... a performance of Mozart's Variations on "Twinkle, Twinkle, Little Star," performed on a replica of the *pianoforte* that Mozart purchased in 1783, online.

The Advent of the Piano and Piano Style

Finally, the newly affluent middle class was not content merely to attend concerts and operatic performances; they also wished to make their own music at home. Most of this domestic music making centered around an instrument that first entered public consciousness in the Classical period: the piano. Invented in Italy about 1700, the piano gradually replaced the harpsichord as the keyboard instrument of choice—and with good reason, for the piano could play at more than one dynamic level (hence, the original name ***pianoforte***, meaning "soft-loud"). Compared with the harpsichord, the piano could produce gradual dynamic changes, more subtle, yet rapid, contrasts, and—ultimately—more power.

Those who played this new domestic instrument were mostly amateurs, and the great majority of these were women (Figure 10.6). A smattering of French, an eye for needlepoint, and some skill at the piano—these were signs of status and gentility that rendered a young woman suitable for marriage. For the nonprofessional woman to play in the home, however, a simpler, more homophonic style of keyboard music was needed, which would not tax the presumed technical limitations of the performer. The spirit of democracy may have been in the air, but this was still very much a sexist age. It was assumed that ladies would not wish, as one publication said, "to bother their pretty little heads with counterpoint and harmony" but would be content with a tuneful melody and a few rudimentary chords to flesh it out. Collections such as *Keyboard Pieces for Ladies* (1768) were directed at these new musical consumers.

Typical of the piano music Mozart created for his amateur students is a work he wrote in 1788, titled "Short Keyboard Sonata for Beginners" (Example 10.2). It is likely that you've heard this piece. It begins with two balanced phrases, each two measures in length. The texture is homophonic: melody plus accompanying chords. Example 10.2A shows the essential structure of this passage as Mozart conceived it. Example 10.2B shows his final product, with the pitches of the chords spread out to provide a continual stream of sound. Such a bass line is called an **Alberti bass**, named after the minor Italian keyboard composer Domenico Alberti (1710–1740). The texture is still light and airy, but the gentle flow of the accompaniment allows the music to sound less clunky (as in Example 10.2A) and more graceful (as in Example 10.2B).

FIGURE 10.6
Marie Antoinette, in 1770 at the age of fifteen, seated at an early piano. In 1774, this Austrian princess became queen of France, but in 1793, at the height of the French Revolution, she was beheaded.

LISTEN TO...

Example 10.2A online.

EXAMPLE 10.2A Melody with chordal accompaniment (hypothetical)

EXAMPLE 10.2B Mozart's melody with Alberti bass

LISTEN TO...
Example 10.2B online.

The Alberti bass serves essentially the same function as the modern "boogie-woogie" bass. It creates an illusion of harmonic activity for those moments when, in fact, the harmony is not changing. In Classical style, the harmony is sometimes even simpler than it seems.

The Dynamic Quality of Classical Style

Balance, symmetry, simplicity, light and airy—these are a few of the terms usually associated with Classical style. And "traveling light" has an advantage: The music can change mood or direction with lightning speed. Recall that, in earlier times, a work by Vivaldi or Bach would establish one "affect," or mood, to be rigidly maintained from beginning to end—the rhythm, melody, and harmony all progressing in a continuous, uninterrupted flow. Such a uniform approach to expression is part of the single-mindedness of Baroque art. Now, with Haydn, Mozart, and the young Beethoven, an energetic theme in rapid notes might be followed by a second one that is slow, lyrical, and tender. What had been a walking bass might now alternate between a plodding and a sprinting one, or no bass at all. Similarly, textures might change quickly from light and open to dense and more contrapuntal, thereby adding tension and excitement. For the first time, composers began to specify crescendos and diminuendos, gradual increases or decreases of the dynamic level, so that the volume of sound might continually fluctuate. When skilled orchestras made use of this technique, audiences were fascinated and rose to their feet. Keyboard players, too, now took up the crescendo and diminuendo, assuming that the new, multidynamic piano was at hand in place of the older, less flexible harpsichord. These rapid changes in mood, texture, color, and dynamics give to Classical music a new sense of urgency and drama. The listener feels a constant flux and flow, not unlike the natural swings of mood that we all experience.

Vienna: Home to Classical Composers

New Orleans jazz, Hollywood film music, and the Broadway musical of New York—all suggest that a particular city gave rise to a distinctive kind of music. So, too, with the Viennese Classical style. The careers of Haydn, Mozart, Beethoven, and the young Franz Schubert all unfolded in Vienna, and from Vienna radiated their powerful musical influence. For that reason, we often refer to them collectively as the **Viennese School** and say that their music epitomizes the "Viennese Classical style."

Vienna was then the capital of the old Holy Roman Empire, a huge expanse covering much of Western and Central Europe (Figure 10.7). In 1790, the heyday of

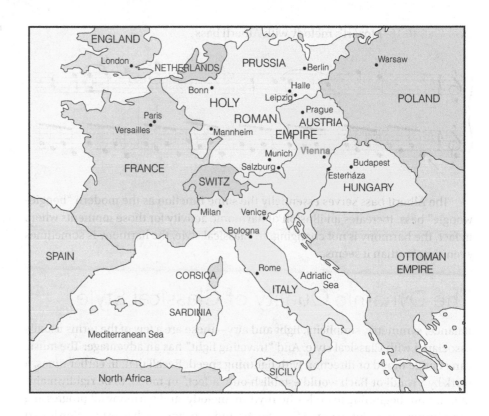

Haydn and Mozart, Vienna had a population of 215,000, which made it the fourth-largest city in Europe, after London, Paris, and Naples. Surrounded by vast farmlands ruled by an aristocratic gentry, it served as a cultural mecca, especially during the winter months when there was little agricultural work to be supervised. Vienna boasted a greater percentage of noblemen among its population than did London or Paris, and here the aristocratic hold on high culture loosened only gradually—but loosen it did. Haydn was a court employee, but Mozart and Beethoven became independent operators. And, while Viennese nobles still patronized music, they often enjoyed it with middle-class citizens at public concerts. There were theaters for German and Italian opera, concerts in the streets on fine summer nights, and ballroom dances where as many as 2,000 couples might sway to a minuet or a waltz by Mozart or Beethoven.

With money to be earned and much to be learned, Vienna attracted musicians from throughout Europe. Haydn moved there from Lower Austria; Mozart, from Upper Austria; his rival, Antonio Salieri, from Italy; and Beethoven, from Bonn, Germany. Later, in the nineteenth century, in addition to native-born Franz Schubert, outsiders such Johannes Brahms and Gustav Mahler would spend their most productive years there. Even today, tourists wandering the streets of Vienna are besieged by hawkers dressed as Haydn or Mozart, selling tickets to a variety of classical concerts that night.

Franz Joseph Haydn (1732–1809)

Joseph Haydn (Figure 10.8) was the first of the great Classical composers to move to Vienna, and his life offers something of a "rags-to-riches" story. Haydn was born in 1732 in a farmhouse in Rohrau, Austria, about twenty-five miles east of Vienna.

His father, a wheelwright, played the harp but could not read music. When the choir director of St. Stephen's Cathedral in Vienna happened to be scouting for talent in the provinces, he heard the boy soprano Haydn sing and brought him back to the capital. Here, Haydn remained as a choirboy, studying the rudiments of composition and learning to play the violin and keyboard. After nearly ten years of service, his voice broke and he was abruptly dismissed. For most of the 1750s, Haydn eked out a "wretched existence," as he called it, much like a freelance musician or aspiring actress might in New York City today. But, in 1761, Haydn's years of struggle ended when he was engaged as director of music for the court of Prince Nikolaus Esterházy (1714–1790).

The **Esterházy family** were wealthy aristocrats who wintered in Vienna and summered on their extensive landholdings to the southeast (see Figure 10.7). At the family's magnificent court at Esterháza (see Figure 10.9), Prince Nikolaus ruled much like a benevolent dictator. But the prince was an autocrat with a fondness for music, maintaining an orchestra, a chapel for singing religious works, and a theater for opera. As was typical of the period, the musician Haydn was considered a servant of his prince and even wore the garb of the domestic help, as can be seen in his portrait. As a condition of his appointment in 1761, Haydn signed a contract stipulating that all the music that he composed belonged not to him but to his aristocratic master.

FIGURE 10.8
Portrait of Joseph Haydn (c. 1762–1763) wearing a wig and the blue livery of the Esterházy court

For a period of nearly thirty years, Haydn served Nikolaus Esterházy at his remote court on what is today the border of Austria and Hungary. In 1790, Prince Nikolaus died, leaving Haydn a pension for life and freedom to travel. Heeding the call of an enterprising impresario, Johann Solomon—and the promise of a substantial fee—Haydn journeyed to London in 1791. For performances in this city, then the largest and richest in Europe, Haydn wrote his last twelve symphonies, called the **London Symphonies**. He himself conducted the premiere of each symphony in a series of concerts at the Hanover Square Rooms, a new public concert hall that catered to the growing middle-class demand for classical music (see Figure 12.2). By the time he returned to Vienna in 1795, Haydn had earned a total of 24,000 Austrian gulden, the equivalent of about $2.1 million today—not bad for the son of a wheelwright. Haydn died on May 31, 1809, at the age of seventy-seven, the most respected composer in Europe.

FIGURE 10.9
The palace of the Esterházy family southeast of Vienna, where Joseph Haydn lived until 1790. The elements of Neo-classical architectural style include the triangular pediment over the entryway, the columns, and the Ionic capitals atop the flat columns.

Haydn's long life, commitment to duty, and unflagging industry resulted in an impressive number of musical compositions: 106 symphonies, about 70 string quartets, nearly a dozen operas, 52 piano sonatas, 14 Masses, and 2 oratorios. He began composing before the death of Bach (1750) and did not put down his pen until about the time Beethoven set to work on his Symphony No. 5 (1808). Thus, Haydn not only witnessed but also, more than any other composer, helped to create the mature Classical style. Yet, although keenly aware of his own musical gifts, he was quick to recognize talent in others, especially Mozart: "Friends often flatter me that I have some genius, but he [Mozart] stood far above me."

Wolfgang Amadeus Mozart (1756–1791)

Indeed who, except possibly Bach, could match Mozart's diversity, breadth of expression, and perfect formal control? Wolfgang Amadeus Mozart (Figure 10.10) was born in 1756 in the mountain town of **Salzburg**, Austria, then a city of about 20,000 residents. His father, Leopold Mozart, was a violinist in the orchestra of the ruling archbishop of Salzburg and the author of a best-selling introduction to playing the violin. Leopold was quick to recognize the musical gifts of his son, who by the age of six was playing the piano, violin, and organ, as well as composing. In 1762, the Mozart family embarked on a nearly four-year-long tour of Europe that included extended stops in Vienna, Munich, Brussels, Paris (Figure 10.11), and London. In Vienna, Wolfgang played for Empress Maria Theresa, in Paris for King Louis XV, and in London for King George III—the boy wonder was indeed the marvel of the age. Eventually, the Mozarts made their way back to Salzburg. In 1769, father and son were off on a grand tour of Italy, including Rome, where, on July 8, 1770, Pope Clement XIV dubbed Wolfgang (see Figure 10.12) a Knight of the Order of the Golden Spur.

Although the aim of all this globe-trotting was to acquire fame and fortune, the result was that Mozart, unlike Haydn, was exposed at an early age to a wealth of musical styles: French Baroque, English choral, German polyphonic, and Italian

FIGURE 10.11
The child prodigy Mozart at the keyboard, with his sister, Nannerl, and his father, Leopold, in Paris in 1764 during their nearly four-year tour of Europe. Note how the youngster's feet dangle far from the floor.

vocal. His extraordinarily keen ear absorbed them all, and his creative mind synthesized them into a new, international style. Today, Mozart is still widely recognized as "the most universal composer in the history of Western music."

A period of relative stability followed Mozart's youthful travels: For much of the 1770s, he resided in Salzburg, where he served as violinist and composer to the reigning archbishop, Colloredo. The archbishop was a stern, frugal man who had little sympathy for Mozart, genius or not (the composer referred to him as the "Archboobie"). Mozart was paid modestly and, like the servant-musicians at the court of Esterházy, ate with the cooks and valets. For a Knight of the Golden Spur who had hobnobbed with kings and queens across Europe, this was humble fare indeed, and Mozart chafed under this system of aristocratic patronage. But he couldn't just quit—servants of the court had to obtain a release from their employer before they could move on. So, in the spring of 1781, Mozart precipitated several unpleasant scenes, forcing the archbishop to fire him. Establishing himself in Vienna, twenty-five-year-old Mozart then did something that no musician before him had accomplished: make his fortune as a freelance artist.

Mozart chose Vienna because the city had a vibrant musical life and a passion for the two things he did best: compose and play the keyboard. In a letter to his sister in the spring of 1782, Mozart spells out how he juggled his time between composition, teaching, and performing.

> My hair is always done by six o'clock in the morning and by seven I am fully dressed. I then compose until nine. From nine to one I give lessons. Then I lunch, unless I am invited to some house where they lunch at two or even three o'clock.... I can never work before five or six o'clock in the evening, and even then I am often prevented by a concert. If I am not prevented, I compose until nine.

The years 1784–1787 witnessed the peak of Mozart's success in Vienna and the creation of many of his greatest works. He had a full complement of pupils, played several concerts a week, and enjoyed lucrative commissions as a composer. Piano concertos, string quartets, symphonies, and operas flowed from his enormously active pen. During his best years, Mozart made a great deal of money, about $325,000 annually by one estimate. But money flew out the door as fast as it came in—he lived well and loved fine clothes, in particular. When a war with the Turkish (Ottoman) Empire broke out in 1788 and a Europe-wide recession ensued, Mozart's income plummeted. For a time, he was reduced to begging discreetly from well-to-do friends. Eventually, by 1791, the economy and Mozart's prospects revived. He received handsome commissions for a new opera for the emperor and for a Requiem Mass.

Such good fortune, however, was to be tragically short-lived. Indeed, the Requiem Mass became Mozart's own requiem when he died unexpectedly on December 5, 1791, at the age of thirty-five. The precise reason for his death has never been determined, though rheumatic fever and kidney failure, made worse by needless bloodletting, are the most likely causes. No single event in the history of music is more regrettable than the premature loss of Mozart. He produced as much as the long-lived Handel and Haydn, but in about half the time!

FIGURE 10.12
Young Mozart proudly wearing the collar of a Knight of the Order of the Golden Spur, an honor conferred upon him for his musical skills by Pope Clement XIV in July 1770

WATCH... "Mozart" presented to the Emperor Joseph II and improvising, from the film *Amadeus*, online.

MOZART: THE GOLD STANDARD OF GENIUS

The CBS program *60 Minutes* describes the world's number one chess player, Magnus Carlsen, as "the Mozart of Chess." Tennis great Roger Federer is referred to as "the Mozart of tennis." Even painter Pablo Picasso was called "the Mozart of painting." But when it comes to genius, why is Mozart the standard against whom all others are compared? To answer this question, we must inquire into the nature of genius. Is it enough to possess an immense gift for cognitive processing? In other words, must a genius add up figures at a grocery checkout as fast as a computer, like Kim Peek, the real-life subject of the film *Rainman*, or play (and win) ten games of chess simultaneously while blindfolded, as can the twenty-four-year-old Carlsen? Or must a genius create something truly significant—a painting, a poem, a symphony, a new drug, or a scientific theory—that changes the lives of others? Suppose you could do both: process information with lightning speed *and* produce innovative creations that influence society. Then, presumably, you would be a candidate for the A list of geniuses, at the top of which sits Mozart.

This still from the spectacularly good Academy Award–winning film *Amadeus* (1985) shows "Mozart" composing at a billiard table. Mozart did, in fact, keep a billiard table in his bedroom. But, in most other ways, the portrayal of Mozart in *Amadeus* is largely fictitious. Mozart was not an irresponsible idiot-savant who died penniless, but a highly intelligent entrepreneur whose income fluctuated wildly from year to year; moreover, he was not poisoned by his rival, composer Antonio Salieri (1750–1825). But *Amadeus* does pose an intriguing question: What does a mediocre or even gifted person (Salieri) do when faced with an absolute genius (Mozart)?

Indeed, according to these measures of genius, Mozart had it all. He was precocious, composing at the age of five, and his cognitive skills were extraordinary. As a child, he could identify the notes played in any chord, judge the pitch of an instrument within a quarter of a tone, or pick out a wrong note in a musical score while crawling on his back across a table. At the age of fourteen, he heard a polyphonic motet sung in the Sistine Chapel in Rome and wrote it down by memory, note for note. How much music can we remember on first hearing it—four or five seconds of the melody? Obviously, Mozart could store and process a great deal of music in his "mind's ear." And not just music, but other sounds as well. Mozart was a superb mimic, and he learned to speak several foreign languages almost upon first hearing them.

With the gifts of genius, however, came peculiarities of personality—by definition, geniuses are rarely "normal." Mozart often fidgeted and made childish jokes and puns—but eternal childlike thinking, as Einstein and Picasso attest, is often the mark of genius. Until the age of ten or so, Mozart was terrified by the sound of a trumpet, and out-of-tune instruments brought physical pain to his ears. Was he slightly autistic? At parties, he often seemed to be in his own world, and his financial affairs were sometimes chaotic.

What, then, allowed Mozart to create so many masterpieces? Among the factors were a prodigious memory and enormous powers of concentration, two characteristics common to all top-tier geniuses. While the external world around him might have been frenetic and unruly, he had the capacity to create in his mind a world of music that was all balance, order, and perfection. Once all had been arranged there, writing it down was easy.

KEY WORDS

Enlightenment (142)
comic opera (143)
opera buffa (143)

pianoforte (146)
Alberti bass (146)

Viennese School (147)
Esterházy family (149)

London Symphonies (149)
Salzburg (150)

 Join us on Facebook at Listening to Music with Craig Wright

PRACTICE ... your understanding of this chapter's concepts by comparing the Checklist of Musical Style for all historic eras and working once more with the chapter's Active Listening Guides online.

DO ... online multiple-choice and critical thinking quizzes that your instructor may assign for a grade.

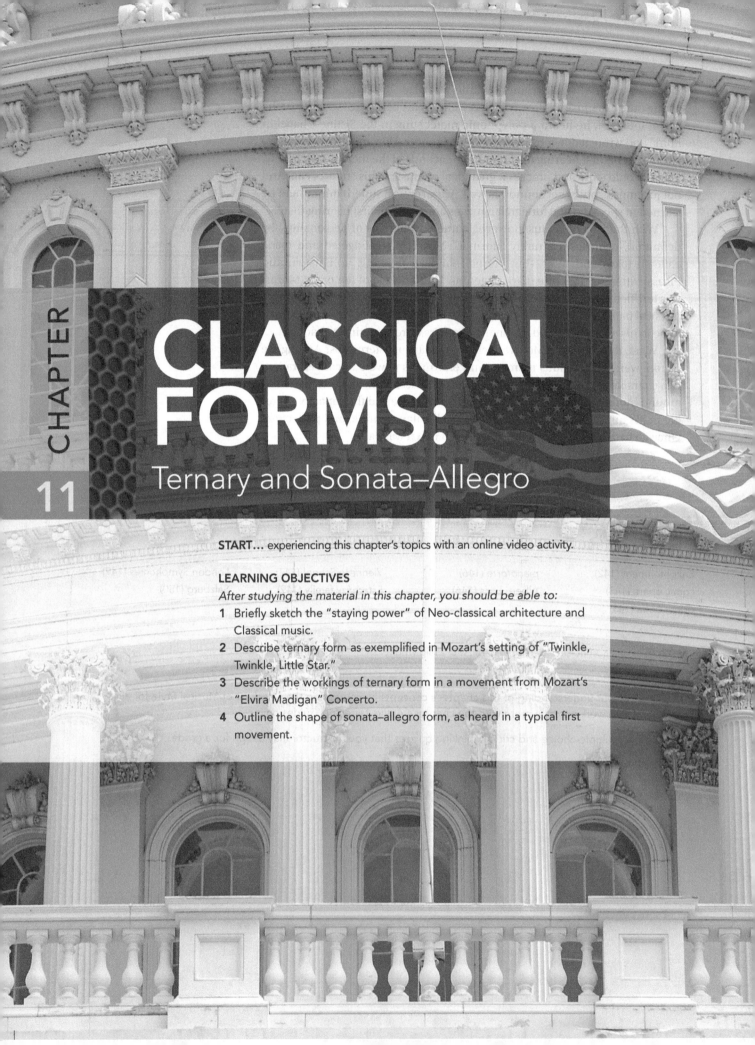

CLASSICAL FORMS:
Ternary and Sonata–Allegro

START... experiencing this chapter's topics with an online video activity.

LEARNING OBJECTIVES

After studying the material in this chapter, you should be able to:

1 Briefly sketch the "staying power" of Neo-classical architecture and Classical music.
2 Describe ternary form as exemplified in Mozart's setting of "Twinkle, Twinkle, Little Star."
3 Describe the workings of ternary form in a movement from Mozart's "Elvira Madigan" Concerto.
4 Outline the shape of sonata–allegro form, as heard in a typical first movement.

READ... the complete chapter text in a rich, interactive online platform.

When we use the term *form*, whether we're discussing a building or a piece of music, we refer to that artifact's shape in visual or aural space. The forms of Classical architecture were consistent and widespread. Around 1800, for example, buildings might have looked much the same in Vienna as in Virginia. Moreover, the forms of Classical architecture are still very much with us today. Consider, for example, the windows in the ballroom at the emperor's court in Vienna (see Figure 11.1), where Mozart and his wife often waltzed. Windows of precisely this design still can be seen in much of the architecture of Washington, D.C. (the U.S. Capitol in this chapter's opening photo), the concert hall of your author's university, and even his living room. Look for others the next time you walk around your campus.

Musical form during the Classical period was similarly well traveled. A few musical designs shaped most Classical music, no matter who the composer or where the concert. Some of these forms predated the Classical period, and some were created during it. And, as in architecture, these forms have proved timeless, serving composers to the present day.

But how do composers make a "form" out of music—something you hear but cannot see? They do so, as mentioned in Chapter 3, by arranging musical events in patterns over the course of a work, making use of four basic procedures: statement, repetition, contrast, and variation.

FIGURE 11.1
A ball at the Redoutensaal (grand ballroom) in the emperor's palace in Vienna, c. 1800. Mozart, Haydn, and, later, Beethoven composed minuets and "German dances" for these events, which sometimes attracted nearly 4,000 fee-paying dancers. Originally, the balls were closed to all but the nobility and military, but Emperor Joseph II (r. 1765–1790) opened them to all citizens—part of the democratization of music in the late eighteenth century. The orchestra can be seen in the gallery to the left. The Redoutensaal still provides a venue for concerts. If you visit Vienna, continue a Classical tradition by buying a ticket and going in.

Ternary Form

In **ternary (ABA) form**, the idea of statement–contrast–repetition is obvious. Think of this design as a kind of musical "home-away-home" if you wish. To demonstrate the point in the simplest possible terms, consider again the French folksong known to us as "Twinkle, Twinkle, Little Star." Wolfgang Amadeus Mozart came to know the melody when he toured France as a youth, and he composed a setting for keyboard that begins as in Example 11.1.

EXAMPLE 11.1 "Twinkle, Twinkle, Little Star"

Notice that both units (**A** and **BA**) are repeated (see repeat sign ⫶| in musical example). Observe also that **A** is in the tonic, **B** hints at a contrasting key (here, the dominant), and the returning **A** is again in the tonic (these harmonies are indicated by the roman numerals I and V). If a piece in ternary form is in major, often **B** will be in minor, and vice versa. Frequently, the switch is to what is called the **relative minor** (or **relative major**, going minor to major). Of course, most pieces in ternary form are more complex than "Twinkle, Twinkle, Little Star." Most have more contrast of melody, key, and/or mood between the **B** section and the surrounding units of **A**.

A more complex example of ternary form can be heard in the famous slow (second) movement of Mozart's Piano Concerto in C major (1786; see Listening Guide). Known popularly as the "Elvira Madigan" Concerto (it was the theme for the 1967 film of that name), these Mozartian sounds still drift through coffee-houses, airports, and shopping malls today, an unseen monument to the staying power of a Classical classic.

Let's start with the melody. Generally speaking, melodies in the Classical style are simple and short, with balanced phrases organized into antecedent-consequent or "question–answer" pairs. **Antecedent phrases** and **consequent phrases** (Figure 11.2) are musical units that operate together: One opens, and the other closes. The melody that opens section **A** of the Piano Concerto in C major consists of an antecedent-consequent unit, each phrase of which is three bars long (see Example 11.2). Notice, too, the pulsing **triplets** (groups of three notes with the number 3 above them) that animate and enrich the accompaniment.

EXAMPLE 11.2 Antecedent and consequent phrases

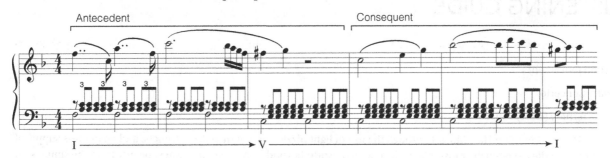

As Mozart progresses, he unfolds three additional themes in a similar manner, which together form section **A**. As is typical of a concerto in Classical style, the **A** material is presented twice: once by the orchestra and then again by a soloist, here the pianist. Mozart, having an ever-creative mind, never met a repetition that he didn't try to vary. Thus, in the pianist's repeat of **A** (at 1:36), the composer inserts a momentary diversion to the relative minor key (2:28). The **B** section (at 3:40), too, is in minor, again favoring the relative minor. And the repeat of **A** (at 4:50) holds a surprise as well. The themes return in a major key but not the tonic key, sliding back to that tonic only at the end. Once there, just to make sure we know we're really home, Mozart adds a few concluding chords as a short **coda** (Italian for "tail")—a section added to the end of a composition to wrap things up. That's all we need to know about this movement in ternary form.

Actually, nothing could be further from the truth. Analysis, like that above, provides only an introduction to the listening experience. Far more important is emotional engagement with the music. Who, for example, could not be moved by the hauntingly beautiful melody (theme 1)? It tugs at the heart because, below it, the accompaniment sounds exactly like that—a gently pulsing heart. Who could not be agitated by the rising melodic sequence and deep dives of the next melody (theme 2)? Who could not feel a sense of both release and relief in the sublimely falling sequence (theme 3)? Have we reached the final tonic yet? No; a deceptive cadence (theme 4) frustrates our arrival, but a full cadence soon brings ultimate satisfaction and closure. By using analysis to unlock feeling, we come to understand the *why* of our emotions.

Having now mastered ternary form (**ABA**), let's proceed to a far greater challenge: hearing sonata–allegro form.

FIGURE 11.2
Many major artists of the eighteenth century journeyed to Rome to absorb the ancient classical style. What they created in painting and architecture we now call Neo-classicism. Among such classically inspired painters was the English-woman Angelica Kauffmann (1741–1807), whose painting *The Artist [Angelica Kauffmann] in the Character of Design Listening to the Inspiration of Poetry* (1782), shows classical balance (two women and two columns). Not coincidentally, the complementary figures in this painting function as do antecedent-consequent phrases in classical music: They are somewhat different, but they balance each other.

LISTENING GUIDE

Wolfgang Amadeus Mozart, Piano Concerto in C major (1786), K. 467   Download 33 (6:58)

Second movement

Genre: Concerto

Form: Ternary (**ABA**) with coda

WHAT TO LISTEN FOR: How Mozart, through the use of light pizzicatos, gently pulsing triplets, and an endless supply of beautiful melodies, seemingly transports the listener to a world beyond—creating the greatest beauty from the simplest of materials.

0:00	**A**	Orchestra sets duple meter with triplet subdivision; violins add theme 1 (antecedent–consequent).
0:29		Violins play theme 2, a two-step ascending melodic sequence, with deep dive.
0:45		Violins play theme 3, a five-step descending melodic sequence.
1:06		Woodwinds present theme 4, a deceptive and then a final-sounding cadence.
1:36		Piano enters with theme 1.
2:00		Piano expands theme 2 (two-step ascending sequence).
2:28		Contrasting section in minor
2:58		Piano ornaments theme 3 (five-step descending sequence).
3:17		Piano leads into theme 4 (deceptive and then final-sounding cadence).
3:40	**B**	Shift to minor key and dramatic rising scale in piano
4:24		Theme 3 starts descent in minor.
4:40		Extended transition leads back to themes of part **A.**
4:50	**A**	Theme 1 returns but in a slightly higher key.
5:12		Theme 2 returns.
5:27		Theme 3 returns.
5:48		Theme 4 returns.
6:12		Reprise of theme 2
6:35	**Coda**	Wistful pitches of tonic triad signal the end.

LISTEN TO ... this selection streaming online.

WATCH ... an Active Listening Guide of this selection online.

DO ... Listening Exercise 11.1, Mozart, Piano Concerto in C major, online.

Sonata–Allegro Form

Most stories, plays, and films have a stereotypical form: setup, complication, resolution. So, too, with sonata–allegro form, which, like a great play, has the potential for dramatic presentation (**A**), conflict (**B**), and resolution (**A**). Sonata–allegro form is the most complex of all musical stories, and it tends to result in the longest pieces. Yet, it is also the most important: In the Classical era, more movements of symphonies, quartets, and the like were written in this form than in any other, and its popularity endured throughout the nineteenth century as well.

First, however, an important distinction: the difference between the *genre* called sonata and the *form* called sonata–allegro. A sonata is a *genre* of music usually involving a solo instrument; **sonata–allegro form**, however, is a *form* giving structure to a single movement within any one of several genres: a sonata, string quartet, serenade, symphony, even a one-movement overture.

To see how this works, consider the movements in two different works in two different genres, Mozart's serenade, *Eine kleine Nachtmusik*, and Haydn's Symphony No. 94 (see Table 11.1). Each work is comprised of four movements, and each movement has its own form. We get the term *sonata–allegro form* from the fact that most sonatas employ this form in the first movement, and the first movement almost always goes fast, or "allegro."

TABLE 11.1 Two works using sonata–allegro form

Mozart, *Eine kleine Nachtmusik* (1787)			
Movement	**1**	**2**	**3**	**4**
Tempo	Fast	Slow	Minuet and trio	Fast
Form	Sonata–allegro	Rondo	Ternary	Rondo
Haydn, Symphony No. 94 (1791)			
Movement	**1**	**2**	**3**	**4**
Tempo	Fast	Slow	Minuet and trio	Fast
Form	Sonata–allegro	Theme and variations	Ternary	Sonata–allegro

The Shape of Sonata–Allegro Form

Let's say that you've just arrived at a concert hall, and the orchestra is about to play the first movement of a symphony. How will things unfold? It's likely that the music will proceed along the lines suggested by Figure 11.3. Not every sonata–allegro

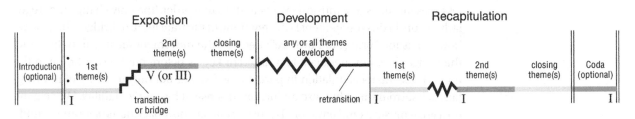

FIGURE 11.3
Sonata–allegro form

movement follows this model in all particulars, but having this roadmap for listening will add to your enjoyment. It will allow you to understand where you have been and anticipate what to expect next.

In its broad outline, sonata–allegro form looks much like ternary form. It consists of an **ABA** plan, with the **B** section providing contrast in mood, key, and thematic treatment. Again, think of a play or film with its setup, complication, and resolution. The initial **A** in sonata–allegro form is called the exposition; the **B**, the development; and the return to **A**, the recapitulation. Let's examine each of these sections in turn and see what we are likely to experience.

Exposition

In the **exposition**, the composer presents the main themes (or musical personalities) of the movement. It begins with the first theme or theme group, which is always in the tonic key. Next comes the **transition**, or **bridge**, as it is sometimes called, which carries the music from the tonic to a new key, usually the dominant, and prepares for the arrival of the second theme. The second theme typically contrasts in character with the first; if the first theme is rapid and assertive, the second theme may be more languid and lyrical. The exposition usually concludes with a closing theme, often simply oscillating between dominant and tonic chords—not much is happening harmonically, so we must be near the end. After the final cadence, the exposition is repeated in full.

Now we've met all the "characters" of the piece; let's see how things develop.

Development

If sonata–allegro is a dramatic musical form, most of the drama comes in the **development**. As the name indicates, a further working out, or "developing," of the thematic material occurs here. The themes can be extended and varied, or wholly transformed; a character we thought we knew can turn out to have a completely different personality. Dramatic confrontation can occur, as when several themes sound together, fighting for our attention. Not only are developments dramatic; they are also unstable and unsettling, the harmony typically modulating quickly from one key to the next. Only toward the end of the development, in the passage called the **retransition**, is tonal order restored, often by means of a stabilizing pedal point on the dominant note. When the dominant chord (V) finally gives way to the tonic (I), the recapitulation begins.

Recapitulation

After the turmoil of the development, the listener greets the recapitulation with a double sense of relief: The first theme returns, and so does the tonic key. Though the **recapitulation** is not an exact, note-for-note repetition of the exposition, it nonetheless presents the same musical events in the same order. The only change that regularly occurs in this restatement is the rewriting of the transition, or bridge. This bridge, however, is the "bridge to nowhere": Because the movement must end in the tonic, the bridge does not modulate to a different key as before but stays at home in the tonic. Thus, the recapitulation imparts to the listener not only a feeling of return to familiar surroundings but also an increased sense of harmonic stability. We've gone on a great musical (and emotional) journey and are now back home safe and sound.

The following two elements—introduction and coda—are optional to sonata–allegro form, functioning something akin to a preface and an epilogue.

Introduction

About half of the mature symphonies of Haydn and Mozart have a brief introduction, like a curtain-raiser before the real drama begins. Introductions are, without exception, slow and stately, and usually are filled with puzzling chords designed to get listeners wondering what sort of musical excursion they are about to take.

Coda

As we have seen, a coda is used to wrap things up. Like their Italian namesake, "tails," codas can be long or short. Haydn and Mozart wrote relatively short codas. Beethoven, however, was inclined to compose lengthy codas, sometimes introducing new themes even at the end of the movement. But, no matter how long the coda, most will end with a final cadence in which the harmonic motion slows down to just two chords, dominant and tonic, played over and over, as if to say, "the end, the end, the end, THE **END**." The more these repeat, the greater the feeling of conclusion.

Hearing Sonata–Allegro Form

Why all this attention to sonata–allegro form? First, it is absolutely central to the core repertoire of Classical music and beyond. Haydn, Mozart, Beethoven, Schubert, Tchaikovsky, Brahms, Mahler, Stravinsky, and Shostakovich all used it. Second, sonata–allegro form is the most complex and difficult of the classical forms to follow. A sonata–allegro movement tends to be long, lasting anywhere from four minutes in a simple composition from the Classical period to twenty minutes or more in a full-blown movement of the Romantic era.

How does the listener meet this musical challenge? First, be sure to memorize the diagram of sonata–allegro form given in Figure 11.3. Equally important, think carefully about the four distinctive musical styles found in sonata–allegro form: thematic, transitional, developmental, and cadential (ending). Each has a distinctive sound. A thematic passage has a clearly recognizable melody, often a singable tune. The transition is full of motion, with melodic sequences and rapid chord changes. The development sounds active, perhaps confusing; the harmonies shift quickly, and the themes, while recognizable, often pile one atop the other in a dense, contrapuntal texture. Finally, a cadential passage, coming at the end of a section or at the end of the piece, sounds repetitive because the same chords are heard again and again in a harmony that seems to have stopped moving forward. Each of these four styles has a specific function within sonata–allegro form: to state, to move, to develop, or to conclude. The ultimate aim of this process is to sway our emotions, but to do so in a way that is under control—formal control.

To test your ability to follow a movement composed in sonata–allegro form, turn to the first movement of Mozart's *Eine kleine Nachtmusik* (Figure 11.4). As the translated title, "A Little Night Music," suggests, this is a **serenade**, a light, multimovement piece for strings alone or a small orchestra, intended for an evening's entertainment and often performed outdoors. Although we do not know the precise occasion for which Mozart composed it, we might well imagine

FIGURE 11.4
Comedian, jazz artist, and improvisational singer Bobby McFerrin conducting the St. Paul Chamber Orchestra. McFerrin has conducted orchestras around the world and issued several recordings of Mozart, including *Eine kleine Nachtmusik*, discussed here.

Eine kleine Nachtmusik providing the musical backdrop for a torch-lit party in a formal Viennese garden.

Would Mozart's listeners have paid attention to the music or merely chatted and wandered about? Would Mozart have cared? Indeed, yes! Contemporary documents show that he demanded attentive listening to his music. Look at the highly detailed Listening Guide that follows. The cursory reader might engage only the essential section headings. But the true Mozart fan will read every word and follow along with the music—read-listen, read-listen, and so on. It is likely that this movement, one of the favorites in the Classical repertoire, will seem like an old friend. You've heard its elegant sounds in countless TV and online commercials where the ad intends to suggest that a particular product is "high end"—sophisticated music for you, the sophisticated consumer.

LISTENING GUIDE

Wolfgang Amadeus Mozart, *Eine kleine Nachtmusik* **(1787)**   Download 34 (5:40)

First movement, *Allegro* (fast)

Genre: Serenade

Form: Sonata–allegro

WHAT TO LISTEN FOR: The various structural divisions of sonata–allegro form

EXPOSITION

First Theme Group ([ ] = repeats)

0:00	[1:37]	The movement opens aggressively with a leaping, fanfare-like motive. It then moves on to a more confined, pressing melody with sixteenth notes agitating beneath, and it ends with a relaxed, stepwise descent down the scale, which is repeated with light ornamentation.	

Transition

0:30	[2:08]	This starts with two quick turns and then races up the scale in repeating sixteenth notes. The bass is at first static, but when it finally moves, it does so with great urgency, pushing the modulation forward to a cadence. The stage is then cleared by a brief pause, allowing the listener an "unobstructed view" of the new theme that is about to enter.	0:30 [2:08] Rapid scales 0:40 [2:18] Bass moves 0:45 [2:21] Cadence and pause

Second Theme

0:48   [2:24]   With its *piano* dynamic level and separating rests, the second theme sounds soft and delicate. It is soon overtaken by a light, somewhat humorous closing theme.

Closing Theme

1:01   [2:37]   The light quality of this melody is produced by its repeating note and the simple rocking of dominant-to-tonic harmony below. Toward the end, more substance is added when the music turns *forte*, and counterpoint appears in the bass. The bass's closing theme is then repeated, and a few cadential chords are tacked on to bring the exposition to an end.

1:07 [2:44] Loud; counterpoint in bass

1:14 [2:51] Closing theme repeated

1:33 [3:09] Cadential chords

1:37   The exposition is now repeated.

DEVELOPMENT

3:13   Just about anything can happen in a development, so the listener had best be on guard. Mozart begins with the fanfare-like first theme again in unison, as if this were yet another statement of the exposition. But abruptly the theme is altered and the tonal center slides up to a new key. Now the closing theme is heard, but soon it, too, begins to slide tonally, down through several keys that sound increasingly remote and bizarre. From this arises a unison scale (all parts move up stepwise together) in a dark-sounding minor key. The dominant note is held, first on top in the violins and then in the bass (3:46). This is the retransition. The mode changes from dark minor to bright major, and the first theme returns forcefully in the tonic key, signaling the beginning of the recapitulation.

3:13 First theme developed

3:17 Quick modulation

3:20 Closing theme developed

3:29 More modulations

3:37 Rising scale in unison

3:45 Retransition: held note (dominant) in violins and then bass

RECAPITULATION

3:48   It is this "double return" of both the tonic key and the first theme that makes the arrival of this and all recapitulations so satisfying. We expect the recapitulation to more or less duplicate the exposition, and this one holds true to form. The only

3:48 Loud return of first theme

4:18 Transition much abbreviated

4:32 Second theme

4:44 Closing theme

(Continued)

change comes, as usual, in the transition, or bridge, where the modulation to the dominant is simply omitted—there's no need to modulate to the dominant, since tradition demands that the second theme and the closing theme appear in the tonic.

4:59 Closing theme repeated

5:26 Cadential chords that ended the exposition are heard again.

CODA

5:28

A brief coda begins. It makes use of a fanfare motive strongly resembling that of the opening theme, but this one is supported below by a pounding tonic chord that drives home the feeling that the movement has come to an appropriate end.

LISTEN TO ... this selection streaming online.

WATCH ... an Active Listening Guide of this selection online.

WATCH ... a special animation of this selection online.

DO ... Listening Exercise 11.2, Mozart, *Eine kleine Nachtmusik*, I, online.

What we have just heard is an example of sonata–allegro form in miniature. Rarely has this musical form been produced in less time or space, and almost never as artfully.

But if sonata–allegro form applies only to instrumental genres such as the symphony and serenade, how can it appear in an opera? It can, in fact, work its way into an opera within the instrumental overtures that open Classical operas. A case in point is Mozart's overture to *Don Giovanni* (1787; see Listening Guide). Mozart begins this dramatic overture with a slow introduction in a minor key that incorporates some of the musical motives that we hear later in the opera. This slow, almost frightening beginning soon changes to a fast tempo, major key, and lighter mood at the start of the exposition—another lightning-quick transition in Classical music.

A discussion of another Classical movement in sonata–allegro form (Mozart's Symphony No. 40 in G minor, first movement) can be found in Chapter 13, along with a Listening Guide and an online Listening Exercise.

Finally, if you like the exciting overture to *Don Giovanni*, you'll love the opera itself (see Chapter 14, "Mozart and Opera"). The central character, Don Giovanni, is full of frightening ambiguities and in many ways served as the model for the Phantom in *Phantom of the Opera* (see Figure 14.2).

LISTENING GUIDE

Wolfgang Amadeus Mozart, Overture to *Don Giovanni* (1787)   Download 35 (5:58)

Genre: Opera overture

Form: Sonata-allegro

WHAT TO LISTEN FOR: Radically contrasting musical moods (and major and minor modes)—befitting an opera that is hugely dramatic and exciting—all unfolding within the tight confines of sonata-allegro form

INTRODUCTION

0:00	Slow, sinister chords give way to twisting chromaticism and finally to writhing scales, all of which suggest the evil nature of Don Giovanni.

EXPOSITION

1:57	First theme moves ahead rapidly.	
2:20	Transition starts with scalar theme presented in melodic sequence.	
2:30	Transition continues with unstable chords that build tension.	
2:35	Transition ends with strong cadence.	
2:39	Second theme marked by scalar descent and "bird-like fluttering" in woodwinds	
3:00	Light closing theme	

Because this is an opera overture, not a symphony, the exposition is not repeated.

DEVELOPMENT

3:18	Themes from exposition are heard in unexpected order: second theme, then first theme.
4:15	Retransition: gradual return to first theme

RECAPITULATION

4:23	Themes return in same order as in exposition.

CODA

5:43	No loud cadential chords to produce "big bang" ending; rather, orchestral fade out designed to coincide with raising of curtain and beginning of first scene

LISTEN TO ... this selection streaming online.

WATCH ... an Active Listening Guide of this selection online.

DO ... Listening Exercise 11.3, Mozart, Overture to *Don Giovanni*, online.

KEY WORDS

ternary (ABA) form (156)

relative major (minor) (156)

antecedent phrase (156)

consequent phrase (156)

triplet (156)

coda (157)

sonata–allegro form (159)

exposition (160)

transition (bridge) (160)

development (160)

retransition (160)

recapitulation (160)

serenade (161)

 Join us on Facebook at Listening to Music with Craig Wright

PRACTICE ... your understanding of this chapter's concepts by comparing Checklists of Musical Style for all historic eras and working once more with the chapter's Active Listening Guides online.

DO ... online multiple-choice and critical thinking quizzes that your instructor may assign for a grade.

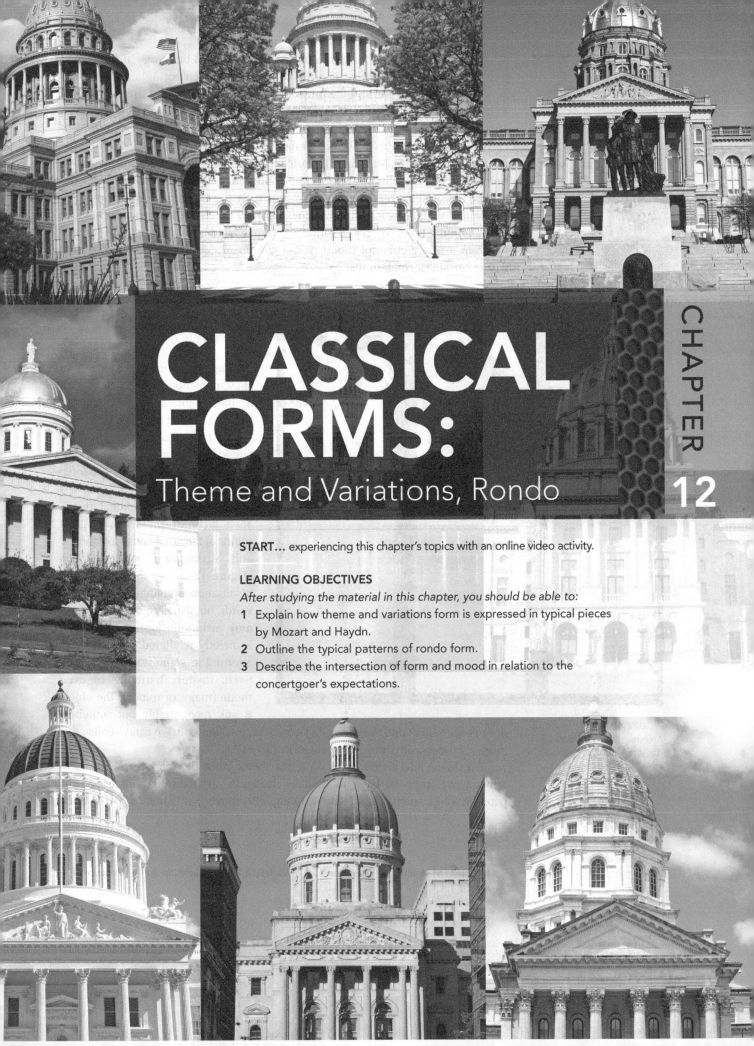

CLASSICAL FORMS:
Theme and Variations, Rondo

START… experiencing this chapter's topics with an online video activity.

LEARNING OBJECTIVES
After studying the material in this chapter, you should be able to:

1 Explain how theme and variations form is expressed in typical pieces by Mozart and Haydn.
2 Outline the typical patterns of rondo form.
3 Describe the intersection of form and mood in relation to the concertgoer's expectations.

READ... the complete chapter text in a rich, interactive online platform.

Did you ever notice that almost all state capitol buildings in the United States look more or less the same? The circular rotunda, topped by a solitary figure, and the projecting portico with columns are common to all, as they are to the capitols in this chapter's opening photo montage. These buildings likely look the same because the Founding Fathers viewed Neo-classical architecture as a way to symbolize and reinforce unity and traditional values within society. Musicians historically have valued traditional forms as well. Indeed, theme and variations form and rondo form have been around since the Middle Ages—since recorded time, for music. By the Classical period, a piece in theme and variations form might show just how inventive a composer could be with a popular tune, whereas a rondo was often called upon to send the audience home in a newly cheerful mood. Yes, a composer could be original—but only within certain (formal) limits.

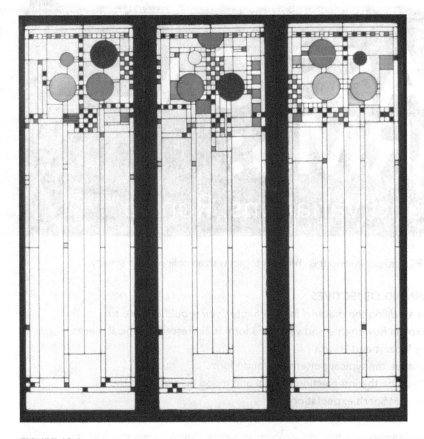

FIGURE 12.1
Architect Frank Lloyd Wright demonstrated the creative artist's age-old desire to vary a theme when he fashioned these stained-glass windows for a children's school in Illinois in 1912. These are only three of a dozen such windows he created, all very similar, yet different.

Theme and Variations

In the film *Amadeus*, Mozart is shown composing variations on a theme of another composer (Salieri), tossing them off effortlessly like a magician pulling handkerchiefs from his sleeve. The compulsion to endlessly reimagine a song, an object, or a grammatical phrase is called the "transformational imperative," an urge expressed by the great minds of Mozart, Leonardo da Vinci, and Shakespeare, among others (Figure 12.1). In music, the object of variation is neither an image nor words, but usually a melody. **Theme and variations** form occurs when a melody is altered, decorated, or adorned in some way by changing pitch, rhythm, harmony, or even mode (major or minor). The object is still recognizable but somehow doesn't seem to sound the same. As we've seen in Chapter 3, we can visualize this musical process with the scheme shown in Table 12.1.

For theme and variations to work, the theme must be well known or easy to remember. Composers have traditionally chosen to vary folksongs and, especially, patriotic songs, such as "God Save the King" (Beethoven) or "America" (Ives). Such

TABLE 12.1 Theme and Variations Form

Statement of theme	Variation 1	Variation 2	Variation 3	Variation 4
A	A^1	A^2	A^3	A^4

tunes are popular, in part because they are simple, and this, too, is an advantage for the composer. Melodies that are spare and uncluttered can more easily be dressed in new musical clothing.

Broadly speaking, a musical variation can be effected in either of two ways: (1) by changing the theme itself or (2) by changing the context around that theme (the accompaniment). Sometimes, these two techniques are used simultaneously. The two examples that follow—one by Mozart and one by Haydn—illustrate a number of techniques for varying a melody and its context. In a set of variations, whether in the fine arts or music, the farther one moves from the initial theme, the more obscure it becomes. For the listener, the primary task is to keep track of the tune as it is altered in increasingly complex ways.

Mozart: Variations on "Twinkle, Twinkle, Little Star" (c. 1781)

In the Classical period, it was common for a composer/pianist to improvise in concert a set of variations on a well-known tune, perhaps one that was requested spontaneously by the audience. Contemporary reports tell us that Mozart was especially skilled in this type of improvisation. In the early 1780s, Mozart wrote down a set of such improvised variations built on the French folksong, "Ah, vous dirai-je, Maman," the melody of which we know today as "Twinkle, Twinkle, Little Star" (see Listening Guide). With such a well-known tune as this, it is easy to follow the melody, even as it becomes increasingly ornamented and its accompaniment altered in the course of twelve variations. (Only the first eight bars of the theme are given in Example 12.1; the complete tune is given in Example 11.1. The music through the first five variations can be heard in Download 6 or in the Active Listening Guide in both Chapter 3 and Chapter 12.)

EXAMPLE 12.1A "Twinkle, Twinkle, Little Star," basic theme (0:00)

LISTEN TO...
Example 12.1A online.

Variation 1 (Example 12.1B) ornaments the theme and almost buries it beneath an avalanche of sixteenth notes. Would you know that "Twinkle, Twinkle, Little Star" lurks herein (see the asterisks) if you did not have the tune securely in your ear?

EXAMPLE 12.1B Variation 1 (0:31)

LISTEN TO...
Example 12.1B online.

In variation 2 (Example 12.1C), the rushing ornamentation is transferred to the bass (the accompaniment is changed), and the theme surfaces again rather clearly in the upper voice.

LISTEN TO...

Example 12.1C online.

EXAMPLE 12.1C Variation 2 (0:57)

In variation 3 (Example 12.1D), triplets in the right hand alter the theme, which is now only recognizable by its general contour.

EXAMPLE 12.1D Variation 3 (1:24)

LISTEN TO...

Example 12.1D online.

After the same technique has been applied to the bass (variation 4; 1:52), a thematic alteration again occurs in variation 5 (Example 12.1E). Here, the rhythm of the melody is "jazzed up" by placing part of it off the beat, in syncopated fashion.

EXAMPLE 12.1E Variation 5 (2:20)

LISTEN TO...

Example 12.1E online.

Of the remaining seven variations, some change the tune to minor, while others add Bach-like counterpoint against it. The final variation presents this duple-meter folk tune reworked into a triple-meter waltz! Yet, throughout all of Mozart's magical embroidery, the theme remains audible in our internal ear, so well ingrained is "Twinkle, Twinkle, Little Star" in our musical memory.

Haydn: Symphony No. 94 (the "Surprise" Symphony, 1792), Second Movement

Mozart composed his set of variations on "Twinkle, Twinkle, Little Star" as a free-standing, independent piece. Joseph Haydn (1732–1809) was the first composer to take theme and variations form and use it for a movement within a symphony. To be sure, Haydn was an innovative artist—he could "surprise" or "shock" as no other composer of the Classical period. In his "Surprise" Symphony, the shock comes in the form of a sudden *fortissimo* chord inserted, as we shall see, into the second movement in the middle of an otherwise serene theme. When Haydn's

Wolfgang Amadeus Mozart, Variations on "Twinkle, Twinkle, Little Star" Download 6 (2:58)

Genre: Keyboard movement

Form: Theme and variations

WHAT TO LISTEN FOR: The theme, or its accompaniment, is varied from one statement to the next, each presentation lasting about thirty seconds.

0:00	**A**	Tune played without ornamentation; melody above, harmony below
0:31	**A¹**	Variation 1: Tune above decorated with florid, fast-moving figurations
0:57	**A²**	Variation 2: Tune above undecorated; florid, fast-moving figurations now in bass
1:24	**A³**	Variation 3: Tune above decorated with graceful arpeggios
1:52	**A⁴**	Variation 4: Tune above with chords; fast-moving triplets in bass
2:20	**A⁵**	Variation 5: Tune syncopated above

LISTEN TO ... this selection streaming online.

WATCH ... an Active Listening Guide of this selection online.

Symphony No. 94 was first heard in London in 1792 (Figure 12.2), the audience cheered this second movement and demanded its immediate repetition. Ever since, this surprising movement has been Haydn's most celebrated composition.

The famous opening melody of the second movement (*Andante*) is written in binary form, a simple **AB** arrangement. Here, **A** is an eight-bar antecedent (opening) phrase, and **B** is an eight-bar consequent (closing) phrase—a prime example of Classical balance. Notice how the beginning of the theme (see Listening Guide) is

FIGURE 12.2
The Hanover Square Rooms in London, the hall in which Haydn's "Surprise" Symphony was first performed in 1792. Designed for an audience of 800 to 900, nearly 1,500 people crowded in for the performances of these London Symphonies.

shaped by laying out in succession the notes of a tonic triad (I) and then a dominant chord (V). The triadic nature of the tune accounts for its folk-song-like quality and makes it easy to remember during the variations that follow. These first eight bars (**A**) are stated and then repeated quietly. And just when all is ending peacefully, the full orchestra, including a thunderous timpani, comes crashing in with a *fortissimo* chord (see asterisk in Listening Guide), as if to shock the drowsy listener back to attention. What better way to show off the latent dynamic power of the larger Classical orchestra? The surprise *fortissimo* chord leads into the **B** section of the theme, which also is repeated. With the simple yet highly attractive binary theme now in place, Haydn proceeds to compose four variations on it, adding a superb coda at the end. In his memoirs, dictated in 1809, Haydn explains that he included the surprise blast as something of a publicity stunt, "to make a début in a brilliant manner," and thereby call further attention to his concerts in London.

Listening to this theme and variations movement by Haydn (Figure 12.3) requires hearing discrete units of music. Each block (variation) is marked by some new treatment of the theme or the accompaniment. In the Classical period, all the units are usually the same size—that is, they have the same number of measures. The variations become progressively more complicated as more ornamentation and transformation are applied, but each unit remains the same length. The addition of a coda after the last variation gives extra weight to the end, so the listener feels that the set of variations has reached an appropriate conclusion. If such extra bars were not appended, the audience would be left hanging, expecting yet another variation to begin.

FIGURE 12.3
A portrait of Joseph Haydn at work. His left hand is trying an idea at the keyboard while his right is ready to write it down. Haydn said about his compositional process: "I sat down at the keyboard and began to improvise. Once I had seized upon an idea, my whole effort was to develop and sustain it."

LISTENING GUIDE

Joseph Haydn, Symphony No. 94, the "Surprise" Symphony (1791)   Download 7 (6:25)

Second movement, *Andante* (moving)

Genre: Symphony

Form: Theme and variations

WHAT TO LISTEN FOR: The seemingly endless number of ways in which a master composer such as Haydn can vary a very simple tune

THEME

0:00   **A** First part of theme

0:17   **A** repeated softly, with second violins adding
         chords to accompaniment and then *fortissimo*
         chord at end

| 0:33 | **B** Second part of theme |

| 0:50 | **B** repeated, with flute and oboe added |

VARIATION 1

| 1:06 | **A** played by second violins while first violins and flute add counterpoint above |

1:24	**A** repeated
1:41	**B** with counterpoint continuing above in first violins and flutes
1:57	**B** repeated

VARIATION 2

| 2:14 | **A** played loud and in minor key; shift (2:23) to a rich major chord |

2:30	**A** repeated (variation of **B** omitted)
2:46	Full orchestra develops **A** in minor key
3:14	First violins alone, playing in unison

VARIATION 3

| 3:23 | **A** ornamented rapidly by oboe |
| 3:39 | **A** repeated; melody in strings, with oboe and flute ornamenting above |

| 3:56 | **B** now in strings, with oboe and flute ornamenting above |
| 4:13 | **B** repeated |

VARIATION 4

| 4:29 | **A** loud, in full orchestra, with violins playing running arpeggios |
| 4:45 | **A** repeated, with theme rhythmically varied |

5:03	**B** varied further by violins
5:20	**B** repeated loudly by full orchestra
5:37	Transition to coda; pause (5:45)

(Continued)

5:51   Reminiscences of theme in its original form

LISTEN TO ... this selection streaming online.

WATCH ... an Active Listening Guide of this selection online.

WATCH ... a unique visual animation of this selection online.

DO ... Listening Exercise 12.1, Haydn, Symphony No. 94, the "Surprise" Symphony, II, online.

FIGURE 12.4
A natural trumpet fabricated in Germany around 1800. On such an instrument musicians could play a full scale only in the higher part of the register—and even then only with difficulty.

Rondo Form

Of all musical forms, the rondo is perhaps the easiest to hear, because a single, unvaried theme (the refrain) returns again and again. The rondo is also one of the oldest musical forms, having originated in the Middle Ages. The Baroque era made frequent use of rondo principles, and even contemporary pop songs occasionally employ this form (see the rondo by Sting at the end of this chapter). A true Classical **rondo** must have at least three statements of the refrain (**A**) and at least two contrasting sections (at least **B** and **C**). Often the placement of the refrain creates symmetrical patterns, such as **ABACA**, **ABACABA**, or even **ABACADA**. When Haydn and Mozart set about writing a rondo, they incorporated some of the same musical processes that they used when writing in sonata–allegro form, specifically transitional and developmental writing. They thereby created a more elastic, flexible rondo in which the refrain (**A**) and the contrasting sections (**B**, **C**, or **D**) might develop and expand dramatically.

The rondo is typically light, quick, and jovial in nature. Classical composers most often chose the rondo form for the last movement, the **finale** (Italian for "end") of a sonata, quartet, or symphony. The carefree tune and the easily grasped digressions lend to the rondo finale an "upbeat" feeling, the musical equivalent of a happy ending.

Haydn: Trumpet Concerto in E♭ major (1796), Third Movement (Finale)

Listening to Haydn's Trumpet Concerto in E♭ major (see Listening Guide) makes us think about the construction of the trumpet—and the French horn as well—around the turn of the nineteenth century. Before 1800, both the trumpet and the horn were natural instruments, without valves (Figure 12.4). On them musicians could play successive intervals of an octave and fifth, and even those of a triad, by "overblowing" (as you can overblow an octave on a recorder, for example). But even great virtuosos had difficulty playing all the notes of a scale perfectly in tune. Moreover, because *over*blowing produces only higher pitches, not lower ones, the trumpet could play very few low notes.

To remedy these deficiencies, a Viennese trumpeter and friend of Haydn, Anton Weidinger (1767–1852), came up with a new design for his instrument. He had the brass of the trumpet pierced with holes that could be covered with movable keypads, anticipating the approach used on woodwinds today. In 1796, Haydn wrote a concerto for Weidinger and his new trumpet. Judging from the reviews of the first performance, the sound of Weidinger's instrument was muffled and unpleasant. In fact, this "covering keypad" approach was soon abandoned; the trumpet thereafter remained "natural" until around 1830, when a wholly new valve-type mechanism was invented for it—and the French horn as well (see Figure 16.2). Yet, because his concerto exploits the full range of our modern instrument, Haydn must have intuited that Weidinger was headed in the right direction and that technology would catch up with his innovative idea.

Not only has the trumpet changed since Haydn's day, so, too, have trumpeters. Yes, the jaunty, irrepressible rondo theme dominates the movement, and its placement creates an **ABABACABA** form (see Listening Guide). But notice toward the end of the movement how the driving orchestra reaches a point of arrival and then holds a chord (at 4:08). Haydn surely intended this sustained chord to be a platform from which the soloist would launch into a flashy cadenza (a brilliant technical display by the soloist alone), as was the custom of the day. However, Haydn left no music for the cadenza. He assumed that any good performer could, and would want to, improvise his own. Today, such improvisation by classical performers is a lost art, and the soloist in the Listening Guide, Wynton Marsalis, simply leaves a few seconds of silence. If you are so inclined, when you get to that spot, hum a few bars to fill in—Haydn's spirit would applaud your creativity!

LISTENING GUIDE

Franz Joseph Haydn, Trumpet Concerto in E♭ major (1796)

Download 36 (4:34)

Third movement, *Allegro* (fast)

Genre: Concerto

Form: Rondo

WHAT TO LISTEN FOR: Who can miss the constant return of the rondo theme as it gradually forms an **ABABACABA** structure?

Time	Description	Section
0:00	**A** (refrain) played first by strings and then by full orchestra	A
0:22	**B** played by full orchestra	B
0:39	**A** played by trumpet	A
1:08	**B** played by trumpet with trills added	B
1:52	After a slight pause, trumpet plays.	A
2:14	Quick modulations to new minor keys	C
2:40	**A** returns in trumpet.	A
2:57	**B** returns in trumpet.	B
3:55	String tremolos build tension, leading to pause	
4:09	Return of **A** accelerates and drives to end.	A

(Continued)

LISTEN TO ... this selection streaming online.

WATCH ... an Active Listening Guide of this selection online.

WATCH ... a trumpeter play the cadenza of this selection—and interrupt to propose marriage to his girlfriend.

DO ... Listening Exercise 12.2, Haydn, Trumpet Concerto in E♭ major, online.

Form, Mood, and the Listener's Expectations

In many ways, going to a concert of classical music is like going to an art museum—except that the musical exhibition is given only at a particular day and time. Today, when we attend a concert to hear an overture by Mozart, a symphony by Haydn,

A RONDO BY STING

Although the rondo form has existed in what we call "classical music" since the Middle Ages, it appears often in the realm of folk and popular music as well. For example, the pop tune "Every Breath You Take," composed by Sting and recorded in 1983 by his New Wave group, The Police, produces a rondo pattern (**ABA-CABA**) that in its symmetrical, indeed palindromic, shape would do any Classical composer proud. This song has now been around for more than thirty years and has been the object of more than fifty "covers," extending to almost every pop idiom, including rap in a version by Puff Daddy. It has even crossed over into the classical-pop repertoire, having been recorded by both the London Philharmonic Orchestra and the Royal Philharmonic Orchestra.

Every breath you take ...	**A**
Can't you see ...	**B**
Every move you make ...	**A**
Since you've gone ...	**C**
[Instrumental interlude to **A** music]	**A**
Can't you see ...	**B**
Every move you make ...	**A**

WATCH... The Police's "Every Breath You Take," a rondo by Sting, online.

TABLE 12.2 Four-movement symphony

Movement	1	2	3	4
Tempo	Fast	Slow	Lively	Fast
Form	Sonata– allegro	Large ternary, theme and variations, or rondo	Minuet and trio in ternary form	Sonata–allegro, theme and variations, or rondo
Mood	Serious and substantive despite fast tempo	Lyrical and tender	Usually light and elegant; sometimes spirited	Bright, lighthearted; sometimes humorous

or a concerto by Beethoven, we revisit music that the orchestra has played in that hall many times over the years. These favorite overtures, symphonies, and concertos belong to the **canon** (standard repertoire, or "chestnuts") of Western classical music.

When concertgoers stepped into a hall in the late eighteenth century, however, they expected all of the music to be new and up to date—why would anyone want to hear old music? But, while the late-eighteenth-century audience didn't know the pieces in advance, listeners did come with certain expectations, not only about the musical form, but also about the mood of the music. For the Classical period, we might summarize these as in Table 12.2.

As we shall see, Ludwig van Beethoven (1770–1827) and later composers of the Romantic era (1820–1900) modified somewhat this conventional format. Yet, the Classical model of what was good and worthy of repeated performance—the Classical canon—continued to gain force among music listeners. Succeeding generations not only wanted to hear "new" music but also increasingly demanded a return to certain tried-and-true works of Haydn, Mozart, and their later contemporary, Beethoven. Oddly, a similar sort of canon has developed for pop music today. At pop concerts, the audience gets most revved up hearing, not the featured artist's new songs, but rather the artist's beloved signature tunes. When the canon sounds at either venue, classical or popular, the crowd feels a collective sense of excitement: This is part of history. This has lasting value. This is what we came for!

KEY WORDS

theme and variations (168)   rondo (174)   finale (174)   canon (of Western music) (177)

f Join us on Facebook at Listening to Music with Craig Wright

PRACTICE ... your understanding of this chapter's concepts by comparing Checklists of Musical Style for all historic eras and working once more with the chapter's Active Listening Guides online.

DO ... online multiple-choice and critical thinking quizzes that your instructor may assign for a grade.

CLASSICAL GENRES:

Instrumental Music

START... experiencing this chapter's topics with an online video activity.

LEARNING OBJECTIVES

After studying the material in this chapter, you should be able to:

1 Understand the makeup of a typical symphony orchestra during the Classical period.

2 Describe how a string quartet ensemble differs from a symphony orchestra and differentiate the kind of music written for each.

3 Explain how sonata–allegro form expands to provide a framework for the first movement of a concerto.

n music, the term *genre* means simply the type or class of music to which we listen (see also Chapter 1). The string quartet is a genre of music, just as are the opera overture, country music ballad, twelve-bar blues piece, military march, and rap song. When we listen to a piece of music, we come armed with expectations as to how it will sound, how long it will last, and how we should behave in response to it. We may even go to a special place—an opera house or a bar—and dress a certain way—in gown and diamond earrings or in black leather jacket and nose rings, for example. It all depends on the genre of music we expect to hear. To hear a Mozart symphony, it's best not to go to a bar.

In the age of Haydn and Mozart, there were five main genres of art music: the instrumental genres of symphony, string quartet, sonata, and concerto, and the vocal genre of opera. Whereas the sonata, concerto, and opera emerged during the Baroque era, the symphony and string quartet were entirely new to the Classical period. Thus, we begin our exploration of Classical genres with the instrumental symphony and quartet.

The Symphony and the Symphony Orchestra

A **symphony** is a multimovement composition for orchestra, lasting from about twenty-five minutes in the Classical period to nearly an hour in the Romantic era. The origins of the symphony go back to the late-seventeenth-century Italian opera house, where an opera began with an instrumental *sinfonia* (literally, "a harmonious sounding together"). Around 1700, the typical Italian *sinfonia* was a one-movement instrumental work in three sections: fast–slow–fast. Soon, Italian musicians and foreigners alike took the *sinfonia* out of the opera house and expanded it into three separate and distinct movements. A fourth movement, the minuet, was inserted by composers north of the Alps beginning in the 1740s. Thus, by midcentury, the symphony had assumed its now-familiar four-movement format: fast–slow–minuet–fast (see "Form, Mood, and the Listener's Expectations" in Chapter 12). While the movements of a symphony are usually independent with regard to musical themes, all are written in a single key (or set of closely related keys).

As public concerts became more common during the Classical period, the symphony increased in popularity. The larger public halls accommodated more people, and the bigger audiences enjoyed the more robust, colorful sound of the Classical orchestra. The four-movement symphony was the best format in which to convey that sound. The fact that Haydn composed so many (106), and Mozart (given his short life) an even more astonishing number (41), shows that by the end of the eighteenth century, the symphony had become the foremost instrumental genre, the showpiece of the concert hall. All but a few of Haydn's last twenty symphonies were composed for public performance in Paris and London, and Mozart's last four symphonies were intended for public concerts that he himself produced. His famous G minor symphony (1788), for example, was apparently first performed in a casino in central Vienna (Figure 13.1)—that's where the people were, and that's where the money was. So dominant did the genre of the "symphony" become that it gave its name to the concert "hall" and the performing "orchestra," thus creating our terms *symphony hall* and *symphony orchestra*.

FIGURE 13.1
The New Market in Vienna, painted by Canaletto in 1760. In the distance is the spire of the cathedral of St. Stephen (where Mozart was married); the large building to the right housed the city casino (today the Ambassador Hotel). Here, in 1788, Mozart premiered his G minor symphony. Even today, famous musicians, such as Yo-Yo Ma and Taylor Swift, perform in casinos, because that's where the money is!

The Classical Symphony Orchestra

As the symphony orchestra moved from private court to public auditorium, the ensemble increased in size to satisfy the demands of its new performance space—and expanding audience. During the 1760s and 1770s, the ensemble at the court of Haydn's patron, Prince Nikolaus Esterházy, was never larger than twenty-five musicians, and the audience at this court was often only the prince and his staff (Figure 13.2). But, when Haydn went to London in 1791, his concert promoters provided him with an orchestra of nearly sixty players in the Hanover Square Rooms (see Figure 12.1). Although this hall normally accommodated 800 to 900 persons, for one concert in the spring of 1792 nearly 1,500 eager listeners crowded in to hear Haydn's latest works.

Mozart's experience in Vienna was similar. For the public concerts that he mounted in the casino in the mid-1780s, he engaged an orchestra of about thirty-five players. But, in a letter from 1781, he mentions an orchestra of eighty instrumentalists, including forty violins, ten violas, eight cellos, and ten double basses. Although this was an exceptional ensemble, brought together for a special charity benefit concert, it shows that at times a very large group could be assembled. It also reveals that a large number of string players could be assigned to play just one string part—as many as twenty might "double" each other on the first violin line, for example.

To balance the growth in the string section and to increase the variety of color in the orchestra, more winds were added. By the 1790s, a typical symphony orchestra in a large European city might include the instrumentalists listed below. Compared to the Baroque orchestra, this ensemble of up to forty players was larger, more colorful, and more flexible. Moreover, within the Classical orchestra, each instrumental family had a specific assignment: The strings presented the bulk of the musical material; the woodwinds added richness and colorful counterpoint; the French horns sustained a sonorous background; and the trumpets and percussion provided brilliance when a magnificent sound was needed (see Table 13.1).

FIGURE 13.2
A watercolor from 1775 shows Haydn leading the small orchestra at the court of the Esterházy princes during a performance of a comic opera. The composer is seated at the keyboard, surrounded by the cellos. The higher strings and woodwinds are seated in two rows at the desk.

Mozart: Symphony No. 40 in G minor (1788), K. 550

In his short lifetime, Mozart wrote 41 symphonies and more than 650 compositions in all. To help us keep track of this enormous amount of music, a nineteenth-century musicologist, Ludwig von Köchel, published a list of Mozart's works in approximately chronological order, assigning each a **Köchel (K) number**. The need for such a numbering system is obvious because Mozart actually wrote two symphonies in G minor: a short, early one (which accompanies the opening of the film *Amadeus*), K. 183, and a longer, later symphony in G minor, K. 550, to which we now turn.

Mozart's celebrated Symphony in G minor requires all the full instrumental sound and disciplined playing that the late-eighteenth-century orchestra could muster. This is not a festive composition (hence, no trumpets and drums) but, rather, an intensely brooding work that suggests tragedy and despair. Though we might be tempted to associate the minor key and despondent mood with a specific event in Mozart's life, apparently no such causal relationship exists. This was one of three symphonies that Mozart produced in the short span of six weeks during the summer of 1788, and the other two are sunny, optimistic works. Rather than responding to a particular disappointment, it is more likely that Mozart invoked the tragic muse in this G minor symphony by drawing on a lifetime of disappointments and a premonition—as his letters attest—of an early death.

To get the most out of the following discussion, have the diagram of sonata-allegro form (Figure 11.3) firmly in mind.

TABLE 13.1 The Classical symphony orchestra

Strings	1st violins, 2nd violins, violas, cellos, double basses (about 27 players in all)
Woodwinds	2 flutes, 2 oboes, 2 clarinets, 2 bassoons
Brasses	2 French horns, 2 trumpets (for festive pieces)
Percussion	2 timpani (for festive pieces)

First Movement (*Molto Allegro*)

Exposition Mozart begins his G minor symphony with a textbook example of Classical phrase structure (four-bar antecedent, four-bar consequent phrases; Example 13.1). Yet, an unusual sense of urgency is created immediately by a throbbing accompaniment and the repeating, insistent eighth-note figure in the melody. This melodic motive, the most memorable aspect in the movement, is a falling half step (here E♭ to D), a tight interval used throughout the history of music to denote pain and suffering.

LISTEN TO...

Example 13.1 online.

EXAMPLE 13.1 Antecedent–consequent phrase structure

Less immediately audible but still contributing equally to the sense of urgency is the accelerating rate of harmonic change. At the outset of the movement, chords are set beneath the melody at an interval of one chord every four measures, then one every two bars, then one every measure, then two chords per measure, and finally four. Thus, the "harmonic rhythm" is moving sixteen times faster at the end of this section than at the beginning! This is how Mozart creates the sense of drive and urgency that we all feel yet may be unable to explain.

After this quickening start, the first theme begins once again but soon veers off course, initiating the transition. Transitions take us somewhere, usually by means of running scales, and this one is no exception. But a new motive is inserted, one so distinctive that we might call it a "transition theme" (see the example in the following Listening Guide). As if to reciprocate for an extra theme here, Mozart dispenses with one toward the end of the exposition, at the point where we would expect a closing theme to appear. To end, Mozart simply alludes to the feverish motive of the first theme to round off the exposition. Then comes the question: "To repeat or not repeat"—although Mozart wished his performers do so, today the decision to repeat the exposition is left to the conductor.

Development Developments develop, and this one is no exception. Here, Mozart subjects the first theme—and only the first theme—to a variety of musical alterations. First, he pushes it through several distantly related keys, then shapes it into the subject of a brief fugue, then sets it as a descending melodic sequence, and finally turns the motive on its head (Example 13.2)—what went down now goes up!

LISTEN TO...

Example 13.2 online.

EXAMPLE 13.2 The motive inverted

The retransition (journey back to the main theme and tonic key) is suddenly interrupted by *sforzandi* (loud attacks). But soon a dominant pedal point sounds in the bassoons, and above it the flute and clarinets descend, cascading gradually like a waterfall back to the tonic pitch. This use of colorful, solo woodwinds in the retransition is a hallmark of Mozart's symphonic style.

Recapitulation As expected, the recapitulation offers the themes in the same order in which they appeared in the exposition. But there are changes in the recapitulation: The transition is greatly extended, becoming something akin to a second development, and the sweet second theme returns (as it should) in tonic minor but now sounds somber, even depressive. Because the repeating motive of the first theme rounds off the recapitulation by way of a closing theme, only the briefest coda is needed to end this passionate, haunting movement.

LISTENING GUIDE

Wolfgang Amadeus Mozart, Symphony No. 40 in G minor (1788), K. 550   Download 37 (7:19)

First movement, *Molto allegro* (very fast)

Genre: Symphony

Form: Sonata–allegro

WHAT TO LISTEN FOR: While the divisions within sonata–allegro form are important to hear, in this movement Mozart wants to convey a feeling of anxiety, even despair, through his use of the minor mode and the "painful" half-step theme.

EXPOSITION ([ ] = REPEAT)

0:00	[1:49]	Urgent, insistent first theme
0:21	[2:10]	First theme begins to repeat but is cut short.
0:30	[2:18]	Transition
0:36	[2:23]	Rapid, ascending scales
0:44	[2:32]	Strong cadence ending transition; pause to clear air
0:47	[2:35]	Lyrical second theme and major key contribute to brighter mood.
0:57	[2:44]	Second theme repeated with new orchestration
1:07	[2:54]	Crescendo leads to closing material (taken from first theme); abrupt stop

DEVELOPMENT

3:34	First theme modulates through several distant keys.
3:51	First theme used as fugue subject in fugato in basses and then violins
4:12	First theme reduced to just opening motive
4:32	*Sforzandi* (loud attacks) give way to retransition.
4:39	Retransition: dominant pedal point in bassoons as music cascades downward

(Continued)

RECAPITULATION

4:45	First theme returns.
5:06	First theme begins to repeat but is cut off by transition.
5:15	Transition theme returns but is greatly extended.
5:41	Rapid, ascending scales
5:49	Cadence and pause
5:53	Second theme now in (tonic) minor
6:01	Second theme repeated with new orchestration
6:12	Return of crescendo, which leads to closing material (taken from first theme)

CODA

6:51	Begins with rising chromatic scale
6:56	Opening motive returns, then three final chords.

LISTEN TO ... this selection streaming online.

WATCH ... an Active Listening Guide of this selection online.

DO ... Listening Exercise 13.1, Mozart, Symphony No. 40 in G minor, I, online.

Second Movement (*Andante*)

After the feverish excitement of the opening movement, the slow, lyrical *Andante* comes as a welcome change of pace. What makes this movement exceptionally beautiful is the extraordinary interplay between the light and dark colors of the woodwinds against the constant tone of the strings. If no thematic contrast and confrontation can be found here, there is, nonetheless, heartfelt expression brought about by Mozart's masterful use of orchestral color.

Third Movement (*Menuetto: Allegretto*)

We expect the aristocratic minuet to provide elegant, graceful dance music. But much to our surprise, Mozart returns to the intense, somber mood of the opening movement. This he does, in part, by choosing to write in the tonic minor key—a rare minuet in minor. This again demonstrates how the minuet had changed from "dance music" to "listening music."

Fourth Movement (*Allegro Assai*)

The finale starts with an ascending "rocket" that explodes in a rapid, *forte* flourish—and only carefully rehearsed string playing can pull off the brilliant effect of this opening gesture. As the movement proceeds, compression takes hold: There is no retransition, only a pregnant pause before the recapitulation; the return dispenses with the repeats built into the first theme; and a coda is omitted. This musical foreshortening produces the same psychological effect experienced at the very beginning of the symphony—a feeling of urgency and acceleration to the very end.

The String Quartet

The symphony is the ideal genre for the public concert hall, for it aims to please a large number of listeners by employing a large musical ensemble. The **string quartet**, on the other hand, typifies chamber music—music for the small concert hall, for the private chamber, or just for the enjoyment of the performers themselves (Figure 13.3). Like the symphony, the string quartet normally has four movements, all unified by a common key. But, unlike the symphony, which might have a dozen violinists joining on the first violin line, the string quartet features only one player per part: first violinist, second violinist, violist, and cellist. Such an intimate ensemble has no need for a conductor; all performers function equally and communicate directly among themselves. No wonder the German poet Johann Wolfgang von Goethe (1749–1832) compared the string quartet to a conversation among four rational people.

Joseph Haydn is rightly called "the father of the string quartet." In the 1760s and 1770s, he began to compose music for four string instruments requiring a new, more agile kind of interaction. From the old Baroque model, Haydn removed the heavy *basso continuo*, replacing it with a more melodically active bass played by a nimble cello alone. He also enriched the middle of the texture by adding a viola, playing immediately above the cello. If Baroque music had a "top- and bottom-heavy" texture (see Figure 6.7), the newer, Classical string quartet style showed a texture covered evenly by four agile instruments, each of which participated more or less equally in a give-and-take of theme and motive—musical democracy at its best (Example 13.3).

EXAMPLE 13.3 Equality within the quartet

The chance to play string quartets together gave rise to a lasting friendship between Haydn and Mozart. During 1784 and 1785, the two men met in Vienna, sometimes at the home of an aristocrat and at other times in Mozart's own apartment. In their quartet, Haydn played first violin, and Mozart played viola. As a result of this experience, Mozart was inspired to dedicate a set of his best works in this genre to the older master, which he published in 1785 (Figure 13.4). Yet, in this convivial, domestic music-making, Haydn and Mozart merely joined in the fashion of the day. For whether in Vienna, Paris, or London, aristocrats and members of the well-to-do middle class were encouraged to play quartets with friends, as well as to engage professional musicians to entertain their guests.

FIGURE 13.4
Title page of six string quartets by Mozart, which Mozart dedicated to Haydn (1785). Mozart offers them to Haydn as "six children," asking Haydn to be their "father, guide, and friend."

LISTEN TO...

Example 13.4 online.

FIGURE 13.5
Franz II (1765–1835), last Holy Roman Emperor and first emperor of Austria. Haydn composed "The Emperor's Hymn" in his honor.

Haydn: Opus 76, No. 3, the "Emperor" Quartet (1797)

Haydn's "Emperor" Quartet, written in Vienna during the summer of 1797, numbers among the best works of the string quartet genre. Known as the "Emperor," it makes liberal use of "The Emperor's Hymn," a melody that Haydn composed in response to the military and political events of his day.

In 1796, the armies of Napoleon invaded the Austrian Empire, which ignited a firestorm of patriotism in Vienna, the Austrian capital. But the Austrians were at a musical disadvantage: The French had their "Marseillaise," and the English their "God Save the King," but the Austrians had no national anthem. To this end, the ministers of state approached Haydn, who quickly fashioned one to the text, "Gott erhalte Franz den Kaiser" ("God Preserve Franz the Emperor"; Example 13.4), in honor of the reigning Austrian Emperor Franz II (Figure 13.5). Called "The Emperor's Hymn," it was first sung in theaters throughout the Austrian realm on the emperor's birthday, February 12, 1797. Later that year, Haydn took the tune and worked it into a string quartet.

EXAMPLE 13.4 "Gott erhalte Franz den Kaiser"

In truth, when Haydn fashioned quartet Opus 76, No. 3, he made use of his imperial hymn, not in all four movements, but only in the slow second movement (see Listening Guide). Here, it serves as the basis of a theme and variations set. The noble theme is first presented by the first violin and is harmonized in simple chords. Thereafter, four variations ensue, and each instrument has its turn at presenting the melody. In successive variation, the accompaniment (context) changes, but the theme remains unaltered. Presumably, one did not tinker with the musical personification of the emperor.

The popularity of "The Emperor's Hymn" did not end with the defeat of Napoleon in 1815 or the death of Emperor Franz II in 1835. So alluring is Haydn's melody that with altered text it became a Protestant hymn ("Glorious Things of Thee Are Spoken") as well as the

LISTENING GUIDE

Franz Joseph Haydn, String Quartet, Opus 76, No. 3, the "Emperor" Quartet (1797)   Download 38 (7:39)

Second movement, *Poco adagio cantabile* (rather slow, song-like)

Genre: String quartet

Form: Theme and variations

WHAT TO LISTEN FOR: Emperor's theme, followed by four variations in which the second violin, cello, viola, and first violin present the theme. Can you tell which one has the theme at a given moment?

THEME

    0:00   Theme played slowly in first violin; lower three parts provide chordal accompaniment.

VARIATION 1

    1:20   Theme in second violin while first violin ornaments above

VARIATION 2

    2:29   Theme in cello while other three instruments provide counterpoint against it

VARIATION 3

    3.47   Theme in viola; other three instruments enter gradually.

VARIATION 4

    5:04   Theme returns to first violin, but now accompaniment is more contrapuntal than chordal.

LISTEN TO ... this selection streaming online.

WATCH ... an Active Listening Guide of this selection online.

WATCH ... a video of this selection online.

DO ... Listening Exercise 13.2, Haydn, "Emperor" Quartet, II, online.

---

national anthem of Austria (1853) and Germany (1922). It was also Haydn's own favorite piece, and he played a piano arrangement of it every night before retiring. In fact, "The Emperor's Hymn" was the last music Haydn played before he died in the early hours of May 31, 1809 (Figure 13.6).

The Sonata

Most children who study a Western musical instrument (piano, flute, violin, or cello, for example) will play a sonata at one time or another. A **sonata** (Italian for "something to be sounded") is a genre of chamber music played on a solo instrument or a solo instrument accompanied by piano. Although it originated at the beginning of the Baroque period, the sonata took its definitive shape during the Classical era. The usual format

FIGURE 13.6

Haydn's home in the suburbs of Vienna, which he purchased in 1793 with the proceeds from his London Symphonies. It was here that he composed "The Emperor's Hymn," which he played for himself at the piano every night before retiring. He died here in 1809.

was three movements (fast–slow–fast), and each movement might be in any one of the preferred Classical forms: sonata–allegro, ternary, rondo, or theme and variations.

According to publishers' inventories from the end of the eighteenth century, more sonatas were printed than any other genre of music. The explanation for this sudden vogue is tied to the equally sudden popularity of the piano. Indeed, the word *sonata* has become so closely associated with the piano that, unless otherwise qualified as "violin sonata," "cello sonata," or the like, we usually assume that "sonata" refers to a three-movement work for piano.

Who played this flood of new sonatas for the piano? Amateur musicians, mostly women, who practiced and performed for polite society in the comfort of their own homes. (Oddly, men in this period usually played, not the piano, but string instruments such as the violin or cello.) In Mozart's time, the ability to play the piano, to do fancy needlework, and to utter a few selected words of French were thought by male-dominated society all that was necessary to be a cultured young lady.

To teach the musical handicraft, instructors were needed. Mozart, Haydn, and Beethoven all served as piano teachers in fashionable circles early in their careers. Their piano sonatas were not intended to be played in public concert halls. Instead, they served two functions: The easier ones provided students with material they might practice at home to develop technique, and the more difficult ones were to be showpieces for the composers themselves, with which they could impress in the homes of wealthy patrons. Among the thirty-two splendid piano sonatas that Beethoven composed, for example, only one was ever performed at a public concert in Vienna during his lifetime.

(A discussion of a Classical piano sonata by Beethoven, his *"Pathétique"* Sonata, is found in Chapter 15, along with the chapter's first Listening Guide.)

The Concerto

With the genre of the **concerto**, we leave the salon or private chamber and return to the public concert hall. The Classical concerto, like the symphony, was a large-scale, multimovement work for instrumental soloist and orchestra that was intended for a public audience. While the symphony might have provided the greatest musical substance at a concert, audiences were often lured to the concert hall by the prospect of hearing a virtuoso play a concerto. Then, as now, listeners were fascinated with the virtuosity and derring-do that a stunning technical display might bring. Gone was the Baroque tradition of the concerto grosso in which a group of soloists (concertino) stepped forward. From this point forward, the concerto was a **solo concerto**, usually for piano but sometimes for violin, cello, French horn, trumpet, or woodwind. In the new concerto, a single soloist commanded all the audience's attention: It was showtime!

Mozart: Piano Concerto in A major (1786), K. 488

During the years 1785–1786, Mozart was at the top of his game and near the top of his fame. He lived in an expensive apartment in the center of Vienna, hobnobbed with royalty and luminaries such as Joseph Haydn, made a lot of money from his concerts, and had a clutch of talented piano students, most of whom were women. Among his star pupils was Barbara Ployer, for whom Mozart wrote his Piano Concerto in A major in 1786.

Mozart composed twenty-three piano concertos, many among the best ever written, establishing his reputation as the inventor of the modern piano concerto. Mozart's motivation, however, was not enduring fame, but money. At each of the public concerts he produced, Mozart offered one or two of his latest concertos. But he had to do more: He was responsible for renting the hall, hiring the orchestra, leading rehearsals, attracting an audience, transporting his piano to the hall (Figure 13.7), and even selling tickets from his apartment (Figure 13.8)—all this in addition to composing the music and appearing as solo virtuoso. But, when all went well, Mozart could make a killing, as a music journal of March 22, 1783, reported:

> Today the celebrated Chevalier Mozart gave a musical concert for his own benefit at the Burgtheater in which pieces of his own music, which was already very popular, were performed. The concert was honored by the presence of an extraordinarily large audience and the two new concertos and other fantasies which Mr. Mozart played on the Forte Piano were received with the loudest approval. Our Monarch [Emperor Joseph II], who contrary to his custom honored the entire concert with his presence, joined in the applause of the public so heartily that one can think of no similar example. The proceeds of the concert are estimated at sixteen hundred gulden.

Sixteen hundred gulden was the equivalent of about $160,000 today and more than four times the annual salary of Mozart's father. With a take such as this, young Mozart could, at least for a time, indulge his expensive tastes.

We derive our term *concerto* from the Italian word *concertare*. It means above all else "to strive together," but it also resonates with a sense of "to struggle against." In a piano concerto, the piano and orchestra engage in a spirited give-and-take of thematic material. The orchestra will throw out a theme, and the piano will try to do it one better.

First Movement (*Allegro*)

As with all of Mozart's concertos, this one is in three movements (there is never a minuet in a concerto). And, as is invariably the case, the first movement is written in sonata–allegro form. Here, however, the form is expanded to meet the special demands and opportunities of the concerto. What results is **double exposition form** (Figure 13.9), in which the orchestra plays one exposition and the soloist

FIGURE 13.7
Mozart's own piano, preserved in the house of his birth in Salzburg, Austria. The keyboard spans five octaves, and the black-and-white color scheme of the keys is reversed, both typical features of the late-eighteenth-century piano. Mozart purchased the instrument in 1784, two years before he composed his A major piano concerto.

FIGURE 13.8
In this period, composers, including Mozart and Haydn, customarily sold tickets to their concerts, not through ticket agencies (they didn't exist), but from their own homes. A few of these have survived for Haydn's concerts in London and for Mozart's concerts in Vienna, as we see here.

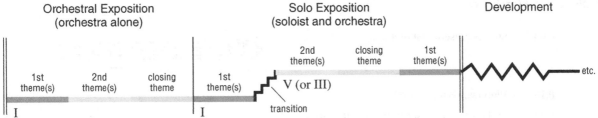

FIGURE 13.9
Double exposition form

FIGURE 13.10

A young woman performs a keyboard concerto in 1777. When Mozart moved to Vienna in 1781, he was forced to earn a living, so he gave composition lessons (mostly to men) and piano lessons (mostly to women). Among his best female students was Barbara Ployer (1765–1811), for whom he wrote the Piano Concerto in A major (K. 488), discussed in the Listening Guide.

then plays another. First, the orchestra presents the first, second, and closing themes, all in the tonic key. Then the soloist enters and, with orchestral assistance, offers the piano's version of the same material but modulating to the dominant before the second theme. Then a surprise: Just when we expect this second exposition to end, Mozart inserts a lyrical new melody in the strings. This is another feature of the Classical concerto—a melody held back for last-minute presentation, a way of keeping the listener "on guard" as the music unfolds.

Finally, after the development and recapitulation, the orchestra suddenly comes to rest on a single chord for several moments. Using this chord as a springboard, the pianist plunges headlong into a flight of virtuosic fancy: the cadenza. More showtime! On the spot, the pianist improvises, mixing rapid runs, arpeggios, and snippets of previously heard themes into a fantasy-like creation. Normally, Mozart, like Haydn, didn't write out the cadenza, in part because he improvised it, and never the same way twice. But, because Mozart intended this concerto for his pupil, Barbara Ployer (see Figure 13.10), he notated what she should play, and thus his cadenza survives today.

Toward the end of this virtuosic razzle-dazzle, Mozart calls for a trill, the traditional signal to the orchestra to reenter the competition. From here to the end, the orchestra holds forth, making use of the original closing theme. There is much to absorb in the long Listening Guide that follows, but the glorious music of Mozart will amply reward the attentive listener.

LISTENING GUIDE

Wolfgang Amadeus Mozart, Piano Concerto in A major (1786), K. 488   Download 39 (11:46)

First movement, *Allegro* (fast)

Genre: Concerto

Form: Double exposition sonata–allegro

WHAT TO LISTEN FOR: The harmonious give-and-take—"concerto"—between soloist and orchestra

EXPOSITION 1 (orchestra)

0:00   Strings present first theme.

0:16   Woodwinds repeat first theme.

0:34   Full orchestra presents first theme, part **b.**

| 0:59 | Strings present second theme, part **a**. |

| 1:15 | Woodwinds repeat second theme, part **a**. |
| 1:30 | Strings present second theme, part **b**. |

| 1:35 | Strings present closing theme, part **a**. |

| 2:02 | Woodwinds present closing theme, part **b**. |

EXPOSITION 2 (piano and orchestra)

2:11	Piano enters with first theme.
2:40	Orchestra plays first theme, part **b**.
3:11	Piano plays second theme, part **a**.
3:27	Woodwinds repeat second theme, part **a**.
3:44	Piano plays and ornaments second theme, part **b**.
3:53	Piano and orchestra in dialogue play closing theme, part **a**.
4:24	Piano trill heralds return of first theme, part **b**.
4:39	Strings quietly offer lyrical new theme.

DEVELOPMENT

5:05	Woodwinds transform new theme as piano interjects scales and then arpeggios.
5:35	Woodwinds offer new theme in imitative counterpoint.
5:49	Pedal point on dominant note in low strings signals beginning of retransition.
6:04	Piano takes over dominant pedal point.
6:18	Piano flourish above sustained dominant chord leads to recapitulation.

RECAPITULATION

| 6:30 | Orchestra plays first theme, part **a**. |
| 6:47 | Piano repeats first theme, part **a**. |

(Continued)

7:00	Orchestra plays first theme, part **b.**
7:10	Scales in piano signal beginning of transition.
7:30	Piano plays second theme, now in tonic, part **a.**
7:46	Woodwinds repeat second theme, part **a.**
8:02	Piano plays second theme, part **b.**
8:06	Piano and orchestra divide closing theme, part **a.**
8:35	Piano plays new theme.
8:48	Woodwinds play new theme while piano offers scales and arpeggios against it.
9:17	Trill in piano announces return of first theme, part **b.**
9:46	Orchestra stops and holds chord.
9:50	Cadenza for piano
10:55	Trill signals reentry of orchestra.
11:08	Orchestra plays closing theme, parts **a** and **b.**
11:30	Final cadential chords

LISTEN TO ... this selection streaming online.

WATCH ... an Active Listening Guide of this selection online.

WATCH ... a YouTube video of the physicality involved in performing this Mozart concerto for piano and orchestra, online.

Second Movement (*Andante*)

The essence of this movement rests in Mozart's exquisitely crafted lines and coloristic harmonies. This is the only work the Viennese master ever wrote in the remote key of F♯ minor, and the daring harmonic changes that it contains prefigure those of the Romantic era. Musicians who have lived with Mozart's music from childhood to old age continue to be profoundly moved by this extraordinary movement. It is at once sublimely beautiful and distantly remote, and its ending is as cold and desolate as death itself.

Third Movement (*Presto*)

There *is* life after death! A boisterous rondo refrain on the piano suddenly breaks the sublime pessimism of the preceding movement. Concertos (and concerts) should end, not with gloom, but joyfully, and it's the job of the usually lighthearted rondo to do just that. In this rondo, Mozart's audience got more than it bargained for; the soloist and orchestra do not simply "speak in turn" but, rather, banter back and forth in the most playful and pleasing way: "Anything you can do, I can do better," "No you can't," "Yes I can," the antagonists seem to say. In Mozart's contest between interactive forces, there is no winner—except the listener.

KEY WORDS

symphony (179)	Köchel (K) number (181)	sonata (187)	solo concerto (188)
sinfonia (179)	string quartet (185)	concerto (188)	double exposition form (189)

 Join us on Facebook at Listening to Music with Craig Wright

PRACTICE ... your understanding of this chapter's concepts by comparing Checklists of Musical Style for all historic eras and working once more with the chapter's Active Listening Guides online.

DO ... online multiple-choice and critical thinking quizzes that your instructor may assign for a grade.

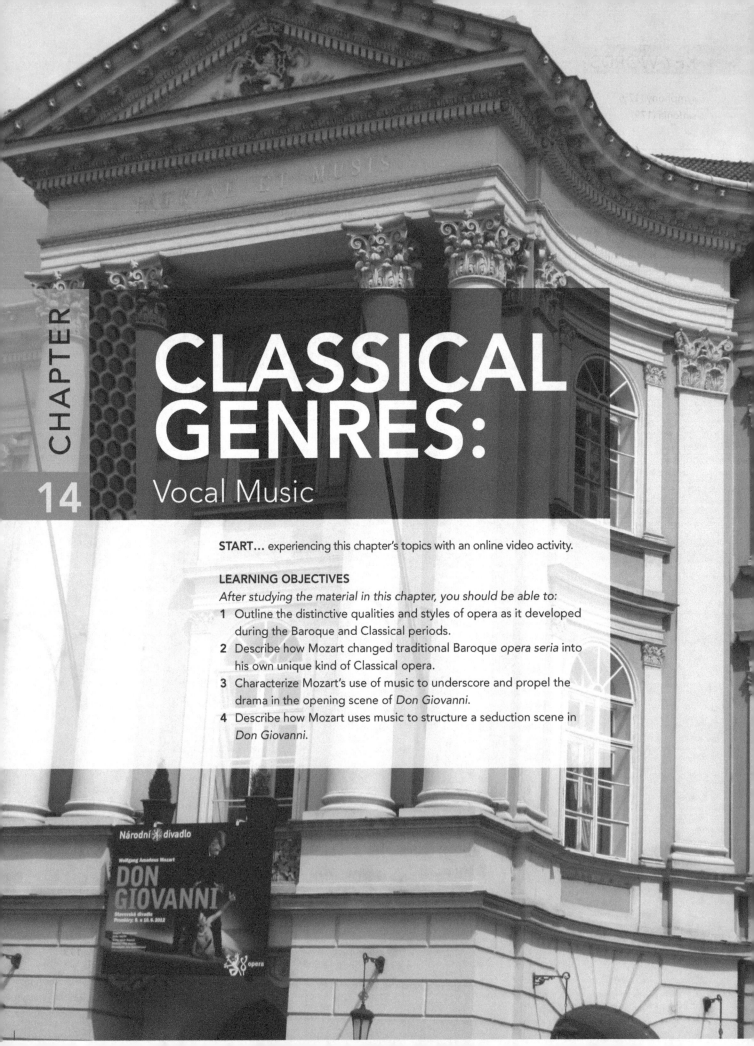

CLASSICAL GENRES:

Vocal Music

START... experiencing this chapter's topics with an online video activity.

LEARNING OBJECTIVES

After studying the material in this chapter, you should be able to:

1 Outline the distinctive qualities and styles of opera as it developed during the Baroque and Classical periods.

2 Describe how Mozart changed traditional Baroque *opera seria* into his own unique kind of Classical opera.

3 Characterize Mozart's use of music to underscore and propel the drama in the opening scene of *Don Giovanni*.

4 Describe how Mozart uses music to structure a seduction scene in *Don Giovanni*.

S inging, which involves music and words, is the oldest and most natural mode of expression. Over the course of human evolution, people in the West have increasingly come to sing in an organized, regulated, and ultimately stylized way, creating first songs and eventually opera, the most unnatural of all genres of art. But, from the Baroque era to the present day, this unnatural, "high-end" form of Western culture has maintained a fanatical following because it combines drama, beautiful music, glamour, star appeal, and all the excitement of the theater.

READ… the complete chapter text in a rich, interactive online platform.

Opera is indeed drama, but drama propelled by music. In the Classical period, opera maintained the essential features that it had developed during the Baroque era. It still began with an overture, was divided into two or three acts, and made use of a succession of arias and recitatives, along with an occasional choral number. And, of course, it was still performed in a theater large enough to accommodate both an orchestra and elaborate stage sets.

Central to the development of opera in the eighteenth century was the rise of comic opera (*opera buffa*), a powerful voice for social change during the Enlightenment (see Chapter 10). The statue-like gods, goddesses, emperors, and queens of the old Baroque *opera seria* gradually exited the stage, making room for more natural, realistic characters drawn from everyday life—a barber and a maid, for example. Whereas Baroque opera poses magnificently, Classical opera moves fluidly. Arias and recitatives flow easily from one to another, and the mood of the music changes rapidly to reflect the quickly moving, often comic, events on stage.

Comic opera introduces a new element into the opera house, the **vocal ensemble**, which allows the plot to unfold more quickly. Instead of waiting for each character to sing in turn, three or more characters can express their own particular emotions simultaneously, singing together. One might sing of her love, another of his fear, another of her outrage, while a fourth pokes fun at the other three. If an author attempted this in a spoken play (everyone talking at once), an incomprehensible jumble would result. In opera, however, this works if the composer creates harmonious music. Composers often placed vocal ensembles at the ends of acts to help spark a rousing conclusion in which all the characters might sing together on stage. The vocal ensemble typifies the more democratic spirit and better dramatic pacing of the late eighteenth century.

Mozart and Opera

The master of Classical opera, and of the vocal ensemble in particular, was Wolfgang Amadeus Mozart (1756–1791). Although Haydn wrote more than a dozen operas and conducted others (see Figure 13.2), he lacked Mozart's instinct for what was effective in the theater and what was not. Beethoven wrote only one opera, *Fidelio*, and he labored mightily on it, working through several revisions over the course of nearly ten years. Neither Haydn nor Beethoven had Mozart's talent for giving each character a distinctly personal set of musical attributes and for lightning-quick changes in mood. Mozart's music is inherently dramatic because, like human emotions, it can change in an instant.

Mozart—the most versatile of composers—wrote all types of opera: Baroque-style *opera seria*, more modern *opera buffa* (comic opera), and a special style of German comic opera called *Singspiel*, which in German means "singing play." Like a Broadway musical, a **Singspiel** is made up of spoken dialogue (instead of recitative), topical humor, and songs. Mozart's best work of this type is *Die Zauberflöte* (*The Magic Flute*, 1791). But, more important, Mozart created a new kind of opera that mixed serious and comic elements to powerful effect. His *Le nozze di Figaro* (*The Marriage of Figaro*, 1786; see Chapter 10) is a domestic comedy that also examines betrayal, adultery, and, ultimately, compassion; his *Don Giovanni* (1787; see below) sets hilarious moments of comic buffoonery within a story of rape, murder, and, ultimately, damnation. In these two masterpieces, both set to texts (libretti) by Lorenzo da Ponte (1749–1838; see box), Mozart's quickly changing music evokes laughter and tears in almost equal measure.

Mozart: *Don Giovanni* (1787), K. 527

Don Giovanni has been called not only Mozart's greatest opera but also the greatest opera ever written. It tells the tale of an amoral philanderer who seduces and murders his way across Europe before being pursued and finally dragged down to Hell by the ghost of a man he has killed. Because this seducer and mocker of public law and morality is a nobleman, *Don Giovanni* is implicitly critical of the aristocracy, so Mozart and da Ponte danced quickly to avoid the wrath of the imperial censor before production.

Mozart's opera was first performed on October 29, 1787, in Prague, Czech Republic (Figure 14.1), a city in which his music was especially popular. As fate would have it, the most notorious Don Juan of the eighteenth century, Giacomo Casanova, was in the audience that first night in Prague because he had had a hand in helping his friend da Ponte shape the libretto. Don Juan, Casanova, and Don Giovanni were all the same.

Although Don Giovanni is charming and clever, the rape and murder that he perpetrates are far from funny. The comedy in *Don Giovanni* emanates not from the sinister Don but, rather, from his worldly-wise servant, Leporello, who points out the contradictions (the basis of all humor) in his master's life and in society in general.

As the curtain rises, we find the reluctant accomplice, Leporello, keeping watch outside the house of Donna Anna, while his master is inside attempting to satisfy his sexual appetite. Grumbling as he paces back and forth, Leporello sings that he would gladly trade places with the fortunate aristocrat ("Notte e giorno faticar," or "I would like to play the gentleman"; see Listening Guide). Immediately, Mozart establishes Leporello's musical character.

He sets this opening aria in F major, a traditional musical key for peasants and peasant life, showing that Leporello is a rustic fellow; Mozart gives him a narrow vocal range without fancy ornaments; and Mozart has him sing quick, repeated pitches, almost as if stuttering. This last technique, **patter song**, is a stock device used to depict low-caste, inarticulate characters in comic opera.

As Leporello concludes his complaint, the masked Don Giovanni rushes onstage, chased by the virtuous Donna Anna (Figure 14.2). Here, the strings rush up the scale and the music modulates upward (see Listening Guide at 1:43) to signify that we are now dealing with the high-born. The victim of Don Giovanni's unwanted sexual assault, Donna Anna, wants her assailant captured and unmasked. While the nobleman and lady carry on a musical tug-of-war in long notes above, servant Leporello patters away fearfully below. This excellent example of vocal ensemble makes clear the conflicting emotions of each party. Older Baroque opera would have had these three emotions come in successive, separate units; Mozart's newer Classical opera accelerates the drama by means of simultaneous action.

FIGURE 14.1

The Estates Theater in Prague, constructed in 1783, four years before Mozart conducted the first performance of *Don Giovanni* there. Much of the film *Amadeus* was filmed here. Note the Neo-classical architecture and window design. Note also that *Don Giovanni* is still popular in Prague, as the banner advertising an evening performance (lower left middle and chapter opener) suggests.

FIGURE 14.2

Don Giovanni (Roderick Williams) tries to seduce Donna Anna (Suzannah Glanville) at the beginning of a 2005 British production of Mozart's *Don Giovanni*. Note the similarity in approach to *The Phantom of the Opera* by Andrew Lloyd Webber. Lloyd Webber drew heavily from Mozart's *Don Giovanni*. For example, the opera that the Phantom composes in Act II is called *Don Juan [Giovanni] Triumphant*, which tries to tell this timeless tale of seduction from Don Juan's point of view.

Now, Donna Anna's father, the Commandant, enters to confront Don Giovanni. Mozart's music tells us that this bodes ill—there is a troubling tremolo in the strings, and the mode (and mood) shifts from major to minor. Our fear is immediately confirmed as the Don, after first refusing to duel, draws his sword and attacks the aging Commandant. In the brief exchange of steel, Mozart depicts the rising tension by means of ascending chromatic scales and tight, tense chords. At the very moment Don Giovanni's sword pierces the Commandant, the action stops and the orchestra holds on a painful **diminished chord**—a tension-filled chord comprised entirely of minor thirds. Here, again, Mozart underscores the action on stage through an expressive musical gesture. He then clears the air of discord with a simple texture and accompaniment as Don Giovanni and Leporello gaze in horror on the dying Commandant.

Finally, a magical moment occurs which perhaps only Mozart could have created. We have a vocal ensemble in which three very different sentiments are conveyed simultaneously: surprise and satisfaction (Don Giovanni), the desire to flee (Leporello), and the pain of a violent death (Commandant). At the end, the listener can feel the Commandant expire, his life slipping away with the slow descent of a chromatic scale. In its intensity and compression, only the opening scene of Shakespeare's *King Lear* rivals the beginning of *Don Giovanni*.

LISTENING GUIDE

Wolfgang Amadeus Mozart, Opera, *Don Giovanni* (1787), K. 527   Download 40 (5:23)

Act I, Scene 1

Characters: Don Giovanni, a rakish lord; Leporello, his servant; Donna Anna, a virtuous noblewoman; the Commandant, her father, a retired military man

WHAT TO LISTEN FOR: Leporello's simple aria, followed by a vocal ensemble, leading to a duel and another vocal ensemble, underscoring the death of the Commandant

ARIA			Leporello
0:00	The pacing Leporello grumbles as he awaits his master, Don Giovanni.	Notte e giorno faticar, per chi nulla sa gradir, piova e il vento sopportar, mangiar male e mal dormir. Voglio far il gentiluomo e non voglio più servir ... (Leporello continues in this vein.)	On the go from morn 'til night for one who shows no appreciation, sustaining wind and rain, without proper food or sleep. I would like to play the gentleman and no more a servant be ...
1:43	Violins rush up the scale, and the music modulates upward as Don Giovanni and Donna Anna rush in.		

VOCAL ENSEMBLE (TRIO)			Donna Anna
1:48	Donna Anna tries to hold and unmask Don Giovanni while Leporello cowers on the side.	Non sperar, se non m'uccidi, ch'io ti lasci fuggir mai.	Do not hope you can escape, unless you kill me.

Don Giovanni

Donna folle, indarno gridi,
chi son io tu non saprai.

Crazy lady, you scream in vain,
you will never know who I am.

Leporello

Che tumulto, oh ciel,
che gridi il padron in nuovi guai.

What a racket, heavens,
what screams, my master in a new
scrape.

Donna Anna

Gente! Servi! Al traditore!
Scellerato!

Everyone! Help! Catch the traitor!
Scoundrel!

Don Giovanni

Taci et trema al mio furore!
Sconsigliata!

Shut up and get out of my way!
Fool!

Leporello

Sta a veder che il malandrino mi
farà recipitar. ...

We will see if this malefactor will
be the ruin of me. ...

(The trio continues in this manner with liberal repeats of text and music.)

| 3:04 | String tremolo and shift from major to minor as the Commandant enters |

VOCAL ENSEMBLE (TRIO)

| 3:11 | The Commandant comes forward to fight; Don Giovanni first refuses and then duels; Leporello tries to flee. |

Commandant

Lasciala, indegno!
Battiti meco!

Let her go, villain!
Fight with me!

Don Giovanni

Va! Non mi degno di pugnar teco!

Away! I wouldn't deign to fight with
you!

Commandant

Così pretendi da me fuggir?

So you think you can get away
thus?

Leporello (aside)

Potessi almeno di qua partir!

If I could only get out of here!

Don Giovanni

Misero! Attendi se vuoi morir!

You old fool! Get ready then, if you
wish to die!

| 3:50 | Musical duel (running scales and tense diminished chords) |

(*Continued*)

4:00	Climax on intense diminished chord (the Commandant falls mortally wounded) and then a pause		

VOCAL ENSEMBLE (TRIO)

Commandant

4:06	Don Giovanni and Leporello look upon the dying Commandant; a "ticking" sound in the strings freezes time.	Ah, soccorso, son tradito. L'assassino m'ha ferito, e dal seno palpitante sento l'anima partir.	Ah, I'm wounded, betrayed. The assassin has run me through, and from my heaving breast I feel my soul depart.

Don Giovanni

		Ah, gia cade il sciagurato, affannoso e agonizzante, già del seno palpitante veggo l'anima partir.	Ah, already the old fool falls, gasping and writhing in pain, and from his heaving breast I can see his soul depart.

Leporello

		Qual misfatto! Qual eccesso! Entro il sen dallo spavento palpitar il cor mi sento. Io non so che far, che dir.	What a horrible thing, how stupid! I can feel within my breast my heart pounding from fear. I don't know what to say or do.

5:02	Slow, chromatic descent as last breath seeps out of the Commandant		

LISTEN TO ... this selection streaming online.

WATCH ... an Active Listening Guide of this selection online.

WATCH ... a performance of this selection online.

DO ... Listening Exercise 14.1, Mozart, *Don Giovanni*, Act I, Scene 1, online.

When we next meet the unrepentant Don Giovanni, he is in pursuit of the country girl Zerlina. She is the betrothed of another peasant, Masetto, and the two are to be married the next day. Don Giovanni quickly dismisses Masetto and turns his charm on the naive Zerlina. First, he tries verbal persuasion, carried off in simple recitative (the harpsichord is still used to accompany simple recitatives in Classical opera, a vestige of the older Baroque practice). Zerlina, he says, is too lovely for a country bumpkin like Masetto. Her beauty demands a higher state: She will become *his* wife!

Simple recitative now gives way to more passionate expression in the charming duet, "Là ci darem la mano" ("Give me your hand, o fairest"). During this duet, Don Giovanni persuades Zerlina to extend her hand (and the prospect of a good deal more). He begins with a seductive melody (**A**), cast squarely in the Classical mold of two four-bar, antecedent–consequent phrases (see the following Listening Guide). Zerlina repeats and extends this, but she still sings alone and untouched. The Don becomes more aggressive in a new phrase (**B**), and Zerlina, in turn, becomes flustered, as her quick sixteenth notes reveal. The initial melody (**A**) returns but is now sung together by the two principals, their voices intertwining—musical union accompanies the act of physical touching that occurs on stage. Finally, as if to further affirm this coupling through music, Mozart adds a concluding section (**C**) in which the two characters skip off, arm in arm ("Let's go, my treasure"), their voices linked together in parallel-moving thirds to show unity of feeling and purpose. These are the means by which a skilled composer like Mozart can underscore, through music, the drama unfolding on the stage.

LISTENING GUIDE

Wolfgang Amadeus Mozart, Opera, *Don Giovanni* (1787), K. 527   Download 41 (5:01)

Act I, Scene 7

Characters: Don Giovanni and the peasant girl Zerlina

Situation: Don Giovanni apparently succeeding in the seduction of Zerlina

WHAT TO LISTEN FOR: The stylistic distinction between recitative and aria (duet), and the gradual joining of the voices, signaling a mutual desire

RECITATIVE

0:00

	Don Giovanni
Alfin siam liberati, Zerlinetta gentil,	At last, gentle Zerlina,
da quel scioccone.	we are free of that clown.
Che ne dite, mio ben, sò far pulito?	And say, my love, didn't I handle it well?
	Zerlina
Signore, è mio marito.	Sir, he is my fiancé.
	Don Giovanni
Chi? Colui?	Who? Him?
Vi par che un onest'uomo,	Do you think that an honorable man,
un nobil cavalier, qual io mi vanto,	a noble cavalier as I believe I am,
possa soffrir che quel visetto d'oro,	could let such a golden face,
quel viso inzuccherato,	such a sweet beauty,
da un bifolcaccio vil sia strapazzato?	be profaned by that clumsy oaf?
	Zerlina
Ma, signor, io gli diedi parola di sposarlo.	But sir, I have already given my word to marry him.
	Don Giovanni
Tal parola non vale un zero.	Such a promise counts for nothing.
Voi non siete fatta per esser paesana;	You were not made to be a peasant girl;
un altra sorte vi procuran quegli	a higher fate is in store for those mischievous
occhi bricconcelli, quei labretti sì belli,	eyes, those beautiful lips, those milky,
quelle dituccia candide e odorose,	perfumed hands,
par me toccar giuncata e fiutar rose.	so soft to touch, scented with roses.

(Continued)

	Zerlina
Ah! ... Non vorrei ...	Ah! ... I do not wish ...
	Don Giovanni
Che non vorreste?	What don't you wish?
	Zerlina
Alfine ingannata restar.	In the end to be deceived.
Io sò che raro colle donne voi altri cavalieri	I know that rarely are you noblemen honest
siete onesti e sinceri.	and sincere with women.
	Don Giovanni
Eh, un'impostura della gente plebea! La	A vile slander of the low classes!
nobiltà ha dipinta negli occhi l'onestà.	Nobility can be seen in honest eyes.
Orsù, non perdiam tempo;	Now let's not waste time.
in questo istante io ti voglio sponsar.	I will marry you immediately.
	Zerlina
Voi?	You?
	Don Giovanni
Certo, io. Quell casinetto è mio.	Certainly, I. That villa over there is mine.
Soli saremo, e là, gioiello mio,	We will be alone, and there, my little jewel,
ci sposeremo.	we will be married.

ARIA (DUET)

0:00	**A**	Là ci darem la mano,	Give me your hand, o fairest,
		là mi dirai di sì.	whisper a gentle "yes."
		Vedi, non è lontano:	See, it's not far:
		partiam, ben mio, da qui.	let's go, my love.

		Zerlina
0:20	Vorrei, e non vorrei,	I'd like to but yet I would not,
	mi trema un poco il cor;	my heart will not be still;
	felice, è ver, sarei,	'tis true, I would be happy,
	ma può burlarmi ancor.	yet he may deceive me still.

Don Giovanni

0:45	**B**	Vieni, mio bel diletto!	Come with me, my pretty one!

Zerlina

Mi fa pietà Masetto!	May Masetto take pity!

Don Giovanni

Io cangierò tua sorte!		I will change your fate!

Zerlina

Presto, non son più forte.		Quick then, I can no longer resist.

1:15	A'	Repeat of first eight lines but with Don Giovanni's and Zerlina's parts moving closer together
1:43	B'	Repeat of next four lines
2:09	C	Change of meter to dance-like as principals skip off together

Together

Andiam, andiam mio bene,	Let's go, let's go, my treasure,
a ristorar le pene	to soothe the pangs
d'un innocente amor!	of innocent love!

LISTEN TO ... this selection streaming online.

WATCH ... an Active Listening Guide of this selection online.

WATCH ... a performance of this selection online.

WATCH ... a YouTube video of the exciting conclusion of *Don Giovanni*, online.

In the end, the frightful ghost of the dead Commandant confronts Don Giovanni and orders him to repent. Ever defiant, Don Giovanni cries, "No, no!" and is dragged down to Hell to the sounds of Mozart's most demonic music—the music with which he began the opera overture (see Chapter 11). In sum, the mixture of sublime beauty and sinister power—the heavenly and the hellish—makes *Don Giovanni* a masterpiece of the highest order. No wonder Andrew Lloyd Webber (see Figure 14.2) paid homage to it in his long-running *Phantom of the Opera*.

KEY WORDS

| vocal ensemble (195) | *Singspiel* (195) | patter song (197) | diminished chord (198) |

---

f Join us on Facebook at Listening to Music with Craig Wright

---

PRACTICE ... your understanding of this chapter's concepts by comparing Checklists of Musical Style for all historic eras and working once more with the chapter's Active Listening Guides online.

DO ... online multiple-choice and critical thinking quizzes that your instructor may assign for a grade.

BEETHOVEN:
Bridge to Romanticism

CHAPTER

15

START... experiencing this chapter's topics with an online video activity.

LEARNING OBJECTIVES
After studying the material in this chapter, you should be able to:

1 Characterize Beethoven's music as it has traditionally been divided
   into three periods.
2 Explain why Beethoven's music can be heard as representative of the
   Classical period and of the early Romantic era as well.
3 Describe Beethoven's piano music from the early years, as typified by
   his "*Pathétique*" Sonata.
4 Elaborate on the symphonies from Beethoven's "heroic" period,
   using his Symphonies No. 3 and No. 5 as examples.
5 Characterize Beethoven's final years, using his Symphony No. 9 as
   an example.

When we think of the image of an artist, what does the artist look like? Usually, someone distracted, a bit of a rebel, perhaps a loner unconcerned about his or her appearance, maybe even behaving bizarrely. Where did we get this notion of the artist? In a word, from Beethoven. Similarly, think of what is arguably the most iconic moment in all of classical music—indeed, the piece with which our book began. First to come to mind is the opening of Beethoven's Symphony No. 5: "duh-duh-duh-DUHHH." Beethoven is deeply ingrained in our collective psyche, both for what he came to represent—the archetype of the artist—and for his extraordinary music.

But Beethoven was lucky. The period of his maturity (the early nineteenth century) coincided with a new Romantic spirit, one of rebellion, independence, and eccentricity. By 1840, the now-dead Beethoven had come to be seen as the greatest artist of the age (Figure 15.1). If the universally admired Beethoven—an angry, self-absorbed loner who walked around wildly humming and scribbling notes—had become the model of greatness, that must be the new norm. And so it was that Beethoven came to be the poster boy for "the artist as eccentric genius." But he alone reached this level of public recognition. He alone transformed the image of the composer from Classical servant to Romantic visionary. When he died in March 1827, 20,000 citizens of Vienna turned out for the funeral—nearly one in every ten inhabitants. Schools closed, and the army was mobilized to control the crowd. An artist—and a musician, no less—had become a cult figure (Figure 15.2).

Today, Beethoven's music continues to enjoy great popular favor—his symphonies, quartets, and sonatas are performed more frequently than those of any other classical composer, slightly more than Mozart's. But what makes Beethoven's music so eternally compelling? Perhaps trite to say, it speaks to us. If Mozart's sublime music seems to communicate universal truths, Beethoven's seems to tell us

FIGURE 15.1

In this work, painted in 1840 (after Beethoven's death) by artist Josef Danhauser, a bust of Beethoven looms godlike over the scene as pianist Franz Liszt and other artists of the day look up with reverential respect. For the nineteenth century, Beethoven came to personify the divinely inspired genius, perhaps because Beethoven himself said that he "conversed with God." It is largely from Beethoven, and the stories about him, that we derive our image of "the artist as genius."

FIGURE 15.2
In this *Peanuts* cartoon strip, a bust of Beethoven sits atop Schroeder's piano as Lucy looks on in admiration—just as in Figure 15.1, where a bust of Beethoven sits atop Franz Liszt's piano as famous artists look on in admiration. Since the early Romantic period, Beethoven has remained an icon of popular culture.

about Beethoven, his struggles, and ultimately the struggles of all of us. As was true of his own personality, Beethoven's music is full of extremes: sometimes tender and sometimes violent. And just as Beethoven the composer triumphed over personal adversity—his growing deafness—so his music imparts a feeling of struggle and, ultimately, heroic victory. It has a sense of rightness, even morality, about it. It seems to speak to the humanity in all of us.

Historians have traditionally divided Beethoven's music into three periods: early, middle, and late. Early Beethoven sounds in many ways like late Haydn and Mozart. Yet, beginning with his middle period (1803–1813), Beethoven projects a new spirit, one that foreshadows the musical style of the Romantic era (1820–1900). An intense lyrical expression is heard in his slow movements, while his allegros abound with pounding rhythms, strong dynamic contrasts, and startling orchestral effects. Although he adheres to Classical musical forms (sonata–allegro, rondo, and theme and variations), so great is his urge for personal expression that Beethoven pushes their formal boundaries to the breaking point. Though a pupil of Haydn and a lifelong admirer of Mozart, he nevertheless elevated music to new heights of both lyricism and dramatic power. For this reason, he can rightly be called the prophet of Romantic music.

The Early Years (1770–1802)

Like Bach and Mozart before him, Beethoven came from a family of musicians. His father and grandfather were performers at the court at Bonn, Germany, on the Rhine River, where Beethoven was baptized on December 17, 1770. Seeing great musical talent in his young son, Beethoven's father, a violent alcoholic, forced him to practice the piano at all hours, day or night. Soon he tried to exploit his son as a child prodigy, a second Mozart, telling the world that the diminutive boy was a year or two younger than he actually was. When Beethoven died in 1827, he thought he was 55—he was actually 57!

In 1792, Beethoven moved to Vienna, then the musical capital of Europe, and began to study with the world's most respected composer, Joseph Haydn. Beethoven also bought new clothes, located a wig maker, and found a dancing instructor. His aim was to gain acceptance into the homes of the wealthy of the Austrian capital, and this he soon achieved, owing not to his woeful social skills, but to his phenomenal ability as a pianist. As a journal of the day reported, "Beethoven, a musical genius, has chosen Vienna as his residence for the past two years. He seems already to have entered into the inner sanctuary of music, distinguishing himself for his precision [in playing], feeling and taste; consequently his fame has risen considerably."

Beethoven played the piano louder, more forcefully even more violently than anyone the Viennese nobility had ever heard. He possessed an extraordinary technique—even if he did hit occasional wrong notes—and this he put to good use, especially in his fanciful improvisations. One of Beethoven's pupils observed, "He knew how to produce such an impression on every listener that frequently there was not a single dry eye, while many broke out into loud sobs, for there was something magical about his playing."

The aristocracy was captivated. One patron put a string quartet at Beethoven's disposal, another made it possible for the composer to experiment with a small orchestra, and all showered him with gifts. He acquired well-to-do pupils; he sold his compositions ("I state my price and they pay," he said with pride in 1801); and he requested and eventually received an annuity (allowance for life) from three noblemen so that he could work undisturbed. The text of this arrangement includes the following provisions:

> It is recognized that only a person who is as free as possible from all cares can consecrate himself to his craft. He can only produce these great and sublime works which ennoble Art if they form his sole pursuit, to the exclusion of all unnecessary obligations. The undersigned have therefore taken the decision to ensure that Herr Ludwig van Beethoven's situation shall not be embarrassed by his most necessary requirements, nor shall his powerful Genius be hampered.

What a contrast between Beethoven's contract and the one signed by Haydn four decades earlier (see Chapter 10, "Franz Joseph Haydn…")! Music was no longer merely a craft and the composer a servant. It had now become an exalted Art, and the great creator a Genius who must be protected and nurtured—a new, Romantic notion of the value of music and the importance of the composer. Beethoven himself promoted this belief that the artistic genius was cut from a different cloth than the rest of humanity. He claimed he spoke with God. And, when one patron demanded that he play for a visiting French general, Beethoven stormed out of the salon and responded by letter: "Prince, what you are, you are through the accident of birth. What I am, I am through my own efforts. There have been many princes and there will be thousands more. But there is only one Beethoven!" What Beethoven failed to realize, of course, is that he, too, owed much of his success to "the accident of birth"—coming from a long line of musicians, he had been born with a huge musical talent.

Piano Sonata, Opus 13, the "*Pathétique*" Sonata (1799)

The bold originality in Beethoven's music can be heard in one of his most celebrated compositions, the **"*Pathétique*" Sonata**. A Classical sonata, as we have seen (Chapter 13, "The Sonata"), is a multimovement work for solo instrument or solo instrument with keyboard accompaniment. This particular sonata, for solo piano, is identified as Beethoven's Opus 13, denoting that it is the thirteenth of 135 works that Beethoven published. (Composers often use the term **opus**—Latin for "work"—with a number to identify their works.) But Beethoven himself also supplied the sonata with its descriptive title—"*Pathétique*" ("Plaintive")—underscoring the passion and pathos he felt within it. Its great drama derives in large part from the juxtaposition of extremes. There are extremes of dynamics (from *fortissimo* to *pianissimo*), tempo (*grave* to *presto*), and range (from very high to very low). The piece also requires of the pianist more technical skill and stamina than had any piano sonata of Mozart or Haydn. Displaying his virtuosity, Beethoven frequently performed the "*Pathétique*" in the homes and palaces of the Viennese aristocracy.

First Movement

Contemporaries recount how Beethoven the pianist played with superhuman speed and force, and how he once banged the keys so hard that he broke six strings. The crashing C minor chord that opens the "*Pathétique*" Sonata suggests Beethoven's sometimes violent approach to the instrument (see Listening Guide). After this startling opening gesture, Beethoven the dramatist takes over, juxtaposing music of wildly differing moods: The *sforzando* chord is immediately followed by the quietest sort of lyricism, only to be interrupted by another chordal thunderbolt (Example 15.1). This slow introduction is probably a written-out version of the sort of improvisation that gained Beethoven great fame in Vienna.

EXAMPLE 15.1 Opening contrasts

LISTEN TO…

Example 15.1 online.

The dramatic introduction leads to a racing first theme that rises impetuously in the right hand. The sense of anxiety that the listener feels is amplified by the throbbing bass, where the left hand of the pianist plays broken octaves (the alternation of two tones an octave apart), reminiscent of the rumbling thunder of an approaching storm (Example 15.2).

EXAMPLE 15.2 Tempestuous first theme

LISTEN TO…

Example 15.2 online.

The remainder of the movement now plays out as a contest between the impetuous, racing themes and the stormy chords. But, while there is much passion and intensity here, there is also Classical formal control. The crashing chords come back at the beginning of both the development and the coda in this sonata–allegro form movement. Thus, these chords provide useful auditory signposts for the listener, while they hold the racing theme in check. Beethoven's music often conveys a feeling of struggle: Classical forms gave Beethoven something to struggle against.

LISTENING GUIDE

Ludwig van Beethoven, Piano Sonata, Opus 13, the *"Pathétique"* Sonata (1799)   Download 42 (8:35)

First movement, *Grave; Allegro di molto e con brio* (grave; very fast and with gusto)

Genre: Sonata

Form: Sonata–allegro

WHAT TO LISTEN FOR: The drama created not only within the opening chords but also between the chords and the racing main theme. Here, contrast is the name of the game: loud against soft, slow against fast, high against low.

INTRODUCTION

0:00	Crashing chords alternate with softer, more lyrical ones.
0:33	Softer chords are continually cut off by crashing chords below.
0:50	Melody builds to climax and then rapid descent.

EXPOSITION ([ ] = repeats)

1:24	[3:08]	**First theme:** Rising, agitated melody in right hand against broken octaves in left

1:43	[3:27]	Transition modulates to new key, thinner texture.
1:56	[3:40]	**Second theme:** Bass, followed by treble, initiates "call and response."

2:29	[4:12]	**Closing theme, part 1:** Right and left hands race in opposite directions.
2:49	[4:32]	**Closing theme, part 2:** Rapid scales in right hand above simple chords in left
2:56	[4:39]	Reminiscence of first theme

DEVELOPMENT

4:54	Crashing chords and softer chords from introduction
5:30	First theme extended and varied
6:11	Rapid, twisting descent played by right hand leads to recapitulation.

RECAPITULATION

6:17		**First theme:** Rising, agitated melody in right hand
6:28		Transition

6:38	**Second theme:** Call and response between bass and treble
7:05	**Closing theme, part 1:** Hands move rapidly in opposite directions.
7:25	**Closing theme, part 2:** Scale runs in right hand
7:31	Reminiscence of first theme

CODA

| 7:49 | Recall of chords from introduction |
| 8:21 | Reminiscence of first theme leads to drive to final cadence. |

LISTEN TO ... this selection streaming online.

WATCH ... an Active Listening Guide of this selection online.

DO ... Listening Exercise 15.1, Beethoven, "*Pathétique*" Sonata, online.

Second Movement

Eyewitnesses who heard Beethoven at the piano remarked on the "legato" (long and lyrical) style of his playing and contrasted it with Mozart's staccato (light and detached) style. Beethoven himself remarked in 1796 that "one can sing on the piano, so long as one has feeling." We can hear Beethoven sing through the legato melodic line that dominates the slow second movement of the "*Pathétique*" Sonata. Indeed, the expression mark that he gave to the movement is *cantabile* (songful). The singing quality of the melody seems to have appealed to classically trained pop star Billy Joel, who borrowed this theme for his song "This Night": The verses are doo-wop, the chorus pure Beethoven.

WATCH... "This Night" online.

Third Movement

A comparison of the second and third movements of the "*Pathétique*" Sonata shows that musical form doesn't always determine musical mood. Although both the *Adagio* and the fast finale are in rondo form, the first is a lyrical hymn and the latter, a passionate, but slightly comical, chase. The finale has hints of the crashing chords and stark contrasts of the first movement, but the earlier violence and impetuosity have softened into a mood of impassioned playfulness.

From Amateur to Virtuoso

In all he touched, Beethoven was an agent of change. The eighteenth-century piano sonata had been essentially chamber music—music that a composer-teacher like Mozart or Haydn would write for a talented amateur pupil, to be played as entertainment in the home. Beethoven took the modest, private piano sonata and infused it with the technical dazzle of the public stage. The louder sound, wider range, and greater length of Beethoven's thirty-two piano sonatas made them appropriate for the increasingly larger concert halls—and pianos—of the nineteenth century. Beginning in the Romantic period, Beethoven's piano sonatas became—and remain—a staple of the professional virtuoso's repertoire. But there

WATCH... a musical animation (with both graphics and an active keyboard) of one of the most virtuosic of all Beethoven's works for piano, the finale of the "Moonlight" Sonata.

was a downside: Sonatas that had originally been created for all amateurs to play were now becoming too difficult. The virtuoso had begun to hijack the amateur's music, a development that would continue throughout the nineteenth century.

Beethoven Loses His Hearing

Beethoven cut a strange, eccentric figure as he wandered the streets of Vienna, sometimes humming, sometimes mumbling, and sometimes jotting on music paper. Dogs barked, and street kids, knowing nothing about genius, sometimes threw stones—which he threw back. Adding to the difficulties of his somewhat unstable personality was the fact that Beethoven was gradually losing his hearing—a serious handicap for any person, but a tragic condition for a musician (Figure 15.3). Just imagine a blind painter.

FIGURE 15.3
A fanciful, yet in many ways accurate, depiction of Beethoven, the creative artist, in the midst of chaos. Beethoven's domestic surroundings were always in disarray, as we see from the music on and under his piano. But toward the end of his life, owing to his deafness, Beethoven wrote down his compositions, not at a piano, but at a small walnut desk in an adjoining room. Ultimately, he heard his music not externally, but internally.

Beethoven first complained about his hearing and a ringing in his ears (tinnitus) in the late 1790s, and he suffered considerable anguish and depression. His increasing deafness did not stop him from composing—most people can hear simple melodies inside their heads, and the gifted Beethoven could generate complex melodies and harmonies in his "inner ear" without need of external sound. As he himself said in 1801, "In my playing and composing my defect [deafness] matters least; but it matters a great deal in social interaction." In truth, growing deafness gradually affected both his social relations and his capacity to perform; he became a recluse and stopped appearing as a pianist because he could no longer gauge how hard to press the keys.

By late 1802, Beethoven recognized that he would ultimately suffer a total loss of hearing. In despair, he wrote something akin to a last will and testament, today called the **Heiligenstadt Testament** after the Viennese suburb in which he penned it. In this confessional document for posterity, the composer admits that he considered suicide: "I would have ended my life; it was only *my art* that held me back." Beethoven emerged from this personal crisis with renewed resolve to fulfill his artistic destiny—he would now, despite his deafness, "seize Fate by the throat."

The "Heroic" Period (1803–1813)

It was in this resurgent, defiant mood that Beethoven entered what we call his **"heroic" period** of composition (1803–1813; also termed simply his "middle period"). His works became longer, more assertive, and full of grand gestures. Simple, often triadic, themes predominate, and these are repeated, sometimes incessantly, as the music swells to majestic proportions. When these themes are played *forte* and given over to the brass instruments, a heroic, triumphant sound results.

As we are coming to see, Beethoven is all about sound. And then, as now, the best way to project the biggest sound in acoustic music is through the symphony orchestra. Beethoven wrote nine symphonies in all, six of them during his "heroic" period. Beethoven's symphonies are few in number because they are so much longer and more complex than those of his predecessors. Beginning with No. 3, his symphonies sometimes go on for forty-five minutes or more, twice the duration of any symphony of Haydn or Mozart. Beethoven's works set the standard for the epic, narrative symphony of the nineteenth century.

Symphony No. 3 in E♭ major ("Eroica"; 1803)

As its title suggests, Beethoven's **"Eroica" ("Heroic") Symphony** epitomizes the grandiose, heroic style. More than any other single orchestral work, it changed the historical direction of the symphony. It assaults the ear with startling rhythmic effects and chord changes that were shocking to early-nineteenth-century listeners. It makes mountains of sound out of the simplest triads by repeating them with ever-increasing volume. Most novel, the work has biographical content, for the hero of the "Eroica" Symphony, at least originally, was Napoleon Bonaparte (Figure 15.4).

Austria and the German states were at war with France in the early nineteenth century. Yet the German-speaking Beethoven was taken with the enemy's revolutionary call for liberty, equality, and fraternity. Napoleon Bonaparte became his hero, and the composer dedicated his third symphony to him, writing on the title page "*intitolata Bonaparte*." But, when news that Napoleon had declared himself emperor reached Beethoven, he flew into a rage, saying, "Now he, too, will trample on all the rights of man and indulge his ambition." Taking up a knife, he scratched so violently to erase Bonaparte's name from the title page that he left a hole in the paper (Figure 15.5). When the work was published, Napoleon's name had been removed in favor of the more general title "Heroic Symphony: To Celebrate the Memory of a Great Man." Beethoven was not an imperialist; he was a revolutionary.

Symphony No. 5 in C minor (1808)

We all know the opening of Beethoven's iconic symphony No. 5 (see Figure 15.6; also Chapter 1), but what about the rest? Be assured, the remainder is as startling as the beginning. In the course of four interrelated movements, Beethoven takes us on an eventful psychological journey. An imaginative listener

FIGURE 15.4
As a young officer, Napoleon Bonaparte seized control of the government of France in 1799. He established a new form of republican government that emphasized the revolutionary ideals of liberty, equality, and fraternity. After Napoleon elevated himself to emperor in 1804, Beethoven changed the title of his Symphony No. 3 from "Bonaparte" to "Eroica." The portrait by Jacques-Louis David shows the newly crowned Napoleon in full imperial regalia. Liberator had become oppressor.

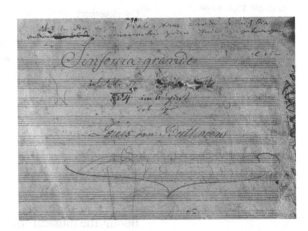

FIGURE 15.5
The title page of the autograph of Beethoven's "Eroica" Symphony: *Sinfonia grande intitolata Bonaparte*. Note the hole in the center where Beethoven took a knife and scratched out the name "Bonaparte."

FIGURE 15.6
Interior of the Theater-an-der-Wien, Vienna, where Beethoven's Symphony No. 5 premiered on December 22, 1808. This all-Beethoven concert lasted four hours, from 6:30 until 10:30 P.M., and presented eight new works, including his Symphony No. 5. During the performance of the symphony, the orchestra sometimes halted because of the difficulties in playing Beethoven's radically new music. Notice the horses on stage. Beethoven lived during a time of transition, when theaters were used for both public spectacles and music-only concerts.

will experience the following sequence of events: (1) a fateful encounter with elemental forces, (2) a period of quiet soul-searching, followed by (3) a further wrestling with the elements, and, finally, (4) a triumphant victory over the forces of Fate. Beethoven himself is said to have remarked with regard to the famous opening motive of the symphony: "There Fate knocks at the door!"

The rhythm of the opening—the famous "duh-duh-duh-DUHHH" motive—animates the entire symphony. Not only does it dominate the opening *Allegro*, but it also reappears in varied form in the three later movements, binding the symphony into a unified whole (Example 15.3).

EXAMPLE 15.3 A rhythm that pervades all movements

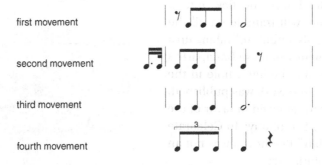

LISTEN TO...

Example 15.3 online.

First Movement

Boom! The musical equivalent of an explosion jolts the listener to attention. What an odd beginning to a symphony—a blast of three short notes and a long one yields to the same three shorts and a long, all now a step lower. Yet, oddly, despite its force, the music can't quite get going. It starts and stops, then seems to lurch forward and gather momentum. And where is the melody? This three-shorts-and-a-long pattern is less a melody than a motive, striking by virtue of its power and compactness. As the movement unfolds, the actual pitches of the motive prove to be of secondary importance. Beethoven is obsessed with its rhythm. He wants to demonstrate the enormous latent force lurking within even the most basic rhythmic atom, a power waiting to be unleashed by a composer who understands the secrets of rhythmic energy.

To control the sometimes violent forces that will explode, the music unfolds within the traditional confines of sonata–allegro form. The basic four-note motive (Example 15.4) provides all the musical material for the first theme area.

EXAMPLE 15.4 The motive of the first movement

LISTEN TO...
Example 15.4 online.

The brief transition played by a solo French horn is only six notes long and is formed simply by adding two notes to the end of the basic four-note motive (Example 15.5). As expected, the transition carries us tonally from the tonic (C minor) to the relative major (E♭ major).

EXAMPLE 15.5 The motive extended to end transition

LISTEN TO...
Example 15.5 online.

The second theme offers a moment of escape from the rush of the "Fate" motive, but even here the pattern of three shorts and a long lurks beneath like a ticking time bomb (Example 15.6).

EXAMPLE 15.6 Second theme with motive beneath

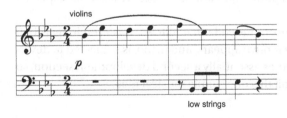

LISTEN TO...
Example 15.6 online.

The closing theme, too, is none other than the motive once again, now presented in a more heroic guise (Example 15.7).

EXAMPLE 15.7 Closing theme

LISTEN TO...
Example 15.7 online.

In the development, the opening motive returns, recapturing, and even surpassing, the force it had at the beginning. Beethoven now inverts the motive—he makes it go up as well as down, though the rhythmic shape remains the same (Example 15.8).

LISTEN TO...

Example 15.8 online.

EXAMPLE 15.8 Motive developed

As the motive rises, so does the musical tension. A powerful rhythmic climax ensues and then gives way to a brief imitative passage. Soon Beethoven reduces the six-note motive of the transition to merely two notes and then just one, passing these figures around *pianissimo* between the strings and winds (Example 15.9).

EXAMPLE 15.9 Transition "decomposed"

Beethoven was a master of the process of thematic penetration—stripping away all extraneous material to get to the core of a musical idea. Here, in this mysterious *pianissimo* passage, he presents the irreducible minimum of his motive: a single note. In the midst of this quiet, the original four-note motive tries to reassert itself *fortissimo*, yet at first cannot do so. Its explosive force, however, cannot be held back. A thunderous return of the opening pitches signals the beginning of the recapitulation.

No sooner do the motive and tonic key reassert themselves than they are suddenly interrupted. Out of the blue, Beethoven interjects a slow, languid solo for oboe. Why did he do this? Think of an overheated pressure cooker about to explode; the unexpected oboe cadenza gently releases the steam. Once musical equilibrium is restored, the recapitulation can, and does, resume its expected course.

What is unexpected is the enormous coda that follows. It is even longer than the exposition! A new form of the motive appears, and it, too, is subjected to development. In fact, this coda constitutes essentially a second development section, so great is Beethoven's urge to exploit this one simple musical idea.

LISTENING GUIDE

Ludwig van Beethoven, Symphony No. 5 in C minor (1808)   Download 43 (7:37)

First movement, *Allegro con brio* (fast with gusto)

Genre: Symphony

Form: Sonata–allegro

WHAT TO LISTEN FOR: How much energy and how many startling effects Beethoven extracts from a simple four-note motive, owing to his extraordinary creative powers. In one form or another, the motive dominates almost every moment of this first movement.

EXPOSITION ([ ] = repeats)

0:00	[1:26]	Two statements of "Fate" motive

0:06	[1:33]	Motive builds momentum in crescendo, working up to climax and three chords, the last of which is held.
0:22	[1:49]	Transition begins and builds to climax using rhythmic motive.
0:43	[2:11]	End of transition played by solo French horn

0:45	[2:14]	Quiet second theme in new major key (relative major), motive below

1:01	[2:27]	Crescendo
1:07	[2:35]	Loud string passage prepares arrival of closing theme.
1:17	[2:44]	Closing theme

DEVELOPMENT

2:54	Motive played *fortissimo* by horn and strings, then passed back and forth between woodwinds and strings
3:16	Another crescendo or "Beethovenian swell"
3:22	Rhythmic climax in which motive is pounded incessantly
3:30	Short passage of imitative counterpoint using transition motive
3:40	Two notes of transition motive passed back and forth
3:51	Single note passed back and forth between winds and strings; gets quiet
4:03	Basic four-note motive tries to reassert itself loudly.
4:11	Motive reenters insistently.

RECAPITULATION

4:17	Return of motive
4:26	Motive gathers momentum and cadences with three chords.

(Continued)

4:37	Unexpected oboe solo

4:51	Motive returns and moves hurriedly to climax.
5:15	Quiet second theme with motive below
5:31	Crescendo leading to closing theme
5:50	Closing theme

CODA

5:59	Motive pounded *fortissimo* on one note, then again a step higher
6:15	Imitative counterpoint
6:30	Rising quarter notes form new four-note pattern.

6:40	New four-note pattern alternates between strings and woodwinds.
7:00	Pounding on single note, then motive as at beginning
7:21	Succession of I–V–I chords brings movement to abrupt end.

LISTEN TO ... this selection streaming online.

WATCH ... an Active Listening Guide of this selection online.

WATCH ... a Stephen Malinowski animation of this selection online.

DO ... Listening Exercise 15.2, Beethoven, Symphony No. 5 in C minor, I, online.

Second Movement

After the pounding that we experienced in the explosive first movement, the calm of the noble *Andante* comes as a welcome change of pace. The mood is at first serene, and the melody is expansive—in contrast to the four-note motive of the first movement, the opening theme here runs on for twenty-two measures. The musical form is also a familiar one: theme and variations. But this is not the simple, easily audible theme and variations of Haydn and Mozart (see Chapter 12). There are two themes: the first lyrical and serene, played mostly by the strings; and the second quiet, then triumphant, played mostly by the brasses (Figure 15.7). By means of this "double" theme and variations, Beethoven demonstrates his ability to add length and complexity to a standard Classical form. He also shows how it is possible to contrast within one movement two starkly opposed expressive domains—the intensely lyrical (theme 1) and the brilliantly heroic (theme 2).

FIGURE 15.7
Original autograph of Beethoven's work on the score of the second movement of his Symphony No. 5. The many corrections in different-colored inks and red pencil suggest the turmoil and constant evolution involved in Beethoven's creative process. Unlike Mozart, to whom finished musical ideas came quickly, Beethoven's art was a continual struggle.

LISTENING GUIDE

Ludwig van Beethoven, Symphony No. 5 in C minor (1808)   Download 44 (10:00)

Second movement, *Andante con moto* (moving with purpose)

Genre: Symphony

Form: Theme and variations

WHAT TO LISTEN FOR: The emotional tension that results from engaging in succession two themes that are very different in mood

THEMES

0:00	Violas and cellos play beginning of theme 1.	
0:24	Woodwinds play middle of theme 1.	
0:36	Violins play end of theme 1.	
0:52	Clarinets, bassoons, and violins play theme 2.	
1:14	Brasses play theme 2 in fanfare style.	
1:30	Mysterious *pianissimo*	

(Continued)

VARIATION 1

1:58	Violas and cellos vary beginning of theme 1 by adding sixteenth notes.	
2:18	Woodwinds play middle of theme 1.
2:31	Strings play end of theme 1.
2:48	Clarinets, bassoons, and violins play theme 2.
3:10	Brasses return with fanfare (theme 2).
3:26	More of mysterious *pianissimo*

VARIATION 2

3:52	Violas and cellos overlay beginning of theme 1 with rapidly moving ornamentation.	
4:27	Pounding repeated chords with theme below in cellos and basses
4:44	Rising scales lead to fermata (hold).
5:04	Woodwinds play fragments of beginning of theme 1.
5:50	Fanfare (theme 2) now returns in full orchestra.
6:36	Woodwinds play beginning of theme 1 detached and in minor key.

VARIATION 3

7:17	Violins play beginning of theme 1 *fortissimo.*
7:43	Woodwinds play middle of theme 1.
7:52	Strings play end of theme 1.

CODA

8:08	Tempo quickens as bassoons play reminiscence of beginning of theme 1.
8:23	Violins play reminiscence of theme 2.
8:34	Woodwinds play middle of theme 1.
8:48	Strings play end of theme 1.
9:11	Ends with repetitions of rhythm of very first measure of movement

LISTEN TO ... this selection streaming online.

WATCH ... an Active Listening Guide of this selection online.

DO ... Listening Exercise 15.3, Beethoven, Symphony No. 5 in C minor, II, online.

Third Movement

In the Classical period, the third movement of a symphony or quartet was usually a graceful minuet and trio (see Table 12.2). Haydn and his pupil Beethoven wanted to infuse this third movement with more life and energy, so they often wrote a faster, more rollicking piece and called it a **scherzo**, meaning "joke" in Italian. And, though there's nothing particularly humorous about the mysterious and sometimes threatening sound of the scherzo of Beethoven's Symphony No. 5, this movement is very far removed from the elegant world of the courtly minuet. In ghostly pizzicatos, the conclusion disappears rather than ends.

Now, a stroke of genius. Beethoven links the third and fourth movements by means of a musical bridge. Holding a single pitch as quietly as possible, the violins create an eerie sound, while the timpani beats menacingly in the background. A three-note motive grows from the violins and is repeated over and over; the interest lies in, not the melody, harmony, or rhythm, but only in a growing volume. This is called a **Beethovenian swell**, a repetitive wave of sound that emerges ever larger and ever louder from the orchestra. With enormous force, the wave finally crashes down, and from it emerges the triumphant beginning of the fourth movement—one of the grandest special effects in all of music.

LISTENING GUIDE

Ludwig van Beethoven, Symphony No. 5 in C minor (1808)   Download 45 (5:30)

Third movement, *Allegro* (fast)

Genre: Symphony

Form: Ternary

WHAT TO LISTEN FOR: This scherzo is no joke. Instead of Beethoven's usually rollicking, jocular scherzo, listen here to the sometimes frightening contrast between sinister strings and deafening French horns.

SCHERZO A

0:00	Cellos and basses creep in with theme 1 and pass it on to higher strings.	
0:09	Repeat	
0:20	French horns *fortissimo* enter with theme 2.	
0:40	Cellos and basses return with theme 1.	
0:55	Crescendo	
1:03	Full orchestra again plays theme 2 *fortissimo.*	
1:25	Development of theme 1	
1:52	Ends with theme 2 *fortissimo*, then *piano*	

(Continued)

TRIO B

1:59	Cellos and basses present subject of fugato.	

Violas and bassoons enter with subject.

Second violins enter with subject.

First violins enter with subject.

2:14   Repeat of imitative entries

2:36   Subject enters imitatively again: Cellos and basses, violas and bassoons, second violins, first violins, and then flutes are added.

3:04   Subject enters imitatively again in same instruments, and flutes extend it.

SCHERZO A

3:30   Quiet return of theme 1 in cellos and basses

3:39   Pizzicato (plucked) presentation of theme 1 in cellos accompanied by bassoons

3:50   Ghostly return of theme 2 in short notes in winds and pizzicato in strings

BRIDGE TO FOURTH MOVEMENT

4:47   Long note held *pianissimo* in strings with timpani beating softly below

5:02   Repeating three-note pattern emerges in first violins.

5:23   Great crescendo leads to fourth movement.

LISTEN TO ... this selection streaming online.

WATCH ... an Active Listening Guide of this selection online.

Fourth Movement

When Beethoven arrived at the finale, he was faced with a nearly impossible task. The last movement of a symphony had traditionally been a light send-off for the audience. How to write a conclusion that would relieve the tension of the preceding musical events yet provide an appropriate, substantive balance to the weighty first movement? To this end, Beethoven created a finale that is longer and beefier than the first movement. To bulk up the orchestra, Beethoven added three trombones, a contrabassoon (low bassoon), and a piccolo (high flute), the first time any of these instruments had been called for in a symphony. He also wrote big, bold, and, in most cases, triadic themes, assigning them most often to the powerful brasses. In these themes and instruments, we hear the "heroic" Beethoven at his best. The finale projects a feeling of affirmation, a sense that superhuman will has triumphed over adversity.

LISTENING GUIDE

Ludwig van Beethoven, Symphony No. 5 in C minor (1808)   Download 46 (8:28)

Fourth movement, *Allegro* (fast)

Genre: Symphony

Form: Sonata–allegro

WHAT TO LISTEN FOR: See if you don't experience a change in mood as you listen to Beethoven's triumph over Fate. Do you not feel a sense of surging exhilaration from beginning to end?

EXPOSITION

0:00	Full orchestra with prominent brasses plays first theme.	
0:33	French horns play transition theme.	
0:59	Strings play second theme.	
1:25	Full orchestra plays closing theme.	

(Repeat of exposition omitted)

DEVELOPMENT

1:56	Loud string tremolo (fluttering)
2:01	Strings and woodwinds pass around fragments of second theme in different keys.
2:24	Double basses begin to play countermelody against second theme.
2:31	Trombones play countermelody.
2:59	Woodwinds and brasses play countermelody above dominant pedal point in cellos and basses.
3:15	Climax and pause on dominant triad
3:35	Ghostly theme from scherzo (third movement) with four-note rhythm

RECAPITULATION

4:09	Full orchestra plays first theme *fortissimo*.
4:42	French horns play transition theme.

(Continued)

| 5:13 | Strings play second theme. |
| 5:38 | Woodwinds play closing theme. |

CODA

6:09	Violins play second theme.
6:19	Brasses and woodwinds play countermelody from development.
6:32	V–I, V–I chords sound like final cadence.
6:40	Bassoons, French horns, flutes, clarinets, and then piccolo continue with transition theme.
7:07	Trill high in piccolo
7:23	Tempo changes to *presto* (very fast).
7:47	Brasses recall first theme, now twice as fast.
7:55	Almost excessive V–I, V–I cadence, then prolonged repeat of final tonic chord

LISTEN TO ... this selection streaming online.

WATCH ... an Active Listening Guide of this selection online.

DO ... Listening Exercise 15.4, Beethoven, Symphony No. 5 in C minor, IV, online.

What was Beethoven's great gift to music, as we hear in his "heroic" symphonies? He discovered sound! Beethoven realized that the newly enlarged orchestra could create great waves of sound. What had been a fleeting, momentary sound in Mozart's day was in Beethoven's hands expanded, by means of volume, and extended, by means of time. Once he hit upon a chord or color he liked, Beethoven would wallow in it, repeating it again and again. At these moments, nothing happens melodically, yet everything happens sonically. Intuitively, we all experience these Beethovenian moments of sonic grandeur with feelings of exaltation. This was revolutionary stuff for Beethoven—and still is for us today. Moods and emotions could be manipulated by sonority alone.

BEETHOVEN THE ECCENTRIC

How would you have characterized Beethoven had you met him? Probably as either a strong-willed or a strange character. Of course his disability (deafness) contributed to his social isolation and seemingly aberrant behavior. But, aside from the issue of hearing, many stories about Beethoven's strange conduct might lead us to ask: Did he not see the world as the rest of us do, or did he simply not care what the world thought of him?

• • •

Here are only a few examples of the composer's unusual behavior:

1. When Beethoven was composing indoors, should it be too hot and his brain become "overheated," he would pour over his head pitchers of water, which would seep through the floorboards into the apartment below, causing unneighborly rows.

2. When composing outdoors (again, in the heat), he would strip down to his underwear, tie his clothes to a pole slung over his shoulder, and walk on, humming and scribbling music as he went.

3. When engaged in an animated conversation (difficult for the deaf composer), he would often mistake a mirror for an open window and spit *on* the former rather than *out* the latter.

4. Upon arriving at a local restaurant, Beethoven once sat and composed for a long time, with such concentration, that he demanded the waiter bring him the bill for his dinner, not realizing that he had neither ordered nor consumed anything.

An engraving of Beethoven, age forty-four, suggesting something of his unpredictable personality. In almost all images of Beethoven, the artist tidies him up, making the composer appear more presentable than he really was.

For his fellow citizens of Vienna, Beethoven was an endless source of both amazement (for his genius) and amusement (for his eccentricities).

The Final Years (1814–1827)

By 1814, Beethoven had lost his hearing entirely and withdrawn from society. His music, too, took on a more remote, inaccessible quality, placing heavy demands on performer and audience alike. In his music of the "heroic" period, Beethoven often seemed to tell a story that the listener could follow. Now, in his late period (Figure 15.8), Beethoven's story seems fragmented, and the listener must put the pieces together, engaging in

FIGURE 15.8
A generally accurate depiction of Beethoven's music room, as drawn by J. N. Hoechle three days after the composer's death. In truth, this room contained two grand pianos. Note the mess still on the piano and the fact that the instrument is filled with broken strings. The spire seen out the window is that of St. Stephen's Cathedral; the bust on the other windowsill is that of Beethoven himself.

long-term listening by tying together melodies or rhythms whose relationships are not immediately obvious. Beethoven seems to have intended this music, not for the audience of his day, but, rather, for future generations. Whether such "difficult" late music was due to Beethoven's internal artistic vision or his total deafness—or both—we shall never know.

Most of Beethoven's late works are piano sonatas and string quartets—intimate, introspective chamber music. But two pieces, the Mass in D major (*Missa Solemnis*, 1823; held in the composer's hands in the chapter opening image) and Symphony No. 9 (1824), are large-scale compositions for full orchestra and chorus. In these later works, Beethoven strives once again to communicate directly to a broad spectrum of humanity.

Symphony No. 9 in D minor (1824)

Beethoven's Symphony No. 9, his last, was the first symphony in the history of music to include a chorus. In the fourth and final movement, he turned to choral voices to add an immediate, human appeal, requiring them to sing a poem in honor of universal brotherhood, Friedrich von Schiller's *An die Freude* (**Ode to Joy**). For more than twenty years, Beethoven had struggled to craft just the right melody for Schiller's text. Example 15.10 gives the final result: Beethoven's complete melody with the poem in English. Observe the direct, foursquare phrase structure of the melody: antecedent, consequent, extension, consequent, or **abcb**, form. Notice also that nearly every pitch is adjacent to the next; there are almost no leaps. Everyone can sing this melody—and that was exactly Beethoven's wish.

LISTEN TO...

Example 15.10 online.

EXAMPLE 15.10 *Ode to Joy*

Having fashioned this simple but inspiring melody, Beethoven used it as the centerpiece of the symphony's finale—indeed, what proved to be Beethoven's own finale in the realm of orchestral music. Here, *Ode to Joy* becomes the thematic foundation of a magnificent set of variations. Beethoven first sets the melody for instruments alone, beginning with the low strains of the double basses and cellos. The theme is repeated three more times, in successively higher registers, gathering force. In each variation, Beethoven changes the surrounding context, rather than the melody itself. This passage demonstrates again how Beethoven, like no composer before him, exploited the power of sound alone, detached from the usual concerns of rhythm, melody, or harmony. When the full orchestra with brilliant brasses presents the theme a fourth time, we feel the power of an overwhelming sonic force.

With this *fortissimo* statement of the theme, the orchestra has done all that it can do alone. Beethoven now bids the chorus to join in, singing Schiller's liberating text. From here to the end of the movement, chorus and orchestra speak with one exalted voice, pressing the tempo, volume, and the range of the pitches to the limits of the performers' abilities. Their message is Beethoven's message: Humanity will be victorious if it strives together, as it does here, to experience great art. In the course of time, Beethoven's hope has been realized: *Ode to Joy* has been sung at all of the Olympic Games since 1956 and currently serves as the official anthem of the European Union. Most encouragingly, *Ode to Joy* flash mobs have popped up around the world and are reproduced on YouTube for millions to enjoy. Beethoven would have loved these—humanity at its best. He embraced all humanity, but only in his music.

WATCH... a YouTube video of an *Ode to Joy* flash mob online.

LISTENING GUIDE

Ludwig van Beethoven, *Ode to Joy* from Symphony No. 9 in D minor (1824)　　　Download 47 (3:04)

Fourth movement (instrumental excerpt only)

Genre: Symphony

Form: Theme and variations

WHAT TO LISTEN FOR: Beethoven's noble melody grows in magnificence from statement in basses and cellos, to variation 1 with bassoon counterpoint, to variation 2 with melody in first violins, to variation 3 with brasses leading the full orchestra.

THEME

0:00　　Theme begins quietly in cellos and double basses.

0:33　　Parts **c** and **b** of the theme are repeated, as in subsequent variations.

VARIATION 1

0:49　　Theme moves higher to second violins; bassoon plays beautiful counterpoint.

VARIATION 2

1:36　　Theme moves higher to first violins; lower strings provide accompaniment.

VARIATION 3

2:22　　Theme moves to high woodwinds and prominent brasses; full orchestra plays loudly.

LISTEN TO ... this selection streaming online.

WATCH ... an Active Listening Guide of this selection online.

WATCH ... a Stephen Malinowski animation of this selection online.

DO ... Listening Exercise 15.5, Beethoven, *Ode to Joy*, online.

What Is Forward Looking in Beethoven's Music?

Beethoven was a cult figure during his own lifetime, and his image continued to tower over all the arts throughout the nineteenth century. He had shown how personal expression might push against and break free of the confines of Classical form. He had expanded the size of the orchestra by calling for new instruments and had doubled the length of the symphony. He had given music "the grand gesture," stunning effects like the crashing introduction to the *"Pathétique"* Sonata and the gigantic crescendo leading to the finale of Symphony No. 5. And, perhaps most important, he had shown that pure sound—sound divorced from melody, harmony, and rhythm—could be glorious in and of itself. The power and originality of his works became the standard against which composers, indeed all artists, of the Romantic era measured their worth. The painting shown earlier in this chapter (see Figure 15.1) depicts Franz Liszt at the piano surrounded by other writers and musicians of the mid-nineteenth century. A larger-than-life bust gazes down from Olympian heights. It is Beethoven, the prophet and high priest of Romanticism.

KEY WORDS

"Pathétique" Sonata (208)	Heiligenstadt Testament (212)	"Eroica" ("Heroic") Symphony (213)	Beethovenian swell (221)
opus (208)	"heroic" period (212)	scherzo (221)	*Ode to Joy* (226)

 Join us on Facebook at Listening to Music with Craig Wright

PRACTICE ... your understanding of this chapter's concepts by comparing Checklists of Musical Style for all historic eras, completing a Musical Style Quiz for the Classical period, and working once more with the chapter's Active Listening Guides online.

DO ... online multiple-choice and critical thinking quizzes that your instructor may assign for a grade.

CHECKLIST OF MUSICAL STYLE *Classical: 1750–1820*

REPRESENTATIVE COMPOSERS

Mozart	Haydn	Beethoven	Schubert

PRINCIPAL GENRES

symphony	opera	sonata	solo concerto
string quartet			

Melody	Short, balanced phrases create tuneful melodies; melody is more influenced by vocal than instrumental style; frequent cadences produce light, airy feeling
Harmony	The rate at which chords change (harmonic rhythm) varies dramatically, creating a dynamic flux and flow; simple chordal harmonies made more active by an "Alberti" bass
Rhythm	Departs from regular, driving patterns of Baroque era to become more stop-and-go; greater rhythmic variety within a single movement
Color	Orchestra grows larger; woodwind section of two flutes, oboes, clarinets, and bassoons becomes typical; piano replaces harpsichord as principal keyboard instrument
Texture	Mostly homophonic; thin bass and middle range, hence light and transparent; passages in contrapuntal style appear sparingly and mainly for contrast
Form	A few standard forms regulate much of Classical music: sonata–allegro, theme and variations, rondo, ternary (for minuets and trios), and double exposition (for solo concerto)

part FIVE

ROMANTICISM, 1820–1900

ROMANTICISM

| 1820 | 1825 | 1830 | 1835 | 1840 | 1845 | 1850 | 1855 |

1818
Mary Shelley writes *Frankenstein*

1826
Felix Mendelssohn composes *Overture to A Midsummer Night's Dream*

1831
Victor Hugo writes *The Hunchback of Notre Dame*

1830
Hector Berlioz composes *Symphonie fantastique*

1830
Revolution of 1830 in Europe

1838
Robert Schumann composes "Dreaming"

1845
Edgar Allen Poe writes poem "The Raven"

1848
Revolution of 1848 in Europe

1848
Karl Marx writes *The Communist Manifesto*

1853
Giuseppe Verdi composes opera *La traviata*

1853–1876
Richard Wagner works on his cycle *Der Ring des Nibelungen*

Today we think of a "romantic" as an idealistic person, a dreamer, sometimes fearful, always hopeful, and perpetually in love. This view resonates with and emerges from the values of the Romantic era (1820–1900), when reason gave way to passion, objective analysis to subjective emotion, and "the real world" to a realm of imagination and dreams. If a single theme dominated the era, it was love; indeed, from the word *romance* we derive the term *romantic*. Nature and the natural beauty of the world also fascinated the Romantics. But the Romantic vision had its dark side as well, for these same artists expressed a fascination with the occult, the supernatural, and the macabre. This was the age not only of Robert Schumann's piano reverie "Dreaming" but also of Mary Shelley's nightmare novel *Frankenstein*.

What was music in the Romantic era? To critic Charles Burney, writing in 1776, music was "an innocent luxury, unnecessary, indeed, to our existence." But to Beethoven, writing in 1812, music was the most important of the arts "that would raise men to the level of gods." Clearly, the very concept of music—its purpose and meaning—had undergone a profound change in thirty-six years. No longer seen merely as entertainment, music now could point the way to previously unexplored realms of the spirit. Beethoven led the way, and many others—Berlioz, Wagner, and Brahms among them—followed in his footsteps. When the German author E. T. A. Hoffmann wrote that Beethoven's Symphony No. 5 "releases the flood gates of fear, of terror, of horror, of pain, and arouses that longing for the eternal which is the essence of Romanticism," he prophesied much Romantic music to come.

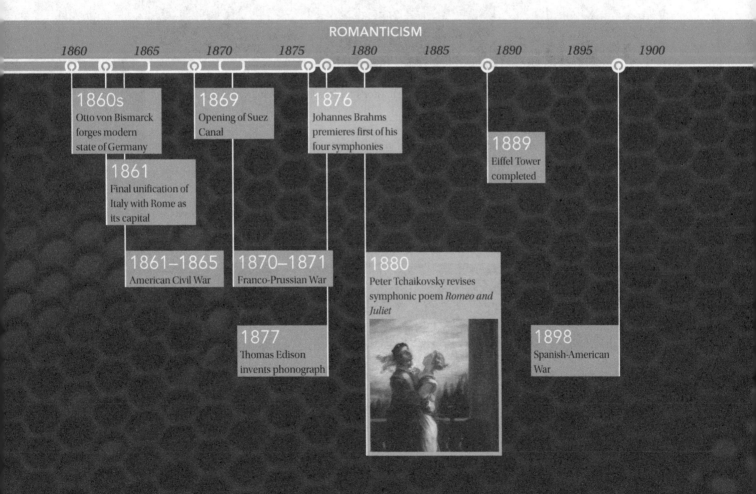

ROMANTICISM

1860 1865 1870 1875 1880 1885 1890 1895 1900

1860s
Otto von Bismarck forges modern state of Germany

1869
Opening of Suez Canal

1876
Johannes Brahms premieres first of his four symphonies

1889
Eiffel Tower completed

1861
Final unification of Italy with Rome as its capital

1861–1865
American Civil War

1870–1871
Franco-Prussian War

1880
Peter Tchaikovsky revises symphonic poem *Romeo and Juliet*

1877
Thomas Edison invents phonograph

1898
Spanish-American War

Introduction to
ROMANTICISM

START... experiencing this chapter's topics with an online video activity.

LEARNING OBJECTIVES

After studying the material in this chapter, you should be able to:

1 Characterize the Romantic era and the musician's place in it.
2 Describe the style of Romantic music in terms of its essential elements.
3 Discuss the growth of the orchestra during the nineteenth century.
4 Trace the advent of the conductor and the virtuoso soloist.

The mature music of Beethoven, with its powerful crescendos, pounding chords, and moments of sonic grandeur, announces the arrival of the Romantic era in music. The transition from musical Classicism to Romanticism in the early nineteenth century coincides with similar stylistic changes in the novels, plays, poetry, and paintings of the period. In all the arts, revolutionary sentiments were in the air: a new desire for liberty, bold action, passionate feeling, and individual expression. Just as the impatient Beethoven finally cast off the wigs and powdered hair of the eighteenth century, many other Romantic artists gradually cast aside the formal constraints of the older Classical style.

READ... the complete chapter text in a rich, interactive online platform.

Romantic Inspiration, Romantic Creativity

Romanticism is often defined as a revolt against the Classical adherence to reason and tradition. Whereas artists of the eighteenth century sought to achieve unity, order, and balance, those of the nineteenth century leaned toward self-expression, striving to communicate with passion no matter what bizarre imbalance might result. If Classical artists drew inspiration from the monuments of ancient Greece and Rome, those of the Romantic era looked to the human imagination and the wonders of nature. The Romantic artist exalted instinctive feelings—not those of the masses, but individual, personal ones. As the American Romantic poet Walt Whitman said, "I celebrate myself, and sing myself."

If a single feeling or sentiment pervaded the Romantic era, it was love. Indeed, "romance" is at the very heart of the word *romantic*. The loves of Romeo and Juliet (as seen in the chapter opening photo) and Tristan and Isolde, for example, captured the public's imagination in the Romantic era. The endless pursuit of an unattainable love became an obsession that, when expressed as music, produced the sounds of longing and yearning heard in so many Romantic works.

Nature, too, worked her magic on the minds of the Romantics (Figure 16.1). Beethoven proclaimed in 1821, "I perform most faithfully the duties that Humanity, God, and Nature enjoin upon me." In his "Pastoral" Symphony (Symphony No. 6), the first important Romantic "nature piece," Beethoven seeks to capture both nature's

FIGURE 16.1

The Dreamer (1840), by German Romantic artist Caspar David Friedrich (1774–1840). The painting suggests two forces dear to the hearts of the Romantics: the natural world and the world of dreams. Here, timeless nature, creator and destroyer of all things human, surrounds a dreamer lost in solitary contemplation. Notice how the tree to the left is squarely centered within the "window" on the left, as if an altar has been erected in honor of nature. In Chapter 19, we will meet Robert Schumann and his composition "Dreaming," which captures this dream world in music.

LOVE AND LUNACY AMONG THE ARTISTS

Just as Romantic music is regarded as the emotional core of classical music generally, so the poetry of the English Romantics (Wordsworth, Keats, Byron, and Shelley) is commonly seen as the heart and soul of poetry in the English language. The eccentric behavior of many of these creators inspired the notion that artists are somehow above "the common cloth" and therefore need not conform to societal norms. Were the musicians and poets of the period free spirits blindly following their creative muse, or were they just self-indulgent—or both? Composers Berlioz, Wagner, and Liszt led lives that were considered scandalous, as did poets George Gordon Byron (1788–1824) and Percy Bysshe Shelley (1792–1822).

Mary Godwin and Percy Bysshe Shelley

Byron—famous today for having swum the Hellespont and having died young while fighting for Greek independence—had a string of affairs and illegitimate children, as well as an incestuous relationship with his half-sister. Shelley was expelled from Oxford, abandoned his first wife (who later drowned herself in the center of London), and ran off with (and eventually married) Mary Godwin (1797–1851). In the summer of 1816, Percy and Mary, along with best friend Byron, lived as neighbors in the Swiss Alps, where, as an evening entertainment, she conceived her gothic novel *Frankenstein*.

Percy Shelley died at age thirty when caught in a sudden storm while sailing on the Italian coast—a fittingly Romantic end. Shelley's poem "Love's Philosophy" (1819), written for Mary, suggests the "lunar" spell under which these capricious English Romantics had fallen.

The fountains mingle with the river
   And the rivers with the ocean,
The winds of heaven mix for ever
   With a sweet emotion;
Nothing in the world is single;
   All things by a law divine
In one spirit meet and mingle.
   Why not I with thine?—
See the mountains kiss high heaven
   And the waves clasp one another;

●●●

> No sister-flower would be forgiven
>   If it disdained its brother;
> And the sunlight clasps the earth
>   And the moonbeams kiss the sea:
> What is all this sweet work worth
>   If thou kiss not me?

In these final lines, we experience the perfect Romantic synthesis of love and nature.

tranquil beauty and its destructive fury. Schubert's "Trout" Quintet, Schumann's *Forest Scenes*, and Strauss's "Alpine" Symphony are just a few of the many musical works that continued this tradition.

Finally, whenever the Romantics embraced subjects like love or nature, or any other, moderation was in short supply. Despair, frenzy, exaltation, and excess of all sorts mark the music and poetry of the Romantic era, as well as the lives of the artists who created it. In Romantic music, for example, the range of expression was broadened by means of "expression marks," such as *espressivo* (expressively), *dolente* (sadly), *presto furioso* (fast and furious), *con forza e passione* (with force and passion), *misterioso* (mysteriously), and *maestoso* (majestically). Not only do these directives explain to the performer how a passage ought to be played, they also reveal what the composer wished the listener to feel while experiencing the music.

The Musician as "Artist," Music as "Art"

We owe to the Romantics the notion that music is more than mere entertainment and the composer more than a hired employee. Bach had been a civil servant, and Haydn and Mozart (mostly) musical domestics in the homes of the great lords of Europe. But Beethoven began to break the chains of servitude. He was the first to demand, and receive, the respect due a great creative spirit. For the composer Franz Liszt (1811–1886), who deeply admired Beethoven, the duty of the artist was nothing less than "the upbringing of mankind." Never was the position of the creative musician loftier than in the mid-nineteenth century.

Just as the musician was elevated from servant to artist, so the music that he or she produced was transformed from entertainment to art. Classical music had been created for the immediate gratification of patron and audience, with little thought given to its lasting value. With the Romantics came the advent of "high art." Symphonies, quartets, and piano sonatas sprang to life, not to give immediate pleasure to listeners, but to satisfy a deep-seated creative urge within the composer. They became extensions of the artist's inner personality. These works might not be understood by the creator's contemporaries, but they would be understood by posterity, by future generations of listeners. The idea of "art for art's sake"—art free of all immediate functional concerns—was born of the Romantic spirit.

Romantic Ideals Change the Listening Experience

Why is everyone so serious in a concert hall? Blame it on the Romantics. Prior to 1800, a concert was as much a social event as a musical experience. People talked, drank, ate, played cards, flirted, and wandered about. Dogs ran freely on the ground floor, and armed guards roamed the theater to maintain at least some order. When people turned to the music, they were loud and demonstrative. They hummed along with the melody and tapped the beat to music they liked. If a performance went well, people applauded, not only at the ends of the pieces, but also between movements. Sometimes they demanded an immediate encore; at other times, they hissed their disapproval.

Around 1840, however, a sudden hush came over the concert hall—rendering it more like a church or temple. With the revered figure of the Romantic artist-composer now before them, the audience sat in respectful silence. A concertgoer who was not distracted socially became a listener who was engaged emotionally. More was expected of the audience, because symphonies and sonatas were now longer and more complex. But the audience, in turn, expected more from the music. The concert was no longer an entertaining event but an emotionally satisfying encounter that would leave the attentive listener exhausted yet somehow purified and uplifted by the artistic experience.

Romanticism has kept its grip on the Western imagination. Belief in the artist as superhero, reverence for the object as a "work of art," and expectations of silence and even formal dress at a concert all developed in the Romantic period. What's more, the notion that a particular group of pieces merited repeated hearings gained currency at this time. Prior to 1800, almost all music was disposable: It was written as entertainment for the moment and then forgotten. But the generation following Beethoven began to consider his finest symphonies, concertos, and quartets, as well as those of Mozart and Haydn, as worthy of preservation and repeated performance (see the end of Chapter 12). These and the best works of succeeding generations came to form a **canon**—indeed, a museum—of classical music, and they constitute the core of today's concert repertoire. The term *classical music* itself was a creation of the early nineteenth century. Thus, what we think about the composer, how we view the work of art, what we can expect to hear at a concert, and even how we dress and behave during the performance are not eternal ideals, with us since time immemorial, but, rather, values created during the Romantic period.

The Style of Romantic Music

Why is film music so often written in the Romantic style? Why are collections of "classical favorites" or "classical moods" filled mostly with music, not of the Classical period, but of the Romantic era? In brief, it's because Romantic music hits an emotional "sweet spot." We love its long, surging melodies and rich harmonies—rendered all the more powerful when delivered by the large and colorful Romantic orchestra. The sound is lush, often sensuous, with little of the aggressive dissonance of more modern music. Because Romantic music is luxuriant and consonant in tone, our psyches cannot resist the Romantic pull.

In truth, however, the works of Romantic composers represent not so much a *revolution* against earlier Classical ideals as an *evolution* beyond them. Composers still wrote symphonies, concertos, string quartets, and sonatas in the Romantic period. But the symphony now grows in length, embodying the most extreme range of expression, while the concerto becomes increasingly virtuosic, as a heroic soloist does battle against an orchestral mass. Romantic composers introduced no new musical forms and only two new genres: the art song (see Chapter 17) and the tone poem (see Chapter 18). Instead, they made music more sonorous, more colorful, and, in some cases, more bizarre.

Romantic Melody

Romantic melodies move beyond the neat, symmetrical units (two plus two, four plus four) inherent in the Classical style, becoming longer, rhythmically more flexible, and increasingly irregular in shape. At the same time, they continue a trend that had developed in the late eighteenth century, in which themes become vocal in conception, more singable or lyrical. Countless melodies of Schubert, Chopin, and Tchaikovsky have been turned into popular songs and movie themes— Romantic music is perfectly suited to the romance of film—because these melodies are so profoundly expressive. Example 16.1 shows the well-known theme from Tchaikovsky's *Romeo and Juliet*. As the brackets indicate, it rises passionately and falls, only to rise higher again, a total of seven times, on the way to a *fortissimo* climax. If we think of music as the sound track for our life, we don't do our laundry to such Romantic melodies; we fall in love!

LISTEN TO...

Example 16.1 online.

EXAMPLE 16.1 Love theme from *Romeo and Juliet*

Colorful Harmony

Part of the emotional intensity of Romantic music was generated by a new, more colorful harmony. Classical music had, in the main, made use of chords built on only the seven notes of the major or minor scale. Romantic composers went further by creating **chromatic harmony**, adding chords constructed on the five remaining notes (the chromatic notes) within the full twelve-note chromatic scale. This gave more colors to their harmonic palette, allowing for the rich, sensuous sounds we associate with Romantic music. Example 16.2 shows a passage with quick-changing chromatic chords, found in a nocturne of Chopin discussed in Chapter 19. The many sharps and flats signal the twisting chromatic movement.

EXAMPLE 16.2 Chromatic harmony

LISTEN TO...

Example 16.2 online.

Chromatic harmony opened up the tonal landscape, encouraging bold shifts between distant chords. Such striking harmonic juxtapositions allowed composers to express a wider range of feeling. In Example 16.3, from another nocturne of Chopin, a chord with four sharps jumps to one with four flats! While such a startling jump violates all the rules of eighteenth-century harmony, our modern ears, accustomed to more bracing harmonies, hear the shift only as pleasing.

EXAMPLE 16.3 Bold harmonic shift

LISTEN TO...
Example 16.3 online.

Finally, nineteenth-century composers gave a "romantic feel" to music by means of dissonance. In fact, longing, pain, and suffering traditionally have been expressed in music by dissonance. According to the traditional rules of composition, all musical dissonance must resolve to consonance. But the longer the dissonance holds, the greater the pain and the desire for resolution. Delaying resolution intensifies feelings of anxiety, longing, and searching, all sentiments appropriate to music that deals with love or loneliness. The very end of Gustav Mahler's orchestral song *Ich bin der Welt abhanden gekommen* (*I Am Lost to the World*) offers a double dissonance–consonance resolution. Violins and then English horn (low oboe) hold a dissonant pitch (see arrows) that resolves downward (see asterisks), dying away (*morendo*) to the final consonant tonic.

EXAMPLE 16.4 Romantic longing expressed through prolonged dissonance

LISTEN TO...
Example 16.4 online.

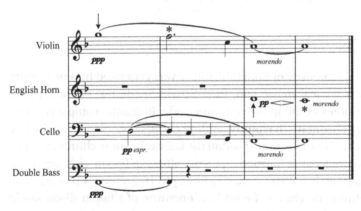

Romantic Tempo: *Rubato*

In keeping with an age that glorified personal freedom and tolerated eccentric behavior, tempo in Romantic music was cut loose from the constraints of a regular beat. The term coined for this was **rubato** (in Italian, literally, "robbed"), a tempo mark that the composer wrote into the score for the benefit of the performer. A performer playing tempo *rubato* "stole" some time here and gave it back there, moving faster or slower so as to create an intensely personal performance. This free approach to tempo was often reinforced by fluctuating dynamic levels that likewise exaggerated the flow of the music. Whatever excesses might result could be excused under the license of artistic freedom.

Bigger Is Better: Greater Length, More Volume and Color

Arts and ideas almost always march in step, and this is true of the notion of length as experienced by the Romantics. Charles Darwin (*On the Origin of Species*, 1859) posited that the earth was not merely 7,000 years old, as the Bible suggested, but several million. Victor Hugo's *Les Misérables* (1862) runs 1,463 pages in the original edition, a scant 8 pages more than Leo Tolstoy's *War and Peace* (1869). And look again at Caspar David Friedrich's *The Dreamer* (Figure 16.1), in which vines overgrowing the ruins of a medieval church suggest the slow, yet inexorable passing of the ages.

Time also passes more slowly in the music of the Romantic era—or at least its pieces last longer. Mozart's G minor symphony (1788) runs about twenty minutes, depending on the tempo of the conductor. But Berlioz's *Symphonie fantastique* (1830) takes nearly fifty-five minutes, and Mahler's Symphony No. 2 (1894) lasts nearly an hour and a half. Perhaps the longest of all musical works is Richard Wagner's four-opera *Ring* cycle (1853–1876), which runs some *seventeen hours* over the course of four evenings—the nineteenth-century equivalent of a miniseries.

Music was getting not only longer but also louder. Whereas the range of music in the Classical era was only *pp* (*pianissimo*) to *ff* (*fortissimo*), now exaggerated "hypermarks" such as *pppp* and *ffff* appear. To create sounds as loud as *ffff*, a larger orchestra and bigger piano were needed. Technology soon obliged to provide them.

The Romantic Orchestra

Does music change technology, or does technology change music? History says the latter. The advent of the phonograph record (1877) ended the monopoly of the live performance; the fidelity wasn't as good as live music, but millions of new listeners would soon enjoy it nonetheless. In the 1940s, the advent of the electric guitar sounded the death knell of swing music and made head-banging rock music possible decades later. In our day, the digital delivery of sound on YouTube and other streaming sites has changed how we receive music as well as its quality. And, just as the digital revolution has altered our contemporary musical landscape, so did technological advancements lead to the modern symphony orchestra.

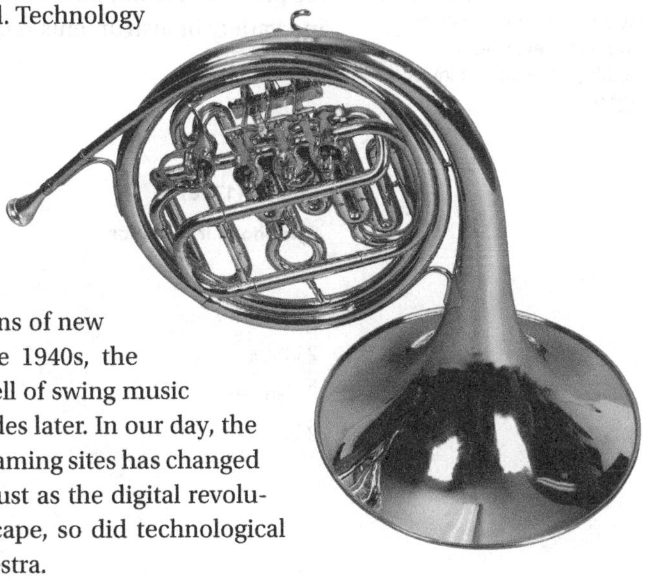

In many ways, the symphony orchestra that we hear today was a product of the nineteenth-century Industrial Revolution. Around 1830, several existing orchestral instruments received mechanical enhancements. The wood of the flute, for example, was replaced by silver, and the instrument was given a new fingering mechanism that added to its agility and made it easier to play in tune. Similarly, the trumpet and French horn were provided with valves that improved technical facility and accuracy of pitch in all keys (Figure 16.2). The French horn, in particular, became an object of special affection during the Romantic period. Its rich, dark tone and its traditional association with the hunt of the forest—and, by extension, all of nature—made it the Romantic instrument par excellence. Even the

FIGURE 16.2
A modern French horn with valves, as invented in France in the 1820s. Before then, the instrument was known in the English-speaking world as simply the "horn" but, after this French innovation, as the "French horn." The valves allow the performer to engage different lengths of tubing instantly and thereby play a full chromatic scale.

FIGURE 16.3
A satirical engraving suggesting the public's impression that Berlioz's (center) vastly enlarged symphony orchestra would harm the audience and might even lead to death (note coffin at lower right).

traditional violin was altered, its fingerboard lengthened and its animal-gut strings replaced with metal wire. This gave the instrument a brighter, more penetrating sound.

Entirely new instruments were added to the Romantic orchestra as well. Beethoven had expanded its range both higher and lower. In his famous Symphony No. 5 (1808; see Chapter 15), he called for a piccolo (a high flute), trombones, and a contrabassoon (a bass bassoon)—the first time any of these had been heard in a symphony. In 1830, Hector Berlioz went even further, requiring an early form of the tuba, an English horn (low oboe), a cornet, and two harps in his *Symphonie fantastique*.

Berlioz, a composer who personified the Romantic spirit, had a typically grandiose notion of what the ideal symphony orchestra should contain. He wanted no fewer than 467 performers, including 120 violins, 40 violas, 45 cellos, 35 double basses, and 30 harps! Such a gigantic instrumental force (Figure 16.3) was never actually assembled, but Berlioz's utopian vision indicates the direction in which Romantic composers were headed. By the second half of the nineteenth century, orchestras with nearly 100 players were not uncommon. Compare, in Table 16.1, for example, the number and variety of instruments required for a typical eighteenth-century performance

TABLE 16.1 Growth of the Symphony Orchestra

Mozart (1788)	Berlioz (1830)	Mahler (1889)
Symphony in G minor	***Symphonie fantastique***	**Symphony No. 1**
	Woodwinds	
1 flute	1 piccolo	3 piccolos
2 oboes	2 flutes	4 flutes
2 clarinets	2 oboes	4 oboes
2 bassoons	1 English horn	1 English horn
	2 B♭ clarinets	4 B♭ clarinets
	1 E♭ clarinet	2 E♭ clarinets
	4 bassoons	1 bass clarinet
		3 bassoons
		1 contrabassoon
	Brasses	
2 French horns	4 French horns	7 French horns
	2 trumpets	5 trumpets
	2 cornets	4 trombones
	3 trombones	1 tuba
	2 ophicleides (tubas)	

Strings		
1st violins (8)*	1st violins (15)*	1st violins (20)*
2nd violins (8)	2nd violins (14)	2nd violins (18)
violas (4)	violas (8)	violas (14)
cellos (4)	cellos (12)	cellos (12)
double basses (3)	double basses (8)	double basses (18)
	2 harps	1 harp
Percussion		
	timpani	timpani (2 players)
	bass drum	bass drum
	snare drum	triangle, cymbals
	cymbals and bells	tam-tam
Total: 36	*Total:* 89	*Total:* 129

*Number of string players estimated according to standards of the period

WATCH... Berlioz's colossal *Grande Messe des morts*, Op. 5 (Requiem), *Dies irae*, "Tuba mirum," online.

DO... Listening Exercise 16.1, Comparing Classical and Romantic Orchestral Works, online.

of Mozart's Symphony in G minor (1788) with the symphony orchestra needed for Berlioz's *Symphonie fantastique* (1830) and for Gustav Mahler's Symphony No. 1 (1888; first performed 1889; published 1906). In the course of 100 years, the orchestra had more than tripled in size. But it went no further: The symphony orchestra that we hear today is essentially that of the late nineteenth century.

Our reaction to the Romantic orchestra today, however, is very different from the response of nineteenth-century listeners. Modern ears have been desensitized by an overexposure to electronically amplified sound, but imagine the impact of an orchestra of 100 players before the days of amplification. Apart from the military cannon and the steam engine, the nineteenth-century orchestra produced the loudest sonic level of any human contrivance. The big sound—and the big contrasts—of the nineteenth-century orchestra were new and startling, and audiences packed ever-larger concert halls to hear these impressive "special effects."

FIGURE 16.4
A large orchestra depicted at Covent Garden Theater, London, in 1846. The conductor stands toward the middle, baton in hand, with strings to his right and woodwinds, brass, and percussion to his left. It was typical in this period to place all or part of the orchestra on risers, which allowed the sound to project more fully.

The Conductor

As the streets of London became more congested with wagons in the mid-nineteenth century, traffic cops appeared, waving red and green flags, and then lanterns at night. So, too, as the Romantic symphony orchestra became larger and more complex, a musical "traffic cop" was needed: the conductor waving a baton (Figure 16.4). In Mozart's day, the leader of the orchestra was one of the

FIGURE 16.5
Composer Carl Maria von Weber conducting with a rolled sheet of music, to highlight the movement of his hand

FIGURE 16.6
Niccolò Paganini

FIGURE 16.7
Paganini sleeping while the devil teaches him to play the violin. In his day, Paganini was thought to be both daredevil and devil—that only a deal with Satan could account for his extraordinary violin-playing powers. Among the stories that circulated: The highest string of Paganini's violin was made of the intestine of his mistress, whom he had murdered with his own hands. The fanciful story continues today in the film *The Devil's Violinist* (2015), with violin rock star David Garrett in the role of Paganini.

performers, either a keyboardist or the first violinist, who led by moving his head and body. But Beethoven, at least toward the end of his life, stood before the orchestra with his back to the audience and waved his hands "like a madman," contemporaries said, gesturing how the music should go. Conductors might also lead with a rolled-up piece of paper, a violin bow, a handkerchief, or a wooden baton, the chosen object intending to clarify the meter and speed of the beat (Figure 16.5). Sometimes the leader merely banged the beat on a music stand. Gradually during the nineteenth century, however, this leader evolved from a mere time beater into an interpreter, and sometimes a dictator, of the musical score. The modern conductor had arrived.

The Virtuoso

Appropriate for an era that glorified the individual, the nineteenth century was the age of the solo **virtuoso**. Of course, instrumental virtuosos had been on the scene before: Bach on the organ and Mozart on the piano, to name just two. Now, though, many musicians began to expend enormous energy striving to raise their performing skills to unprecedented heights. Pianists and violinists, in particular, spent long hours practicing technical exercises—arpeggios, tremolos, trills, and scales played in thirds, sixths, and octaves—to develop showstopping hand speed on their instrument. Naturally, some of what these wizards played was lacking in musical substance, little more than tasteless displays of showmanship designed to appeal immediately to the audiences that packed the ever-larger concert halls.

Franz Liszt (1811–1886) sometimes played at the keyboard with a lighted cigar between his fingers. The Italian Niccolò Paganini (1782–1840; Figures 16.6

and 16.7) secretly tuned the four strings of his violin in ways that would allow him to negotiate with ease extraordinarily difficult, rollercoaster-like passages (Example 16.5). So great was his fame that Paganini became the "celebrity spokesperson" of the day, his picture appearing on napkins, ties, pipes, billiard cues, and powder boxes. Celebrity marketing had arrived, and it started with virtuoso musicians.

EXAMPLE 16.5 Paganini, Caprice, Opus 1, No. 5

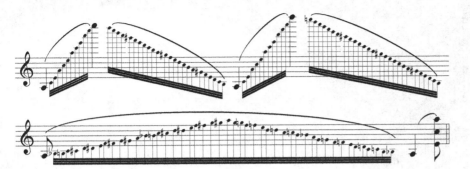

WATCH... a YouTube video of a modern, if fanciful, take on the life of Paganini, online.

KEY WORDS

Romanticism (233)   chromatic harmony (237)   *rubato* (238)   virtuoso (242)
canon (236)

---

f Join us on Facebook at Listening to Music with Craig Wright

---

PRACTICE ... your understanding of this chapter's concepts by comparing Checklists of Musical Style for all historic eras and working once more with the chapter's Active Listening Guides online.

DO ... online multiple-choice and critical thinking quizzes that your instructor may assign for a grade.

ROMANTIC MUSIC:
The Art Song

START... experiencing this chapter's topics with an online video activity.

LEARNING OBJECTIVES
After studying the material in this chapter, you should be able to:

1 Describe what an art song is.
2 List three or four important things about the life of Franz Schubert.
3 Sketch the lives of Robert and Clara Schumann.
4 Differentiate two through-composed songs—one in strophic form and one in strophic variation form.

The decade 1803–1813 stands as perhaps the most auspicious in the history of Western music. In this short span of time were born the composers Hector Berlioz (1803), Felix Mendelssohn (1809), Frédéric Chopin (1810), Robert Schumann (1810), Franz Liszt (1811), Giuseppe Verdi (1813), and Richard Wagner (1813). Add to these the shining figures of Franz Schubert (born 1797) and Clara Schumann (born 1819), and this brilliant galaxy of Romantic musical stars is complete. We call them Romantics because they were part of—indeed, they created—the Romantic movement in music. Perhaps, not surprisingly, they were all very unconventional people. Their lives typify all that we have come to associate with the Romantic spirit: self-expression, passion, a love of nature and literature, occasional excess, and sometimes even a bit of lunacy (see Chapter 16, "Love and Lunacy Among the Artists"). Not only did they create great art, but life and how they lived it also became an art.

READ... the complete chapter text in a rich, interactive online platform.

The Art Song

Popular song became all the rage during the nineteenth century, in America as well as in Europe. In those days, a music lover couldn't listen to a radio or stream an MP3, but he or she could sing, and do so at home from printed sheet music. The popularity of domestic singing was fed by the expansion of printing and by the growing middle-class desire to own a piano (see Chapter 19). Mass production had lowered piano prices, allowing families to buy a modest, upright instrument (see Figure 17.4), put it in the parlor, and gather around it to sing. But what ended in America with the beloved parlor songs of Stephen Foster ("My Old Kentucky Home," "Oh! Susanna," "Beautiful Dreamer") had begun earlier in Europe with a slightly more elevated genre: the art song. An **art song** is a song for solo voice and piano accompaniment, with high artistic aspirations. Because it was cultivated most intensely in German-speaking lands, it is also called the *Lied* (pronounced "leet"; pl., *Lieder*; German for "song").

A song, of course, embodies two art forms: poetry (the lyrics) and music. We never call a piece a "song" unless it has lyrics. In the early nineteenth century, publishers churned out odes, sonnets, ballads, and romances by the thousands. This was the great age of the Romantic poets: among them, Wordsworth, Keats, Shelly, and Byron in England; Hugo in France; and Goethe and Heine in Germany. Many of their poems quickly became song lyrics for young Romantic composers, with the prolific Franz Schubert writing the largest number. His special talent was to fashion music that captured not only the broad spirit but also the small details of the text, creating a sensitive mood painting. Schubert remarked, "When one has a good poem, the music comes easily, melodies just flow, so that composing is a real joy."

Franz Schubert (1797–1828)

Franz Schubert (Figure 17.1) was born in Vienna in 1797. Among the great Viennese masters—Haydn, Mozart, Beethoven, Schubert, Brahms, and Mahler—only he was native-born to the city. Because his father was a schoolteacher, young Franz was groomed for that profession. Yet the boy's obvious musical talent made it imperative that he also take music lessons; his father taught him to play the violin, and his older brother, the piano. At the age of eleven, Schubert was admitted

FIGURE 17.1
Franz Schubert

as a choirboy in the emperor's chapel, a group that is still well known today as the Vienna Boys' Choir.

After his voice changed in 1812, young Franz left the court chapel and enrolled in a teachers' college. He had been spared compulsory military service because he was below the minimum height of five feet, and his sight was so poor that he was compelled to wear the spectacles that are now familiar from his portraits. By 1815, he had become a teacher at his father's primary school. But he found teaching demanding and tedious, and so, after three unpleasant years, Schubert quit his "day job" to give himself over wholly to music.

"You lucky fellow; I really envy you! You live a life of sweet, precious freedom, can give free rein to your musical genius, can express your thoughts in any way you like." This was Schubert's brother's view of the composer's newfound freedom. But, as many Romantics would discover, the reality was harsher than the ideal. Aside from some small income that he earned from the sale of a few songs, he lacked financial support. For most of his adult life, Schubert lived like a bohemian, moving from café to café and helped along by the generosity of his friends, on whose couches he slept when he was broke. A true Romantic, Schubert had traded security for artistic opportunity.

Attending Schubert's decision was a broader change in how and where audiences heard music. As he was reaching artistic maturity, the era of the great aristocratic salon (entertainment hall) was drawing to an end, its role now filled by the middle-class parlor or living room. Here, in less formal surroundings, groups of men and women with a common interest in music, novels, drama, or poetry would meet to read and discuss the latest fashions in these arts. The gatherings at which Schubert appeared, and at which only his compositions were played, were called **Schubertiads** by his friends. In small, purely private assemblies such as these (Figure 17.2), rather than in large public concerts, most of Schubert's best songs had their first performance.

In 1822, disaster befell the composer: Schubert contracted syphilis, a venereal disease that, before the advent of antibiotics, was tantamount to a death sentence. Although he completed a great C minor symphony (1828), a more lyrical one in B

FIGURE 17.2

A small, private, upper-middle-class assembly known as a Schubertiad, named after the composer, at which artists presented their works. The singer before the piano is Johann Vogl, accompanied by the diminutive Schubert at the piano, immediately to Vogl's left. Who's missing? Members of the nobility.

minor—appropriately called the "Unfinished Symphony"—was left incomplete at his death. When Beethoven died in 1827, Schubert served as a torchbearer at the funeral. The next year, he, too, was dead, the youngest of the great composers. The epitaph for his tombstone reads, "The art of music here buried a rich treasure, but even fairer hopes."

Although Schubert composed symphonies, piano sonatas, and even operas in the course of his brief career, he was known in his day almost exclusively as a writer of art songs (*Lieder*). Indeed, he composed more than 600 works in this genre, many of which are minor masterpieces. In a few cases, Schubert chose to set several texts together in a series. In so doing, he created what is called a **song cycle** (something akin to today's "concept album")—a tightly structured group of individual songs that tell a story or treat a single theme. *Die schöne Müllerin* (*The Pretty Maid of the Mill;* twenty songs) and *Winterreise* (*Winter Journey;* twenty-four songs), both of which relate the sad consequences of unrequited love, are Schubert's two great song cycles.

Erlkönig (1815)

Like Mozart, Schubert was a child prodigy. To get an idea of his precocious talent, we need only listen to his song *Erlkönig* (*Elf King*), written when he was just eighteen years old (see Listening Guide). According to a friend's account, Schubert was pacing back and forth, reading a book of poetry by the renowned Johann von Goethe. Suddenly, he reached for a pen and began writing furiously, in one creative act, setting all of Goethe's ballad, *Erlkönig*, to music. A folk **ballad** is a dramatic, usually tragic, story told by a narrator (today's "country music ballad" is a distant descendant of such European folk ballads). In Goethe's *Erlkönig*, an evil Elf King lures a young boy to his death, for legend had it that whomever the Elf King touched would die (Figure 17.3). This tale exemplifies the Romantic fascination with the supernatural and the macabre.

FIGURE 17.3
The ballad of the Elf King, depicted by Schubert's friend Moritz von Schwind. The artist had heard Schubert perform the song at many Schubertiads; indeed, in Figure 17.2, he stands in a crowd of gentlemen next to the door (upper right-hand corner).

The opening line of the poem sets the frightening nocturnal scene: "Who rides so late through night and wind?" With his feverish son cradled in his arms, a father rides at breakneck speed to an inn to seek help. Schubert captures both the general sense of terror in the scene and the detail of the galloping horse; he creates an accompanying figure in the piano (Example 17.1) that pounds on relentlessly, just as fast as the pianist can make it go.

EXAMPLE 17.1 Furious, frightening piano opening

The specter of death, the Elf King, beckons gently to the boy. He does so in seductively sweet tones, in a melody with the gentle lilt and folksy "um-pah-pah" accompaniment of a popular tune (Example 17.2).

EXAMPLE 17.2 The alluring Elf King

Du lie - bes Kind, komm, geh' mit mir!

(Thou dearest boy, come go with me!)

The frightened boy cries out to his father in an agitated line that culminates in a tense, chromatic ascent (Example 17.3).

EXAMPLE 17.3 The frightened boy

chromaticism

Mein Va - ter, mein Va - ter, und hö - rest du nicht, was Er - len - kö - nig mir lei - se ver - spricht?

(Dear father, my father, say, did'st thou not hear the Elf King whisper promises in my ear?)

The boy's cry is heard again and again in the course of the song, each time at a successively higher pitch and with increasingly dissonant harmonies. In this way, the music mirrors the boy's growing terror. The father tries to calm the boy in low tones that are steady, stable, and repetitive. The Elf King at first charms in sweet, consonant tones but then threatens in dissonant ones, as seduction gives way to abduction. Thus, each of the three characters of the story is portrayed with distinct musical qualities (although all are sung by a single voice). This is musical characterization at its finest; the melody and accompaniment not only support the text but also intensify and enrich it. Suddenly the end is reached: The hand of the Elf King (Death) has touched his victim. Anxiety gives way to sorrow as the narrator announces in increasingly somber (minor) tones, "But in his arms, his child was dead!"

LISTENING GUIDE

Franz Schubert, Erlkönig (1815)   Download 48 (4:13)

Genre: Art song

Form: Through-composed

WHAT TO LISTEN FOR: Onomatopoeic music—music that sounds out its meaning at every turn. In this art song, Schubert takes the changing expressive elements of the text (galloping horse; steady, reassuring tones of the father; sweet enticements of the Elf King; increasingly frantic cries of the boy) and provides each with characteristic music. Done today, such a treatment would likely be cartoon music; done by a master songwriter like Schubert, it is great art.

0:00   Piano introduction: pounding triplets in right hand and ominous minor-mode motive in left hand

Narrator

0:23		Wer reitet so spät	Who rides so late
		durch Nacht und Wind?	through night and wind?
		Es ist der Vater	A loving father
		mit seinem Kind.	with his child.
		Er hat den Knaben wohl	He clasps his boy close
		in dem Arm,	with his arm,
		er fasst ihn sicher,	he holds him tightly
		er hält ihn warm.	and keeps him warm.

Father

| 0:56 | | Mein Sohn, was birgst | My son, what makes you |
| | | du so bang dein Gesicht? | hide your face in fear? |

Son

| 1:04 | With disjunct leaps but no agitation | Siehst, Vater, du den Erlkönig nicht? Den Erlenkönig mit Kron' und Schweif? | Father don't you see the Elf King? The Elf King with crown and shroud? |

Father

| 1:20 | In low, calming tones | Mein Sohn, es ist ein Nebelstreif. | My son, it's only some streak of mist. |

(*Continued*)

1:31	With seductive melody in major key	Du liebes Kind, komm, geh' mit mir! gar schöne Spiele spiel' ich mit dir; manch' bunte Blumen sind an dem Strand, meine Mutter hat manch' gülden Gewand.	**Elf King** You dear child, come along with me! I'll play some very fine games with you; where varied blossoms are on meadows fair, and my mother has golden garments to wear.
1:54	Growing agitation depicted by tight chromatic movement in voice	Mein Vater, mein Vater, und hörest du nicht, was Erlenkönig mir leise verspricht?	**Son** My father, my father, do you not hear how the Elf King whispers promises in my ear?
2:07	In low, steady pitches	Sei ruhig, bleibe ruhig, mein Kind, in dürren Blättern säuselt der Wind.	**Father** Be calm, stay calm, my child, Through wither'd leaves the wind blows wild.
2:18	With happy, lilting tune in major key	Willst, feiner Knabe, du mit mir geh'n? Meine Töchter sollen dich warten schön, meine Töchter führen den nächtlichen Reih'n, und wiegen und tanzen und singen dich ein.	**Elf King** My handsome young lad, will you come with me? My beauteous daughters wait for you, With them you would join in the dance every night, and they will rock and dance and sing you to sleep.
2:35	Intense chromatic notes, but now a step higher and with minor key, suggesting panic	Mein Vater, mein Vater, und siehst du nicht dort Erlkönigs Töchter am düstern Ort?	**Son** My Father, my father, don't you see at all the Elf King's daughters over there in the dusk?
2:48	Low register, but more leaps (agitation) than before	Mein Sohn, mein Sohn, ich seh' es genau, es scheinen die alten Weiden so grau.	**Father** My son, my son, the form you there see, is only the aging gray willow tree.
3:05	Music starts seductively but then turns minor and menacing.	Ich liebe dich, mich reizt deine schöne Gestalt; und bist du nicht willig, so brauch' ich Gewalt!	**Elf King** I love you, I'm charmed by your fine appearance; And if you're not willing, I'll seize you by force!

			Son	
3:17	Piercing cries in highest range	Mein Vater, mein Vater, jetzt fasst er mich an! Erlkönig hat mir ein Leids gethan!	My father, my father, now he's got me! The Elf King has seized me by his trick!
			Narrator	
3:31	With rising and then falling line	Dem Vater grausets; er reitet geschwind, er hält in den Armen das ächzende Kind. Erreicht den Hof mit Müh' und Noth:	The father shudders; he rides headlong, holding the groaning child in his arms. He reaches the inn with toil and dread:
3:47	Piano slows down and stops; then recitative	in seinen Armen das Kind war todt!	but in his arms his child was dead!

LISTEN TO ... this selection streaming online.

WATCH ... an Active Listening Guide of this selection online.

WATCH ... various interpretations of this selection online.

DO ... Listening Exercise 17.1, Schubert, *Erlkönig*, online.

Just as the tension in Goethe's poem rises incessantly from the beginning to the very end, Schubert's music unfolds continually, without significant repetition. Such a musical composition featuring ever-changing melodic and harmonic material is called **through-composed**, and Schubert's *Erlkönig*, accordingly, is termed a through-composed art song. For lyric poems, as opposed to dramatic ballads like *Erlkönig*, however, **strophic form** is usually preferred. In strophic form, a single poetic mood or emotion is maintained from one stanza, or strophe, of the text to the next, and the music is repeated. Most pop songs are written in strophic form, each strophe consisting of a verse and chorus. For a very familiar example of a nineteenth-century art song in strophic form, revisit the famous Brahms *Lullaby* (Download 5).

Clara Wieck Schumann (1819–1896)

The nineteenth century had few "power couples" because, for the most part, there were few woman with any power (see box, "Where Were the Women?"). One exception, however, was the duo of Robert and Clara Schumann. We will get to know Robert better in Chapter 19. But when Clara met Robert in 1830, he was a nobody and she a star. Robert Schumann had just dropped out of law school and moved to Leipzig, Germany, to begin the study of piano under the tutelage of the renowned Friedrich Wieck (1785–1873). Wieck just happened to have a beautiful

WHERE WERE THE WOMEN?

You may have noticed that female composers are poorly represented in this book. We have explored the works of Hildegard of Bingen and the Countess of Dia (Chapter 4), and later we will meet those of Ellen Taaffe Zwilich (Chapter 27) and Caroline Shaw (Chapter 28). But, in general, although women have been actively engaged as performers of secular music since the Middle Ages, only rarely have they become composers. Nor have women become poets or painters in any number. To answer the question, "Why not?" we turn to the insights of the famous novelist Virginia Woolf.

In a brilliant essay entitled "A Room of One's Own" (1929), Woolf first pointedly identified two causes that had "disabled" creative women over the centuries: lack of opportunity and lack of encouragement. Had Shakespeare had a talented sister named Judith, she couldn't have become a playwright. Daughters were almost never given lessons in musical composition or painting, and female authors were forced to disguise their gender through pen names such as George Sand (Aurore Dudevant) and George Elliot (Mary Ann Evans).

Two examples from Paris, a major artistic capital, typify the difficulty that women had in learning the rules of the game. Although founded in 1793, the Paris Conservatory did not admit women into classes in advanced music theory and composition until almost a century later; women might study piano, but according to a decree of the 1820s, they had to enter and leave by a separate door. Similarly, the state-sponsored Academy of Fine Arts in Paris did not admit women painters until 1897; even then, they were barred from nude anatomy classes, instruction crucial to the figural arts, because their presence was thought "morally inappropriate." Only in those exceptional cases in which a daughter received an intensive musical education at home did a woman have a fighting chance to become a musical creator.

Even among "home-schooled" women, however, opposition and self-doubt existed. As Clara Schumann wrote in her diary, "I once believed that I possessed creative talent, but I have given up this idea; a woman must not desire to compose. There has never yet been one able to do it. Should I expect to be that one?" And Fanny Mendelssohn Hensel (1805–1847), the gifted sister of composer Felix Mendelssohn, received this mandate from her father when she was fifteen years old and was considering music as a profession: "What you wrote to me about your musical occupations, and in comparison to those of Felix, was rightly thought

Fanny Mendelssohn in 1829, in a sketch by her husband-to-be, Wilhelm Hensel

and expressed. But though music will perhaps become his profession, for you it can and must only be an ornament, never the core of your existence.... You must become more steady and collected, and prepare yourself for your real calling, the only calling for a young woman—*the state of a housewife!* [emphasis added]."

Times have changed. That two of the three most recent winners of the Pulitzer Prize for musical composition are women does not reflect political correctness. The musical scores are judged anonymously.

daughter, Clara, a child piano prodigy, who at the age of eleven had already turned heads in Paris. Within a few years, Robert and Clara had fallen in love; he was then twenty-four, she fifteen. But father Friedrich adamantly opposed their marriage, and in those days a girl needed her father's consent. Robert seemed to have no prospects, especially after an injury to his right hand had ended all hopes of a career as a concert pianist. Only after a protracted legal battle and a court decree did Robert and Clara wed, on September 12, 1840 (Figure 17.4). The day Robert Schumann won his court victory for the hand of Clara, he wrote in his diary, "Happiest day and end of the struggle."

But their struggles had just begun. Clara Wieck Schumann had been one of the great piano virtuosos of the nineteenth century. After her marriage, she assumed the role of wife to Robert and mother to the eight children she soon bore him. Clara, too, had tried her hand at musical composition, writing mostly art songs and other forms of chamber music. But as her children grew more numerous—and Robert's mental health deteriorated (see "Lives of Tragedy and Fidelity" below)—her compositions became fewer, and her concert tours were curtailed. Self-doubt made things worse, as she came to question the capacity of any woman to excel as a creative artist (see box, "Where Were the Women?"). Thus, Clara's most productive period as a composer coincided with the very early years of her marriage to Robert.

FIGURE 17.4
Robert and Clara Schumann in 1850, from an engraving constructed from an early photograph. Notice that they stand next to a small upright piano rather than a grand piano. In a grand piano, the strings run parallel with the ground; in an upright piano, they run at right angles to the ground. An upright fits better in a modest, middle-class living room and is less expensive to manufacture.

"Liebst du um Schönheit" (1841)

Clara Schumann composed her *Lied*, "Liebst du um Schönheit" ("If You Love for Beauty"), in 1841, the year after her wedding. Expressing the optimism of a newlywed, the playful four-stanza text by Friedrich Rückert sets forth three reasons (stanzas 1–3) why the lady should *not* be loved—not for beauty, youth, or money (all three of which Clara actually possessed)—but one (last stanza) for which she *should* be loved—for love alone. Although the melodic and accompanimental figures presented in the first strophe prevail in subsequent ones, Clara varies the musical setting on each occasion, thereby producing what is called **modified strophic form** (the music of each strophe changes slightly from one to the next). Here, a form represented as **AA'A''A'''** results. Example 17.4 shows the melody of strophe 1 and how it is modified in strophe 2. The ever-evolving music gives this art song its remarkable freshness. Had you not known, would you have guessed that this song was composed by a woman? Does such a thing as a "female sound" exist?

EXAMPLE 17.4 Strophe 2 modifies strophe 1

Strophe 1

Liebst du um Schön-heit, o nicht mich lie-be! Lie - be die Son-ne, sie trägt ein gold-nes Haar!

(If you love for beauty, don't love me! Love the sun, with her golden hair!)

Strophe 2

Liebst du um Ju-gend, o nicht mich lie-be! Lie-be den Früh-ling der ist je-des Jahr!

(If you love for youth, don't love me! Love the spring, which is young each year!)

LISTENING GUIDE

Clara Schumann, "Liebst du um Schönheit" (1841)　　　　　　Download 49 (2:32)

Genre: Art song

Form: Modified strophic (**AA'A''A'''**)

WHAT TO LISTEN FOR: The ever-so-slight changes in the vocal line and accompaniment from one stanza to the next; the musical freshness and sparkle that can perhaps be created only by a young person in love

			Strophe 1	
0:00	A	Liebst du um Schönheit, o nicht mich liebe!	If you love for beauty, don't love me!
		Liebe die Sonne, sie trägt ein gold'nes Haar!	Love the sun, with her golden hair!

			Strophe 2	
0:34	A'	Liebst du um Jugend, o nicht mich liebe!	If you love for youth, don't love me!
		Liebe den Frühling, der jung ist jedes Jahr!	Love the spring, which is young each year!

			Strophe 3	
1:00	A''	Liebst du um Schätze, o nicht mich liebe!	If you love for money, don't love me!
		Liebe die Meerfrau, sie hat viel Perlen klar!	Love the mermaid, she has many pearls!

			Strophe 4	
1:27	A'''	Liebst du um Liebe, o ja—mich liebe!	If you love for love, oh yes—love me!
		Liebe mich immer, dich lieb' ich immerdar!	Love me for always, and I will love you eternally!
2:04		Brief coda for piano alone	

LISTEN TO ... this selection streaming online.

WATCH ... an Active Listening Guide of this selection online.

DO ... Listening Exercise 17.2, Clara Schumann, "Liebst du um Schönheit," online.

Lives of Tragedy and Fidelity

From his earliest years, Robert Schumann had been afflicted with what psychiatrists now call bipolar disorder. His moods swung from energetic euphoria to suicidal depression. In some years, he produced a torrent of music; in others, virtually nothing. As time progressed, Schumann's condition worsened. He began to hear voices, both heavenly and hellish, and warned Clara that he might harm her. One morning, pursued by demons within, he jumped off a bridge into the Rhine River. Nearby fishermen pulled him to safety, but from then on, by his own request, he was confined to an asylum, where he died of dementia in 1856 at the age of forty-six.

Clara Schumann outlived Robert by forty years. She raised the children, and to pay the bills, she gradually resumed her career as a touring piano virtuoso. Always dressed in black mourning ("widow's weeds," as they were called), she played across Europe into the 1890s. After Robert's death, Clara never composed again and never remarried. Proving that life sometimes imitates art, Clara remained true to the pledge made in her song "Liebst du um Schönheit": "I will love you eternally." Today, the Schumanns rest side by side in a small cemetery in Bonn, Germany—two souls exemplifying Romantic faith in eternal love.

KEY WORDS

art song (245)	Schubertiad (246)	ballad (247)	strophic form (251)
Lied (pl. *Lieder*) (245)	song cycle (247)	through-composed (251)	modified strophic form (253)

 Join us on Facebook at Listening to Music with Craig Wright

PRACTICE ... your understanding of this chapter's concepts by comparing Checklists of Musical Style for all historic eras and working once more with the chapter's Active Listening Guides online.

DO ... online multiple-choice and critical thinking quizzes that your instructor may assign for a grade.

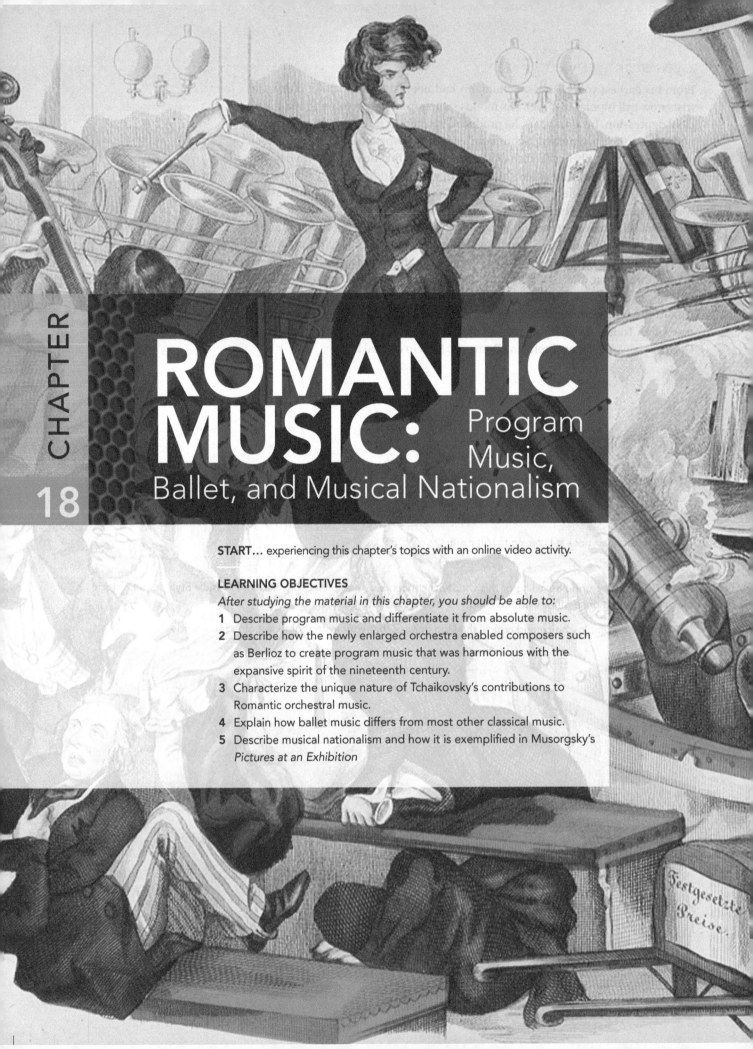

ROMANTIC MUSIC: Program Music, Ballet, and Musical Nationalism

START... experiencing this chapter's topics with an online video activity.

LEARNING OBJECTIVES

After studying the material in this chapter, you should be able to:

1 Describe program music and differentiate it from absolute music.

2 Describe how the newly enlarged orchestra enabled composers such as Berlioz to create program music that was harmonious with the expansive spirit of the nineteenth century.

3 Characterize the unique nature of Tchaikovsky's contributions to Romantic orchestral music.

4 Explain how ballet music differs from most other classical music.

5 Describe musical nationalism and how it is exemplified in Musorgsky's *Pictures at an Exhibition*

Program Music

READ... the complete chapter text in a rich, interactive online platform.

The Romantic love of literature stimulated interest not only in the art song (see Chapter 17) but also in program music. Indeed, the nineteenth century can fairly be called the "century of program music." True, there had been earlier isolated examples of program music—in Vivaldi's *The Four Seasons*, for example (see Chapter 7). But Romantic composers believed that music could be more than pure, abstract sound—that musical sounds alone (without a text) could tell a story. Most important, they now had the power and color of the newly enlarged orchestra to help tell the tale.

Program music is instrumental music that seeks to re-create in sound the events and emotions portrayed in some extramusical source: a story, legend, play, novel, even a historical event. Almost always, program music is composed for a symphony orchestra because its distinctive instrumental sounds can tell a story in the most colorful, vivid detail. Similarly, specific musical gestures empower program music because they, too, evoke particular feelings and associations. A lyrical melody may spur memories of love, harshly dissonant chords may imply conflict, or a rising trumpet call may suggest the arrival of the hero, for example. By stringing together such musical gestures in a convincing sequence, a composer can tell a story through music. Program music is fully harmonious with the strongly literary spirit of the nineteenth century, when the short story and the novel became commonplace.

Some Romantic composers, notably Johannes Brahms (1833–1897), resisted the allure of program music and continued to write what came to be called **absolute music**—symphonies, sonatas, quartets, and other instrumental music without extramusical or programmatic references (see Chapter 23). The composer of *absolute music* left it to the listener to infer whatever "meaning" he or she wished. The composer of *program music*, however, told the listener what to experience by crafting a sequence of sounds that implied a narrative. In 1850, composer Franz Liszt got to the heart of the matter when he observed that a program "provided a means by which to protect the listener against a wrong poetical interpretation and to direct his attention to the poetical idea of the whole."

The three most common types of program music are the following:

- **Dramatic overture** (to an opera, a play, or even a festival): a one-movement work, usually in sonata–allegro form, that portrays through music a sequence of dramatic events. Many overtures became audience favorites and are today performed at concerts without the opera or play that originally inspired them. Examples include Rossini's overture to his opera *William Tell* (1829), and Mendelssohn's *Overture* (1826) to Shakespeare's play *A Midsummer Night's Dream*, as well as Tchaikovsky's *1812 Overture* (1882), written to commemorate Russia's victory over Napoleon.

- **Tone poem** (also called **symphonic poem**): a one-movement work for orchestra that gives musical expression to the emotions and events associated with a story, play, political event, or personal experience. Examples include Tchaikovsky's *Romeo and Juliet* (1869; revised 1880), Musorgsky's *Night on Bald Mountain* (1867), and Strauss's *Also sprach Zarathustra* (1896). In fact, the tone poem and the dramatic overture differ very little: Both are one-movement orchestral works with programmatic content intended for the concert hall.

- **Program symphony**: a symphony with the usual three, four, or five movements, which together depict a succession of specific events or scenes drawn from an extramusical story or event. Examples include Berlioz's *Symphonie fantastique* (1830) and Liszt's "Faust" Symphony (1857).

Hector Berlioz (1803–1869) and the Program Symphony

FIGURE 18.1
Hector Berlioz at the age of twenty-nine

Hector Berlioz (Figure 18.1) was one of the most unusual figures in the history of music. He was born in 1803 near the mountain city of Grenoble, France, the son of a local doctor. As a youth, Berlioz studied mainly the sciences and ancient Roman literature. Although local tutors taught him to play the flute and guitar, he had no systematic training in music theory or composition and little exposure to classical music. Among the major composers of the nineteenth century, he was the only one without fluency at the keyboard. He never studied piano and could do no more than bang out a few chords.

At the age of seventeen, Berlioz was sent off to Paris to study medicine, his father's profession. For two years, he pursued a program in the physical sciences, earning a degree in 1821. But Berlioz found the medical dissecting table horrific— "rats in the corners gnawing on bleeding vertebrae"—and the allure of the concert hall irresistible. After a period of soul-searching over the choice of a career, he vowed to become "no doctor or apothecary but a great composer."

If you told your parents that you'd dropped out of medical school to become a composer, how would they react? Berlioz's father did the predictable. He immediately cut off his son's living stipend, leaving young Berlioz to ponder how he might support himself while studying composition at the Paris Conservatory (the French national school of music). Other composers had relied on teaching as a means to earn a regular income. But with no particular skill at any instrument, what music could Berlioz teach? Instead, he turned to music criticism, writing reviews and articles for literary journals and newspapers—both very much on the rise in the more literate society of the nineteenth century. Berlioz was the first composer to earn a livelihood as a music critic, and it was criticism, not composition, that remained his primary source of income for the rest of his life.

Perhaps it was inevitable that Berlioz would turn to writing about music, for in his mind, a connection had always existed between music and the written word. As a student, Berlioz encountered the works of Shakespeare, and the experience changed his life: "Shakespeare, coming upon me unawares, struck me like a thunderbolt. The lightning flash of that discovery revealed to me at a stroke the whole heaven of art." Berlioz devoured Shakespeare's plays and based musical compositions on four of them: *The Tempest, King Lear, Hamlet*, and *Romeo and Juliet*. The common denominator in the art of both Shakespeare and Berlioz is range of expression. Just as no dramatist before Shakespeare had portrayed the full spectrum of human emotions on the stage, so no composer before Berlioz, not even Beethoven, had undertaken to create such a wide range of moods through sound.

To depict wild swings of mood in music, Berlioz called for enormous orchestral and choral forces—hundreds and hundreds of performers (see Figure 18.2 and Chapter 16, "Bigger Is Better: Greater Length, More Volume and Color"). He also experimented with new instruments: the **ophicleide** (an early form of the tuba), the **English horn** (a low oboe), the harp (an ancient instrument that he brought into the symphony orchestra for the first time), the **cornet** (a small, trumpet-like instrument with valves, borrowed from the military band), and even the newly invented saxophone. In 1843, Berlioz wrote a textbook on **orchestration**—the art of arranging a composer's music for just the right instruments—that is still used today in colleges and conservatories around the world. The boy who couldn't play the piano had become a master of the orchestra!

Berlioz's approach to musical form was equally innovative; he rarely used such standard forms as sonata–allegro or theme and variations. Instead, he preferred to create forms that flowed from the particular narrative of the story at hand. His French compatriots called his seemingly formless compositions "bizarre" and "monstrous," and thought him something of a madman. Subscribing to the adage "No man is a prophet in his own land," Berlioz took his progressive music to London, Vienna, Prague, and even Moscow, introducing such works as *Symphonie fantastique* and *Romeo and Juliet*. He died in Paris in 1869, isolated and embittered, the little recognition he received in his native France having come too late to boost his career or self-esteem.

Symphonie fantastique (1830)

Berlioz's most celebrated composition, then and now, is his *Symphonie fantastique*, perhaps the single most radical example of musical Romanticism. Here, musical form and orchestration are progressive; the programmatic content is revolutionary. Over the course of five movements, Berlioz tells a story, thus creating the first program symphony—in today's terms, a musical miniseries with five episodes. True to its name, the story surrounding *Symphonie fantastique* is more fantastical—more Hollywood—than fiction.

In September 1827, impressionable Hector Berlioz went to the theater in Paris, specifically to see a troupe of English actors present Shakespeare's *Romeo and Juliet* and then *Hamlet*. Though he understood little English, Shakespearean drama overwhelmed Berlioz with its human insights, touching beauty, and sometimes bloody onstage actions. But Berlioz not only fell in love with Shakespeare's work, he was also smitten with the leading lady who played Ophelia to Hamlet and Juliet to Romeo—Harriet Smithson (Figure 18.3). As a crazed young man might stalk a Hollywood starlet today, Berlioz wrote passionate letters and chased after Smithson. Eventually, his ardor cooled—for a time, he even became engaged to someone else. But the experience of an all-consuming love, the despair of rejection, and the vision of darkness and possible death furnished the stimulus—and story line—for an unusually imaginative symphony.

Symphonie fantastique derives its title, not because it is "fantastic" in the sense of "wonderful" (though it is), but because it is a fantasy: Over the course of a symphony, Berlioz fantasizes about his relationship with Harriet Smithson. The thread that binds the five disparate movements is a single melody that personifies the beloved. Berlioz called this theme his ***idée fixe***

FIGURE 18.2
A caricature of Berlioz conducting in mid-nineteenth-century Paris, in what became known as "monster concerts" because of the massive forces the composer required. Berlioz would have liked several hundred performers for the premiere of his *Symphonie fantastique* in 1830, but the printed program suggests that he had to settle for about 100.

FIGURE 18.3
The actress Harriet Smithson became an obsession for Berlioz and the source of inspiration for his *Symphonie fantastique*. Eventually, Berlioz did meet and marry Smithson (see box below, "The Real End of the Program").

("fixed idea," or musical fixation); the melody is always present—like Harriet, an obsession in Berlioz's tortured mind. However, as his feelings about Harriet change from movement to movement, the composer transforms the fundamental melody, altering the pitches, rhythms, and instrumental color. To make sure the listener could follow this wild progression of emotional states, Berlioz prepared a written program (quoted below) to be followed as the music was performed. This, too, was radical, for program notes at concerts at this time were nonexistent. Berlioz's episodic tale unfolds like a bad romance: unrequited love, attempted suicide by drug overdose, murder of a starlet, and a hellish revenge.

First Movement: Reveries, Passions

> Program: A young musician...sees for the first time a woman who embodies all the charms of the ideal being he has imagined in his dreams....The subject of the first movement is the passage from this state of melancholy reverie, interrupted by a few moments of joy, to that of delirious passion, with movements of fury, jealousy, and its return to tenderness, tears, and religious consolation.

A slow introduction ("this state of melancholy reverie") prepares the way for the first vision of the beloved, who is represented by the first appearance of the main theme, the *idée fixe* (Example 18.1).

EXAMPLE 18.1 The *idée fixe*

The movement progresses in something akin to sonata–allegro form. The "recapitulation," however, doesn't so much repeat the *idée fixe* as transform the melody to reflect the artist's feelings of sorrow and tenderness.

Second Movement: A Ball

> Program: The artist finds himself ... in the midst of the tumult of a party.

A lilting waltz now begins, but it is interrupted by the unexpected appearance of the *idée fixe* (the beloved has arrived), its rhythm changed to accommodate the triple meter of the waltz. Four harps add a graceful accompaniment when the waltz returns, and, toward the end, there is even a lovely solo for cornet. The sequence of waltz-*idée fixe*-waltz creates a ternary form.

Third Movement: Scene in the Country

> Program: Finding himself one evening in the country, the artist hears in the distance two shepherds piping....He reflects upon his isolation and hopes that soon he will no longer be alone.

The dialogue between the shepherds (artist and beloved perhaps?) is presented by an English horn and an oboe, the latter played offstage to give the effect of a distant response. The unexpected appearance of the *idée fixe* in the woodwinds suggests that the artist has hopes of winning his beloved. But has she falsely encouraged him? In response to the lonely petition of an English horn, we now hear only silence. She loves me, she loves me not.

Fourth Movement: March to the Scaffold

> Program: Having realized that his love goes unrecognized, the artist poisons himself with opium. The dose of the narcotic, too weak to kill him, plunges him into a sleep accompanied by the most horrible visions. He dreams that he has killed the one he loved, that he is condemned, led to the scaffold, and now witnesses his own execution.

This drug-induced nightmare—opium was the drug of choice of the Romantics—centers on the march to the scaffold where the artist is to be executed. The steady beat of the low strings and the muffled bass drum sound the steps of the procession. Near the end, the image of the beloved returns in the clarinet, only to be suddenly cut off by a *fortissimo* crash by the full orchestra. The guillotine has fallen and with it the lover's head.

Berlioz grew up during the aftermath of the French Revolution and Napoleonic Wars, when troops and military bands marched through the streets. "March to the Scaffold" begins with a "gloomy and wild" march, followed by a "brilliant and grand" one. Periodically, powerful, low brass instruments blare forth (see Listening Guide), led by the new ophicleide (tuba). Equally striking, at 2:12, Berlioz assigns to each and every note of a descending scale a different instrumental color. And he writes his climax—drum roll, please—with a crescendo and snare drum announcing the fall of the guillotine (see Figure 18.4). So graphically does Berlioz orchestrate this moment that we hear the severed head of the lover thud on the ground—a musical first (and last).

FIGURE 18.4
The iconic moment of the French Revolution was the beheading of Marie Antoinette (see Figure 10.6) at the guillotine in 1793, as accurately depicted in this contemporary illustration. Public executions then made great spectator sport, as the large crowd here suggests. Remarkably, Berlioz captured many of these details (march to scaffold by military troops, descending guillotine, severed head, cheering crowd) through the "special effects" of his program music.

LISTENING GUIDE

Hector Berlioz, *Symphonie fantastique* (1830)   Download 50 (4:48)

Fourth movement, "March to the Scaffold"

WHAT TO LISTEN FOR: Rousing marches and an execution at the guillotine—program music at its most graphic—all brought off by a brilliantly inventive orchestration. At the end, repeated brass chords signal the cheer of the crowd—executions were once spectator sports.

0:00	Drums announce quiet introduction.
0:28	Loud first march commences (condemned led to the scaffold).

0:41	March theme repeats with bassoon counterpoint.
1:40	New, loud march theme (the crowd roars)

2:05	Low brass, including ophicleide (tuba)
2:12	Descending scales, each note with distinctive orchestration
2:23	New march theme and descending scales repeated and extended
2:47	Low brass, including ophicleide (tuba)
2:54	Descending scales, each note with distinctive orchestration
3:44	End of new march theme goes faster (the crowd presses forward).
4:16	Clarinet plays *idée fixe* (lover's last vision of beloved).

4:25	Sudden crashing chord, then pizzicatos (head is severed and falls to ground)
4:28	Loud, brassy final chords (the crowd cheers)

LISTEN TO ... this selection streaming online.

WATCH ... an Active Listening Guide of this selection online.

DO ... Listening Exercise 18.1, Berlioz, *Symphonie fantastique*, "March to the Scaffold," online.

Fifth Movement: Dream of a Witches' Sabbath

Program: He sees himself at the witches' sabbath surrounded by a troop of frightful shadows, sorcerers, and monsters of all sorts, gathered for his funeral. Strange noises, groans, bursts of laughter, distant cries echoed by others. The "beloved" melody returns again, but it has lost its noble, modest character and is now only base, trivial, and grotesque. An outburst of joy at her arrival; she joins in the devilish orgy.

With our protagonist now dead—headless, in fact—that should be the end of the story. Instead, to conclude, Berlioz appends a monstrous finale, his vision of a soul tormented in hell. A crowd of witches emerges to dance around the corpse of the artist on its way to the inferno. Eerie sounds are produced by the strings, using mutes, and by the high woodwinds and French horn, playing glissandos. A piercing clarinet enters with a horrid parody of the *idée fixe* (Example 18.2), as Harriet Smithson, now in the frightful garb of a wicked old hag, comes on stage.

EXAMPLE 18.2 The *idée fixe* made ugly

LISTEN TO...
Example 18.2 online.

Smithson is greeted by a joyous *fortissimo* outburst by the full assembly, as all dance to the now-perverted *idée fixe*. Suddenly, the music becomes ominously quiet, and in one of the most strikingly original moments in all classical music, great Gothic church bells sound—another Berlioz "special effect." The bells introduce a melody known to all citizens of the day, the burial hymn of the medieval Church, the **Dies irae** (Example 18.3), here played by ophicleides and bassoons. (In recent years, the *Dies irae* has been used to signal doom in movie thrillers, including *The Nightmare Before Christmas*, *Sleeping with the Enemy*, and *The Shining*.)

EXAMPLE 18.3 *Dies irae* chant

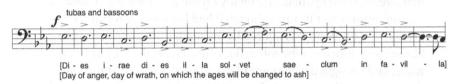

[Di - es   i - rae di - es   il - la sol - vet   sae - clum   in   fa - vil - la]
[Day of anger, day of wrath, on which the ages will be changed to ash]

LISTEN TO...
Example 18.3 online.

Not only is the orchestration sensational, but also the musical symbolism is sacrilegious. Just as the painter Francisco de Goya (Figure 18.5) parodies the Catholic Mass in his *Witches' Sabbath*—making babies serve as communion wafers—so Berlioz creates a mockery of one of the most venerable Gregorian chants of the Catholic Church. First, the *Dies irae* is played by the horns twice as fast (a process called rhythmic **diminution**). Then the sacred melody is transformed into a jazzed-up dance tune, played by a shrill, high clarinet, the entire scene now becoming a blasphemous black mass. At one point, Berlioz instructs the violins to play *col legno* (Italian for "with the wood")—to strike

FIGURE 18.5
Witches' Sabbath by Francisco de Goya (1746–1828) bears the same title as the finale of Berlioz's *Symphonie fantastique*. Both create images of the bizarre and macabre so dear to the hearts of Romantic artists.

WATCH... a YouTube video of the finale of Berlioz's *Symphonie fantastique* online.

the strings, not with the usual front of the bow, but with the wooden back, creating a noise that is evocative of the crackling of hellfire.

To the audience that first heard the *Symphonie fantastique* on December 5, 1830, all of this must have seemed incomprehensible: new instruments, novel playing effects, simultaneous melodies in different keys, and a form that is not traditional, like sonata–allegro or rondo, but rather grows out of the events in a program that reads like the screenplay for a horror film. But it all works. Here, again,

THE REAL END OF THE PROGRAM

How did the story of Berlioz and his beloved Harriet Smithson really end? In truth, Berlioz did meet and marry Harriet, but the two lived together miserably ever after—the Romantic ideal was often just that. He complained about her increasing weight, she about his infidelities. Harriet died in 1854 and was buried in a small graveyard in Paris. In 1864, that cemetery was to be closed and the remains of all the deceased transferred to a new, larger burial ground. It fell to widower Berlioz to remove Harriet's corpse to the new cemetery, as he recounts in his *Memoirs*:

> One dark, gloomy morning I set forth alone for the sad spot. A municipal officer was waiting, to be present at the disinterment. The grave had already been opened, and on my arrival the gravedigger jumped in. The coffin was still entire, though it had been ten years underground; the lid alone was injured by the damp. The man, instead of lifting it out, tore away the rotten lid, which cracked with a hideous noise, and brought the contents of the coffin to light. He then bent down, took up the crowned, decayed head of the poor *Ophelia*—and laid it in a new coffin awaiting it at the edge of the grave. Then, bending down a second time, he lifted with difficulty the headless trunk and limbs—a blackish mass to which the shroud still adhered, resembling a heap of pitch in a damp sack. I remember the dull sound ...

and the odor. (Hector Berlioz, *Memoirs*)

Berlioz had begun by playing Romeo to Harriet's Juliet and ended by playing Hamlet to her Ophelia. He cast his music, and his life, in terms of Shakespearean drama. And so, too, did the twentieth century. In 1969, during the centenary commemorating Berlioz's death, Romantic enthusiasts repositioned the remains of star-crossed Hector and Harriet. Today, they lie side by side in the Parisian cemetery of Montmartre.

is an instance of a creator, a genius, breaking the rules and stepping outside the box of conventional art; yet, he does so in a way that produces a wholly integrated, unified, and ultimately satisfying work. The separate special effects may be revolutionary and momentarily shocking, but they are consistent and logical among themselves when heard within the total artistic concept. Had Berlioz never written another note of music, he would still be justly famous for this single masterpiece of Romantic invention.

Peter Tchaikovsky (1840–1893): Tone Poem and Ballet Music

The Romantic passion for program music continued throughout the nineteenth century, most notably in the tone poems of Peter Tchaikovsky (Figure 18.6). As defined earlier in this chapter, a tone poem is a one-movement work for orchestra that captures the emotions and events of a story through music. Thus, a tone poem is really no different from a program symphony, except that everything happens in just one movement. Because Tchaikovsky was less a motivic symphonist and more a musical narrator, he excelled at program music—he always had a story to tell.

Tchaikovsky was born in 1840 into an upper-middle-class family in provincial Russia. He showed a keen ear for music in his earliest years and by the age of six could speak fluent French and German. (An excellent musical ear and a capacity to learn foreign languages often go hand in hand, as both involve processing patterns of sound primarily in the temporal lobe of the brain.) As to his career, his parents determined that law would provide the safest path to success. But, like Robert Schumann before him, Tchaikovsky eventually realized that music, not law, fired his imagination, so he made his way to the Saint Petersburg Conservatory of Music. When he graduated in 1866, Tchaikovsky was immediately offered a position at the newly formed Moscow Conservatory, that of professor of harmony and musical composition.

In truth, it was not his conservatory job in Moscow that supported Tchaikovsky during most of his mature years but, rather, a private arrangement with an eccentric patroness, Madame Nadezhda von Meck (Figure 18.7). This wealthy, music-loving widow furnished him with an annual income of 6,000 rubles (about $40,000 U.S. today) on the condition that she and the composer never meet—a requirement not always easily fulfilled, because the two sometimes resided at the same summer estate. In addition to this annuity, in 1881, Tsar Alexander III awarded Tchaikovsky an annual pension of 3,000 rubles in recognition of his importance to Russian cultural life. Now a man of independent means, Tchaikovsky traveled extensively in Western Europe, and even to America. He enjoyed the freedom that so many artists find necessary to creative activity.

Although Tchaikovsky excelled in all genres of classical music, today he is best known for his program music and ballets. For example, his programmatic *The 1812 Overture* (1882), which commemorates the Russian defeat of Napoleon in 1812, is heard in the United States on the Fourth of July, with Tchaikovsky's musical pyrotechnics usually accompanied by fireworks in the night sky. By the end of the nineteenth century, Tchaikovsky was the world's most popular orchestral composer, the "big name" brought from Europe to America when star appeal was needed to add luster

FIGURE 18.6
Peter Tchaikovsky

FIGURE 18.7
Nadezhda von Meck was the widow of an engineer who made a fortune constructing the first railroads in Russia during the 1860s and 1870s. She used her money, in part, to support composers such as Tchaikovsky and, later, Claude Debussy.

to the opening of Carnegie Hall in 1891. He died suddenly in 1893, at the age of fifty-three, after drinking unboiled water during a cholera epidemic.

Tone Poem *Romeo and Juliet* (1869; revised 1880)

Tchaikovsky termed his most overtly programmatic works "overture," "overture fantasy," or "symphonic fantasy." Today, we would call each simply a tone poem. Like Berlioz before him, Tchaikovsky had fallen under the spell of Shakespeare, and he, too, composed tone poems inspired by *Hamlet* and *Romeo and Juliet*.

In *Romeo and Juliet* (see Listening Guide), Tchaikovsky aimed to capture the spirit, not the letter, of Shakespeare's play. The play, of course, develops as a continuous linear story. Tchaikovsky's tone poem, however, unfolds within the confines of sonata–allegro form, which gives the music a recursive shape: presentation, confrontation, resolution. The play lasts about three hours; the tone poem, only about twenty minutes. Thus, to distill the dramatic material to its musical essence, Tchaikovsky focuses on only three themes: the compassionate music of the kindly Friar Laurence, whose plan to unite the lovers goes fatally awry; the fighting music, which represents the feud between the Capulets and the Montagues; and the famous love theme, which expresses the passion of Romeo and Juliet.

Tchaikovsky begins slowly with a musical introduction featuring solemn religious music, pointing to a succession of mysterious chords strummed on a harp, as if a medieval priest or a bard were about to narrate a long, tragic tale (see opening image for Chapter 21). Suddenly, out rush angry percussive sounds, racing strings, and syncopated cymbal crashes: We have joined the violent world of the Capulets and Montagues. And, just where we would expect a lyrical second theme to appear in sonata–allegro form, on cue steps forth the love theme. As appropriate for a pair of lovers, this one has two parts (Examples 18.4A and 18.4B), each of which grows and becomes more passionate when pushed upward in ascending melodic sequence.

EXAMPLE 18.4A Love theme, part 1

viola and English horn

EXAMPLE 18.4B Love theme, part 2

violins

The brief development section pits the feuding families against the increasingly adamant pleas of Friar Laurence. The recapitulation, true to sonata–allegro form, begins with the feud music but moves quickly to an expanded, more ecstatic presentation of the love theme (part 2 first, then part 1). Here, Tchaikovsky followed the dictum, "save your best for last." In the exposition, the love theme first appeared in a low woodwind and middle strings; in the recapitulation, however, the composer places the final statement of the theme on high in the violins, all now surging forward with a powerful but warm vibrato—the quintessential expression of Romantic love in music.

But all does not end well, as a foreboding roll on the timpani suggests at the beginning of the coda. The steady drumbeats of a funeral procession and fragments of the broken love theme tell us that Romeo and Juliet are dead. Yet, suddenly, in a transformative moment, celestial, hymn-like sounds imply that the lovers have been reunited in some higher realm. All that remains is to bring the curtain down on the story of the star-crossed lovers, which Tchaikovsky does with seven *fortissimo* hammer strokes for full orchestra, all on the tonic chord.

Shakespeare wrote *Romeo and Juliet* as a tragedy: "For never was a story of more woe/Than this of Juliet and her Romeo," say the final lines of the play. By incorporating a "celestial conclusion" into his coda—a hymn-like choir of angelic woodwinds, followed by the transformed love theme on high in the violins—Tchaikovsky has changed the final import of the play. True child of the Romantic age, he suggests that the love–death of Romeo and Juliet is, in fact, not a tragedy, but a spiritual triumph.

LISTENING GUIDE

Peter Tchaikovsky, Romeo and Juliet (1869; revised 1880)   Download 51 (19:25)

Genre: Tone poem

Form: Sonata–allegro

WHAT TO LISTEN FOR: As the music unfolds, focus on the three main sonic groups—Friar Laurence, the feuding Capulets and Montagues, and the love of Romeo and Juliet—and you'll be able to follow the story line of Tchaikovsky's version of this timeless tale.

INTRODUCTION

0:00	Friar Laurence theme sounding organ-like in woodwinds	

0:37	Anguished, dissonant sound in strings and French horn
1:29	Harp alternates with flute solo and woodwinds.
2:11	Friar Laurence theme returns with new accompaniment.
2:36	Anguished sound returns in strings with French horn.
3:23	Harp strumming returns.
3:56	Timpani roll and string tremolos build tension; hints of Friar Laurence theme in woodwinds.
4:32	Anguished sound again returns, then yields to crescendo on repeating tonic chord.

(Continued)

EXPOSITION

5:16   Feud theme in agitated minor; angry rhythmic motive in woodwinds, racing scales in strings

6:04   Crashing syncopations (with cymbal) running against scales

6:38   Gentle transition, with release of tension, to second theme

7:28   Love theme (part 1) played quietly by English horn and viola

7:50   Love theme (part 2) played quietly by strings with mutes

8:32   Love theme (part 1) returns with growing ardor in high woodwinds while French horn plays counterpoint against it.

9:34   Lyrical closing section in which cellos and English horn engage in dialogue against backdrop of gently plucked chords in harp

DEVELOPMENT

10:36   Feud theme against which horn soon plays Friar Laurence theme

10:56   String syncopations, again against Friar Laurence theme

11:20   Feud theme and Friar Laurence theme continue in opposition.

12:03   Cymbal crashes signal climax of development as trumpet blares forth with Friar Laurence theme.

RECAPITULATION

12:35   Feud theme in woodwinds and brasses against racing strings

12:58   Love theme (part 2) softly in woodwinds

13:35   Love theme (part 1) sounds ecstatically with all its inherent force and sweep.

14:14   Love theme begins again in strings, with counterpoint in brasses.

14:30   Fragments of love theme in strings, then brasses

14:55   Love theme begins again but is cut off by feud theme; syncopated cymbal crashes.

15:14   Feud theme and Friar Laurence theme build to a climax.

16:12   Timpani roll announces coda.

CODA

16:24   Timpani beats funeral march while strings play fragments of love theme.

17:19   Love theme (part 2) transformed into sound of heavenly chorale played by woodwinds

18:20   Transcendent love theme sounds from on high in violins.

18:55   Timpani roll and final chords

LISTEN TO ... this selection streaming online.

WATCH ... an Active Listening Guide of this selection online.

DO ... Listening Exercise 18.2, Tchaikovsky, *Romeo and Juliet*, online.

Tchaikovsky's Ballets

Ballet, like opera, calls to mind "high-end" culture. Indeed, the origins of ballet and opera go back to the French royal court of Louis XIV (who reigned 1643–1715). Throughout the eighteenth century, no serious opera was complete without a ballet or two to provide a pleasant diversion. By the early nineteenth century, however, this dance spectacle had separated from opera and moved onstage as the independent genre we know today. A **ballet** is a dramatic dance in which the characters, using various stylized steps and pantomime, tell a story. Music expresses the emotions of the story through patterns of sound, while dance does the same through patterns of physical movement. Although ballet first developed in France, it gradually gained universal popularity, indeed an adopted homeland, in Russia. Even today, the terms *Russian* and *ballerina* seem inextricably linked—and so are ballet and Tchaikovsky.

Early in his career, Tchaikovsky realized that ballet required precisely the compositional skills that he possessed. Unlike Bach, Mozart, and Beethoven, Tchaikovsky was not a "developer"—he was not good at teasing out intricate motivic relationships over long spans of time. Instead, his gift was to create one striking melody and mood after another—to create one vivid scene and then move on to the next. And this is precisely what **ballet music** requires—not motivic manipulation or contrapuntal intricacy, but short bursts of tuneful melody and pulsating rhythm, all of which are intended to capture the emotional essence of the scene. *Short* is the operative word here; because dancing in a ballet is exhausting, neither the principals nor the *corps de ballet* hold center stage for more than three minutes at a time. Tchaikovsky's "short-segment" style proved perfect for the demands of ballet. From his pen flowed *Swan Lake* (1876), *Sleeping Beauty* (1889), and *The Nutcracker* (1892; Figure 18.8), arguably the three most popular works in the entire repertoire of grand Romantic ballet.

Who doesn't know some of the ballet music from *The Nutcracker* (1892), a holiday ritual as traditional as caroling and gift giving? The story, typical of Romantic-era narratives, springs from a fairy-tale fantasy. After a Christmas Eve celebration, an exhausted young girl, Clara, falls asleep and dreams of people from exotic places and toys that come to life. Fantastical characters parade before us, not merely accompanied, but literally brought to life, by the music. In "Dance of the Reed Pipes" (see Listening Guide), sleeping Clara imagines she sees shepherds dancing in a meadow. Because shepherds since time immemorial had played "pan pipes," Tchaikovsky orchestrated this scene in a way that featured flutes. (The tableau is also called the "Dance of the Toy Flutes.") The rhythm of the music, first duple and slow, then duple and fast, propels the dancing shepherds. Indeed, ballet music must not only create evocative moods through colorful orchestration,

FIGURE 18.8
A recent production of *The Nutcracker* by the Royal Ballet, showing a *pas de deux* (steps for two principals). Limiting the length of scenes, as is necessary in ballet, allows the dancers literally to "stay on their toes."

LISTENING GUIDE

Peter Tchaikovsky, "Dance of the Reed Pipes" from *The Nutcracker* (1891)   Download 8 (2:34)

Situation: In this portion of the ballet, Clara's dream takes her and the Handsome Prince to exotic places around the globe (China, Arabia, Russia, and Spain among them), and for each, Tchaikovsky creates music that sounds evocative of a foreign locale, at least to Western ears. While in China, we encounter a group of dancing shepherds playing reed pipes—hence, the prominence of the flutes.

Genre: Ballet music

Form: Ternary (**ABA'**)

WHAT TO LISTEN FOR: Not only the charming sound of the flutes but also the clear-cut ternary form (**ABA'**): flutes in major, followed by soft trumpets in minor (1:22), and a return (1:57) to the flutes at the end.

0:00		Flutes play melody above low string pizzicato.
0:35	**A**	English horn and then clarinet add counterpoint.
0:51		Melody repeats with violins now adding counterpoint.
1:22	**B**	Change to minor mode: Trumpets play melody above two-note bass ostinato.
1:36		Violins join melody.
1:57	**A'**	Return to flute melody (with violin counterpoint) in major mode

LISTEN TO ... this selection streaming online.

WATCH ... an Active Listening Guide of this selection online.

WATCH ... a video of another part of *The Nutcracker* online.

DO ... Listening Exercise 18.3, Tchaikovsky, "Dance of the Reed Pipes," online.

---

it must also project a strong, clear metrical pulse to animate—indeed, regulate—the steps of the dancers. Whether the music is ballet or hip-hop, if you can't hear the beat, you can't dance to the music.

Finally, it is important to keep in mind that ballet music is not program music. Program music is a purely instrumental genre in which sounds alone create the narrative. In ballet music, on the other hand, music is an adjunct: The movements, facial expressions, and gestures of the dancers tell the story.

Music and Nationalism

Today, we are witnessing a globalization of music and of culture generally. Companies such as Apple, Google, and Facebook covertly encourage the adoption of English as a universal language and overtly promote economic ties that cross borders. The various nations of Europe have formed a European Community, and we in the United States participate in the North America Free Trade Agreement (NAFTA). University students are encouraged to spend a semester studying abroad. Thousands of students around the world can take a single course simultaneously online through providers such as Coursera and edX. Everyone, it seems, is looking and learning outward.

In the nineteenth century, however, things were very different. People were looking inward, often for a force that would liberate them from political oppression. At a time when people of one language were frequently ruled by foreign emperors who spoke another, Europe's ethnic groups came to realize that their ethnicity might be an agent of liberation. Driven by the unifying force of group identity, the Greeks threw off the Turks and formed their own country (1820s), the French-speaking Belgians rebelled against the Dutch (1830s), the Finns against the Russians (1860s), and the Czechs against the German-speaking Austrians (1870s). (Some of this move toward national independence persists today, as the Ukrainians try to remove the controlling hand of Russia.) Before the nineteenth century, French, German, and Russian were the dominant languages of Europe; thereafter, literary works published in Czech, Hungarian, Norwegian, and Finnish, among other languages, were not uncommon.

Music played an important part in this ethnic awakening, sounding out cultural differences and providing a rallying point in a movement called **musical nationalism**. National anthems, native dances, protest songs, and victory symphonies all evoked through music the rising tide of national identity. "The Star-Spangled Banner" (U.S. national anthem), the "Marseillaise" (French national anthem), and "Italian Brothers, Italy Has Arisen" (Italian national anthem), for example, were all products of this patriotic zeal.

But how did a composer create music that sounded ethnic or national? He or she did so by incorporating indigenous folksongs, native scales, dance rhythms, and local instrumental sounds. Ethnic sentiments could also be conveyed by the use of national subjects—the life of a national hero, for example—as the basis of an opera or a tone poem. Among Romantic compositions with overtly nationalistic titles are Liszt's *Hungarian Rhapsodies*, Rimsky-Korsakov's *Russian Easter Overture*, Dvořák's *Slavonic Dances*, Smetana's *Má vlast (My Fatherland)*, and Sibelius's *Finlandia*. For all these composers, a musical signifier (a folksong, for example) served as a badge of both personal identity and ethnic pride.

Russian Nationalism: Modest Musorgsky (1839–1881)

Before the nineteenth century, Russia was a cultural backwater—at least in the eyes of the West. Gradually, it assimilated the traditions of German orchestral music, French ballet, and Italian opera, and then went further, developing its own ethnic high art. An early use of Russian subject matter in opera can be heard in Mikhail Glinka's *A Life for the Tsar* (1836). As a review of the first performance reported: "All were enthralled with the sounds of the native, Russian national music. Everyone showed complete accord in the expression of enthusiasm that the patriotic content of the opera aroused." Glinka's nationalist spirit was passed to a group of young composers whom contemporaries dubbed the "Mighty Handful" or, less grandiosely, the **Russian Five**: Alexander Borodin (1833–1887), César Cui (1835–1918), Mily Balakirev (1837–1910), Nikolai Rimsky-Korsakov (1844–1908), and Modest Musorgsky (1839–1881). They created a national art by taking the sophisticated traditions of Western classical music and incorporating therein simple elements of Russian folk and religious music. Of the Russian Five, the most original and least Western in musical style was Modest Musorgsky (Figure 18.9).

As with most members of the Russian Five, Musorgsky (pronounced "moo-SORG-ski") did not at first seem destined for a career in music. He was trained

to be a military officer and for a period of four years was commissioned in the Russian army. He resigned his appointment in 1858 in favor of a minor post as a civil servant and more free time to indulge his avocation, musical composition. The next year he said, "I have been a cosmopolitan [Western classical composer], but now there's been some sort of regeneration. Everything Russian is becoming dear to me." Unfortunately, his brief, chaotic life was marked by increasing poverty, depression, and alcoholism, a development evident in the one surviving portrait of him. During his few periods of creative productivity, Musorgsky managed to compile a small body of work which includes a boldly inventive tone poem, *Night on Bald Mountain* (1867; used prominently in Walt Disney's *Fantasia*); an imaginative set of descriptive pieces called *Pictures at an Exhibition* (1874); and an operatic masterpiece, *Boris Godunov* (1874), based on the life of a popular sixteenth-century Russian tsar. Many of Musorgsky's works were left unfinished at the time of his death in 1881.

Pictures at an Exhibition (1874)

The genesis of *Pictures at an Exhibition* can be traced to the death of Musorgsky's close friend, the Russian painter and architect Victor Hartmann, who had died suddenly of a heart attack in 1873. As a memorial to Hartmann, friends mounted an exhibition of his paintings and drawings in Moscow the following year. Musorgsky was inspired to capture the spirit of Hartmann's works in a series of ten short pieces for piano. To provide unity within the sequence of musical pictures, the composer hit on the idea of incorporating a recurring interlude, which he called *Promenade*. This gave listeners the impression of enjoying a leisurely stroll into and through a gallery, moving from one of Hartmann's images to the next each time the *Promenade* music sounded.

Today, *Pictures at an Exhibition* is best known in the brilliantly orchestrated version by Maurice Ravel (1875–1937), completed in 1922. (Perhaps by coincidence, the first attempts at making color motion pictures occurred about this same time.) Whether fulfilling Musorgsky's original intent or going beyond it, Ravel's version greatly enhances the impact of the music by replacing the "black-and-white" sounds of the piano with the radiant color of the full late-Romantic orchestra.

With the *Promenade* (see Listening Guide and Example 18.5), we enter not just any gallery but one filled with purely Russian art. The tempo is marked "Fast but resolute, in the Russian manner"; the meter is irregular, as in a folk dance, with alternating five- and six-beat measures. Generally speaking, Western art music is symmetrical and repetitious; Western and Eastern folk music, however, is more irregular and unpredictable. Finally, the melody here is built on a **pentatonic scale**, which uses only five notes instead of the usual Western scale of seven notes—here Bb, C, D, F, and G. Throughout the world, indigenous folk cultures use the pentatonic (five-note) scale. To Western ears, then, *Promenade*, like Russia itself, seems both familiar and strange.

WATCH… a demonstration of the pentatonic scale online.

LISTEN TO… Example 18.5 online.

EXAMPLE 18.5 *Promenade* theme

LISTENING GUIDE

Modest Musorgsky, *Promenade* from *Pictures at an Exhibition* (1874)   Download 52 (1:36)

Orchestrated by Maurice Ravel (1922)

WHAT TO LISTEN FOR: The alternation of texture between monophony (brilliant trumpet) and homophony (full brasses). Also, try conducting with the music and you'll notice how the meter continually shifts—a characteristic of folk music.

0:00	Solo trumpet begins *Promenade* theme.
0:10	Full brasses respond.
0:18	Trumpet and full brasses continue to alternate.
0:33	Full strings and then woodwinds and brasses enter.
1:22	Brasses briefly restate *Promenade* theme.

LISTEN TO ... this selection streaming online.

WATCH ... an Active Listening Guide of this selection online.

Having entered the musical picture gallery, the visitor now focuses in turn on a musical evocation of each of ten paintings: first a depiction of an elf-like gnome, then an old castle, and so on. As we walk from image to image, the *Promenade* theme accompanies us. Finally, we arrive at the tenth and last picture, Musorgsky's musical rendering of a grand and glorious gate (see Listening Guide). This final scene is based on Hartmann's *The Great Gate of Kiev* (Figure 18.10), the painter's vision of a triumphant gate to the Ukrainian city of Kiev (then controlled by Russia). Think of the *Arc de Triomphe* in Paris or the Arch of Constantine in Rome, through which victorious armies returned home in triumph. Hartmann's painting is impressive, but Musorgsky's music is more so. Using the rondo form (here **ABABCA**), Musorgsky arranges his thematic material to depict a grand parade passing beneath the giant gate. Its majesty is first evoked through the impressive sound of the full brasses (theme **A**). Suddenly, the music shifts to solemn woodwinds quietly playing a harmonized chant from the liturgy of the Russian Orthodox Church (**B**), thereby suggesting a procession of Russian clergy or pilgrims. Even the composer–viewer seems to walk beneath the gate as the *Promenade* theme (**C**) appears, before a final return to a panoramic view of the gate (**A**), now with Hartmann's bells ringing triumphantly.

FIGURE 18.10
Victor Hartmann's vision, *The Great Gate of Kiev*, which inspired the last of the musical paintings in Musorgsky's *Pictures at an Exhibition*. Note the bells in the tower, a motif that is featured prominently at the very end of Musorgsky's musical evocation of this design.

Modest Musorgsky, *The Great Gate of Kiev*, from *Pictures at an Exhibition* (1874)   Download 53 (4:46)

Orchestrated by Maurice Ravel (1922)

Form: Rondo **(ABABCA)**

WHAT TO LISTEN FOR: Three distinctively different kinds of music: **A** (brasses and full orchestra at 0:00), **B** (woodwinds at 0:56), and **C** (*Promenade* theme at 2:42). **A** sounds Western; **B** and **C** sound more Russian. Most important, listen to how Musorgsky makes the gate theme (**A**) sound more grand with each appearance.

0:00	**A**	Gate theme in full brasses; major scale and regular meter
0:56	**B**	Pilgrims' hymn sounds in woodwind choir.

1:23	**A**	Gate theme in brasses, with running scales in strings
1:53	**B**	Pilgrims' hymn reappears in woodwinds.
2:18	**X**	Exotic sounds
2:42	**C**	*Promenade* theme returns in trumpet.
3:07	**A**	Gate theme in full glory

LISTEN TO ... this selection streaming online.

WATCH ... an Active Listening Guide of this selection online.

DO ... Listening Exercise 18.4, Musorgsky, *Pictures at an Exhibition*, online.

program music (257)	ophicleide (258)	*Dies irae* (263)	ballet music (269)
absolute music (257)	English horn (258)	diminution (263)	musical nationalism (271)
dramatic overture (257)	cornet (258)	*col legno* (263)	Russian Five (271)
tone (symphonic) poem (257)	orchestration (259)	ballet (269)	pentatonic scale (272)
program symphony (258)	*idée fixe* (259)		

 Join us on Facebook at Listening to Music with Craig Wright

PRACTICE ... your understanding of this chapter's concepts by comparing Checklists of Musical Style for all historic eras and working once more with the chapter's Active Listening Guides online.

DO ... online multiple-choice and critical thinking quizzes that your instructor may assign for a grade.

Romantic Music:
PIANO
Music

START... experiencing this chapter's topics with an online video activity.

LEARNING OBJECTIVES

After studying the material in this chapter, you should be able to:

1 Describe how the construction of the piano changed during the nineteenth century.
2 Describe a character piece of the Romantic era.
3 Compare the careers of good friends Frédéric Chopin and Franz Liszt.
4 Differentiate a nocturne for piano from an etude for piano.

We've all banged away on a piano at one time or another. Some of us may have had piano lessons requiring endless finger exercises, accompanied by our mother's prediction: "Someday you'll thank me for this." But did you ever stop to think about how the piano came to be?

The first piano was constructed around 1700 as an alternative to the harpsichord, as a way of giving more dynamics and shading to the musical line. Mozart was the first composer to use the piano exclusively, beginning around 1770. His was a small instrument with only 61 keys, a frame made of wood, and a weight of only 187 pounds (see Figure 13.7). A century later, spurred by the new technology of the Industrial Revolution, the piano had grown into the 88-key, cast-iron–framed, 1,000-pound grand monster that we know today (Figure 19.1). Iron had replaced wood, strings had become thicker and stronger, and foot pedals had been added. On the right side was the **sustaining pedal**, which enabled strings to continue to sound after the performer had lifted his or her hand from the corresponding keys. On the left side was the **soft pedal**, which lessened the dynamic level by shifting the position of the hammers relative to the strings. Finally, in the 1850s, the Steinway Company of New York began **cross-stringing** the piano, overlaying the lowest-sounding strings across those of the middle register, thereby producing a richer, more homogeneous sound (Figure 19.2). By the mid-nineteenth century, all the essential features of the modern piano were in place. The essential design of the piano hasn't changed in 150 years.

As the piano grew larger and more expressive, it became something of a home entertainment center. In the days before television and video games, the family could gather around the piano to while away the evening hours. Every aspiring middle-class home had to have a piano, both for family enjoyment and as a status symbol—the high-art instrument in the parlor signified to visitors that they had entered a cultured home. Parents made sure their children, especially the girls, received lessons, and publishers, eager to profit from the new enthusiasm for the piano, turned out reams of sheet music for pianists of all skill levels.

Spurred by the sudden popularity of

FIGURE 19.1
A large concert grand piano once owned by Franz Liszt, now in the Liszt Museum in Budapest, Hungary. The instrument was made by the Chickering Piano Company of Boston (the largest U.S. piano manufacturer before the appearance of the Steinway Company) and shipped overseas to Liszt in 1872 as a marketing tool: "If Liszt plays a Chickering, so, young American, should you!"

FIGURE 19.2
Looking inside a Steinway piano made in New York in 1867, now in the Yale Collection of Musical Instruments, we see the cast-iron frame and support bars running parallel with the strings. Note also the "overstringing," in which the bass strings come at an angle, up and across those of the middle register, helping to produce a richer, more homogenous sound. The fact that both of these cutting-edge pianos were produced in the United States demonstrates the ascendant position that country came to occupy in industrial manufacturing during the nineteenth century.

the piano, a host of virtuoso performers descended upon the concert halls of Europe. What they played—rapid octaves, blazing chromatic scales, thundering chords—was usually more a display of technical virtuosity than a demonstration of musical substance. Today, these entertainers would be entirely forgotten had not several also been gifted composers. Over time, we forget the performers but remember the composers.

Robert Schumann (1810–1856)

We met Robert Schumann, as well as Clara Schumann and Franz Schubert, in our discussion of the nineteenth-century art song (see Chapter 17). All three composers wrote extensively for the piano. Clara Schumann was one of the great virtuosos of the nineteenth century. Robert Schumann tried to become one, but his career on the instrument ended with a self-inflicted hand injury. Thereafter, he concentrated on composition.

Robert Schumann was something of a manic composer, his "streaks" being perhaps manifestations of his bipolar personality. During the 1830s, Robert occupied himself mainly with the composition of collections of pieces for piano. Among these is *Kinderszenen* (*Scenes from Childhood*, 1838), a set of thirteen short, intimate pieces appropriate for the middle-class parlor. Despite the title, these are not pieces intended for children. Rather, they are musical recollections of events and sensations from childhood—"reminiscences of a grown-up for grown-ups," the composer called them. Congruent with the Romantic fondness for the world of the imagination, the most famous of the set is a piece about dreaming.

"Träumerei" ("Dreaming"; 1838)

Did you ever daydream about your childhood? Of course—and that's what Robert Schumann's "Träumerei" ("Dreaming") does in music. The piece is as short and fleeting—and as perfect—as a pleasant childhood memory. "Träumerei" also demonstrates an important principle of melodic construction: What goes up, must come down. Melodies that involve large leaps upward invariably descend in the opposite direction, usually by smaller steps—think of the leaps and gradual declines in "Over the Rainbow," for example. "Träumerei" begins with an opening gesture that spans an octave—tonic to tonic an octave higher (see example in Listening Guide at asterisks)—and gradually falls back to the tonic. Thereafter, it spins out a succession of similar, higher ascents and declines, each creating brief alternations of excitement (quick ascent into the unknown) and satisfaction (slow descent back home).

Not only is Robert Schumann's "Träumerei" part of the nineteenth-century aesthetic that brought dreams to the forefront of the Romantic consciousness (see Friedrich's painting, *The Dreamer*, Figure 16.1), but it also represents a musical genre new to the nineteenth century: the character piece. A **character piece**, usually written for piano, is a short instrumental work that tries to capture the essence of a single mood, sentiment, or emotion. Because the character piece passes by in the twinkling of an eye, it was sometimes given a whimsical title, such as bagatelle (a trifle), humoresque, arabesque, musical moment, caprice, romance, or impromptu. Although the character piece "Träumerei" is real, the fleeting nature of the listening experience forces an engagement with the imagination.

Robert Schumann, "Träumerei" ("Dreaming"), from *Kinderszenen* (1838)   Download 54 (2:44)

Genre: Character piece

Form: Ternary (**ABA'**)

WHAT TO LISTEN FOR: The rapid ascents and gradual declines of the melody. The pianist here is Vladimir Horowitz, arguably the greatest piano virtuoso of the twentieth century, who played "Träumerei" as an encore at each of his concerts. This recording is from a live performance.

0:00	**A**	Dream-like melody rises and falls, and then rises to a higher climax and falls.

0:35	**A**	Repeat of opening section
1:11	**B**	Melody extended as it rises and falls
1:28		Melody rises to highest pitch level.
1:49	**A'**	Dream-like melody returns, but climax is set to a new harmony.

LISTEN TO ... this selection streaming online.

WATCH ... an Active Listening Guide of this selection online.

FIGURE 19.3
A superbly Romantic portrait of Chopin by the famous French painter, Eugène Delacroix (1799–1863), who, like Franz Liszt, was a friend and admirer of Chopin.

Frédéric Chopin (1810–1849)

The Beatles or the Stones, Yankees or Red Sox, Liverpool or Manchester United—whether it's music or sports, every fan has his or her favorite. So, too, opinions were passionately divided regarding the two great virtuoso composers of the Romantic era: Frédéric Chopin and Franz Liszt.

Frédéric Chopin (Figure 19.3) was born in Warsaw, Poland, to a French father and a Polish mother. His father taught French—then the universal language of the aristocracy—at an elite secondary school for the sons of Polish nobility. As a student there, young Frédéric not only gained an excellent general education but also acquired aristocratic friends and tastes. Fearing that Warsaw was too small and provincial, the fledgling composer moved first to Vienna and then, in September 1831, to Paris. That very year, Poland's fight for independence was crushed by Russian troops—such tension still echoes today in Poland's neighbor, Ukraine. Becoming an expatriate voice for Polish musical nationalism (for nationalism, see Chapter 18), Chopin never returned to his homeland.

Although Chopin's concerts caused something of a sensation when he arrived in Paris, he wasn't cut out for the life of the public showman. Unlike Franz Liszt, Chopin was introverted, physically slight, and somewhat sickly. Consequently, he chose to play at private *musicales* (musical evenings) in the homes of the aristocracy and to give lessons for a fee that only the very rich could afford. As he said within a year of his arrival, "I hobnob with ambassadors, princes, and ministers. I can't imagine what miracle is responsible for all this because I really haven't done anything to bring it about."

In October 1836, Chopin met Baroness Aurore Dudevant (1803–1876), a writer who, under the pen name George Sand, poured forth a steady stream of Romantic novels roughly akin to today's Silhouette Romances. Sand, a bisexual, was an ardent individualist with a predilection for wearing men's clothing and smoking cigars (see Sand seated behind Liszt in Figure 15.1 and in Figure 19.4). Six years Chopin's senior, Sand became his lover and protector. Many of the composer's best works were written at Nohant, her summer residence that was 150 miles south of Paris. After their relationship ended in 1847, Chopin undertook a taxing concert tour of England and Scotland. While this improved his bank account, it weakened his delicate health. He died in Paris of tuberculosis at the age of thirty-nine.

Chopin was a rarity among Romantic composers—he wrote only works for solo piano or ensemble pieces (including songs) in which the piano figures prominently. His works for solo piano include those in the Polish national style (called mazurkas and polonaises), three piano sonatas, a set of twenty-four preludes (one in each of the major and minor keys), twenty-four etudes (technical studies), and twenty-one nocturnes. Far better than the other genres for piano, the nocturnes embody the essence of musical Romanticism.

WATCH... a fanciful peek into the lives of pianists Chopin and Liszt, writer Sand, and painter Delacroix, online.

FIGURE 19.4
Novelist Aurore Dudevant (George Sand) by Eugène Delacroix. Both the painter Delacroix and the composer Chopin often stayed at her summer estate in Nohant in the south of France.

Nocturne in E♭ major, Opus 9, No. 2 (1832)

Can music be painfully beautiful? If so, such music surely can be found in this Chopin nocturne. A **nocturne** (night piece) is a slow, dreamy genre of piano music that came into favor in the 1820s and 1830s. It suggests moonlit nights, romantic longing, and a certain wistful melancholy, all evoked through slightly chromatic melodies and softly strumming harmonies. To set a nocturnal mood, Chopin usually lays out a very regular accompaniment, either as an arpeggio going up and down or as chords going low-middle-high, both of which give the sense of a harp or guitar strumming softly in the night. Above this support, he places a sensuous melody that plays around and against the very square accompaniment, as we see in his Nocturne in E♭ major (Example 19.1).

EXAMPLE 19.1 Melody in Chopin's Nocturne

Once this melody is in place, Chopin repeats it and varies it twice, with each variation more florid than the last. Between presentations comes an interlude of rich chromatic harmony (see Listening Guide). Note in Example 19.1 how Chopin carefully specifies the use of the sustaining pedal. "Ped." here means to depress the sustaining (right) pedal; the asterisk means to release it. In this way, the lowest bass notes can be sustained (while the left hand moves up for the next two chords), thereby creating a richer, more sonorous sound.

Where did Chopin derive this nocturnal style? Oddly enough, from the arias found in the Italian *bel canto* opera ("beautiful singing" opera; see Chapter 20) that he heard when he first arrived in Paris in 1831. In the Nocturne in E♭ major, we have essentially a song or an aria without words, and the beautiful melody always sounds in the top (soprano) register. At the end, Chopin adds an elaborate, vocal cadenza that leads to the final tonic chord. Then, as this chord softly repeats, the nocturnal world dissolves.

LISTENING GUIDE

Frédéric Chopin, Nocturne in E♭ major, Opus 9, No. 2 (1832)   Download 55 (4:26)

Genre: Nocturne

Form: Theme and variations

WHAT TO LISTEN FOR: The gradual unfolding of a beautiful, song-like melody. The performance here is by Polish-born pianist Arthur Rubinstein (1887–1982), universally recognized as the greatest interpreter of the music of his countryman, Chopin.

Theme

0:00	"Vocal" melody (**a**) set above solid "low-middle-high" chordal accompaniment
0:29	Melody **a** repeated with ornaments
0:58	Melody extended (**b**) through ...
1:04	... bold harmonic shifts, and then ...
1:20	... chromatic harmony

Variation 1

| 1:27 | Melody **a** returns but is now more ornate. |
| 1:56 | Extension **b** is lightly ornamented. |

Variation 2

| 2:24 | Melody **a** returns with new ornamentation. |
| 2:54 | Extension **b** elongated to reach climax |

Coda

| 3:49 | "Vocal" cadenza of rapidly repeating pattern sounding akin to a trill |
| 4:06 | Final strumming of accompaniment on tonic chord |

LISTEN TO ... this selection streaming online.

WATCH ... an Active Listening Guide of this selection online.

Franz Liszt (1811–1886)

WATCH... a wonderful example of Liszt's virtuosity applied to Schubert's art song, *Erlkönig*, in what is called a "piano transcription," online.

Franz Liszt wasn't merely a composer and pianist—he was a phenomenon, perhaps the most flamboyant artistic personality of the entire nineteenth century. Handsome, supremely talented, and equally self-confident, he strutted across the stage as the musical sex symbol of the Romantic era (Figure 19.5). Born in Hungary of German-speaking parents, Liszt was a child prodigy, a *Wunderkind*, who had his first music published at the age of twelve. But Liszt was an unusual prodigy; he not only relied on his natural gifts but also practiced maniacally, four to five hours a day. Tremolos, leaps, double trills, glissandos, and simultaneous octaves in both hands, all played at breakneck speed, became part of the repertoire that he soon brought to the stage as a touring concert virtuoso.

In 1833, Liszt's career as a concert pianist took an unexpected turn. He met the Countess Marie d'Agoult (at his feet in Figure 15.1, and in Figure 19.6) and gave up the life of the performing artist in exchange for what he thought would be the love of his life. Although she was already married and the mother of two children, Marie and Liszt eloped, first to Switzerland and then to Italy. Residing in these countries for four years, the couple had three illegitimate children of their own. Their youngest daughter would become the wife of Richard Wagner (see Figure 21.3). Then, as now, a touch of scandal only fueled a successful stage career.

Beginning in 1839 and continuing until 1847, Liszt once more took to the road as a touring virtuoso. He played more than 1,000 concerts: from Ireland to Turkey, from Sweden to Spain, from Portugal to Russia. Everywhere he went, the handsome pianist was greeted with the sort of mass hysteria that today is reserved

FIGURE 19.5
The young, charismatic Franz Liszt, preeminent pianist of the Romantic era

FIGURE 19.6
Countess Marie d'Agoult in 1843. She was a novelist in her own right, and some of the tracts on music that appeared under Liszt's name were probably penned by her. Like many female writers of the day, including George Sand and George Eliot, she wrote under a masculine *nom de plume*: Daniel Stern.

FIGURE 19.7
Lisztomania, as depicted in 1842. A recital by Liszt was likely to create the sort of sensation that a concert by a rock star might generate today. Women fought for a lock of his hair, a broken string from his piano, or a shred of his velvet gloves.

for rock stars. Audiences of 3,000 crowded into the larger halls (Figure 19.7). Women tried to rip off his silk scarf and white gloves, and they fought for a lock of his hair. **Lisztomania** swept Europe.

Despite their obvious sensationalism, Liszt's concerts in the 1840s established the format of our modern-day piano **recital**. Liszt was the first to play entire programs from memory (not reading from music). He was the first to place the piano parallel with the line of the stage so that neither his back nor his full face, but rather his extraordinary side profile, was visible to the audience. He was the first to perform on the stage alone—up to that point, concerts traditionally had included numerous performers on the program. These solo appearances were called first "soliloquies" and then "recitals," suggesting that they were like personal dramatic recitations. As Liszt modestly claimed in his adopted French, "Le concert, c'est moi!"

In 1861, Liszt again surprised the world: He moved to Rome, entered Holy Orders in the Roman Catholic Church, and took up residence in the Vatican! The composer now styled himself "Abbé Liszt"; thereafter, he was always photographed or depicted wearing a long clerical robe. He died at the age of seventy-five in Bayreuth, Germany, where he had gone to hear the latest opera of his son-in-law, Richard Wagner.

Judging from contemporary accounts, Liszt was the greatest pianist who ever lived, certainly with regard to technical facility. He had large hands and unusually long fingers, with very little web-like connective tissue between them, which allowed him to make wide stretches with relative ease. He could play a melody in octaves when others could play only the single notes of the line. If others might execute a passage in octaves, Liszt could dash it off in more impressive-sounding tenths (octave plus third). So, he wrote daredevil music full of virtuosic display, as we see in Example 19.2, which goes lightning fast.

EXAMPLE 19.2 A typical moment in a Liszt piano piece. It looks difficult—and it is!

The preceding example comes from one of Liszt's etudes. An **etude** is a short, one-movement composition designed to improve a particular aspect of a performer's technique—more rapid note repetition, surer leaps, or faster chromatic scales, as throughout the example. The more advanced of these techniques require almost superhuman technical skill. Ironically, such "study pieces" by Liszt and Chopin are not useful for the average pianist—to practice them you must already be a virtuoso!

LISTEN TO...

Example 19.2 online.

Concert Etude No. 3, "Un sospiro" ("A Sigh"; 1848)

Blazing technique, however, could also accompany great beauty. Such is the case in Concert Etude No. 3, nicknamed "Un sospiro" ("A Sigh"). Liszt liked such poetic names because they suggested that the music aspired to a higher realm, one beyond mere technique building.

From within a welter of arpeggios arises a radiant melody. To build technique—and dazzle an audience—Liszt includes (1) rapid arpeggios in both hands; (2) chromatic scales in parallel sixths, executed as fast as possible (see Example 19.2); and (3) abundant cross-hand playing. **Cross-hand playing** (moving the left hand over the right hand to play a high melody line) becomes necessary in the nineteenth century because performers had to quickly traverse a greater span on the keyboard (sixty-one keys were gradually increased to eighty-eight). As the example in the Listening Guide demonstrates, by using the sustaining pedal, the left hand (l.h.) holds the bass notes and then quickly jumps over the right hand to play part of the melody. Liszt was famous for this gambit, which came to be called "the three-hand trick"; in Figure 19.8, he appears to have eight. The challenge to the performer is to make the melody radiate while negotiating the dangers of the accompaniment—to be both artist and wizard.

FIGURE 19.8
The aged Abbé Liszt, dressed as a clergyman with halo above, fingers blazing, appears to have, not just two or three hands, but eight!

LISTENING GUIDE

Franz Liszt, Concert Etude No. 3, "Un sospiro" ("A Sigh"; 1848)   Download 56 (5:37)

Genre: Etude

Form: Theme and variations

WHAT TO LISTEN FOR: Take your pick: technical glitz, radiant melody, or boldly shifting harmonies, especially at the end. You can also play a game of auditory "Where's Waldo?": Is the melody in the bass, middle, or treble of the texture?

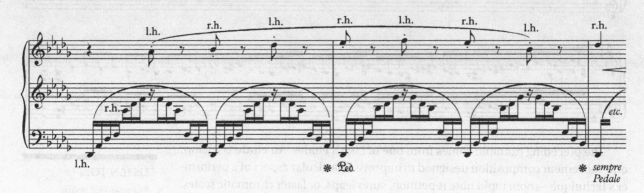

0:00	Rippling arpeggios, shared by both hands, establish accompaniment.
0:07	Melody arises from arpeggios using cross-hand playing.
0:44	Melody now ornamented by broken octaves
1:21	Melody transferred to bass, then treble (top)
1:42	Melody moves progressively toward bass.
2:09	Rapid descent of chromatic scale played in sixths (see Example 19.2)
2:27	Melody returns in thirds in treble, set to new harmonies.
2:42	Bold harmonic shifts in harmony
3:08	Rapid descent of major scale played in sixths
3:17	Melody returns in middle part of texture.
4:06	Melody continues but is supported by unexpected chord changes.
4:36	**Coda:** All ranges of piano exploited; final chord progression of striking harmonic shifts

LISTEN TO ... this selection streaming online.

WATCH ... an Active Listening Guide of this selection online.

DO ... Listening Exercise 19.1, Liszt, "Un sospiro," online.

KEY WORDS

sustaining pedal (276)   character piece (277)   Lisztomania (282)   etude (283)
soft pedal (276)   nocturne (279)   recital (282)   cross-hand playing (283)
cross-stringing (276)

 Join us on Facebook at Listening to Music with Craig Wright

PRACTICE ... your understanding of this chapter's concepts by comparing Checklists of Musical Style for all historic eras and working once more with the chapter's Active Listening Guides online.

DO ... online multiple-choice and critical thinking quizzes that your instructor may assign for a grade.

Romantic Opera:
ITALY

START… experiencing this chapter's topics with an online video activity.

LEARNING OBJECTIVES

After studying the material in this chapter, you should be able to:

1 Identify what characterizes *bel canto* opera and which composers created it.
2 Trace the biography of Giuseppe Verdi and place him within the political events of the mid-nineteenth century.
3 Identify aspects of Verdi's dramaturgy that make him the most performed of all opera composers.
4 Describe how Verdi's *La traviata* typifies Italian Romantic opera.

The nineteenth century is often called the "golden age of opera." It is the century of Rossini, Bellini, Verdi, Wagner, Bizet, and Puccini. Notice that the four opera composers whose names end in "i" are, of course, Italian. The Italian language, with its evenly spaced, open vowels, is perfectly suited for singing, and the people of Italy seem to have an innate love of melody. Perhaps for this reason, opera began in Italy around 1600 (see Chapter 6). Thereafter, Italian opera dominated the European stage. When Handel wrote opera for London in the 1720s and Mozart wrote it for Vienna in the 1780s, they did so using mainly the language and traditions of Italian opera. Even today, Italian remains the language that is most frequently heard in opera houses around the world, from La Scala in Milan to the Metropolitan Opera in New York.

READ... the complete chapter text in a rich, interactive online platform.

In the early nineteenth century, the primacy of Italian opera was maintained almost single-handedly by Gioachino Rossini (1792–1868), the composer of *The Barber of Seville* (1816). Surprising as it may now seem, Rossini was the most celebrated musician in Europe during the 1820s, exceeding even Beethoven in fame. Why this "Rossini fever," as it was called? Because Rossini wrote operas—not symphonies or string quartets—and opera was then the leading genre of musical entertainment. Indeed, during Rossini's lifetime, opera captured the popular imagination in much the same way that film does today.

Rossini's best-known opera is comic, an *opera buffa*, titled *Il barbiere di Siviglia* (*The Barber of Seville*), which has never disappeared from the stage since its premiere in 1816. Even casual music lovers know a little of this enduring work in the form of the "Figaro, Figaro, Figaro" call from the opening aria of the resourceful barber, Figaro. Rossini could also write in a more serious style, exemplified in his last opera, *William Tell* (1829). This stormy drama, too, has achieved a measure of immortality, the overture providing the theme music for the radio and film character of the Lone Ranger. It's the ultimate "action" music.

Italian *Bel Canto* Opera

Rossini and his younger contemporaries pioneered a style of opera in which attention focused exclusively on the solo voice—on the art of beautiful, sometimes extravagant singing, called **bel canto** (Italian for "beautiful singing"), a term coined by Rossini himself. After Rossini, the two most gifted of the early creators of *bel canto* opera were Gaetano Donizetti (1797–1848) and Vincenzo Bellini (1801–1835). In their works, the orchestra provides merely a simple harmonic support for the soaring, sometimes divinely beautiful, lines of the voice. Look at the opening of the famous aria, "Casta diva," from Bellini's *Norma* (1831), in which the heroine sings a prayer to a distant moon goddess (Example 20.1). Here, the orchestra functions like a giant guitar. Simple chords are fleshed out as arpeggios by the strings while an even simpler bass line is plucked below. With the orchestra having little to do, all of the interest rests in the rapturous sound of the human voice as it spins out an expansive melody. For Italians, music and voice are almost one and the same.

HOW TO BECOME A DIVA: PRACTICE AND PERSIST

Glamorous opera star Renée Fleming appears to have been born a diva, a queen descended from operatic royalty. But actually she was once just a teenager at public Churchville-Chili High School in suburban Rochester, New York. Like so many others, she went to college at a large state university, only later making her way into high-powered music conservatories: first, the Eastman School of Music (back in Rochester) and then the Juilliard School in New York City. To pay the bills along the way, Fleming sang jazz and took on church gigs. Who would have known that, of the thousands of hopeful singers in music conservatories at the time, she would become the diva?

Fleming had talent, good teaching, and persistence. "As much as I struggled with my fears, it never occurred to me to just stop trying. My parents had drilled into me the code of Never Give Up," she says in *The Inner Voice: The Making of a Singer*. Lessons with a famous soprano in Germany and parts in a Juilliard opera, and then an opera in Mozart's city of Salzburg, preceded her big break. In 1988, at the age of twenty-nine, she won the operatic equivalent of TV's *The Voice*: the Metropolitan Opera National Council Auditions. Pushing to develop her talent all the while, Fleming thereafter worked her way up to ever-more-important roles in ever-more-important opera houses: Omaha, Houston, Seattle, and, finally, a much-coveted debut at America's most prestigious venue: New York's Metropolitan Opera. Her biggest audience, however, watched her sing "The Star-Spangled Banner" at the 2014 Super Bowl. The TV audience alone numbered a record 111.5 million.

The reigning opera diva, Renée Fleming, of Rochester, New York, specializes in *bel canto* opera.

Ultimately, two factors mark Renée Fleming's claim to being the preeminent classical diva: her exceptional vocal control—the product of long hours of practice—and her talent as an actress, which comes from acting in Broadway plays. Yes, she does that, too. What's the professional life span of a diva, or any singer, for that matter? A career normally ends at about age sixty-five. Vocal cords are muscles, like any others, and when they go, so does the vocal career.

WATCH ... Renée Fleming singing "Casta diva," online.

EXAMPLE 20.1 "Casta diva"

Ca - sta Di - va, ca - sta Di - va, che i - nar-

(Chaste goddess, who does bathe in silver light these hallowed, ancient trees)

gen - ti que - ste sa - cre, que - ste sa - cre, que - ste sa - cre anti - che pian - te,

Not surprisingly, by placing such importance on the voices of the leading singers, *bel canto* opera fostered a star system among the cast. Usually, the lyric soprano—heroine and **prima donna** (Italian for "first lady")—held the most exalted position in the operatic pantheon. By the 1880s, she would also be called a **diva**, which, as in the aria "Casta diva," means "goddess" in Italian. Indeed, the diva and her beautiful voice would rule Italian *bel canto* opera throughout the nineteenth century and even down to the present day.

As to the men, the castrato finally disappeared from the operatic stage in 1821. The romantic lead was now sung by a man with a high, but natural, voice. Replacing the heroic castrato with the equally heroic male tenor was part of a general nineteenth-century operatic evolution away from the artificial and "effeminate" and toward greater realism. This male voice lived on in the powerful, but lyrical, style of singing made famous by Enrico Caruso (1873–1921) and Luciano Pavarotti (1935–2007), the most commercially successful operatic singer of all time.

Giuseppe Verdi (1813–1901)

The name Giuseppe Verdi (VAIR-dee) is virtually synonymous with Italian opera. For six decades, from the time of *Nabucco* in 1842 until *Falstaff* in 1893, Verdi had almost no rival for the affections of the opera-loving public in Italy and throughout Europe. Even today, the best-loved of his twenty-six operas are more readily available—in opera houses, TV productions, DVDs, and HD broadcasts—than those of any other composer.

Verdi was born near Busseto in northern Italy in 1813, the son of a tavern keeper. He was no musical prodigy: At the age of eighteen, Verdi was rejected for admission to the Conservatory of Music in Milan because he was already too old and his piano technique was faulty. Indeed, not before the age of twenty-nine did he finally achieve musical success, with the opera *Nabucco* (1842). A surprise

FIGURE 20.1
La Scala Opera House about 1830. It was here that Bellini's *Norma*, with its signature aria, "Casta diva," premiered in 1831 and here, too, that Verdi's first four and last two operas had their premieres. It remains today the foremost opera house in Italy.

hit when premiered at La Scala Opera House in Milan (Figure 20.1), *Nabucco* launched Verdi's career in Europe and eventually in North and South America as well.

Today, Giuseppe Verdi (Figure 20.2) would be characterized variously as a political leftist, rebel, or revolutionary. He worked for the overthrow of the Austrian government, which then ruled most of northern Italy. By coincidence, the name "Verdi" ("Green" in Italian) had the same letters as **V**ittorio **E**manuele **R**e **d**'Italia, the people's choice to lead a free and unified Italy. Verdi willingly capitalized on this association of his name with the nationalist Green Party. During the 1840s, popular cries of "Viva Verdi" ("Long Live the Green [Nationalist] Party") echoed in support of Italian unification. Yet, it was not only Verdi's name but also his music that connected the composer to Italian nationalism. In *Nabucco*, for example, Verdi honors a suppressed people (in this case, the Jews), who groan under the rule of a cruel foreign power (the Babylonians). Sensitive listeners heard Verdi's choruses as "protest music," singable street songs urging the expulsion of foreign rulers (in this case, the Austrians from northern Italy). In 1849, however, much to Verdi's dismay, the nationalist revolution failed, crushed by Austrian troops.

Disillusioned with Italian politics, in 1850 Verdi temporarily moved to Paris and turned his attention from national to personal drama. In quick order, he composed a trio of works without which no opera house today could function: *Rigoletto* (1851), *La traviata* (1853), and *Il trovatore* (1853). Upon his return to Italy in 1857, the number, but not the quality, of Verdi's operas declined.

FIGURE 20.2
A photograph of Giuseppe Verdi, taken about 1885, on an early published score of his opera *La traviata*.

He composed only when the subject was of special interest or the money so great that he couldn't refuse. His opera *Aida* (1871), commissioned to celebrate the opening of the Suez Canal, brought him an astonishing fee—the equivalent of about $720,000 today. Verdi had become wealthy, and he retired to his estate in Italy, which by 1871 had become a single, unified nation. The plan was to lead the life of a country squire—or so he thought.

But, like a performer who feels he owes the audience more or has something more to prove to himself, Verdi returned to the theater, composing the critically acclaimed *Otello* (1887) and *Falstaff* (1893), both based on plays of Shakespeare. Of all artists, musical or otherwise, late-bloomer Verdi created quality works at the most advanced age: *Falstaff* was composed in his eightieth year.

Verdi's Dramaturgy and Musical Style

When the curtain goes up on a Verdi opera, the listener will find elements of dramaturgy—construction of the drama—and musical style that are unique to this composer. For Giuseppe Verdi, conflict should inform every scene, and he expressed that conflict, whether personal or national, by juxtaposing self-contained, clearly contrasting units of music. A rousing march, a patriotic chorus, a passionate recitative, and a lyrical aria might follow in quick succession. The composer aims not at musical and dramatic subtlety but, rather, at banner headlines of emotion. The psychic states of the characters are so clearly depicted, sometimes exaggerated, that the drama comes perilously close to melodrama, reliant on sentimentality and sensationalism at the expense of subtle character development. But it is never dull. There is action, passion, and intensity, all the things that give an opera mass appeal. In 1854, Verdi said, "There is one thing the public will not tolerate in the theater: boredom."

How does Verdi generate this feeling of intense passion and nonstop action? He does so by creating a new kind of recitative and a new style of aria. As before, the recitative still narrates the action, and the aria still expresses the character's emotional states, but Verdi now replaces a simple recitative, accompanied only by *basso continuo* (bass plus harpsichord chords), with an orchestrally accompanied **recitativo accompagnato**. This allows the action to flow smoothly from orchestrally accompanied aria to orchestrally accompanied recitative and back without a jarring change of texture. As for the aria, Verdi brings to it a new intensity or, as the Italians call it, *forza*. Verdi is a composer who is squarely in the tradition of Italian *bel canto* opera. He focuses his attention on the solo voice and on a lyrical, beautiful vocal line. Indeed, no composer had a greater gift for writing simple, memorable melodies that the audience could whistle on the way out of the theater. Yet, Verdi also adds intensity and passion to these arias by pushing singers to the upper reaches of their range. The thrilling moments in which the hero (the tenor) or the heroine (the soprano) go right to the top are literally the high points of any Verdi opera.

La traviata (1853)

We may measure the passionate intensity in Verdi's operas by listening to a portion of his *La traviata*, written in Paris in 1853. *La traviata* means literally "The Woman Gone Astray." The wayward woman here is the sickly Violetta Valery, a courtesan, or high-class prostitute, who first resists and then succumbs to the love of young Alfredo Germont. Then, without explanation, Violetta deserts Alfredo,

FIGURE 20.3
Marie Duplessis. The end of her brief, scandalous life is the subject of Giuseppe Verdi's opera *La traviata*. So notorious had she become by the time of her death at age twenty-three that no less a figure than Charles Dickens said, "You would have thought her passing was a question of the death of a hero or a Joan of Arc."

in truth so that her scandalous reputation will not bring disgrace on his respectable family. The hot-tempered Alfredo now publicly insults Violetta, fights a duel with her new "protector," and is banished from France. When the nature of Violetta's sacrifice is revealed, Alfredo rushes back to Paris, but it is too late! She is dying of tuberculosis—her fate dictated by an operatic convention that requires the heroine to sing one last show-stopping aria and then expire.

Verdi based the libretto of *La traviata* on a play that he had seen in Paris in 1852: *Camille*, by Alexandre Dumas the younger. (His father, Alexandre Dumas senior, wrote *The Count of Monte Cristo* and *The Three Musketeers*.) *Camille* tells the story of real-life figure Marie Duplessis (Figure 20.3), mistress of the playwright Dumas and, for a short time, of the composer-pianist Franz Liszt as well (see Chapter 19). Verdi renamed her Violetta and had her serve as the model for the courtesan in his opera *La traviata*. Like many people in this period, Marie died young of tuberculosis at the age of twenty-three.

We join *La traviata* toward the end of the first act. A gala party is in progress in a fashionable Parisian salon, and here the dashing Alfredo has finally managed to cut Violetta away from the crowd to profess his love. He does so in the aria "Un dì felice" ("One Happy Day"), which is lovely yet somber in tone (see Listening Guide). The seriousness of Alfredo's intent is underscored by the slow, square, even plodding accompaniment of the orchestra. When Violetta enters, she is supported by the same accompaniment, but the mood of the aria changes radically, becoming light and carefree. Witness Verdi's characterization by means of musical contrast: Alfredo's slow melody with a hint of minor is replaced by Violetta's flighty sound of high, rapidly moving pitches. Eventually, the two join together: he below, somberly proclaiming the mysteries of love; she above, making light of them. What started as a solo aria has become a duet, the voices—and hands—of the principals now intertwined. Once again, music enhances drama by replicating in its own language the action onstage.

LISTENING GUIDE

Giuseppe Verdi, "Un dì felice," *La traviata* (1853)   Download 57 (3:27)

Characters: Alfredo, a young man of good standing; Violetta, a kept woman leading a wanton life in Paris

Situation: A party in a Parisian salon around 1850; Alfredo professes his love to Violetta, who at first rejects him

WHAT TO LISTEN FOR: A somber, minor-tinged solo for tenor, followed by a bright, flighty one for soprano, and finally the conjunction of the voices in a pleasing duet

ARIA   **Alfredo (tenor)**

0:00	Tenor solo above "um-pah-pah" orchestral accompaniment	Un dì felice, eterea,	One happy day,
		Mi balaneste innante.	you appeared to me.
		E da quel dì tremante	And from this day, trembling,
		Vissi d'ignoto amor,	I have lived in that unspoken love,
		Di quell'amor ch'è palpito	in that love which animates
		Dell'universo intero,	the world,
	Shift to minor	Misterioso, altero,	mysterious, proud,
		Croce e delizia al cor.	pain and delight to the heart.

		Violetta (soprano)	
1:22	Violetta changes aria to a lighter mood through faster tempo and shorter notes.	Ah, se ciò è ver, fuggitemi. Solo amistade io v'offro; Amar non so, nè soffro Un cosi eroico amore. Io sono franca, ingenua; Altra cercar dovete; arduo troverete. Dimenticarmi allor.	If that's true, leave me. Only friendship I offer you; I don't know how to love or suffer such a heroic love. I'm being honest and sincere; you must find another; it won't be difficult. Just leave me.

DUET

Alfredo

1:50	Alfredo and Violetta together in rapturous duet	Oh amore! Misterioso, altero, Croce e delizia al cor.	Oh love! Mysterious, proud, pain and delight to the heart.

Violetta

		Non arduo troverete. Dimenticarmi allor.	It won't be difficult. Just leave me.
2:51	Exuberant vocal flourishes for both, but orchestra is silent	Ah!	Ah!

LISTEN TO ... this selection streaming online.

WATCH ... an Active Listening Guide of this selection online.

DO ... Listening Exercise 20.1, Verdi, *La traviata*, "Un dì felice," online.

Alfredo kisses Violetta's hand and departs, leaving her alone onstage to ponder her future. After singing a slow, reflective aria, she has come to a decision. Forget love, live for pleasure, she says, in an increasingly impassioned accompanied recitative: "Follie! Follie!" ("Folly! Folly!"). As Violetta's emotional barometer rises, so does her music, climaxing at the end of the recitative on the word *gioire* (*enjoy*). Through this high-flying music, Verdi defines the dangerous "live-for-the-moment" side of Violetta's character. Indeed, something about the height and intensity of the pitch (which is piercing enough to shatter a glass) suggests that Violetta is out of control. This is the fast and dazzling side of *bel canto* singing.

Recitative leads to aria, and the scene concludes with "Sempre libera" ("Always free"), one of the great showpiece arias for soprano voice (see Listening Guide). "Sempre libera" typifies a general type of aria called a **cabaletta**: a fast display piece that allows the singer to make an emphatic declaration and, with it, a dramatic exit—a showstopper in every sense, as a scene or act comes to an end. Here, the soprano must project an emotional state bordering on hysteria yet maintain absolute control over the pitch in her singing. Violetta's declaration of independence is briefly broken by the offstage voice of Alfredo, who reminds her of the seductive power of love (Figure 20.4). This, too, Violetta brushes aside as she repeats her

FIGURE 20.4

As writer Mark Evan Bonds has pointed out, the romantic comedy *Pretty Woman* (1990), starring Richard Gere and Julia Roberts, is a cinematic remake of the story of *La traviata*—respectable businessman meets call girl. An important difference, however, is that, in Verdi's treatment, as often happens in opera, no Hollywood ending prevails: The tragic heroine dies at the end.

pledge to remain a free woman. But, of course, our heroine does not remain free; otherwise, we would have no opera. She falls hopelessly in love with Alfredo, as Acts II and III reveal. Listen now to the end of Act I of Verdi's *La traviata*.

LISTENING GUIDE

Giuseppe Verdi, "Follie! Follie!" and "Sempre libera," *La traviata* (1853)   Download 58 (4:38)

Characters: Violetta and Alfredo (outside her window)

Situation: Violetta, having wondered if Alfredo might be the passionate love she has long sought, rejects that notion, vowing to remain free.

Form: Accompanied recitative followed by two-strophe aria

WHAT TO LISTEN FOR: The switch from accompanied recitative to aria, indeed an emphatic type of final aria called a cabaletta

RECITATIVE			Violetta
0:00	Accompanied by orchestra	Follie! Follie!	Folly! Folly!
		Delirio vano è questo! Povera donna, sola,	What sort of crazy dream is this! Poor woman, alone,
		abbandonata, in questo popoloso deserto	abandoned, in this populated desert
		che appellano Parigi.	that they call Paris.
		Che spero or più?	What hope have I?
		Che far degg'io?	What can I do?
0:55	Flights of vocal fancy as she thinks of pleasure	Gioire!	Pleasure!
		Di voluttà ne' vortici perir!	Perish in a whirl of indulgence!
		Gioire!	Enjoy!
1:06	Introduction to cabaletta		

CABALETTA

1:17		Sempre libera degg'io	Always free I must remain
		Folleggiare di gioia in gioia,	to reel from pleasure to pleasure,
		Vo' che scorra il viver mio	running my life
		Pei sentieri del piacer.	along the paths of joy.
		Nasca il giorno, o il giorno muoia,	From dawn to dusk
		Sempre lieta ne' ritrovi,	I'm always happy finding
		A diletti sempre nuovi	new delights that make
		Dee volare il mio pensier.	my spirit soar.

Alfredo

1:58	Echoes of his previous aria	Amor è palpito	Love that animates
		Dell'universo intero,	the world,
		Misterioso, altero,	mysterious, proud,
		Croce e delizia al cor.	pain and delight to the heart.

Violetta

2:34	Extravagant flourishes	Follie! Follie!	Folly! Folly!
		Gioire! Gioire!	Enjoy! Enjoy!

CABALETTA RETURNS

3:03	This time even more brilliant in its showy, superficial style	Sempre libera …	Always free …

LISTEN TO … this selection streaming online.

WATCH … an Active Listening Guide of this selection online.

WATCH … a performance of this selection online.

DO … Listening Exercise 20.2, Verdi, *La traviata*, "Follie! Follie!" online.

KEY WORDS

bel canto (287)	diva (289)	cabaletta (293)
prima donna (289)	*recitativo accompagnato* (291)	

---

f Join us on Facebook at Listening to Music with Craig Wright

---

PRACTICE … your understanding of this chapter's concepts by comparing Checklists of Musical Style for all historic eras and working once more with the chapter's Active Listening Guides online.

DO … online multiple-choice and critical thinking quizzes that your instructor may assign for a grade.

Romantic Opera:
GERMANY

START... experiencing this chapter's topics with an online video activity.

LEARNING OBJECTIVES

After studying the material in this chapter, you should be able to:

1 Sketch the history of Nordic fantasy literature from Richard Wagner to *Game of Thrones*.

2 Identify the ways in which Wagner's music dramas differ from the traditional Italian operas of Verdi.

3 Describe Wagner's Ring cycle and how it relates to Nordic fantasy literature.

4 Discuss Wagner's system of musical leitmotifs and how they inform the seventeen hours of music that constitute the Ring cycle.

When we go to the opera today, we usually see supertitles in English but hear singing in one of two languages: Italian or German. Before 1820, opera was mainly an Italian affair. First created in Italy around 1600, it then, over the next 200 years, was exported to all parts of Europe. With the onset of the nineteenth century, however, other people, driven by an emerging sense of national pride (see "Music and Nationalism" in Chapter 18), developed idiomatic opera in their native tongues. Although Italian opera remained the dominant style, it now had to share the stage with newer forms of opera written in French, Russian, Czech, Swedish, and especially German—all languages found north of the Alps.

READ ... the complete chapter text in a rich, interactive online platform.

Germany and Nordic Fantasy Literature

Historical periods often seem to look to earlier times for inspiration. The Renaissance and the Classical era, for example, embraced elements of Greek and Roman antiquity. The Romantic imagination, however, chose to model itself on the Middle Ages. A nostalgic fondness for a dimly understood "dark ages" developed early in the nineteenth century, especially north of the Alps. In these years, philologists (scholars of language) began to rediscover and publish "lost" medieval sagas and epic poems: the Anglo-Saxon *Beowulf* (1815), the German *Song of the Nibelungs* (1820), and the Finnish *Kalevala* (1835) among them. These were not medieval historical records but, rather, flights of poetic fancy in which a bard told stories of dark castles, fair maidens, heroic princes, and fire-breathing dragons. They were also markers of nineteenth-century nationalism in that each was written in an early form of an indigenous national language.

Inspired by these stories, Romantic artists such as John Martin (1789–1854) envisioned neo-medieval landscapes in paint (see chapter-opening image of his *The Bard*); novelists and poets such as Alfred, Lord Tennyson (1809–1892) fantasized about the knights of the Round Table; and composers, most notably Richard Wagner, constructed operas around a superhero named Siegfried. The popularity of such fantasy genres continues today. Think of the success of C. S. Lewis's *The Chronicles of Narnia*, J. R. R. Tolkien's *The Hobbit* and *The Lord of the Rings*, J. K. Rowling's Gothic *Harry Potter* series, and, most recently, the long-running *Game of Thrones* TV series, based on George R. R. Martin's book series, *A Song of Ice and Fire*. These are wonderful authors in the literal sense, yet they all owe a debt of gratitude to the past master of the epic fantasy series: Richard Wagner.

Richard Wagner (1813–1883)

The discovery of a deeply rooted German literature went hand in hand with the development of a national tradition of German opera, led by Richard Wagner (REEK-hard VAHG-ner; Figure 21.1). Before Wagner, German composers rarely wrote operas in their native language. Wagner, on the other hand, not only set German librettos exclusively but also wrote them himself, the only major opera composer to do so. Indeed, Wagner was a poet, philosopher, propagandist, self-publicist, and visionary who believed that operas—his operas—would revolutionize society. Understandably, many of his contemporaries were skeptical, and even today, opinion about Wagner is strongly divided. Some people are left cold, believing Wagner's music to be long-winded and his operatic plots devoid of realistic

FIGURE 21.1
Richard Wagner, as photographed in 1871

human drama. (In this camp was Mark Twain, who quipped famously: "Wagner's music is not nearly as bad as it sounds!") Some, knowing of Wagner's rabid anti-Semitism and Adolf Hitler's adoration of Wagner, refuse to listen at all. (Wagner's music is still unofficially banned in Israel.) But others are converted into adoring Wagnerites at the first sound of the composer's superhero themes and powerful orchestral climaxes.

Who was this controversial artist who has stirred such mixed feelings within the musical public for 150 years? A native of Leipzig, Germany, who studied a bit of music at the church where Bach had worked (see Figure 8.7), Wagner was largely self-taught in musical matters—his idol was Beethoven, and he studied Beethoven's scores on his own. After a succession of jobs as an opera director in several small German towns, Wagner moved to Paris in 1839 in hopes of seeing his first opera produced there. But, instead of meeting acclaim in Paris, as had Liszt and Chopin before him, Wagner was greeted with deafening indifference. No one would produce his work. Reduced to poverty, he spent a brief stint in debtor's prison.

When Wagner's big break came, it was not in Paris but back in his native Germany, in the city of Dresden. His opera *Rienzi* was given a hearing there in 1842, and Wagner was soon offered the post of director of the Dresden Opera. During the next six years, he created three additional German Romantic operas for the Dresden stage: *Der fliegende Holländer* (*The Flying Dutchman*, 1844), *Tannhäuser* (1845), and *Lohengrin* (1848)—the source of the famous wedding march, "Here Comes the Bride." All three involve plots situated in some ill-defined "Middle Ages." In the aftermath of the political revolution that swept much of Europe in 1848, Wagner was forced to flee Dresden, though in truth he took flight as much to avoid his creditors as to escape a repressive government.

Wagner found safe haven in Switzerland, which was to be his home, on and off, for the next dozen years. Having read the recently published edition of the Germanic epic entitled *Niebelungenlied* (*Song of the Nibelungs*), Wagner began to imagine a complex set of music dramas on a vast and unprecedented scale. What he ultimately created was *Der Ring des Nibelungen (The Ring of the Nibelungs)*, a set of four operas, now called the **Ring cycle**, which was intended to be performed during the course of four successive evenings. As with Tolkien's trilogy, *The Lord of the Rings*, Wagner's Ring cycle involves wizards, goblins, giants, dragons, and sword-wielding superheroes. Both sagas also revolve around a much-coveted ring, which affords its possessor unparalleled power but also carries a sinister curse. And, as with Tolkien's tale, Wagner's story is of epic length. *Das Rheingold*, the first opera, lasts two and a half hours; *Die Walküre* and *Siegfried* each runs nearly four and a half hours; the finale, *Götterdämmerung (Twilight of the Gods)*, goes on for no less than five and a half hours. Wagner began the Ring cycle in 1853 and didn't finish until 1874, perhaps the longest-running project by a single creator in the history of art.

Most composers make music to fit the context (performance space) in which it is to be heard. But Wagner was no ordinary composer. When producers refused to mount his epic, fantastical operas, megalomaniac Wagner solicited money from a king and built his own performance opera house at Bayreuth, Germany (Figure 21.2). His was the first hall to have an orchestral pit, the first to dim the lights during a performance, and the first to use special effects like smoke and steam. And Wagner would suffer no distractions from his art—he was also the first not to admit latecomers to their seats.

The first performance of Wagner's Ring cycle took place at Bayreuth in August 1876, the first time these operas had been heard as a group. Following Wagner's death in 1883, his remains were interred on the grounds of the Wagner villa in Bayreuth. Still controlled today by descendants of Wagner, the **Bayreuth Festival** continues to stage annually the music dramas of Wagner—and only Wagner. Tickets cost upwards of $500 apiece, and the wait to get them can stretch from five to ten years. Yet, each summer, nearly 60,000 Wagnerites make the pilgrimage to this theatrical shrine, to venerate one of art's most determined, and ruthless, visionaries.

FIGURE 21.2
In the foreground, we see Richard Wagner greeting Kaiser (King) Wilhelm I at the newly constructed Bayreuth Festival Theater. Completed in 1876, Bayreuth still serves as a home for the music dramas of Wagner—and only Wagner. To Wagner's right is his now-aged father-in-law, Franz Liszt (who was actually much taller than Wagner). This image is both a celebrity makeover and another example of celebrity marketing, the practice of using famous musicians to promote a product. The advertising card here was one of an assortment of "free gifts" that came with a beef bouillon product called Liebig Meat Extract. As can be seen by the text, the product was marketed in Italy and France as well as Germany.

Wagner's "Music Dramas"

Wagner and Verdi were born in the same year (1813), but their approach to opera was very different. Wagner wanted his opera to be radically new, so he gave it a new name: "music drama." A **music drama** for Wagner was a musical work for the stage in which all the arts—poetry, music, drama, mime, dance, and scenic design—are of equal importance and function harmoniously together. Wagner referred to such an artistic union as a *Gesamtkunstwerk* (German for "total art work"). If Verdi's opera is overwhelmingly a singer's opera, that of Wagner can be called a full cast and orchestra opera.

Wagner's music drama differs from traditional Italian opera in three important ways. First, Wagner did away with the Italian "separate numbers" opera, in which closed units of aria, recitative, and chorus are stitched together. Instead, he wrote a nonstop stream of solo singing and declamation that goes through an entire act, what is now called **endless melody**. Second, in his vocal writing, Wagner avoided repetition, symmetry, and regular cadences—all things that can make a melody catchy. Instead, he wanted his melodic line to spring forth directly from the rise and fall of the words, avoiding showy vocal fireworks generally. Third, and finally, as Wagner decreased the importance of the traditional vocal aria, he increased the importance of the orchestra.

With Wagner, the orchestra is everything. It sounds forth the main musical themes, develops and exploits them, and thereby plays out the drama through purely instrumental music. As Beethoven and Berlioz had done before him, Wagner continued to expand the size of the orchestra. The number of instruments that he required for the premiere of the Ring cycle, for example, was a gargantuan 125, including a massive brass section: 4 trumpets, 4 trombones, 8 horns (four doubling on tuba), and a contrabass (very low) tuba. If Wagner's music sounds powerful, it is the heavy artillery of brasses that makes it so.

A bigger orchestra demanded, in turn, more forceful singers. To be heard above an orchestra of 125 players, specially trained voices of great stamina were needed: the so-called Wagnerian tenor and Wagnerian soprano. The voice types that typically dominate the operatic stage today—with their powerful sound and wide vibrato—were first developed in Wagner's music dramas.

Wagner's *Ring* and *Die Walküre*
(*The Valkyrie*, 1856; first performed 1870)

Richard Wagner conceived his Ring cycle not only as a timeless fantasy adventure but also as a timely allegory for nineteenth-century German society. Through his libretto, Wagner explores power, greed, heroism, and race. These were then important issues in Germany, which was striving to become a unified nation (unity came in 1861) and which was rapidly industrializing. The curse-bearing "ring" at the center of the cycle, for example, represents (capitalist) power; characters fight to possess it, for whoever wears the ring rules the world.

The plot of the *Ring* is long and maddeningly complicated. To simplify greatly: Wotan, the chief god, rules over a fantasy world of heroes and villains, of natural and supernatural creatures. Wotan is well intentioned but has many weaknesses. Like some leading politicians today, he lies, cheats, and breaks promises in an attempt to maintain traditional values as well as his personal power. Although married, he has sired many children of uncertain maternity, among them the Valkyries, nine high-flying, hard-riding women warriors. Wotan's favorite offspring is the Valkyrie Brünnhilde, who gives the name "The Valkyrie" to the title of the drama.

At the beginning of Act III, the Valkyries ride away furiously, carrying the bodies of fallen heroes toward Wotan's mountaintop fortress, Valhalla. Their music is the famous "Ride of the Valkyries" in which these daughters of Wotan sing their war cry, "Hojotoho! Heijaha!" Wagner's music pushes them forward. The hard-charging main motive (Example 21.1) is triadic in construction, rising heroically as it proceeds.

LISTEN TO...

Example 21.1 online.

EXAMPLE 21.1 Valkyries leitmotif

As more and more Valkyries ride onstage, they greet one another with their familiar war cry (Example 21.2).

LISTEN TO...

Example 21.2 online.

EXAMPLE 21.2 Valkyries' vocal leitmotif

Ho-jo - to - ho !   Hei-a -   ha !

Wagner's associates (Figure 21.3) came to call his Valkyries motive and others like it leitmotifs. A **leitmotif** (signature tune) is a brief, distinctive unit of music designed to represent a character, object, or idea; they return repeatedly as sonic signposts to show the listener how the drama is unfolding. Wagner's leitmotifs are usually not sung but, rather, played by the orchestra. In this way, an element of the subconscious can be introduced into the drama: The orchestra can give a sense of what a character is thinking even when he or she is singing about something else. By developing, extending, varying, contrasting, and resolving these representational leitmotifs, Wagner is able to play out the essence of the drama almost without recourse to his singers. In *Die Walküre*, Wagner employs more than thirty

FIGURE 21.3
Cosima Wagner (daughter
of Franz Liszt and Marie
d'Agoult), husband Rich-
ard Wagner, and Liszt at
Wagner's villa in Bayreuth in
1880. At the right is a young
admirer of Wagner, Hans von
Wolzogen, who first coined
the term *leitmotif*.

leitmotifs and—although art is rarely an exact science—one critic has counted that
they sound 405 times!

Wagner knew that he was onto a good thing with "Ride of the Valkyries"
and thus created a purely instrumental version (see Listening Guide)—a sure-
fire crowd-pleaser and moneymaker—that could be performed in concert or
even outdoors. In this form, Wagner's fame spread. "Ride of the Valkyries" was
among the pieces played at an all-Wagner concert in Central Park, New York
City, in September 1872, the first time Wagner's music was publicly performed in
the United States. Subsequently, that same piece was used as an early film score
(*Birth of a Nation*, 1915), in war movies (*Apocalypse Now*, 1979; *Valkyrie*, 2009),
and in Nazi war propaganda. Initially associated with warrior women, "Ride of the
Valkyries" has become a sonic icon for all militaristic music, even available as an
especially assertive ring tone for your phone.

LISTENING GUIDE

Richard Wagner, "Ride of the Valkyries," *Die Walküre*
(1856; first performed, 1870; orchestral version 1870)

Download 59 (5:29)

Characters: The Valkyries

Situation: With music that pushes continually forward for more than five minutes, the warrior maidens carry the corpses of
fallen heroes to Valhalla, the home of the gods.

(Continued)

WHAT TO LISTEN FOR: How the hard-charging motive pushes the music continually forward, nonstop from beginning to end. Notice that the voices for the Valkyries vocal leitmotif ("Hojotoho! Heijaha!") have been replaced by violins in this purely instrumental version.

0:00	Opening call to attention with trills in high strings and woodwinds
0:25	Entrance of the Valkyries leitmotif in French horns and trombones

0:39	Entrance of the Valkyries leitmotif in trumpets
0:53	Brasses continue to present and share all or parts of the motive.
1:13	Bass trombones present motive, adding gravity to the sound.
1:30	Valkyries vocal leitmotif played by violins and woodwinds

1:57	Brasses continue with Valkyries leitmotif played *fortissimo*.
2:34	Dramatic descents in the strings and woodwinds
3:09	Bold, chromatic chord changes rising by half step
3:25	Valkyries leitmotif returns, quietly at first.
4:07	Cymbal sounds on the downbeat; tubas are audible beneath.
4:42	Valkyries vocal leitmotif returns in strings.
5:11	Rising scale and sudden end

LISTEN TO ... this selection streaming online.

WATCH ... an Active Listening Guide of this selection online.

WATCH ... a sung version of this selection online.

DO ... Listening Exercise 21.1, Wagner, "Ride of the Valkyries," online.

Despite the heroic excitement of "Ride of the Valkyries," all is not well in the land of the gods. Brünnhilde, the leader of the Valkyries' pack, has disobeyed Wotan. She has encouraged an incestuous love between two of Wotan's other children, twin brother and sister Siegmund and Sieglinde, respectively, from whom the superhero Siegfried will be born. (We said this plot was complicated.) Punishment comes in the form of humiliation: Brünnhilde is to be "demoted" from god to mortal and made to sleep upon a rock until some pedestrian male comes along and claims her as his wife (Figure 21.4). Brünnhilde recoils in horror, and Wotan agrees to reduce her sentence: He will surround her slumbering body with a ring of fire that only a deserving figure—ultimately, the superhero Siegfried—can penetrate. Clutching her in his arms, Wotan bids Brünnhilde farewell, knowing that they will never meet again.

Wotan is more than sad at the loss of Brünnhilde; he is destroyed, for, among all his children, she is his favorite. At the heart of this climactic scene is one of the drama's central conflicts: Wotan is torn between love (for Brünnhilde) and power (enforcing his authority). By choosing the latter, he loses not only Brünnhilde but also any illusion that he can really shape the world as he sees it. The intense physical attraction demonstrated onstage between father and daughter causes the audience to wonder: Had Wotan and Brünnhilde already extended to themselves license for incestuous love? The composer suggests as much in this supercharged final scene.

FIGURE 21.4
Wotan punishes Brünnhilde. Note Wotan's spear, on which are written the covenants that will govern society. Because she has encouraged free love, Brünnhilde has violated one of those rules.

LISTENING GUIDE

Richard Wagner, "Wotan's Farewell," *Die Walküre*
(1856; first performed 1870), first of two parts

Download 60 (4:55)

Characters: Wotan, chief of the gods, and Brünnhilde, leader of the Valkyries

Situation: Wotan bids eternal farewell to his beloved daughter, Brünnhilde, at the outset of the final scene of the drama.

WHAT TO LISTEN FOR: In addition to Wotan's huge bass-baritone voice and an even richer orchestral sound, three new leitmotifs: the first signifying the long slumber that Brünnhilde must now endure; the second, the ring of fire that will surround her; and the third, a prefiguration of hero Siegfried, who will rescue our Valkyrie in the next music drama.

0:00   Return of Valkyries leitmotif, signifying the
        presence of Brünnhilde

0:15   Brief introduction featuring "slumber"
        leitmotif

0:21   Leb'wohl, du kühnes, herrliches Kind!   Farewell, brave, splendid child!
        Du meines Herzens heiligster Stolz!   You, my heart's most holy possession!
        Leb'wohl! Leb'wohl! Leb'wohl!   Farewell! Farewell! Farewell!

(Continued)

1:06	Wotan suddenly drops to *pianissimo* and becomes more passionate.	
	Muss ich dich meiden	Must I reject you
	und darf nicht minnig	and must I no longer lovingly
	mein Grüss dich mehr grüssen,	greet you with my greeting,
	sollst du nun nicht mehr neben mir reiten	shall you no longer ride next to me
	noch Met beim Mahl mir reichen;	or bring me my mead at dinner;
	muss ich verlieren dich, die ich liebe	must I send you away, the one whom I love,
	du lachende Lust meines Auges?	laughing joy of my eyes?
1:58	Magic fire leitmotif sounds in violins	

	Ein bräutliches Feuer soll dir nun brennen	A bridal fire shall now burn
	wie nie einer Braut es gebrannt,	as one has never burned before,
	flammende Gluth umglühe den Fels;	a flaming threat shall flare round the rock;
	mit zehrenden Schrecken	with withering terror
	scheuch'es den Zagen;	it will frighten the weak;
	der Feige fliehe Brünnhildes Fels!	the fainthearted will flee Brünnhilde's rock!
2:29	Siegfried as hero leitmotif	

2:35	Denn einer nur freie die Braut	For a hero alone will win the bride,
	der freier als ich, der Gott!	one who is freer than I, the god!
3:04	"Slumber" leitmotif returns in violins.	
4:09	Orchestral climax led by surging strings, then long, gradual fadeout	

LISTEN TO … this selection streaming online.

WATCH … an Active Listening Guide of this selection online.

WATCH … this scene portrayed with soloist James Morris, perhaps the finest of the most recent Wotans, online.

DO … Listening Exercise 21.2, Wagner, "Wotan's Farewell," online.

WAGNER GOES TO THE MOVIES

Who are the Richard Wagners of today? One might say John Williams and Howard Shore—film composers for the *Star Wars* and *Lord of the Rings* series, respectively. Williams and Shore, however, likely would not be quick to compare themselves to Wagner, for he created not only the music, but everything else. Wagner was fund-raiser, theater builder, scriptwriter, composer,

●●●

conductor, drama coach, producer, and much more. But Williams and Shore knew of Wagner—both were classically trained—and they borrowed heavily from his leitmotif technique.

When John Williams wrote the music for the original trilogy of *Star Wars, The Empire Strikes Back,* and *The Return of the Jedi,* he composed for each main character (and theme or force) a particular musical motive. At the end of this box are two of Williams's leitmotifs, the first signifying the hero Luke Skywalker and the second (merely an insistent rhythm), the evil Darth Vader. Williams sets these leading motives in the orchestra, thereby telling the audience what the character is thinking or what the future may hold.

To see an opera/film parallel, recall "Wotan's Farewell," in which Wagner signals to the audience that a superhero will, in his next opera, rescue Brünnhilde. He does so by calling upon the powerful Siegfried leitmotif to surge up in the brasses. Compare, then, the moment in *Star Wars* when we learn that farm boy Luke Skywalker will, in the next film, become a Jedi warrior: when the orchestra plays the heroic "Force" leitmotif in the background.

In fact, *Star Wars,* conceived and created by George Lucas, has more than just leitmotifs in common with Wagner's music dramas. Both Wagner and Lucas started with a core of three dramas and added a fourth as a preface or "prequel." (*Das Rheingold* was prefixed to the *Ring,* and *The Phantom Menace* was prefixed to *Star Wars.*) Lucas, of course, added two further episodes to his saga, and recently Walt Disney Pictures, Lucasfilm, and Bad Robot have produced a seventh (*The Force Awakens,* 2015). The leitmotifs, however, remain the same. Like Wagner's Ring cycle, *Star Wars* and *The Lord of the Rings* play out a series of epic battles between larger-than-life heroes and villains, mythical forces for good and evil, warring throughout cosmic time. Modern cinematography is now greatly enhanced by computer graphics; the music, however, remains entirely within the older, Romantic tradition of Wagnerian opera.

Luke's Theme

Darth Vader's Theme

Finally, although Richard Wagner was a ruthless, unscrupulous human being, no one can deny his artistic greatness. Within all the arts, Wagner was the most revolutionary creative force of the nineteenth century, more so than Beethoven. Wagner built his own all-encompassing theater, put a massive orchestra deep in a pit, turned out the lights, invented new visual effects for the stage, and created an evolving dramatic series with characters who emerge, grow, and disappear over time. Wagner's literary bent initiated the modern epic fantasy series. His theatrical mind wanted, 100 years ago, what only today's modern technology would allow: the gigantic home entertainment center and the IMAX Theater. Here, as at Bayreuth, the audience would sit in the dark, with no distractions, and watch a lengthy dramatic series unfold on a large screen, driven by powerful, yet unseen music. Can one despise the man, yet love the artistic vision?

KEY WORDS

Ring cycle (298)
Bayreuth Festival (299)

music drama (299)
Gesamtkunstwerk (299)

endless melody (299)
leitmotif (300)

 Join us on Facebook at Listening to Music with Craig Wright

PRACTICE ... your understanding of this chapter's concepts by comparing Checklists of Musical Style for all historic eras and working once more with the chapter's Active Listening Guides online.

DO ... online multiple-choice and critical thinking quizzes that your instructor may assign for a grade.

Nineteenth-Century
REALISTIC
OPERA

START… experiencing this chapter's topics with an online video activity.

LEARNING OBJECTIVES
After studying the material in this chapter, you should be able to:

1 Differentiate nineteenth-century realistic opera from traditional
   bel canto opera, using the operas of Bizet and Puccini as examples.
2 Recount the career of "late bloomer" Giacomo Puccini.
3 Discuss how the plots of *Carmen* and *La bohème* define them as
   representative of realistic opera.

READ... the complete chapter text in a rich, interactive online platform.

Romantic opera, much like contemporary film, is largely an escapist art. The stage is populated by larger-than-life characters or by the well-to-do, people of leisure who are untroubled by mundane concerns or financial worries. During the second half of the nineteenth century, however, a contrasting type of opera developed in Europe, one more in tune with the social truths of the day. Simultaneously, the "start time" for opera moved from late afternoon to early evening. Why? Because people had to work during the day; opera was no longer only for the leisure class. And when the populace arrived, it often witnessed **realistic opera**, a new genre treating issues of everyday life in a realistic way. Poverty, physical abuse, industrial exploitation, and crime—afflictions of the lower classes, in particular—are presented onstage for all to see. In realistic opera, rarely is there a happy ending.

Realistic opera was part of an artistic reaction to the ill effects of the nineteenth-century Industrial Revolution, an economic transformation that brought with it great prosperity for some but oppressive factory conditions and social disintegration for others. Science played a role, too, for the nineteenth century witnessed the emergence of the theory of evolution. First popularized in Charles Darwin's *On the Origin of Species* (1859), evolutionary theory suggests a dog-eat-dog world in which only the fittest survive. Painters such as Jean-François Millet (1814–1875) and the young Vincent van Gogh (1853–1890) captured on canvas the life of the downtrodden (Figure 22.1). Writer Charles Dickens (1812–1870) did the same in realistic novels, such as *Oliver Twist* (1838) and *Bleak House* (1852). These artists aimed to transform the mundane and commonplace into art, to find the poetic and heroic in even the most ordinary aspects of human experience.

Must art imitate life? Composers of realistic opera thought so and thus embraced the gritty and unsavory facets of nineteenth-century society. The plots of their operas read like tabloid headlines: "Knife-Wielding Gypsy Girl Arrested in Cigarette Factory" (Bizet's *Carmen*, 1875); "Jealous Clown Stabs Wife to Death" (Leoncavallo's *Pagliacci*, 1892); "Abused Singer Murders Chief of Police" (Puccini's *Tosca*, 1892). If traditional Romantic opera is usually sentimental, nineteenth-century realistic opera is sensational.

FIGURE 22.1
The Potato Eaters (1885). During his youth, Vincent van Gogh chose to live and work in the coal-mining region of eastern Belgium. This grim painting records his impressions of life within a mining family and the evening meal of potatoes and tea.

Georges Bizet's *Carmen* (1875)

The first important realistic opera is *Carmen* (1875) by Georges Bizet (bee-SAY). Bizet (1838–1875), who spent his short life entirely in Paris, was primarily an opera composer, and *Carmen* is his masterpiece. Set in nineteenth-century Spain, *Carmen* centers on a sensual young gypsy woman known only as Carmen (Figure 22.2). Though her day job seems to be little more than part-time worker in a cigarette factory, this sexually assertive, domineering woman holds the populace in her sway. By means of alluring dance and song, she seduces a naïve army corporal, Don José. Falling hopelessly in love, Don José deserts his military post, "marries" Carmen, and takes up with her gypsy bandit friends. But Carmen, who refuses to belong to any man, soon abandons Don José to give herself to the handsome bullfighter Escamillo. Having lost all for nothing, the emasculated Don José stabs Carmen to death in a bloody ending.

This violent conclusion highlights the stark realism of *Carmen*. The heroine is a woman of easy virtue who makes herself available to every man, albeit on her own terms. She lives for the moment, surrounded by social outcasts (gypsies), prostitutes, and thieves. All this was shocking stuff for the Parisian audiences of Bizet's day. During the first rehearsals in 1875, the women of the chorus threatened to strike because they were asked to smoke and fight on stage. Critics called the libretto "obscene." Bizet's producers asked him to tone down the more lurid aspects of the drama (especially the bloody ending)—to make it more acceptable as family entertainment—but he refused.

Carmen is full of alluring melodies, including the well-known Toreador Song and the even more beloved Habanera. In fashioning these tunes, Bizet borrowed phrases from several Spanish popular songs, folksongs, and **flamenco** melodies (songs of southern Spain infused with gypsy elements). The Habanera, which introduces the character Carmen, makes use of a then-popular Spanish song.

Literally, **habanera** means "the thing from Havana." Musically, it is a type of dance-song that developed in Spanish-controlled Cuba during the early nineteenth century. African and Latin influences on its musical style can perhaps be seen in the descending chromatic scale and certainly in the static harmony (the downbeat of every measure is a D in the bass), as well as in the insistent, repetitious rhythm (♩♫♩ | ♩♫♩). The infectious rhythm of the habanera gives it its irresistible quality—we all want to get up and join the dance. But the habanera is a sensual dance—like its descendant, the tango, with the same rhythm—and this sensual quality contributes greatly to Carmen's seductive aura.

The structure of Bizet's Habanera is straightforward (see Listening Guide). At first, Carmen sings a descending chromatic line of four 4-bar phrases ("Love is like an elusive bird"). By their nature, fully chromatic melodies have no tonal center. This one, too, is musically noncommittal and slippery, just as Carmen herself is both ambiguous and evasive. The chorus immediately repeats the chromatic melody, but now Carmen voluptuously glides above it, singing the single word *L'amour* (*Love*). As her voice soars, like the elusive bird of love, the tonality brightens from minor to major. To this is then added a refrain ("Love is like a gypsy child") in which the melody alternates between a major triad and a minor one. Against this refrain, the chorus shouts, "Watch out!" warning of Carmen's destructive potential. This same structure—a chromatically descending melody, followed by the triadic refrain with choral shouts—then repeats. Bizet wanted his Habanera

FIGURE 22.2
Beyoncé Knowles poses with the red dress that she wore in *Carmen: A Hip Hopera*.

to establish the character of Carmen as a sensual enchantress. In every way, the music *is* Carmen. And, like Carmen, once this seductive melody has us in its spell, it will never let go.

LISTENING GUIDE

Georges Bizet, Habanera from *Carmen* (1875)   Download 61 (4:34)

Situation: The scantily clad gypsy woman, Carmen, exuding an almost primeval sexuality, dances before Don José, soldiers, and other gypsies.

Form: Strophic (verse and chorus/refrain)

WHAT TO LISTEN FOR: The sultry habanera rhythm, then Carmen's sensuous melody, and finally her soaring voice on the word *L'amour* (*Love*). A second stanza repeats the same formal plan.

0:00   Bass ostinato with habanera rhythm; minor mode

Stanza 1

0:06   Carmen enters with enticing descending melody.

L'amour est un oiseau rebelle	Love is like an elusive bird
Que nul ne peut apprivoiser;	That cannot be tamed;
Et c'est bien en vain qu'on l'appelle,	You call it in vain,
S'il lui convient de refuser.	If it decides to refuse.
Rien n'y fait, menace ou prière,	Neither threat nor prayer will prevail,
L'un parle bien, l'autre se tait;	One man talks a lot, the other is silent;
Et c'est l'autre que je préfère,	And it's the latter I prefer,
Il n'a rien dit; mais il me plaît.	He hasn't said a word, but he pleases me.

0:41   Change to major mode; chorus repeats melody;
            Carmen soars above on *L'amour*.

Refrain

0:57   Carmen sings refrain.

L'amour est enfant de Bohème,	Love is like a gypsy child,
Il n'a jamais connu de loi,	Who has never known constraint,

	Si tu ne m'aimes pas, je t'aime,	If I love you, and you don't love me,
	Si je t'aime, prends garde à toi!	Watch out!
1:14	Chorus shouts, "Prends garde à toi!"	Watch out!
1:37	Chorus sings refrain with Carmen.	
2:14	Bass ostinato with habanera rhythm	

Stanza 2

2:21	Carmen enters with enticing chromatic melody.	
	L'oiseau que tu croyais surprendre	The bird you thought you'd surprised
	Battit de l'aile et s'envola;	Beat its wings and flew away;
	L'amour est loin, tu peux l'attendre;	Love is far away, but expect it;
	Tu ne l'attends plus, il est là!	You don't expect it, but there it is!
	Tout autour de toi, vite,	All around you, quick!
	Il vient, s'en va, puis il revient;	It comes, it goes, and then it returns;
	Tu crois le tenir, il t'évite;	You think you've trapped it, it escapes;
	Tu crois l'éviter, il te tient!	You think you've escaped it, it traps you!
2:55	Change to major mode; chorus repeats melody; Carmen soars above on *L'amour*.	

Refrain

3:12	Carmen, chorus (3:51), and then Carmen (4:09) again sings refrain.

LISTEN TO ... this selection streaming online.

WATCH ... an Active Listening Guide of this selection online.

WATCH ... a performance of this selection online.

DO ... Listening Exercise 22.1, Bizet, Habanera from *Carmen*, online.

At its premiere in Paris on March 3, 1875, *Carmen* was a flop—the realistic subject matter was thought too degrading. Despondent over this poor reception, composer Georges Bizet suffered a fatal heart attack exactly ninety days later.

As the nineteenth century progressed and theatrical subjects became increasingly realistic, however, the appeal of *Carmen* grew. Now arguably the world's most popular opera, parts of the *Carmen* story have appeared in some seventy films, including an early silent movie (1915) and an Academy Award–winning production (1984). In addition, the most popular melodies of *Carmen* serve as background music in countless TV commercials and cartoons, and they are sometimes the object of parody (witness the Muppets' spoof of the Habanera on YouTube). In an early episode of *The Simpsons*, the family goes to the opera, where it hears— what else?—*Carmen*, and Bart and Homer sing along. *Carmen* has also been refashioned into an African opera set in Senegal (*Karmen Geï*, 2001), an African American Broadway musical (*Carmen Jones*, 1954), and an MTV special (*Carmen: A Hip Hopera*, starring Beyoncé Knowles, 2001; Figure 22.2). Not surprisingly for a realistic opera, *Carmen* is a work that transcends race and class, a quality that accounts in part for its lasting popularity.

WATCH... a YouTube video of the Muppets' spoof of the Habanera, online.

WATCH... a YouTube video of the Habanera from Bizet's *Carmen*, as it appears in Beyoncé's *Carmen: A Hip Hopera*, online.

HIGH ART, HIGH TICKET PRICES: WHY DOES OPERA COST SO MUCH?

Today, if you go to the New York Metropolitan Opera or the Chicago Lyric Opera, you will pay upward of $500 for a front row seat. Why is opera so expensive? Opera is, to borrow from Richard Wagner, a *Gesamtkunskwerk* (German for "total art work"), involving scenery, lighting, actors/singers, sometimes dancers, usually a chorus, and always a full symphony orchestra with conductor. In all, the Metropolitan Opera employs nearly 4,000 workers, represented by sixteen separate labor unions.

Take a single opera, such as *La bohème*, for example. While it may be a realistic opera in regard to subject matter, the expense of mounting it can make it anything but. A Met production involves the following: an orchestra of 72, a chorus of 80, 35 children and 106 extras for street scenes, a 12-piece stage band, 94 stagehands, a horse, and a donkey. And don't forget the soloists, the best of whom receive up to $17,000 per performance. Even a member of the chorus—a demanding job because of all the rehearsals—earns $200,000 annually plus benefits. If the Met sells all 3,800 seats for a production of *La bohème*, it will still lose money, the loss being covered by donors and endowments.

How to beat the high ticket prices? Take advantage of technology and go to a local movie theater in your city. Now both the Metropolitan Opera and the Royal Opera Company of London beam HD broadcasts around the world (for the schedule, just google "Metropolitan Opera HD" or "Royal Opera Live Cinema Season"). The Met now streams to 1,900 movie theaters in sixty-four countries. These broadcasts are not films of operas but, rather, live performances in which you see and hear Renée Fleming or Plácido Domingo as they perform. For the audience, the advantages to the HD broadcasts are obvious: The listener can sit right up front and, given the high quality of cinema-house audio speakers, enjoy sound of the highest quality. All this for the price of a movie ticket!

Giacomo Puccini's *La bohème* (1896)

Italian realistic opera of the late nineteenth century goes by its own special name, **verismo** opera (*verismo* is Italian for "realism"). Yet, though it enjoys a separate name, *verismo* opera in Italy was little different from realistic opera elsewhere. Although many Italian composers wrote *verismo* operas, by far the best known today is Giacomo Puccini (Figure 22.3).

Giacomo Puccini (1858–1924) was the scion of four generations of musicians from the northern Italian town of Lucca. Both his father and his grandfather had written operas, and his forebears before them had composed religious music for the local cathedral. But Puccini, like Verdi, was no child prodigy. For a decade following his graduation from the Milan Conservatory, he lived in poverty as he struggled to develop a distinctive operatic style. Not until the age of thirty-five did late-blooming Puccini score his first triumph, the *verismo* opera *Manon Lescaut* (1893). Thereafter, successes came in quick order: *La bohème* (1896), *Tosca* (1900), and *Madama Butterfly* (1904). Growing famous, wealthy, and a bit complacent, Puccini worked less and less frequently. His last, and many believe his best, opera, *Turandot*, was left unfinished at the time of his death from throat cancer in 1924.

Puccini's best-known opera—indeed the most famous of all *verismo* operas—is *La bohème* (*Bohemian Life*, 1896). The realism of *La bohème* rests in the setting and characters: The principals are bohemians—unconventional artists living in abject poverty. The hero, Rodolfo (a poet), and his pals Schaunard (a musician), Colline (a philosopher), and Marcello (a painter), inhabit an unheated attic on the Left Bank of Paris. The heroine, Mimi, their neighbor, is a poor seamstress with tuberculosis. Rodolfo and Mimi meet and fall in love. He grows obsessively jealous while she becomes progressively ill. They separate for a time, only to return to each other's arms immediately before Mimi's death. The historical importance of *La bohème* rests in the fact that it was the first opera to foreground city life—with all its wealth, poverty, and disease—in the plot of an opera.

In truth, the plot to *La bohème* is neither deep nor philosophical, and there is little character development. Instead, the glorious sound of the human voice (*bel canto* singing again) carries the day. Puccini continues the nineteenth-century tendency to lessen the distinction between recitative and aria. His solos typically start syllabically (no more than one note per syllable), as if the character is beginning a conversation. As the speaker's ardor grows, the voice gains intensity and becomes more expansive, with the strings doubling the melody to add warmth and expression. Verbal semantics yield to musical sensations. When Rodolfo, for example, sings of Mimi's frozen little hand in the aria "Che gelida manina" ("Ah, What a Frozen Little Hand"; see Listening Guide), we move imperceptibly from recitative to aria, gradually transcending the squalor of the Left Bank garret and soaring to a better world far beyond. The contrast between the dreary stage setting and the transcendental beauty of the music is the great paradox of realistic opera.

FIGURE 22.3
Giacomo Puccini

LISTENING GUIDE

Giacomo Puccini, "Che gelida manina," *La bohème* (1896)   Download 62 (4:29)

Characters: The poor poet Rodolfo and the equally impoverished seamstress Mimi

Situation: Mimi has knocked on Rodolfo's door to ask for a light for her candle. Charmed by the lovely stranger, he naturally obliges. The wind again blows out Mimi's candle, and amid the confusion, she drops her key. As the two search for it in the darkness, Rodolfo by chance touches her hand and, then holding it, seizes the moment to tell her about himself and his hopes.

Performer: Renowned tenor Plácido Domingo

(Continued)

0:00	Rodolfo begins conversationally, much as in recitative.	Che gelida manina se la lasci riscaldar. Cercar che giova? Al buio non si trova. Ma per fortuna è una notte di luna, e qui la luna l'abbiamo vicina. Aspetti, signorina, le dirò con due parole	Ah, what a frozen little hand, let me warm it up. What's the good of searching? We won't find it in the dark. But by good luck there is moonlight tonight, and here we have the moon nearby. Wait, young lady, I will tell you in two words
1:03	Voice increases in range, volume, and intensity, as Rodolfo explains who he is and what he does.	chi son, e che faccio, come vivo. Vuole? Chi son? Sono un poeta. Che cosa faccio? Scrivo. E come vivo? Vivo!	who I am, and what I do, how I live. Would you like this? Who am I? I'm a poet. What do I do? I write. How do I live? I live!
1:55	Return to conversational style	In povertà mia lieta scialo da gran signore rime et inni d'amore. Per sogni et per chimere e per castelli in aria, l'anima ho milionaria.	In my delightful poverty I grandiosely scatter rhymes and songs of love. Through dreams and reveries and through castles in the air, I have the soul of a millionaire.
2:27	Voice grows more expansive with longer notes and higher range; orchestra doubles voice in unison.	Talor dal mio forziere ruban tutti i gioelli gli due ladri: occhi belli. V'entrar con voi pur ora, ed i miei sogni usati e i bei sogni miei tosto si dileguar! Ma il furto non m'accora, poichè v'ha preso stanza la speranza!	Sometimes from the strongbox two thieves steal all the jewels: two pretty eyes. They came in with you just now, and my usual dreams, my lovely dreams vanish at once! But the theft doesn't bother me, because their place has been taken by hope!
3:25	Orchestra sounds melody alone and then is joined by voice for climactic high note on *speranza*!		
3:47	As music diminishes, Rodolfo asks for a response from Mimi.	Or che mi conoscete, parlate voi, deh! parlate. Chi siete? Vi piaccia dir!	Now that you know who I am, tell me about yourself, speak! Who are you?

LISTEN TO ... this selection streaming online.

WATCH ... an Active Listening Guide of this selection online.

WATCH ... a performance of this selection online.

DO ... Listening Exercise 22.2, Puccini, "Che gelida manina," *La bohème*, online.

KEY WORDS

realistic opera (308)   flamenco (309)   habanera (309)   *verismo* opera (312)

 Join us on Facebook at Listening to Music with Craig Wright

PRACTICE ... your understanding of this chapter's concepts by comparing Checklists of Musical Style for all historic eras and working once more with the chapter's Active Listening Guides online.

DO ... online multiple-choice and critical thinking quizzes that your instructor may assign for a grade.

Late Romantic
ORCHESTRAL
Music

START... experiencing this chapter's topics with an online video activity.

LEARNING OBJECTIVES

After studying the material in this chapter, you should be able to:

1 Describe how the symphony hall, housing a symphony orchestra, reached its zenith as a "music-only" concert venue during the late Romantic period.

2 Describe the difficulty that Brahms and other late Romantic composers faced when attempting to write a symphony "post-Beethoven."

3 Describe how a composer from Prague, Antonín Dvořák, came to write one of America's best-known orchestral works in New York City and Spillville, Iowa.

4 Enumerate the ways in which the symphonies of Gustav Mahler exemplify the enormously expanded symphony of the late nineteenth century.

The symphony orchestra reached its full potential in the late nineteenth century, developing into a colorful, powerful force of more than 100 players. It became, in a phrase, one of the greatest glories of Western culture. But, to hear an orchestra, listeners had to make a special trip to a large concert hall; computers, smartphones, and electronically amplified sounds were still far in the future. Today, of course, streaming classical music is only a click away. But accessibility has come at a price; the recent revolution in digitally disseminated music has been accompanied by a general decline in the quality of sound. Listening to Beethoven or Wagner via compressed MP3 or M4A files gives only a vague approximation of the nineteenth-century original. Good headphones can help. But to experience a symphony orchestra at its best, as did listeners in the late Romantic era, we must journey to a large concert hall with great architecture, ambience, and acoustics. Many still exist.

Romantic Values and Today's Concert Hall

Look closely at the chapter-opening photograph. Here we see the front of world-famous Carnegie Hall, built in New York in 1891. Notice, in the bottom left corner over the door, the inscription "MUSIC HALL," followed by "FOUNDED BY ANDREW CARNEGIE." Now recall Figure 15.5, which shows the music theater of the early Romantic period in Vienna in which Beethoven's Symphony No. 5 premiered in 1808. Notice, again, the horses on stage (lower left). Between the early and late nineteenth century, the concert hall underwent a transformation: What had been a multipurpose theater, in which a concert of classical music one night would be followed by an opera the next, and then perhaps by a circus or a horse show, was succeeded by a new kind of auditorium, a "music-only" sanctuary.

Indeed, the late Romantic era was the high point in widespread construction of large, music-specific halls in Europe, and North and South America as well. Auditoriums in several major cultural cities of the world—Vienna (Musikverein, 1870), Leipzig (Second Gewandhaus, 1884), New York (Carnegie Hall, 1891), Boston (Symphony Hall, 1900), and Chicago (Symphony Hall, 1904)—first saw the light of day then and remain among the best ever constructed, in terms of sight lines and acoustics. The new Walt Disney Concert Hall in Los Angeles (2003) and the Schermerhorn Symphony Center in Nashville (2006) continue this tradition. Indeed, the Schermerhorn Symphony Center copies many of the architectural features of Vienna's nineteenth-century Musikverein (compare Figure 1.6 with Figure 23.1). All of these auditoriums were built to be large concert halls, seating 1,800 to 2,800 listeners, devoted exclusively to high-attention, undistracted listening.

Did the late nineteenth century mark the apex of classical music in the West? Indeed, one might rightly claim that Western symphonic music reached its zenith then, owing to the unequaled size of the orchestra, the acoustic quality of the new large concert halls, and the prestige that the general public accorded to high-end classical music. True or not, the institutions and values formed during the late Romantic era still hold sway today.

Prior to 1800, almost all music was disposable—popular music, in a sense. It was composed as entertainment for the moment and then forgotten. And well into the early decades of the nineteenth century, a concert was likely to be a variety show of popular favorites, both vocal and instrumental. A single movement of a

FIGURE 23.1

The Musikverein (Music Center) of Vienna, initiated by admirers of Beethoven and often performed in by Brahms, who lived only a few doors away. It set the standard throughout the Western world for a "music-only" sanctuary, a temple for classical music. And just as at religious services, people tended to dress up and sit quietly to hear the divine message.

symphony would be followed by an opera aria, perhaps a dramatic reading from a play, a polka, an operatic trio, a concerto, and finally the finale of yet another symphony. Gradually, however, the new "music-only" concert hall came to serve mainly as an "instrumental-music-only" hall, or "symphony hall" as it was soon called, and the instrumental music performed there adhered mostly to the standard canon of classical music (see the end of Chapter 12)—the great works of Haydn, Mozart, Beethoven, and Schubert.

The Romantic era had made classical music a conservative art (indeed, the term *music conservatory* originated then) in the sense that it conserved the greats. And, still today, what the concertgoer experiences doesn't differ much from what listeners of the late Romantic period experienced. Today's concert hall is about the same size (average 2,500 seats), and the symphony orchestra that performs there includes about the same number of musicians (90 to 105 players at full strength). So, too, the music on the program has remained largely unchanged, as listeners revisit a musical museum and enjoy the works of the classical masters. But, throughout the nineteenth century, the canon continued to expand and would soon include masterpieces by Brahms, Dvořák, and Mahler.

Johannes Brahms (1833–1897)

It took courage for a late Romantic composer such as Johannes Brahms (Figure 23.2) even to contemplate the creation of a large, multimovement symphony or concerto. How could one possibly top the monumental works of Beethoven? Wagner asked why anyone after Beethoven bothered to write symphonies at all, given the dramatic impact of Beethoven's Third, Fifth, and Ninth symphonies. Wagner himself wrote only one symphony, and Verdi wrote none. Some composers, notably Berlioz and Liszt, turned to a completely different sort of symphony, the program symphony (see Chapter 18), in which an external scenario determined the nature and order of the musical events. Not until the late Romantic period—nearly fifty years after the death of Beethoven—did Johannes Brahms emerge to assume the role of Beethoven's successor.

Brahms was born in the north German port city of Hamburg in 1833. He was given the Latin name Johannes to distinguish him from his father, Johann, a street musician and beer hall fiddler. Although Johannes's formal education never went beyond primary school, his father saw to it that he received the best training on the piano and in music theory, with the works of Bach and Beethoven given pride of place. While he studied these masters by day, by night Brahms earned money playing out-of-tune pianos in "stimulation bars" on the Hamburg waterfront. (During 1960–1962, The Beatles went to Hamburg to play in the descendants of these strip joints.) To get his hands on better instruments, Brahms sometimes practiced in the showrooms of local piano stores.

Brahms first caught the public's attention in 1853, when Robert Schumann published a highly laudatory article proclaiming him a musical messiah, the heir apparent to Haydn, Mozart, and Beethoven. Brahms, in turn, embraced Robert and his wife, Clara (see Figure 17.4), as his musical mentors. After Robert was confined to a mental institution in 1854, Brahms became Clara's confidant, and his respect and affection for her ripened into love, despite the fact that she was fourteen years his senior. Whether owing to his unconsummated love for Clara or for other reasons, Brahms remained a bachelor all his life.

Disappointed first in love and then in his attempt to gain a conducting position in his native Hamburg, Brahms moved to Vienna in 1863. He supported his modest lifestyle—very "un-Wagnerian," he called it—by performing and conducting. His fame as a composer increased dramatically in 1868 with performances of his *German Requiem*, which was soon sold to amateur choruses around the world. In this same year, he composed what is today perhaps his best-known piece, the simple yet beautiful art song *Wiegenlied*, known among English speakers as "Brahms's Lullaby" (see Chapter 3 and Download 5). Honorary degrees from Cambridge University (1876) and Breslau University (1879) attested to his growing stature. After Wagner's death in 1883, Brahms was generally considered the greatest living German composer. His own death, from liver cancer, came in the spring of 1897. He was buried in the central cemetery of Vienna, thirty feet from the graves of Beethoven and Schubert.

Vienna was (and remains) a musical yet conservative city, fiercely protective of its rich cultural heritage. That Brahms should choose it as his place of residence is not surprising—Vienna had been the home of Haydn, Mozart, Beethoven, and Schubert, and the conservative Brahms found inspiration in the music of these past masters (Figure 23.3). Again and again, he returned to traditional genres, such as the symphony, concerto, quartet, and sonata, and to conventional forms, such as sonata–allegro and theme and variations. Most telling, Brahms composed no program music. Instead, he chose to write **absolute music**, chamber sonatas, symphonies, and concertos without narrative or "storytelling" intent. The music of Brahms unfolds as patterns of pure, abstract sound within the tight confines of traditional forms. Although Brahms could write sweeping Romantic melodies, he was at heart a "developer" of small motives in the tradition of Bach and Beethoven. Indeed, in 1877, a music critic eternally linked Brahms to his

FIGURE 23.3
Brahms's composing room in Vienna, where he lived from 1871 until his death in 1897. On the wall, looking down on the piano, is a bust of Beethoven. The spirit of Beethoven loomed large over the entire nineteenth century (see also Figure 15.1) and over Brahms, in particular.

predecessors by coining the expression "the three Bs" of classical music: Bach, Beethoven, and Brahms.

Violin Concerto in D major (1878)

In 1870, Brahms wrote, "I shall never compose a symphony! You have no idea how the likes of us feel when we hear the tramp of a giant like him behind us." That "giant," of course, was Beethoven, and Brahms, like other nineteenth-century composers, was terrified by the prospect of competing with his revered predecessor. But Brahms did go on to write a symphony—indeed, four of them, first performed, in turn, in 1876, 1877, 1883, and 1885. In the midst of this symphonic activity, Brahms also wrote his only violin concerto, which rivals the earlier violin concerto of Beethoven.

How do you write a concerto for an instrument that you can't play? How do you know how to make the instrument sound good and what to avoid? Brahms, who was trained as a pianist and not a violinist, did as composers before and after him. He turned to a virtuoso on the instrument—in this case, his friend, Joseph Joachim (1831–1907). When the concerto was premiered in 1878, Joachim played the solo part while Brahms conducted the orchestra.

One technical "trick" that Joachim surely insisted that Brahms employ is the art of playing **double stops**. Usually, we think of the violin as a monophonic instrument, capable of playing only one string and thus only one pitch at a time. But a good violinist can hold (stop) two and sometimes more strings simultaneously and sweep across them with the bow. This imparts a richer, more chordal sound to the soloist's part. Example 23.1 shows how Brahms incorporates double stops (here, two or four pitches played simultaneously) into the melody of the last movement of his concerto.

EXAMPLE 23.1 Double stops

When he arrived at the finale of his Violin Concerto, Brahms the conservative turned to a form traditionally used in the last movement of a concerto: the rondo. Recall that a rondo centers on a single theme that serves as a musical refrain (see Chapter 3, "Rondo Form"). Here, the refrain has the flavor of a gypsy tune, like the Hungarian dances Brahms often heard in Viennese cafés as he sipped beer, smoked a cigar, and chatted with friends. What animates this refrain is its lively rhythm (Example 23.2).

LISTEN TO...

Example 23.1 online.

EXAMPLE 23.2 Brahms Violin Concerto rhythm

Above this foot-tapping motive, the violin sometimes soars with difficult passage work (scales, arpeggios, and double stops). The makers of the Academy Award–winning *There Will Be Blood* (2007) featured this movement by Brahms in the sound track of the film, perhaps to represent the tug of war (concerto) between the greedy oil man (played by Daniel Day-Lewis) and the landowners. Indeed, the nineteenth-century solo concerto was not only a "concerted" effort by all participants but also a contest between soloist and orchestra. One musician of the day recognized the tension when he said that Brahms had written a concerto not "for the violin but against it," to which another replied, "Brahms's concerto is not against the violin, but for the violin and against the orchestra—and the violin wins." Needless to say, the sight of the final victorious bows of a soloist appealed to listeners in the Romantic age, who had a penchant for hero worship. In the case of our recording (see Listening Guide), however, our hero is a heroine: virtuosa violinist Hilary Hahn (Figure 23.4). Times have changed.

FIGURE 23.4
American-born violin virtuosa and two-time Grammy winner Hilary Hahn, whose spirited and beautifully clear performance is heard on Download 63. She made this recording at the age of twenty-two.

LISTENING GUIDE

Johannes Brahms, Violin Concerto in D major (1878)   Download 63 (7:39)

Third movement, Allegro giocoso, ma non tropo vivace (fast and playful, but not too lively)

Genre: Concerto

Form: Rondo

WHAT TO LISTEN FOR: The exchanges between the soloist and the orchestra, and the "anything you can do, I can do better" spirit that develops. The constantly returning rondo theme (Example 23.1) is easy to recognize, no matter who performs it.

0:00	**A**	Refrain played by violin and then by orchestra
0:50		Transition: racing scales in violin
1:10	**B**	New theme moves up, and then down, a major scale.
1:54	**A**	Violin returns with refrain; orchestra repeats it.
2:30	**C**	Violin plays more lyrical theme built on arpeggio.
3:28	**B**	Rising scale in violin, answered by falling scale in orchestra
4:15		Elaboration of rhythm of refrain
4:33	**A**	Orchestra plays refrain *fortissimo.*
4:59		Violin plays very brief cadenza; then rhythm of refrain is developed.
6:03		Another brief cadenza
6:17	**Coda**	Rhythm of refrain becomes march-like.

LISTEN TO ... this selection streaming online.

WATCH ... an Active Listening Guide of this selection online.

DO ... Listening Exercise 23.1, Brahms, Violin Concerto in D major, online.

A Requiem for the Concert Hall:
Brahms's *Ein Deutsches Requiem* (1868)

We have said that, during the nineteenth century, the "music-only" concert hall became something akin to a temple for the engagement of high-art music. Accordingly, during this period, sacred music—Masses, for example—entered the concert hall, and music lovers thought this move from church to concert hall not the least bit sacrilegious. In the Romantic era, Bach's B minor Mass and Mozart's Requiem Mass made the transition from one venue to the other with ease.

When we think of a "Requiem," what first comes to mind is a Latin Mass, performed in the Catholic Church for the burial of the dead. In writing his *Ein Deutsches Requiem* (*A German Requiem*), however, Brahms created music for neither a Catholic Mass—nowhere is heard the voice of God on the Day of Judgment—nor a Protestant funeral service. Instead, Brahms composed his *Ein Deutsches Requiem* as an ecumenical profession of faith, in his native German, that extends sounds of solace to all who have suffered the loss of a loved one. For Brahms personally, the inspiration for the work seems to have stemmed from the death of his mentor, Robert Schumann, and the more recent loss of his mother.

The emotional core of this hour-long, seven-movement work is found in its fourth movement. "Wie lieblich sind deine Wohnungen" ("How lovely is Thy dwelling place"), says the text of Psalm 84, and before us looms an image of the heavenly House of the Lord. Imitating the blissful souls in heaven, a four-part chorus sings praises to God in a skillful blend of homophonic and polyphonic textures. This is religious orchestral music. Indeed, the orchestra does not merely accompany the chorus but, rather, engages in a dialogue with it. The opening phrase played by the woodwinds descends peacefully but is immediately answered by the sopranos, who sing the mirror inversion of the line in ascending form (see Listening Guide). Composing an inverted version of a melody requires great contrapuntal skill. Brahms perfected his counterpoint through the study of Bach, and this technique lies at the heart of Brahms's compositional style.

LISTENING GUIDE

Johannes Brahms, *Ein Deutsches* Requiem (1868)   Download 64 (5:26)

Fourth movement, "Wie lieblich sind deine Wohnungen"

Text: Psalm 84, verses 1, 2, and 4

WHAT TO LISTEN FOR: Intricate counterpoint enriching the soothing sound of the Romantic chorus and orchestra

0:00   Woodwinds play peaceful melody.

0:08   Sopranos respond in same mood.   Wie lieblich sind deine Wohnungen, Herr Zebaoth!   How lovely is Thy dwelling place, O, Lord of Hosts!

(*Continued*)

0:46	Tenors sing same text; basses, altos, and sopranos follow in imitative counterpoint.		
1:26	More imitative counterpoint is sung with strong accents in orchestra.	Meine Seele verlanget und sehnet sich nach den Vorhöfen des Herrn;	My soul longs and thirsts for the courts of the Lord;
1:59	Chorus sings homophony with strong accents in orchestra.	Mein Leib und Seele freuen sich in dem Lebendigen Gott.	My body and soul rejoice in the living God.
2:33	Return of opening music in orchestra and then chorus	Wie lieblich ...	How lovely ...
3:19	Chorus quietly sings chordal homophony.	Wohl denen, die in deinem Hause wohnen,	Blessed are they who dwell in Thy house,
3:41	Chorus declaims its praise of the Lord in forceful imitative counterpoint.	die loben Dich immerdar.	Where they praise You ever after.
4:29	Return of opening music and text	Wie lieblich ...	How lovely ...

LISTEN TO ... this selection streaming online.

WATCH ... an Active Listening Guide of this selection online.

Antonín Dvořák (1841–1904)

"There is no doubt that he is very talented. He is also very poor." Thus wrote Johannes Brahms to the music publisher Simrock in 1876, describing then-unknown Czech symphonist Antonín Dvořák. The son of a butcher, Dvořák was a native of Bohemia, an area of the Czech Republic south of Prague. He, too, passed an apprenticeship to be a butcher, but a prosperous uncle saw musical talent in the teenager and sent him to study the organ in Prague for a year. Thereafter, for nearly two decades, Dvořák eked out a living as a freelance violist and organist in Prague, playing in dance bands, the opera orchestra, and church. All the while, he composed tirelessly—operas, symphonies, string quartets, and songs, almost all of which went unheard.

Then the breakout moment—as when an unknown author gets that first blockbuster novel published. In 1878, music publisher Simrock issued Dvořák's *Slavonic Dances* (1878), a set of eight pieces for piano duet that incorporated the spirit of the folk dances of the Czechs (a subset of the Slavs). These "you-too-can-play-them-at-home" pieces were wildly popular, and Dvořák was soon known throughout Europe. Now even his more ambitious "high-art" works were given performances in London, Berlin, Vienna, Moscow, Budapest, and even the United States, in Cincinnati—which then included a large German and Czech contingent among its population.

In the spring of 1892, Dvořák received an offer he couldn't refuse. He was promised the astonishing sum of $15,000 per year (more than twenty-five times what he made in Prague) to become director of the newly founded National Conservatory of Music in New York City. And so, on September 17, 1892, Dvořák set sail for America, in first class, and took up residence at 327 East 17th Street. Here, he immediately began work on his "American" Quartet and his Symphony No. 9, "From the New World." Instead of returning to Prague that summer, Dvořák and his family traveled, mostly by train, to Spillville, Iowa. Spending three months among the mainly Czech-speaking people of this rural farming community, he finished his ninth and last symphony.

Symphony No. 9 in E minor, "From the New World" (1893)

The symphony "From the New World" proved to be the capstone of Dvořák's career and remains by far his best-known work. It received a rousing premiere in New York at America's most prestigious new concert venue, Carnegie Hall (see chapter-opening photograph), on December 16, 1893. On the program was Mendelssohn's incidental music to *A Midsummer Night's Dream* and Brahms's Violin Concerto (see above), with Dvořák's new symphony sandwiched in the middle. As Dvořák reported to his publisher Simrock the following week:

> The success of the symphony was tremendous. The papers write that no composer has ever had such a triumph [Figure 23.5]. I was in a box. The hall was filled with the best New York audience. The people clapped so much that I had to thank them from the box like a king! You know how glad I am if I can avoid such ovations, but there was no getting out of it, and I had to show myself [to take bows] like-it-or-not.

The title Dvořák gave to this symphony, "From the New World," might suggest that he incorporated musical elements that are distinctly American. Yet, although Dvořák showed a keen interest in the indigenous music of African-Americans and American Indians, none of the many tuneful melodies heard in the symphony has yet been identified as a preexisting folksong. But in general the composer seems to have re-created the spirit of his American experience, writing a moving tribute to the memory of some distant home.

Typical of the Classical and Romantic symphony, Dvořák's "From the New World" has four movements in the usual sequence of (1) fast, (2) slow, (3) minuet or scherzo, and (4) fast. Although an energetic first movement and a powerful finale frame the symphony, the slow second movement is the emotional soul of the work. A mood of calm strength envelops the opening, a memorable moment for players of brass instruments and listeners alike. Once this solidly serene atmosphere is established, a haunting melody emerges from the English horn (Example 23.3 and Figure 23.6). Throughout the Romantic period, the English horn was used to suggest feelings of distance and nostalgia—to create the effect of looking back on a time, a place, and people (friends, relatives, countrymen) that exist no longer. Although the genesis of this theme remains unclear, we do know that it came to represent "home" in the psyche of many turn-of-the-century Americans; a publisher extracted this signature tune from the symphony and printed it as a song under the title "Goin' Home."

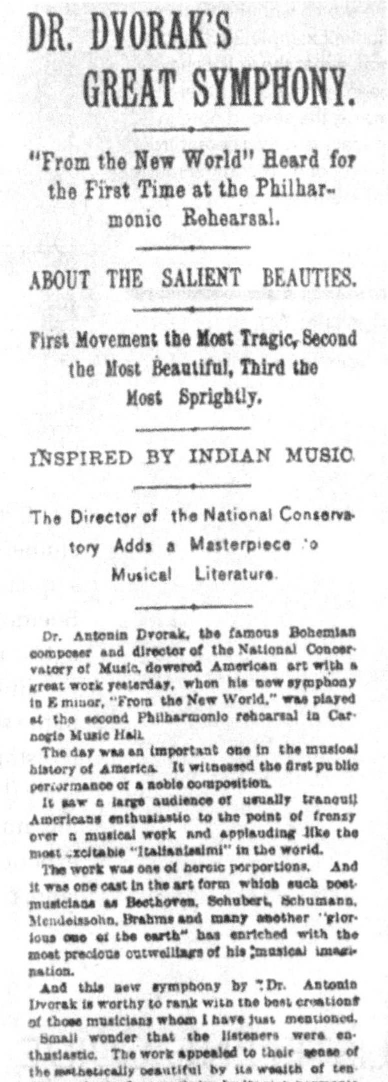

DR. DVORAK'S GREAT SYMPHONY.

"From the New World" Heard for the First Time at the Philharmonic Rehearsal.

ABOUT THE SALIENT BEAUTIES.

First Movement the Most Tragic, Second the Most Beautiful, Third the Most Sprightly.

INSPIRED BY INDIAN MUSIC

The Director of the National Conservatory Adds a Masterpiece to Musical Literature.

Dr. Antonin Dvorak, the famous Bohemian composer and director of the National Conservatory of Music, dowered American art with a great work yesterday, when his new symphony in E minor, "From the New World," was played at the second Philharmonic rehearsal in Carnegie Music Hall.

The day was an important one in the musical history of America. It witnessed the first public performance of a noble composition.

It saw a large audience of usually tranquil Americans enthusiastic to the point of frenzy over a musical work and applauding like the most excitable "Italianissimi" in the world.

The work was one of heroic porportions. And it was one cast in the art form which such poet-musicians as Beethoven, Schubert, Schumann, Mendelssohn, Brahms and many another "glorious one of the earth" has enriched with the most precious outwellings of his musical imagination.

And this new symphony by "Dr. Antonin Dvorak is worthy to rank with the best creations of those musicians whom I have just mentioned.

Small wonder that the listeners were enthusiastic. The work appealed to their sense of the aesthetically beautiful by its wealth of tender, pathetic, fiery melody; by its rich harmonic clothing; by its delicate, sonorous, gorgeous, ever varying instrumentation. . . . . .

FIGURE 23.5
A rave review of the premiere of the symphony "From the New World" in the *New York Herald*, December 17, 1893. The author actually reviewed the public dress rehearsal the preceding day, a practice still common today.

FIGURE 23.6

A diplomatic facsimile of an autograph sketch of the famous English horn theme from the second movement of Dvořák's symphony "From the New World." The tempo was later changed from *andante* to *largo* and some of the notes altered to emphasize the pentatonic scale, a traditional signifier of "the folk." For example, compare the beginning of the sketch with the final version in Example 23.3, and notice that the G flats have been removed. In other words, the second note in the facsimile is different from the second note in the musical example.

LISTEN TO...

Example 23.3 online.

EXAMPLE 23.3 "Goin' Home" melody

If the listener—every listener—feels comfortable with the melody "Goin' Home," part of the reason is its very familiar musical structure: antecedent, consequent, extension, consequent (think of Stephen Foster's "Oh! Susanna" or Beethoven's *Ode to Joy*). With the concluding consequent phrase elevated an octave to the tonic pitch above, we are brought tonally and emotionally back home.

But back to *whose* home? Is this a melody composed from scratch by Dvořák in the style of a folksong, or is it one taken from an African-American colleague? Is it distinctly American or Czech? In truth, the melody is built around a pentatonic scale (here, D♭ E♭ F, A♭ B♭), which, as we have seen (Chapter 18), is characteristic of folk music around the world. But such is the power of music: Each listener can experience in this movement the memories and emotions of his or her own homeland, no matter where it is.

LISTENING GUIDE

Antonín Dvořák, Symphony No. 9 in E minor, "From the New World" (1893)   Download 65 (12:25)

Second movement, *Largo* (very slow and broad)

Form: **ABCA'**

WHAT TO LISTEN FOR: The initial fullness of the brass, projecting a sense of a vast horizon, and then the slow, mournful tune of the English horn, the signature song of the movement, seeming to recall a distant past

A section

0:00   Solemn introductory chords in low brass choir, then timpani

0:40   English horn solo, the "Goin' Home" melody

1:06   Clarinet joins English horn, then strings join as well.

2:20   Introductory chords now played by high woodwinds and French horn, concluded by brasses and timpani

2:48   Strings repeat and extend "Goin' Home" melody.

3:44   Melody returns to English horn and is completed by woodwinds and strings.

4:25   French horn echoes the melody.

B section

4:48   Faster tempo and new theme (**B1**) in flute and oboe

5:20   Second new theme (**B2**) in clarinets above bass pizzicato

6:10   Melody **B1** played more insistently by violins

7:25   Melody **B2** played more intensely by violins

C section

8:28   Oboe introduces chirping of flute and clarinet.

8:54   Brasses play *fortissimo* recall of first theme of first movement.

9:10   Diminuendo and lovely transition back to **A**

A section

9:23   English horn brings back "Goin' Home" melody.

9:47   Pairs of violins and violas play melody but break off, as if choked by emotion.

10:18   Solo cello and solo violin play melody, then full strings join.

10:54   Quiet soliloquy by violins

11:22   Final return and extension of opening chords

LISTEN TO … this selection streaming online.

WATCH … an Active Listening Guide of this selection online.

DO … Listening Exercise 23.2, Dvořák, Symphony No. 9 in E minor, 2nd movement, online.

Gustav Mahler (1860–1911)

With whom would you like to have a cup of coffee—Brahms, Dvořák, or Mahler? Interesting company all, surely: Brahms was a conservative person (but with a highly acerbic tongue); Dvořák was the son of a butcher and raised pigeons as a hobby; Mahler, however, looked and behaved every bit like the temperamental artist, a demanding, tyrannical, self-absorbed personality. Mahler's life was one of living and suffering for his art, and his music is both extravagant and idiosyncratic. The extravagance is typical of late-nineteenth-century music; the idiosyncrasies derive from Mahler's unusual personality.

Gustav Mahler was born in 1860 into a middle-class Jewish family living in Moravia, now encompassed by the Czech Republic. As did many other gifted Czechs at that time, however, Mahler moved to a larger, more cosmopolitan German city to advance his career. At the age of fifteen, he enrolled in the prestigious Vienna Conservatory of Music, where he studied composition and conducting. Mahler felt that his mission in life was to conduct—to interpret—the works of the masters ("to suffer for my great masters," as he phrased it). Like many young conductors, he began his career with positions in provincial towns, hoping to work his way back to the big city.

In May 1897, Mahler returned triumphantly to his adopted city of Vienna as director of the Vienna Court Opera, a position Mozart had once coveted. The next year he also assumed directorship of the Vienna Philharmonic, then and now one of the world's great orchestras. But Mahler was, in today's terms, a "control freak," a tyrant in search of an artistic ideal; he filled his scores with countless small expression marks and then insisted that the orchestra do exactly as he prescribed. That he drove himself as hard as he pushed others was little comfort to the singers and instrumentalists who had to endure his wrath during rehearsals. After ten stormy but artistically successful seasons (1897–1907), Mahler was dismissed from the Vienna Court Opera. About this time, he accepted an offer from New York to take charge of the Metropolitan Opera, and eventually he conducted the New York Philharmonic as well. (The first season alone he earned $350,000 in today's money for three months' work.) Here, too, both acclaim and controversy coexisted. And here, too, at least at the Met, his contract was not renewed after two years, though he stayed on longer, until February 1911, with the Philharmonic. He died in Vienna in May 1911 of a lingering streptococcal infection that had attacked his weak heart—a tragic end to an obsessive and somewhat tormented life.

Gustav Mahler was the last in the long line of great German symphonists that extends back through Brahms, Schubert, and Beethoven to Mozart and, ultimately, to Haydn. What had begun as a modest instrumental genre with a limited emotional range had grown in the course of the nineteenth century into a monumental structure, the musical equivalent, in Mahler's view, of the entire cosmos.

In all, Gustav Mahler completed nine symphonies. As he once said, "The symphony is the world; it must embrace everything." And so he tried to embrace every sort of music within his symphonic writing. Folk dances, popular songs, military marches, off-stage bands, bugle calls, and even Gregorian chant all sound at various points in his symphonies (Figure 23.7). Most important, Mahler made use of songs—his own songs—in seven of his nine symphonies.

FIGURE 23.7
A satire of Gustav Mahler conducting one of his colossal symphonies. As the cartoonist suggests, his symphonies contain the whole world of sound, from bird songs and nursery rhymes to bells and whistles to military music. And he required a large orchestra. Mahler's Symphony No. 2, for example, calls for ten horns and eight trumpets, and lasts an hour and a half. The first performance of his Symphony No. 8 in Munich in 1910 involved 858 singers and 171 instrumentalists! With good reason, it has been nicknamed the "Symphony of a Thousand."

Symphony No. 1 (1888; revised until 1906)

Mahler is unique among composers in that he wrote only symphonies and orchestral songs. An **orchestral song** (or **orchestral *Lied***) is an art song in which the full orchestra replaces the piano as the medium of accompaniment. Mahler's first composition was an orchestral *Lied* cycle of five songs, titled *Lieder eines fahrenden Gesellen* (*Songs of a Traveling Lad*, 1883–1885), which consists of five poems about a young man experiencing life and lost love for the first time, just as was Mahler. Mahler himself was the poet; below is his text of the fifth and final poem.

Auf der Straße steht ein Lindenbaum,	On the road there was a linden tree
Da hab' ich zum ersten Mal	that provided rest for me
im Schlaf geruht!	and for the first time sleep!
Unter dem Lindenbaum,	Beneath that linden tree
Der hat seine Blüten	snowed down upon me
über mich geschneit,	its blooms.
Da wußt' ich nicht, wie das Leben tut,	I had no idea the nature of life,
War alles, alles wieder gut!	All seemed good, all good!
Alles! Alles, Lieb und Leid	All! All is love and suffering
Und Welt und Traum!	And world and dream!

Over the years, Mahler's early songs provided a wellspring of inspiration, and when he turned to write his first symphony in 1888, he went back to that well. Specifically, he returned to the music associated with the lines "All is love and suffering/And world and dream!," a sentiment that summed up the Romantics' view of the world generally, and Mahler's, in particular.

Mahler labored over his Symphony No. 1 mightily, perhaps obsessively, for almost twenty years. What we now call the third movement (see Listening Guide) caused the composer the most difficulty. The same was true for audiences who first heard this music, which they found an inexplicable jumble. To know why, we must understand the importance that Mahler placed on dreams in the act of creativity, for listening to Mahler's instrumental works is often like experiencing life as a dream through music. Dreams differ from reality in that they are devoid of plausible contexts and of events that come in logical sequence. "How did that get here? Why does it look like that? How very strange! How grotesque!" Mahler called this third movement "Funeral March," but this is no ordinary funeral. It is one of dreams and the imagination (Figure 23.8). Perhaps not coincidentally, Mahler was living in Vienna when another Czech expatriate, Sigmund Freud, developed his

FIGURE 23.8
During the long gestation of Symphony No. 1, Mahler described the sort of funeral procession he envisaged in the third movement: "The beasts of the forest accompany a dead hunter's coffin to the grave, with hares carrying a small banner, with a band of Bohemian musicians in front, and the procession escorted by music-making cats, toads, crows, etc." Clearly, this idea came to him from a popular 1850 woodcut by Schubert's friend, Moritz von Schwind (Chapter 17 opener and Figure 17.2). Note how the smoke from the torches is made to curl like a double bass scroll, a deer plays the cello, and a cat leads the way on the violin.

theory of psychoanalysis based on dreams. In 1910, Mahler consulted Freud, but Freud refused to treat him for fear of destroying the composer's creative process.

With the lugubrious sounds of a low drum, the funeral cortège begins, slowly and in a minor key. But wait—something's wrong. This once-happy music, the child's round "Frère Jacques" ("Are You Sleeping?"), has now been made sad (Example 23.4) by lowering the third degree of the scale, turning major into minor.

EXAMPLE 23.4 "Frère Jacques" in minor

Now things get stranger. Suddenly a village band blares forth with what sounds like a rollicking folk dance, Jewish Klezmer music of the sort Mahler knew from his youth and we will meet again in Chapter 33. Is this a funeral or a folk dance? As the sounds of the folk band disappear, a vision of a lovesick lad dreaming under a linden tree passes by as Mahler recalls the lovely music from the end of his *Songs of a Traveling Lad*. Reality, memory, or dream? At the end, all musical images blur into one kaleidoscopic coda, before the funeral cortège pulls away and disappears in the distance.

LISTENING GUIDE

Gustav Mahler, Symphony No. 1 (1888; revised until 1906)

Download 66 (10:18)

Third movement, Funeral March

Form: **ABC, composite coda**

WHAT TO LISTEN FOR: The presentation and the bizarre, dream-like assemblage of themes as a funeral procession is made to appear and disappear—move through time and space—through music

Part A

0:00	Low drum (timpani) signals beginning of procession.
0:08	Solo double bass plays sad "Frère Jacques."
0:28	Solo bassoon plays "Frère Jacques."
0:38	Other low instruments enter with theme.
1:03	Oboe plays sprightly countersubject.
1:16	Woodwinds continue with theme and counterpoint.
1:53	Funeral cortège slows down.

Part B

2:11	Oboes enter with first dance-like tune.

2:55	Strings slow down dance-like tune.
3:26	Clarinets introduce variation of dance-like tune.

4:14	Fragments of "Frère Jacques" and its counterpoint
4:21	Timpani and low strings quietly signal beat of funeral cortège.
4:40	Fade-out of funeral cortège

Part C

5:00	Harp provides introductory accompaniment.
5:10	Song from *Traveling Lad* enters in violin and other instruments.

5:50	Oboe varies song, ending with chromatic descent.
6:45	Low gong signals transition.

Composite coda (themes joined as conclusion)

7:03	"Frère Jacques" returns, but woodwinds sound increasingly ugly.
7:38	Trumpets play new counterpoint against "Frère Jacques."

8:01	Shrill clarinets play variation of dance-like theme.
8:19	"Frère Jacques," trumpet counterpoint, and dance-like theme sound together.
9:01	Violins play song from *Traveling Lad* with warm vibrato, joining three other themes.
9:31	"Frère Jacques" theme disintegrates as vision of funeral disappears in distance.
10:00	Gong suggests vague haze.

LISTEN TO ... this selection streaming online.

WATCH ... an Active Listening Guide of this selection online.

DO ... Listening Exercise 23.3, Mahler, Symphony No. 1, 3rd movement, Funeral March, online.

Gustav Mahler was a visionary—with strange musical visions—but he was also a practical musician. He knew how to make the imaginary funeral procession move before our eyes because he understood a basic principle of acoustics: longer sound waves (hence lower pitches) travel farther than shorter waves (higher pitches). That is why we hear the bass drum and tubas of an approaching marching band long before we hear the higher trumpets and clarinets. Mahler starts this movement with drums (timpani), then adds a low double bass, then a low bassoon, and gradually—as the procession moves before us—higher instruments and greater volume. To make the procession move in the other direction and disappear, all he has to do is reverse the process—thus, bassoon, double bass, and finally drums at the very end.

KEY WORDS

absolute music (319)   double stops (320)   orchestral song (orchestral *Lied*) (329)

 Join us on Facebook at Listening to Music with Craig Wright

PRACTICE ... your understanding of this chapter's concepts by comparing Checklists of Musical Style for all historic eras, completing a Musical Style Quiz for the Romantic era, and working once more with the chapter's Active Listening Guides online.

DO ... online multiple-choice and critical thinking quizzes that your instructor may assign for a grade.

CHECKLIST OF MUSICAL STYLE   *Romantic: 1820–1900*

REPRESENTATIVE COMPOSERS

Beethoven	Clara Schumann	Wagner	Tchaikovsky
Schubert	Chopin	Bizet	Musorgsky
Berlioz	Liszt	Brahms	Mahler
Mendelssohn	Verdi	Dvořák	Puccini
Robert Schumann			

PRINCIPAL GENRES

symphony	tone poem (symphonic poem)	orchestral song (orchestral *Lied*)	character piece for piano
program symphony			ballet music
dramatic overture	opera	solo concerto	
concert overture	art song (*Lied*)		

Melody	Melody is more flexible and irregular in shape than in the Classical period; long, singable lines with powerful climaxes and chromatic inflections for expressiveness
Harmony	Greater use of chromaticism makes the harmony richer and more colorful; sudden shifts to remote chords for expressive purposes; heightened dissonance conveys feelings of anxiety and longing
Rhythm	Rhythms are free and relaxed, occasionally obscuring the meter; tempo can fluctuate greatly (tempo *rubato*) and sometimes slow to a crawl to allow for "the grand gesture"
Color	The orchestra becomes enormous, reaching upward of 100 performers: trombone, tuba, contrabassoon, piccolo, and English horn added to the ensemble; experiments with new playing techniques for special effects; dynamics vary widely to create extreme levels of expression; piano becomes larger and more powerful
Texture	Predominantly homophonic but dense and rich because of larger orchestras and orchestral scores; sustaining pedal on the piano also adds to density
Form	No new forms created; rather, traditional forms (strophic, sonata–allegro, and theme and variations, for example) used and extended in length; traditional forms also applied to new genres, such as tone poem and art song

MODERN
and Postmodern Art Music,
1880–Present

part SIX

MODERNISM AND POSTMODERNISM

1880   1890   1900   1910   1920   1930   1940

1912
Arnold Schoenberg composes *Pierrot lunaire*

1905
Charles Ives finishes *Variations on America*

1907
Pablo Picasso paints *Les Demoiselles d'Avignon*

1936
Samuel Barber composes *Adagio for Strings*

1894
Claude Debussy composes *Prelude to The Afternoon of a Faun*

1914–1918
World War I

1939–1945
World War II

1913
Igor Stravinsky composes *The Rite of Spring*

1929
Beginning of Great Depression

Although historians like things neat and tidy, trends nevertheless overlap, making it difficult to identify the end of an old style and the appearance of a new one. Setting the dates of "Modernism" and "Postmodernism" is a particularly difficult task. Until recently, historians have usually referred to "modern" music simply as "twentieth-century" music. But modern musical idioms appeared in some Impressionist music of the late nineteenth century, whereas aspects of musical Romanticism continue to exist even today, particularly in film scores. Similarly, "Postmodernism" may have begun as early as the 1930s and continues to develop during our own times. Understanding, then, that the terms *Modern* and *Postmodern* together connote one long, overlapping musical period, what are a few of the features that mark this epoch?

Toward the beginning of the twentieth century, composers increasingly turned against the warm sentimentality that was characteristic of nineteenth-century music, replacing this Romantic aesthetic with an increasingly harsh, percussive, impersonal sound. Melodies became more angular, and harmonies, more dissonant. Piercing woodwinds now often replaced emotive strings as the main carriers of melody. Over the decades, the massive compositions of the late Romantic period—perhaps best represented by Gustav Mahler's "Symphony of a Thousand" (1910)—yielded to smaller, less extravagant works. An abstract, "nonexpressive," and "nonrepresentational" style of music emerged and was most clearly evident in Arnold Schoenberg's rigid twelve-tone music.

In the 1960s, however, a reaction against the formal abstractions of Schoenberg and his disciples contributed to the increasing popularity of musical Postmodernism. Composers and the listening public had rebelled, choosing to embrace a variety of musical styles—electronic music, chance music, and Minimalism, for example. Viewed broadly, Modernism turned and did battle with traditional musical styles. Postmodernism, on the other hand, dispenses entirely with conventional musical forms and processes, saying, in effect: "Any creator can apply whatever artistic methods and values he or she wishes."

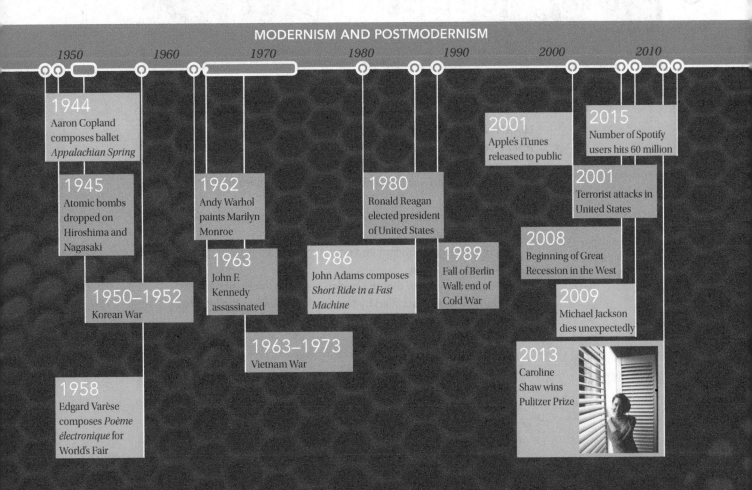

MODERNISM AND POSTMODERNISM

1950   1960   1970   1980   1990   2000   2010

1944
Aaron Copland composes ballet *Appalachian Spring*

1945
Atomic bombs dropped on Hiroshima and Nagasaki

1950–1952
Korean War

1958
Edgard Varèse composes *Poème électronique* for World's Fair

1962
Andy Warhol paints Marilyn Monroe

1963
John F. Kennedy assassinated

1963–1973
Vietnam War

1980
Ronald Reagan elected president of United States

1986
John Adams composes *Short Ride in a Fast Machine*

1989
Fall of Berlin Wall; end of Cold War

2001
Apple's iTunes released to public

2001
Terrorist attacks in United States

2008
Beginning of Great Recession in the West

2009
Michael Jackson dies unexpectedly

2013
Caroline Shaw wins Pulitzer Prize

2015
Number of Spotify users hits 60 million

From
IMPRESSIONISM
to Modernism

START... experiencing this chapter's topics with an online video activity.

LEARNING OBJECTIVES
After studying the material in this chapter, you should be able to:

1 Describe how Impressionism evolved as a reaction against German Romanticism and how Impressionist art is different from traditional Western art.

2 Articulate how the music of Claude Debussy differs from its German Romantic predecessors.

3 Describe musical Exoticism and how it manifested itself in the music of Debussy and Ravel.

4 Explain how we know that the bridge between Impressionism and Modernism was personified by two seminal figures in the history of music: Debussy and Stravinsky.

The evolution of musical style is a constant "yin and yang" driven by changing public tastes. Creativity (the new) challenges the status quo (the old), and ultimately a synthesis results, which, over time, becomes the new status quo. In the late Middle Ages, a musical style emerged that contemporaries called the *Ars nova* (New Art), which they then contrasted with the previous *Ars antiqua* (Old Art). At the beginning of the Baroque era (around 1600), music theorists juxtaposed the new music of the day, which they called *Stile moderno*, with the previous one, called *Stile antico*. So, too, at the turn of the twentieth century, progressive artists—musicians, painters, poets, and writers—gradually turned away from Romanticism toward a style called Modernism. Coterminous with this transition, however, was yet a third "ism": Impressionism.

Impressionism

All good things must come to an end. Romantic music reached its apotheosis during the late nineteenth century in the grand works of Wagner, Tchaikovsky, Brahms, and Mahler, all of whom were German speaking or composed in a Germanic style. By 1900, however, this German-dominated musical empire had started to weaken. Not surprisingly, the strongest challenge to the hegemony of the Germans came from their traditional enemies, the French. French composers began to ridicule the sentimentality of Romanticism, in general, and the grandiose structures of the German style, in particular. German music was said to be too heavy, too pretentious, and too bombastic, like one of Wagner's Nordic giants from the *Ring* cycle. Meaningful expression, it was believed, could be communicated in more subtle and decorative ways, in something other than sheer volume of sound and epic length. What the French created, musical Impressionism, was a middle ground between the lush sounds of Romanticism and the bombshells of Modernism that were to come.

Impressionism in Painting and Music

The artistic movement that arose in France in opposition to German Romantic music has been given the name **Impressionism**. We are, of course, more familiar with this term as a designation for a school of late-nineteenth-century painters working in and around Paris, including Claude Monet (1840–1926; Figure 24.1), Auguste Renoir (1841–1919), Edgar Degas (1834–1917), Camille Pissarro (1830–1903), and the American Mary Cassatt (1844–1926).

You can see the painting that gave the epoch its name—Monet's *Impression: Sunrise* (1873)—at the beginning of this chapter. There, the ships, rowboats, and other elements in the early morning light are more suggested than fully rendered. In 1874, Claude Monet submitted this painting to be exhibited at the Salon of the French Academy of Fine Arts, but it was rejected. One critic, Louis Leroy, derisively said: "Wallpaper in its most embryonic

READ... the complete chapter text in a rich, interactive online platform.

FIGURE 24.1
Claude Monet, *Woman with Umbrella* (1886). The Impressionist canvas is not a finished surface in the traditional sense. Rather, the painter breaks down light into separate dabs of color and juxtaposes them for the viewer's eye to reassemble. Here, bold brushstrokes convey an astonishing sense of movement, freshness, and sparkling light. Sunlight is everywhere, and everything shimmers. Who is the woman? We have no idea—this is an impression of a person, not a portrait, and less a photograph.

state is more finished than that seascape." In the uproar that followed, Monet and his fellow artists were disparagingly called "impressionists" for the seemingly crude, imprecise quality of their art. The painters accepted the name, partly as an act of defiance against the establishment, and soon the term was universally adopted.

What irony! French Impressionism, which once generated such controversy, is now the most beloved of all artistic styles. Indeed, judging by museum attendance and reproductions sold, there is an almost limitless enthusiasm for the art of Monet, Degas, Renoir, and their associates—precisely the paintings that the artists' contemporaries mocked and jeered. But what is it about the Impressionist style that initially caused such a furor? What was new and modern about it?

The Impressionists saw the world as awash in vibrant rays of light and sought to capture the aura that sun-dappled objects created in the eyes of the beholder. To accomplish this, they covered their canvases with small, dab-like brushstrokes in which light was broken down into spots of color, thereby creating a sense of movement and fluidity. Shapes are not clearly defined but blurred, more suggested than delineated. Minor details disappear.

For their part, musicians found inspiration in the Impressionist art of the day. They, too, began to work with dabs of color to create fleeting sensations. Claude Debussy, whose compositions most consistently displayed the Impressionist style in music, was delighted to be grouped with the Impressionist painters. "You do me great honor by calling me a pupil of Claude Monet," he told a friend in 1916. Debussy gave some of his compositions such artistic titles as *Sketches, Images*, and *Prints*. Rare are the moments in history when the aesthetic aims of painters and musicians were as closely allied.

Claude Debussy (1862–1918)

Debussy (see Figure 24.2) was born in 1862 into a modest family living in a small town outside Paris. As neither of his parents was musical, it came as a surprise when their son demonstrated talent at the keyboard and an extraordinary musical ear. At the age of ten, prodigy Debussy entered the Paris Conservatory for lessons in piano, composition, and music theory. Owing to his skill as a performer, he was soon engaged for summer work in the household of Nadezhda von Meck (see Figure 18.7), a wealthy patroness of the arts and the principal supporter of Tchaikovsky. This employment took him, in turn, to Italy, Russia, and Vienna. In 1884, he won the Prix de Rome, an official prize in composition funded by the French government, which required a three-year stay in Rome. But Debussy, like Berlioz before him, was not happy in then-sleepy Rome. He preferred Paris, which was becoming in every way a modern metropolis, with motorcars, a subway, and avant-garde art.

Returning to Paris more or less permanently in 1887, the young Frenchman continued to study his craft and to search for his own independent voice as a composer. He had some minor successes, and yet, as he said to a colleague in 1893, "There are still things that I am not able to do—create masterpieces, for example." But the next year, in 1894, he did just that. With the completion of *Prélude à l'Après-midi d'un faune (Prelude to The Afternoon of a Faun)*, he gave to the public what has become his most enduring orchestral work. Debussy's later compositions, including his opera *Pelléas et Mélisande* (1902), the symphonic poem *La mer* (*The Sea*, 1905), and his two books of *Préludes* for piano, met with less popular favor.

FIGURE 24.2
Claude Debussy at the age of twenty-two, at the time he won the Prix de Rome

Critics complained that Debussy's works were lacking in traditional form, melody, and forward motion—in other words, they had characteristics of the Modernism that was to come. Illness and the outbreak of World War I in 1914 brought Debussy's innovations to a halt. He died of cancer in the spring of 1918 while the guns of the German army were shelling Paris from the north.

Prelude to The Afternoon of a Faun (1894)

Debussy spent more of his time in the company of poets and painters than with musicians. His orchestral *Prelude to The Afternoon of a Faun*, in fact, was written to precede a stage reading of the poem *The Afternoon of a Faun* by his friend and mentor, Stéphane Mallarmé (Figure 24.3), the leader of a progressive group of poets called the **Symbolists**. The faun of Mallarmé's poem is not a young deer but a satyr (a mythological beast that is half man, half goat), who spends his days in lustful pursuit of the nymphs of the forest. On this afternoon, we see the faun, exhausted from the morning's escapades, reclining on the forest floor in the still air of the midday heat (Figure 24.4). He contemplates future conquests while blowing listlessly on his panpipes. The following passage from Mallarmé's poem suggests the dream-like mood, vague and elusive, that Debussy sought to re-create in his musical setting:

> No murmur of water in the woodland scene,
> Bathed simply in the sounds of my flute.
> And the only breeze, except for my two pipes,
> Blows itself empty long before
> It can scatter the sound in an arid rain.
> On a horizon unmoved by a ripple
> This sound, visible and serene,
> Mounts to the heavens, an inspired wisp.

Not wishing to compose narrative programmatic music in the tradition of Berlioz or Tchaikovsky, Debussy made no effort to follow closely the events in Mallarmé's poem; he wanted a succession of sonic sensations rather than a musical story. As Debussy said at the time of the first performance of *Prelude* in December 1894, "My *Prelude* is really a sequence of mood paintings, throughout which the desire and dreams of the Faun move in the heat of the midday sun."

FIGURE 24.3
The symbolist poet Stéphane Mallarmé, author of "The Afternoon of a Faun," as painted by the great predecessor of the Impressionists, Edouard Manet (1832–1883). Mallarmé was a friend and artistic mentor of the composer Debussy.

FIGURE 24.4
Mallarmé's *The Afternoon of a Faun* created something of a sensation among late-nineteenth-century artists. This painting by Pal Szinyei Merse (1845–1920) is just one of several such representations of the faun and woodland nymphs. Notice that he holds classical panpipes, which Debussy transformed into the sound of the flute.

When Mallarmé heard the music, he, in turn, said the following about Debussy's musical response to the poem: "I never expected anything like it. The music prolongs the emotion of my poem and paints its scenery more passionately than colors could."

Note that both musician and poet refer to *Prelude to The Afternoon of a Faun* in terms of painting. But how does one create a painting in music? Here (see Listening Guide), a musical tableau is depicted by using the distinctive colors of the instruments, especially the woodwinds, to evoke vibrant moods and sensations. The flute has one timbre, the oboe another, and the clarinet yet another. Debussy said, in effect: "Let us focus on the color-producing capacity of the instruments, let us see what new shades can be elicited from them, let us try new registers, let us try new combinations." Thus, a solo flute begins in its lowest register (the pipes of the faun), followed by a harp glissando and then dabs of color from the French horn. These tonal impressions swirl, dissolve, and form again but don't seem to progress. No strong-beat rhythms or clear-cut meters push the music forward; instead of a singable melody as we know it, we hear a twisting, undulating swirl of sound (see example in Listening Guide). All is languid beauty, a music that is utterly original and shockingly sensual.

LISTENING GUIDE

Claude Debussy, *Prelude to The Afternoon of a Faun* (1894)   Download 67 (9:40)

Genre: Symphonic poem (tone poem)

Form: Ternary (**ABA´**)

WHAT TO LISTEN FOR *(AND WHAT YOU WON'T HEAR)*: How colors and textures are of primary importance, while clear-cut melodies and foot-tapping rhythms are largely absent

A

0:00   Solo flute plays undulating line.

0:18   Harp glissandos and dabs of color from French horns

0:43   Flute continues with melody, then (1:01) passes it to oboe.

1:13   Crescendo that disappears before it can climax

1:35   Return of melody to flute

B

2:48   Clarinet and then flute play rapid chromatic arabesques.

3:45   Crescendo that melts into clarinet solo (4:14)

| 4:33 | Sweeping Romantic theme in woodwinds |
| 5:07 | Sweeping theme repeated in violins, then solo horn (5:53), clarinet, and violin |

A′

6:22	Solo flute, then oboe (7:00) return with twisting chromatic line.
7:39	Solo flute plays theme again above string tremolo (shimmering effect) with solo violin high above.
8:19	Solo viola in low range of instrument plays chromatic line.
8:45	Oboe offers complement to line.

CODA

9:04	Ostinato in harps
9:14	Violins and French horns move up and down in lockstep (parallel motion).
9:24	Dabs of sound in various instruments

LISTEN TO ... this selection streaming online.

WATCH ... an Active Listening Guide of this selection online.

DO ... Listening Exercise 24.1, Debussy, *Prelude to The Afternoon of a Faun*, online.

Debussy's *Prelude to The Afternoon of a Faun* might be called an example of "stealth Modernism"—it sneaks up on the listener. His undulating lines and consonant harmonies are so pleasing that we scarcely notice the novelty: a radically new approach to line and color. Debussy replaced the German primacy of theme with an Impressionist primacy of color. For him, color might exist independent of melody and, perhaps, overshadow it.

Think back to the orchestral music of Beethoven, Brahms, and Tchaikovsky. In these earlier works, new themes are generally introduced by a new instrument or group of instruments. Instrumental color thus works hand in hand with melody, alerting us to the fact that what we hear *is* a new melody. With Debussy, by contrast, instruments enter with a distinct color but no easily discernible melodic profile. Thus, colors—and textures to some degree—begin to replace melody and harmony as the primary agents of musical expression. Debussy's approach is a thoroughly modern one, which will later be adopted by the most revolutionary of Modernists, including Americans Charles Ives, Edgard Varèse, and John Cage (see Chapters 26 and 27). Not coincidentally, progressive painters, such as van Gogh (see Figure 24.5), Matisse, and Picasso, began to separate color from line as well.

FIGURE 24.5
Vincent van Gogh's *The Night Café* (1888), the Café de l'Alcazar, where van Gogh took his meals when he was in Arles, France. Here, the colors red and green are intensified and made to clash, and light itself (emanating from the gas lanterns) shimmers in a ghastly, ghostly yellow. The creation of eye-popping color gives the painting its emotional intensity.

Préludes for Piano (1910, 1913)

Orchestras are colorful, but pianos are just black and white—or, at least, monochromatic in sound. How, then, does a composer create evocative musical sensations with the more limited palette of the piano? This was the challenge that Claude Debussy assumed when he began to compose two books of *Préludes* for piano, which he ultimately published in 1910 and 1913. The titles of some of these short pieces allude to their evocative, sometimes mysterious qualities: *Steps in the Snow, The Sunken Cathedral, What the West Wind Saw*, and *Sounds and Perfumes Swirl in the Night Air.*

How does a composer make perfume swirl through music? That Debussy would attempt to "evoke" such an external sensation by means of an expressive musical gesture demonstrates a very traditional approach to music, which is well within the aesthetic of Romanticism. The means by which Debussy achieves his aims at the piano, however, bring us to the forefront of Modernism. His approach at the keyboard doesn't involve color but, instead, alters the basic elements of music: scales, chords, and counterpoint.

Voiles (Sails), from the first book of *Préludes* (1910), takes us to the sea (Figure 24.6). As we hear a fluid descent, mostly in parallel motion, we imagine sails flapping listlessly in the breeze. The hazy, languid atmosphere is created in part by the special scale that Debussy employs, the **whole-tone scale** (Example 24.1), in which all the pitches are a whole step apart.

LISTEN TO...

Example 24.1 online.

EXAMPLE 24.1 Whole-tone scale

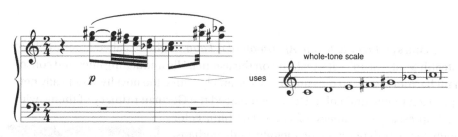

FIGURE 24.6
Claude Monet's *Sailboats* (1874). The rocking of the boats is suggested by the exaggerated reflections on the water.

Because in the whole-tone scale each note is the same distance from its neighbor, no one pitch is heard as the tonal center—all pitches seem equally important. The composer can stop on any note of the scale, and it will sound no more central, or tonic-like, than any other pitch. The music floats without a tonal anchor. Next, Debussy creates a gentle rocking motion by inserting a four-note ostinato into the texture (Example 24.2).

EXAMPLE 24.2 Ostinato

LISTEN TO...
Example 24.2 online.

Frequently used by Impressionist composers, ostinatos lend a static quality to the music—repetition stops any forward motion. In contrast to the forward-moving functional chord progressions created by traditional German composers Bach, Beethoven, and Brahms, these French ostinatos make musical time stand still. To see the difference, consider the musical framework of a well-known piece that marches along in a well-directed chord progression (Example 24.3), from "The Star-Spangled Banner."

EXAMPLE 24.3 Beginning of "The Star-Spangled Banner": Contrary motion

LISTEN TO...
Example 24.3 online.

Notice another aspect of this traditional anthem, the use of **contrary motion**, a musical process in which the soprano and the bass go in opposite directions. For every move upward or downward by the soprano, the bass does the opposite. For five hundred years in the West, contrary motion had been the rule for good counterpoint—and what we teach in music theory classes still today. Yet, here, in the middle of *Voiles*, Debussy creates a progression of four-pitch chords that consistently move in what is called parallel motion (Example 24.4). In **parallel motion**, all parts progress together, locked in step, in the same direction—a very untraditional sound.

LISTEN TO...
Example 24.4 online.

EXAMPLE 24.4 Parallel motion

left
hand

Parallel motion was an innovation of Debussy, and it was one way in which he expressed his opposition to the German school, which was so deeply steeped in counterpoint.

Movement seems to return to the sailing ships as the pianist races through a harp-like **glissando**, a rapid rise up or down the scale. This scale, however, is different from the preceding whole-tone scale. It is a pentatonic scale (Example 24.5). The octave is divided into five notes, here corresponding to the black keys on the piano. The pentatonic scale is often found in folk music (see Chapters 18 and 23); Debussy first encountered it in the Southeast Asian music he heard at the Paris World's Fair of 1889 (see "West Meets East: Removing Cultural Borders").

EXAMPLE 24.5 Pentatonic scale and glissando

Following this energized whirl around the pentatonic scale, the nautical scene regains its placid demeanor with the return of the whole-tone scale. At the end, Debussy directs the pianist to push down and hold the sustaining pedal (the rightmost pedal). Once the sustaining pedal is pressed and held, all notes sounded thereafter will blur into vagueness, like the hazes and mists that envelop many Impressionist paintings (see chapter-opening photo).

In sum, in his piano piece *Voiles* (see Listening Guide), Debussy introduces novelties that run contrary to the tradition of Western classical music: (1) a whole-tone scale that lessens the sense of the tonic and tonality; (2) ostinatos that seem to cause the forward harmonic motion to stop; (3) parallel motion that destroys the traditional structural framework of Western music, namely counterpoint; and (4) a non-Western (pentatonic) scale. All this in a single short piece!

LISTENING GUIDE

Claude Debussy, *Voiles*, from *Préludes*, Book I (1910)   Download 68 (3:52)

Form: Ternary (**ABA′**)

WHAT TO LISTEN FOR: How the composer has used unusual scales and techniques (whole-tone scale, ostinato, parallel motion, and pentatonic scale) to create a new aesthetic that is different in style from any German-tradition work we have heard

0:00	**A**	Descending parallel thirds using whole-tone scale
0:10		Bass pedal point enters.
1:01		Ostinato enters in middle register.
1:38		Ostinato moves into top register; chords move in parallel motion in middle register.
2:09	**B**	Harp-like glissandos using pentatonic scale
2:23		Chords moving in parallel motion above pedal point
2:46		Glissandos now employing whole-tone scale

| 3:16 | A′ | Descending thirds return. |
| 3:28 | | Glissandos blur through use of sustaining pedal. |

LISTEN TO ... this selection streaming online.

WATCH ... an Active Listening Guide of this selection online.

WEST MEETS EAST: REMOVING CULTURAL BORDERS

At the turn of the twentieth century, Paris was the cultural capital of the Western world, but oddly, its citizens were eager to turn their eyes and ears to the East. In 1889, the French government sponsored an *Exposition universelle* (World's Fair), which featured Far Eastern art. Here, painter Paul Gauguin (1848–1903) first became enamored with the tropical colors of the Pacific. Claude Debussy, too, made several visits. Not only did he see the newly completed Eiffel Tower and newfangled inventions like electric lighting and electric-powered elevators, but he also heard for the first time the exotic sounds of Southeast Asia. Colonial governments, including those of Cambodia, Vietnam, and Indonesia, had sent small ensembles of instrumentalists, singers, and dancers to perform in newly constructed pavilions. The Cambodian pagoda seems to have been the inspiration for a later piano piece called *Pagodes* (*Pagodas*, 1903). Debussy also encountered a colorful gamelan orchestra from Indonesia, as he recalled to a friend some years later: "Do you not remember the Javanese (Indonesian) music that was capable of expressing every nuance of meaning, even unmentionable shades, and makes our tonic and dominant sounds seem weak and empty?" This experience inspired Debussy to incorporate into his own music the sounds of the East: ostinatos, static harmonies, pentatonic and whole-tone scales, delicately layered textures, and shimmering surfaces. Thus, many of the most progressive aspects of Debussy's compositional style—his Modernist tendencies—were stimulated by his contacts with music from the East.

Exoticism in Music

One of the magical qualities of music is its capacity to transport us to distant lands. Far-off places can be experienced in our minds, if only through the strange and mysterious sounds we associate with them. Composers at the turn of the twentieth century delighted in such vicarious journeys, and their music is brimming with the "exotic." Claude Debussy was strongly influenced by the art of the Far East (see "West Meets East: Removing Cultural Borders"), and so, too, were the famous painters of the time. Impressionist Claude Monet lined the walls of his home in Giverny, France, not with his own canvases, but with prints and watercolors from Japan. Their influence can be seen in the startling portrait of his wife in traditional Japanese costume (Figure 24.7). Finally, look ahead at the photo of Debussy and Stravinsky taken in Debussy's apartment in 1910 (Figure 24.9), and notice on the wall a copy of *The Great Wave* by Japanese artist Katsushika Hokusai. For Debussy, as for Monet, *à la mode* (stylishly modern) meant art from the Far East.

The exotic in fashion, furniture, and art is easy to recognize, but how does this play out in music? Musical **Exoticism** is communicated by any sound drawn from outside the traditional Western European musical experience. A non-Western scale, a folk rhythm, or a passage in parallel motion (the antithesis of Western counterpoint) is enough to suggest "the other." Even a single blow on a strange percussion instrument—a Chinese gong, for example—can magically transport us half a world away.

The Exotic of Spain: Ravel's *Bolero* (1928)

Although not as distant as China or Japan, Spain was nonetheless considered an exotic place by Northern Europeans in the late nineteenth and early twentieth centuries. The culture of southern Spain in particular, only thirty miles from the tip of North Africa, offered the mysterious allure of the Near East. As French poet Victor Hugo (1802–1885) said: "Spain is still the Orient; Spain is half African, and Africa is half Asiatic." Like the poets and painters of France, French composers created art with a would-be Spanish character. Debussy composed an orchestral piece (*Ibéria*, 1908) and a piano work (*Evening in Grenada*, 1902) using Spanish melodies. Maurice Ravel wrote his first orchestral work (*Spanish Rhapsody*, 1907) and his last ballet (*Bolero*, 1928), as well as an opera (*The Spanish Hour*, 1911), on Spanish subjects. Yet, ironically, neither Debussy nor Ravel ever set foot in Spain. As a friend of Ravel remarked: "He was the eternal traveler who never went there."

Indeed, Maurice Ravel (1875–1937) spent almost all of his life in Paris, a modest music teacher and composer earning a modest living. (Within his otherwise sedentary life of the imagination can be noted a single exception: a wildly successful tour of the United States undertaken in 1928.) For the most part, then, Ravel was content to conjure far-off lands through his exotic music, as he did in his final "voyage" to Spain—a modern-style ballet titled *Bolero*.

A **bolero** is a sultry Spanish dance in a slow tempo and triple meter. For the first performance in Paris, on November 22, 1928, Ravel set the stage to look like a Spanish inn. A single light shone down on a female gypsy dancer, as in John

Sargent's painting, *Spanish Dancer* (Figure 24.8). Around the room, male dancers sat listlessly, a few holding guitars as if to accompany the lone ballerina. In a style reminiscent of the seductive gypsy Carmen in the opera of that name (see Chapter 22), the female dancer begins, moving with ever-increasing passion. The men, one by one, rise and join in the dance of seduction. The sound gets louder and louder. With growing abandon, the entire company begins to sway to the repetitive, hypnotic music, moving inexorably toward a frenzied climax. After about fifteen minutes, the melody suddenly rises in pitch, breaking the hypnotic spell, and the work comes to a crashing conclusion.

FIGURE 24.8
John Singer Sargent (1856–1925), *El Jaleo: Spanish Dancer*. Sargent was an American painter working in Paris who got caught up in the European enthusiasm for all things Spanish at the end of the nineteenth century.

Most of the audience that first night in Paris cheered Ravel and his new work, but at least one woman yelled, "He's mad!" What excited the crowd's passions was that Ravel had written an extended work with only a single melody. The two versions of this theme—one a major-like form, and the other minor-like—are repeated again and again. Ravel himself was somewhat ambivalent about his creation: "I have written only one masterpiece. That is the *Bolero*. Unfortunately, it contains no music."

What Ravel meant by this paradoxical statement is that the piece has no development of the traditional German sort. As with the orchestral music of Debussy, what makes Ravel's ballet score effective is the foregrounding of color, texture, and volume, at the expense of melody and harmony (see Listening Guide). In fact, the melody and supporting harmony do not develop but are simply repeated again and again by different instruments over the duration of fourteen to seventeen minutes, depending on the tempo the conductor chooses. This music is modern in two senses: for listeners of today, *Bolero*'s spellbinding repetitions seem to distantly prefigure electronic dance/trance music; for listeners of Ravel's day, the crashing, dissonant, final chords said that music had left the realm of Impressionism and entered the sometimes shocking new world of Modernism.

LISTENING GUIDE

Maurice Ravel, *Bolero* (1928)

Download 69 (15:29)

Genre: Ballet

Form: **AABBAABB**, etc.

WHAT TO LISTEN FOR: By writing a two-part melody (**A** and **B**) that does nothing but repeat, Ravel forces the listener to concentrate on the kaleidoscopic changes of instrumental color. All the while, a consistent, albeit slow, dance beat pounds in the background, leading to a shockingly Modernist ending.

0:00   Snare drum (imitating castanets) and low strings begin two-bar rhythmic ostinatos.

(Continued)

0:11	Flute enters quietly with melody **A**.	
1:00	Clarinet presents melody **A**.	
1:50	Bassoon enters with melody **B**; harp is added to accompaniment.	
2:40	High clarinet presents melody **B**.	
3:25	Bassoon joins with snare drum in playing rhythmic ostinato.	
3:31	Low oboe plays melody **A**.	
4:20	Trumpet (with mute) and flute together play melody **A**.	
5:10	Saxophone plays melody **B**.	
6:00	High saxophone repeats melody **B**.	
6:50	Two flutes, French horn, and celesta (keyboard instrument producing bell-like sound) together play melody **A**.	
7:40	Several woodwind instruments play melody **A**.	
8:29	Trombone plays melody **B**.	
9:19	Woodwinds and French horn play melody **B** loudly.	
10:02	Timpani added to accompaniment	
10:08	First violins and woodwinds play melody **A**.	
10:56	First and second violins and woodwinds play melody **A**.	
11:44	Violins, woodwinds, and trumpets play melody **B**.	
12:32	Violins, violas, cellos, woodwinds, and trumpets play melody **B**.	
13:20	First violins, trumpets, and piccolos play melody **A**.	
14:08	Same instruments, now with trombone added, play melody **A**.	

14:50	Musical climax; melody **B** moves to higher pitch level and is extended.
15:11	Melody settles back down to original pitch level.
15:23	End: no melody, just rhythmic ostinato and cymbal crashes

LISTEN TO ... this selection streaming online.

WATCH ... an Active Listening Guide of this selection online.

DO ... Listening Exercise 24.2, Ravel, *Bolero*, online.

From Impressionism to Modernism

Impressionism was not the mother of Modernism—more like its aunt. It possessed some, but by no means all, of the musical DNA of the later, more radical Modernist style. To review, the Impressionist style included repetitive, ostinato-like melodies and harmonies that avoided a well-defined goal, as well as instrumental color just for the sake of color. Ostinatos, color, texture, and materials taken from non-Western music were the materials favored by the Impressionists, as Romantic narrative music gave way to pure Modernist soundscapes. Indeed, how music sounded became what music was. This is a very Modernist aesthetic—one that even anticipates Postmodernism. But first things first: on to Modernism.

To point the way, consider, finally, the remarkable historical document seen in Figure 24.9, a photo taken in 1910 that personifies the link between Impressionism and Modernism. Here, in the Paris apartment of Claude Debussy, the composer stands at ease. Behind him hang reproductions of two Japanese paintings, including (top painting) *The Great Wave*, by Katsushika Hokusai, physical evidence demonstrating the importance of the exotic in the lives of Western artists at this time. Seated is Igor Stravinksy, looking every bit the dapper, confident young lion that he was. Debussy and Stravinsky would meet again in Paris in 1912, when the two would play, four-hands at the piano, the almost-finished score of Stravinsky's *The Rite of Spring*, the opening salvo in the battle of Modernism in all the arts.

FIGURE 24.9
Debussy (standing) and Stravinsky (seated) captured at a moment in time: the transition between Impressionism and Modernism

KEY WORDS

Impressionism (337) whole-tone scale (342) parallel motion (343) Exoticism (346)

Symbolists (339) contrary motion (343) glissando (344) bolero (346)

 Join us on Facebook at Listening to Music with Craig Wright

PRACTICE ... your understanding of this chapter's concepts by comparing Checklists of Musical Style for all historic eras and working once more with the chapter's Active Listening Guides online.

DO ... online multiple-choice and critical thinking quizzes that your instructor may assign for a grade.

CHECKLIST OF MUSICAL STYLE *Impressionist: 1880–1920*

REPRESENTATIVE COMPOSERS

Debussy Ravel

PRINCIPAL GENRES

tone poem (symphonic poem)	orchestral song	character piece for piano
string quartet	opera	ballet music

Melody	Varies from short dabs of sound to long, free-flowing lines; melodies are rarely tuneful or singable but, instead, twist and turn rapidly in undulating patterns
Harmony	Purposeful chord progressions replaced by static harmony; chords frequently proceed in parallel motion; use of nontraditional scale patterns (whole-tone, pentatonic) confuses sense of tonal center
Rhythm	Usually free and flexible with irregular accents, making it difficult to determine meter; rhythmic ostinatos used to give feeling of stasis rather than movement
Color	More emphasis on woodwinds and brasses and less on violins as primary carriers of melody; more soloistic writing to show that the color of the instrument is as important as, or more important than, the melody line it plays
Texture	Can vary from thin and airy to heavy and dense; sustaining pedal of the piano often used to create a wash of sound; glissandos run quickly from low to high or high to low
Form	Traditional forms involving clear-cut repetitions less frequent, although ternary form is not uncommon; composers try to develop a form unique and particular to each new musical work

Early-Twentieth-Century
MODERNISM

START... experiencing this chapter's topics with an online video activity.

LEARNING OBJECTIVES
After studying the material in this chapter, you should be able to:
1 Define Modernism, and differentiate Modernist music from the music of the Romantic period.
2 Describe how the Modernist styles of Cubism and Expressionism differ from one another, and from photographic realism.
3 List some of the new approaches to melody and harmony that are audible in Modernist music.
4 Describe the ways in which Stravinsky's *The Rite of Spring* exemplifies both Primitivism and Modernism in art.
5 Explain what atonal music is and how it came to be.
6 Explain how Schoenberg's twelve-tone music works and how it solved a problem that Schoenberg himself had created.

n truth, previous changes in musical style (Classical to Romantic, for example) were more evolutionary than revolutionary. But the transition from Romanticism to Modernism was something different, more like an explosion, indeed a shockingly radical departure—and, to many people, simply outrageous. Below is a Modernist verse by American poet Gertrude Stein (1874–1946), describing a piano in *Tender Buttons* (1914). Can you make sense of it?

> **A PIANO.** If the speed is open, if the color is careless, if the selection of a strong scent is not awkward, if the button holder is held by all the waving color and there is no color, not any color.

Stein, a mentor to painter Pablo Picasso (1881–1973) and novelists F. Scott Fitzgerald (1896–1940) and Ernest Hemingway (1899–1961), was an early promoter of Modernism, a style that was easy to recognize but difficult to define. Simply put, **Modernism** was a movement in the arts between 1900 and 2000 that promoted a bracing, progressive style antithetical to the traditional values of Romanticism.

Modernism: An Anti-Romantic Movement

Today, Modernist art is no longer "modern" in a chronological sense; some of it is now more than 100 years old. But, if "modern" means a radical departure from traditional values, then this description remains apt. It still shocks us more intensely than does the more recent art of the Postmodernist period (1945–present). As we just saw, Modernism took the usual requirements for a poem—that it make sense as a narrative or image and possess proper grammar and syntax—and turned them upside down. So, too, with Modernist music, the concertgoer's expectations for what makes a good melody, pleasing harmony, and regular meter were confounded. Listeners of the early twentieth century were just as baffled by the Modernist sounds of Stravinsky and Schoenberg as they were by the poetry of Gertrude Stein.

Why did such a radically different kind of expression emerge shortly after 1900? In part, because of a violent social disruption that shook Europe and (to a far lesser degree) North America: the run-up to, and outbreak of, World War I. For the Western world, the first two decades of the twentieth century constituted a social earthquake of the highest magnitude. World War I (1914–1918) left 9 million soldiers dead on the battlefields—27,000 French infantry in a single day on a single field. Shocked by the carnage, intellectuals turned away from the predominantly idealistic, sentimental aesthetics of Romanticism—how could one think of love and beauty in the face of wholesale destruction? For writers, painters, and composers alike, disjunction, anxiety, even hysteria became valid artistic sentiments that reflected the realities of the day. The epicenter of this upheaval was, again, France and Germany.

As early as 1870, France and Germany had fought what we now call the Franco-Prussian War, and tensions simmered ominously throughout the decades that followed. Developments in the arts mirrored the unsettled times. In *fin-de-siècle* (end-of-nineteenth-century) Paris, we saw how the Impressionists, led by Debussy, mounted a quietly sensual protest against the extremes of German Romanticism. Shortly thereafter, Modernism—in the hands of the revolutionary Russian expatriate Igor Stravinsky—arrived in Paris in full force. In the German-speaking lands, the Expressionists, including Arnold Schoenberg, staged the most disruptive revolt of all against tonality and tradition, conveying their anxiety through radical dissonance. With Modernism, shock began to replace beauty as the defining component of musical art.

Not all listeners were pleased with this Modernist approach. Schoenberg's early experiments with dissonance were at first received with hoots from a hostile public in Vienna in 1913; that same year, Stravinsky's *Le Sacre du printemps* (*The Rite of Spring*) caused a riot at its Parisian premiere. But Modernist artists like Stein, Stravinsky, and Schoenberg were determined to issue the public a wake-up call, to yank it away from Romantic idealism and back to harsh reality. So, too, were the painters.

Modernist Painting and Music: The Rejection of Representational Art

Photography, as we have seen, was invented in France around 1830, and, by the end of the nineteenth century, photographic images had become commonplace. Perhaps there was a connection between the appearance of a machine that could

exactly duplicate the visual world and the sudden disinclination of painters to do so. Whatever the cause, representational art began to disappear, pushed aside first by Impressionism and then by a more disruptive new style, emanating from Paris in the early 1900s and called **Cubism**. In a Cubist painting, the artist fractures and dislocates formal reality into geometrical blocks and planes, as in the famous *Les Demoiselles d'Avignon* (Figure 25.1), created in 1907 by Pablo Picasso (1881–1973), where the female form has been recast into angular, interlocking shapes. Here, Picasso emphasizes two-dimensional abstraction (geometric trapezoids, squares, and triangles) instead of three-dimensional realism.

In Germany, Austria, and Scandinavia, a different, yet equally unconventional, style of art—**Expressionism**—developed around this time. The aim of Expressionism was not to depict objects as the eye sees them but to express the strong emotion that these objects generated in the artist. In brief, Expressionism is art "inside out." Clashing colors and distorted shapes can be used to signify the pain and anxiety of a subject crying out to an unsympathetic world, as we see in Edvard Munch's early Expressionist work *The Scream* (Figure 25.2).

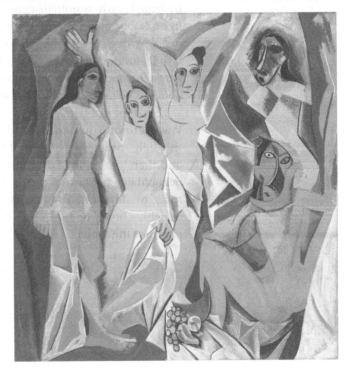

FIGURE 25.1

One of the first statements of Cubist art, Picasso's *Les Demoiselles d'Avignon* (1907). The ladies of the evening are depicted by means of geometric shapes on a flat, two-dimensional plane. Like much avant-garde music of the time, Cubist paintings reject the emotionalism and decorative appeal of nineteenth-century art. The painting was so radical that Picasso refused to exhibit it for nearly a decade.

Modernist painters and musicians were heading in the same direction, not by coincidence, but in a real and personal way. Picasso and Stravinsky socialized in Paris and sometimes collaborated on theater works. And Schoenberg, himself a talented painter (see Figure 25.9), exhibited his art with an Expressionist group whose

WATCH... a film on Cubism as four-dimensional art, online.

WATCH... a sequence of early Expressionist paintings by Edvard Munch, accompanied by a dissonant, chromatic string quartet of Arnold Schoenberg, online.

LISTEN TO...

Example 25.1 online.

members included Wassily Kandinsky (see Figure 25.8). In the works of these artists, traditional "themes," whether visual or aural, were becoming distorted to the point of being unrecognizable.

Melody: More Angularity and Chromaticism

Just as the conventional figure vanished from avant-garde painting (see Picasso, Figure 25.1, and Munch, Figure 25.2), so, too, the traditional (singable) melody disappeared from early Modernist music. Indeed, there are very few themes in twentieth-century music that the listener goes away humming. If Romantic melody is generally smooth and conjunctive in motion (moving more by steps than by leaps), early-twentieth-century melody tends to be fragmented and angular, like a Cubist painting. The young avant-garde composers went to great lengths to *avoid* writing conjunctive, stepwise lines. Rather than moving up a half step from C to D♭, for example, they were inclined to jump down a major seventh to the D♭ an octave below. Avoiding a simple interval for an agonizingly distant one an octave above or below is called **octave displacement**; it is a feature of Modernist music.

So, too, the heavy use of chromaticism, which developed with Liszt and Wagner toward the end of the nineteenth century, is a feature of Modernist music. In a fully chromatic scale, all the pitches are an equal distance (half step) apart, and therefore none stands out as the home pitch. In Example 25.1 by Arnold Schoenberg, notice how the melody makes large leaps where it might more easily move by steps and also how several sharps and flats are introduced to produce a highly chromatic line. Octave displacement obscures the tune; chromaticism obscures the tonic.

EXAMPLE 25.1 Octave displacement and chromaticism

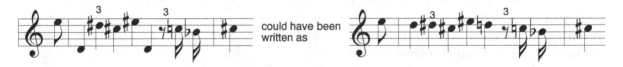

Harmony: The "Emancipation of Dissonance" and New Chords

Since the late Middle Ages, the basic building block of Western music had been the triad—a consonant, three-note chord (see Chapter 2, "Harmony"). A composer might introduce dissonance (a nontriad tone) for variety and tension, yet the rules of consonant harmony required that a dissonant pitch move (resolve) immediately to a consonant pitch (a member of the triad). Dissonance was subordinate to, and controlled by, the triad. By the first decade of the twentieth century, however, composers such as Arnold Schoenberg were using so much dissonance that the triad lost its adhesive force. Schoenberg famously referred to this development as "the emancipation of dissonance," meaning that dissonance was now liberated from the requirement that it resolve into a consonant triad. Dissonance had been sprung and could now go about terrorizing unwary listeners!

Indeed, shocked audiences at first rebelled when they heard Schoenberg's dissonance-filled scores. Ultimately, however, Schoenberg succeeded in "raising the bar" for what the ear might tolerate, thereby preparing listeners for a much higher level of dissonance in both classical and popular music. Indeed, the work of Schoenberg and like-minded composers paved the way, albeit indirectly, for the heavy dissonances of today's progressive jazz and the dissonant "metal" styles of Metallica, Kiss, Anthrax, Slayer, and countless others.

Early-twentieth-century composers created dissonance not only by obscuring or distorting the triad but also by introducing new chords. One technique for creating new chords was the superimposition of more thirds above the triad itself (Example 25.2). Thus, there emerged not only the **seventh chord** (a seventh chord spans seven letters of the scale, from A to G, for example) but also the **ninth chord** and the **eleventh chord**. The more thirds that were added on top of the basic triad, the more dissonant the sound of the chord. The more such dissonant chords are placed in succession, the more the music sounds like Stravinsky or Metallica.

EXAMPLE 25.2 New chords

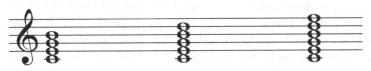

seventh chord   ninth chord   eleventh chord

LISTEN TO...
Example 25.2 online.

The most extreme new chord was the **tone cluster**, the simultaneous sounding of a number of pitches only a whole step or a half step apart. Example 25.3 shows a tone cluster created by the American Modernist Charles Ives (1874–1954). You, too, can create this high-dissonance chord simply by striking a group of adjacent keys on the piano with your fist or forearm. Try it.

EXAMPLE 25.3 Tone cluster

LISTEN TO...
Example 25.3 online.

Chromaticism, unresolved dissonance, and new chords all weakened the force of tonality, the "cohesive gravity" that pulled and held together traditional music. But early-twentieth-century Modernist composers devised substitutes to provide musical cohesion and unity, as we shall now see.

Igor Stravinsky (1882–1971)

Despite his diminutive stature, Igor Stravinsky (Figure 25.3) was a protean warrior for the avant-garde who commanded attention—and an audience—wherever he went. (As a student in 1966, this author had a lengthy, but confusing, conversation

FIGURE 25.3
Igor Stravinsky may have looked studious, but he enjoyed life among the glitterati of twentieth-century art and culture. The film *Coco and Igor* (2009) links him romantically with French fashion designer Coco Chanel, founder of the House of Chanel.

FIGURE 25.4
Sergei Diaghilev in New York in 1916. Diaghilev's creation, the modern dance company he called *Ballets Russes*, has been immortalized by the award-winning film *Ballets Russes* (2005).

with him—was the composer too old, or was the student too young?) Possessing an uncanny ear for sonority, Stravinsky created masterpieces in many genres: opera, ballet, symphony, concerto, church Mass, and cantata. His versatility was such that he could set to music a classical Greek drama (*Oedipus Rex*, 1927) one day and write a ballet for elephants (*Circus Polka*, 1942) the next. Throughout his long life, he traveled with the fashionable set of high art. Although reared in St. Petersburg, Russia, he later lived in Paris, Venice, Lausanne, New York, and Hollywood. Forced to become an expatriate because of the Russian Revolution (1917), he took French citizenship in 1934, and then, having moved to the United States at the outbreak of World War II, he became an American citizen in 1945. He counted among his friends painter Pablo Picasso (1881–1973), poet T. S. Eliot (1888–1965), and fashion designer Coco Chanel (1883–1971). On his eightieth birthday, in 1962, Stravinsky was honored by President John F. Kennedy at the White House and, later in the same year, by Russian premier Nikita Khrushchev in the Kremlin. When he died in New York at the age of eighty-eight, cosmopolitan Stravinsky was the world's most famous composer, perhaps the last "high-art" composer to receive such worldwide recognition.

Stravinsky rose to international fame as a composer of ballet music. In 1908, his early scores caught the attention of Sergei Diaghilev (1872–1929; Figure 25.4), the legendary **impresario** (producer) of Russian opera and ballet. Diaghilev knew he could make money by exporting Russian ballet to Paris, which at that time was the artistic capital of the world. So he formed a dance company, called the ***Ballets Russes*** (Russian Ballets), and hired, over the course of time, the most progressive artists he could find: Pablo Picasso and Henri Matisse for scenic design, and Debussy, Ravel, and Stravinsky, among others, as composers. Stravinsky soon became the principal composer of the company, and the *Ballets Russes* became the focus of his musical activity for the next ten years. Accordingly, the decade 1910–1920 has become known as Stravinsky's Russian ballet period.

With the onset of World War I and the temporary disappearance of large symphony orchestras in Europe, Stravinsky, along with others, developed a style called **Neo-classicism**, which emphasized classical forms and smaller ensembles of the sort that had existed in the Baroque and Classical periods. Stravinsky's Neo-classical period extended from 1920 until 1951, when he adopted the twelve-tone technique of Arnold Schoenberg (see "Arnold Schoenberg (1874–1951)" near the end of this chapter), which he continued to pursue until his death.

Although Stravinsky's style continually evolved over the course of his nearly seventy-year career, his particular brand of Modernism—the "Stravinsky sound"—is always recognizable. In simple terms, his music is lean, clean, and bracing. He downplays warm strings, preferring instead the tones of piercing winds and brittle percussion. While his orchestra can be large and colorful, its sound is rarely lush or sentimental. Most important, rhythm is the vital element in Stravinsky's compositional style. His beat is strong, but often irregular, and he builds complexity by requiring independent meters and rhythms to sound simultaneously (see "Irregular Accents" below). All of these stylistic traits can be heard in his ballet *The Rite of Spring*. This watershed of musical Modernism,

Stravinsky's most famous work, stunned and angered the audience at its explosive 1913 premiere.

Le Sacre du Printemps (The Rite of Spring, 1913)

Igor Stravinsky composed three important early ballet scores for Diaghilev's dance company: *The Firebird* (1910), *Petrushka* (1911), and *The Rite of Spring* (1913). All are built on Russian folktales—a legacy of musical nationalism (see Chapter 18)—and all make use of the large, colorful orchestra of the late nineteenth century. Yet, the choreography for these Russian ballets required not the refined, graceful gestures of Romantic ballet—the elegant sort that we associate with Tchaikovsky's *Swan Lake* and *The Nutcracker* (see Chapter 18). Instead, these are modern dances with angular poses and abrupt, jerky motions, as can be seen in the original costumes for *The Rite of Spring* (Figure 25.5). The dancers do not soar in tutus; they stomp in primitive attire. Indeed, here Stravinsky adopts the aesthetic of **Primitivism**, a style that attempts to capture the unadorned lines, raw energy, and elemental truth of non-Western art and apply it in a Modernist context. (Picasso's *Les Demoiselles d'Avignon*—see Figure 25.1—inspired by African sculpture, is also an example of Primitivism.) In *The Rite of Spring*, Stravinsky expresses these elements through pounding rhythms, almost brutal dissonance, and a story that takes us back to the Stone Age.

The Premiere

Although *The Rite of Spring* (see Listening Guide) has been called *the* great masterpiece of Modernism, at its premiere it provoked not admiration but a riot of dissent. This premiere, the most notorious in the history of Western music, took place on an unusually hot evening, May 29, 1913, at the newly built Théâtre Champs-Élysées in the most fashionable section of Paris. With the very first sounds of the orchestra, many in the packed theater voiced, shouted, and hissed their displeasure. Some, feigning auditory pain, yelled for a doctor; others, for two. There were arguments and flying fists as opponents and partisans warred over this Russian brand of Modernism. To restore calm, the curtain was lowered momentarily and the house lights were turned on and off. All in vain. The musicians still could not be heard, and, consequently, the dancers had difficulty staying together. A sense of the chaotic scene comes through in a review by a visiting critic of the *New York Press*:

FIGURE 25.5
Dancers wearing re-creations of the "primitive" dress of Slavic tribes, as they appeared in the original production of Stravinsky's *The Rite of Spring* (1913). The costumes and scenic design for this premiere were by Russian artist Nicholas Roerich (1874–1947).

> I was sitting in a box in which I had rented one seat. Three ladies sat in front of me and a young man occupied the place behind me. He stood up during the course of the ballet to enable himself to see more clearly.

The intense excitement under which he was laboring, thanks to the potent force of the music, betrayed itself presently when he began to beat rhythmically on the top of my head with his fists. My emotion was so great that I did not feel the blows for some time. They were perfectly synchronized with the beat of the music!

In truth, the violent reaction to *The Rite of Spring* was not only a response to the music but also to the Modernist choreography, which sought to obliterate any trace of classical ballet: The dance was just as "primitive" as Stravinsky's Modernist score. But what aspects of Stravinsky's music shocked so many in the audience that night?

Percussive Orchestra

First, there is a new percussive—one might say "heavy-metal"—approach to the orchestra. The percussion section is enlarged to include four timpani, a triangle, a tambourine, a guiro, cymbals, antique cymbals, a bass drum, and a tam-tam. Even the string family, the traditional provider of warmth and richness in the symphony orchestra, is required to play percussively, attacking the strings with repeated down-bows at seemingly random moments of accent. Instead of warm, lush sounds, we hear bright, brittle, almost barbaric ones pounded out by scraping strings, percussion, heavy woodwinds, and brasses.

Irregular Accents

Stravinsky intensifies the effect of his harsh, metallic sounds by placing them where they are not expected, on unaccented beats, thereby creating explosive syncopation, something he had learned to appreciate by listening to American jazz. Notice, in Example 25.4, the famous beginning of "Augurs of Spring," how the strings accent (>) the second, fourth, and then first pulses of subsequent four-pulse measures. In this way, Stravinsky destroys ordinary 1-2-3-4 meter and forces us to hear, in succession, groups of 4, 5, 2, 6, 3, 4, and 5 pulses—a conductor's nightmare, and a dancer's as well!

EXAMPLE 25.4 Irregular accents

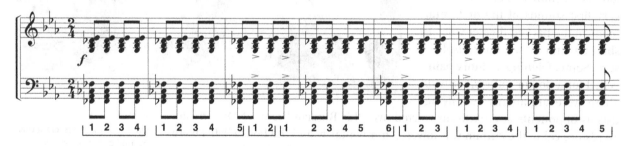

Polymeter

The rhythm of *The Rite of Spring* is complex because Stravinsky often superimposes two or more different meters simultaneously. Notice in Example 25.5 that the oboe plays in $\frac{6}{8}$ time and the E♭ clarinet plays in $\frac{7}{8}$ time, while the B♭ clarinet plays in $\frac{5}{8}$ time. This is an example of **polymeter**—two or more meters sounding simultaneously.

WATCH... an online video of what the premiere of *The Rite of Spring* must have been like.

LISTEN TO...
Example 25.4 online.

WATCH... a demonstration of how various meters can be combined, online.

EXAMPLE 25.5 Polymeter

Polyrhythm

Not only do individual parts often play separate meters, but they also sometimes project two or more independent rhythms simultaneously. Look at the reduced score given in Example 25.6. Every instrument seems to be doing its own thing! In fact, six distinct rhythms can be heard, offering a good example of **polyrhythm**—two or more rhythms sounding simultaneously.

EXAMPLE 25.6 Polyrhythm

Ostinato Figures

Notice also in Examples 25.5 and 25.6 that most of the instruments play the same motive over and over at the same pitch level. Such a repeating musical figure, as we have seen, is called an ostinato. In this instance, we hear multiple ostinatos.

Stravinsky was not the first twentieth-century composer to use ostinatos extensively. Debussy had done so earlier in his Impressionist scores. But Stravinsky employs them more often and for longer spans than did his predecessors. They give structure to the music. In *The Rite of Spring*, ostinatos also give the music its incessant, motorized quality, especially in the sections with fast tempos.

Dissonant Polychords

The harsh, biting sound that is heard throughout much of *The Rite of Spring* is often created by two triads, or a triad and a seventh chord sounding at once. What results is a **polychord** (Figure 25.6)—the simultaneous sounding of one triad or seventh chord with another. When the individual chords of a polychord are only a whole step or a half step apart, the result is especially dissonant. In Example 25.7, the passage from the beginning of "Augurs of Spring," a seventh chord built on E♭ is played simultaneously with a major triad built on F♭. This single chord succinctly expresses the primitive brutality of the pagan world that Stravinsky imagined.

LISTEN TO...

Example 25.7 online.

EXAMPLE 25.7 Polychord

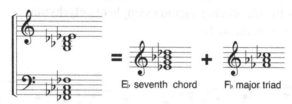

E♭ seventh chord   F♭ major triad

The Plot

The subtitle of *The Rite of Spring* sets the context: *Pictures of Pagan Russia*. In Part 1, "The Adoration of the Earth," a primitive Slavic tribe celebrates pagan springtime

FIGURE 25.6
In his *Schemes of Painting* (1922), the artist Albert Gleizes demonstrates that a Cubist work can be created by rotating a figure or line against itself, and then again and again until visual dissonance results. Similarly, a polychord is created by placing two or more triads or seventh chords off center and against one another, thereby creating aural dissonance.

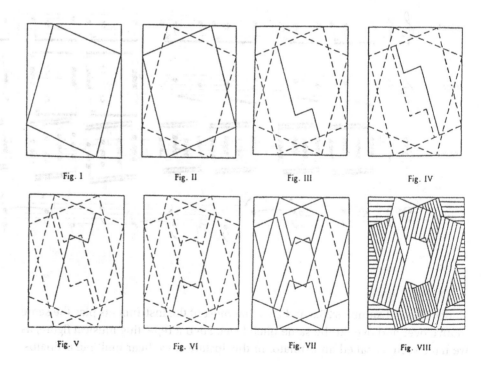

Fig. I   Fig. II   Fig. III   Fig. IV

Fig. V   Fig. VI   Fig. VII   Fig. VIII

rituals; in Part 2, "The Sacrifice," a virgin dances herself to death as an offering to the god of spring (Figure 25.7). Before the curtain rises on Part 1, however, the huge orchestra plays an Introduction in total darkness. Inexorably, the music unfolds from soft to loud, from one line to many, and from tranquil to cacophonous, suggesting all the creepy-crawly things of the earth coming to riotous life in early spring. As the curtain rises, primitive dancers pound onto the stage (Scene 1: "Augurs of Spring:

Dance of the Adolescents"), energized by jarring accents (see Example 25.4) and ear-splitting dissonance (see Example 25.7). To soften the blows, Stravinsky occasionally incorporates folk music, whether quoting authentic Russian songs or (more commonly) creating his own melodies with a folk flavor. Despite the folkloric content, however, the bulk of the composition came from within. As Stravinsky declared, "I had only my ears to guide me. I heard and I wrote what I heard. I am the vessel through which *The Rite of Spring* passed."

LISTENING GUIDE

Igor Stravinsky, *Le Sacre du printemps* (1913)   Download 70 (6:56)

Introduction and Scene 1 ("Augurs of Spring: Dance of the Adolescents")

Genre: Ballet music

WHAT TO LISTEN FOR: In the Introduction, a growing cacophony of writhing woodwinds, which seem to be crawling out of the earth. In Scene 1 (3:36), an elemental pounding of dissonant string chords (see Example 25.4), punctuated by blasts from French horns and trumpets—"primitive Modernism" at its best

Introduction

0:00	Bassoon writhing in high register

0:21	Other winds (bass clarinet, English horn, another bassoon, high clarinet) gradually enter.
1:40	Flutes play in parallel motion.
1:56	Writhing woodwinds continue.
2:40	Ostinato in bass supports gradual orchestral crescendo.
3:03	Bassoon melody returns; clarinet trills.

(Continued)

"Augurs of Spring: Dance of the Adolescents"

(Youthful dancers pound onto stage; male and female groups entice one another; attention shifts to more folk-like dances of girls.)

3:36   Elemental pounding of dissonant string chords, punctuated by blasts from French horns and trumpets

4:25   Bassoons and then trombones play stepwise motive.

4:56   *Fortissimo* chords and timpani blows

5:20   French horn plays folk-like melody.

5:41   Flute plays melody.

5:56   Trumpets play new folk-like melody.

6:32   Gradual orchestral crescendo

LISTEN TO ... this selection streaming online.

WATCH ... an Active Listening Guide of this selection online.

WATCH ... a superb re-creation of the original music and choreography of *The Rite of Spring*, by Robert Joffrey and Milicent Hodson, online.

DO ... Listening Exercise 25.1, Stravinsky, *Le Sacre du printemps*, online.

Following the scandalous success that attended the premiere of *The Rite of Spring*, Stravinsky extracted the music from the ballet itself and presented it as a multimovement work for orchestra alone. The music itself was now recognized as an important, if controversial, statement of the musical avant-garde. Later, in 1940, the score of *The Rite of Spring* furnished the music for an important segment of Walt Disney's early, full-length animated film *Fantasia*. Disney made Modernism mainstream.

Arnold Schoenberg (1874–1951)

The second face of early musical Modernism was that of Arnold Schoenberg (1874–1951). Ironically, his brand of radicalism emerged in Vienna, the city of Mozart and Brahms, long known for its cultural conservatism. In the early twentieth century, a trio of native Viennese musicians—Schoenberg, along with his pupils Alban Berg (1885–1935) and Anton Webern (1883–1945)—stretched musical Romanticism to and beyond the breaking point. The close association of these three innovative composers has come to be called the **Second Viennese School** (the first, of course, consisted of Mozart, Haydn, and Beethoven—see Chapter 10, "Vienna: Home to Classical Composers").

Arnold Schoenberg, the leader of this group, almost single-handedly thrust musical Modernism upon a reluctant Viennese public. Schoenberg was from a Jewish family of modest means and was largely self-taught as a musician. He came to know the music of Wagner, Brahms, and Mahler mostly by playing their scores and attending concerts. Like many college students today, Schoenberg reached the age of twenty-one still lacking a clear professional direction. He had a "day job" as a bank teller, but at night he satisfied his curiosity through the study of literature, philosophy, painting, and musical composition. Eventually, his musical scores began to be heard in Vienna, though they were usually not well received.

Schoenberg's earliest compositions were written in the late Romantic style, with rich harmonies, chromatic melodies, and programmatic content. But, by 1908, his music had begun to evolve in unexpected directions. Strongly influenced by Wagner's chromatic harmonies, Schoenberg started to compose works with no tonal center. If Wagner could write winding chromatic passages that temporarily obscured the tonic pitch, why not go all the way and create fully chromatic pieces in which there is no tonic pitch? This Schoenberg did, and in so doing, created what is called **atonal music**—music without tonality, without a key center.

Schoenberg's contemporaries found his atonal music difficult to understand. After all, this was the period in which all of Vienna was dancing to the tuneful waltzes of Johann Strauss. Not only did Schoenberg's music have no tonal center, but his melodies were highly disjunctive, his harmonies exceedingly dissonant, and his rhythms undanceable. Some performers refused to play his music, and, when others did, the audience's reaction was occasionally violent. At one concert on March 31, 1913, the police had to be called in to restore order. Fortunately for Schoenberg, he possessed a characteristic typical of innovative geniuses throughout history: self-confidence. As he said, "One must be convinced of the infallibility of one's own fantasy; one must believe in one's own creative spirit."

Pierrot lunaire (Moonstruck Pierrot, 1912)

Pierrot lunaire (Moonstruck Pierrot), Schoenberg's best-known composition, is an exemplary work of Expressionist art (Figure 25.8). Schoenberg aimed to create an intimate chamber work for small ensemble and female singer, who declaims twenty-one poems by Albert Giraud. Here, we meet Pierrot, a sad clown from the world of traditional Italian pantomime and puppet shows—always in love but never successful. In this Expressionist poetry, the clown has fallen under the sway of the moon and has changed into an alienated

FIGURE 25.8
Impression 28 (2nd version, 1912), created by Arnold Schonberg's fellow artist, Wassily Kandinsky, is an early example of Abstract Expressionism. Kandinsky's painting and Schoenberg's *Pierrot lunaire*, discussed here, were both created in 1912. In fact, the art and music of this movement can be described in rather similar terms. The bold, clashing colors, disjointed shapes, and jagged lines of the painters have their counterparts in the harsh dissonances, asymmetrical rhythms, and angular, chromatic melodies of Schoenberg and his followers.

modern artist. Pierrot projects his inner anxiety by means of **Sprechstimme** (German for "speech-voice"; indicated by an "x" in the Listening Guide), a technique that requires the vocalist to declaim the text rather than to sing it. The singer must execute the rhythmic values exactly, but once the singer hits a pitch, he or she should quit the tone immediately, sliding away in either a downward or an upward direction. This creates the exaggerated, sometimes hysterical declamation that one might hear from a lunatic, which is appropriate for Pierrot, given the lunar spell cast upon him. Indeed, some translate the title as *Pierrot Insane*.

Poem 6, *Madonna*, of *Pierrot lunaire* (see Listening Guide) depicts the clown's tormented, hallucinatory vision of the suffering Madonna (Mother of Christ) at the cross. (See also Figure 25.9.) Note that the poet builds a refrain (boldface) into the text: *O Mutter aller Schmerzen* ("O Mother of all sorrows"). Traditionally, composers had taken the appearance of a textual refrain as a cue to repeat the melody as well, thereby creating musical unity over the course of the work. However, Schoenberg, ever the iconoclast, avoids any and all repetition. Instead, his music unfolds in a continuum of ever-new sounds. For the listener, this creates a difficulty: The human psyche finds an unending series of new things—sounds or otherwise—very unsettling. Thus, the listener's first reaction to the dissonant continuum of pitches in *Pierrot lunaire* may be decidedly negative. Yet, with repeated hearings, the force of the jarring elements of the atonal style begins to lessen, and a bizarre, eerie sort of beauty emerges, especially if the listener is sensitive to the meaning of the text.

FIGURE 25.9
Arnold Schoenberg, then unsure whether he wanted to be a painter or a musician, painted *Red Gaze* in 1910. Notice that line six of the poem *Madonna* in the Listening Guide— "Gleichen Augen, rot und offen" ("Like eyes, red and open")—seems to express Schoenberg's own fears and anxiety. The aim of Expressionist art was to convey the innermost feelings of the artist and even the subconscious.

LISTENING GUIDE

Arnold Schoenberg, *Pierrot lunaire* (1912)   Download 71 (2:03)

Number 6, *Madonna*

Genre: Art song

Form: Through composed

WHAT TO LISTEN FOR: The dissonant harmonies and disjunctive vocal melody delivered in an almost-hysterical style, called *Sprechstimme*. The accompanying chamber ensemble includes flute, bass clarinet, violin, cello, and piano. Try to sing the tonic (home) pitch. It's impossible, for this is atonal music.

Steig, O Mutter aller Schmerzen
Auf den Altar meiner Verse!
Blut aus deinen magern Brüsten
Hat des Schwertes Wut vergossen.
Deine ewig frischen Wunden

Arise, O Mother of all sorrows
On the altar of my verse!
Blood from your thin breast
Has spilled the rage of the sword.
Your eternally fresh wounds

Gleichen Augen, rot und offen,	Like eyes, red and open,
Steig, O Mutter aller Schmerzen	**Arise, O Mother of all sorrows**
Auf den Altar meiner Verse!	**On the altar of my verse!**
(1:15) In den abgezehrten Händen	In your thin and wasted hands
Hältst du deines Sohnes Leiche	You hold the body of your Son
Ihn zu zeigen aller Menschheit,	To show him to all mankind,
Doch der Blick der Menschen meidet Dich,	Yet the look of men avoids You,
O Mutter aller Schmerzen.	**O Mother of all sorrows**.

LISTEN TO ... this selection streaming online.

WATCH ... an Active Listening Guide of this selection online.

Twelve-Tone Music

When Schoenberg created atonal music, as heard in *Pierrot lunaire*, he also created a serious artistic problem. Having removed the traditional building blocks of music (consonant triads, tonal chord progressions, and tonal centers), what musical structures would replace them? If all twelve notes of the chromatic scale are equally important, as is true in atonal music, why choose any one pitch or another at a given moment? What was needed was a system. As composer Leonard Bernstein said about Schoenberg and this moment in music history: "A German has to have a system!"

By 1923, Schoenberg had solved the problem of "formal anarchy"—the absence of form caused by total chromatic freedom. He discovered a new way of creating music that he called "composing with twelve tones." **Twelve-tone composition** is a method of writing atonal music that uses each of the twelve notes of the chromatic scale set in a fixed, predetermined order. The composer begins by arranging the twelve notes of the chromatic scale in a sequence of his or her choosing, forming a "tone row." Throughout the composition, these twelve notes must appear in the same order. Music in which elements such as pitch, timbre, or dynamics come in a fixed series is called **serial music**. In twelve-tone music, the twelve-note series may unfold not only as a melody but also as a melody with accompaniment, or simply as a progression of chords, because two or more notes in the row may sound simultaneously. Moreover, in addition to appearing in its basic form, the row might go backward (retrograde) or upside down (inversion), or both backward and upside down at the same time (retrograde inversion). While such arrangements might seem wholly artificial and very unmusical, we should remember that composers such as Johann Sebastian Bach in the Baroque era and Josquin Desprez in the Renaissance sometimes subjected their melodies to similar permutations. The purpose of Schoenberg's twelve-tone method was to create musical unity by basing each piece on a single, orderly arrangement of twelve tones, thereby guaranteeing the perfect equality of all pitches so that none would seem like a tonal center.

WATCH... a quick tutorial on the structure of twelve-tone music, online.

Trio from *Suite for Piano*, Opus 25 (1924)

Schoenberg's first steps along this radical twelve-tone path were tentative, and the pieces he created were very short. Among Schoenberg's first serial compositions was his *Suite for Piano*, a collection of seven brief dance movements, including the

Minuet and Trio, discussed below. The tone row for *Suite for Piano*, along with its three permutations, is as follows:

Row												Retrograde											
E	F	G	D♭	G♭	E♭	A♭	D	B	C	A	B♭	B♭	A	C	B	D	A♭	E♭	G♭	D♭	G	F	E
1	2	3	4	5	6	7	8	9	10	11	12	12	11	10	9	8	7	6	5	4	3	2	1

Inversion												Retrograde-inversion											
E	E♭	D♭	G	D	F	C	F♯	A	G♯	B	B♭	B♭	B	G♯	A	F♮	C	F	D	G	D♭	E♭	E
1	2	3	4	5	6	7	8	9	10	11	12	12	11	10	9	8	7	6	5	4	3	2	1

Schoenberg allows the row or any of its permutations to begin on any pitch, as long as the original sequence of intervals is maintained. Notice in the Trio, for example, that the row itself begins on E♭ but is also allowed to start on B♭ (see Listening Guide). In the second part, measures 6–9, the exact serial progression of the row breaks down slightly. The composer explained this as a "justifiable deviation," owing to the need for tonal variety at this point. Notice also that the rhythms may also be changed for the sake of variety. As you listen to the Trio, see if you can follow the unfolding of the row and all its permutations by following the numbers. Listen many times—the piece is only fifty-one seconds long! Its aesthetic effect is similar to that of a constructivist painting by an artist like Theo van Doesburg (see Figure 25.10). If you like the abstract mechanical precision of the painting, you'll likely enjoy Schoenberg's twelve-tone piano piece as well.

FIGURE 25.10
Artist Theo van Doesburg (1883–1931) often fashioned designs in retrograde motion, in which the pattern proceeding downward from the top left was the same as that moving upward from the bottom right. One can simulate the same effect by comparing his *Rhythms of a Russian Dance* (1918) in upright and rotated orientations.

Arnold Schoenberg, Trio, from *Suite for Piano* (1924)

Download 72 (0:53)

Genre: Twelve-tone piano music

WHAT TO LISTEN FOR: Listen several times (it's a very short piece); with each hearing, the disjunction and dissonance will recede, leaving a sense of an abstract sonic space, which is free of emotional commitment.

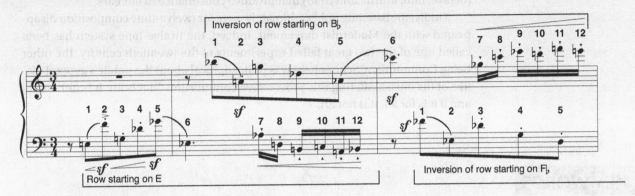

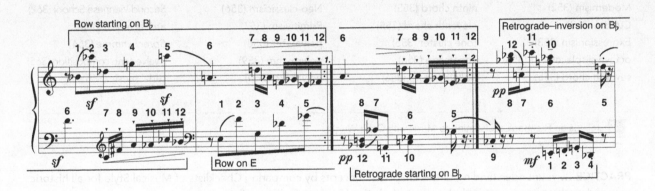

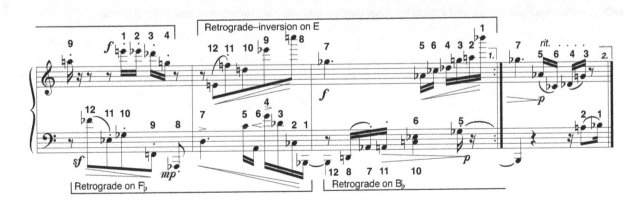

LISTEN TO ... this selection streaming online.

WATCH ... an Active Listening Guide of this selection online.

Although the twelve-tone process became the rage among Modernist composers—even Stravinsky came under its sway—audiences never fully embraced it. Why would anyone write music that is mechanistic and not pretty? For Schoenberg, "pretty" was not the point; as this piano piece proves, the job of art is to stimulate as well as satisfy. Nevertheless, most music lovers continued to find Schoenberg's twelve-tone style inaccessible. Audiences intuited that twelve-tone music is unnatural because it is not based on the sounds of the primary overtones (octave, fifth, fourth, and triad) that produce consonance to our ears.

Oddly, the listening public ultimately won, for twelve-tone composition disappeared with the Modernist movement. Indeed, the twelve-tone system has been called one of the two great failed experiments of the twentieth century, the other being Communism. Schoenberg was philosophical about the public's general dislike of his music, offering this provocative conundrum: "If it is art, it is not for all, and if it is for all, it is not art."

KEY WORDS

Modernism (352)	ninth chord (355)	Neo-classicism (356)	Second Viennese School (362)
Cubism (353)	eleventh chord (355)	Primitivism (357)	atonal music (363)
Expressionism (353)	tone cluster (355)	polymeter (358)	*Sprechstimme* (364)
octave displacement (354)	impresario (356)	polyrhythm (359)	twelve-tone composition (365)
seventh chord (355)	*Ballets Russes* (356)	polychord (360)	serial music (365)

 Join us on Facebook at Listening to Music with Craig Wright

PRACTICE ... your understanding of this chapter's concepts by comparing Checklists of Musical Style for all historic eras and working once more with the chapter's Active Listening Guides online.

DO ... online multiple-choice and critical thinking quizzes that your instructor may assign for a grade.

AMERICAN
Modernism

START... experiencing this chapter's topics with an online video activity.

LEARNING OBJECTIVES
After studying the material in this chapter, you should be able to:

1 Describe the ways in which Charles Ives's music anticipated many of the salient features of European Modernism.

2 Explain why the sounds of Samuel Barber's iconic *Adagio for Strings* put it on so many lists of sad classical music.

3 Outline how Aaron Copland's music blends Americana with European Modernism.

4 Describe how Ellen Taaffe Zwilich has established a dialogue with the past in her Neo-classical compositions.

The year 2015 marked the 130th anniversary of the arrival of the Statue of Liberty in New York City, a gift from the people of France, symbolizing the freedom and opportunity that awaited immigrants arriving in the United States of America. Indeed, the United States has evolved into a highly pluralistic society, home to Native Americans as well as recent and not-so-recent arrivals of almost every ethnic group. Offering a "free market" for the exchange of artistic ideas and benefiting from the creativity spurred by ethnic diversity, the United States has come to enjoy the most vibrant musical culture in the world. Among the popular musical traditions to originate in the United States are gospel, blues, ragtime, jazz, rock and roll, hip-hop, Appalachian bluegrass, zydeco, and country and western.

American art music of the past 100 years has been equally varied but different. At first, American "high-art" composers labored under the influence of European Modernism, specifically atonal and twelve-tone music, represented by Stravinsky and Schoenberg, both of whom immigrated to the United States. But American art music gradually threw off the "anxiety of influence" of European Modernism, to create uniquely American Modernist and then Postmodernist styles that were less abstract and systematic, and more tune based and "listener friendly."

Charles Ives (1874–1954)

Charles Ives (Figure 26.1) was an American original, arguably the greatest—and certainly the most experimental—of American Modernist composers. He was born in Danbury, Connecticut, the son of George Ives (1845–1894), a bandleader in the Union army who had served with General Ulysses S. Grant during the Civil War. The senior Ives gave his son a highly unorthodox musical education, at least by European standards. The obligatory study of the three B's (Bach, Beethoven, and Brahms); instruction in harmony and counterpoint; and lessons on the violin, piano, organ, cornet, and drums were all included. But young Ives also learned, as he put it, to "stretch his ears." In one exercise, for example, he was made to sing "Swanee River" in E♭ while his father accompanied him on the piano in the key of C—a useful lesson in **polytonality** (two or more keys sounding simultaneously).

Because his forebears had gone to Yale, it was decided that Charles should enroll there, too. At Yale, he took courses in music with Horatio Parker (1863–1919), a composer who had studied in Germany. But Ives's youthful, independent ideas about how music should sound clashed with Parker's traditional European training in harmony and counterpoint. The student learned to leave his more audacious musical experiments—which included, for example, a fugue with a subject entering in four different keys—outside Parker's classroom. Ives became heavily involved in extracurricular activities, playing on the baseball team and joining a fraternity (Delta Kappa Epsilon) as he maintained a D+ average (a "gentleman's" mark before the days of grade inflation).

When he graduated in 1898, Ives decided not to pursue music as a profession, realizing that the sort of music he heard in his head was not the kind the public would pay to hear. Instead, he headed for New York City and Wall Street, and, in 1907, he and a friend formed the company of Ives and Myrick, an agency that sold insurance as a subsidiary of Mutual of New York (MONY). Ives and Myrick became the largest insurance agency in the United States, and, in 1929, the year in which Ives retired, the company had sales of $49 million.

FIGURE 26.1
Young Charles Ives in the baseball uniform of Hopkins Grammar School, New Haven, Connecticut. A better ball player than student, Ives needed an extra year between high school and college to prepare for Yale.

But Charles Ives led two lives: high-powered insurance executive by day, prolific composer by night. During the twenty years between his departure from Yale (1898) and the American entry into World War I (1917), Ives wrote the bulk of his 43 works for orchestra (including 4 symphonies), 41 choral pieces, approximately 75 works for piano solo or various chamber ensembles, and more than 150 songs. Almost without exception, they went unheard. Ives made little effort to get his music performed—composition was for him a very private matter. By the 1930s, however, word of his unusual creations had spread among a few influential performers and critics. In 1947, he was awarded the Pulitzer Prize in music for his Third Symphony, which he had written forty years earlier! Having become a gruff, grumpy eccentric, Ives told the members of the Pulitzer committee, "Prizes are for boys. I'm grown up."

Ives's Music

Charles Ives was an idiosyncratic man with an equally idiosyncratic aesthetic; his extreme Modernist music is unlike that of any other composer. Between 1898 and 1917, Ives independently devised the same radical compositional techniques—including atonality, polymeter, polyrhythm, and tone clusters—that would only later begin to appear in the works of Schoenberg, Stravinsky, and the other European Modernists. Moreover, Ives was the first composer to use polytonality extensively, and he even experimented with **quarter-tone** music, in which the smallest interval is not the chromatic half step (the smallest division that the modern piano can play) but *half* of a half step. Ives's music places great demands on both performer and listener alike. It is full of grinding dissonances and dense, complex textures. At the same time, however, it contains many simple, popular musical elements, incorporating patriotic songs, marches, hymns, dance tunes, fiddle tunes, rags, and football cheers; this was Ives's musical America. Ives often combined these familiar musical idioms with melodies of his own, piling one tune on top of another to form a new composite. What results is a jarring kind of **collage art**: art made up of disparate materials taken from very different places. In a manner akin to that of a progressive artist, such as William Harnett, who reinterprets fragments of reality in surprising ways (Figure 26.2), Ives takes the familiar and "defamiliarizes" it, thereby making the old sound very modern.

Variations on America (1892–ca. 1905)

Ives took an important step toward collage art in one of his earliest works, *Variations on America* for organ, which he began in 1892 at the age of seventeen. As the title indicates, this is a set of variations on the patriotic tune known in the United States as "America" or "My Country 'Tis of Thee" (in Canada and England, it's known as "God Save the Queen [King]").

The work opens with a conventional introduction (see Listening Guide), followed by a statement of the well-known theme. Variation 1 is filled with increasingly chromatic figuration in the right hand but otherwise seems tame enough.

WATCH... a YouTube video of Ives's brand of American Modernism and collage art at their most extreme, online.

FIGURE 26.2
William Harnett's *Music and the Old Cupboard Door* (1889) creates a satisfying collage of Americana by melding various objects from a closet and the world of music.

Thereafter, however, Ives lets loose, building a "mashup" of outside musical references with the original melody. Variation 2 ends with the close chromatic harmony that was popular with turn-of-the-century barbershop quartets, while Variation 3, with its quick puffs of sound, is reminiscent of a calliope, or steam organ, at a county fair. Variation 4 introduces the most foreign element: a Polish polonaise (traditional dance). The fifth and final variation features a Bach-like walking bass to be played by the pedals "as fast as they can go." The collage in this piece, then, consists of a patriotic tune melded with allusions to a barbershop quartet, steam whistles, a Polish polonaise, and a Baroque organ toccata.

Sometime during the first decade of the twentieth century, when Ives was an insurance agent in New York City, he revisited his *Variations on America* and inserted two interludes. Both are remarkable for their extensive use of polytonality. In the first interlude, for example, the right hand plays the melody in F major; against this, the left hand and the pedal perform the same music, but in the clashing key of Db! The same theme is set against itself, as happens in the visual arts (see the chapter-opening photo, a 1958 collage created by Jasper Johns). Ives was the first composer in the history of music to employ polytonality consistently, and the result is bracingly dissonant. "America" had never sounded like this before. Indeed, America wasn't ready for Ives's ear-splitting sonorities. Not until 1949, more than fifty years after Ives began *Variations on America*, did he find a publisher that was willing to print it.

LISTENING GUIDE

Charles Ives, *Variations on America* (1892–ca. 1905)   Download 73 (7:07)

Genre: Organ work

Form: Theme and variations

WHAT TO LISTEN FOR: The discrepancy in sound between the variations

Introduction

0:00	Hints of theme to come
0:54	Theme "America" in chordal homophony

Variation 1

1:24	Theme in left hand as rapid figuration in right hand becomes increasingly chromatic

Variation 2

2:18	Dark, descending chromatic harmonies cover the theme.

Interlude 1

3:08	Dissonant polytonality; right hand plays tune in F major, and left hand and pedal play in Db major.

Variation 3

    3:31   Meter changes from triple to duple.

    4:01   New, fast-moving counterpoint added in left hand

Variation 4

    4:32   Theme set as a snappy polonaise (Polish dance) in minor
                 key and triple meter

Interlude 2

    5:19   More polytonality; right hand plays in A♭, and left hand
                 plays in F major

Variation 5

    5:32   Steady, Bach-like walking bass played rapidly in the pedal

Coda

    6:25   Recall of introduction; pedal plays beginning of theme as
                 final flourish.

LISTEN TO... this selection streaming online.

WATCH... an Active Listening Guide of this selection online.

Samuel Barber (1910–1981)

Is there music that we simply love even though it teaches us almost nothing? Is it all right to just enjoy music and not be challenged by it, staying well inside our musical comfort zone? The music of Samuel Barber requires an affirmative answer to both questions.

Samuel Barber was reared in a traditional home (Figure 26.3), in a traditional American town (West Chester, Pennsylvania), and he composed mostly in a traditional musical style (Romantic-Modernist). Being something of a musical prodigy, he was sent to a traditional music school, the prestigious Curtis Institute of Music in Philadelphia. Thereafter, commissions and composition awards, including two Pulitzer Prizes, came at regular intervals. He had both money and acclaim. What was there not to be happy about?

Barber seems to have been unhappy from an early age and to have battled depression throughout his life. Indeed, his first composition, written at the age of six,

FIGURE 26.3
The solidly American boyhood home of Samuel Barber in West Chester, Pennsylvania. Notice the relentlessly symmetrical, or traditional palindromic, design.

is a twenty-three measure piano piece in C minor (of course) entitled *Sadness*. At the age of nine, he wrote a confessional letter to his mother, asking that she forgive him for not being an athlete and not wanting to play football, and enjoining her not to concern herself with that "worrying secret … because it is neither yours nor my fault."

Was Barber's lifelong depression related to the fact that he was gay and (like Schubert and Tchaikovsky before him) forced to be secretive at a time when homosexuality still carried legal sanctions and social stigmas? Attempts to draw a direct connection between personal experience and musical expression are generally misguided, but it is of interest that Barber's *Adagio for Strings* shows up in almost every search for sad classical music, be it in the "Sublime Sad Classical Collection" or "The Saddest Music in the World."

Adagio for Strings (1938)

What makes the iconic *Adagio for Strings* sound so sad? A slow tempo, steady pulse, generally reduced volume, and heavy dose of low strings all contribute. The music slowly rises but then falls, and, as the mournful melody appears in successive presentations, it moves down (through violins, violas, and then cellos), not up, as Beethoven's would in a triumphant moment. But, oddly, *Adagio for Strings* privileges minor chords no more than major ones and actually ends on a major chord, which is an anomaly for a sad piece.

What makes *Adagio for Strings* (see Listening Guide) Modernist music? At first, it sounds anything but. Indeed, one can rightly call *Adagio for Strings* an example of **Neo-Romanticism**, a style that starts with the musical elements of Romantic music but reimagines them with an awareness of Modernist musical processes. Barber uses few biting dissonances, no melodic disjunction (his melody moves mostly stepwise), no atonality (the home key is B♭ minor), and no brittle woodwinds or pounding strings. What we hear are the warm, lush sounds of the strings—up to a point.

That point arrives at the very middle of the piece, when a giant string crescendo begins and works its way upward, pitch by pitch and decibel by decibel, to an ear-splitting dissonance and mind-bending intensity. During this crescendo, we pass from a Neo-Romantic to a Modernist style, for the dissonance and anxiety of the modern mentality are now what Barber wishes to express. By way of analogy, this climactic moment in which the tortured soul cries out for understanding can be experienced once again by revisiting Munch's famous *The Scream* (Figure 25.2), an example of early Expressionism. The shattering climax of *Adagio for Strings* is Barber's scream, and, once passed, the exhausted music settles back to its original melancholic low. The listener can experience this piece as **ABA'**, or sadness (depression)-scream-sadness.

LISTENING GUIDE

Adagio for Strings (1938)   Download 74 (9:03)

Genre: A slow (*Adagio*) movement

Form: **ABA'**

WHAT TO LISTEN FOR: A slow, sad meditation that seems to be wandering until it rises to a mind-shattering climactic intensity

0:00	Violins move the theme slowly, mostly by step, up the scale.	
0:38	Violins gradually fall to a lower pitch level.	
1:04	Violins rise and leap to a higher pitch level at the end of the phrase.	
1:41	Violas enter at a lower pitch level with the theme and lead it up and then back down.	
2:37	Violas depart again with the theme and leap to a higher pitch level at end of phrase.	
3:11	Violas and violins engage in contrapuntal dialogue.	
3:48	Cellos enter with the theme.	
4:43	Cellos depart again with the theme and leap to a higher pitch level at end of phrase.	
5:10	Violins and then cellos begin slow, gradual ascent in pitch, with rising volume, dissonance, and intensity.	
6:10	Music reaches peak of intensity.	
6:27	Deafening silence	
6:32	Homophonic chords in low register	
7:01	Theme rises again, much as at the beginning.	
8:16	Music seems to disintegrate but struggles slowly to the end.	

LISTEN TO ... this selection streaming online.

WATCH ... an Active Listening Guide of this selection online.

Aaron Copland (1900–1990)

Until the twentieth century, the United States was a cultural backwater of a European tide. European symphonic scores, for example, dominated the repertoire of symphony orchestras in New York, Boston, Cincinnati, and Chicago, among other places, in post–Civil War America. During the twentieth century, however, as the presence of the United States grew increasingly large on the world stage, American composers provided the emerging nation with its own distinctive musical character—one that was not only attuned to the Modernist style then prevalent in Europe but also that sounded truly American. The composer who best captured the spirit of the American heartland was Aaron Copland (Figure 26.4), who, ironically, spent much of his life within the confines of New York City.

Aaron Copland was born in Brooklyn, New York, to Jewish immigrant parents. After a rudimentary musical education in New York, he set sail for Paris to broaden his artistic horizons. In this he was not alone, for the City of Light at

FIGURE 26.4
Aaron Copland

this time attracted young writers, painters, and musicians from around the world, including Igor Stravinsky (1882–1974), Pablo Picasso (1881–1973), James Joyce (1882–1941), Gertrude Stein (1874–1946), Ernest Hemingway (1898–1961), and F. Scott Fitzgerald (1896–1940). After three years of study, Copland returned to the United States, determined to compose in a distinctly American style. Like other young expatriate artists during the 1920s, Copland had to leave his homeland in order to learn what made it unique: "In greater or lesser degree," he remarked, "all of us discovered America in Europe."

During the late 1920s and early 1930s, Copland sought to forge an American style by incorporating into his music elements of jazz, a distinctly American product. This was, as novelist F. Scott Fitzgerald dubbed it, the Jazz Age, when American jazz was a craze that swept the world. But the Jazz Age ended with the Great Depression, so Copland then turned his attention to a series of projects with rural and western American subjects. The ballet scores *Billy the Kid* (1938) and *Rodeo* (1942) are set in the West and make use of classic cowboy songs like "Goodbye, Old Paint" and "The Old Chisholm Trail." Another ballet, *Appalachian Spring* (1944), re-creates the ambience of the Pennsylvania farm country, and his only opera, *The Tender Land* (1954), is set in the corn belt of the Midwest. In 2009, Ken Burns featured Copland's music prominently in the sound track of his TV miniseries *The National Parks: America's Best Idea*. What could be more American than the wide-open sounds of Aaron Copland?

Copland's Music

Copland evokes a sense of space in his music by means of a distinctive kind of orchestration called **open scoring**. He typically creates a solid bass, a very thin middle texture, and a top of one or two high, clear tones, such as those of the clarinet, flute, or trumpet. This separation and careful spacing of the instruments create the fresh, uncluttered sound that is so pleasing in Copland's music. Another characteristic element of Copland's style is the use of Americana; although he uses the dissonant harmonies and disjunct melodies of European Modernism, he incorporates American folk and popular songs to soften the impact. Copland's melodies tend to be more stepwise and major/minor than those of other twentieth-century composers, perhaps because Western folk and popular tunes are conjunct (have few skips) and nonchromatic. His harmonies are almost always tonal and often change slowly in a way that can evoke the vastness and grandeur of the American landscape. The triad, too, is still important to Copland, perhaps for its stability and simplicity, and dissonance unfolds slowly against it, rather than in a jarringly abrupt, Modernist fashion. Spatial clarity, folksongs, and a conservative approach to dissonance, then, mark Copland's "listener-friendly" scores.

The clarity and simplicity of Aaron Copland's music is not accidental. During the Great Depression of the 1930s, he became convinced that the gulf between modern music and the ordinary citizen had become too great—that dissonance and atonality had little to say to most music lovers: "It made no sense to ignore them [ordinary listeners] and to continue writing as if they did not exist. I felt that it was worth the effort to see if I couldn't say what I had to say in the simplest possible terms." Thus, he not only wrote appealing new tonal works like *Lincoln Portrait* (1941) and *Fanfare for the Common Man* (1942) but also incorporated simple, traditional tunes such as "The Gift to Be Simple," which he uses in *Appalachian Spring*.

Appalachian Spring (1944)

Appalachian Spring (Figure 26.5) is a one-act ballet that tells the story of "a pioneer celebration of spring in a newly built farmhouse in the State of Pennsylvania in the early 1800s." A new bride and her farmer husband express through dance the anxieties and joys of life in pioneer America. The work was composed in 1944 for the great American choreographer Martha Graham (1893–1991), and it won Copland a Pulitzer Prize the following year. The score is divided into eight connected sections that differ in tempo and mood (see Listening Guide). Copland provided a brief description of each of these orchestral scenes.

Section 1

"Introduction of the characters one by one, in a suffused light." The quiet beauty of the land at daybreak is revealed (Example 26.1) as the orchestra slowly presents, one by one, the notes of the tonic and dominant triads.

EXAMPLE 26.1 A musical dawn

FIGURE 26.5
A scene from Martha Graham's ballet, *Appalachian Spring*, with music by Aaron Copland. Here, Katherine Crockett dances the role of the Bride (New York, 1999).

While this overlapping presentation of two triads constitutes a polychord of the sort created by Stravinsky (see Chapter 25, "Dissonant Polychords"), the effect is only mildly dissonant because of the slow, quiet way in which the notes of the two chords are introduced. The serene simplicity of the introduction sets the tone for the entire work.

LISTEN TO…
Example 26.1 online.

Section 2

"A sentiment both elated and religious gives the keynote of this scene." The early calm is suddenly broken by a lively dance with a salient rhythm, played aggressively by the strings (Example 26.2). The dance has all the modern rhythmic vigor of Stravinsky's music but none of its extreme polymeter (see Chapter 25, "Polymeter"). As the dance proceeds, a more restrained hymn-like melody emerges in the trumpet (Example 26.3). The juxtaposition of these contrasting themes could not better illustrate the sonic difference between European Modernism and American folk simplicity.

EXAMPLE 26.2 Modernist-style dance

LISTEN TO…
Example 26.2 online.

LISTEN TO...

Example 26.3 online.

EXAMPLE 26.3 American-hymn style

Sections 3–6

Section 3 is a dance for the two principals, a *pas de deux* in ballet parlance, accompanied by lyrical writing for strings and winds. Sections 4 and 5 are musical depictions of the livelier aspects of country life, with Section 4 including a toe-tapping hoedown, while Section 6 recalls the quiet calm of the opening of the ballet.

Section 7

"Calm and flowing. Scenes of daily activity for the Bride and her Farmer-husband." For this section, Copland chose to make use of a traditional tune of the Shakers, an extreme religious sect that prospered in the Appalachian region in the early nineteenth century and whose members expressed their spiritual intensity in frenzied singing, dancing, and shaking. Today, this tune is famous, having been featured, among other places, in a John Williams piece for Barack Obama's inauguration in 2009. But the melody has become well known only because Copland featured it in *Appalachian Spring*. In fact, the composer plucked it from an obscure book of folksongs in 1944 because he thought the simple, scalar tune (Example 26.4) fit well with the American character of the ballet and because the text of the Shaker song is harmonious with what occurs on stage: "scenes of daily activity."

LISTEN TO...

Example 26.4 online.

EXAMPLE 26.4 Shaker tune

WATCH... an homage to Copland by John Williams, with this famous Shaker tune as played by Yo-Yo Ma and others, online.

'Tis the gift to be simple,
'Tis the gift to be free,
'Tis the gift to come down where we ought to be,
And when we find ourselves in the place just right,
'Twill be in the valley of love and delight.

In the five variations that follow, *The Gift to Be Simple* is not so much varied as it is clothed in different instrumental attire.

Section 8

"The Bride takes her place among her neighbors." Serenity returns to the scene as the strings play a slow, mostly stepwise descent, as Copland says, "like a prayer." The hymn-like melody from Section 2 is heard again in the flute, followed by the quiet "landscape music" from the beginning of the ballet. Darkness has again descended on the valley, leaving the young pioneer couple "strong in their new house" and secure in their community.

LISTENING GUIDE

Aaron Copland, *Appalachian Spring* (1944)

Sections 1, 2, and 7

Genre: Ballet music

WHAT TO LISTEN FOR: Section 1 (Download 75): The distinctly Copland sound caused by an orchestration that clearly separates low supporting strings from high solo woodwinds. Section 2 (Download 76): Percussive, dissonant Modernism soon made to contrast with a lyrical hymn-like tune in the trumpet. Section 7 (Download 77): The inventive use of theme-and-variations form in which the composer changes the feeling associated with the theme from irrepressibly cheerful to, at the end, triumphant.

SECTION 1 (Download 75)

0:00	Quiet unfolding of ascending triads by clarinet and other instruments
0:53	Soft melody descends in woodwinds and strings.
1:34	More ascending triads in woodwinds and trumpet, and then flute melody (1:46)
2:01	Oboe and then bassoon solos
2:49	Clarinet plays concluding ascending triad.

SECTION 2 (Download 76)

0:00	Percussive rhythm in strings and rising woodwinds
0:17	Rhythm gels into sprightly dance.

0:43	Trumpet plays hymn-like melody above dance.

1:13	Rhythmic motive scattered but then played more forcefully
2:10	Hymn played quietly in strings, with flute counterpoint above
2:45	Rhythmic motive skips away in woodwinds.

SECTION 7 (Download 77)

0:00	Clarinet presents Shaker tune.

0:33	Variation 1: Oboe and bassoon play tune.
1:02	Variation 2: Violas and trombones play tune at half its previous speed.
1:49	Variation 3: Trumpets and trombones play tune at fast tempo.
2:12	Variation 4: Woodwinds play tune more slowly.
2:30	Variation 5: Final majestic statement of tune by full orchestra

LISTEN TO ... this selection streaming online.

WATCH ... an Active Listening Guide of this selection online.

DO ... Listening Exercise 26.1, Copland, *Appalachian Spring*, online.

AARON COPLAND (1900–1990) • **379**

Ellen Taaffe Zwilich (b. 1939)

FIGURE 26.6
Ellen Taaffe Zwilich

By the end of World War II, American composers such as Charles Ives and Aaron Copland had given European Modernism a uniquely American voice. Consequently, American composers thereafter no longer felt obliged to forge a national style. Paraphrasing what Ellen Taaffe Zwilich (Figure 26.6) said in 2007 about the "mindset" of American composers during the last century: "There was a time, in the 1920s with the music of Copland, for example, when we were searching for an American voice. Then we went beyond that stage. Our musical interests are now really quite all over the map."

The daughter of an airline pilot, Zwilich was born in 1939 in Miami, Florida, and was educated at The Florida State University, to which she has recently returned to occupy a professorship in musical composition. In 1960, Zwilich moved to New York City, where she played violin in the American Symphony Orchestra, studied composition at the Juilliard School, and worked for a time as an usher at Carnegie Hall. Her "big break" came in 1983, when she became the first woman to win the Pulitzer Prize in music. During 1995–1998, she was the first person of either gender to occupy the newly created Composer's Chair at Carnegie Hall—the usher had become the director. As to honors, Zwilich has been elected to two "halls of fame" for artistic and academic excellence—the American Academy of Arts and Sciences and the American Academy of Arts and Letters—and has been the recipient of no fewer than six honorary doctorates from various universities.

Concerto Grosso 1985 (1985)

Just how far ranging, forward and backward, Zwilich's musical vision extends can be heard in her *Concerto Grosso 1985* (see Listening Guide). Commissioned by the Washington Friends of Handel, this work honors the composer George Frideric Handel (see Chapter 9), a leading exponent of the concerto grosso. Here, Zwilich follows a twentieth-century musical procedure generally called **Neo-classicism**—the use of the genres, forms, and aesthetics of the Baroque (1600–1750) or Classical (1750–1820) periods to inform a new, Modernist composition. As opera composer Giuseppe Verdi had said earlier, "Let us go back to the old—it will be a step forward."

In *Concerto Grosso 1985*, Zwilich embraces several elements of Baroque musical style: a regular rhythmic pulse, a repeating bass pedal point, a walking bass, terraced dynamics, and a harpsichord. Most directly, she incorporates a Baroque melody, borrowed from Handel's Violin Sonata in D major (Example 26.5A), at the opening of each movement of her concerto. Yet, Zwilich throws in a modern touch, adding twisting chromaticism (Example 26.5B) and a biting, dissonant harmony to Handel's original theme. Further, she demands an insistent, pounding style of playing that would have shocked the eighteenth-century master. Is this music Baroque or Modernist? Mostly the latter—here, music of the past inspires but does not overwhelm the present.

EXAMPLE 26.5A Handel

mp

Handel's original melody

LISTEN TO...

Example 26.5A online.

EXAMPLE 26.5B Zwilich

mp

Zwilich's modernization of it

LISTEN TO...

Example 26.5B online.

LISTENING GUIDE

Ellen Taaffe Zwilich, *Concerto Grosso 1985* (1985)

Download 78 (4:44)

Third movement, *Largo* (slow and broad)

Genre: Concerto grosso

WHAT TO LISTEN FOR: A predominantly Modernist style, infused with elements of the Baroque era. To understand how the generally consonant "American" style of Copland contrasts with the more dissonant Modernism of Zwilich, listen again to a bit of Copland (Download 77) before moving on to Zwilich.

0:00	Bass pedal point begins.
0:05	Melody rises in English horn, and then oboe and violins.
0:29	Bass finally begins to "walk" to lower pitches.
0:59	Violins play melody *forte*, with dissonant chords added by harpsichord.
1:04	French horns provide dissonant melodic counterpoint.
1:39	Dissonant chords repeated *forte*.
2:10	Cellos play melody above dissonant chords faintly heard in harpsichord.
2:42	Violins and violas play melody above soft dissonant chords and bass pedal point.
3:33	Bass and chordal accompaniment become more fragmented.
3:52	Violins play melody quietly above fragmented chords.

LISTEN TO ... this selection streaming online.

WATCH ... an Active Listening Guide of this selection online.

DO ... Listening Exercise 26.2, Zwilich, *Concerto Grosso 1985*, online.

KEY WORDS

polytonality (370)   collage art (371)   open scoring (376)

quarter tone (371)   Neo-Romanticism (374)   Neo-classicism (380)

 Join us on Facebook at Listening to Music with Craig Wright

PRACTICE ... your understanding of this chapter's concepts by comparing Checklists of Musical Style for all historic eras, completing a Musical Style Quiz for the Modern era, and working once more with the chapter's Active Listening Guides online.

DO ... online multiple-choice and critical thinking quizzes that your instructor may assign for a grade.

CHECKLIST OF MUSICAL STYLE   *Modern: 1900–present*

REPRESENTATIVE COMPOSERS

Stravinsky   Ives   Barber

Schoenberg   Copland   Zwilich

PRINCIPAL GENRES

symphony   string quartet   ballet music

solo concerto   opera   choral music

Melody	Wide-ranging disjunctive lines, often chromatic and dissonant; angularity accentuated by use of octave displacement
Harmony	Highly dissonant, marked by chromaticism, new chords, and tone clusters; dissonance no longer must move to consonance but may move to another dissonance; sometimes two conflicting but equal tonal centers sound simultaneously (polytonality); sometimes no audible tonal center is present (atonality)
Rhythm	Vigorous, often asymmetrical rhythms; conflicting simultaneous meters (polymeter) and rhythms (polyrhythm) make for temporal complexity
Color	Color becomes agent of form and beauty in and of itself; composers seek new sounds from traditional, acoustical instruments and innovative singing techniques from electronic instruments and computers, and from noises in environment
Texture	As varied and individual as the men and women composing music
Form	A range of extremes: sonata–allegro, rondo, theme and variations benefit from Neo-classical revival; twelve-tone procedure allows for almost mathematical formal control; forms and processes of classical music, jazz, and pop music begin to influence one another in exciting new ways

POSTMODERNISM

START... experiencing this chapter's topics with an online video activity.

LEARNING OBJECTIVES

After studying the material in this chapter, you should be able to:

1 Define Postmodernist art, and explain how it differs from Modernist art.

2 Trace the development of electronic music and its impact on popular, film, and video game music.

3 Identify some of the provocative ways in which composer John Cage expressed his brand of Postmodernist art.

4 Describe Minimalism as a movement in music and the visual arts.

5 Speculate about the future of classical music, if composer Caroline Shaw is any indication.

6 Complete a capstone listening activity, describing an unfamiliar piece of music.

READ... the complete chapter text in a rich, interactive online platform.

WATCH... Yo-Yo Ma participate in the creation of a Postmodernist piece embracing Bach, bluegrass, and the sounds of Beijing, online.

FIGURE 27.1
Jeff Koons's figure of a woman hugging a toy, Pink Panther, provokes an argument, as does much Postmodernist art: What is art? What makes a work of genius? While some may say that Koons's porcelain figure *Pink Panther* (1988) is not art, it sold at auction on May 10, 2011, for $16.8 million. But does artistic value equate with money? To think further about what makes art—and great art, in particular— consider another sculpture shown earlier in this book, Michelangelo's *David* (see Figure 5.4).

The "isms" seem to be spreading like a virus: Impressionism, Expressionism, Modernism, Neo-classicism, and now Postmodernism. But how to describe the music being composed today? We are modern people, so we might rightly assume that our art belongs to the Modernist style. But Modernism, it turns out, is no longer modern in the sense of being cutting edge. In the years since World War II, Modernism has been superseded by what we call **Postmodernism**. Seen narrowly, if Modernism distorted traditional melody, Postmodernism abandons it. Viewed more broadly, whereas Modernism was reactive, playing off the musical elements from previous Western historical periods, Postmodernism leaves all musical traditions behind.

Postmodernists instead favor an inclusive, "anything goes" approach to art. For Postmodernists, art is for everyone, not just an elite few, and all art is of equal potential. Andy Warhol's paintings of Campbell's Soup cans or of Marilyn Monroe (see the chapter-opening photo), for example, are just as worthy a subject as Michelangelo's *David*. Jeff Koons's blonde (Figure 27.1) is just as meaningful as Leonardo da Vinci's *Mona Lisa*. Consequently, there is no "high" or "low" art, no "good" or "bad" art, only *art*.

Regarding the proper subjects of art, the boundary separating acceptable from unacceptable has been removed in the Postmodern period. In 1952, Francis Bacon, whose paintings now sell for upwards of $140 million, attached slabs of beef to his torso and photographed himself; in 2010, Lady Gaga shocked the crowd at the Video Music Awards in a dress made entirely of raw meat. These adventurous artists aim to show that any object can be transformed into a bold creative statement.

Finally, the Postmodern world is a pluralistic one, in which one culture or orientation is just as important as the next. Indeed, cultural differences are shrinking due to globalization, a process of homogenization made inevitable by instant mass-media communication. Postmodernism is also refreshingly egalitarian when it comes to gender, affirming a belief that the creations of, say, gay living black women are just as important as those of straight dead white men.

Postmodernist principles apply to music as well as to art, architecture, and fashion. If all art holds equal potential, then it is no longer necessary to separate classical from popular music—the two styles can even coexist within the same composition, as they do, for example, in recent works of Paul McCartney and Wynton Marsalis. No longer, according to Postmodernism, need there be distinctions between "highbrow" and "lowbrow" music; all music—classical, country, hip-hop, folk, rock, and all the rest—is to be prized in equal measure. John Williams's film music is as important as Igor Stravinsky's ballet scores; Eminem is as worthy of our attention as Mozart. People can listen to whatever they want.

In today's Postmodernist musical culture, amplified instruments and electronic music are commonplace in symphony hall and rock arena alike. Traditional acoustic instruments share the spotlight with newer electronic ones. Yo-Yo Ma's Stradivarius cello may be a cultural treasure, but so, too, is Jimi Hendrix's electric guitar. Postmodernism embraces an egalitarian, pluralistic musical world in which technology plays an important role. Today, unlike the past, it is impossible to predict where a performance of new "art" music will take place, whether concert hall or street corner, or what the audience will hear.

Edgard Varèse (1883–1965) and Electronic Music

The origins of musical Postmodernism can be traced to the 1930s and the experimental compositions of Edgard Varèse (Figure 27.2). Varèse was born in France but immigrated to the United States in 1915 in search of a less traditional artistic environment. After an accidental fire caused the loss of some of his scores brought from Paris, he destroyed the rest intentionally, thereby obliterating all traces of his European musical past. Already an extreme Modernist, Varèse showed himself eager to step beyond the boundaries of the Western musical tradition and embrace the Postmodernist age. But for the 1930s, Varèse was a pioneer far ahead of his time—Postmodernism didn't reach full force until the 1960s. As with many other artistic and cultural movements, Modernism and Postmodernism overlapped for decades. Indeed, in some ways, the two styles are still doing battle today.

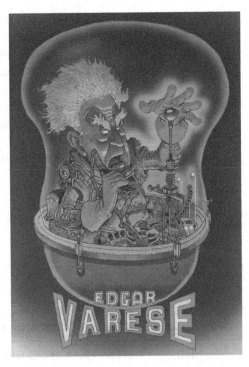

Significantly, Varèse titled his first work written in the United States *Amériques* (1921), suggesting not only a new geography but also a new world of musical sound. Besides the usual strings, brasses, and woodwinds, the orchestra for *Amériques* also required a battery of new percussion instruments, including sirens and sleigh bells, most of which had never been heard in a symphony orchestra. In earlier centuries, composers had typically called on percussion to provide accentuation. The thuds, bangs, and crashes of these instruments helped to delineate the outline of the musical structure. Like road signs, they pointed the way but did not constitute the essence of the musical journey. By the 1930s, however, Varèse had radically altered the traditional role of the percussion family. In *Ionization* (1931), the orchestra consists of nothing but percussion instruments, including two sirens, two tam-tams, a gong, cymbals, anvils, three different sizes of bass drum, bongos, various Cuban rattles and gourds, slap-sticks, Chinese blocks, sleigh bells, and chimes. Here, percussive sounds don't just reinforce the music; they *are* the music.

But this music is very different. With percussion in the forefront, traditional melody and harmony all but disappear. What remains are rhythm, color, and texture. Yet Varèse wanted more. As he said in a lecture in 1936, "When new instruments allow me to write music as I conceive it, [then my shifting sound-masses] will be clearly perceived." Two decades later, the "new instruments" Varèse had envisioned—electronic instruments—became available.

Poème électronique (1958)

Most traditional music around the world is played on acoustic instruments (those made of natural materials). Shortly after World War II, however, new technology led to the development of **electronic music** produced by a **synthesizer**—a machine that can produce, transform, and combine (synthesize) sounds by means of electronic circuitry. Varèse's *Poème électronique* (1958) is an early landmark of electronic music. In this piece, the composer combined new electronic sounds generated by a synthesizer using bits of *musique concrète*. **Musique concrète** was the French expression for sounds that came from our real-world environment, captured by a tape recorder and sometimes manipulated in some imaginative way. These might be a siren, a plate crashing to the floor, an organ, church bells, or a human voice. For *Poème électronique*, Varèse incorporated both *musique concrète* and newly created electronic sounds. In 1958, his "poem for the electronic age" provided a soundscape for a multimedia exhibition at the Brussels World's Fair. Varèse's eight-minute creation was recorded on tape and then played back over 425 speakers, again and again, to the 15,000–16,000 people who walked through the structure daily. While the music played, a video montage was projected on the inside walls of the building.

LISTENING GUIDE

Edgard Varèse, *Poème électronique* (1958)　　　　　　　　　　　　　Download 79 (3:28)

Opening

Genre: Electronic music

WHAT TO LISTEN FOR: A brave new sonic world, comprised of prerecorded sounds from everyday life (*musique concrète*), sometimes manipulated electronically, and new sounds generated by purely electronic means

0:00	Large bell, squibbles and zaps, sirens
0:41	Drip-like noise, squawks
0:56	Three-note chromatic ascent sounded three times
1:11	Low sustained noise with rattle, siren, and more squawks
1:33	Three-note chromatic ascent, squawks, and chirps
2:03	Percussion instruments, siren (2:12)
2:34	Large bell returns, sustained tones
2:58	More drips, large low crescendo, rattles, and zaps

LISTEN TO ... this selection streaming online.

WATCH ... an Active Listening Guide of this selection online.

DO ... Listening Exercise 27.1, Varèse, *Poème électronique*, online.

ELECTRONIC MUSIC: FROM THOMAS EDISON TO BEATS MUSIC

The application of modern technology to music began in 1877 when Thomas Edison patented the phonograph. Around 1920, sounds of the phonograph became harnessed to electromagnetic wave diffusion, leading to the radio (ironically, it was Edison's archrival, Nicola Tesla, who promoted the radio). The principal content of the radio broadcast was music, some of which was live but most of which was played from phonograph records. Ultimately, electronic sound transmission evolved into the streamed MP3 and MP4 files of today.

●●●

To hear music, it is no longer necessary to learn to play an instrument or go to a concert; just turn on your phone.

The monopoly of acoustic instruments dissolved shortly after World War II, when musicians began tinkering with radios, tape recorders, and then computers to produce new sounds and a new kind of music: electronic music. Not only could music be radio broadcast, but also, using this same sort of technology involving tubes, oscillators, and amplifiers, it could be *created*. The pioneer here was Edgard Varèse, who promoted the early synthesizer. A synthesizer takes the overtones of a pitch and transforms them; with a synthesizer, the sound of a piano, for example, can be changed into that of a trumpet, or a clarinet, or an entire 110-piece orchestra. Soon, computer processors were storing and transforming sound as digital information, thereby creating **computer music**. Finally, by the 1980s, microprocessors had become small enough to place a keyboard within the computer, creating an all-in-one synthesizer. Henceforth, any aspiring rock musician or garage band could own the hardware required to produce digital audio, to be disseminated by affixing it to a disc or streamed online. Serious art composers and rock musicians were now literally on the same wavelength.

While Haydn and Brahms—indeed, most "preelectronic" composers—created at the piano, a composer today is more likely to do so in a home electronic recording studio. Martin O'Donnell, creator of the music for the *Halo* video game series, says that he works with "keyboards, synths, and samplers as well as digital recording equipment controlled by computers." Indeed, video music of all sorts—for video games, TV shows, and films—is predominantly electronic or acoustic music manipulated digitally. For example, the opening theme of the perennially popular *The Simpsons*, written by Danny Elfman (1953–), is electronically based computer music that makes use of interpolated acoustic sounds as well.

Likewise with pop music, new processes have made new sounds possible. In the 1980s, rap and hip-hop artists began using a technique called **sampling**, whereby the rapper or producer extracts a small portion of prerecorded music and then mechanically repeats it over and over as a musical backdrop to the text being rapped. In **scratching**, which is something of a retro technique that is popular in rap and hip-hop, a creative DJ with one

Composer Danny Elfman, seen here in an electronic recording studio, blends electronic music and traditional acoustic sounds in his film scores, among them *Good Will Hunting*, *Milk*, *Terminator*, *Batman*, *Men in Black* (I, II, and III), *Silver Linings Playbook*, and *American Hustle*.

or more turntables manipulates the needles, scratching on the vinyl of the record while other prerecorded sounds loop continually in the background.

For the best of Postmodernist electronic music, one might well turn to Trent Reznor, front man for industrial rock project Nine Inch Nails and creative director of the new streaming-music service Beats Music (now a subsidiary of Apple). Reznor and his collaborator, Atticus Ross, have crafted award-winning scores for the films *The Social Network* (2010) and *Gone Girl* (2014). If you listen to a bit of the sixty-six-minute sound track for *The Social Network*, you'll enjoy hearing an exciting mix of traditional scales and melodies (along with inversions), electronic dance rhythms, electric funk bass, Minimalist patterns (see later in this chapter), and electronic distortion. "Eclectic electric" fairly captures the diversity of this Postmodernist music. Are these thought-provoking tracks classical or pop, a symphony or a film score, a classical suite or an industrial rock concept album? One thing is certain: They're all electronic.Ultimately, the true measure of the ascendancy of electronic music (or of any musical style) is that it has been embraced by "the academy" (university music programs and music conservatories). Thirty years ago, a college student would walk into the office of a professor of composition and sit at a piano to play a newly created score. Today, both student and professor meet in an electronic studio like that pictured here, where sound is produced and recorded by synthesizers and digital processors, and synced with video monitors. Where are these young composers headed in the Postmodernist age? Less often to a performance in a traditional concert hall and more often to Madison Avenue (for television) and Hollywood (for film and video games). Music and entertainment are once again as united as they were in the eighteenth century, when performances were not so much "art" as "entertainment."

LISTEN TO... the film score for *The Social Network*, online.

One of two electronic music studios for teaching undergraduate composition at Yale University. Visible are MIDI (musical instrument digital interface) keyboards and iMac computers.

John Cage (1912–1992) and Chance Music

If everything is more or less of equal value, as Postmodernists would say, why not just leave art to chance? This is essentially what American composer John Cage (Figure 27.3) decided to do. Cage was born in Los Angeles, California, the son of an inventor. He graduated as valedictorian of Los Angeles High School and spent two years at nearby Pomona College before going to Europe to learn more about art, architecture, and music. Arriving in New York City in 1942, he worked variously as a wall washer at the YWCA, a teacher of music and mycology (the science of mushrooms) at the New School for Social Research, and a music director of a modern dance company.

From his earliest days as a musician, Cage had a special affection for percussion instruments and the unusual sounds they could create. His *First Construction (in Metal)* (1939) has six percussionists playing the piano, metal thunder-sheets, ox bells, cowbells, sleigh bells, water gongs, and brake drums, among other things. By 1941, he had collected 300 percussion objects of this kind—anything that might make an unusual noise when struck or shaken. Cage's tinkering with percussive sounds led him to invent the **prepared piano**—a grand piano outfitted with screws, bolts, washers, erasers, and bits of felt and plastic all inserted between the strings. This transformed the piano into a one-person percussion band that could produce a great variety of sounds and noises—twangs, zaps, rattles, thuds, and the like—no two of which were exactly the same in pitch or color. In creating the prepared piano, Cage was merely continuing along the experimental trail blazed by his spiritual mentor, Edgard Varèse: "Years ago, after I decided to devote my life to music, I noticed that people distinguished between noises and sounds. I decided to follow Varèse and fight for noises, to be on the side of the underdog."

Cage's glorification of everyday noise began in earnest during the 1950s. Rather than engage in a titanic struggle to shape the elements of music, as had Beethoven, he decided to sit back, relax, and simply allow noises to occur around him. In creating this sort of intentionally purposeless, undirected music, Cage invented what has come to be called chance music, the ultimate Postmodernist experimentation. In **chance music**, musical events are not carefully predetermined by the composer but occur instead in an unpredictable sequence as the result of such nonmusical decisions as following astrological charts, tossing coins, throwing dice, or randomly shuffling the pages of music to be played. The musical "happening" that results is the sort of spontaneous group experience that flowered during the 1960s. For example, in Cage's work *0'00"* (1962), performed by the composer himself that year, he sliced and prepared vegetables at an onstage table, put them through a food processor, and then drank the juice, all the while amplifying and broadcasting the sound of these activities to the audience (including your author). Cage's declaration that the ordinary noise made by food processing can be "art" is virtually identical in intent to Andy Warhol's glorification of the Campbell's Soup can: Both typify the kind of radical art fashioned during the 1960s in New York City, the epicenter of Postmodernism.

Naturally, music critics called Cage a joker and a charlatan. Most would agree that his "compositions," in and of themselves, are not of great musical value in traditional terms. Nevertheless, by raising profound questions regarding the relationships between human activity, sound, and music, his compositions eloquently articulate his own musical philosophy. By focusing on the chance appearance of ordinary noise, Cage aggressively asks us to reevaluate the basic principles that underlie most Western music: Why must sounds of similar range and color occur one after the other? Why must music have form and unity? Why must it have a

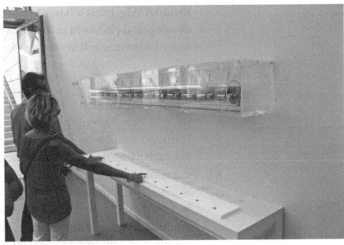

FIGURE 27.3
John Cage's exhibit *Extended Lullaby* (1994) at the Louis Vuitton Foundation art museum in Paris. Visitors passing by create chance music as they press buttons to activate one of twelve mechanical music boxes (at top). The random order of the melodies and the intervals of time between starts always create a new composition. Is this a work of art, a musical composition, or both?

WATCH... a video of a prepared piano, online.

WATCH... John Cage play amplified cacti and other plant matter with a feather, online.

melody? Why must it have "meaning"? Why must it express anything? Why must it develop and climax in some organized way? Why must it be goal oriented, as is so much of human activity in the West?

4'33" (1952)

Cage's "composition" that causes us to focus on these questions most intently is his *4'33"* (see Listening Guide). Here, one or more performers carrying any sort of instrument come on stage, seat themselves, open the "score," and play ... nothing. For each of the three carefully timed movements, there is no notated music, only the indication *Tacet* ("It is silent"). But, as the audience soon realizes, "absolute" silence is virtually impossible to attain, except in outer space. With no organized sound to be heard during the four minutes and thirty-three seconds that follow, the listener gradually becomes aware of the background noise in the hall—a creaking floor, a passing car, a dropped paper clip, an electrical hum. Cage asks us to embrace these random everyday noises—to tune our ears in innocent sonic wonder. Are these sounds not of artistic value, too? What is music? What is noise? What is art?

Needless to say, we haven't asked you to download or stream four minutes and thirty-three seconds of background noise. You can create your own, and John Cage would have liked that. Sit in a "quiet" room for that length of time, and notice what you hear. Perhaps this experiment will make you more aware of how important willful organization is to the art we call music. If nothing else, Cage makes us realize that music is, above all, a form of organized communication between one person and the next and that random background noise can do nothing to communicate human perceptions and feelings.

LISTENING GUIDE

John Cage, *4'33"* (1952)   **No Download (4:33)**

Genre: Chance music

WHAT TO LISTEN FOR: Nothing, except the ambient background noise of the room and whatever external noise may intrude by chance

---

John Adams (b. 1947) and Minimalism

Western classical music—the music of Bach, Beethoven, and Brahms—is typically built from large, carefully placed units. The music has themes (melodies), and as they develop, the listener's emotional response evolves and usually peaks with the climax of the work. A compelling sequence of events leads to a desired end. But what would happen if composers reduced the music to just one or two simple motives and repeated them again and again? What would happen if they focused on what things *are* rather than on what these things might *become*? Such is the approach taken by a group of American Postmodernist composers called the Minimalists.

Minimalism is a style of Postmodernist music, originating in the 1960s, that takes a very small musical unit and repeats it over and over to form a composition.

A three-note melodic cell, a single arpeggio, two alternating chords—these are the sort of "minimal" elements that a composer might introduce, reiterate again and again, modify or expand, and then begin to repeat once more. The basic material is usually simple, tonal, and consonant. By repeating these minimal elements incessantly, at a steady pulse, the composer creates a hypnotic effect; "trance music" is the name sometimes given to this style. The trance-like quality of Minimalist music has influenced rock musicians (The Velvet Underground, Talking Heads, Nine Inch Nails, and Radiohead) and has led to a new genre of pop music variously called "techno," "rave," or "electronic dance music." Minimalism, in both art and music, has been mainly an American movement. Its most successful musical practitioners are Steve Reich (b. 1936), Philip Glass (b. 1937), and John Adams (b. 1947; Figure 27.4).

FIGURE 27.4
John Adams. In 2003, New York City's Lincoln Center held an eight-week "Absolutely Adams" festival to go along with its annual "Mostly Mozart" program.

WATCH... an expansive example of John Adams's Minimalist style.

John Adams (no relation to the presidents) was born in Worcester, Massachusetts, in 1947 and was educated at Harvard. As a student there, he was encouraged to compose in the twelve-tone style of Arnold Schoenberg (see Chapter 25). But, if Adams counted twelve-tone rows by day, he listened to The Beatles in his dorm room at night. After moving to San Francisco after graduation, Adams developed his own eclectic musical style, which blended the learned with the popular and added increasing amounts of Minimalism, then gaining popularity in California. Some of Adams's early scores of the 1980s are strictly Minimalist works, but later ones become more all-embracing; from time to time, vocal chant or a funky bass line, for example, will sound forth within a context of constantly repeating, minimal sonorities. In 2003, Adams received the Pulitzer Prize and three Grammys for his *On the Transmigration of Souls*, which commemorated those killed at the World Trade Center in 2001. Ironically, although Adams is a Minimalist composer, he has been able to extend his ever-repeating blocks of sound into "maximalist" (lengthy) operas, the best known being *Nixon in China* (1987) and *Doctor Atomic* (2005). His most recent composition, the oratorio entitled *The Gospel According to the Other Mary* (2012), runs nearly two and a half hours. As a creature of the Postmodernist age, Adams feels squeezed between the rich classical tradition and the all-powerful world of pop culture:

> I have bad days when I really feel that I'm working in an art form [classical music] that's just not relevant anymore, that had its peak in the years from Vivaldi to Bartók, and now we are just fighting over the crumbs. A really good recording of mine might sell 50,000 copies; that's very rare in classical music. For a rock group, 50,000 CDs sold would be a disaster. (*Harvard Magazine*, 24 July 2007).

Short Ride in a Fast Machine (1986)

To experience Postmodern Minimalism quickly, we turn to an early work by John Adams, commissioned in 1986 by the Pittsburgh Symphony. *Short Ride in a Fast*

Machine is scored for a full orchestra and two electronic keyboard synthesizers. Example 27.1 shows how the music is composed of short (mostly four-note) motives that are continually repeated. This work has five sections (we'll call them laps). In each lap, the machine seems to accelerate, not because the tempo gets faster, but because more and more repeating motives are added. The effect created is that of a powerful, twentieth-century engine firing on all cylinders. Notice how the score, which is used to generate musical sounds, also creates an example of Minimalist art!

EXAMPLE 27.1 Minimalism, musical and visual

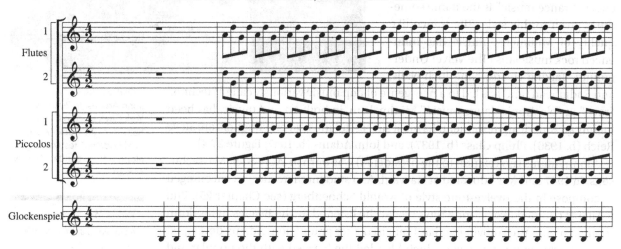

LISTENING GUIDE

John Adams, *Short Ride in a Fast Machine* (1986)   Download 80 (4:01)

Delirando (with exhilaration)

WHAT TO LISTEN FOR: To make a Minimalist suggestion: short, repeating motives

0:00	**Lap 1:** Woodblock, woodwinds, and keyboard synthesizers begin; brasses, snare drum, and glockenspiel are gradually added.
1:04	**Lap 2:** Bass drum "backfires"; motives rise in pitch and become more dissonant.
1:43	**Lap 3:** Starts quietly with sinister repeating motive in bass; syncopation and dissonance increase.
2:30	**Lap 4:** Two-note falling motive in bass
2:53	**Lap 5:** Trumpets play fanfare-like motives (this is the "victory lap").
3:50	Musical vehicle begins another lap but suddenly breaks down.

LISTEN TO ... this selection streaming online.

WATCH ... an Active Listening Guide of this selection online.

DO ... Listening Exercise 27.2, Adams, *Short Ride in a Fast Machine*, online.

Caroline Shaw (b. 1982) and a New Model for Classical Music

Up to this point in our exploration of classical music, we have discussed the music of the past—the past 1,500 years, to be more precise. But what will be the music of the future? Who will be the next Mozart? Where will we find him or her—writing symphonies or video game music? Will it be a Taylor Swift, a Trent Reznor of Beats Music, a Matthew Aucoin who will have an opera premiered at the Metropolitan Opera House in New York City at age twenty-five, or a Caroline Shaw, who won the Pulitzer Prize for Music for her *Partita for 8 Voices* at the age of thirty, the youngest person ever to do so? The unfolding career of Caroline Shaw (Figure 27.5) might suggest a new course of evolution for classical music and a change in the very notion of a composer.

Ironically, prize-winning composer Shaw had no intention of being a composer. Her training in music (at Rice and at Yale) was on the violin, and her aim was to join a resident string quartet or a symphony orchestra. Along the way, she discovered that she could sing at a professional level. So, after graduation from music school in 2008, she moved to New York City to be a freelance musician (by definition, unemployed but willing to work). There, she performed with instrumental, vocal, and dance groups, as an anonymous backup musician for Paul McCartney, and as an occasional busker on the city streets. But most of her time was spent as a singer and composer for the Grammy-winning a cappella ensemble, Roomful of Teeth. Shaw's life, like that of most freelancers, personifies the eclectic pluralism of the Postmodernist musician.

Most societies around the world have no concept of "the composer"—someone who sits waiting for a "eureka" moment and then creates a work of art, fixed forever in notation, for others to perform. The composer-dominated process for Western classical music emerged in the thirteenth century, when musicians were first able to control both pitch and rhythm by recording them in written notation. In most other musical cultures, new compositions emerge out of the processes of group improvisation and performance. Creator and performers are one and the same.

Caroline Shaw, with her performance-rich background, exemplifies this other approach. She doesn't see the composer as musical architect and the performer as mere humble carpenter. Her music often depends on the players at hand and the performance space available, inside or outside. Indeed, Shaw puts very little emphasis on the work of art notated for all time; some of her compositions, such as *Ritornello* (no date), remain intentionally unfinished so that they will continue to evolve through performance. The composition for which she won the Pulitzer Prize was submitted, not as a score, but rather as a live performance in recorded form. To this day, a score of the work is not commercially available.

FIGURE 27.5
Caroline Adelaide Shaw, a violinist, singer, and composer whose music grows out of group performance

Thus, we turn to a recording of "Passacaglia," movement 4, of a set of pieces entitled *Partita for 8 Voices* (see Listening Guide). The term *passacaglia* refers to a dance of the early Baroque era; *partita*, too, takes us back to the Baroque, when it denoted a suite (collection) of dances (see Chapter 9, "Handel and the Orchestral Dance Suite"). But the Baroque influences in Shaw's *Partita for 8 Voices* extend only to the title and no further. Rather, it is an a cappella work for eight solo voices, including her own, in which Shaw attempts to extract new vocal sounds from herself and her fellow singers.

Singing is a collaborative art that has been with us since the dawn of humanity. Is it really possible for a young composer to create *new* sounds through such music? Listen and decide. Shaw's sounds are pure sound; they carry no text. Mixed in are several verbal lines, but, again, these "words" are not what they seem. They carry no real meaning because they are not part of a process of verbal communication. The opening harmony, both social and musical, grows increasingly dissonant, crying out for attention; verbal unity (one speaker) becomes verbal "dyscommunication," in which no one is listening to anyone else. Is this piece simply an exploration of new sounds, or is it a metaphor for modern urban life?

LISTENING GUIDE

"Passacaglia," from *Partita for 8 Voices* (2013)   Download 81 (5:55)

Genre: A cappella choral work

Form: Ternary (**ABA'**)

WHAT TO LISTEN FOR: Whispers, shouts, cries, feigned electronic sounds, nonsensical words; there seem to be as many new sounds here as there are people singing.

0:00	**A**	Eight a cappella voices sing major triads that gradually expand to seventh chords.
0:40		Chords repeat, but at a louder volume and level of intensity.
1:14		Chords become cries.
1:48		Oscillating two-pitch ostinato emerges as dissonance grows around it.
2:34	**B**	Speaking voice enters: "The eighty-sixth, eighty-seventh, and eighty-eighth points...."
3:04		Other speaking and singing voices enter, with increasingly chaotic "dyscommunication."
3:32		Speaking voices alone, interrupted for a moment by echoing silence
3:50		Singing voices begin to reenter.
4:32		Crescendo of voices that sounds like electronic distortion
4:39	**A'**	Vocal cries return.
5:15		Consonant triads return and then dissolve.
5:38		Final sound incorporates bass re-creation of Mongolian throat singing.

LISTEN TO ... this selection streaming online.

WATCH ... an Active Listening Guide of this selection online.

WATCH ... the premiere performance of this selection online.

Contemporary artists don't hear or see things the way the rest of us do. By the act of creation, they ask us to embrace their vision of the human experience. They invite us to think outside the box by shifting the position of the box, hoping that succeeding generations will agree to that change as we, over time, have come to love the art, for example, of Monet and Picasso, and the novels of Virginia Woolf. Walk into any museum of contemporary art, and you will find some works that are inspiring and others that are truly laughable. What about "Passacaglia"? Will Shaw's work endure, or will she be only a "youngest to win Pulitzer Prize" footnote to music history? Who will decide if she remains in the museum of musical performance? You, the informed listening public.

A Bonus Work and a Test: Christopher Rouse, Flute Concerto, Fifth Movement, *Amhrán* (1993)

Up to this point on our tour of the history of Western classical music, works have been described and their meaning suggested to you. Now it's your turn to be both music critic and author. Information about the following piece by American composer Christopher Rouse will not be provided, except to say that it is the fifth movement of a concerto for flute, commissioned jointly by flutist Carol Wincenc, of the Juilliard School of Music, and the Detroit Symphony Orchestra. Wincenc performs in this recording.

The point of this exercise is to apply your listening skills to a work that is new to you. Listen to the piece, and focus first on the technical aspects and broader stylistic issues. What instruments are playing? What creates the mood? Does the melody seem modular (antecedent–consequent phrases, for example), or does it just wander? Are the harmonies consonant or dissonant? What is the texture? Does the style seem Classical, Romantic, Modernist, or a mixture? Is this classical or popular music? Is this music from the Western or Eastern tradition?

More important, listen emotionally, asking yourself questions such as these: Do I like this piece? What do I feel as I listen? Do memories come to mind? (If so, of what? Of people? Of places?) Do I feel myself transported? (If so, where?) Do I see colors? What is the composer trying to communicate to me, and do I want to hear it? Do I want to listen to this piece again?

Instead of giving you a Listening Guide, you are asked to create one, using the framework here. The online Active Listening Guide will ask you additional questions that will help you complete your own guide.

LISTENING GUIDE

Christopher Rouse, Concerto for Flute (1993)   Download 82 (5:42)

Fifth movement, *Amhrán* (*Song*)

WHAT TO LISTEN FOR: Identify the major events of the piece, and prepare a timed chart or guide describing what occurred in the music to make you hear them as important points of articulation.

LISTEN TO ... this selection streaming online.

WATCH ... an Active Listening Guide of this selection online.

Of course, if you're still curious about the piece, you can search for Rouse's own interpretation online.

And yet, a composer's explanation may not be the final word as to how the music works its magic: Some things about music simply cannot be explained. If they could, the magic wouldn't be magical.

KEY WORDS

Postmodernism (384)

electronic music (385)

synthesizer (385)

musique concrète (385)

computer music (387)

sampling (387)

scratching (387)

prepared piano (389)

chance music (389)

Minimalism (390)

 Join us on Facebook at Listening to Music with Craig Wright

PRACTICE ... your understanding of this chapter's concepts by comparing Checklists of Musical Style for all historic eras, completing a Musical Style Quiz for the Modern era, and working once more with the chapter's Active Listening Guides online.

DO ... online multiple-choice and critical thinking quizzes that your instructor may assign for a grade.

CHECKLIST OF MUSICAL STYLE   *Postmodern: 1945–present*

REPRESENTATIVE COMPOSERS

Varèse

Cage

Glass

Reich

Adams

Shaw

Rouse

PRINCIPAL GENRES

No common genres; each work of art creates a genre unique to itself

Nearly impossible to generalize in terms of musical style; major stylistic trends not yet discernible

Barriers between high art and low art removed; all art judged to be of more or less equal value—symphony orchestras play video game music

Experimentation with electronic music and computer-generated sound

Previously accepted fundamentals of music, such as discrete pitches and division of octave into twelve equal pitches, often abandoned

Narrative music (goal-oriented music) rejected

Chance music permits random "happenings" and noises from the environment to shape a musical work

Introduction of visual and performance media into the written musical score

Instruments from outside the tradition of Western classical music (for example, electric guitar, sitar, kazoo) prescribed in the score

Experimentation with new notational styles within musical scores (for example, sketches, diagrams, prose instructions)

AMERICAN POPULAR Music

part SEVEN

AMERICAN POPULAR MUSIC

1880　　*1890*　　*1900*　　*1910*　　*1920*　　*1930*　　*1940*

1880s–1890s
Songs of Stephen Foster enjoy popularity

1880s–1890s
Blues originates in the South

1890–1910
Tin Pan Alley becomes center for creation of popular songs

1890s
Scott Joplin's ragtime music becomes the rage

1925
Louis Armstrong makes his first jazz recording in Chicago

1925
F. Scott Fitzgerald publishes *The Great Gatsby*

1924
Bessie Smith makes her first blues recording in New York

1924
George Gershwin composes *Rhapsody in Blue*

1920s
"Roaring Twenties," or "Jazz Age"

1935
George Gershwin premieres *Porgy and Bess*

1900–1920
Classic New Orleans–style jazz originates

1929
Stock market crash; beginning of Great Depression

1914–1918
World War I

Every nation has its popular music—the music that all the people, not merely an educated few, know and love. Today, downloads of popular music outsell those of classical music by more than twenty to one. For the most part, popular music is simple and direct, and the listener needs little or no formal training to appreciate it. Popular music is intended to be enjoyed in the moment, without particular concern for lasting artistic value.

The United States is among the most heterogeneous populations in the world, and American popular music reflects this richness and diversity. Folk ballads, fiddle tunes, Native American songs, country songs, cowboy songs, blues, ragtime, gospel hymns, military band marches, parlor songs, Broadway show tunes, jazz, swing, film and video game music, rhythm and blues, rock, hip-hop, electropop, and rap—these are but some of the many musical genres that originated here to form the rich American vernacular tradition. With the advent of jazz in the early twentieth century, American popular music gained prominence throughout the world. Even classical composers such as Debussy, Ravel, and Stravinsky were captivated, incorporating the infectious rhythms of jazz into their "learned" scores. Today, American—and American-influenced—popular music continues to dominate the airwaves around the globe. Although now French rappers and Korean remakes of Michael Jackson-style pop songs have come on the scene, the original designers of these styles, and many more, were, in the words of Bruce Springsteen, "Born in the USA."

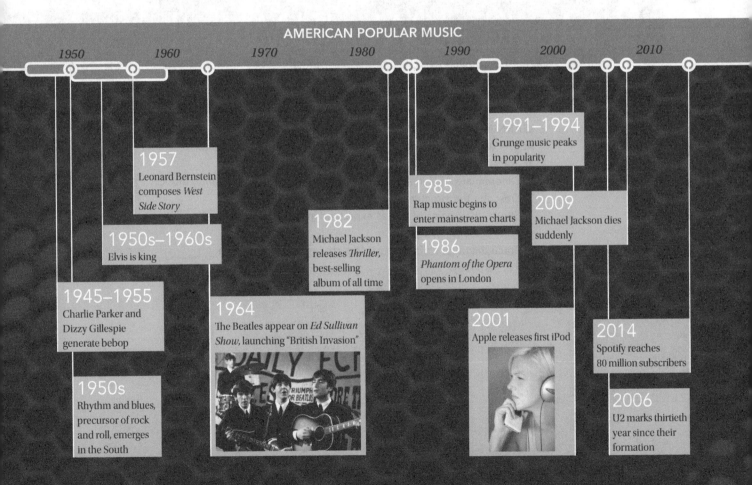

AMERICAN POPULAR MUSIC

1950   1960   1970   1980   1990   2000   2010

1991–1994
Grunge music peaks in popularity

1957
Leonard Bernstein composes *West Side Story*

1985
Rap music begins to enter mainstream charts

2009
Michael Jackson dies suddenly

1982
Michael Jackson releases *Thriller*, best-selling album of all time

1950s–1960s
Elvis is king

1986
Phantom of the Opera opens in London

1945–1955
Charlie Parker and Dizzy Gillespie generate bebop

1964
The Beatles appear on *Ed Sullivan Show*, launching "British Invasion"

2001
Apple releases first iPod

2014
Spotify reaches 80 million subscribers

1950s
Rhythm and blues, precursor of rock and roll, emerges in the South

2006
U2 marks thirtieth year since their formation

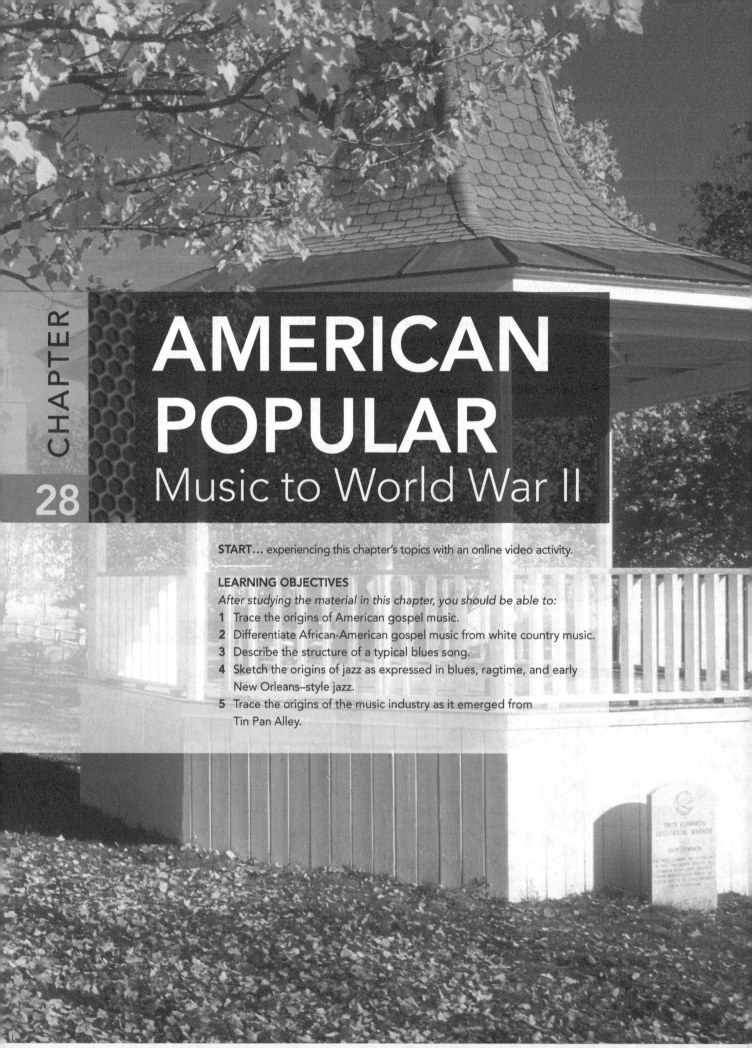

AMERICAN POPULAR
Music to World War II

START… experiencing this chapter's topics with an online video activity.

LEARNING OBJECTIVES
After studying the material in this chapter, you should be able to:
1 Trace the origins of American gospel music.
2 Differentiate African-American gospel music from white country music.
3 Describe the structure of a typical blues song.
4 Sketch the origins of jazz as expressed in blues, ragtime, and early New Orleans–style jazz.
5 Trace the origins of the music industry as it emerged from Tin Pan Alley.

Early American Psalms, Hymns, and Gospel Singing

America was settled in the early seventeenth century by passionate, devout people who were seeking freedom for their particular religious beliefs. They were serious folk, and the music they brought with them, both written and aural, was mostly religious music. Of course, people sang and played what we call "secular" popular music—fiddle tunes, sea shanties, work songs, and ballads, for example—but this kind of popular music wasn't published in America until the early nineteenth century. People may have sung everywhere, but the one place in which they sang from written scores was church.

Among the earliest books, musical or otherwise, to be published in America was the **Bay Psalm Book** (Cambridge, Massachusetts, 1640), a **Psalter** (Book of Psalms) to which homophonic and polyphonic settings of psalm texts were affixed in later editions. During the eighteenth century, the old psalm tunes of New England were gradually replaced by newer hymns, accompanied by church organs. These hymns gradually journeyed south and west, more or less following the path of the Appalachian Trail. As they migrated, new hymns were added to the common repertoire. Prior to the American Civil War (1861–1865), these tunes were sung not only in free white churches but also within enslaved African-American communities, providing a springboard for spirituals and gospel music. Whites generally sang from books; blacks, from an unwritten oral tradition.

Such a bicultural mode of performance can be seen in the history of the American gospel hymn "Amazing Grace." Although known by all, "Amazing Grace" has a generally unknown history, owing largely to the complexity of the story. The words originated in the British Isles in 1748, the product of seaman John Newton, who penned them as the result of a spiritual conversion he experienced after being rescued from a violent storm. Originally a slave trader, Newton went on to become a clergyman and an abolitionist. The text of Newton's hymn made its way to America, where in 1835 South Carolinian William Walker supplied it with a new melody, a tune that Walker adopted and adapted from a well-known New England song called "New Britain." (Supplying a new text with an old tune was commonplace in early-nineteenth-century America; that's how "The Star-Spangled Banner" came about in 1814.) Eventually, Englishman Newton's text with American southerner Walker's borrowed melody was published in *The Southern Harmony* in New Haven, Connecticut, in 1835 and thereafter became a beloved favorite (Figure 28.1). If this sounds like the script for a film or a Broadway show, you're right. The film *Amazing Grace* appeared in 2006, and a show with the same name opened on Broadway in 2015.

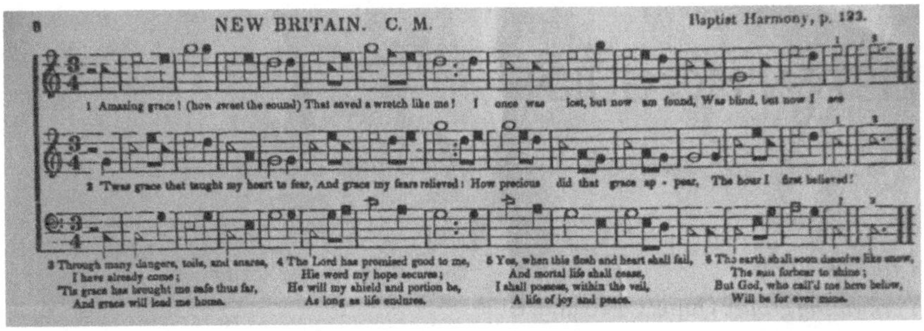

But the story continues. Although "Amazing Grace" has been published countless times, the music continues to evolve.

FIGURE 28.1

A photo of "Amazing Grace" as it appeared in *The Southern Harmony*, 1835. The odd shape of the notes engendered what is called shape note singing, a process widespread among semimusically literate congregations in early America. If singers could recognize the shape of the note and knew musical solfège (do-re-mi, and so on), they wouldn't have to read a clef. "Amazing Grace" has six stanzas, or strophes, all of which are given on the page.

Because this tune was disseminated partly through oral tradition, regional dialects have emerged and will continue to do so. Recall the version of the tune you have in your head, find it on the Internet, or watch a YouTube video of President Barack Obama (who appears to have his own version) singing it, and compare them with the original printed version from 1835 in Example 28.1.

EXAMPLE 28.1 "Amazing Grace"

A - ma - zing grace, how sweet the sound, that saved a wretch like me. I

once was lost but now am found, was blind but now I see. see.

What accounts for the power, indeed the staying power, of "Amazing Grace" (see Listening Guide)? Why have generations loved this melody? First of all, the tune is simple but not square; it consists of two *seven*-bar phrases—unusual for a popular song. In range it outlines exactly an octave, and the tonic triad is strongly present. In terms of a scale, the melody is pentatonic (here G, A, C, D, E, [G]), the sound of which takes us from the classical realm to the world of folk music. The tempo is slow, and the meter is triple (weak *strong*, weak *strong*), which adds a comforting, lilting quality to the listening experience. Finally, not only do words such as "sweet the sound" add emotional impact (music sung to a text has the capacity for a "double whammy" of musical and syntactical perception), there are also verbal disjunctions ("lost" and "blind") that resolve (to "found" and "see") as a musical dissonance might resolve to consonance. Pun intended, this is an amazing tune—so simple, so elevating, and so eternally perfect.

LISTENING GUIDE

"Amazing Grace" (text, John Newton, 1748; music, William Walker, 1835)   Download 83 (4:33)

Genre: Hymn

Form: Strophic

Performing group: Quire, Cleveland, Ohio

WHAT TO LISTEN FOR: You know the tune, but does your version agree with the 1835 original that is sung here?

Stanza 1

0:00	Soprano soloist	Amazing grace! (how sweet the sound)
		That saved a wretch like me!

I once was lost, but now am found,

Was blind, but now I see.

Stanza 2

0:45	Choir in homophony	'Twas grace that taught my heart to fear,
		And grace my fears relieved;
		How precious did that grace appear,
		The hour I first believed!

Stanza 3

1:30	Tenor soloist	Through many dangers, toils, and snares,
		I have already come;
		'Tis grace has brought me safe thus far,
		And grace will lead me home.

Stanza 4

2:15	Choir	The Lord has promised good to me,
		His word my hope secures;
		He will my shield and portion be,
		As long as life endures.

Stanza 5

3:01	Unison (monophony)	Yes, when this flesh and heart shall fail,
		And mortal life shall cease,
		I shall possess, within the veil,
		A life of joy and peace.

Stanza 6

3:47	Choir in homophony	The earth shall soon dissolve like snow,
		The sun forbear to shine;
		But God, who call'd me here below,
		Will be for ever mine.

LISTEN TO ... this selection streaming online.

WATCH ... an Active Listening Guide of this selection online.

Hymns such as "Amazing Grace" became deeply embedded in the oral memory of Americans, particularly in the South. Among African-Americans before the Civil War, social gatherings and certain musical instruments were controlled or proscribed, for fear they would foment rebellion within this enslaved population. The singing of hymns in churches, however, was permitted, and hymns became the core of the musical, social, and spiritual experience of blacks in the South. When sung in a black community, texts that referred to "crossing on over the river Jordan" or that enjoined "let my people go" would be heard as encouragement, or at least hope, of a release from the slavery of this life. In black communities, the hymn might be "Africanized" in several ways: The words might be parsed out between leader and chorus in "call and response" style (see below under "Blues"), the tune might be syncopated or "jazzed up," or the accompaniment might be converted to a blues harmony, and, in the end, all would be sung with joyous hand-clapping, foot-stomping enthusiasm. In printed form, this is a hymn; when Africanized in this fashion, the hymn becomes **gospel music**. In the course of time, "The Star-Spangled Banner" (1814) became America's official national anthem and "Amazing Grace" (1835), its unofficial gospel hymn.

Yet, such is the protean power of music that the same "Amazing Grace" would sound very different in a white Appalachian church or outdoor revivalist meeting. Supplied with two counter voices—one a harmony-implying bass below and the other a "close-harmony" voice, within an octave around the melody, above—and accompanied by a guitar or fiddle, the tune stuck closer to its published original (see Example 28.1). This style of Appalachian-hill country singing has been called, since the 1940s, country music.

Country Music

Country music can be defined as the traditional repertoire of religious and folk music flourishing in the Appalachian region of America. The songs, mostly about love and life's disappointments, came mainly from the Anglo-Irish settlers. They were mostly folk **ballads**, narrative songs in strophic form that told a (usually sad) tale in an unemotional way. Appalachian ballads were at first sung by voice alone or voice accompanied by a **fiddle** (an inexpensive violin played without much vibrato). Sometimes a mountain dulcimer or an autoharp might also be used or a **banjo**, a four- or five-string plucked folk instrument of African-American origin. Eventually, all of them were replaced by one or more guitars, an instrument with greater resonance and range.

The style of country music usually involves a vibrato-less voice, which imparts a "lonesome" quality. The singer often slides between pitches, a musical gesture that seems congruous with the many diphthongs (two sounds on one vowel) of a typical southern drawl. Harmonies are uncomplicated in the extreme, usually consisting of only two (I and V) or three (I, IV, and V) chords. This harmonic simplicity likely derived from the rudimentary skills of early country singers, who could strum only these chords on the banjo or guitar. Unlike African-American gospel music, rarely is there a strong beat or drums in traditional country music.

From rural roots in the Appalachian Mountains, country music has grown into a mega-industry. There are country music stars, country radio stations, and a country music city (Nashville) with a Country Music Hall of Fame. While CD sales of almost all genres of music—pop as well as classical—have steadily declined in recent years in favor of digital downloads, those of country music have actually increased. Garth Brooks, for example, has sold 150 million albums. Each week, according to a recent survey, more than 77 million adults tune in to a country music station.

Whatever one's response to country music—people seem either to love it or to hate it—the explosion of the genre has had one undeniable consequence: It has elevated the female vocalist to a position of primacy as a recording artist. The process began with Sara Carter (1898–1979), the lead singer of the influential Carter family, and continued with June Carter Cash (1929–2003; wife of Johnny Cash), Loretta

Lynn (1935–), Dolly Parton (1945–), Reba McEntire (1955–), Shania Twain (1965–), Carrie Underwood (1983–), and Taylor Swift (1989–). Oddly, the same ascent has happened with gospel singers, for the majority of the best of them have been women. Whether in the context of the white Appalachian barn dance or the African-American church service, women were on an equal footing with men regarding access to education, opportunity, and encouragement, and, in this domain of popular music, they came to receive, in the word of Aretha Franklin (1942–), "R-E-S-P-E-C-T."

Blues

Why, where, and how the blues originated is a story that will probably never be fully told. We cannot even hazard a guess as to who named this style of singing "the blues," though the expression "the blue devils" had been used to describe a melancholy mood since Shakespeare's time. All that can be said with certainty is that the **blues** is a form of black folksong that originated in the South sometime during the 1880s and 1890s. Like all true folk music, the blues was passed along by oral tradition, with one performer learning directly from another without benefit of written notation. Despite having nothing written or recorded, tracing the ancestry of the blues leads to two very different sources. First, and most important, was the African work song and field holler (or cry) of the black laborers, which bequeathed to the blues a wailing vocal style, a particular scale (see Example 28.2), and a body of subjects or topics for singing the blues. The second was the Anglo-American folk ballad, which imparted the regular, predictable pattern of chord changes that characterizes the blues. Blues was first printed as sheet music in 1912 ("The Memphis Blues" and "The Dallas Blues"), and the first blues recordings, most of which were made by black artists, were cut in 1920.

A singer sings the blues to relieve a melancholic soul and to give vent to feelings of pain and anger. Poverty, loneliness, oppression, family troubles, infidelity, and separation are typical subjects of the blues. The lyrics are arranged in a succession of stanzas (usually three to six in a song), and each stanza is made up of three lines. The second line normally repeats the first line, and the third line rounds off the idea and concludes with a rhyme. At the end of each line, an instrument inserts a short response, called an **instrumental break**, as a way of replying to the cry of the voice. Thus, the blues perpetuates the age-old African performing style of **call and response**, the form of which is shown in the following stanza from the "Preaching Blues":

Call	Response
The blues is a lowdown, achin' heart disease,	(instrumental break)
The blues is a lowdown, achin' heart disease,	(instrumental break)
It's like consumption, killin' you by degrees.	(instrumental break)

By the 1920s, the guitar had become the accompanying instrument favored by blues singers. It could supply not only a solid harmonic support but also an expressive "second voice" to answer the previous call of the singer. "Bending" the guitar strings at the frets produced a moaning, mournful sound in keeping with the general feeling of the blues.

The object of the blues is not so much to tell a story, as in the white folk ballad of country music, as to express pure emotion—verbal meaning is less important than vocal expression. The voice sometimes moans and sometimes shouts, is often hoarse and raspy, and always twists and bends the pitch. Instead of hitting a tone directly, the singer usually approaches it by sliding from above or below. In addition, a particular scale (Example 28.2), called the **blues scale**, is used in place of a major or a minor scale. The blues scale has seven notes, but the third, fifth, and seventh notes are sometimes flat, sometimes natural, and sometimes in between. The three "in-between" notes are called **blue notes**. The blues scale is an integral part of virtually all African-American folk music, including the work song and the spiritual, as well as the blues.

LISTEN TO...

Example 28.2 online.

EXAMPLE 28.2 Blues scale

⌐ = blue note

Good blues singers indulge in much spontaneous expression, adding and removing text and improvising around the basic melody as the spirit moves them. Such liberties are possible because these mournful songs are usually built upon the bedrock of the twelve-bar blues harmonic pattern that repeats, over and over, one statement for each stanza of text. Singing the blues most often involves singing vocal lines in a slow $\frac{4}{4}$ above this simple I–IV–I–V–I chord progression in the following manner:

Vocal Lines:	Line 1			Break		Line 2		Break		Line 3			Break
Chord:	I———————————				IV———		I———		V———			I
Measure:	1	2	3	4	5	6	7	8	9	10	11	12	

Sometimes additional chords are inserted between the basic ones for greater harmonic interest. Yet, the simplicity of the pattern is its greatest strength. Thousands of tunes have been constructed over this basic harmonic progression, by solo singers, solo pianists, New Orleans–style jazz combos, and rock and roll bands.

Bessie Smith (1894–1937)

Although there have been and are many great blues singers—Blind Lemon Jefferson, Lead Belly, Nina Simone, and B. B. King, to name just a few—perhaps the greatest of them all was Bessie Smith (Figure 28.2), called the "Empress of the Blues." A native of Chattanooga, Tennessee, Smith was "discovered" singing in a bar in Selma, Alabama, and was brought to New York to record for Columbia Records. The blues recordings she made between 1924 and 1927 catapulted her to the top of the popular music world. In her first full year as a recording artist, her disks sold more than 2 million copies, and she became the highest-paid black artist, male or female, of the day. In fact, all of the great blues singers who achieved recording success during the 1920s were women, perhaps because so many blues texts have to do with male-female relations and are written from the woman's perspective. Tragically, Smith's career was cut short by a fatal automobile accident in 1937.

"Lost Your Head Blues" (see Listening Guide), recorded in 1926 in New York, reveals the huge, sweeping voice of Bessie Smith. (Perhaps the closest modern

FIGURE 28.2
Bessie Smith, the "Empress of the Blues," was a physically powerful woman with an exceptionally flexible, expressive voice.

equivalents are Adele and Amy Winehouse.) She was capable of great power, even harshness, one moment and then in the next breath could deliver a phrase of tender beauty. She could hit a note right on the head if she wanted to, or bend, dip, and glide into the pitch, as she does, for example, on the words *days*, *long*, and *nights* in the last stanza of "Lost Your Head Blues." In this recording, Bessie Smith is backed by Fletcher Henderson (piano) and Joe Smith (trumpet). The piece begins with a four-bar introduction, after which the voice enters and the twelve-bar blues harmony starts up, with one full statement of the pattern for each of the five stanzas of text. Smith continually varies her melody above the repeating bass by means of vocal inflections and off-key shadings. Her expressive vocal line, the soulful, improvised responses played by the trumpet, and the repeating twelve-bar harmony carried by the piano are the essence of the blues.

LISTENING GUIDE

"Lost Your Head Blues"

Download 84 (2:57)

Sung by Bessie Smith (recorded 1926)

Genre: Twelve-bar blues

Form: Strophic

WHAT TO LISTEN FOR: As jazz musicians say, "Follow the chord changes," which is possible here because the blues harmony changes slowly and in a regular pattern.

0:00	Four-bar introduction	
0:11	Line 1: I was with you baby when you did not have a dime. (trumpet)	
	Chords: I _____	
0:22	Line 2: I was with you baby when you did not have a dime. (trumpet)	
	Chords: IV _____ I_____	
0:32	Line 3: Now since you got plenty money you have throw'd your good gal down. (trumpet)	
	Chords: V _____ I_____	

For the next three stanzas, the chord changes and instrumental breaks continue as above; in the last stanza, the breaks come in the middle of the lines as well as at the end.

0:44   Once ain't for always, two ain't for twice.

Once ain't for always, two ain't for twice.

When you get a good gal, you better treat her nice.

1:16   When you were lonesome, I tried to treat you kind.

When you were lonesome, I tried to treat you kind.

But since you've got money, it's done changed your mind.

1:49   I'm gonna leave baby, ain't gonna say goodbye.

I'm gonna leave baby, ain't gonna say goodbye.

But I'll write you and tell you the reason why.

(Continued)

2:20   Days* are lonesome, nights are long*.

Days are lonesome, nights are so long.

I'm a good ol' gal, but I've just been treated wrong.

*Note the vocal "slides" here.

LISTEN TO ... this selection streaming online.

WATCH ... an Active Listening Guide of this selection online.

DO ... Listening Exercise 28.1, Bessie Smith, "Lost Your Head Blues," online.

To say that the blues has had a great impact on popular music is tantamount to saying that the ocean is large. Besides blues specialists, such as Robert Johnson (1911–1938) and B. B. King (1925–2015), virtually every pop singer has embraced or borrowed the conventions of the genre at one time or another. So, too, have all the jazz greats, from Louis Armstrong ("Gut Bucket Blues") at the beginning of the twentieth century to Wynton Marsalis (*Marsalis and Clapton Play the Blues*) at the beginning of the twenty-first. Equally important, it was from the blues and its off-spring, rhythm and blues, that rock and roll was born.

Early Jazz

Jazz has been called "America's classical music." Like America itself, jazz is an amalgam, a mixture of many different influences. Foremost among these, of course, are the traditional musical practices of Africa, as manifested in the gospel music and blues of African-Americans in the South. But jazz also contains European elements: marches and hymns, in addition to fiddle tunes and dances from the British Isles, as preserved in the folk music of white Appalachia. The complex rhythms, percussive sounds, and bending vocal style of African-American music merged with the four-square phrasing and strong, regular harmonies of the Anglo-American tradition to produce a dynamic new sound.

Jazz is a lively, energetic music with pulsating rhythms and scintillating syncopations, usually played by either a small instrumental ensemble (a combo) or a larger group (a big band). Jazz originated as African-American popular music, much of it improvised spontaneously. And, like most pop music today, musicians learned jazz by listening to others play it (in this case, in cafés and clubs) or from recordings, but not from written notation. Yet, during the twentieth century, jazz came to demand great technical virtuosity and developed its own body of music theory and historical criticism—both hallmarks of an art in a mature "classical stage." For this reason, jazz is now often called "America's classical music." Today, there are concert halls to hear jazz, such as Preservation Hall in New Orleans and Rose Hall in Lincoln Center, New York, a bastion of traditional classical music. Even the archetypical jazz club, the Blue Note Café in downtown New York City, now has multiple outlets stretching from Milan to Tokyo. What began about 1910 as an alternative-culture music produced by minority outsiders has, over a century later, gone mainstream and engendered a global audience.

Ragtime: A Precursor of Jazz

Ragtime music was an immediate precursor of jazz and shares with it many of the same rhythmic features. For black musicians, "to rag" meant to play or sing music in a heavily syncopated, jazzy style—with "ragged time." Ragtime music originated in brothels, saloons, and dance halls during the 1890s, and the jaunty, upbeat sound of ragtime captured the spirit of that age. Most rags were written by black pianists who played in houses of ill repute because it was almost impossible in those years for black musicians to find employment elsewhere. First published in 1897, piano rags took America by storm, with more than 2,000 titles appearing in print by the end of World War I. Sold as sheet music of a thin page or two, piano rags moved quickly from the saloon into middle-class homes, where musically literate amateurs played them on the upright parlor piano.

The undisputed "King of Ragtime" was Scott Joplin (1868–1917) (Figure 28.3). The son of a slave, Joplin managed to acquire for himself a solid grounding in classical music while he earned a living playing in honky-tonk bars in and around St. Louis, Missouri. In 1899, he published "Maple Leaf Rag," which sold an astonishing 1 million copies. Though he went on to write other immensely popular rags, such as "The Entertainer" and "Peacherine Rag," Joplin gradually shed the image of barroom pianist and moved to New York to compose rag-based opera.

"Maple Leaf Rag," which was immensely popular at the turn of the twentieth century, is typical of the style of Joplin and his fellow ragtime composers. Its form is similar to that of an American military march of those same years, consisting of a succession of phrases (strains), each sixteen bars in length. The harmony, however, is distinctly European, moving in purposeful chord progressions with slight chromatic inflections—Joplin knew his Schubert and Chopin! Yet, what makes ragtime so infectious is its bouncy, syncopated rhythm. Syncopation, of course, is the momentary displacement of an accent from on the beat to off the beat. In piano ragtime, the left hand keeps a regular "um-pah, um-pah" beat, usually in duple meter, while the right hand lays on syncopations against it. In the following example from "Maple Leaf Rag," syncopation (**S**) occurs when long notes (either an eighth note or two sixteenth notes tied together) sound off (between) the steady eighth-note beats of the bass.

EXAMPLE 28.3 Syncopation in "Maple Leaf Rag"

As you follow the Listening Guide, you may be interested to know that "Maple Leaf Rag" is performed here by composer Scott Joplin himself. This recording was originally made in 1916—not on a vinyl record, but on a mechanical piano roll, and only later transferred to vinyl and ultimately to digital format. You'll likely be surprised by the slow tempo, but as Joplin warned in one of his publications, "Never play ragtime fast."

LISTENING GUIDE

Scott Joplin, "Maple Leaf Rag" (1899)   Download 85 (3:21)

Genre: Ragtime

Form: **AABBACCDD**

WHAT TO LISTEN FOR: A listening experience on two planes: Hear the march-like regularity of the left hand as opposed to the syncopated abandon of the right.

0:00	**A** stated and repeated
0:44	**B** stated and repeated
1:29	**A** returns.
1:50	**C** stated and repeated
2:34	**D** stated and repeated

LISTEN TO ... this selection streaming online.

WATCH ... an Active Listening Guide of this selection online.

New Orleans Jazz

Although jazz sprang up almost simultaneously in towns up and down the Mississippi River, its focal point and probable place of origin was New Orleans. This city was the home of many early jazz greats—King Oliver (1885–1938), Jelly Roll Morton (1890–1941), and Louis Armstrong (1901–1971)—and it also boasted an exceptionally dynamic and varied musical life that encouraged the development of new musical styles. Culturally, New Orleans looked more toward France and the Caribbean than it did toward the Anglo-American North. The city air was filled not only with opera tunes, marches, and ballroom dances from imperial France but also with African-American blues and ragtime, as well as Cuban dance rhythms. The end of the Spanish-American War (1898) brought a flood of used military band instruments into secondhand shops in New Orleans (then the closest American city to Cuba) at prices that were affordable even to impoverished blacks. Musicians, black and white alike, found ready employment in ballrooms of the well-to-do, in the bars and brothels of Storyville (a thirty-eight-square-block red-light district in the center of the city), and at parades, picnics, weddings, and funerals associated with the many New Orleans societies and fraternal orders. Music was everywhere. And so, today, whether in the middle of the street, in jazz clubs, or in Preservation Hall, New Orleans–style jazz remains ubiquitous.

What marks the sound of **New Orleans jazz**? Syncopation combined with a free treatment of melody. A given march, rag, blues, or popular melody is played with off-beat accents and a spontaneous sliding into and around the pitches of the tune. The rag had strains of sixteen bars; many popular songs of the period had four four-bar phrases; and the traditional blues, as we have seen, consisted of a steady stream of twelve-bar units. Within the square, formal confines of these four-, eight-, twelve-, and sixteen-bar patterns, the New Orleans jazz combo found a security that allowed solo instruments the greatest sort of freedom of expression. The melody was usually played in some jazzed-up way by a cornet or trumpet; a clarinet supported this lead instrument and further embellished the tune; a trombone added counterpoint against the melody in a lower range; down below, a tuba set the harmonies if the group was marching, but if it did not, that job was handed over to a string bass, piano, banjo, and/or guitar. These same instruments (tuba, string bass, piano, banjo, and guitar), along with the drums, formed the **rhythm section** because they not only set the harmony but also helped the drums give out the beat in a steady fashion. Finally, New Orleans–style bands, then and now, rarely play from written music. Instead, they count, or feel, when the chords must change, and they improvise and refashion the tune to make it fit those changes.

Louis Armstrong (1901–1971)

When the U.S. government closed the brothels and gambling houses of Storyville in 1917, many places of employment for jazz musicians disappeared. Performers began to look elsewhere for work—in New York, Chicago, even Los Angeles. One of those who eventually made his way to Chicago was Louis "Satchmo" (short for "Satchelmouth") Armstrong (Figure 28.4). Armstrong was born in New Orleans in 1901, and, in 1923, he followed his mentor, King Oliver, to Chicago to join the latter's Creole Jazz Band. By this time, Armstrong was already recognized by his peers as the best jazz trumpeter alive. He soon formed his own band in Chicago, the Hot Five, to make what became a series of landmark recordings. When the vogue of classic New Orleans–style jazz gave way to the sound of the swing band about 1930, Armstrong moved to New York, where he fronted (played as featured soloist in) a number of large bands. He was an early practitioner of "scat singing"—singing nonsense syllables in jazz style—and eventually became known as much for the gravelly sound of his voice, in songs such as "Hello Dolly" and "Mack the Knife," as for his trumpet playing. His last years were spent in almost continual travel, sent around the world by the U.S. State Department as "Ambassador Satchmo." He died at his home in Queens, New York, in 1971.

Although cut in Chicago, Armstrong's early discs are classics of New Orleans–style jazz. The tune "Willie the Weeper" was recorded by Armstrong's expanded band, his Hot Seven, in 1927 in Chicago. We'll never know who "composed" the piece. Like much folk music, and African-American music, in particular, "Willie the Weeper" was worked out by the entire group, following two basic chord progressions—the first in a major key and the second in a minor key. Certainly, none of "Willie the Weeper" was ever written down in musical notation. As Armstrong's drummer, Baby Dodds, said, "We weren't a bunch of fellows to write down anything."

Instead, Armstrong and his Hot Seven relied on "head arrangements," a combination of aural memory (remembering the tune and the harmony) and spontaneous improvisation, in which each member of the group took his turn as soloist. Here, the tune in major is sixteen bars long, while the contrasting one in minor lasts eight bars. In a jazz piece of this sort (see Listening Guide), each presentation of the tune is called a **chorus** (different from a chorus in a song), whether played by a soloist or the entire ensemble. The underlying chord progressions and the outline of the melody provide a framework for the spontaneous improvisations of the players during each chorus. Call it what you will—precise abandon, bonded independence, controlled chaos—the joyful exuberance of these extraordinary musicians cannot be denied.

LISTENING GUIDE

"Willie the Weeper"   Download 86 (3:14)

Performed by Louis Armstrong and his Hot Seven (recorded 1927)

Genre: New Orleans jazz

WHAT TO LISTEN FOR: How these skilled instrumentalists play with precise spontaneity, their free improvisations kept in check by the rigid structure of eight- or sixteen-bar phrases

0:00	Four-bar introduction
0:05	Chorus 1 (16 bars): Full ensemble; trumpet (Armstrong) and trombone play the tune.
0:25	Chorus 2: Armstrong varies tune.
0:46	Minor chorus 1 (8 bars): Trombone and tuba play tune.
0:57	Minor chorus 2: Trombone and tuba repeat tune.
1:07	Chorus 3: Trombone solo
1:28	Chorus 4: Extraordinary clarinet solo
1:49	Minor chorus 3: Trumpet solo
1:59	Minor chorus 4: Piano solo
2:09	Chorus 5: Guitar solo
2:29	Chorus 6: Armstrong carries tune.
2:49	Chorus 7: Trumpet, trombone, and clarinet improvise around tune with wild abandon.

LISTEN TO ... this selection streaming online.

WATCH ... an Active Listening Guide of this selection online.

DO ... Listening Exercise 28.2, Armstrong, "Willie the Weeper," online.

Big Bands and Swing

The recordings of Louis Armstrong and his Hot Seven sold as fast as they could be pressed. Jazz became the rage of the 1920s, just as ragtime had been the craze at the turn of the century. It was, in the words of novelist F. Scott Fitzgerald, the "Jazz Age." So popular had jazz become that it was now performed in ballrooms, large dance

FIGURE 28.5
Duke Ellington (seated at the piano) and his band in 1943. Although you see no music or music stands in this staged photograph, Ellington's band, which he called the Duke Ellington Orchestra, used them in performance. Because it was a *big* band, written notation was needed to coordinate the greater number of instruments.

halls, and movie theaters, in addition to the smaller bars and supper clubs where New Orleans–style jazz had its home. And, just as the small supper club gradually gave way to the ballroom, so, too, did the small jazz combo cede pride of place to the big band. To be heard above the stomping and swaying of many hundreds of pairs of feet, an ensemble larger than the traditional New Orleans combo of five or seven players was needed. Thus was born the big-band era—the glory days of the bands of Duke Ellington (1889–1974), Benny Goodman (1909–1986), Count Basie (1904–1984), and Glenn Miller (1904–1944).

Though not "big" by the standard of today's marching band, the **big band** of the 1930s and 1940s was at least double the size of the New Orleans–style jazz combo. In 1943, for example, Duke Ellington's orchestra consisted of four trumpets, three trombones, five reed players (men who played both clarinet and saxophone), plus a rhythm section of piano, string bass, guitar, and drums—a total of sixteen players (Figure 28.5). Most big-band compositions were worked out ahead of time and set down in written arrangements called "charts." The fact that jazz musicians now for the first time had to play from written notation suggests a desire for a more disciplined, polished, orchestral sound. The addition of a quintet of saxophones gave the ensemble a smoother, more blended quality. The new sound had little of the sharp bite and wild syncopation of the earlier New Orleans–style jazz. Rather, the music was mellow, bouncy, and flowing. In a word, it "swings." **Swing**, then, can be defined as a popular style of jazz played by a big band in the 1930s and 1940s. The recent revival of "swing dancing" shows that an elegant yet distinctly jazzy dance style can enjoy enduring popularity.

WATCH... a YouTube video of Duke Ellington's classic, "Take the A Train," online.

WATCH... a YouTube video of Benny Goodman's big band playing swing music in 1937, online.

From Tin Pan Alley to Broadway

Today, the music business is a global industry, with publishing houses, big-time stars, recording contracts, licensing deals, concert tours, and streaming music services. The point of origin of the business, however, can be seen by dropping a pin on a Google map at the intersection of Broadway and West 28th Street in New York City. Here, beginning around 1900, the music publishing industry arose as a business opportunity to serve and profit from Americans hungry for the latest popular songs.

FIGURE 28.6
The origins of the music business in America can be seen in this early-twentieth-century photo of Tin Pan Alley. George Gershwin got his first job at Jerome H. Remick & Company (top center).

FIGURE 28.7
George Gershwin

Imagine music before the phonograph, radio, and streaming music. How would you have heard what was new and have chosen the songs you liked? Songs could be sampled, not on your phone, but rather by going to a music store where a **song plugger**, like young George Gershwin, for example, peddled (plugged) them by singing and playing the piano. If you liked what you heard, you could buy a printed copy and take the song home to try out on your piano.

But songs needed to be created and printed, and these all-in-one music stores provided those services, too. Songwriters sold new songs under contract to the store, which then printed them as sheet music and sold them to the public. So numerous did these stores become west of Broadway on 28th Street that the stretch came to be nicknamed **Tin Pan Alley** because the song pluggers sounded like a crowd banging on tin cans. Look at Figure 28.6, and you can see the music stores crowded cheek by jowl. Look closely at the bottom right, where you'll see "William Morris."

Fast forward to the present. That very same William Morris store, founded in 1898, became William Morris Agency, grew until it merged with Endeavor Talent Agency in 2009, and, ultimately, in 2013, bought media giant IMB for $2.3 billion. Today, William Morris Agency represents, among other singer/songwriters, Taylor Swift, Usher, Justin Timberlake, and Bruno Mars. From humble beginnings, this small shop on West 28th Street has grown into a media powerhouse.

So, too, with Broadway. Those same music stores that published songs also booked singers and comedians at the theaters being built north along Broadway. This nexus of music stores and theaters became the show business center of New York City, with its epicenter at Times Square, the junction of 42nd Street and Broadway.

Jazz on Broadway: George Gershwin (1898–1937)

Jazz, classical, Broadway, opera, Tin Pan Alley songs—George Gershwin (1898–1937) could compose them all. Gershwin (Figure 28.7) was born to Jewish immigrant parents, Rose and Morris Gershovitz, in New York on September 26, 1898. His mother did what many upwardly mobile middle-class matrons then did in America: She bought her family an upright piano on an installment plan. But, of all the family members, only young George could play the instrument, picking out every sort of rag, march, and show tune by ear. Soon he was taking formal lessons in classical music, studying Mozart, Chopin, and Debussy. By the age of fifteen, music had become Gershwin's life, so he quit high school and took a job as a song plugger on Tin Pan Alley, earning fifteen dollars a week. In 1919, Gershwin stopped plugging the music of others and began to promote his own. With his hit song "Swanee," he became both rich and famous at the age of twenty-one.

Mother Gershovitz hadn't wasted her money on classical piano lessons. Although son George wrote numerous Broadway shows during the 1920s, he increasingly turned his attention to traditionally classical genres. In three large-scale orchestral compositions (*Rhapsody in Blue*, 1924; *Piano Concerto in F*, 1925; and *An American in Paris*, 1928), he created something called **symphonic jazz**, a fusion of jazz idioms with the textures and forms of the classical symphony. Later, in 1935, he extended this fusion of jazz and classical to the genre of opera with *Porgy and Bess*. But the venue for the New York premiere of the "opera" in October 1935 was not an opera house but a Broadway theater. Called an opera, *Porgy and Bess* takes the conventions of opera (sung, rather than spoken, recitatives, for example) and mixes in Broadway show tunes and jazz idioms. Its signature song is "Summertime."

Porgy and Bess revolves around aspects of African-American life in a fictitious section of Charleston, South Carolina, called "Catfish Row." Throughout the opera, "Summertime" (see Listening Guide) functions as a musical *idée fixe* (see Chapter 18)—a tune that just won't go away. It sounds first and most memorably as a lullaby that Clara sings to her child, and then as a counterpoint during the explosive craps game. It is reprised in Acts II and III. Folk elements include the suggestion of a pentatonic scale (here, A, C, D, E, G), the absence of a leading tone (a leading tone gives music a Western "classical" sound), and perhaps the minor mode as well. To the extent that an element of jazz is audible, it depends on the performance, and on how much liberty the singer and players take with the rhythm and with sliding between the pitches—that is, on how much they jazz it up.

LISTENING GUIDE

George Gershwin, "Summertime" (1935)   Download 87 (2:53)

Performed by Lena Horne

Genre: Something between opera aria and Broadway show tune

Form: Strophic

Situation: As the opera opens, the stage is set for a summer evening in "Catfish Row." Clara, a fisherman's wife, sings a lullaby to her infant.

WHAT TO LISTEN FOR: How Lena Horne belts out a Broadway sound backed by a big band featuring muted trumpet. ("Summertime" has been interpreted in many ways by many singers.)

0:00	Instrumental introduction

Strophe 1

0:12	Summertime ...

Strophe 2

1:03	One of these mornings ...
1:54	Variation of Strophe 2 added by performers in jazz style

LISTEN TO ... this selection streaming online.

WATCH ... an Active Listening Guide of this selection online.

Although George Gershwin died suddenly in Hollywood at the age of thirty-nine, his music endures. From his purely instrumental symphonic tone poem *An American in Paris* emerged a story line for a film (1951) and a Broadway show (2014), both of which had that same name. Mixed in among instrumental dances are favorite Gershwin show tunes, including "I've Got Rhythm" and "'S Wonderful." Although the shows may be about an American in Paris, the music is entirely that of Broadway, discussed in Chapter 29.

KEY WORDS

Bay Psalm Book (401)	banjo (404)	jazz (408)	big band (413)
Psalter (401)	blues (405)	ragtime (409)	swing (413)
gospel music (404)	instrumental break (405)	New Orleans jazz (410)	song plugger (414)
country music (404)	call and response (405)	rhythm section (411)	Tin Pan Alley (414)
ballad (404)	blues scale (406)	chorus (412)	symphonic jazz (415)
fiddle (404)	blue note (406)		

 Join us on Facebook at Listening to Music with Craig Wright

PRACTICE ... your understanding of this chapter's concepts by working once more with the chapter's Active Listening Guides online.

DO ... online multiple-choice and critical thinking quizzes that your instructor may assign for a grade.

POSTWAR
Jazz and Broadway

START... experiencing this chapter's topics with an online video activity.

LEARNING OBJECTIVES

After studying the material in this chapter, you should be able to:

1 Explain bebop and how it differs from previous jazz styles, namely New Orleans–style jazz and swing.
2 Describe how the approach to harmony in modal jazz differs from previous kinds of jazz.
3 Explain how a Broadway musical differs from an opera.
4 Differentiate *West Side Story*, *Sweeney Todd*, and *Phantom of the Opera* based on the extent of influences of Modernist and Romantic music in each.

For the United States of America, the first half of the twentieth century was an "age of anxiety" marked by two world wars and the Great Depression. By contrast, the second half of the century was an "age of prosperity" in which the income of most Americans increased greatly. For jazz, however, the opposite held true. The popular big bands of the 1930s thrived during the Great Depression and at the beginning of World War II, but, when the war ended and America's GIs returned home to their families, they gradually turned to another kind of music: rock and roll. Jazz musicians, too, headed in a different direction, creating a new style called "bebop." Ironically, bebop was popular music that wasn't all that popular. It was intended instead for a niche audience of connoisseurs.

Bebop

By the end of the Swing Era, about 1945, many of the best young performers felt that playing from written big-band charts limited their creativity. They wanted to return to a style in which improvisation was more important than composition and in which the performer, not the composer or arranger, was king. Choosing their playing partners carefully, they "jammed" in small, select groups in nightclubs in midtown Manhattan and in Harlem, and in so doing created a new, virtuosic style of jazz.

Bebop, or "bop," is angular, hard-driving jazz played by a small combo without written music. It derives its name from the fact that the fast, snappy melody sounds like the words *bebop*, *bebop* said quickly. A typical bebop ensemble consists of a quintet of trumpet, saxophone, piano, double bass, and drums—many fewer players than in a big band. The best soloists, among them saxophonist Charlie Parker (1920–1955) and trumpeter Dizzy Gillespie (1917–1993), had astonishing technique and played at breakneck speed. They also ornamented the melody with so much embellishment that the original tune soon became unrecognizable. Finally, bebop introduced much more complex accompaniments. In place of the basic triads of the scale, accompanists now used seventh, ninth, and eleventh chords, making the harmony obscure and dissonant.

Not all big-band musicians had the ability or the interest to play this new style—to "make the (chord) changes," as they called it. Bebop was for an elite few. But its small audience was less interested in *what* was being played than in *how* it was being played.

Charlie "Bird" Parker (1920–1955)

Perhaps the most gifted of the bebop artists was Charlie "Yardbird," or "Bird," Parker (Figure 29.1), the subject of Clint Eastwood's film *Bird* (1988) and most recently the chamber opera *Yardbird* (2015). Parker was a tragic figure, a drug-addicted, alcoholic, antisocial man whose skills as an improviser and performer were nonetheless greater than those of any other jazz musician save Louis Armstrong. Indeed, the lives of Armstrong and Parker make an interesting comparison. Both were born into the extreme poverty of the ghetto—Armstrong, in New Orleans, and Parker, in Kansas City—and both rose to the top of their profession through extraordinary talent and hard work. But Armstrong, an extrovert, viewed himself as a public entertainer as much as an artist. Parker, in contrast, didn't care if people liked his music and managed to alienate everyone around him, including, finally, his longtime friend and playing partner, Dizzy Gillespie.

He would die of the effects of his many excesses, alone and broke, at the age of thirty-four. Parker's personal life may have been a mess, but his inventive style of playing irrevocably changed the history of jazz.

In 1950, Parker teamed up with another bebop icon, Dizzy Gillespie, to create their version of a sentimental love song called "My Melancholy Baby" (1912), which by then had become a standard. A **standard** is a tune so influential that it inspires other musicians to record their own interpretations of it, each new version being what is called a **cover**. It isn't uncommon for a standard to be recorded by more than 100 different artists. By creating and recording what became a string of standards, Parker and Gillespie solidified bebop as a legitimate form of jazz. They wanted to be wildly original; the standard provided the listener a clear base from which to appreciate their originality.

"My Melancholy Baby," a tune written on Tin Pan Alley in 1912, is typical of the standards of the early twentieth century (see Listening Guide). Like most standards, its structure is straightforward: a sixteen-bar melody divided into four, four-measure phrases (**ABAC**). After a four-bar introduction by pianist Thelonious Monk, Charlie Parker plays the tune more or less "straight," with only moderately complex elaborations. But, when Dizzy Gillespie enters for the second chorus, the ornamentation becomes more complex, with racing thirty-second notes. The complexity continues through the third and final chorus, which Monk and Parker divide. What results is a music more for listening than for dancing. Bebop is the "chamber music" of jazz, a style designed to appeal to only a small number of knowledgeable listeners.

FIGURE 29.1
Charlie "Bird" Parker (left) and Dizzy Gillespie

LISTENING GUIDE

"My Melancholy Baby" (1912)   Download 88 (3:25)

Performed by Charlie Parker, saxophone; Dizzy Gillespie, trumpet; Thelonious Monk, piano; Curly Russell, bass; Buddy Rich, drums (recorded in New York City, 1950)

Genre: Bebop

Form: Strophic (each strophe in jazz is called a chorus)

WHAT TO LISTEN FOR: Listen to the tune in chorus 1, and then track how the trumpet, piano, and saxophone improvise on it in choruses 2 and 3.

INTRO

    0:00   Four-bar piano introduction

CHORUS 1

    0:13   **A**   Saxophone improvises lightly around tune.

    0:30   **B**

(Continued)

0:46	A		
0:59	C		

CHORUS 2

1:14	A	Trumpet (with mute)	
1:29	B	Wildly complex variation of **B**	
1:44	A		
1:58	C		

CHORUS 3

2:15	A	Piano	
2:31	B	Piano	
2:43	A	Saxophone	
2:59	C	Saxophone, with ritard at end	

TAG

3:14		Tag (short coda) by saxophone and trumpet playing a whimsical "Christmas Is Coming (The Geese Are Getting Fat)"

LISTEN TO ... this selection streaming online.

WATCH ... an Active Listening Guide of this selection online.

DO ... Listening Exercise 29.1, Parker, "My Melancholy Baby," online.

Other Jazzes: Cool and Modal

By 1950, jazz was no longer young; indeed, it had been around for nearly fifty years. Moreover, by mid-twentieth century, one could no longer speak of "jazz" and mean one specific style. The general term *jazz* might refer to one of three subgenres: New Orleans–style jazz, swing, or bebop. Bebop was at the vanguard, but it was not loved by all—with its fast tempos and biting attacks, bebop was almost too hot to handle. An immediate reaction appeared in the form of **cool jazz**, which sought to soften bebop's hard-driving sound with a more relaxed feel and less frenzied solos. Its leader was trumpeter Miles Davis and his seminal album, *Birth of the Cool* (1949). Davis played in a low range, with a more lyrical tone and softer dynamics. Seated alongside Davis during much of the late 1950s was John Coltrane, who initiated yet another kind of jazz, called modal jazz.

Modal jazz is a complex style that grew out of the extended harmonic language used in bebop accompaniments. Most traditional music, whether classical, pop, or early jazz, revolved around chord progressions moving sequentially through the basic triads (tonic, subdominant, dominant, for example) of the major or minor scale. So deeply ingrained are those progressions that we don't even notice them, other than to subconsciously think, "Yes, that's the way music ought to go." Modal jazz, however, changes the supporting harmonies in three ways: It uses modes (scales other than major or minor); it emphasizes chords other than dominant and subdominant (although the tonic remained primary); and it slows down the rate of harmonic change compared to the frenetically fast chord changes in bebop. Because they were less constrained to make one or two chord changes every bar, as in bebop, performers of modal jazz felt freer to extend the melody line on whatever chord or scale they happened to be.

John Coltrane (1926–1967)

The high priest of modal jazz was John Coltrane (Figure 29.2). "High" is the appropriate word here, because not only is Coltrane thought by jazz aficionados to have been the greatest of the great jazz creators, but also he, Parker, and Davis were heroin addicts whose lives were cut short by that drug. Like Parker, Davis, and most other New York jazz artists at the time, Coltrane demonstrated musical originality by crafting new pieces out of standards. Thus, on his pathbreaking album of modal jazz entitled *My Favorite Things* (1960), Coltrane improvised entirely on preexisting tunes by Broadway greats Richard Rodgers, George Gershwin, and Cole Porter, creating an entire album of nothing by covers. America was singing tunes such as Rodgers's "My Favorite Things" and Gershwin's "Summertime." What Coltrane did with them, however, was very different from what listeners expected.

FIGURE 29.2
John Coltrane performs in Paris in 1960.

One of the hit tunes in Rodgers and Hammerstein's *The Sound of Music* (1959; see later in this chapter) is "My Favorite Things," immortalized by Julie Andrews. The song consists of an initial melody (**A**) with three similar phrases, beginning with "Raindrops on roses and whiskers on kittens," followed by the refrain, "These are a few of my favorite things." After three such stanzas, a contrasting fourth stanza of not-favorite things ("When the dog bites, when the bee stings") provides a brief minor-key foil (melody **B**), which turns to cheery major at the end with the triumphant words, "but then I don't feel so bad."

Then came the Coltrane transformation: What had been a delightfully simple, upbeat Broadway song became under his fingers a darker, unpredictable series of abstract embroideries, influenced by the practices of Indian sitar music (Coltrane had studied the sitar and named his son, Ravi, in honor of Ravi Shankar; see Chapter 32, "An Indian Raga for the Sitar"). As we join Coltrane's long improvisation (see Listening Guide), we hear his soprano saxophone play a recognizable version of the tune, supported by chord changes in the piano, although those chords are no longer simple triads but more complex seventh and ninth chords. Thereafter, Coltrane overlays increasingly elaborate arabesques above a repeating harmony of just two chords, one built on the tonic and the other built on the supertonic (the second degree) of what is called a Dorian mode, set here on the pitch E. But forget the complicated music theory, and just listen to the music.

LISTENING GUIDE

Original tune by Richard Rodgers (1959)

Performed by John Coltrane, soprano saxophone; McCoy Tyner, piano; Steve Davis, bass; Elvin Jones, drums (recorded in New York 1960)

Genre: Modal jazz

Form: Theme (Richard Rodgers) and variations (John Coltrane)

WHAT TO LISTEN FOR: The contradiction between the simple alternation of two chords in the piano harmony and the astonishing sheets of scalar sounds emanating from Coltrane's soprano saxophone. You can hear the modal chords repeating as an ostinato in the piano. The original of this track was 13:41, but we focus only on the last four minutes.

0:00	**A**		Tune in saxophone; original harmony audible but enriched with seventh and ninth chords
0:18			Accompanying chords in piano come in sequence of 1, 2, **3** (II, II, **I**) chords repeated beneath melody.
0:50			Accompanying chords in piano come in sequence of 1, 2, **3**, but third chord in pattern is altered.
1:30			Accompanying chords move into higher range, but pattern remains the same; sax goes to top of range.
1:45			Accompanying chords drop in range; range of sax drops.
2:35			Sax brings back recognizable version of tune.
2:51	**B**		Contrasting melody **B** finally enters.
3:10	**Coda**		Coda in which arabesque-like fragments of the melody climax and gradually fade away

LISTEN TO ... this selection streaming online.

WATCH ... an Active Listening Guide of this selection online.

Jazz-Fusion and Beyond

During the 1960s, beatniks used to say "far out, man," and that piece of modal jazz by Coltrane is indeed far out—an example of the most free and experimental type of jazz ever created. But, in subsequent decades, jazz went from being "far out" to "close in"—closer to the mainstream of music. During the 1970s, what was selling was not jazz but rock, so jazz musicians, such as Miles Davis, added an electric bass and strong drumming with a backbeat to create **jazz-fusion**, a blend of jazz and rock. The moral of the story as it pertained to jazz and its listening audience is this: any popular music without a catchy tune or a finger-snapping beat won't be popular for long.

No sooner did jazz-fusion try to bring a beat back to jazz than **smooth jazz** removed it, first with the legato sounds of saxophonist Kenny G in the 1980s and 1990s, and more recently with the mellow tones of trumpeter Chris Botti, beginning around 2000. Thus, the pendulum for jazz continues to swing between hot and cool, heavy beat and weak beat, choppy and smooth. To bebop or not to bebop still seems to be the question.

The Broadway Musical

"Broadway," New York, isn't just a state of mind or a musical style, but a real place, a neighborhood of theaters. Originally connected to Tin Pan Alley (see Chapter 28, "From Tin Pan Alley to Broadway") at 28th Street, the strip of nearly forty theaters runs up the West Side along Broadway as far as 54th Street. Some of these theaters are home to dramatic plays and comedies, but about forty theaters regularly host Broadway musicals.

The Broadway **musical** (also known as the Broadway show) is a form of American popular musical theater that emerged shortly after 1900. A musical is based on a "book" (the libretto) that contains the lyrics (the rhyming verse used in the songs). Most of the dialogue in a musical is spoken, but the emotional high points are sung. In musical genealogy, then, the Broadway musical is a distant cousin of the eighteenth-century comic opera, which also had spoken dialogue. The earliest Broadway musicals were written by native-born Americans—most notably, George M. Cohan (*Little Johnny Jones*, 1906, which included "Give My Regards to Broadway") and Jerome Kern (*Showboat*, 1927). The oft-revived *Showboat*, with its signature song "Ol' Man River," is especially noteworthy in that it includes strains of uniquely American music: specifically, blues, jazz, and the Negro spiritual (Africanized hymn).

The collaboration between composer Richard Rodgers (1902–1979) and lyricist Oscar Hammerstein (1895–1960) marked the beginning of a golden era for American musical theater. In a span of less than two decades, this gifted team produced a succession of blockbuster musicals, beginning with *Oklahoma!* (1943); continuing with *Carousel* (1945), *South Pacific* (1949), and *The King and I* (1951); and concluding with *The Sound of Music* (1959). Their success was unparalleled at that time: *Oklahoma!* originally ran for 2,248 performances, and *The King and I* ran for 4,625 performances. Rodgers and Hammerstein struck gold by blending tasteful (if sentimental) lyrics with uplifting (if square-cut) melodies. "Broadway songbooks" (printed collections of musical theater standards) are filled with such hits as "Oh, What a Beautiful Mornin'" (*Oklahoma!*), "You'll Never Walk Alone" (*Carousel*), "Some Enchanted Evening" (*South Pacific*), "Getting to Know You" (*The King and I*), and "My Favorite Things" (*The Sound of Music*)—all Rodgers and Hammerstein creations.

We usually think of the "British Invasion" as the arrival of The Beatles and their fresh sound in America in 1963. But a second musical invasion came just a few years later with the arrival on Broadway of the megahits of Englishman Andrew Lloyd Webber (*Jesus Christ Superstar, Evita, Cats*, and *Phantom of the Opera*). These showcased not only sweeping melodies and lush, Romantic orchestrations, but also dazzling scenic effects—Broadway as spectacle.

Today, diversity seems to be the watchword on Broadway. Although *Phantom of the Opera* continues to play nightly, theatergoers can also see revivals of earlier American musicals (*The King and I* and Bernstein's *On the Town*); works in the traditional mold (*Chicago* and *Wicked*); adaptations of popular movies (Disney's *Aladdin* and *The Lion King*); musicals built from earlier pop music (*Jersey Boys, Beautiful*, and *Mamma Mia!*); and even musicals with religious themes (*Book of Mormon* and *Amazing Grace*). To get to the core of the Broadway musical, let's examine three of the most critically acclaimed and financially successful shows of the second half of the twentieth century, three Broadway classics.

Leonard Bernstein (1918–1990) and *West Side Story* (1957)

Leonard Bernstein, educated at Harvard and at the Curtis Institute in Philadelphia, was one of the great composer–conductor–interpreters of the twentieth century. As a composer, the protean Bernstein created symphonies and ballets, as well as a film score and four musicals. As a conductor, he was affiliated with the acclaimed New York Philharmonic for nearly half a century. And, as a virtuoso pianist, educator, and advocate for the arts, he even influenced presidents, especially John F. Kennedy. America has never enjoyed a more dynamic musical leader than the lionesque Bernstein.

When Bernstein's *West Side Story* premiered on Broadway in 1957, it became the musical sensation of the decade. The show succeeds by mixing old and new: Standard Broadway numbers are infused with Modernist music, and an ancient tale gets a modern, urban setting. In Bernstein's retelling of the Romeo and Juliet story, the feuding Montagues and Capulets are replaced by New York street gangs—the all-American Jets and the Puerto Rican Sharks. The star-crossed lovers are Tony, former leader of the Jets, and Maria (Figure 29.3), sister of the Sharks' leader. They meet at a dance held in a high school gym. Afterward, they rendezvous on Maria's fire escape (Juliet's balcony) and sing the show-stopping duet "Tonight" (see Listening Guide). In the lyrics of "Tonight," the past, present, and future seem to converge in a world made suddenly beautiful by the presence of the beloved. The heartbeats of the young couple are transformed into music; the tempo continually fluctuates, as slower, lyrical phrases rapidly quicken with intense emotion and then slow down again. At times, the melodies are underscored by punchy, syncopated accompaniment in the brass and strings, evoking Latin musical styles in a reference to Maria's heritage. The two lovers take turns singing to each other and then sing together in unison, illustrating their perfect compatibility. Like Romeo and Juliet, Tony and Maria may love each other with ardent passion, but they are destined for tragedy. At the end of the next day, Tony is killed after an ill-fated attempt to make peace between the gangs, leaving Maria to grieve over his body.

FIGURE 29.3
Natalie Wood in the role of Maria in the film version (1961) of Leonard Bernstein's *West Side Story*

LISTENING GUIDE

Leonard Bernstein, "Tonight," from *West Side Story* (original cast recording, 1957)   Download 90 (3:54)

Characters: Tony and Maria

Situation: Tony and Maria, who met and fell in love at a dance earlier in the evening, sing a duet on the fire escape outside her apartment.

WHAT TO LISTEN FOR: The song is sung once by Maria and then again, almost exactly the same way, as Tony joins in unison.

0:00	Recitative-like exchange	**Maria**
		Only you ...*
		Ever.
		Tony
		And there's nothing for me....
0:48	"Tonight" melody enters in the strings; first strophe is sung by Maria.	**Maria**
		Tonight, tonight ...
1:59	Second strophe is sung by Tony and Maria together in unison.	**Tony and Maria**
		Tonight, tonight ...
3:14	Brief reprise of "Tonight" melody	Good night ...

*Full text not given for reasons of copyright

LISTEN TO ... this selection streaming online.

WATCH ... an Active Listening Guide of this selection online.

WATCH ... a performance of this selection online.

DO ... Listening Exercise 29.2, Bernstein, "Tonight," online.

Stephen Sondheim (1930–) and *Sweeney Todd* (1979)

Who wrote the *lyrics* for Bernstein's *West Side Story*? Surprisingly, Stephen Sondheim, who would go on to become a leading composer of the *music* of many productions on Broadway. A private student of both Broadway legend Oscar Hammerstein and twelve-tone Modernist Milton Babbitt, Sondheim has a talent for weaving the witty verbal utterances that are characteristic of good musical theater into the intricate musical textures found in symphonic music. He is widely credited with raising the quality of American musical theater in the late twentieth century by seamlessly combining Modernist musical techniques with his own pithy type of poetry. Sondheim's musicals vary widely in style, incorporating everything from Gershwin-inspired jazz harmonies, to Stravinsky-like dissonance, to Viennese waltzes, in addition to the standard Broadway tune.

Although Sondheim is the creator of several important musicals, among them *A Funny Thing Happened on the Way to the Forum* (1962) and *Into the Woods* (1987), one show in particular, *Sweeney Todd, the Demon Barber of Fleet Street* (1979), is touted as a musical masterpiece of operatic proportions. The book is based on a nineteenth-century "penny dreadful" story of a demonic barber who cuts the

throats of his clients and then bakes them into meat pies. Sondheim's version of the popular thriller is especially elaborate; it has been likened to opera (and, indeed, performed by opera companies) and was successfully adapted for film in 2007 (directed by Tim Burton and starring Johnny Depp; Figure 29.4). Atypical for Broadway, the three-hour tragedy contains very little spoken dialogue, places great technical demands on the singers, and incorporates dissonant, Modernist musical elements. Sondheim's operatic musical is complex in a variety of ways: It calls for elaborate stage machinery (a giant, multilevel, revolving barbershop/pie shop), and the dramatic structure interweaves intricate subplots about subsidiary characters whom Todd has met throughout his life. But stage effects and dramatic complexity seem almost secondary to the brilliance of the music.

FIGURE 29.4
Johnny Depp as Sweeney in the 2007 film version of *Sweeney Todd*

The score of *Sweeney Todd* adroitly leads the audience through Sweeney's grisly story. The ghostly curtain raiser, "The Ballad of Sweeney Todd," is a chilling chorus sung directly to the audience. The melody of the choral refrain ("Swing your razor") employs the opening pitches of the *Dies irae*, the Gregorian chant used for the Mass of the Dead (see Chapter 4, Example 4.1). This is just one of many subtle references to other musical genres and traditions that Sondheim deftly folds into his monumental score. Slowly, out of these initial snippets of text and Minimalist fragments of melody, the composer begins to unify motives, instruments, and singers into massive walls of sound for both chorus and orchestra.

LISTENING GUIDE

Stephen Sondheim, "The Ballad of Sweeney Todd," from *Sweeney Todd, the Demon Barber of Fleet Street* (1979) \
Download 91 (3:34)

Genre: Broadway musical chorus

Form: Strophic with insertions

Situation: Members of the cast preview the story of Sweeney Todd, the murderous barber of London's Fleet Street.

WHAT TO LISTEN FOR: An opening Broadway chorus full of Modernist elements (dissonance, ostinatos, brittle woodwinds, and so on)

0:00	Dissonant prelude played by organ
0:34	Musical "scream"
0:40	Chromatic two-note buzzing ostinato provides background.
0:48	**Strophe 1**
	Attend the tale ...*

1:14	Shrill woodwinds added to accompanying ostinato		**Strophe 2** He kept a shop ...
1:41	Chorus, dissonant and percussive		Swing your razor wide!
			Strophe 3
2:02	Divided among members of cast		His needs were few ...
2:24	Chorus grows in intensity, dissonance, and rhythmic disjunction.		Inconspicuous Sweeney ...
			Strophe 4
2:58	Loud ostinato gradually diminishes, leading to quiet, and then percussive end.		Attend the tale ...

*Full text not given for reasons of copyright

LISTEN TO ... this selection streaming online.

WATCH ... an Active Listening Guide of this selection online.

Andrew Lloyd Webber (1948–) and *Phantom of the Opera* (1986)

No review of Broadway would be complete without a more thorough discussion of Andrew Lloyd Webber, the most successful of all musical-theater composers, at least in terms of profit and public recognition. The list of blockbuster musicals by Lloyd Webber is even lengthier than that of Rogers and Hammerstein: Among them are *Jesus Christ Superstar* (1970), *Evita* (1976), *Cats* (1981), *Starlight Express* (1984), and *Phantom of the Opera* (1986). Like Leonard Bernstein and Stephen Sondheim, Lloyd Webber was classically trained in music, attending Oxford University and the Royal Academy of Music in London. But, unlike his American competitors, who incorporate elements of Modernism in their scores, Lloyd Webber brings essentially a Romantic sound to his musicals. We all remember "Don't Cry for Me Argentina" (*Evita*), "Memory" (*Cats*), and "The Music of the Night" (*Phantom*) because Lloyd Webber gives us what we want to hear: beautiful, aria-like tunes, and lush, Romantic orchestrations with powerful brasses and surging strings. Combine these with spectacular stage effects created by director Tim Rice, and one has a formula for success.

Indeed, *Phantom of the Opera* has achieved a success unrivaled in the history of musical theater, making its composer a billionaire. Premiering in 1986 in London and then in 1988 in New York, *Phantom of the Opera* is by far the longest running of all Broadway musicals, having enjoyed more than 11,000 consecutive performances before 15.5 million people in New York alone. Indeed, with show-stopping songs such as "The Music of the Night," "Think of Me," and "All I Ask of You," the production has lost none of its popular appeal. Worldwide, the musical has been performed in 145 cities (Helsinki, Hong Kong, and Istanbul were added in 2015) and has grossed nearly $6 billion.

WATCH... a YouTube video of Michael Crawford, the original Phantom, singing "The Music of the Night," online.

Worldwide may be the key word here. Originally, the Broadway musical focused on the problems of the proverbial American man in the street and his "gal," both of whom just happened to live in New York City. Today, the musical has gone global. It is conceived with an eye toward general themes appealing to an international market and is thus another manifestation of the shrinking and homogenization of our musical world.

THE ECONOMICS OF BROADWAY AND THE LISTENING EXPERIENCE TODAY

"Want to do a show? Bring some dough!" That's the mantra of Broadway. To get a show up and running, of course, a theater has to be rented and performers have to be engaged. But, before the show can go on, that theater must be specially equipped and the production must be advertised. The initial advertising budget for a Broadway musical ranges from $15,000 to $100,000 per week. The total cost just to mount (not maintain) the average show is about $7 million, although a technically difficult production such as *Spider-Man: Turn Off the Dark* can reach $75 million.

To cover such expenses, a producer forms a consortium of investors and sells shares of the musical, like shares of stock. If the show does well, the investors divide the profits; if not, they get nothing back. First reviews can be crucial. But, even if the show passes the critical test, weekly production costs must be met, ranging from $350,000 for a midsize show such as *Mamma Mia!* to nearly $600,000 for a large production like *Phantom of the Opera*. A highly successful show can easily recoup its costs. *Phantom* brings in $1.5 million in a good week, and *The Lion King* earns even more, about $2 million, simply because its ticket prices are among the highest on Broadway. (The average

Outside the Majestic Theater in New York, where *Phantom of the Opera* has been playing continuously since 1988. Note the mask, which has become something of a cultural icon.

seat at *Phantom* costs $98, but the top ticket at *The Book of Mormon* will set you back $477.) Even these high prices, however, don't guarantee success for the producers: Only about 30 percent of musicals ever show a profit.

How can a producer generate more revenue and increase the chances of success? Do what the airlines do—put more seats in the existing space. A recent development at Broadway theaters is to remove the musicians from the pit that separates the stage from the audience and fill it with additional seats. The orchestra is still "live"—the musicians' union contract requires it—but the performers are located in a separate room that is two or three floors above the theater, and the electronic sound is pumped through speakers into the theater below. Instead of seeing the conductor's hand in the pit before them, onstage performers see the conductor on a TV monitor. This "off-site" approach maximizes ticket revenue, but theatergoers are left wondering whether the music is live or prerecorded.

KEY WORDS

bebop (418)	cover (419)	modal jazz (420)	smooth jazz (422)
standard (419)	cool jazz (420)	jazz-fusion (422)	(Broadway) musical (423)

 Join us on Facebook at Listening to Music with Craig Wright

PRACTICE ... your understanding of this chapter's concepts by working once more with the chapter's Active Listening Guides online.

DO ... online multiple-choice and critical thinking quizzes that your instructor may assign for a grade.

MUSIC FOR MEDIA:
Film, TV, and Games

START… experiencing this chapter's topics with an online video activity.

LEARNING OBJECTIVES
After studying the material in this chapter, you should be able to:

1 Outline the development of "classical"-style orchestral film scoring between the 1920s and 1940s.

2 Trace the era of experimentation in film scoring between the 1950s and 1970s.

3 Describe the rise of TV music and its interaction with composition for films.

4 Contrast the compilation method with the thematic, orchestral style of film scoring.

5 Describe the evolution of video game music.

6 Appreciate today's blending of music for film, TV, computers, and phones.

A century ago, engaging this book in the way you are doing wouldn't have been possible, because listening to its music would require you to find a live performance or learn to play it yourself. This is, in part, why piano music flourished in the eighteenth and nineteenth centuries, when the piano became the primary means of mechanically reproducing music at home. A music lover couldn't sit at a computer and, at the click of a mouse, hear and see a concerto being performed. Not until the twentieth century did the world see the most radical change in music reproduction yet: the introduction of sound technology. The technological reproduction of sound—of having instant personal access to music—has dramatically altered not only how we listen to music but also how composers create it.

READ... the complete chapter text in a rich, interactive online platform.

Up to this point, the music we've been studying was written to be performed live by a symphony orchestra, ensemble, solo performer, or choir, but now we'll focus specifically on the medium through which that music becomes audible.

Recorded sound, as we saw in Chapter 1, originated in 1877, when Thomas Edison patented the phonograph, which played wax cylinders, and in 1887, when Emile Berliner patented a disc-playing gramophone. But well into the 1910s, this technology remained expensive and seldom applied. The first device to truly democratize music was radio. Affordable radios brought the concert hall into countless American homes in the 1920s and 1930s. Contemporary composers such as Aaron Copland took note, favoring woodwinds and brasses in their symphonic works, in part because the more robust sound of those instruments cut through radio static, or "fuzz," better than that of strings.

Since the 1920s, audio technology has evolved to become not only clearer and richer but also more portable and more accessible. Improvements like long-playing records (LPs) and magnetic tape in the 1950s led to digital technologies—from CDs to MP3s and M4As—in the 1980s and 1990s. We've already seen how concert music changed in response to new sound reproduction technologies, how magnetic tape allowed Edgard Varèse to create *Poème électronique* (1958) and made popular music, like The Beatles' "A Day in the Life" (1967), revolutionary. And we will see in Chapter 31 how digital technologies made entire genres, like hip-hop, possible. Professional equipment like the **digital audio workstation (DAW)**, designed to record, edit, and play digital audio, and software like GarageBand have put sound manipulation at the fingertips of professionals and amateurs alike.

Nowhere has this revolution been more evident than in the audiovisual media that began to flourish at the turn of the twentieth century. The music of film, television, and games has radically shaped the listening experience in the last century.

The Dawn of Film Music

Moving pictures were first introduced in 1897 by the Lumière brothers, Auguste and Louis, in Lyon, France. They used their invention mostly as a novelty, to document life in Lyon and around the globe. But the technology soon took root as entertainment in the United States. By the early 1910s, storefront "nickelodeon" theaters—so named because admission cost a nickel—had sprung up in towns and cities across America. Most early films were short but were not "silent." A musical accompaniment was typically improvised by a pianist, often with a percussionist rendering the sound effects.

The Classical Score: 1920s–1940s

By the early 1920s, most U.S. cities had dedicated movie "palaces," some seating up to several thousand moviegoers. As films grew in popularity, they also expanded in length and complexity of plot. The stars of the day were early cinematic greats, such as Charlie Chaplin, Buster Keaton, and Lillian Gish, and directors D. W. Griffith, Fritz Lang, and Sergei Eisenstein, among others. In the movie palaces especially, film sound was elaborate, with a prepared score compiled from bits of existing orchestral works played live by a large theater orchestra or by an organ equipped with special sound effects.

Talking pictures were introduced in 1926, when the Vitaphone company experimented with synchronizing a phonograph with the film projector. Because this format was unstable and easily desynchronized, it was soon replaced with a format that encoded both sight and sound together, permanently fixed in the film-strip itself. The new technology also allowed filmmakers for the first time to create a sound track that contained three elements: dialogue, sound effects, and music. A desire for realism drove the integration of dialogue and sound effects. But, without a visible source of sound, such as a piano or an orchestra, music seemed an "unnatural" addition.

Although it had been heard continuously in silent movies, music in the early sound film was initially confined to pockets of uncontested space during which people weren't speaking—credit sequences, chases, or action sequences. Music written for these sections in films were called **cues**. A **film score** could be made up of any number of individual cues that could last any length of time, usually until a scene change. As audiences became accustomed to synchronized sound and music being integrated into the cinematic experience, composers like Max Steiner and Erich Korngold began to develop **underscoring**, expanding the presence of music so that it could be heard even under dialogue.

By the late 1930s, cues had become longer and more frequent. Often a **thematic cue** was attached to specific people, places, or ideas and repeated like a Wagnerian leitmotif throughout the film to emphasize or contribute to the story line. The classic Hollywood score was also *orchestral*, because the orchestra lent an aura of class to a medium that was still struggling to shed its reputation as cheap entertainment. Orchestral sound also registered well in theaters when it was projected through speakers that might be of uneven quality. Many composers and musicians working in Hollywood in the 1930s and 1940s were European émigrés well versed in concert-hall genres, especially opera. They adjusted the instrumentation of their film scores as opera composers did: quieter under dialogue, fuller and louder in stretches without it.

A classic example of a Golden Age Hollywood film score is Max Steiner's for David O. Selznick's *Gone with the Wind* (1939), a highly acclaimed Civil War epic based on Margaret Mitchell's best-selling novel. The score has many important "classical" features, heard during nearly three hours of film and including over ninety cues, a dozen themes, and an overture, almost all of it in late-Romantic style. Within the first twenty minutes of the film, one theme (see Listening Guide) is prominently presented in the opening credits and then clearly attached, like a leitmotif, to a place: the Southern plantation Tara, around which most of the action takes place. As it soars again from beneath the dialogue between two of the film's central characters, Scarlett O'Hara and her father, the music establishes the importance of Tara in the emerging narrative (Figure 30.1).

Movie poster for *Gone with the Wind* shows not only the two romantic leads, Vivien Leigh and Clark Gable, but also the opening scene between Scarlett and her father, in which they look out over their land to the strains of Tara's Theme.

All of the music in *Gone with the Wind* is composed in the style of Neo-Romanticism. By its very nature, then, the score by Max Steiner is retrospective, its sounds calling to mind the comfortable ones of the good old days—Romantic nostalgia. But of course, the old days in the antebellum South were not so good for a third of the population, African-American slaves. Many African-American groups opposed the production of *Gone with the Wind* because it projected an almost cartoon vision of reality, one in which pain and suffering was literally whitewashed. In the case of the film, stereotypical images of blacks happily singing "Swing Low, Sweet Chariot" went hand in hand with stereotypical Romantic music.

LISTENING GUIDE

Max Steiner, Tara's Theme, *Gone with the Wind* (1939)   Download 92 (3:04)

Genre: Orchestral film score

Form: **ABA**

WHAT TO LISTEN FOR: The classical feel of this overture with its fanfares and themes.

0:00		Church bell music and elaborate fanfare of the Selznick International trademark music (by composer Alfred Newman) raise the curtain, as the theater lights dim.
0:19		Quoted Civil War–era tune sets the scene.
0:32	**A**	Soaring **A** part of Tara's Theme begins as the movie title and a view of the plantation scroll across the screen.
0:50		**A** repeated, along with cast list
1:08	**B**	**B** part of Tara's Theme accompanies secondary credits.
1:28	**A**	**A** repeats.
1:49	**Coda**	Conclusion incorporating fragments of **A** in a contrasting key leads into the beginning of the film.

LISTEN TO ... this selection streaming online.

WATCH ... an Active Listening Guide of this selection online.

WATCH ... the film's opening scene, with Scarlett and Mr. O'Hara, online.

FIGURE 30.2
Alfred Hitchcock mugs with musical collaborator Bernard Herrmann.

Experimentation: 1950s–1970s

After World War II, the subject matter of films changed dramatically. American cinema, in particular, settled into a gritty style of realism and *film noir*, dark and brooding. Much like realist opera of the late nineteenth century (see Chapter 22), films began to examine the seamier side of life—murder, crime, poverty, and addiction. These themes played especially well to disillusioned Cold War audiences, as did science fiction films that fostered and exploited new fears of atomic energy.

The musical scores for these films changed dramatically, too. *Noir* films, with criminals, detectives, nightclubs, or all of the above—films like *The Big Combo* (1955), *The Man with the Golden Arm* (1955), *Sweet Smell of Success* (1957), and *Touch of Evil* (1958)—featured the hard, bebop jazz of the 1950s nightclub (see Chapter 29). In the 1960s, composer Henry Mancini lightened and Latinized jazz for comedies like *Breakfast at Tiffany's* (1961) and *The Pink Panther* (1963). Sci-fi films of the 1950s and 1960s, such as *The Day the Earth Stood Still* (1955) and *Forbidden Planet* (1956), also turned away from classic orchestral sound by incorporating electronic instruments (see Chapter 27), oscillators, and eerie-sounding theremins into their scores. Bernard Herrmann, who scored *The Day the Earth Stood Still*, went on to collaborate with director Alfred Hitchcock (Figure 30.2), providing musical scores that were either atonal (*Vertigo*, 1958) or persistently dissonant (*Psycho*, 1960) for many of Hitchcock's iconic psychological thrillers. In *Psycho*, Herrmann uses dissonance to create tension in the nervous Prelude (see Listening Guide) and also to literally act as a sound effect, as in the film's famous shower scene (see Listening Guide).

WATCH… a demonstration of the creepy-sounding theremin online.

LISTENING GUIDE

Bernard Herrmann, Prelude from *Psycho* (1960)   Download 93 (2:00)

Genre: Experimental film score

WHAT TO LISTEN FOR: How the music, using only strings, builds a mood of tension from the very start

0:00	Strings play nervous, driving music, punctuated with a quick foreshadowing of the violin "screams" to come in the shower scene.
0:32	Tense melody swirls into the Prelude.
0:46	Foreshadowing violins
0:48	Dissonant driving music continues.
1:07	Tense melody returns.
1:17	Staccato violins continue to build tension.
1:24	Driving music goes on.
1:36	Tense melody returns.
1:46	Brief, swirling figure repeats in rising octaves, until Prelude ends abruptly.

LISTEN TO … this selection streaming online.

WATCH … an Active Listening Guide of this selection online.

Bernard Herrmann, Shower Scene from *Psycho* (1960)   Download 94 (0:58)

Genre: Experimental film score

WHAT TO LISTEN FOR: How the music enhances the on-screen horror by literally screaming for Marion Crane, making this many moviegoers' most memorably terrifying scene.

0:00	Violins "scream" in abrupt upward, dissonant glissandos.
0:08	Lower strings enter, playing screams in imitation.
0:12	Screaming repeats, starting with violins and then lower strings.
0:24	Screaming dies out, as lower strings play slowly fading low notes.

LISTEN TO ... this selection streaming online.

WATCH ... an Active Listening Guide of this selection online.

WATCH ... a performance of this selection online.

Experimental sounds, electronic guitar riffs, bells, ocarinas, human cries, and wordless choirs were also heard in scores, most notably accompanying the popular "spaghetti westerns" of Sergio Leone, including *The Good, the Bad and the Ugly* (1966), scored by Ennio Morricone and informally dubbed "best theme tune ever."

Other new sounds erupted from cinema screens at midcentury, including rock and roll. Although initially confined to "teen pics" like *Rock Around the Clock* (1956) and *Blackboard Jungle* (1955), or films starring Elvis Presley (*Jailhouse Rock*, 1957; *G.I. Blues*, 1960; *Blue Hawaii*, 1961), the trend persisted into the 1960s and 1970s in both B films (*Easy Rider*, 1969) and mainstream dramas (*The Graduate*, 1967; *American Graffiti*, 1973).

The structure of the sound track was modified as well, often displaying a single instrumental theme, or **theme song**, like *The Pink Panther* theme or the theme for James Bond films, beginning with *Dr. No* (1962), instead of the Steiner "leitmotif" model of a separate theme for every character. Because the average length of a film credit sequence, where the theme was introduced, was close to the average length of a pop song (three minutes), this **monothematic format** worked for marketing purposes as well.

LISTEN TO... Ennio Morricone's theme for *The Good, the Bad and the Ugly* online.

LISTEN TO... Monty Norman's theme for *James Bond* online.

The Era of TV Music

In the 1950s and 1960s, as television eroded movie attendance and the 1948 court-ordered divestment of studio-owned theaters decimated studio profits, the studios pushed for films and TV shows with themes that could be marketed and sold separately. Selling stand-alone musical themes, extracted from films and TV productions, and arranged in any number of ways, proved very profitable for the film studios.

Much as the phonograph had made concert music available in the home, TV brought the movies home, too. Television literally recycled films, but it also developed its own programming. Much of it drew on existing film genres—westerns, detective shows, teen dramas—and TV music followed suit. Some shows had jazz-influenced theme music, like Henry Mancini's theme for the detective series *Peter Gunn* (1958-1961). Jazz sounded especially good through the small speakers of the average home TV set, much better than a tinny orchestra.

Film composers frequently wrote for television, importing new cinema sounds to that medium. Electronic instrumentation, too, was introduced to the small screen in the 1950s, in shows like *The Twilight Zone* (1959-1964), whose theme was written by Bernard Herrmann of *Psycho* fame; *My Favorite Martian* (1963-1966); *Lost in Space* (1965-1968); and *Star Trek* (1966-1969), whose theme made longtime film orchestrator Alexander Courage famous. The monothematic formula worked well for television, as music provided continuity between weekly episodes that were different in content.

Film in the TV Era

The film studios continued trying to counter the threat of television with bigger movies, wide-screen formats like Cinerama and Vistavision, and better, louder sound tracks. Magnetic tape offered improved sound quality—a "high-fidelity" sound—but converting the optical sound track to a magnetic one, which required new cameras, projectors, and theater speakers, was too expensive to adopt on a large scale. The magnetic tape revolution did find its way into the film sound track, but not until the late 1960s, and in a very different way.

FIGURE 30.3
The Berlin Philharmonic's 1968 recording of Strauss's Blue Danube Waltz, conducted by Herbert von Karajan, provided the accompaniment to a slow-motion, space-age ballet in *2001: A Space Odyssey*.

When film directors like Stanley Kubrick (*2001: A Space Odyssey*), Dennis Hopper (*Easy Rider*), William Friedkin (*The Exorcist*), and George Lucas (*Star Wars*) began to cut and paste together their own sound tracks from pre-existing and prerecorded music, a radically new method of "composing" film music was born. This **compilation method** profoundly altered the construction of film music by giving directors and music supervisors, rather than composers, the ability to shape a film's music. Kubrick used a mix of classical music—Modernist compositions by Hungarian composer Gyorgi Ligeti (*Requiem, Atmospheres, Lontano, Lux Aeterna*) and some nineteenth- and twentieth-century Romantic orchestral pieces by Richard Strauss (*Also sprach Zarathustra;* see the end of Chapter 1), Johann Strauss (Blue Danube Waltz; Figure 30.3), and Aram Khatchaturian (Suite from the ballet *Gayane*)—in the compilation for *2001: A Space Odyssey* (1968). In contrast, *Easy Rider*'s sound track rocked to the music of ten pop songs, including Steppenwolf's "The Pusher" and "Born to Be Wild."

The Dolby Sound Era: 1980s–2000

Much of the experimentation in film score instrumentation came to an end in the 1970s when a recording engineer, Ray Dolby, introduced high-fidelity recording techniques to cinema. His innovations coincided with a boom in construction of new movie theaters, "multiplexes" now housing eight to sixteen small theaters within a single complex, most of which installed the new Dolby stereo sound equipment. Dolby's new high-fidelity sound was noticeably better and especially good at rendering old "orchestral" sounds.

Return of the Classical Score

When John Williams scored a low-budget, Buck Rogers–style science fiction film with an old-fashioned, classical, Steiner-model score, that film—*Star Wars*—and its nostalgic musical style both became unexpected hits. The classical, orchestral, thematic score and the Steiner model were suddenly popular and marketable again. Williams would score all the films of the initial *Star Wars* trilogy (1977–1983) and all the films in the franchise since (see Listening Guide; see also "Wagner Goes to the Movies" in Chapter 21). Williams also has been involved in the most prolific composer–director partnership in film music history. His collaboration with film-maker Steven Spielberg spans some of the most popular action–adventure films of the last forty years, including *Close Encounters of the Third Kind* (1977), *E.T. the Extra-Terrestrial* (1982), all the *Indiana Jones* films (1981–2008), and the *Jurassic Park* films (1993–2001), as well as such important Spielberg dramas as *Schindler's List* (1993), *Amistad* (1997), *War Horse* (2011), and *Lincoln* (2012).

LISTENING GUIDE

John Williams, Main Theme from *Star Wars* (1977)　　　　　　Download 95 (5:47)

Genre: Orchestral film score

WHAT TO LISTEN FOR: Williams's masterful use of a full orchestra and multiple themes to create a classical, Steiner-model overture

0:00	Brass fanfare as the introduction starts to scroll up the screen: "A long time ago, in a galaxy far, far away. ..."
0:08	*Star Wars* main theme, played twice
0:27	Lyrical interlude in violins, played twice
0:49	Main theme returns with a cymbal crash.
1:10	Momentum builds, violins swirl, as introduction fades to black.
1:27	Outer-space music, with piccolo, as a transition
1:46	Ominous music, heavy with brass, slows the pace.
2:04	Martial music interlude forebodes imperial storm troopers.

(Continued)

2:14	Swirling violins return, reintroducing ...
2:22	... main theme in low brasses.
2:37	Lyrical melody in violins, played twice
2:55	Main theme
3:11	Outer-space music as a transition
3:19	Princess Leia's theme in low strings
4:02	Momentum builds again, bringing back main theme in many guises.
5:17	Celebratory conclusion

LISTEN TO ... this selection streaming online.

WATCH ... an Active Listening Guide of this selection online.

Experimentation

New sounds were heard as film composers began to use the keyboard synthesizer (see Chapter 27) for film scores. The austere sci-fi cityscapes, like those Vangelis scored for *Blade Runner* (1982), were a natural fit for the unconventional pitches and timbres that synthesizers could produce, but synthesizers also refreshed traditional thematic scores with a new, modern sound, as in Vangelis's *Chariots of Fire* (1981). Significantly, Vangelis was a pop musician who used the synthesizer for its lyrical and percussive sounds more than traditional concert composers might.

LISTEN TO... Vangelis's percussive theme for *Chariots of Fire* online.

Compilation Scoring

Compilation scoring—cutting and pasting from preexisting music—also persisted, although only a few directors pursued its original goal of directorial artistry. Instead, most films of the 1980s and 1990s used compilations of popular music mainly to sell sound track albums, which they did at an accelerated clip. Film studios also began to replicate the **music video**, a new visual form of music being pioneered by the twenty-four-hour cable channel MTV. Films could shift editing tempos suddenly to create an "MTV moment," a fast-paced montage of images that were cut to match the beat of the accompanying pop song. Movies like *Flashdance* (1983), *Footloose* (1984), and *Top Gun* (1986) popularized the formula and its powerful synergy of media.

Some directors, however, continued to use compilation for artful purposes. Directors like Martin Scorsese (*Raging Bull*, 1980; *Goodfellas*, 1989) fashioned a new pop sound for the Mafia long before HBO's *The Sopranos* did. Spike Lee (*Do the Right Thing*, 1989; *He Got Game*, 1996) and Woody Allen (*Manhattan*, 1979; *Hannah and Her Sisters*, 1986) continued to "score" their pictures from their own record collections.

A new young voice in compilation scoring emerged in the 1990s. Director Quentin Tarantino has personally compiled all of his sound tracks from a vast collection of popular music styles, TV, and other film scores. His compilation for *Pulp Fiction* (1994) remains a high-water mark among the highest-grossing sound track albums of all time. Some pieces were recycled hits. Tarantino rescued other songs from obscurity and breathed new life into them, including the 1961 surf guitar solo by Dick Dale, "Misirlou," which opens the film. It's almost impossible to listen to this music without hearing the eccentric hit men Vincent Vega (John Travolta) and Jules Winnfield (Samuel L. Jackson) discussing what a McDonald's Quarter Pounder with Cheese is called in Paris.

LISTEN TO... Dick Dale's "Misirlou" from *Pulp Fiction* online.

The Sound of Games

In the late 1970s and early 1980s, a new audiovisual mass medium emerged, first on TV consoles and then on desktop computers: video games. To this day, game sound is dictated by technological limitations, but early games had only enough memory for a few pieces of monophonic synthesized music. *Pong*, an early game for TV consoles, had only synthesized "bleeps." *Pac-Man, Frogger, Donkey Kong*, and *Asteroids*, games from the early 1980s, all had very simple synthesized melodies and in-game music (**looped underscoring**), as did *Tetris* and *Super Mario Bros*.

In the late 1980s and early 1990s, however, as computer power and memory increased, game sound evolved dramatically. Like television, it strained toward the cinematic, and better game sound came to mean orchestral scoring. Nobuo Uematsu's music for *Final Fantasy* (1987) and Shigeru Miyamoto's music for *The Legend of Zelda* (1989) were some of the first games to have full orchestral thematic scores (and the processor power to deliver them). Many games also aimed at the cinematic by incorporating popular music, including Sega's *Michael Jackson's Moonwalker* (1990) and Rockstar's *Grand Theft Auto* (1997), in which car radios are a constant source of popular music.

But one aspect of game music that means it does not and cannot aspire to the level of film music is its interactive structure. Most games have a static window before play begins, for which music is written. **Cut music**, for beginnings and endings, often resembled film and television themes in that it was typically melodic, with a distinctive contour or colorful instrumentation. As game studios' revenues and processing power increased, they began hiring film composers to create cut music, including Danny Elfman (see Chapter 27, "Electronic Music: From Thomas Edison to Beats Music"), Howard Shore (*The Lord of the Rings* series), and Hans Zimmer. Because it had to be flexible and change with player skills and abilities, in-game music developed a different structure. Early games used loops and ostinatos to extend game play. Later, better multichannel sound for PlayStation and Xbox, working through home media centers that had improved sound technology, meant that advancement through levels in the game triggered new layers of sounds, more complex rhythms, and thicker instrumentation. These branching and layering structures formed an alternative to looping, as games began to use musical complexity to signal game-playing success. As text had once engendered related gestures in music, as in word painting, now game plots did the same.

Total Immersion: Music for Film, TV, Computers, and Phones

The visual spectacle and complexity of film and all other audiovisual media have grown significantly since the 1980s and 1990s, especially with the rise of **computer-generated images (CGI)**. The cinematic treatment of comic book characters (*Spiderman, X-Men, Captain America, Avengers,* and *Guardians of the Galaxy* franchises), facilitated by synergies between the comic book and film industries (such as Disney's purchase of Marvel Entertainment in 2004), have made CGI a ubiquitous part of modern filmmaking.

Science fiction and fantasy films have become CGI spectacles, as in Peter Jackson's *The Lord of the Rings* movie trilogy (2001) and *The Hobbit* series (2012). All of these films are packed with long, special effects–driven battle scenes staged to the sounds of orchestral scores. The orchestras in these films, however, are much expanded and louder, so as to be heard above densely complex sound effects, which can occupy upwards of sixty individual tracks. As a result, composers like Howard Shore (*The Lord of the Rings* series, *King Kong,* and the *Twilight* franchise), James Newton Howard (*The Hunger Games* franchise), and Danny Elfman (*Avengers: Age of Ultron*) have made their scores louder and simpler, simply in order to be heard.

The complexity of sound track sound effects has also led composers to collaborate more closely with sound designers. The results are musical scores that are often difficult to distinguish from sound effects. The horror genre and franchises like the *Saw* series (2004–2010), scored by Charlie Clouser, are a good example of the blurring that regularly surfaces between sound design and music scoring. But the phenomenon has found a home in scoring practices for film dramas, too, such as Trent Reznor's and Atticus Ross's work for director David Fincher (*Social Network,* 2010; *Gone Girl,* 2014). Reznor and Clouser both came to film after playing in the popular industrial rock band Nine Inch Nails.

In the last five years or so, the cinema has sustained another revolution, this one involving the medium of film itself. As early as the 1990s, film studios experimented with replacing 35-millimeter celluloid film with digital prints stored on computer hard drives. In 2009, the Digital Cinema Initiative, a cooperative of the six major studios (Disney, Fox, MGM, Sony, Paramount, Universal, and Warner Brothers), theater owners, and cinematographers, pushed to make this conversion happen. As of 2015, most Hollywood films were shot using digital cameras, and nearly all U.S. cinemas have been converted to digital projection. This sweeping change in film production and exhibition is noticeable not only in the explosion of 3-D, HD, and IMAX exhibition venues but also in movie theater sound. Dolby's new Atmos system requires theaters to install speakers on nearly every surface, including floor and ceiling. Moviegoers are surrounded by a dome of sound that gives them a newly immersive sonic experience, available in films such as *Brave* (2012) and *Gravity* (2013). What we've traditionally thought of as a viewing experience has, in large measure, become a musical one as well.

The development of music for this new digital cinema is nowhere more audible than in the work of composers associated with Remote Control Productions (RCP), the collaborative scoring studio run by composer Hans Zimmer. Zimmer maintains one of the largest digital libraries of "sampled sound" in the world.

His scoring method, which he says is more like engineering than composing, begins with the establishment of a sound world for the film, a landscape of individual samples or parts, which he assembles using a digital audio workstation. This material—usually four or five notes, or a few slow-moving chords—is thematicized and repeated, with a layer of instrumentation or a new rhythmic beat added with each repetition. This accumulative process continues until the theme can't get any louder or more complex, at which point the texture is suddenly reduced to just a few isolated sounds. Zimmer has called this new scoring model **Romantic Minimalism**, because a small (minimal) bit of material is repeated extensively but is constantly varied and expanded timbrally and rhythmically in the style of Romantic-era music. Films in which you can hear the Zimmer model include *Gladiator*, *The Dark Knight* trilogy, *Pirates of the Caribbean: At World's End*, *The DaVinci Code*, *Sherlock Holmes*, *Man of Steel*, *Inception* (Figure 30.4), and *Interstellar*. Most of the sound and music samples with which Zimmer works are performed on acoustic instruments and not, for the most part, synthesized. Zimmer maintains the library but invites other composers (many of whom have trained with him as orchestrators) to use it and be a collaborative part of the RCP group. RCP alumni have also spread the sound of Romantic Minimalism to television (*House of Cards'* Jeff Beal and *Game of Thrones'* Djwadi) and to game scores, including *Call of Duty* and *Metal Gear* (Harry Gregson-Williams) and *Assassin's Creed* (Lorne Balfe).

Game scores especially have sought to replicate the new immersive sound of the cinema with ever more complex sound effects and scores. But, with the ubiquity of hand-held tablets and smartphones, game scores have also become nostalgic. Because smartphones currently have limited sound-processing space, some of the most popular games—*Candy Crush Saga, Angry Birds*, and *Two Dots* among them—have joyously self-conscious, 1980s-inspired synthetic themes. For the moment, access has trumped immersion, but that, too, will change as the digital sound revolution of the phone continues.

LISTEN TO... the theme from *Inception* online.

FIGURE 30.4
This M. C. Escher–like poster for *Inception* captures the complexity of both its plot and its score, one full of continually re-formed and recycling units.

KEY WORDS

digital audio workstation (DAW) (431)	underscoring (432)	compilation method (436)	computer-generated images (CGI) (440)
cues (432)	thematic cue (432)	music video (438)	
film score (432)	theme song (435)	looped underscoring (439)	Romantic Minimalism (441)
	monothematic format (435)	cut music (439)	

 Join us on Facebook at Listening to Music with Craig Wright

PRACTICE ... your understanding of this chapter's concepts by working once more with the chapter's Active Listening Guides online.

DO ... online multiple-choice and critical thinking quizzes that your instructor may assign for a grade.

ROCK:
Music of Rebellion

START... experiencing this chapter's topics with an online video activity.

LEARNING OBJECTIVES

After studying the material in this chapter, you should be able to:

1 Outline the popular styles that preceded rock music in the post–World War II era.
2 Describe how rock and roll emerged in the early 1950s.
3 Differentiate rock from rock and roll.
4 Enumerate several rock substyles that developed starting in the 1960s.

Now that you're near the end of this book, you know quite a bit about musical style and the types of composers and compositions that Western history has deemed worthy of study. You now know that, although J. S. Bach toiled in obscurity for much of his career, he ultimately became one of the most revered and studied artists in the classical tradition. You've discovered that Rossini's tuneful operas—rather than Beethoven's now-iconic symphonies—most captivated audiences in the early nineteenth century. And you've learned that Stravinsky's *Le Sacre du printemps* (*The Rite of Spring*), while shocking enough to provoke a riot at its premiere, was quickly folded into the musical mainstream and, within a few decades, studied in every music appreciation class around the world.

As we trace the history of today's popular music, we experience a good number of the same cultural and aesthetic dynamics: Many of the countless substyles of rock music, originating from a culture of rebellion, have nevertheless contributed to the pop mainstream. The study of rock music is complicated by the diversity of the genre as well as by the sheer number of rock composers and musicians who have produced recordings. Of course, rock music possesses a brief history in comparison to that of the Western art tradition; nonetheless, it forces us to consider a large and astonishingly varied body of artists and recorded works. Although we can see the sweep of music history as a wide river, we should also understand that numerous stylistic streams feed into it.

Antecedents of Rock

In post–World War II America, two new musical styles grew from African-American swing music with its roots in Kansas City—namely, that of the Count Basie Orchestra. One was a highly improvisatory, rhythmically frenetic jazz called bebop (see Chapter 29, "Bebop"). The other, **rhythm and blues (R&B)**, descended from a laid-back, riff-based, blues (see Chapter 28, "Blues"). In both styles, a small rhythm section of piano, guitar, bass, and drums accompanied a few saxophones and other "horns" (a general term given by jazz musicians to any sort of brass instrument). However, unlike the instrumentally complex bebop, rhythm and blues (initially called "race music" or "jump blues") was song and dance based. Works in this style characteristically featured a solo vocalist singing about love—or lack thereof—in an unambiguous duple meter: a 4/4 bass pattern that sometimes emphasized the weaker beats (backbeats). The harmonic formula was frequently a twelve-bar blues performed over a walking bass in a style called **boogie-woogie** (driving music in which the bass plays the harmony, not as chords, but as a succession of fast pitches of equal length). This easygoing, popular sound developed in African American musical circles and was first marketed to black audiences. However, in the early 1940s, many of the popular "jump blues" songs of bandleader Louis Jordan began to cross over from the "Harlem Hit Parade" or "race" charts to the overall U.S. market, and, by early 1945, Jordan was producing commercially successful hits like "Caldonia" (1945) and "Choo Choo Ch'Boogie" (1946). Unlike the esoteric bebop, rhythm and blues became wildly popular, particularly among rebellious American youth. Songs like Roy Brown's "Good Rockin' Tonight" (1947) and Jimmy Preston's "Rock the Joint" (1949) pointed the way to a raucous style that was lyrically explicit and instrumentally simple, accentuating repeated riffs and call-and-response patterns.

In 1951, Ike Turner's Kings of Rhythm (recorded as Jackie Brenston and His Delta Cats) laid down the track "Rocket 88" in a small Memphis studio owned by Sam Philips. The song, released on the Chess label, showcased Brenston's loose vocal phrasing, framed by Turner's hammering triplets and syncopated right-hand figures on the piano. The definitive feature of this recording, however, is the walking bass pattern, played on a distinctly fuzzy-sounding electric guitar connected to what turned out to be a damaged amplifier. The booming bass created the first recording that diverged in timbral concept from "horn-band accompanied by rhythm section" to "rhythm section accompanied by horns." And that made all the difference.

WATCH... YouTube videos of early rhythm and blues songs "Choo Choo Ch'Boogie" and "Rocket 88," online.

Rock and Roll

In the early 1950s, the emerging style of rhythm and blues was rechristened **rock and roll** by pioneering radio disk jockey Alan Freed (1921–1965), partially to liberate it from its earlier association with African Americans. Freed disseminated this music through radio broadcasts, first in Cleveland and later in New York, and through concerts and dances that fostered racial integration. The demand for rock and roll was unprecedented, and as other stations incorporated the music into their formats, its records became songs of defiance for the baby boom generation. Furthermore, Freed's transmissions were rebroadcast in Europe, extending rock and roll's popularity to Great Britain and beyond.

Rock and roll was not a new term. The words are found in popular songs as early as the 1920s. Its roots are older still. *Rocking* and *rolling*, old nautical terms referring to the motion of boats, had been used in black English to describe bodily spasms that were experienced not only during religious ecstasy but also during dance (of course, with sexual connotations).

The first great exponent of rock and roll was Elvis Presley (1935–1977; Figure 31.1). Presley began his career performing "hillbilly music," singing gospel music in his Pentecostal church, and listening to blues and jazz in the black neighborhood of Memphis. In his sound, Elvis authentically combined genres of indigenous American black and rural white music. Proof of this lies in his first record, from July 1954. On one side is a cover of a traditional bluegrass song, "Blue Moon of Kentucky," but on the other is the explosive "That's All Right," written by Arthur "Big Boy" Crudup, a black Mississippi Delta blues singer and guitarist. All told, Elvis had 149 songs appear on *Billboard*'s "Hot 100 Pop Chart." He reached iconic status around the globe not only through the unmistakable sound of his voice but also through the projection of his image on television and in over thirty feature films. John Lennon's oft-quoted statement, "Before Elvis, there was nothing," is an exaggeration, of course, but in the world's consciousness of rock and roll, these words still ring true.

Presley's image was cemented in popular consciousness in 1956 with his recording and subsequent TV performances of "Hound Dog." The complicated history of this song is instructive, for it tells us much about how a transformative song might come to be. The composition was written in New York by Jerry Lieber and Mike Stoller, and it was first recorded by Big Mama Thornton in 1952. The Thornton version falls clearly on the R&B side of the fence. Three years later, Freddie Bell and the Bellboys, a local group from Philadelphia, recorded a cover of the song, changing Lieber's lyrics sufficiently to render them innocuous. Instead of

FIGURE 31.1
"The King is dead, long live the King." The hysteria surrounding Elvis has diminished only slightly since his death in 1977. His retrospective album, *Elvis 30 #1 Hits*, released in 2002 on the twenty-fifth anniversary of his death, sold a million copies in the first month. Elvis's estate has generated more income than that of any deceased celebrity ($60 million) except for Michael Jackson ($275 million).

pertaining to a "dog" as a metaphor for a persistent, yet unfaithful male suitor, the song now seemed to be about a canine and only faintly about a romantic interest. The earthy words of R&B had been tidied up. First released on Teen Records in 1955, Bell's record enjoyed only limited distribution in the Philadelphia area. Presley heard the Bellboys' rendition of the song during one of their stage shows in Las Vegas and received permission from Bell to adapt and record this variation. In Presley's unique interpretation, "Hound Dog" went on to achieve phenomenal sales, making Presley's career.

But how did Presley change the original song? Mainly by combining subtle features of both the Thornton and the Bell versions. To the **AAB** text pattern, he added some "uh" sounds, a glottal "crah-in," and assorted "well" and "yeah" calls, thereby roughing up the rhythm. He removed the horns, taking the ensemble away from the early jump sound and pushing it clearly into the rock and roll category. More radical than Presley's music, however, was his mode of performance. Delivered on live television before a predominantly older, white audience, Presley's actions were downright scandalous. With tremulous hands, slip-sliding feet, knees twisting from side to side and—famously—gyrating hips, Presley elicited screams, giggles, and embarrassed laughter from the audience.

The mature style of rock and roll, personified by the music and performances of Elvis Presley, was an amalgam of black R&B and a broad array of urban and rural influences—some African American, some white. Although we might think that the artists themselves wrote the songs of rock and roll, as often as not, the tunes were composed by professional songsmiths working in the music industry. One composer–performer who both directly and indirectly influenced later musical generations was Buddy Holly (and the Crickets). Holly's unique vocal styling and his iconic look set a standard for originality. A song like "Peggy Sue" (1957) betrays none of its African American roots. Essentially a twelve-bar blues, the melody utilizes the major triads and the major scale without blue notes. This, along with the twangy Fender-guitar strumming and the snareless, locomotive drumming, renders the idiom unrecognizable. Many of the other entertainers who emerged during this first era of rock and roll, however, lacked Holly's originality; these artists, such as Pat Boone, spread the popularity of rock and roll through bland but commercially appealing versions of authentic songs composed and first recorded by inspired musicians like "Fats" Domino and "Little Richard" Penniman.

Rock

With the arrival of The Beatles (Figure 31.2) in the United States from England and their appearance on *The Ed Sullivan Show* on February 9, 1964, the full potential of "teen" music was realized. John Lennon (1940–1980), Paul McCartney (1942–), George Harrison (1943–2001), and Ringo Starr (1940–) had a profound effect on the music and culture of the world. Named after Buddy Holly's "Crickets" and influenced by American rock and roll and R&B, The Beatles began by playing and recording **covers**, or interpretations of songs already recorded by others. However, they developed an unprecedented ability to create original, fresh sounds. As inventive as their early work is, it clearly bears the stamp of their stylistic forebears. Soon, however, these four musicians, pushed in part by their classically trained producer George Martin, moved toward radical experimentation in both songwriting and studio recording.

WATCH... a 1956 YouTube video of Presley performing "Hound Dog," online.

WATCH... YouTube videos of early rock and roll songs "That's All Right" and "Peggy Sue," online.

FIGURE 31.2
Although they were together for only ten years (1960–1970), no pop group has ever equaled The Beatles' musical originality and stylistic variety. Each one of their number 1 hits was fresh and wildly different from the last.

First influenced by the folk music revival and the introspective and politically aware Bob Dylan, and then by marijuana and LSD, the songwriting of McCartney and Lennon moved away from the early poppish boy-loves-girl topics and guitar-bass-drums sound, and matured into deeper, musically complex, and verbally intricate poetic expression. By 1966, after several years of playing their music live, the growing intricacies of their songs forced them to withdraw to the studio. Limited neither by the constraints of the performance space nor by the ups and downs of a live show, here The Beatles could avail themselves of the full range of acoustic and electronic recording techniques, including the electronic manipulation of audio tape. They also began to experiment with short promotional films for individual songs. The albums that they fashioned were immediately perceived as masterpieces, marginalizing the three-minute tune and the two-sided single that previously dominated the recording industry.

In 1967, for example, The Beatles put together the psychedelic "Strawberry Fields Forever," a song that incorporated astoundingly innovative instrumentation and Postmodern *musique concrète* (see Chapter 27). They also released a surreal film for the work that is considered the first modern music video. Assembling the album *Sgt. Pepper's Lonely Hearts Club Band* during the same year, The Beatles brought to fruition the thematically unified **concept album**. The lyrics were intended to be regarded as serious poetry, and the album art provided a sophisticated visual accompaniment to electronic studio recording techniques. "A Day in the Life," the final song on side B of *Sgt. Pepper's Lonely Hearts Club Band*, is physically connected to the previous song, "Sgt. Pepper's Lonely Hearts Club Band (Reprise)," much like the third and fourth movements of Beethoven's Symphony No. 5 are linked. The Beatles had significantly raised the "creativity bar" for rock and roll. Subsequent artists were expected to compose the songs that they performed and to release concept albums rather than singles. The Beatles had created sound worlds that were not only new but also widely disparate. Consequently, the sophisticated, varied styles that had emerged from rock and roll required a new name, called simply **rock**.

WATCH... YouTube videos of The Beatles' "A Day in the Life" and "Sgt. Pepper's Lonely Hearts Club Band," online.

In the late 1960s, rock came into its own, and it did so in the form of the so-called British Invasion, spearheaded by bands from the United Kingdom, such as The Rolling Stones, Cream, and Led Zeppelin. They gave the style initiated by The Beatles a harder edge and lengthy instrumental improvisations, bringing the sound of the solo electric guitar to the forefront of rock. They also used the **guitar riff** (an improvisatory flourish that becomes a motive) and the rhythmic ostinato to hold works together. In the Stones' "(I Can't Get No) Satisfaction" (1965), for example, we hear an incessant pounding of a guitar riff that is strung through a vaguely bluesy strophic form pivoting around a tonic hub. We also find examples in rock of straight twelve-bar blues, as in "Crossroads" (1969) by Cream, in which guitarist Eric Clapton adapts an old Robert Johnson blues number, structuring it around an identifying riff.

Perhaps the greatest figure of this era was guitarist, singer, and songwriter Jimi Hendrix (1942–1970), who, like his contemporaries, The Beatles, changed forever the creative potential for the rock artist. An icon of late-1960s fashion, he remains unparalleled in the popular imagination for his unique performance antics, including setting fire to his guitar. Hendrix was arguably the most original guitarist in rock history. He utilized a harmonic vocabulary that ranged from simple blues to complex chords and unusual intervals. Hendrix's most enduring legacy was his genius in expanding the range of the amplified guitar. Instead of using the instrument solely as a melodic and harmonic device, he reimagined it as one that could produce an assortment of noises, vocal effects, and electronic sounds, such as those immortalized in his performance of "The Star-Spangled Banner" at the Woodstock Music and Art Fair in 1969 (see chapter-opening photo). Hendrix's performance can been construed as his commentary on a country torn asunder by race and by the Vietnam War.

Evolving Rock Substyles

Soul, Motown, and Funk

Despite rock's dependence on traditional African American music for its roots and foundation, political, social, and economic circumstances served to isolate much black music during the 1950s and 1960s. Although people of color and female artists have had a significant voice in rock, their influence has sometimes been assessed as peripheral. However, numerous types of music created by these "marginal" artists were important as both commercial and artistic forces, for they repollinated rock with vigorous new ideas.

Late-1950s R&B and doo-wop (see Chapter 2) grew increasingly sophisticated, thanks to the success of record labels like Stax, in Memphis, and Motown Records, in Detroit. **Motown**, through the accomplishments of founder Berry Gordy, organized, polished and marketed not only music but also popular acts. For example, Gordy transformed the earlier girl groups into well-coiffed, costumed, and choreographed ensembles such as Martha and the Vandellas, whose soulful "Dancing in the Street" (1964) projects over a pulsating backbeat of percussion. The most popular of these Motown ensembles were The Supremes, a vocal trio that scored ten number 1 hits from 1964 to 1967. Led by Diana Ross, this group appeared countless times on television variety shows. Ross's softly breathy voice and seductive innocence would serve as a model for many pop singers to come. Motown also nurtured the male counterparts like The Temptations and The Four Tops, whose success was mostly limited to the R&B charts but who nonetheless laid the groundwork for the "boy bands" of subsequent decades.

Soul, the gospel-rooted style of the 1950s and 1960s, saw its popularity confined mainly to African American communities, but many artists broke through into the mainstream. A high level of musical complexity can be found in the arrangements and musicianship among these artists. Unlike the more popular but carefully choreographed Motown act, soul music relied on spontaneity and improvisation in live performance. Among the earliest of these artists to achieve acclaim was Ray Charles, whose "I Got a Woman" (1954) drew directly on gospel songs and whose Latin-tinged "What'd I Say" (1958) entered the mainstream.

The most important figure of the soul movement, however, was James Brown (1933–2006), the self-proclaimed "Godfather of Soul" and "the hardest working man in show business." Brown was the inventor of **funk** (a blend of soul, jazz, and R&B) as well as the musical and choreographic inspiration for future artists like Michael Jackson. First appearing on the R&B charts in 1956, Brown spent a decade honing his stage act before he broke through to a wider audience. In a way similar to Ray Charles, Brown brought black Fundamentalist preaching, shouting, and a free conversational manner to the realm of pop with great dramatic effect. In a song like "It's a Man's Man's World" (1966), we hear Brown's full range as a singer, including his use of the voice as a percussive instrument. His now classic funk tune, "Get Up (I Feel Like Being a) Sex Machine" (1970), conveys a sense of the choreographic energy that Brown bequeathed to Jackson, who as a boy often watched him from backstage.

WATCH... YouTube videos of Ray Charles's "I Got a Woman" and James Brown's "Get Up," online.

Punk Rock and New Wave

A highly politicized **punk rock**—a fast, hard-edged music with short, simple songs and few instruments besides guitars and drums—slithered onto the music scene in the mid-1970s. Punk rock's self-destructive and nihilistic approach offered a welcome alternative, for example, to the mechanistic music and manufactured fabrics of the 1970s disco craze. Instead of using music as a form of escapism, the lyrics of the songs often pointed out the boredom of idle youth and the desperation of the urban poor. Pressed bell-bottoms gave way to torn jeans. Concept albums, extended tracks, and instrumental virtuosity became relics of the past. Like the pre-Beatles artists, if you couldn't say what you wanted to say in less than three minutes, then it wasn't worth saying.

The downtown New York City club music of the Ramones (1976) shaped British derivations like the Sex Pistols (1977) and the more sophisticated music of The Clash, who in 1979 combined their punk aesthetics with the Jamaican music that had been bubbling under the surface in both the United Kingdom and America. These three bands produced seminal albums during the second half of the 1970s. The crude amplified sounds, fast-driving rhythms, unassuming timbres, and simple harmonies helped to renovate rock, propelling it back to its working-class, garage-band roots.

This rudimentary sound of punk did not capture the interest of the general public. Nevertheless, punk went on to inspire the more literate and reflective **New Wave** sound (a more electronic and experimental form of punk rock) of the late 1970s and early 1980s, exemplified by such bands as Elvis Costello and the Attractions, the Police, and the Talking Heads.

Metal

The Kinks' "You Really Got Me" and "All the Day and All of the Night" (both 1964) marked the likely first appearances in popular music of the **power chord** (a "triad" lacking the major or minor third, thus a simple dyad chord of a fifth, 1–5, instead of usual triadic 1–3–5). The guitarist often slides these chords along the neck of the instrument in parallel motion. Used in "heavier" compositions by many of the guitar-bass-drum trios—the so-called power trios—of the late 1960s, this gesture became an integral feature of the louder, chordal sound of the very early 1970s. The lyrics of the new songs incorporated surrealistic themes, paranoid delusions, and dark, dreary subjects, plumbing the depths of adolescent angst. By the late 1980s, the freshest rock sounds were emanating from Metallica and other heavy-metal bands that performed energetic, powerful laments in somber, minor modes.

Rap

Although we think of **rap** music as contemporary, it's really more than forty years old. Rap originated as an African American style in the early 1970s in New York's South Bronx when DJ Kool Herc (Jamaican-born Clive Campbell) developed an imitation of the Jamaican practice of using "sound systems"—that is, mobile stereo equipment—to play music at local parties. Herc would play some of James Brown's early funk records and, using two turntables, discovered that he was able to isolate choice portions of the tracks (called the "break") and loop and extend them while the crowd danced ("break dancing"). Digging deep into black oral traditions, earlier Jamaican DJs would play R&B hits while also "toasting," calling out or metrically chanting for the crowd. Herc served as a toaster or MC (master of ceremonies) as well as DJ. Thus began the hip-hop culture of MCs, DJs, break dancers, and attendant graffiti artists that slowly made its way into the consciousness of America. Although origins are always fuzzy, the first recording with the word *rap* in the title is The Sugarhill Gang's "Rapper's Delight" (1979). The sound exploded in African American communities, and the next year Blondie, a New Wave band, incorporated a rapped section in their song "Rapture." During the decade that followed, rap became a major cultural force.

FIGURE 31.3
Run-DMC

The Queens, New York, group Run-DMC (Figure 31.3)—Joseph "Run" Simmons (1964–), Darryl "D.M.C." McDaniels (1964–), and Jason "Jam Master Jay" Mizell (1965–2002)—were the first rap artists to achieve major commercial success. Largely thanks to Run's brother, promoter and producer Russell Simmons, this group broke genre barriers in their first album with the high-profile inclusion of an electric guitar in "Rock Box" (1984), the video of which was the first of its type to be aired on MTV. Two years later, their collaboration with members of the band Aerosmith on "Walk This Way" brought Run-DMC's sound into heavy rotation on radio and TV. The video demonstrated that, although black and white forms of popular music sometimes seem to have nothing in common, in the end, they are stylistic cousins.

WATCH... a YouTube video of Run-DMC and Aerosmith performing "Walk This Way," online.

Grunge

Members of Generation X, born around 1975 of baby boom parents, became dissatisfied with the aesthetics of the music scene. In and around the city of Seattle and linked to the Sub Pop label, a movement arose that produced the dark, introspective songs of **grunge** (a type of alternative rock inspired by punk). Once again, it fell to a new, still ever-brooding, adolescent population to revitalize the noises and poetics of rock, echoing and redefining its raw essence. Grunge rejected its stylistic parents and grandparents, dumping all the superfluities that 1960s rock propagated: coiffed hair, stage makeup, costumes, ostentatious stage spectacles, synth sounds, self-indulgent sexuality, and virtuosity for its own sake—and that was just for starters.

The greatest figure to come out of the movement was Kurt Cobain. In 1991, his band, Nirvana, produced the classic *Nevermind* (1991). Steeped in a wide assortment of influences, the album is a brilliant mix, containing everything from straight garage-band rock, to metal and punk, to soft acoustic. The mood is sometimes angry but more often simply annoyed, and now and then merely playful. The absurd lyrics are occasionally ironic and quote other songs a few times. Cobain's guitar playing is nonvirtuosic but highly original and even idiosyncratic. In fact, Cobain was adamantly opposed to studio recording "tricks" in general and was once cajoled into adding an extra vocal track only after the producer told him, "John Lennon did it." By eschewing artifice, Cobain was reverting to an unpretentious folk aesthetic, albeit a more irritated and apolitical one. The band's signature song, "Smells Like Teen Spirit," was, according to Cobain, a "teen revolutionary theme," but a single, definitive message is more difficult to pin down. Like most ingenious works, an absolute meaning of the text at its moment of creation is lost to time, and it is therefore the reader who brings significance to the hodgepodge of lyrics.

WATCH... a YouTube video of "Smells Like Teen Spirit," online.

Thriller (1982) and Music Videos

The greatest-selling original album in the United States and by far the largest seller worldwide was the brainchild of a former Motown boy-band prodigy and an arranger twenty-five years his senior. Michael Jackson began his career at the age of five, singing in a band with his four brothers, The Jackson 5. The group's songs first charted in late 1969, inconsequential hits that were juvenile, pleasant bubblegum music, performed in a soft funk style. However, the infectious melodies sung by young Michael were well crafted and delivered with the proportional intensity of a diminutive James Brown. The brothers performed Motown-type choreography while their amazingly cute lead singer projected much of their charisma.

Soon the young Michael took off on his own, but after four solo albums that had little success, he paired with Quincy Jones, an experienced jazz musician, film music arranger, producer, and record executive, to create the highly acclaimed album *Off the Wall* (1979). Cuts from the album generally took the music pop/R&B/disco approach, with added percussive vocal accents from the James Brown tradition. Several composers contributed to the compilation, most notably Stevie Wonder and Paul McCartney.

Three years later, Jackson released *Thriller*. The album, which presented a carefully chosen medley of genres—from disco, to R&B, to pop ballad, to rock—rivals The Beatles albums in its stylistic variety. *Thriller* was consciously fabricated as a crossover tour-de-force, possessing something to appeal to virtually all ages and all tastes. The three videos that were released were especially innovative, unlike many early videos, and actually conformed to their lyrical story lines. The title track overwhelmed all expectations by being realized as a fourteen-minute film, and Jackson became the first African American to have his videos aired on MTV. His appearance on the Motown 25th Anniversary special on March 25, 1983, featuring a breathtaking performance of "Billie Jean" with the famous "moon walk," reintroduced a dynamic, physically transformed, and fully mature Michael Jackson to a national audience.

"Classic" but Ever-Evolving

When rock was young, there were a few artists, about twenty labels screening and developing the talent, and a few performance media in which the public could experience music (live, radio, vinyl, and television). For the first twenty or thirty years of its existence, one could name any rock or pop performers, and it was likely that any teen or young adult would have at least heard of them. However, technological and economic factors over the past twenty years have led to an explosion in the number of aspiring artists. Sound generators and mixing programs are cheap and ubiquitous, allowing tens of thousands of unsigned music makers to record their own material at home. Individual tracks are made readily available for the public to "taste test," to stream on myriad devices, and to download (for money or not). The thirteen-song album seems to have become passé. Today, if a poll of "favorite artists" were taken in a classroom, the chances are that many students would name artists unknown to many others. And maybe, if the class were small, no responses would be duplicated. More than likely, this chapter has snubbed your favorite song, band, and stylistic preference. It is impossible, of course, to include all of the various types of rock and pop that have arisen over the past fifty years and to laud all of the heroes. And, as a means for the distribution of music over the Internet by individual artists only grows, this atomization of rock will only continue.

About popular music, Sting has said, "At its best, it's subversive." Truly, youth music, as part of a general adolescent and postadolescent rebellion, will forever be slippery in style, difficult to label, and rapidly evolving—that is the essence of creativity. Yet, at the same time, rock has begun to take its place next to earlier styles of music in the musical museum. Just as we now have classical conservatories and more than one jazz hall of fame, so, too, there are classic rock stations, which appeal to an older demographic. But rock seems capable of perpetual regeneration. As one group of artists comes of age, another youthful band waits in the wings with its own ideas—and ways of expressing them through music.

KEY WORDS

rhythm and blues (R&B) (444)	cover (446)	Motown (448)	New Wave (449)
boogie-woogie (444)	concept album (447)	soul (449)	power chord (450)
rock and roll (445)	rock (447)	funk (449)	rap (450)
	guitar riff (448)	punk rock (449)	grunge (451)

 Join us on Facebook at Listening to Music with Craig Wright

DO ... online multiple-choice and critical thinking quizzes that your instructor may assign for a grade.

GLOSSARY

: indication to performer to repeat the music

A

absolute music: instrumental music that is free of a text or any preexisting program

a cappella: a term applied to unaccompanied vocal music; originated in the expression *a cappella Sistina*, "in the Sistine Chapel" of the pope, where instruments were forbidden to accompany the singers

accelerando: a tempo mark indicating "getting faster"

accent: emphasis or stress placed on a musical tone or a chord

accidental: a sharp, flat, or natural sign that alters the pitch of a note a half step

accompagnato: see *recitativo accompagnato*

acoustic instrument: instrument that produces sounds naturally when strings are bowed or plucked, a tube has air passed through it, or percussion instruments are struck

acoustic music: music produced by acoustic instruments

adagio: a tempo mark indicating "slow"

Alberti bass: a pattern of accompaniment whereby, instead of having the pitches of a chord sound all together, the notes are played in succession to provide a continual stream of sound

allegretto: a tempo mark indicating "moderately fast"

allegro: a tempo mark indicating "fast"

allemande: a stately dance in $\frac{4}{4}$ meter with gracefully interweaving lines

alto (contralto): the lower of the two female voice parts, the soprano being higher

amygdala: small area in the brain's limbic system associated with emotions

andante: a tempo mark indicating "moderately moving"

andantino: a tempo mark indicating "moderately moving" yet slightly faster than *andante*

antecedent phrase: the opening, incomplete-sounding phrase of a melody; often followed by a consequent phrase that brings the melody to closure

anthem: a composition for chorus on a sacred subject; similar in design and function to a motet

aria: an elaborate lyrical song for solo voice

arioso: a style of singing and a type of song midway between an aria and a recitative

arpeggio: the notes of a triad or seventh chord played in quick succession, up or down

Art of Fugue, The: Bach's last project (1742–1750), an encyclopedic treatment of all known contrapuntal procedures, set forth in nineteen canons and fugues

art song: a genre of song for voice and piano accompaniment, with high artistic aspirations

atonal music: music without tonality; music without a key center; most often associated with the twentieth-century avant-garde style of Arnold Schoenberg

augmentation: the notes of a melody held for longer than (usually double) their normal duration

B

backbeat: a drumbeat or cymbal crash occurring regularly after a strong beat, as on beats 2 and 4 in a measure with four beats

ballad: a traditional song, or folksong, sung by a soloist, which tells a dramatic, usually tragic, tale and is organized by stanzas

ballet: an art form that uses dance and music, along with costumes and scenery, to tell a story and display emotions through expressive gestures and movement

ballet music: music composed to accompany a ballet, with short bursts of tuneful melody and captivating rhythm, all intended to capture the emotional essence of the scene

Ballets Russes: a Russian ballet company of the early twentieth century, led by Sergei Diaghilev

banjo: a five-string, plucked folk instrument of African-American origin

bar: see *measure*

baritone: a male voice part of a middle range, between the higher tenor and the lower bass

bar line: small vertical line used in music notation to separate one bar, or measure, from the next

Baroque: term used to describe the arts generally during the period 1600–1750 and signifying excess and extravagance

basilar membrane: small organ in the cochlea of the inner ear, which recognizes sound patterns by frequency and sends the information, via the auditory nerve, to the brain stem and from there to the brain itself

bas instruments: a class of soft musical instruments, including the flute, recorder, fiddle, harp, and lute, that was popular during the late Middle Ages

bass: the lowest male voice range

bass clef: a sign placed on a staff to indicate the notes below middle C

bass drum: a large, low-sounding drum that is struck with a soft-headed stick

basso continuo: a small ensemble of at least two instrumentalists who provide a foundation for the melody or melodies above; heard almost exclusively in Baroque music

bassoon: a low, double-reed instrument of the woodwind family

basso ostinato: a motive or phrase in the bass that is repeated again and again

bass viol: see *viola da gamba*

Bayreuth Festival: still controlled today by the descendants of Wagner, a festival that continues to stage annually the music dramas of Wagner—and only Wagner—at the Bayreuth Festival Theater, an opera house built especially for that purpose

beat: an even pulse in music that divides the passing of time into equal segments

bebop: a complex, hard-driving style of jazz that emerged shortly after World War II; played without musical notation by a small ensemble

Beethovenian swell: in Ludwig van Beethoven's works, a repetitive wave of sound that emerges ever larger and ever louder from the orchestra

bel canto: (Italian for "beautiful singing") a style of singing and a type of Italian opera developed in the nineteenth century that features the beautiful tone and brilliant technique of the human voice

big band: a mid- to large-size dance band that emerged in the 1930s to play the style of jazz called swing

binary form: a musical form consisting of two contrasting units (**A** and **B**), constructed to balance and complement each other

blue note: the third, fifth, or seventh note of the blues scale that can be altered to be sharper or flatter; helps produce the wail of the blues

blues: an expressive, soulful style of singing that emerged from the African-American spiritual and work song in the South at the end of the nineteenth century; its texts are strophic and its harmonies, simple and repetitive

blues scale: a seven-note scale in which the third, fifth, and seventh notes are sometimes flat, sometimes natural, and sometimes in between

bolero: a popular, suggestive Spanish dance for a soloist or couple, often performed to the accompaniment of castanets

boogie-woogie: driving music in which the bass plays the harmony, not as chords, but as a succession of fast pitches of equal length

Brandenburg Concertos: set of six concerti grossi composed by J. S. Bach between 1711 and 1720, and subsequently dedicated to Margrave Christian Ludwig of Brandenburg

brass family: a group of musical instruments traditionally made of brass and played with a mouthpiece; includes the trumpet, trombone, French horn, and tuba

bridge: see *transition*

bugle: a simple brass instrument that evolved from the valveless military trumpet

C

cabaletta: the concluding fast aria of any two- or three-section operatic scene; a useful mechanism to get the principals off the stage

cadence: the concluding part of a musical phrase or the end of a chordal progression

cadenza: a showy passage for the soloist appearing near the end of the movement in a concerto; usually incorporates rapid runs, arpeggios, and snippets of previously heard themes into a fantasy-like improvisation

call and response: a method of performance in which a soloist sings and a group or another soloist answers; particularly favored in African music and genres of African-American music, such as the blues

canon (of Western music): a core repertoire, or the "chestnuts," of classical music performed at concerts continually since the eighteenth century

canon (round): a contrapuntal form in which the individual voices enter and each in turn duplicates exactly the melody that the first voice played or sang

cantata: a term originally meaning "something sung"; in its mature state, it consists of several movements, including one or more arias, ariosos, and recitatives; cantatas can be on secular subjects and intended for private performance or on religious subjects, such as those of J. S. Bach for the German Lutheran church

caprice: a light, whimsical character piece of the nineteenth century

carol: a song in the local language that marked Christmas, Easter, or even a military victory; most carols use strophic form

castanets: percussion instruments (rattles) of indefinite pitch associated with Spanish music

castrato: a male adult singer who was castrated as a boy to keep his voice from changing so that it would remain in the soprano or alto register

celesta: a small percussive keyboard instrument using hammers to strike metal bars, thereby producing a bright, bell-like sound

cello (violoncello): an instrument of the violin family but more than twice the violin's size; it is played between the legs and produces a rich, lyrical tone

chamber music: music, usually instrumental music, performed in a small concert hall or private residence with just one performer on each part

chance music: music that involves an element of chance (rolling dice, choosing cards, and so on) or whimsy on the part of the performers; especially popular with avant-garde composers

chanson: a French term used broadly to indicate a lyrical song from the Middle Ages into the twentieth century

character piece: a brief instrumental work seeking to capture a single mood, sentiment, or emotion; a genre much favored by composers of the Romantic era

chorale: the German word for the hymn of the Lutheran Church; hence, a simple religious melody to be sung by the congregation

chord: two or more simultaneously sounding pitches

chord progression: a succession of chords changing in a purposeful fashion

chorus: a group of singers, usually including sopranos, altos, tenors, and basses, with at least two and often many more singers on each vocal part; in Tin Pan Alley songs and Broadway tunes, the main melody of the song; jazz musicians often improvised around it

chromatic harmony: harmony utilizing chords built on the five chromatic notes of the scale in addition to the seven diatonic ones; produces rich harmonies

chromaticism: the frequent presence in melodies and chords of intervals only a half step apart; in a scale, the use of notes that are not part of the diatonic major or minor pattern

chromatic scale: a scale that makes use of all twelve pitches, equally divided, within the octave

church cantata: see *cantata*

clarinet: a single-reed instrument of the woodwind family with a large range and a wide variety of timbres within it

classical music: the traditional music of any culture, usually involving a specialized technical vocabulary and requiring many years of training; it is "high art" or "learned," timeless music that is enjoyed generation after generation

clavier: a general term for all keyboard instruments, including the harpsichord, organ, and piano

clef: a sign used to indicate the register, or range of pitches, in which an instrument is to play or a singer is to sing

coda: (Italian for "tail") a final and concluding section of a musical composition

collage art: art made up of disparate materials taken from very different places

collegium musicum: a society of amateur musicians (usually associated with a university) dedicated to the performance of music, nowadays music of the Middle Ages, Renaissance, and Baroque eras

col legno: (Italian for "with the wood") an instruction to string players to strike the strings of the instrument, not with the horsehair of the bow, but with the wood of it

color (timbre): the character or quality of a musical tone produced by a voice or an instrument, as determined by its harmonics and its attack and decay

comic opera: a genre of opera that originated in the eighteenth century, portraying everyday characters and situations, and using spoken dialogue and simple songs

compilation method: a new method of "composing" film music in which directors began to cut and paste together their own sound tracks from preexisting and prerecorded music

computer-generated images (CGI): special effects introduced into films of the 1980s and 1990s

computer music: the most recent development in electronic music; couples the computer with the electronic synthesizer to imitate the sounds of acoustic instruments and to produce new sounds

concept album: an album in which all of the songs treat a single theme or relate to one another in some way

concertino: the group of instruments that function as soloists in a concerto grosso

concerto: an instrumental genre in which one or more soloists play with and against an orchestra

concerto grosso: a multimovement concerto of the Baroque era that pits the sound of a small group of soloists (the concertino) against that of the full orchestra (the tutti)

concert overture: an independent, one-movement work, usually of programmatic content, originally intended for the concert hall and not designed to precede an opera or play

conductor: The orchestra's musical "traffic cop," who directs the performers

conjunct motion: melodic motion that proceeds primarily by steps and without leaps

consequent phrase: the second phrase of a two-part melodic unit that brings a melody to a point of repose and closure

consonance: pitches sounding agreeable and stable

continuo: see *basso continuo*

contrabassoon: a larger, lower-sounding version of the bassoon

contrary motion: a musical process in which the soprano and bass go in opposite directions

contrast: a process employed by a composer to introduce different melodies, rhythms, textures, or moods in order to provide variety and even to create conflict

cool jazz: a style of jazz that emerged in the 1950s that is softer, more relaxed, and less frenzied than bebop

cornet: a brass instrument with valves that looks like a short trumpet; it has a more mellow tone than the trumpet and is most often used in military bands

cornetto: a woodwind instrument, developed during the late Middle Ages and early Renaissance, that sounds like a hybrid of a clarinet and a trumpet

Council of Trent: a two-decades-long (1545–1563) conference at which leading cardinals and bishops undertook the reform of the Roman Catholic Church, including its music

counterpoint: the harmonious opposition of two or more independent musical lines

Counter-Reformation: a movement that fostered reform in the Roman Catholic Church in response to the challenge of the Protestant Reformation and led to a conservative, austere approach to art

country music: repertoire of American songs with lyrics treating the subjects of love and life's disappointments, accompanied primarily by one or more guitars

courante: a lively dance in 6/4 with an upbeat and frequent changes of metrical accent

cover: new version of a standard; interpretation of a song already recorded by others

crescendo: a gradual increase in the volume of sound

cross-hand playing: moving the left hand over the right hand to play a high melody line

cross stringing: a practice popularized by the Steinway Company of New York whereby the lowest-sounding strings of the piano ride up and across those of the middle register,

thereby giving the piano a richer, more homogenous sound

Cubism: early-twentieth-century artistic style in which the artist fractures and dislocates formal reality into geometrical blocks and planes

cue: music written for sections in early films during which people weren't speaking

Cultural Revolution: Chairman Mao Zedong's social and political reformation of the People's Republic of China between 1966 and 1976

cut music: music used for beginnings and endings in video games, often resembling film and television themes in that it is typically melodic, with a distinctive contour or colorful instrumentation

cymbals: a percussion instrument consisting of two metal discs; they are made to crash together in order to create emphasis and articulation in music

D

da capo **aria:** an aria in two sections, with an obligatory return to and repeat of the first; hence, an aria in ternary (**ABA**) form

da capo **form:** ternary (**ABA**) form for an aria, so called because the performers, when reaching the end of **B**, "take it from the head" and repeat **A**

dance suite: a collection of instrumental dances, each with its own distinctive rhythm and character

decrescendo (diminuendo): a gradual decrease in the volume of sound

development: the centermost portion of sonata–allegro form, in which the thematic material of the exposition is developed and extended, transformed, or reduced to its essence; often the most confrontational and unstable section of the movement

diatonic: pertaining to the seven notes that make up either the major or the minor scale

Dies irae: a Gregorian chant composed in the thirteenth century and used as the central portion of the Requiem Mass of the Catholic Church

digital audio workstation (DAW): professional equipment designed to record, edit, and play digital audio

diminished chord: a triad or seventh chord made up entirely of minor thirds and producing a tense, unstable sound

diminuendo: a gradual decrease in the volume of sound

diminution: a reduction, usually by half, of all the rhythmic durations in a melody

disjunct motion: a melodic motion that moves primarily by leaps rather than by steps

dissonance: a discordant mingling of sounds, sounding disagreeable and unstable

diva: (Italian for "goddess") a celebrated female opera singer; a prima donna

Doctrine of Affections: early-seventeenth-century aesthetic theory that held that different musical moods could and should be used to influence the emotions, or affections, of the listener

dominant: the chord built on the fifth degree of the scale

doo-wop: a type of soul music that emerged in the 1950s as an outgrowth of the gospel hymns sung in African-American churches in urban Detroit, Chicago, Philadelphia, and New York; its lyrics made use of repeating phrases sung in a cappella (unaccompanied) harmony below the tune

dotted note: a note to which an additional duration of 50 percent has been added

double bass: the largest and lowest-pitched instrument in the string family

double counterpoint: a counterpoint with two themes that can reverse position, with the top theme moving to the bottom and the bottom theme moving to the top (see **invertible counterpoint**)

double exposition form: a form, originating in the concerto of the Classical period, in which first the orchestra and then the soloist present the primary thematic material

double stops: a technique applied to string instruments in which two strings instead of just one are pressed down and played simultaneously

downbeat: the first beat of each measure; indicated by a downward motion of the conductor's hand and usually stressed

dramatic overture: a one-movement work, usually in sonata–allegro form, that encapsulates in music the essential dramatic events of the opera or play that follows

drone: a continuous sound on one or more fixed pitches

duple meter: a gathering of beats into two beats per measure, with every other beat stressed

dynamics: the various levels of volume, loud and soft, at which sounds are produced in a musical composition

E

electronic instruments: machines that produce musical sounds by electronic means, the most widespread instrument being the electronic keyboard

electronic music: sounds produced and manipulated by magnetic tape machines, synthesizers, and/or computers

eleventh chord: a chord comprising five intervals of a third and spanning eleven letters of the scale

encore: (French for "again") the repeat of a piece demanded by an appreciative audience; an extra piece added at the end of a concert

endless melody: a nonstop stream of solo singing and declamation that goes through an entire act of a Wagnerian music drama

English horn: a low oboe, pitched at the interval a fifth below the oboe, much favored by composers of the Romantic era

Enlightenment: eighteenth-century period in philosophy and letters during which thinkers gave free rein to the pursuit of truth and the discovery of natural laws

episode: a passage of free, nonimitative counterpoint found in a fugue

"Eroica" Symphony: Beethoven's Symphony No. 3 (1803), originally dedicated to Napoleon but published as the "Heroic Symphony"

Esterházy family: the richest and most influential among the German-speaking aristocrats of eighteenth-century Hungary, with extensive landholdings southeast of Vienna and a passionate interest in music; patrons of Haydn

etude: a short, one-movement composition designed to improve a particular aspect of a performer's technique

Exoticism: the use of sounds drawn from outside the traditional Western European musical experience, popular among composers in late-nineteenth-century Europe

exposition: in a fugue, the opening section, in which each voice in turn has the opportunity to present the subject; in sonata–allegro form, the principal section, in which all thematic material is presented

Expressionism: a powerful movement in the early-twentieth-century arts, initially a German-Austrian development that arose in Berlin, Munich, and Vienna; its aim was not to depict objects as they are seen but to express the strong emotion that the object generates in the artist

F

falsetto voice: a high, soprano-like voice produced by adult male singers when they sing in head voice and not in full chest voice

fantasy: a free, improvisatory-like composition in which the composer follows his or her whims rather than an established musical form

fermata: in musical notation, a mark indicating that the performer(s) should hold a note or a chord for an extended duration

fiddle: a popular term for the violin

figured bass: in musical notation, a numerical shorthand that tells the player which unwritten notes to fill in above the written bass note

film score: music for an early film made up of any number of individual cues that could last any length, usually until a scene change

finale: the last movement of a multimovement composition, which usually works to a climax and conclusion

flamenco: a genre of Spanish song and dance, with guitar accompaniment, that originated in southernmost Spain and exhibits non-Western, possibly Arab-influenced, scales

flat: in musical notation, a symbol that lowers a pitch by a half step

flute: a high-sounding member of the woodwind family; initially made of wood, but more recently, beginning in the nineteenth century, of silver or even platinum

folk music: music springing from rural communities and passed along by oral transmission, with one singer learning from another

folk-rock: a mixture of the steady beat of rock with the forms, topics, and styles of singing of the traditional Anglo-American folk ballad

folksong: a song originating from an ethnic group and passed from generation to generation by oral tradition rather than written notation

form: the purposeful organization of the artist's materials; in music, the general shape of a composition as perceived by the listener

forte (f): in musical notation, a dynamic mark indicating "loud"

fortepiano (pianoforte): the original name of the piano

fortissimo (ff): in musical notation, a dynamic mark indicating "very loud"

free counterpoint: counterpoint in which the voices do not all make use of some preexisting subject in imitation

free jazz: a style of jazz perfected during the 1960s in which a soloist indulges in flights of creative fancy without concern for the rhythm, melody, or harmony of the other performers

French horn: a brass instrument that plays in the middle range of the brass family; developed from the medieval hunting horn

French overture: an overture style developed by Jean-Baptiste Lully with two sections, the first slow in duple meter with dotted note values, the second fast in triple meter and with light imitation; the first section can be repeated after the second

fugato: a short fugue set in some other musical form, such as sonata–allegro or theme and variations

fugue: a composition for three, four, or five parts played or sung by voices or instruments; begins with a presentation of a subject in imitation in each part and continues with modulating passages of free counterpoint and further appearances of the subject

full cadence: a cadence that sounds complete, in part because it usually ends on the tonic note

funk: a blend of soul, jazz, and rhythm and blues that emerged in African-American music in the 1960s

fusion: *see jazz-fusion*

G

galliard: a fast, leaping Renaissance dance in triple meter

genre: a type of music; specifically, the quality of musical style, form, performing medium, and place of performance that characterize any one type of music

Gesamtkunstwerk: (German for "total art work") an art form that involves music, poetry, drama, mime, dance, and scenic design; often used in reference to Richard Wagner's music dramas

Gewandhaus Orchestra: the symphony orchestra that originated in the Clothiers' House in Leipzig, Germany, in the eighteenth century

gigue: a fast dance in 6/8 or 12/8 with a constant eighth-note pulse that produces a gallop-like effect

glissando: an effect of sliding up or down the scale very rapidly

globalization: the development of an increasingly integrated global economy

glockenspiel: a percussion instrument made of tuned metal bars that are struck by mallets

gong: a circular, metal percussion instrument of Asian origin

gospel music: a highly rhythmic, often syncopated religious music, sung with call and response, which developed in African-American churches in the American South

Gothic style: a medieval style exemplified by cathedrals possessing such elements as pointed arches, high ceiling vaults, flying buttresses, and richly colored stained glass

grave: a tempo mark indicating "very slow and grave"

great (grand) staff: a large musical staff that combines both the treble and the bass clefs

Gregorian chant (plainsong): a large body of unaccompanied monophonic vocal music, set to Latin texts, composed for the Western Church over the course of fifteen centuries, from the time of the earliest fathers to the Council of Trent (1545–1563)

ground bass: the English term for *basso ostinato*

grunge: a type of alternative rock music, inspired by punk rock and youthful rebellion generally, that originated in the northwestern United States and peaked in popularity around 1990

guitar riff: an improvisatory flourish that becomes a motive

H

habanera: (Spanish for "the thing from Havana") an Afro-Cuban dance song that came to prominence in the nineteenth century, marked by a repeating bass and a repeating, syncopated rhythm

half cadence: a cadence at which the music does not come to a fully satisfying stop but stands as if suspended on a dominant chord

half step: the smallest musical interval in the Western major or minor scale; the distance between any two adjacent keys on the piano

harmony: the sounds that provide the support and enrichment—the accompaniment—for melody

harp: an ancient, plucked-string instrument with a triangular shape

harpsichord: a keyboard instrument, especially popular during the Baroque era (1600–1750), that produces sound by depressing a key that drives a lever upward and forces a pick to pluck a string

hauts instruments: a class of loud musical instruments, including the trumpet, sackbut, shawm, and drum, that was popular during the late Middle Ages

Heiligenstadt Testament: something akin to Beethoven's last will and testament, written in despair when he recognized that he would ultimately suffer a total loss of hearing; named after the Viennese suburb in which he penned it

"heroic" period: a period in Beethoven's compositional career (1803–1813) during which he wrote longer works incorporating broad gestures, grand climaxes, and triadic, triumphant themes

hip hop: a larger genre, encompassing rap music, in which the vocal line is delivered more like speech than like song and in which a wide variety of rhythmic devices are used

homophony: a texture in which all the voices, or lines, move to new pitches at roughly the same time; often referred to in contradistinction to polyphony

horn: a term generally used by musicians to refer to any brass instrument, but most often the French horn

hornpipe: an energetic dance, derived from the country jig, in either $\frac{3}{2}$ or $\frac{2}{4}$ time

humanism: the Renaissance belief that people have the capacity to create many things that are both good and beautiful; it rejoiced in the human form in all its fullness, looked outward, and indulged a passion for invention and discovery

Hundred Years' War (1337–1453): the name given to a century-long series of military conflicts between the French and the English

I

idée fixe: literally, a "fixed idea"; more specifically, an obsessive musical theme as first used in Hector Berlioz's *Symphonie fantastique*

idiomatic writing: a musical composition that exploits the strengths and avoids the weaknesses of particular voices and instruments

imitation: a polyphonic procedure whereby one or more voices, or parts, enter and duplicate exactly for a short period of time the music presented by the previous voice

imitative counterpoint: a type of counterpoint in which the voices or lines frequently use imitation

impresario: a renowned producer

Impressionism: a late-nineteenth-century movement that arose in France; the Impressionists were the first to reject photographic realism in painting, instead trying to re-create the impression that an object produces upon the senses in a single, fleeting moment

incidental music: music to be inserted between the acts or during important scenes of a play to add an extra dimension to the drama

instrumental break: in the blues or in jazz, a short instrumental passage that interrupts and responds to the singing of a voice

intermezzo: (Italian for "between piece") a light musical interlude intended to separate and thus break the mood of two more serious, surrounding movements or operatic acts or scenes

interval: the distance between any two pitches on a musical scale

inversion: the process of inverting the musical intervals in a theme or a melody; a melody that ascends by step, now descends by step, and so on

invertible counterpoint: see *double counterpoint*

J

jazz: a lively, energetic music with pulsating rhythms and scintillating syncopations, usually played by either a small instrumental ensemble (a combo) or a larger group (a big band)

jazz-fusion: a mixture of jazz and rock cultivated by American bands in the 1970s

jazz riff: a short motive, usually played by an entire instrumental section (woodwinds or brasses), that appears frequently, but intermittently, in a jazz composition

K

key: a tonal center built on a tonic note and making use of a scale; also, on a keyboard instrument, one of a series of levers that can be depressed to generate sound

key signature: in musical notation, a preplaced set of sharps or flats used to indicate the scale and key

Köchel (K) number: an identifying number assigned to each of the works of Mozart, in roughly chronological order, by Ludwig von Köchel (1800–1877)

Kyrie: the first portion of the Ordinary of the Mass and, hence, usually the opening movement in a polyphonic setting of the Mass

L

largo: a tempo mark indicating "slow and broad"

La Scala: the principal opera house of the city of Milan, Italy, which opened in 1778

leading tone: the pitch a half step below the tonic, which pulls up and into it, especially at cadences

leap: melodic movement not by an interval of just a step, but usually by a jump of at least a fourth

legato: in musical notation, an articulation mark indicating that the notes are to be smoothly connected; the opposite of staccato

leitmotif: a brief, distinctive unit of music designed to represent a character, object, or idea; a term applied to the motives in the music dramas of Richard Wagner

lento: a tempo mark indicating "very slow"

libretto: the text of an opera

Lied: (German for "song") the genre of art song, for voice and piano accompaniment, that originated in Germany c. 1800

limbic system: primitive subregion of the brain associated with emotions and survival

Lisztomania: the sort of mass hysteria, today reserved for pop music stars,

that surrounded touring Romantic-era pianist Franz Liszt

London Symphonies: the twelve symphonies composed by Joseph Haydn for performance in London between 1791 and 1795; Haydn's last twelve symphonies (Nos. 93–104)

looped underscoring: repetition of simple theme music within video games

lute: a six-string instrument appearing in the West in the late Middle Ages

lyrics: text set to music

M

madrigal: a popular genre of secular vocal music that originated in Italy during the Renaissance, in which usually four or five voices sing love poems

madrigalism: a device, originating in the madrigal, by which key words in a text spark a particularly expressive musical setting

major scale: a seven-note scale that ascends in the following order of whole and half steps: 1–1–½–1–1–1–½

marimba: Mexican percussion instrument similar in construction to the xylophone

Marseillaise, La: a tune written as a revolutionary marching song in 1792 by Claude-Joseph Rouget de Lisle and sung by a battalion from Marseilles as it entered Paris that year; it subsequently became the French national anthem

Mass: the central religious service of the Roman Catholic Church, one that incorporates singing for spiritual reflection or as accompaniment to sacred acts

mazurka: a fast dance of Polish origins in triple meter with an accent on the second beat

measure (bar): a group of beats, or musical pulses; usually, the number of beats is fixed and constant so that the measure serves as a continual unit of measurement in music

melisma: in singing, one vowel luxuriously spread out over many notes

melismatic singing: many notes sung to just one syllable

melodic sequence: the repetition of a musical motive at successively higher or lower degrees of the scale

melody: a series of notes arranged in order to form a distinctive, recognizable musical unit; most often placed in the treble

mensural notation: measured notation that specified rhythm as well as pitch precisely

meter: the gathering of beats into regular groups

meter signature: see *time signature*

metronome: a mechanical device used by performers to keep a steady tempo

mezzo-soprano: a female vocal range between alto and soprano

middle C: the middlemost C on the modern piano

Minimalism: a style of modern music that takes a very small amount of musical material and repeats it over and over to form a composition

minor scale: a seven-note scale that ascends in the following order of whole and half steps: 1–½–1–1–½–1–1

minuet: a moderate dance in ¾ though actually danced in patterns of six steps, with no upbeat but with highly symmetrical phrasing

modal jazz: a style of jazz that developed during the 1950s, in which the melody is constructed around scale patterns other than major and minor, and the chordal harmony emphasizes degrees of the scale other than the traditional subdominant, dominant, and tonic

mode: a pattern of pitches forming a scale; the two primary modes in Western music are major and minor

moderato: a tempo marking indicating "moderately moving"

Modernism: a bracing, progressive style that dominated classical music and the arts generally from the beginning to the end of the twentieth century

modified strophic form: strophic form in which the music is modified slightly to accommodate a particularly expressive word or phrase in the text

modulation: the process in music whereby the tonal center changes from one key to another—from G major to C major, for example

monody: a general term connoting solo singing accompanied by a *basso continuo* in the early Baroque period

monophony: a musical texture involving only a single line of music with no accompaniment

monothematic format: film-scoring format in which a single instrumental theme is used throughout a film

motet: a composition for choir or larger chorus setting a religious, devotional, or solemn text; often sung a cappella

motive: a short, distinctive melodic figure that stands by itself

Motown: record company founded by Berry Gordy and based in Detroit

mouthpiece: a detachable portion of a brass instrument into which the player blows

movement: a large, independent section of a major instrumental work, such as a sonata, dance suite, symphony, quartet, or concerto

music: the rational organization of sounds and silences as they pass through time

musical (musical comedy): a popular genre of musical theater designed to appeal to a general audience by means of spoken dialogue, songs, and energetic dances

musical nationalism: see *nationalism*

musical notation: written music

musical template: set of musical expectations that each of us engages as we listen to a piece; it reminds us how we think the music ought to go, what sounds good and what sounds bad

music drama: a term used for the mature operas of Richard Wagner

music video: a visual form of music pioneered by the twenty-four-hour cable channel MTV

musique concrète: music in which the composer works directly with sounds recorded on magnetic tape, not with musical notation and performers

mute: any device that muffles the sound of a musical instrument; on the trumpet, for example, it is a cup that is placed inside the bell of the instrument

N

nationalism: a movement in music in the nineteenth century in which composers sought to emphasize indigenous qualities in their music by incorporating folk songs, native scales, dance rhythms, and local instrumental sounds

natural: in musical notation, a symbol that cancels a preexisting sharp or flat

Neo-classicism: a movement in twentieth-century music that sought to return to the musical forms and aesthetics of the Baroque and Classical periods

neo-Romanticism: a style that starts with the musical elements of Romantic music but reimagines them with an awareness of Modernist musical processes

New Age music: a style of nonconfrontational, often repetitious music performed on electronic instruments that arose during the 1990s

New Orleans jazz: a style of jazz that originated in that city shortly after 1900, involving a syncopated, improvisatory style of playing built on the tunes and harmonies of blues, parlor songs, rags, and marches

New Wave: a more electronic and experimental form of punk rock

ninth chord: a chord spanning nine letters of the scale and constructed by superimposing four intervals of a third

nocturne: a slow, introspective type of music, usually for piano, with rich harmonies and poignant dissonances intending to convey the mysteries of the night

nonimitative counterpoint: counterpoint with independent lines that do not imitate each other

O

oboe: an instrument of the woodwind family; the highest-pitched of the double-reed instruments

octave: the interval comprising the first and eighth tones of the major and minor diatonic scale; the sounds are quite similar because the frequency of vibration of the higher pitch is exactly twice that of the lower

octave displacement: a process used in constructing a melody whereby a simple, nearby interval is made more distant, and the melodic line more disjunct, by placing the next note up or down an octave

Ode to Joy: *An die Freude* by poet Friedrich von Schiller, set to music by Beethoven as a hymn in honor of universal brotherhood and used in the finale of his Symphony No. 9

open scoring: music with a solid bass, thin middle texture, and penetrating high sound of a flute, clarinet, or trumpet

opera: a dramatic work in which the actors sing some or all of their parts; it usually makes use of elaborate stage sets and costumes

opera buffa: (Italian for "comic opera") a genre of opera featuring light, often domestic subjects, with tuneful melodies, comic situations, and happy endings

opera seria: a genre of opera that dominated the stage during the Baroque era, making use of serious historical or mythological subjects, *da capo* arias, and lengthy overtures

operetta: a light opera with spoken dialogue and numerous dances involving comedy and romance in equal measure

ophicleide: a low brass instrument originating in military bands about the time of the French Revolution; the precursor of the tuba

opus: (Latin for "work") the term adopted by composers to enumerate and identify their compositions

oral tradition: the process used in the transmission of folk songs and other traditional music in which the material is passed from one generation to the next by singing, playing, and hearing without musical notation

oratorio: a large-scale genre of sacred music involving an overture, arias, recitatives, and choruses, but sung, whether in a theater or a church, without costumes or scenery

orchestra: see *symphony orchestra*

orchestral dance suite: a dance suite written for orchestra

orchestral Lied: see *orchestral song*

orchestral score: a composite of the musical lines of all of the instruments of the orchestra and from which a conductor conducts

orchestral song: a genre of music emerging in the nineteenth century in which the voice is accompanied not merely by a piano but by a full orchestra

orchestration: the art of assigning to the various instruments of the orchestra, or of a chamber ensemble, the diverse melodies, accompaniments, and counterpoints of a musical composition

Ordinary of the Mass: the five sung portions of the Mass for which the texts are invariable

organ: an ancient musical instrument constructed mainly of pipes and keys; the player depresses a key, which allows air to rush into or over a pipe, thereby producing sound

organum: the name given to the early polyphony of the Western Church from the ninth through the thirteenth centuries

oscillator: a device that, when activated by an electronic current, pulses back and forth to produce an electronic signal that can be converted by a loudspeaker into sound

ostinato: (Italian for "obstinate") a musical figure, motive, melody, harmony, or rhythm that is repeated again and again

overtone: Extremely faint sound, in addition to the fundamental sound of an instrument, caused by fractional vibrations of a string or air column within a pipe

overture: an introductory movement, usually for orchestra, that precedes an opera, oratorio, or dance suite

P

parallel motion: a musical process in which all of the lines or parts move in the same direction, and at the same intervals, for a period of time; the opposite of counterpoint

part: an independent line or voice in a musical composition; also, a section of a composition

***"Pathétique"* Sonata:** one of Beethoven's most celebrated compositions for piano

patter song: a stock device, employing quick, repeated pitches, almost as if stuttering; used to depict low-caste, inarticulate characters in comic opera

pavane: slow, gliding Renaissance dance in duple meter performed by couples holding hands

pedal point: a note, usually in the bass, sustained or continually repeated for a period of time while the harmonies change around it

pentatonic scale: a five-note scale found often in folk music and non-Western music

phrase: a self-contained portion of a melody, theme, or tune

pianissimo (pp): in musical notation, a dynamic mark indicating "very soft"

piano (p): in musical notation, a dynamic mark indicating "soft"

piano: a large keyboard instrument that creates sound at various dynamic levels when hammers are struck against strings

pianoforte: the original name for the piano

piano transcription: the transformation and reduction of an orchestral score, and a piece of orchestral music, onto the great staff for playing at the piano

piccolo: a small flute; the smallest and highest-pitched woodwind instrument

pickup: a note or two coming before the first downbeat of a piece, intending to give a little extra push into that downbeat

pitch: the relative position, high or low, of a musical sound

pizzicato: the process whereby a performer plucks the strings of an instrument rather than bowing them

plainsong: see *Gregorian chant*

point of imitation: a distinctive motive that is sung or played in turn by each voice or instrumental line

polonaise: a dance of Polish origin in triple meter without an upbeat but usually with an accent on the second of the three beats

polychord: the stacking of one triad or seventh chord on another so they sound simultaneously

polymeter: two or more meters sounding simultaneously

polyphony: a musical texture involving two or more simultaneously sounding lines; the lines are often independent and create counterpoint

polyrhythm: two or more rhythms sounding simultaneously

polytonality: the simultaneous sounding of two keys or tonalities

popular music: a broad category of music designed to please a large section of the general public; sometimes used in contradistinction to more "serious" or more "learned" classical music

Postmodernism: cultural movement that leaves artistic traditions behind in favor of an inclusive, "anything goes" approach to art and music

power chord: a "triad" lacking the major or minor third, thus a simple dyad chord of a fifth, 1–5, instead of the usual triadic

prelude: an introductory, improvisatory-like movement that gives the performer a chance to warm up and sets the stage for a more substantive subsequent movement

prepared piano: a piano outfitted with screws, bolts, washers, erasers, and bits of felt and plastic to transform the instrument from a melodic one to a percussive one

prestissimo: in musical notation, a tempo mark indicating "as fast as possible"

presto: in musical notation, a tempo mark indicating "very fast"

prima donna: (Italian for "first lady") the leading female singer in an opera

primary auditory cortex: area of the brain's temporal lobe that processes sound

Primitivism: artistic mode of expression that attempts to capture the unadorned lines, raw energy, and elemental truth of non-Western art and apply it in a Modernist context

program music: a piece of instrumental music, usually for symphony orchestra, that seeks to re-create in sound the events and emotions portrayed in some extramusical source: a story, a play, a historical event, an encounter with nature, or even a painting

program symphony: a symphony with the usual three, four, or five movements in which the individual movements together tell a tale or depict a succession of specific events or scenes

Proper of the Mass: the sections of the Mass that are sung to texts that vary with each feast day

Psalter: the Book of Psalms

punk rock: fast, hard-edged music, with short, simple songs and minimal instrumentation

Q

quadrivium: a curriculum of four scientific disciplines (arithmetic, geometry, astronomy, and music) taught in medieval schools and universities

quadruple meter: music with four beats per measure

quarter note: unit of musical duration that most often represents the beat; normally moves at roughly the rate of the average person's heartbeat

quarter tone: the division of the whole tone, or whole step, into quarter tones, a division even smaller than the half tone, or half step, on the piano

R

ragtime: an early type of jazz emerging in the 1890s and characterized by a steady bass and a syncopated, jazzy treble

rap: a style of popular music closely associated with hip hop that became popular in the United States in the 1980s, mostly among urban African Americans; it usually involves rapping along with audio processing (sampling and scratching)

realistic opera: a general term for those operas of the nineteenth and early twentieth centuries that deal with everyday, gritty subjects; includes Italian *verismo* opera

rebec: a medieval fiddle

recapitulation: in sonata–allegro form, the return to the first theme and the tonic key following the development

recital: a concert of chamber music, usually for a solo performer

recitative: musically heightened speech, often used in an opera, oratorio, or cantata to report dramatic action and advance the plot

recitativo accompagnato: a recitative accompanied by the orchestra instead of merely the harpsichord; the opposite of simple, or *secco,* recitative

recorder: an end-blown wooden flute with seven finger holes, played straight out instead of to one side

relative major: the major key in a pair of major and minor keys; relative keys have the same key signature, for example, E♭ major and C minor (both with three flats)

relative minor: the minor key in a pair of major and minor keys; see *relative major*

Renaissance: period of intellectual and artistic flowering that occurred first in Italy, then in France, and finally in England, during the years 1350–1600

repetition: process employed by a composer to validate the importance of a section of music by repeating it

rest: a silence in music of a specific duration

retransition: the end of the development section, where the tonality often becomes stabilized on the dominant in preparation for the return of the tonic (and first theme) at the beginning of the recapitulation

retrograde: a musical process in which a melody is played or sung, not from beginning to end, but starting with the last note and working backward to the first

rhythm: the organization of time in music, dividing up long spans of time into smaller, more easily comprehended units

rhythm and blues: a style of early rock and roll c. 1950 characterized by a pounding ⁴⁄₄ beat and a raw, growling style of singing, all set within a twelve-bar blues harmony

rhythm section: the section within a jazz band, usually consisting of drums, double bass, piano, banjo, and/or guitar, that establishes the harmony and rhythm

Ring cycle: a cycle of four interconnected music dramas by Richard Wagner that collectively tell the tale of the Germanic legend *Der Ring des Nibelungen*

ritard: a gradual slowing down of the tempo

ritardando: in musical notation, a tempo mark indicating a slowing down of the tempo

ritornello: a theme in Baroque works that returns again and again; from Italian for "return" or "refrain"

ritornello form: form in a Baroque concerto grosso in which all or part of the main theme—the ritornello (Italian for "return" or "refrain")—returns again and again, invariably played by the tutti, or full orchestra

rock: a type of popular music that emerged from rock and roll in the mid-1960s, marked by amplified singing, electric instruments, and a strong rhythmic drive conducive to dancing

rock and roll: a type of popular music that emerged from rhythm and blues in the 1950s, characterized by amplified singing, acoustic and electric instruments, and a very strong rhythmic drive conducive to dancing

romance: a slow, lyrical piece, or movement within a larger work, for instruments, or instrument and voice, much favored by composers of the Romantic period

Romanticism: A movement in the arts and ideas, roughly coinciding with the nineteenth century, that valued human independence, political freedom, a love of nature, and passionate expression, especially in poetry and music

Romantic Minimalism: a scoring technique pioneered by composer Hans Zimmer, in which a small (minimal) bit of material is repeated extensively, but constantly varied and expanded timbrally and rhythmically in the style of Romantic-era music

rondeau: see *rondo form*

rondo form: classical form with at least three statements of the refrain (**A**) and at least two contrasting sections (at least **B** and **C**); placement of the refrain creates symmetrical patterns such as **ABACA, ABACABA,** or even **ABACADA**

rubato: (Italian for "robbed") in musical notation, a tempo mark indicating that the performer may take, or steal, great liberties with the tempo

Russian Five: a group of young composers (Borodin, Cui, Balakirev, Rimsky-Korsakov, and Musorgsky) centered in St. Petersburg, whose aim was to write purely Russian music free of European influence

S

sackbut: a brass instrument of the late Middle Ages and Renaissance; the precursor of the trombone

Salzburg: mountain town in Austria, birthplace of Mozart

sampling: reusing (and often repeating) portions of a previous sound recording in a new song

Sanctus: the fourth section of the Ordinary of the Mass

sarabande: a slow, elegant dance in $\frac{3}{4}$ with a strong accent on the second beat

scale: an arrangement of pitches that ascends and descends in a fixed and unvarying pattern

scena: a scenic plan in Italian opera involving a succession of separate elements such as a slow aria, a recitative, and a fast concluding aria

scherzo: (Italian for "joke") a rapid, jovial work in triple meter often used in place of the minuet as the third movement in a string quartet or symphony

Schubertiad: a social gathering for music and poetry that featured the songs and piano music of Franz Schubert

score: a volume of musical notation involving more than one staff

scratching: sound processing that involves the rhythmical manipulation of a vinyl record

secco recitative: see *simple recitative*

Second Viennese School: a group of progressive modernist composers that revolved around Arnold Schoenberg in Vienna in the early twentieth century

sequence: a Gregorian chant, sung during the Proper of the Mass, in which

a chorus and a soloist alternate; see also *melodic sequence*

serenade: an instrumental work for a small ensemble originally intended as a light entertainment in the evening

serial music: music in which some important component—pitch, dynamics, rhythm—comes in a continually repeating series; see also *twelve-tone composition*

seventh chord: a chord spanning seven letter names and constructed by superimposing three thirds

sforzando: a sudden, loud attack on one note or chord

sharp: a musical symbol that raises a pitch by a half step

shawm: a double-reed woodwind instrument of the late Middle Ages and Renaissance; the precursor of the oboe

simple recitative: recitative accompanied only by a *basso continuo* or a harpsichord, and not the full orchestra

sinfonia: (Italian for "symphony") a one-movement (later three- or four-movement) orchestral work that originated in Italy in the seventeenth century

Singspiel: (German for "singing play") a musical comedy originating in Germany with spoken dialogue, tuneful songs, and topical humor

Sistine Chapel: the pope's private chapel within his Vatican apartments

smooth jazz: mellow jazz genre that became popular beginning in the 1980s, with the legato sounds of saxophonist Kenny G

snare drum: a small drum consisting of a metal cylinder covered with a skin or sheet of plastic that, when played with sticks, produces the "rat-ta-tat" sound familiar from marching bands

soft pedal: the left pedal of the piano, which, when depressed, shifts the keyboard in such a way that the hammers strike fewer strings, making the instrument sound softer

solo: a musical composition, or portion of a composition, sung or played by a single performer

solo concerto: a concerto in which an orchestra and a single performer in turn present and develop the musical material in the spirit of harmonious competition

solo sonata: a work, usually in three or four movements, for keyboard or other solo instrument; when a solo

melodic instrument played a sonata in the Baroque era, it was supported by the *basso continuo*

sonata: originally, "something sounded" on an instrument as opposed to something sung (a "cantata"); later, a multi-movement work for solo instrument, or instrument with keyboard accompaniment

sonata–allegro form: a dramatic musical form that originated in the Classical period involving an exposition, development, and recapitulation, with optional introduction and coda

song cycle: a collection of several songs united by a common textual theme or literary idea

song plugger: a pianist-vocalist who plugged (peddled) songs in a music store by performing them, thereby allowing the customer to decide which to purchase

soprano: the highest female voice part

soul: gospel-style singing that emerged in African American music during the 1950s and 1960s

sound wave: vibration that reflects differences in air pressure

Sprechstimme: (German for "speech-voice") a vocal technique in which a singer declaims, rather than sings, a text at only approximate pitch levels

staccato: a manner of playing in which each note is held only for the shortest possible time

staff: a horizontal grid onto which are put the symbols of musical notation: notes, rests, accidentals, dynamic marks, etc.

standard: tune so influential as to cause other musicians to record many other interpretations of it

stanza: a poetic unit of two or more lines with a consistent meter and rhyme scheme

statement: presentation of an important musical idea

step: the interval between adjacent pitches in the diatonic or chromatic scale; either a whole step or a half step

stomp: a piece of early jazz in which a distinctive rhythm, with syncopation, is established in the opening bars, as in the opening phrases of the "Charleston"

stop: a knob (or key) on a pipe organ that, when pulled (or pushed), allows a particular group of pipes to sound, thereby creating a distinctive tone color

string bass: see *double bass*

string instruments: instruments that produce sound when strings are bowed or plucked; the harp, the guitar, and members of the violin family are all string instruments

string quartet: a standard instrumental ensemble for chamber music consisting of a single first and second violin, a viola, and a cello; also, the genre of music, usually in three or four movements, composed for this ensemble

strophe: see *stanza*

strophic form: a musical form often used in setting a strophic, or stanzaic, text, such as a hymn or carol; the music is repeated anew for each successive strophe

strophic variation: a form in which the music is slightly varied from one strophe to the next

style: the general surface sound produced by the interaction of the elements of music: melody, rhythm, harmony, color, texture, and form

subdominant: the chord built on the fourth, or subdominant, degree of the major or minor scale

subject: the term for the principal theme in a fugue

suite: an ordered set of instrumental pieces, usually all in one key, intended to be played in a single sitting (see also *dance suite*)

sustaining pedal: the rightmost pedal on the piano; when it is depressed, all dampers are removed from the strings, allowing them to vibrate freely

swing: a mellow, bouncy, flowing style of jazz that originated in the 1930s

syllabic singing: a style of singing in which each syllable of text has only one or two notes; the opposite of melismatic singing

Symbolists: group of poets in late-nineteenth-century Paris whose aesthetic aims were in harmony with those of the Impressionist painters; they worked to create a poetic style in which the literal *meaning* of the word was less important than its *sound* and the associations that the particular sound might produce

symphonic jazz: music (mostly of the 1920s and 1930s) that incorporates idioms of jazz into the genres and forms traditionally performed by the classical symphony orchestra

symphonic poem (tone poem): a one-movement work for orchestra of the Romantic era that gives musical expression to the emotions and events associated with a story, play, political occurrence, personal experience, or encounter with nature

symphony: a genre of instrumental music for orchestra consisting of several movements; also, the orchestral ensemble that plays this genre

symphony orchestra: the large instrumental ensemble that plays symphonies, overtures, concertos, and the like

syncopation: a rhythmic device in which the natural accent falling on a strong beat is displaced to a weak beat or between the beats

synthesizer: a machine that has the capacity to produce, transform, and combine (or synthesize) electronic sounds

tambourine: a small drum, the head of which is hung with jangles; it can be struck or shaken to produce a tremolo effect

tam-tam: an unpitched gong used in Western orchestras

tango: a genre of popular urban song and dance originating in Cuba and Argentina in the nineteenth century; marked by a duple meter with syncopation after the first beat and a slow, sensuous feel

tempo: the speed at which the beats occur in music

tenor: the highest male voice range

ternary form: a three-part musical form in which the third section is a repeat of the first; hence **ABA**

terraced dynamics: a term used to describe the sharp, abrupt dynamic contrasts found in the music of the Baroque era

texture: the density and disposition of the musical lines that make up a musical composition; monophonic, homophonic, and polyphonic are the primary musical textures

theme and variations: a musical form in which a theme continually returns but is varied by changing the notes of the melody, the harmony, the rhythm, or some other feature of the music

thematic cue: film score cue attached to specific people, places, or ideas and repeated like a motive

throughout the film to emphasize or contribute to the storyline

theme song: a single instrumental theme or song used throughout a film

through-composed: a term used to describe music that exhibits no obvious repetitions or overt musical form from beginning to end

timbre: see *color*

time signature (*meter signature*): two numbers, one on top of the other, usually placed at the beginning of the music to tell the performer what note value is carrying the beat and how the beats are to be grouped

timpani (kettle drums): a percussion instrument consisting usually of two, but sometimes four, large drums that can produce a specific pitch when struck with mallets

Tin Pan Alley: a section of New York City near Broadway and West 28th Street where music stores abounded during the early years of the twentieth century; the noise was so cacophonous that it sounded like a crowd banging on tin pans

toccata: a one-movement composition, free in form, originally for solo keyboard but later for instrumental ensemble as well

tonality: the organization of music around a central tone (the tonic) and the scale built on that tone

tone: a sound with a definite, consistent pitch

tone cluster: a dissonant sounding of several pitches, each only a half step away from the other, in a densely packed chord

tone poem: see *symphonic poem*

tonic: the central pitch around which the melody and harmony gravitate

transition (bridge): in sonata–allegro form, the unstable section in which the tonality changes from tonic to dominant (or relative major) in preparation for the appearance of the second theme

treble: the uppermost musical line, voice, or part; the part in which the melody is most often found

treble clef: the sign placed on a staff to indicate the notes above middle C

tremolo: a musical tremor produced on a string instrument by repeating the same pitch with quick up-and-down strokes of the bow

triad: a chord consisting of three pitches and two intervals of a third

trill: a rapid alternation of two neighboring pitches

trio: an ensemble, vocal or instrumental, with three performers; also, a brief, self-contained composition contrasting with a previous piece, such as a minuet or a mazurka; originally, the trio was performed by only three instruments

trio sonata: an ensemble of the Baroque period consisting actually of four performers, two playing upper parts and two on the *basso continuo* instruments

triple meter: gathering of beats into three beats per measure, with every third beat stressed

triplet: a group of three notes inserted into the space of two

trivium: a literary curriculum of three disciplines (grammar, logic, and rhetoric) taught in medieval schools and universities

trobairitz: female poet-musician of medieval southern France

trombone: a brass instrument of medium to low range that is supplied with a slide, allowing a variety of pitches to sound

troubadour: a type of secular poet-musician that flourished in southern France during the twelfth and thirteenth centuries

trouvère: a type of secular poet-musician that flourished in northern France during the thirteenth and early fourteenth centuries

trumpet: a brass instrument of the soprano range

tuba: a brass instrument of the bass range

tune: a simple melody that is easy to sing

tutti: (Italian for "all") the full orchestra or full performing force

twelve-bar blues: a standard formal plan for the blues involving a repeating twelve-measure harmonic support in which the chords can progress I-IV-I-V-I

twelve-tone composition: a method of composing music, devised by Arnold Schoenberg, that has each of the twelve notes of the chromatic scale sound in a fixed, regularly recurring order

U

underscoring: expanding the presence of music in an early film, so that it could be heard even under dialogue

unison: two or more voices or instrumental parts singing or playing the same pitch

upbeat: the beat that occurs with the upward motion of the conductor's hand and immediately before the downbeat

V

variation: process employed by a composer to alter melody or harmony in some way

vaudeville: an early form of American musical theater involving songs and dances, comedy skits, etc.; a precursor of the musical comedy of Broadway

venue: the place where music is performed

verismo opera: "realism" opera; the Italian term for a type of late-nineteenth-century opera in which the subject matter concerns the unpleasant realities of everyday life

verse and chorus: strophic form; in successive strophes, new lines of text come at the beginning of each strophe followed by a textural refrain at the end; in group performance the verse is usually sung by a soloist and the chorus by the chorus, hence the name

vibrato: a slight and continual wobbling of the pitch produced on a string instrument or by the human voice

vielle: medieval fiddle

Viennese School: group of Classical composers, including Haydn, Mozart, Beethoven, and Schubert, whose careers all unfolded in Vienna

viola: a string instrument; the alto member of the violin family

viola da gamba (bass viol): the lowest member of the viol family; a large six- or seven-string instrument played with a bow and heard primarily in the music of the late Renaissance and Baroque eras

violin: a string instrument; the soprano member of the violin family

virtuosity: extraordinary technical facility possessed by an instrumental performer or singer

virtuoso: an instrumentalist or singer with a highly developed technical facility

vivace: in musical notation, a tempo mark indicating "fast and lively"

vocal ensemble: in opera, a group of four or more solo singers, usually the principals

voice: the vocal instrument of the human body; also, a musical line or part

volume: the degree of softness or loudness of a sound

W

walking bass: a bass line that moves at a moderate pace, mostly in equal note values, and often stepwise up or down the scale

waltz: a popular, triple-meter dance of the late eighteenth and nineteenth centuries

Well-Tempered Clavier, The: two sets of twenty-four preludes and fugues compiled by J. S. Bach in 1720 and 1742

whole step: the predominant interval in the Western major and minor scale; the interval made up of two half steps

whole-tone scale: a six-note scale, each pitch of which is a whole tone away from the next

woodwind family: a group of instruments initially constructed of wood; most make their sound with the aid of a single or double reed; includes the flute, piccolo, clarinet, oboe, English horn, and bassoon

word painting: the process of depicting the text in music, be it subtly, overtly, or even jokingly, by means of expressive musical devices

X

xylophone: a percussion instrument consisting of tuned wooden bars, with resonators below, that are struck with mallets.

RECORDING CREDITS

1. Beethoven: Symphony No. 5, I (opening). Cleveland Orchestra; George Szell, conductor. Originally released 1964. All rights reserved by Sony Music Entertainment

2. R. Strauss: *Also sprach Zarathustra*. Chicago Symphony; Fritz Reiner, conductor. Originally released 1954. All rights reserved by Sony Music Entertainment

3. Richards/Williams/Dixon: "Duke of Earl." Gene Chandler. Courtesy of Concord Music Group

4. Handel: "Hallelujah" chorus. *Messiah*. Musica Sacra; Richard Westenburg, conductor. (P) 1983 Sony Music Entertainment

5. Brahms: *Wiegenlied* (*Lullaby*). Angelika Kirchschlager, mezzo-soprano; Helmut Deutsch, piano. (P) 1999 Sony Music Entertainment

6. Mozart: Variations on "Twinkle, Twinkle, Little Star." Philippe Entremont, piano. (P) 1986 Sony Music Entertainment

7. Haydn: Symphony No. 94 (the "Surprise"), II. Cleveland Orchestra; George Szell, conductor. Originally released 1968. All rights reserved by Sony Music Entertainment

8. Tchaikovsky: "Dance of the Reed Pipes." *The Nutcracker*. Philadelphia Orchestra; Eugene Ormandy, conductor. Originally released 1965. All rights reserved by Sony Music Entertainment

9. Mouret: Rondeau from *Suite de symphonies*. Crispian Steele-Perkins, trumpet; English Chamber Orchestra; Donald Fraser, conductor. (P) 1992 Sony Music Entertainment

10. Anonymous: *Dies irae*. Cantores Yalensis; Craig Wright, director

11. Hildegard of Bingen: *O rubor sanguinis*. Hildegard Singers; Rebecca Boyle, soprano. (P) 1996 Wadsworth/Cengage Learning. Courtesy of Wadsworth/Cengage Learning

12. Perotinus: *Viderunt omnes*. Deller Consort; Alfred Deller, director. Courtesy of eOne Entertainment Group

13. Machaut: *Kyrie* from *Messe de Nostre Dame*. Hilliard Ensemble; Paul Hillier, director. (P) 1989 Hyperion Records Ltd. Courtesy of Hyperion Records Ltd.

14. Countess of Dia: *A chantar m'er*. Clemencic Consort; Rene Clemencic, director. (P) 1987 harmonia mundi s.a. Courtesy of harmonia mundi usa

15. Anonymous: Agincourt Carol. Gothic Voices; Christopher Page, director. (P) 1987 Hyperion Records Ltd. Courtesy of Hyperion Records Ltd.

16. Josquin Desprez: *Ave Maria*. La Chapelle Royale; Philippe Herreweghe, director. (P) 1986 harmonia mundi s.a. Courtesy of harmonia mundi usa

17. Palestrina: *Kyrie* of the *Missa Papae Marcelli*. Tallis Scholars; Peter Phillips, conductor. (P) 1994 Gimell Records Ltd. Courtesy of Gimell Records Ltd.

18. Anonymous: Pavane and Galliard. Piffaro. Courtesy of Wadsworth/Cengage Learning

19. Weelkes: *As Vesta Was from Latmos Hill Descending*. Consort of Musicke; Anthony Rooley, director. (P) 1988 Hyperion Records Ltd. Courtesy of Hyperion Records Ltd.

20. Monteverdi: Toccata. *Orfeo*. Laurence Dale, tenor; Concerto Vocale; Rene Jacobs, director. (P) 1995 harmonia mundi s.a. Courtesy of harmonia mundi usa

21. Monteverdi: Prologue, "Del mio Permesso amato." *Orfeo*. Laurence Dale, tenor; Concerto Vocale; Rene Jacobs, director. (P) 1995 harmonia mundi s.a. Courtesy of harmonia mundi usa

22. Purcell: "Thy hand, Belinda" and "When I am laid in earth." *Dido and Aeneas*. Lorraine Hunt Lieberson, soprano; Philharmonia Baroque Orchestra; Nicholas McGegan, conductor. (P) 1994 harmonia mundi s.a. Courtesy of harmonia mundi usa

23. Pachelbel: Canon in D major. Baroque Chamber Orchestra; Ettore Stratta, conductor. (P) 1973 Sony Music Entertainment

24. Vivaldi: Violin Concerto in E major (the "Spring") from *The Four Seasons*, I. Tafelmusik; Jeanne Lamon, violin and conductor. (P) 1992 Sony Music Entertainment

25. Bach: Organ Fugue in G minor. E. Power Biggs, organ. Originally released 1961. All rights reserved by Sony Music Entertainment

26. Bach: Brandenburg Concerto No. 5, I. Le Petite Bande; Sigiswald Kuijken, conductor. (P) 1995 Sony Music Entertainment

27. Bach: *Wachet auf, ruft uns die Stimme*, Cantata No. 140, II. American Bach Soloists; Jeffrey Thomas, director. (P) 1996 Koch International L.P. Courtesy of the American Bach Soloists

28. Bach: *Wachet auf, ruft uns die Stimme*, Cantata No. 140, IV. American Bach Soloists; Jeffrey Thomas, director. (P) 1996 Koch International L.P. Courtesy of the American Bach Soloists

29. Bach: *Wachet auf, ruft uns die Stimme*, Cantata No. 140, VII. American Bach Soloists; Jeffrey Thomas, director. (P) 1996 Koch International L.P. Courtesy of the American Bach Soloists

30. Handel: *Water Music*, Minuet and Trio. RCA Victor Symphony; Leopold Stokowski, conductor. Originally released 1961.

31. Handel: "Behold, a Virgin shall conceive" and "O thou that tellest good tidings to Zion," *Messiah*. Katherine Ciesinski, alto; Judith Blegen, soprano; Musica Sacra; Richard Westenburg, conductor. (P) 1982 Sony Music Entertainment

32. Mozart: "Se vuol ballare," *Le nozze di Figaro*. Michelle Pertusi, baritone; Maggio Musicale; Zubin Mehta, conductor. (P) 1994 Sony Music Entertainment

33. Mozart: Piano Concerto in C major, K. 467, II. English Chamber Orchestra; Murray Perahia, piano and conductor. (P) 1977 Sony Music Entertainment

34. Mozart: *Eine kleine Nachtmusik*, I. St. Paul Chamber Orchestra; Bobby McFerrin, conductor. (P) 1995 Sony Music Entertainment

35. Mozart: *Don Giovanni*, Overture. Paris Opera Orchestra; Lorin Maazel, conductor. (P) 1979 Sony Music Entertainment

36. Haydn: Concerto for Trumpet and Orchestra in E-flat major, III. Wynton Marsalis, trumpet; English Chamber Orchestra; Raymond Leppard, conductor. (P) 1994 Sony Music Entertainment

37. Mozart: Symphony No. 40, I. Chicago Symphony; James Levine, conductor. (P) 1982 Sony Music Entertainment

38. Haydn: String Quartet in C major (the "Emperor"), II. Gewandhaus Quartet. (P) 2005 Membran Music Ltd. Courtesy of New Classical Adventures

39. Mozart: Piano Concerto in A major, K. 488, I. English Chamber Orchestra; Murray Perahia, piano and conductor. (P) 1984 Sony Music Entertainment

40. Mozart: "Notte e giorno faticar," *Don Giovanni*. Rugierro Raimondi; Kiri Te Kanawa; Paris Opera Orchestra; Lorin Maazel, conductor. (P) 1979 Sony Music Entertainment

41. Mozart: "Là ci darem la mano," *Don Giovanni*. Rugierro Raimondi; Kiri Te Kanawa; Paris Opera Orchestra; Lorin Maazel, conductor. (P) 1979 Sony Music Entertainment

42. Beethoven: "*Pathétique*" Sonata, I. Vladimir Horowitz, piano. Originally released 1964.

43. Beethoven: Symphony No. 5 in C minor, I. Cleveland Orchestra; George Szell, conductor. Originally released 1964.

44. Beethoven: Symphony No. 5 in C minor, II. Cleveland Orchestra; George Szell, conductor. Originally released 1964.

45. Beethoven: Symphony No. 5 in C minor, III. Cleveland Orchestra; George Szell, conductor. Originally released 1964.

46. Beethoven: Symphony No. 5 in C minor, IV. Cleveland Orchestra; George Szell, conductor. Originally released 1964.

47. Beethoven: *Ode to Joy* from Symphony No. 9, IV. New York Philharmonic; Leonard Bernstein, conductor. (P) 1969 Sony Music Entertainment

48. Schubert: *Erlkönig*. Dietrich Fischer-Dieskau, baritone; Gerald Moore, piano. Courtesy of Deutsche Grammophon, under license from Universal Music Enterprises

49. Schumann: "Liebst du um Schönheit." Barbara Bonney, soprano; Vladimir Ashkenazy, piano. (P) The Decca Music Group. Courtesy of The Decca Music Group, under license from Universal Music Enterprises

50. Berlioz: *Symphonie fantastique*, IV. New York Philharmonic; Leonard Bernstein, conductor. Originally released 1964.

51. Tchaikovsky: *Romeo and Juliet*. New York Philharmonic; Leonard Bernstein, conductor. Originally released 1963.

52. Musorgsky: *Promenade*, from *Pictures at an Exhibition*. Chicago Symphony; Seiji Ozawa, conductor. Originally released 1967.

53. Musorgsky: *The Great Gate of Kiev*, from *Pictures at an Exhibition*. Chicago Symphony; Seiji Ozawa, conductor. Originally released 1967.

54. Schumann: "Träumerei," from *Kinderszenen*. Vladimir Horowitz, piano. Originally released 1950.

55. Chopin: Nocturne in E-flat major. Arthur Rubinstein, piano. Originally released 1965.

56. Liszt: "Un sospiro." Jorge Bolet, piano. (P) 1972 Sony Music Entertainment

57. Verdi: "Un dì felice," *La traviata*. Carlo Bergonzi, tenor; Montserrat Caballe, soprano; RCA Italiana Opera Orchestra; Georges Pretre, conductor. (P) 1993 Sony Music Entertainment

58. Verdi: "Follie!" and "Sempre libera," *La traviata*. Montserrat Caballe, soprano; RCA Italiana Opera Orchestra; Georges Pretre, conductor. (P) 1993 Sony Music Entertainment

59. Wagner: "Ride of the Valkyries" *Die Walküre*. New York Philharmonic; Zubin Mehta, conductor. (P) 1983 Sony Music Entertainment

60. Wagner: "Wotan's Farewell," *Die Walküre*. René Pape, bass; Mariinsky Orchestra; Valery Gergiev, conductor.

(P) 2013 The Mariinsky Label. Courtesy of The Mariinsky Label

61. Bizet: Habanera from *Carmen*. Leontyne Price, soprano; Vienna State Opera Orchestra; Herbert von Karajan, conductor. Originally released 1963. All rights reserved by Sony Music Entertainment

62. Puccini: "Che gelida manina," *La bohéme*. Montserrat Caballe, soprano; Placido Domingo, tenor; London Philharmonic; Sir Georg Solti, conductor. (P) 1974 Sony Music Entertainment

63. Brahms: Violin Concerto in D major, III. Hilary Hahn, violin; Academy of St. Martin-in-the-Fields; Neville Marriner, conductor. (P) 2001 Sony Music Entertainment

64. Brahms: "Wie lieblich sind deine Wohnungen," *Eine Deutsches Requiem*. Chicago Symphony Orchestra and Chorus; James Levine, conductor. (P) 1984 Sony Music Entertainment

65. Dvořák: Symphony No. 9, "From the New World," II. Chicago Symphony; Fritz Reiner, conductor. Originally recorded 1957. All rights reserved by Sony Music Entertainment

66. Mahler: Symphony No. 1, III. New York Philharmonic; Leonard Bernstein, conductor. Originally released 1967 Sony Music Entertainment

67. Debussy: *Prelude to The Afternoon of a Faun*. Philharmonia Orchestra; Pierre Boulez, conductor. Originally released 1967. All rights reserved by Sony Music Entertainment

68. Debussy: *Voiles*, from *Preludes*, Book I. Paul Crossley, piano. (P) 1993 Sony Music Entertainment

69. Ravel: *Bolero*. New York Philharmonic; Pierre Boulez, conductor. (P) 1983 Sony Music Entertainment

70. Stravinsky: *Le Sacre du printemps*, Introduction and Scene 1. Cleveland Orchestra; Pierre Boulez, conductor. Originally released 1969. All rights reserved by Sony Music Entertainment

71. Schoenberg: *Madonna*, from *Pierrot lunaire*. Yvonne Minton; Ensemble conducted by Pierre Boulez, conductor. (P) 1978 Sony Music Entertainment

72. Schoenberg: *Suite for Piano*, Trio. Courtesy of Wadsworth/Cengage Learning

73. Ives: *Variations on America*. Simon Preston, organ. (P) 1990 The Decca Record Company Ltd. Courtesy of Decca Music Group, under license from Universal Music Enterprises

74. Barber: *Adagio for Strings*. New York Philharmonic; Thomas Schippers, conductor. (P) 1973 Sony Music Entertainment

75. Copland: *Appalachian Spring*, I. Boston Symphony; Aaron Copland, conductor. Originally recorded 1959. All rights reserved Sony Music Entertainment

76. Copland: *Appalachian Spring*, II. Boston Symphony; Aaron Copland, conductor. Originally recorded 1959. All rights reserved Sony Music Entertainment

77. Copland: *Appalachian Spring*, VII. Boston Symphony; Aaron Copland, conductor. Originally recorded 1959. All rights reserved Sony Music Entertainment

78. Zwilich: *Concerto Grosso 1985*, III. New York Philharmonic; Zubin Mehta, conductor. (P) 1989 Recorded Anthology of American Music, Inc. Courtesy of New World Records, Recorded Anthology of American Music, Inc.

79. Varése: *Poéme électronique* (opening). Realized by the composer on magnetic tape. (P) 1972 Sony Music Entertainment

80. Adams: *Short Ride in a Fast Machine*. Borenmouth Symphony; Marin Alsop, conductor. (P) 2004 Naxos Rights International. Courtesy of Naxos of America

81. Shaw: "Passacaglia," from *Partita for 8 Singers*. Roomful of Teeth. (P) 2013 New Amsterdam Records. Courtesy of New Amsterdam Records

82. Rouse: Flute Concerto. V (*Amhrán*). Carol Wincenc, flute; Houston Symphony Orchestra; Christoph Eschenbach, conductor. (P) 2005 Telarc. Courtesy of Concord Music Group

83. Traditional: "Amazing Grace." Quire Cleveland; Ross W. Duffin, Artistic Director. (P) 2014 Quire Cleveland, Ross W. Duffin, Artistic Director

84. B. Smith: "Lost Your Head Blues." Bessie Smith. Originally released 1926. All rights reserved by Sony Music Entertainment

85. Joplin: "Maple Leaf Rag." Scott Joplin. Courtesy of Shout! Entertainment a division of Retropolis LLC.

86. Rymal/Melrose/Bloom: "Willie the Weeper." Louis Armstrong and the Hot Seven. Originally released 1927. All rights reserved by Sony Music Entertainment

87. Heyward/Gershwin/Gershwin: "Summertime." Lena Horne. Originally released 1957. All rights reserved by Sony Music Entertainment

88. Burnett/Parker: "My Melancholy Baby." Charlie Parker, alto saxophone; Dizzy Gillespie, trumpet; Thelonious Monk, piano; Curly Russell, bass; Buddy Rich, drums. Courtesy of the Verve Music Group, under license from Universal Music Enterprises

89. Rodgers/Hammerstein: "My Favorite Things." John Coltrane, saxophone; McCoy Tyner, piano; Steve Davis, bass; Elvin Jones, drums. Courtesy of Atlantic Record Corp. under license from Rhino Entertainment

90. Bernstein: "Tonight," *West Side Story*. Original Broadway Cast. Originally released 1957. All rights reserved by Sony Music Entertainment

91. Sondheim: "The Ballad of Sweeney Todd," from *Sweeney Todd, the Demon Barber of Fleet Street*. Original Broadway Cast, (P) 1979 Sony Music Entertainment

92. Steiner: Tara's Theme, *Gone with the Wind*. National Philharmonic Orchestra; Charles Gerhardt, conductor. (P) 1974 Sony Music Entertainment

93. Herrmann: Prelude from *Psycho*. Los Angeles Philharmonic; Esa Pekka Salonen, conductor. (P) 1996 Sony Music Entertainment

94. Herrmann: Shower Scene from *Psycho*. Los Angeles Philharmonic; Esa Pekka Salonen, conductor. (P) 1996 Sony Music Entertainment

95. Williams: Main Theme from *Star Wars*. Skywalker Symphony; John Williams, conductor. (P) 1990 Sony Music Entertainment

96. Traditional: "Yamato-joshi." Kifu Mitsuhashi, shakuhachi. Courtesy of Celestial Harmonies

97. He Zhanhao/Gang Chen: *The Butterfly Lovers Concerto* (excerpt), I. Guangzhou Symphony Orchestra; Jun Chen, erhu; Yong-yan Hu, conductor. (P) 2000 Naxos International. Under license from Naxos of America, Inc.

98. Shankar: *Raga Bhimpalasi*. Ravi Shankar, sitar. Originally Released 1957. All rights reserved by Sony Music Entertainment

99. Traditional: "Hujan Mas." Gamelan Gong Kebjar. Courtesy of Lyrichord Discs

100. Traditional: "Adhan" (Islamic call to worship). Various. Courtesy of Celestial Harmonies

101. Traditional: *Fun Taschlich*. The Klezmatics. (P) 1990 Rounder Records Corp. Courtesy of Concord Music Group

102. Traditional: *Kasuan Kura*. Alhaji Ibrahim Abdulai & the Master Drummers of Dagbon. Courtesy of Concord Music Group

103. Traditional: "Romántica Mujer." Cachao. (P) 1995 Sony Music Entertainment

104. Jobim/Gimbel/de Morae: "The Girl from Ipanema." Astrud Gilberto, Joao Gilberto, Stan Getz. Courtesy of the Verve Music Group, Under license from Universal Music Enterprises

105. Traditional: "El burro." Mariachi Cobre. Courtesy of Celestial Harmonies

PHOTO CREDITS

Part Opener 1: iStockphoto.com/Klubovy.

Chapter 1: page 2: AP Images/Mark Humphrey; **1.4:** David Redfern/Getty Images; **1.5:** kurt brownell photography; **1.6:** AP Images/Mark Humphrey; **1.7:** Jason Merritt/Getty Images Entertainment/Getty Images; **1.8:** Kevin Mazur/WireImage/Getty Images; **1.9:** Dea/S. Vannini/DeAgostini/Getty Images; **1.10:** © Cengage Learning.

Chapter 2: page 16: iStockphoto.com/Gord Horne; **2.1:** Phil Dent/Redferns/Getty Images; **2.2:** Amy T. Zielinski/Redferns/Getty Images; **2.6:** JPL/NASA; **2.7:** Fine Art Images/Heritage Images/Hulton Fine Art Collection/Getty Images.

Chapter 3: page 32: Art Resource, NY; **3.1:** Christian Steiner/Courtesy Brentano String Quartet; **3.2:** Christian Bertrand/ShutterStock.com; **3.3:** Courtesy of Chelsea Edwards Lane; **3.4a-d:** Conn-Selmer, Inc.; **3.5:** Photograph by Martin Reichenthal courtesy of Opening Day Entertainment for the Canadian Brass Chris Stock/Lebrecht Music & Arts; **3.6:** Chris Stock/Lebrecht Music and Arts Photo Library; **3.7:** Tim Wimborne/Reuters/Corbis; **3.8:** John Haskey; **3.9:** Harpsichord by Pascal Taskin, Paris, 1770. Acc. No. 4866.1957. Gift of Bettina Warburg Grimson in memory of Samuel B. Grimson. Photo Joseph Szaszfai/Carl Kaufman/Courtesy Yale University Collection of Musical Instruments; **3.10:** Steve Thorne/Redferns/Getty Images; **3.12:** Neale Cousland/Shutterstock.com; **3.13:** Digital Image Museum Associates/LACMA/Art Resource, NY; **3.14:** Richard Klune/Encyclopedia/Corbis; **3.15:** Charles & Josette Lenars/Encyclopedia/Corbis.

Part Opener 2: page 50 (t): *David*, 1501-04 (marble), Buonarroti, Michelangelo (1475-1564)/Galleria dell' Accademia, Florence, Italy/Bridgeman Images; **(bc):** Erich Lessing/Art Resource, NY; **(br):** iStockphoto.com/DigiStu; **page 51 (br):** SuperStock; **(bl):** *David*, 1501-04 (marble), Buonarroti, Michelangelo (1475-1564)/Galleria dell' Accademia, Florence, Italy/Bridgeman Images.

Chapter 4: page 52: iStockphoto.com/Tashka/Natalia Bratslavsky; **4.1:** Fine Art Images/Age Fotostock; **4.2:** Erich Lessing/Art Resource, NY; **4.3:** iStockphoto.com/DigiStu; **4.5:** Craig Wright; **4.6:** Biblioth que nationale de France; **4.7:** The Stapleton Collection/Art Resource, NY; **4.8:** Scala/Art Resource, NY.

Chapter 5: page 67: SuperStock; **5.1:** Rhkamen/Moment/Getty Images; **5.2:** *The Lady with the Ermine* (Cecilia Gallerani), 1496 (oil on walnut panel), Vinci, Leonardo da (1452-1519)/© Czartoryski Museum, Cracow, Poland/Bridgeman Images; **5.3:** Virgin and Mary Magdalen at the foot of the Cross, detail from the Isenheim Altarpiece, c.1510-15 (detail of 3706), Grunewald, Matthias (Mathis Nithart Gothart) (c.1480-1528)/Musee d'Unterlinden, Colmar,

France/Bridgeman Images; **5.4:** *David*, 1501-04 (marble), Buonarroti, Michelangelo (1475-1564)/Galleria dell' Accademia, Florence, Italy/Bridgeman Images; **5.5:** UniversalImagesGroup/Universal History Archive/Getty Images; **5.6:** SuperStock; **page 72:** Cott Dom A XVII f.74v Nuns in a choir stall, from the Psalter of Henry VI, Paris, 1400-20 (vellum), French School, (15th century)/British Library, London, UK/© British Library Board. All Rights Reserved/Bridgeman Images; **page 73:** Scala/Art Resource, NY; **5.7:** Scala/Art Resource, NY; **5.8:** Germanisches Nationalmuseum; **5.9:** *The Rustic Concert, the Song* (oil on panel) (pair of 19949), Italian School, (16th century)/Musee de l'Hotel Lallemant, Bourges, France/Bridgeman Images; **5.10:** By kind permission of Viscount De L'Isle from his private collection at Penshurst Place, Kent, England (http://www.penshurstplace.com/).

Part Opener 3: page 82: Dea/A.Dagli Orti/De Agostini Picture Library/Getty Images; **(b):** Craig Wright; **page 83 (bl):** Bpk/Berlin/Art Resource, NY; **(br):** Lebrecht Music and Arts Photo Library.

Chapter 6: page 84: iStockphoto.com; **6.1:** Craig Wright; **6.2:** Craig Wright; **6.3:** Craig Wright; **6.4:** Attivit Culturali/Alinari Archives/Getty Images; **6.5:** © Cengage Learning; **6.8:** World History Archive/SuperStock; **6.9:** Gianni Dagli Orti/The Art Archive/Art Resource, NY; **6.10:** Erich Lessing/Art Resource, NY; **6.11:** Erich Lessing/Art Resource, NY; **6.12:** Bpk/Berlin/Art Resource, NY; **6.13:** Sergio Anelli/Electa/Mondadori Portfolio/Getty Images; **page 97:** Time Life Pictures/DMI/The LIFE Picture Collection/Getty Images.

Chapter 7: page 98: Dea/G. Cigolini/DeAgostini/Getty Images; **7.1:** Violin, by Stradivari, Cremona, 1699 (photo;, Stradivari, Antonio (1644-1737)/Victoria & Albert Museum, London, UK/Bridgeman Images; **7.2:** Scala/Art Resource, NY; **7.3:** Pierre Patel/The Gallery Collection/Fine Art Premium/Corbis; **7.4:** *Portrait of Antonio Vivaldi* (oil on canvas), Italian School, (18th century)/Civico Museo Bibliografico Musicale, Bologna, Italy/Bridgeman Images; **7.5:** Scala/Art Resource, NY.

Chapter 8: page 110: iStockphoto.com/Sieto; **8.1:** Dea/A. Dagli Orti/De Agostini Picture Library/Getty Images; **8.2:** Craig Wright; **8.4:** Kunstmuseum Basel/Gianni Dagli Orti/The Art Archive/Picture Desk; © 2015 The Josef and Anni Albers Foundation/Artists Rights Society (ARS), New York; **8.5:** Lebrecht Music and Arts Photo Library; **8.6:** Craig Wright; **8.7:** Bettmann/Corbis; **8.8:** Lebrecht Music and Arts Photo Library; **8.9:** Johann Sebastian Bach's Gebeine und Antlitz S. Leipzig: S. Hirzel, 1895.

Chapter 9: page 126: Bridgeman-Giraudon/Art Resource, NY; **9.1:** Lebrecht Music and Arts Photo Library; **9.2:** Bridgeman-Giraudon/Art Resource, NY; **9.3:** Photos 12/Alamy; **9.4:** Lebrecht Music and Arts Photo Library;

9.5: DEA/A.Dagli Orti/Getty Images; 9.6: Lebrecht Music and Arts Photo Library; 9.7: Joanne Harris/Lebrecht Music and Arts Photo Library.

Part Opener 4: page 138 (t): iStockphoto.com/Joel Carillet; (bc): Imagno/Hulton Archive/Getty Images; (br): Omikron/Science Source/Getty Images; page 139: Dea/S. Vannini/DeAgostini/Getty Images.

Chapter 10: page 140: iStockphoto.com/Photohoo; 10.1: Lee Boltin/The Life Images Collection/Getty Images; 10.2: © 2017 Cengage Learning; 10.3: Joseph Sohm/Visions of America/Encyclopedia/Corbis; 10.4: Erich Lessing/Art Resource, NY; 10.5: Robbie Jack/Historical/Corbis; 10.6: Archduchess Marie Antoinette Habsburg-Lothringen (1755-93) at the spinnet, fifteenth child of Empress Maria Theresa of Austria (1717-80) and Emperor Francis I (1708-65) wife of Louis XVI of France (1754-93), Wagenschon, Franz Xaver (1726-90)/Kunsthistorisches Museum, Vienna, Austria/Bridgeman Images; 10.7: © Cengage learning; 10.8: Professor Daniel Heartz/University of California Berkeley Department of Music; 10.9: Imagno/Hulton Archive/Getty Images; 10.10: Omikron/Science Source/Getty Images; 10.11: Imagno/Hulton Archive/Getty Images; 10.12: De Agostini/A. Dagli Orti/De Agostini Picture Library/Getty Images; page 152: Saul Zaentz Company/The Kobal Collection/Picture Desk.

Chapter 11: page 154: iStockphoto.com/Joel Carillet; 11.1: Erich Lessing/Art Resource, NY; 11.2: Mary Evans Picture Library/The Image Works; 11.4: Steve Kagan/The LIFE Images Collection/Getty Images.

Chapter 12: page 167 (cr): iStockphoto.com/Dwight Nadig; (tl): iStockphoto.com/sunChan; (cl): iStockphoto.com/Kenneth Wiedemann; (tc): iStockphoto.com/Kenneth Wiedemann; (bl): iStockphoto.com/Slobo; (bc): iStockphoto.com/Davel5957; (br): iStockphoto.com/Eyecrave; (tr): iStockphoto.com/Bruce McIntosh; (c): iStockphoto.com/Uschools; 12.1: SuperStock; 12.2: Private Collection/The Bridgeman Art Library; 12.3: Eileen Tweedy/The Art Archive/Picture Desk; 12.4: Courtesy Yale University Collection of Musical Instruments; Collection purchase, 1957; Accession No. 3650.1957; page 176: George De Sota/Getty Images Entertainment/Getty Images.

Chapter 13: page 178: Imagno/Hulton Archive/Getty Images; 13.1: DeAgostini/G.Nimatallah/Getty Images; 13.2: Joseph Haydn (1732-1809) at the first performance of his opera 'L'Incontro Improvviso' in the Esterhazy theatre, 29th August 1775 (w/c), German School, (18th century)/Deutsches Theatermuseum, Munich, Germany/Bridgeman Images; 13.3: Mozart Museum Villa Bertramka Prague/Gianni Dagli Orti/The Art Archive/Picture Desk; 13.4: The Eda Kuhn Loeb Music Library of the Harvard College Library; 13.5: bpk, Berlin/Art Resource, NY; 13.6: Craig Wright; 13.7: bpk, Berlin/Art Resource, NY; 13.8: Internationale Stiftung Mozarteum (ISM), Salzburg, Austria; 13.10: Graphische Sammlung, Zentralbibliothek Zrich.

Chapter 14: page 194: Craig Wright; page 196: Abigail Lebrecht/ColouriserAL/Lebrecht Music & Arts Photo Library; 14.1: Craig Wright; 14.2: Tristram Kenton/Lebrecht Music & Arts Photo Library.

Chapter 15: page 205: Fine Art Images/SuperStock/Getty Images; 15.1: Heritage Images/Hulton Fine Art Collection/Getty Images; 15.2: PEANUTS (c)1958 Peanuts Worldwide LLC. Dist. By UNIVERSAL UCLICK. Reprinted with permission. All rights reserved.; 15.3: Stock Montage/SuperStock; 15.4: Barney Burstein/Fine Art/Corbis; 15.5: Erich Lessing/Art Resource, NY; 15.6: Museum der Stadt Wien/Dagli Orti/The Art Archive/Picture-desk; 15.7: Bildarchiv Preussischer Kulturbesitz/Art Resource NY; page 224: Yale University; 15.8: De Agostini/De Agostini Picture Library/Getty Images.

Part Opener 5: page 230 (t): Robbie Jack/Corbis Entertainment/Corbis; page 230 (br): Hulton-Deutsch Collection/Historical/Corbis; (bc): The Witches' Sabbath (oil on canvas), Goya y Lucientes, Francisco Jose de (1746-1828)/Museo Lazaro Galdiano, Madrid, Spain/Bridgeman Images; page 231: A.K.G., Berlin/SuperStock.

Chapter 16: page 232: A.K.G., Berlin/SuperStock; 16.1: Superstock; page 234 (tr): Amelia Curran/Getty Images; page 234(tl): John Opie/Getty Images; 16.2: Bob Jacobson/keepsake/Corbis; 16.3: Apic/Hulton Archive/Getty Images; 16.4: Art Resource; 16.5: Lebrecht Music & Arts Photo Library; 16.6: Historical/Corbis; 16.7: Interfoto/Personalities/Alamy.

Chapter 17: page 244: Bpk, Berlin/Art Resource, NY; 17.1: Imagno/Getty Images; 17.2: An Evening at Baron von Spaun's: Schubert at the piano among his friends, including the operatic baritone Heinrich Vogl (1845-1900) (pen & ink on paper), Schwind, Moritz Ludwig von (1804-71)/Wien Museum Karlsplatz, Vienna, Austria/The Bridgeman Art Library; 17.3: Bpk, Berlin/Art Resource, NY; page 252: Mary Evans Picture Library/The Image Works; 17.4: Omikron Omikron/Photo Researchers/Getty Images.

Chapter 18: page 256: Apic/Hulton Archive/Getty Images; 18.1: Scala/Art Resource, NY; 18.2: Concert of the Philharmonic Society, caricature of Hector Berlioz (1803-69) from Le Journal pour Rire, 1850 (engraving) (b/w photo), Dore, Gustave (1832-83) (after)/Private Collection/Archives Charmet/Bridgeman Images; 18.3: Yale Center for British Art, Paul Mellon Collection; 18.4: De Agostini Picture Library/Getty Images; 18.5: The Witches' Sabbath (oil on canvas), Goya y Lucientes, Francisco Jose de (1746-1828)/Museo Lazaro Galdiano, Madrid, Spain/Bridgeman Images; page 264: Erich Lessing/Art Resource, NY; 18.6: Lebrecht Music & Arts; 18.7: Topham/The Image Works; 18.8: Robbie Jack/Corbis Entertainment/Corbis; 18.9: Portrait of Modest Petrovich Moussorgsky (1839-81) 1881 (oil on canvas), Repin, Ilya Efimovich (1844-1930)/Tretyakov Gallery, Moscow, Russia/Bridgeman Images; 18.10: Sketch of a gate in Kiev, one of the "Pictures at an Exhibition" (colour litho),

Gartman (Hartmann), Viktor Aleksandrovich (1834-73)/ Private Collection/RIA Novosti/Bridgeman Images.

Chapter 19: page 275: Heritage Images/Hulton Fine Art Collection/Getty Images; **19.1:** Craig Wright; **19.2:** Craig Wright; **19.3:** Mirosław Kijewski/Getty Images; **19.4:** SuperStock; **19.5:** De Agostini/G. Dagli Orti/Getty Images; **19.6:** Bridgeman-Giraudon/Art Resource, NY; **19.7:** Lebrecht Music & Arts Photo Library; **19.8:** Mary Evans Picture Library/The Image Works.

Chapter 20: page 286: Neil Libbert/Bridgeman Images; **page 288:** Kevin Mazur/WireImage/Getty Images; **20.1:** Scala/Art Resource, NY; **20.2:** Mary Evans Picture Library/The Image Works; **20.3:** Lebrecht Music & Arts Photo Library; **20.4:** Everett Collection.

Chapter 21: page 296: *The Bard*, c.1817 (oil on canvas), Martin, John (1789-1854)/Yale Center for British Art, Paul Mellon Collection, USA/Paul Mellon Collection/The Bridgeman Art Library; **21.1:** Gilmore Music Library/Yale University; **21.2:** *Wagner and Kaiser Wilhem I open the Bayreuth Theatre in 1876* (chromolitho), European School, (19th century)/Private Collection/© Look and Learn/ Rosenberg Collection/Bridgeman Images; **21.3:** Mary Evans Picture Library/The Image Works; **21.4:** Ann Ronan Pictures/Print Collector/Getty Images.

Chapter 22: page 307: iStockphoto.com/Ivan Bastien; **22.1:** DEA PICTURE LIBRARY/DeAgostini/Getty Images; **22.2:** Frank Micelotta/Getty Images Entertainment/Getty Images; **22.3:** Tully Potter/Lebrecht Music and Arts Photo Library.

Chapter 23: page 316: Russellkord.com/Age footstock; **23.1:** Jan Persson/JazzSign/Lebrecht Music & Arts Photo Library; **23.2:** Dea/A. Dagli Orti/De Agostini Picture Library/Getty Images; **23.3:** Alfredo Dagli Orti/The Art Archive/Art Resource, NY; **23.4:** Jemal Countess/Getty Images Entertainment/Getty Images; **23.5:** Lebrecht/The Image Works; **23.6:** Craig Wright; **23.7:** Imagno/Hulton Archive/Getty Images; **23.8:** Heritage Images/ Hulton Archive/Getty Images.

Part Opener 6: page 334 (t): Craig Wright; **(bl):** De Agostini/G. Dagli Orti/De Agostini Picture Library/Getty images; **(bc):** Topham/The Image Works; **page 335:** Alex Lee (2015, Washington, DC).

Chapter 24: page 336: Peter Willi/SuperStock; **24.1:** *Woman with Parasol turned to the Left*, 1886 (oil on canvas), Monet, Claude (1840-1926)/Musee d'Orsay, Paris, France/ Giraudon/The Bridgeman Art Library; **24.2:** De Agostini/G. Dagli Orti/De Agostini Picture Library/Getty images; **24.3:** Erich Lessing/Art Resource, NY; **24.4:** *Faun and Nymph*, 1868 (oil on canvas), Szinyei Merse, Pal (1845-1920)/Hungarian National Gallery, Budapest, Hungary/Bridgeman Images; **24.5:** Yale University Art Gallery; **24.6:** Erich Lessing/ Art Resource, NY; **page 345:** Alinari Archives/The Image Works; **24.7:** Interfoto/Fine Arts/Alamy; **24.8:** The Granger Collection, NYC; **24.9:** Craig Wright.

Chapter 25: page 351: SuperStock; **25.1:** © 2015 Estate of Pablo Picasso / Artists Rights Society (ARS), New York; **25.2:** Photo: Erich Lessing/Art Resource, NY; © 2015 Artists Rights Society (ARS), New York; **25.3:** Archive Pics/Alamy; **25.4:** Lebrecht Music and Arts Photo Library/Alamy; **25.5:** Topham/The Image Works; **25.6:** © Cengage Learning; **25.7:** Robbie Jack/Corbis; **25.8:** SuperStock; **25.9:** Bridgeman Art Library/Artists Rights Society (ARS), New York; © 2015 Belmont Music Publisher, Los Angeles/ARS, New York/ Bildrecht, Vienna; **25.10a-b:** The Museum of Modern Art/ Licensed by SCALA/Art Resource, NY.

Chapter 26: page 369: SuperStock; **26.1:** Lebrecht Music & Arts Photo Library; **26.2:** *The Old Cupboard Door*, 1889 (oil on canvas), Harnett, William Michael (1848-92)/ Sheffield Galleries and Museums Trust, UK/Photo © Museums Sheffield/The Bridgeman Art Library; **26.3:** Craig Wright; **26.4:** AP Images/Martell; **26.5:** Julie Lemberger/ Encyclopedia/Corbis; **26.6:** Florida State University College of Music.

Chapter 27: page 383: Alan Marsh/First Light/Getty Images; **27.1:** Digital Image The Museum of Modern Art/Licensed by SCALA/Art Resource, NY; **27.2:** Alastair Graham/Lebrecht Music and Arts Photo Library; **page 387:** AF Archive/Alamy; **page 388:** Craig Wright; **27.3:** Craig Wright; **27.4:** Ron Scherl/ Getty Images; **27.5:** Alex Lee (2015, Washington, DC).

Part Opener 7: page 398 (t): Lucasfilm/Ronald Grant Archive/Alamy; **(b):** Michael Ochs Archives/Getty Images; **page 399 (bl):** Bob Thomas/Getty Images; **(br):** PictureNet/ keepsake RM/Corbis.

Chapter 28: page 400: Andre Jenny/Alamy; **28.1:** Craig Wright; **28.2:** Historical/Corbis; **28.3:** Michael Ochs Archives/Getty Images; **28.4:** Hulton Archive/Getty Images; **28.5:** Bettmann/Corbis; **28.6:** Hulton Archive/Getty Images; **28.7:** Abigail Lebrecht/ColouriserAL/Lebrecht Music and Arts Photo Library.

Chapter 29: page 417: iStockphoto.com/Jeff deVries; **29.1:** Michael Ochs Archives/Getty Images; **29.2:** Herve Gloaguen/ Getty Images; **29.3:** Mirisch-7 Arts/United Artists/The Kobal Collection/Picture Desk; **29.4:** Dreamworks/Warner Bros/ Gallo, Leah/The Kobal Collection/Picture Desk; **page 428:** JTB Photo/SuperStock.

Chapter 30: page 430: Lucasfilm/Ronald Grant Archive/ Alamy; **30.1:** AF archive/Alamy; **30.2:** Lebrecht Music & Arts Photo Library; **30.3:** Lebrecht Music & Arts Photo Library; **30.4:** Bettmann/Corbis.

Chapter 31: page 443: Dan McCoy/The Image Works; **31.1:** Bettmann/CORBIS; **31.2:** Bob Thomas/Getty Images; **31.3:** Hulton Archive/Getty Images.

Carol, 63–65
Carousel (Rodgers & Hammerstein), 423
Carter, Sara, 404
Casanova, Giocomo, 196, 197
Cash, Johnny, 404
Cash, June Carter, 404
Cassett, Mary, 337
"Casta diva" *(Norma)* (Bellini), 287–289
Castrato voice, 72
   Handel, George Frideric and, 130
   opera seria and, 130
Cathedrals, music of, 57–61
Cats (Lloyd Webber), 423, 427
Cello, 34
Chambord Chateau, France, 48
Chance music, 388–390
Chandler, Gene, "Duke of Earl," 29–30
Chanel, Coco and Stravinsky, Igor, 356
Chansons, 61
Chaplin, Charlie, 432
Character pieces, 277
Chariots of Fire score (Vangelis), 438
Charlemagne, 50
Charles, Ray, 96, 449
Charts for big-band music, 413
Chaucer, Geoffrey, 50
"Che gelida manina" *(La bohème)*
   (Puccini), 313–314
Chicago, 423
Chicago Lyric Opera, 312
Chickering Piano Company, 276
Choirs of Renaissance, 72–73
"Choo choo Ch'Boogie," 444
Chopin, Frédéric, 245, 278–281
   harmonic shift and, 238
   Nocturne in E-flat major, Opus 9, No. 2,
     279–281
Chorales, 119–120
Chord progression, 28
   in "Duke of Earl," 29–30
Chords, 27–28
   in Baroque music, 89–90
   chromatic harmony and, 237–238
   consonance and, 28–29
   defined, 27
   dissonance and, 28–29
   harmony and, 26–27
   in Modernist music, 355
   power chords, 450
Choruses, 63
   strophes and, 44
Christian Ludwig, Margrave of
   Brandenburg, 115
Chromatic harmony, 237–238
Chromaticism, 355
   in *Concerto Grosso 1985* (Zwilich),
     380–381
Chromatic scale, 26
Church cantata, 118
Circus Polka (Stravinsky), 356
Clapton, Eric, 448
Clarinet, 36
The Clash, 449
Classical music, 7, 99

formality of concerts, 10–11
   genres of, 8–9
   language of, 9
   popular music compared, 7–8
   styles of, 48–49
   venues of, 8–9
   on YouTube, 10
Classical period, 137–153
   concerts in, 142–143
   defined, 141
   dynamic quality of style, 147
   forms of, 154–166
   mood and form in, 175–177
   musical styles and, 49
   opera in, 143–144
Classical symphony orchestra, 180–181
Clefs, 23
Clement XIV, Pope, 150, 151
Close Encounters of the Third Kind
   (Spielberg), 437
Clouser, Charlie, 440
C major scale, triads of, 27–28
C minor symphony (Schubert), 246
Cobain, Kurt, 451
Coda, 157
   in *Eine kleine Nachtmusik* (Mozart), 164
   in sonata–allegro form, 161
Cohan, George M., 423
Coldplay, 12
Collage art, 371
Col legno, 263
Colloredo, Archbishop, 151
Color in music, 33
Coltrane, John, 420, 421–422
Columbus, Christopher, 51
Comic opera, 143, 195. *See also Opera
   buffa*
   patter song in, 197
The Communist Manifesto (Marx), 230
Compact discs (CDs), 6, 10
Compilation method, 436
Compilation scoring, 438–439
Complex syncopation, 20
Computer-generated images (CGIs), 440
Computers
   Mac computers, 388
   music and, 387
Concept albums, 447
Concert at the Villa (Visentini), 89
Concert Etude No. 3, "Un Sospiro" ("A
   Sigh") (Liszt), 283–284
Concert halls, 8. *See also* specific halls
   romantic values and, 317–318
Concertino, 104
Concerto for Flute (Rouse), 395–396
Concerto grosso, 104–105
   Brandenburg Concertos (Bach), 115
Concerto Grosso 1985 (Zwilich), 380–382
Concertos, 188–192
   of Baroque period, 104–108
Concerts
   "for profit" concerts, 142–143
   live concerts, 10–11
   Romanticism and, 235–236

Concert spirituel, 142–143
Conducting patterns, 19–20
Conductors, 41
   of Romantic orchestras, 241–242
Consequent phrases, 156–157
Consonance, 28–29
   musical template and, 6
Contrabassoon, 37
   in Romantic orchestra, 240
Contrary motion, 343
Contrast, 44
Contratenor altus, 60
Contratenor bassus, 60
Coolio, 103
Cool jazz, 420–421
Copland, Aaron, 335, 375–379
   Appalachian Spring, 376, 377–379
   ballets of, 376
   and radio music, 431
Corelli, Arcangelo, 86
Cornet
   Berlioz, Hector and, 258–259
   in *Symphonie fantastique* (Berlioz), 240
The Coronation of Poppea
   (Monteverdi), 82
Coronation Service of King George II and
   Queen Caroline (Handel), 127
Corps de ballet, 269
Costello, Elvis, 449
Cöthen, Prince of, 115
Council of Trent, 51, 75
Count Basie, 413
Counterpoint, 42–43
Counter-Reformation, 74–76
   Baroque and, 83
The Count of Monte Cristo (Dumas the
   senior), 292
Country music, 404–405
Country Music Hall of Fame, 11
Courage, Alexander, 436
Coursera, 271
Court music, 61–65
Covent Garden Theater, London, 241
Cover, 446
Cream, 448
Creole Jazz Band, 411
Crescendo, 33
   in Classical style, 147
Crockett, Katherine, 377
Cross-handed playing, 283
"Crossroads" (Cream), 448
Cross-stringing of piano, 276
Crudup, Arthur "Big Boy," 445
Cubism, 353
   Gleizes, Albert on, 360
Cues, 432
Cui, César, 271
Curtis Institute of Music, Philadelphia, 373
Cut music, 439
Cymbals, 39

D

Da capo form, 122
D'Agoult, Marie, 281–282

LISTENING GUIDE INDEX

LISTENING GUIDE INDEX